Lewis Campbell

The Theaetetus of Plato with a revised text and english notes

Lewis Campbell

The Theaetetus of Plato with a revised text and english notes

ISBN/EAN: 9783741178856

Manufactured in Europe, USA, Canada, Australia, Japa

Cover: Foto ©Andreas Hilbeck / pixelio.de

Manufactured and distributed by brebook publishing software (www.brebook.com)

Lewis Campbell

The Theaetetus of Plato with a revised text and english notes

THE THEÆTETUS

OF PLATO,

WITH

A REVISED TEXT AND ENGLISH NOTES,

BY THE

REV. LEWIS CAMPBELL, M. A.

VICAR OF MILFORD, HANTS.

LATE FELLOW AND TUTOR OF QUEEN'S COLLEGE, OXFORD.

OXFORD:

AT THE UNIVERSITY P

M.DCCC.LXI.

TO

EDMUND LAW LUSHINGTON, Esq., M.A.,

PROFESSOR OF GREEK IN THE UNIVERSITY OF GLASGOW,

THIS EDITION OF PLATO'S THEÆTETUS

IS GRATEFULLY INSCRIBED

BY HIS OLD PUPIL

LEWIS CAMPBELL.

May, 1861.

PREFACE.

THE Text of this Edition differs in some respects from that of the Zurich Editors, from which it has in the main been printed.

1. All conjectural emendations have been excluded, except such as appeared to be absolutely required for the correction of mere clerical errors: and these latter have been enclosed within brackets [ ]. The Student is thus at once enabled to distinguish between the (sometimes corrupt) reading that is found in MSS., and that which has been created by the ingenuity of scholars.

The *guesses* even of the highest genius do not pretend to certainty; and the admission of conjectural readings into the text has this disadvantage, that it tends to lull curiosity asleep, and to put an end to conjecture.

Some of the readings which have been thus removed exist in almost all the editions from Stephanus downwards. He appears to have received them on the authority of Cornarius, who, after long study of the ancient medical writers, translated Plato in his old age. In the execution of this work (according to his son, who published it at Basle in 1561) he used the three printed editions then extant, and *one* MS. from the Library of Baron Hassenstein. This MS. was probably destroyed with the others in the same Library before the end of the 16th century.

Unfortunately, in the Eclogæ, or Select Readings, which he appended to each quaternion of dialogues, Cornarius has not distinguished between the readings of this MS. and his own conjectures, of which, as Fischer says (in an Epistle prefixed to his edition of the Eclogæ, Lips. 1771), 'magnam attulit multitudinem.' The formula 'legendum est' appears to serve equally for both. In his remarks on the Theætetus he only once names the MS., and then to differ from it: and in this case (ὑπολαθὼν p. 147) the 'Codex Hassenstenius' is in agreement with the twenty MSS. which have been collated since.

The claim of any single reading of Cornarius to MS. authority, unless supported by other evidence, must be allowed to be very slight indeed. And nothing is known of the value of the MS. in question, beyond what may be gathered from the fact that it was probably bought, towards the middle of the 16th century, for the sum (according to Fischer) of 2000 ducats.

2. Of MS. readings, that of the 'Codex Clarkianus' in the Bodleian Library has, with rare exceptions, been preferred. The value of this MS., which no editor except C. F. Hermann has yet sufficiently appreciated, is evident from the following facts. ' It was written,' (so the last page informs us) ' by the

PREFACE. vii

hand of John,' (well-named) 'Calligraphus, for Arethas the Deacon, of Patræ,' in the year 896. It was brought from Patmos by Dr. Clarke the traveller, from whom it was bought for the Bodleian Library. Thus it is not only considerably superior in known antiquity to any other MS. containing the Theætetus, but has probably been preserved from adverse influences to which others may have been exposed. The two MSS., Vat. Δ. and Ven. Π. (the latter of the 12th century) are very closely related to the Bodleian (though apparently not copied from it), agreeing as they do with it in its peculiar mistakes, and in the lacuna from p. 208, τῶν μὲν οὖν, to p. 210, δοξάζομεν, inclusive. The errors of the Bodleian MS. (which probably did not originate with John Calligraphus) are of a very simple kind, consisting chiefly either of the repetition of a syllable or initial consonant by a sort of memory of the eye, or the substitution of a word apparently from conjecture, or the introduction of a gloss into the text. Here and there a word is dropped or misplaced (though this is less common than in other MSS.) or the accentuation is at fault, or ο and ω, ε and η, ι and ει are confounded. In one or two instances a marginal reading in the ancient hand seems to indicate that the scribe had several texts amongst which to choose.

The notes contain a few readings of this MS. not mentioned by Gaisford. These are due to a collation made in the year 1856, and have since been verified with the kind assistance of some

PREFACE.

friends. Where the readings of all the MSS. appeared corrupt, that of the Bodleian MS. has been printed between obeli. ††.

For a full account of the various readings, the student is referred to the notes of Bekker and Stallbaum, and to Gaisford's Lectiones Platonicæ.

The present editor is under obligations to Heindorf, Stallbaum, Ast, Deycks, Socher, Zeller, Munk, Lassalle, and other scholars and writers, of whose labours he would have availed himself more largely had circumstances permitted. He has not been contented, however, until the data acquired seemed enough to justify him in forming his own opinion on each point.

For valuable information concerning the MSS. of Plato, he begs to express his acknowledgments to the Rev. H. O. Coxe, Bodley's Librarian, Oxford. His thanks are also due to the Rev. Dr. Badham, for having pointed out several difficulties in the text.

INTRODUCTION.

GREEK philosophy had passed through several phases before Plato wrote. The reflective and creative impulse, which had long striven with forms of the imagination, experiences of history, and impressions of Nature, and to which Socrates had added the energy of moral life, found its crowning form and development in his mind; while different tendencies of thought, which had till then seemed independent of each other, became woven by him into a kind of unity. This is not, however, the unity of a plan, foreseen by the author himself: or of a system, into which earlier ideas are moulded; nor even such perfect unity of treatment as would result if previous conceptions were seen and handled from an unaltering point of view: it is rather the common impress given by a growing mind to the various surrounding aspects of inquiry which it has made its own. The philosophy of Plato is one long dialogue, in which Socrates (its moving centre) becomes the pupil of each school, and teaches where he seems to learn. Protagorean scepticism, Eleatic transcendentalism, the mysticism of the Pythagoreans, the rhetoric of Lysias, are alike penetrated and weighed by the same searching spirit, which enters every labyrinth without losing itself in any.

In the Theætetus some earlier and some contemporary theories are made to converge upon the question, What is Knowledge? The method followed in it, and some of the leading thoughts, are akin to the earlier Megarian philosophy; while in itself the dialogue may be considered as a gradual advance from the consciousness of particular and relative impressions towards the contemplation of the universal and absolute Idea. This progress here takes the subjective form of an attempt to define knowledge; and in the course of it sensation and opinion are analysed, and shewn to be wholly indeterminate.

The antithesis between sense and knowledge, opinion and certainty, appearance and truth, the relative and the absolute, has never ceased to exercise the human mind since the dawn of reflection. To Plato, and still more to those who preceded him, the antithesis and the problem which it involves were new. The mind of an educated Athenian in the time of Socrates was subtle, imaginative, comprehensive, in all practical and artistic matters fully awake, curious and ready for inquiry, but little familiar with the study of abstract ideas. The youth, who in this dialogue is presented to us as an embodiment of the philosophic nature, childishly attempts to define knowledge by an enumeration of the arts and sciences. Yet he proves capable of following the most sustained philosophical argument. So from crude beginnings the Greek mind was led onwards to discover for itself, by the light of its own young but noble intelligence, thoughts which its experience had not anticipated.

The endeavour to trace the origin of these thoughts, which have been so fruitful since, resembles the investigation of the sources of mythology. As the Homeric poems present a cycle of mythological ideas, the analysis of which, by the help of known analogies, reveals the dim features of an earlier and simpler cycle, so in the writings of Plato there are left many traces of earlier philosophies, by comparing which with their genuine extant fragments, and with the testimonies of later writers, some light is thrown, perhaps on those earlier philosophies themselves, certainly on the intellectual atmosphere in which Plato lived. The same inquiry brings out and illustrates his position in regard to contemporary opinion.

In the following Essay it is proposed in the first place to view some of these historical elements in connexion with the Theætetus, and to examine what indications this dialogue itself affords of its relation to them.

The answer to this question will be found useful in considering further, (1) the general scope and purpose of the dialogue, (2) its genuineness (if necessary), (3) its position amongst the other dialogues of Plato, (4) its supposed occasion, and the date of its composition; (5) its relation to Aristotle, and (6) to philosophy in general.

§ 1. Contemporary opinions.

Although the chief names mentioned in the Theætetus are older than Socrates, and "the problem has come down to us

INTRODUCTION.   xi

from ancient times," a careful reader is soon led to suspect that the dialogue contains allusions to living men. The 'disciples' of Protagoras, and the 'friends' of Heraclitus, evidently play an important part in it: whilst there are others, the 'hard, repellant,' 'illiterate' persons, who are expressly forbidden to have any share in the discussion. These and the like touches, which may be paralleled from other dialogues, naturally provoke inquiry.

Before entering upon this, it may be noticed generally, that there is a peculiarity in Plato's manner of alluding to the thinkers of his own time. He speaks not of definite schools, but of 'a certain theory,' or of 'certain men.' We do not read of the friends of Antisthenes, or the disciples of Aristippus, or of Euclides and his band (οἱ ἀμφὶ Εὐκλείδην), but 'I have met many such men,' 'there are numbers who keep saying this,' or more familiarly, 'there are certain refined persons, to whom we must shew courtesy.' Allowance must no doubt be made for the natural reticence of Plato, and for the irony of the philosopher, who 'knows nothing of his neighbour.' But it is also reasonable to infer that the schools which claimed affinity with Socrates were only in process of formation, and that their boundaries were not yet well defined. The above remark does not apply to schools already formed, nor to persons contemporary with Socrates himself.—It is from later writers and not from Plato, that we learn which of the other philosophers then living exercised an influence that could survive their age. The chief amongst them in relation to the present subject were three friends or at least companions of Socrates,—Euclides, Aristippus, and Antisthenes.

I. Euclides of Megara, Plato's contemporary and fellow- Euclides. disciple, seems in his method to have combined the negative dialectic of the Eleatics with the cross-questioning and with the ethical definitions of Socrates. The dialogue, written and spoken, seems to have assumed with him something of a controversial form. His ἐριστική must have been more earnest and philosophical than the vulgar ἀντιλογική so often ridiculed by Plato; but it was subject in a less degree to the same defects. We are told further, that he used to attack the conclusion and not the premises of an opponent. — One other fragment of his logic remains. He is said to have objected to

h 2

definition by comparison, because if things are unlike, they should not be compared; and if like, it is better to deal with the thing itself than its resemblances[a].

The centre of his positive teaching was the Good, which he said was one, called by many names, as Wisdom, God, Intelligence; and to what was opposed to this he denied existence. Here also the teaching of Socrates is engrafted on that of Parmenides and Zeno. The One Being, which is above growth and decay, is to be sought for, not in the universe, but in wisdom, the mind, and virtue. The non-existent is that which is opposite to, or other than the Good.

His theory of knowledge was probably less absolute than that of Parmenides, denying reality to the impressions of sense, but relying upon a sort of dialectic and upon certain ideas or forms, amongst which some diversity was allowed, so far at least as they entered into human language.

It is not easy to determine to what extent the teaching of Euclides contained the germs of the sophisms of Eubulides, or of the paradoxes of Diodorus and Stilpo. If it had such a tendency, he must have approached Antisthenes more nearly than would otherwise appear. It seems not unreasonable, however, to suppose that Eubulides may have introduced a new element into the Megarian school. At all events he gave a new and not altogether wholesome impulse to its paradoxical side.

The following are the chief points in which the Theætetus affords indications of its connexion with the school of Megara.

1. Its controversial tone.

Socrates more than once expresses the consciousness of such a tendency. We start indeed with the virtuous determination to conduct the argument, not as professors of word-fencing, but as lovers of knowledge, and yet presently we find ourselves in danger of being on a par with "those skilful men."[b] Protagoras is imagined as reiterating this reproach, and confirming it by the reflection, which is dwelt upon also in the Phædo, that controversy leads to the hatred of inquiry. We are more-

---

[a] Cf. Plat. Rep. p. 476: τὸ δυνατὸν τίσι ἔχει ἐπὶ τοῖσι ὑντίοις, ἄλλο τ' ἐν ὅπερ τις ἰδὼν τὰ ἐγκωμιαζόμενα τὰ ὄμοια τῷ μὴ ὁμοίῳ, ἀλλ' αὐτὸ ἄν τι ἔχῃ τοῦ ὁ ἔστιν. Ar. Eth. N. VI. 3 ἀκριβολογείσθαι, καὶ μὴ ἀποπλανᾶσθαι ταῖς ὁμοιότησι.

[b] Theæt. p. 164.

over oppressed throughout the discussion with the fear of an imaginary adversary, skilled at the same sophistical weapons. And on reflecting, at each stage of the argument, what it is that has ruled throughout, and that remains triumphant, we are compelled to answer 'a negative dialectic.' The first impression of the youth, the maxims of the old philosophers, even our second thoughts and the strained effort of the imagination to substantiate them, are raised, only to be parted from the sphere of knowledge by this sharp weapon; which in another aspect is the liberating though still dividing instrument of the man-midwife Socrates. In this sense the Theætetus may fairly be regarded as an "eristic" or Megarian dialogue; since, although it is no mere sophistical sham-fight, it is characterized by the predominance of that dialectical exercise which consists in refuting theories. This is noticed by Plato himself in the passages just referred to, and is implied in the image of μαιευτική.

And the form of refutation used corresponds to that which is described as characteristic of Euclides. In each case the proof is not impugned, but the thing proved is laid hold of and annihilated. Man is not the measure, for if so, then why not every other creature endowed with sense? Motion cannot be the sole principle, for if so, language would be impossible. Protagoras is made to object to this mode of treatment. Socrates imagines him challenging them to disprove his promises, and complaining that they use only negative proof.

2. Besides this correspondence of method, there are also some coincidences of idea.

a. The turning point of the whole dialogue, the fulcrum, by means of which the mind is finally lifted out of the region of sense, is the mention of the good, expedient, just and honourable, which Theætetus had at first unwarily included amongst the things which are not, but become. The knowledge of what is good cannot be resolved into sensation, nor into those motions on which the doctrine of sense was founded, because it regards the future.

This thought is also the occasion of the eloquent digression, in which a just and holy life accompanied with wisdom (μετὰ φρονήσεως) is set forth as the way from Earth to Heaven. And the form in which this idea of good occurs, is not transcendent, as in the Republic [c], nor, as in the Philebus, arrived at by a process of reasoning upon the combination of finite and infinite in the world. It is more simple and Socratic than in either of these. And while it is conceived of as one, Socrates is not afraid of varying the name, (ἀγαθόν, καλόν, ὠφέλιμον, δίκαιον, ὅσιον, φρόνησις.)

β. In its general aspect the Theætetus affords only a partial escape from the relative world of sense and opinion towards absolute being, terminating with the conception of λόγος as definition by the distinctive difference. Where it may be noticed by the way, that the stress laid upon the perception of individual peculiarities (πρὶν ἡ σμότης αὕτη τῶν ἄλλων σμοτήτων ——διάφορόν τι μνημεῖον——κατάθηται) is parallel to the saying of Euclides, that comparison does not convey knowledge.

This intermediate character of the Theætetus is indicated by Plato's own remark, that we are wavering between two factions, not siding wholly with either. This position is still in harmony with the philosophy of Euclides, who made some attempt to hold unity and diversity in solution together, and who rested ultimately on some form of reasoning (λόγος). It may be added, that the two conceptions with which the dialogue closes, of the separation of a whole into its elementary parts, and of the power of distinguishing the thing in question from all others, belong to the tendency combated in the Sophista, but more or less embodied in the Theætetus, to acquiesce in difference, falling short of the highest unity.

γ. It will appear in the sequel, that the difficulty about false opinion, which fills such an important place in the inquiry, and the distinction between the ἐπιστητά and ἄλογα (p. 201), which occasions the last answer of Theætetus, can be referred with greater probability to the Megarians than to Antisthenes.

3. In one or two points we are reminded of the later Megarian subtilties, and are led to suspect that they may have had their counterpart in the school of Euclides.

The humorous account of the man, from whom there is no escape, who shuts your eye, and asks if you see his cloak with it [d], may be compared with the ἐγκεκαλυμμένος of Eubulides. And when we are asked whether any one ever said to himself,

---

[c] p. 507. ...
[d] p. 165.

INTRODUCTION.

τὸ ἕτερον ἕτερον εἶναι*, we may find a later parallel in the paradox of Stilpo, ἕτερον ἑτέρου μὴ κατηγορεῖσθαι. Such casual hints confirm the suspicion that the tendency already existed at Megara, though in a milder form than afterwards, 'to part everything from everything.' τὸ τῶν ἀπὸ παντὸς ἀποχωρίζειν. A more pleasing instance of the same analytical bias appears in the three φάσματα[f] or axioms of the mind, by which it suffers itself to be bound; or in the repeated difficulty, 'Ἀρ' οἷόν τε τὸν εἰδότα μὴ εἰδέναι, which in fact underlies many of the later paradoxes.

The story that Plato and the other philosophers took refuge with Euclides at Megara, although hardly sufficient ground to build upon, is interesting as illustrating the friendship which clearly existed between Plato and Euclides.

If we add to these coincidences the fact that Plato represents this dialogue as having been preserved by Euclides, and asked for by Terpsion, (the Megarians who were present at the death of Socrates,) and that it is read in the house of the former, we have enumerated the chief points at which the dialogue seems to touch upon Megara.

Perhaps there is no more satisfactory account to be given of variations and inconsistencies in Plato, than that in different dialogues he is consciously approaching and examining different contemporary theories, adopting their tone, putting on their dress, as it were proving their armour, not without a latent confidence in the unaided strength of Mind.

This philosophical side of the dramatic genius of Plato is as real and more important than the poetical. The dialogue is not only a convenient artistic form for bringing out the different aspects of a question; Plato is himself continually holding converse with some one: and dramatic propriety is preserved not only in minute points, but in the tone pervading whole dialogues. Those in which an Eleatic stranger is the chief spokesman may still be Plato's, although they seem pervaded by an almost pedantic consciousness of method not found in others: a similar remark applies to the Parmenides: and even amongst those in which Socrates holds the first place a marked difference is perceivable; which may be accounted for by saying, (1) that Socrates is not Socrates, but Plato becoming all things

* p. 190   [f] p. 155.

to all philosophies: (2) that Socrates is not altogether Plato, but a part-representation, part-creation of Plato's, which he contemplates and converses with, and even criticises: (3) that Socrates himself has different faces, reflected partially in his different followers, the most characteristic of which, the negative 'elenchus,' was reflected in Euclides of Megara.

Aristippus. II. We scarcely need the testimony of later writers to the fact that Euclides and Aristippus were opposed. It is sufficiently obvious from the statements of their doctrine which remain. They were natural enemies on the metaphysical side, as the Cyrenaic and Cynic were on the ethical. Aristippus is mentioned by name only once in Plato. In the Phædo it is emphatically remarked that he was not present at the death of Socrates. If we connect this with the strong language in which the position that pleasure is the chief good (which Aristippus held), is met in the Republic [p. 509. οὐ γὰρ δήπου σύ γε ἡδονὴν αὐτὸ λέγεις. Εὐφήμει, ἦν δ' ἐγώ], it is natural to infer that he was regarded by Plato with little sympathy, and that he was probably one of those who left Socrates too early, and gave themselves the credit of their discoveries. The tone of Xenophon's representation conveys a similar impression. Attending like Socrates to the theory of human life, of knowledge and of the chief good, he seems to have been enabled by the impulse of Socratic inquiry to give a philosophical form to the popular doctrine, to which his easy temper and indolent life inclined him, that the Good is nothing else but pleasure. With this he consistently enough combined the sceptical assertion, The impression of the moment is the only Knowledge. He probably supported both these principles with certain physical and logical theories: adding that nothing was by nature just, but by custom and usage, and that the same word used by different men represents a different idea.

Whether his doctrine had fully developed itself into the distinct form which is given in the Theætetus to the hypothesis, Sense is Knowledge, it is impossible to say. That he is pointedly alluded to amongst the 'disciples of Protagoras,' if not as their chief, there seems little doubt, from what is recorded of his opinions. A comparison of the following extracts tends to establish this: although it must be remembered that the discussion of these questions by Plato and Aristotle may be

INTRODUCTION.

supposed in some degree to modify the statements of later writers:

Diog. L. II. 86. Διὸ πάθη ὑφίστανται, σίνων καὶ ἡδονήν· τὴν μὲν λείαν κίνησιν τὴν ἡδονήν, τὸν δὲ πόνον τραχεῖαν κίνησιν.

Aristocles ap. Euseb. Pr. Ev. XIV. 18. Τρεῖς γὰρ ἔφη καταστάσεις εἶναι κατὰ τὴν ἡμετέραν σύγκρασιν· μίαν μὲν καθ' ἣν ἀλγοῦμεν, ἑτέραν τῷ κατὰ θάλατταν χειμῶνι, ἑτέραν δέ, καθ' ἣν ἡδόμεθα, τῇ λείῳ κύματι ἀφομοιούμενοι· εἶναι γὰρ λείαν κίνησιν τὴν ἡδονήν, οὐρίῳ παραβαλλομένῳ ἀνέμῳ· τὴν δὲ τρίτην μέσην εἶναι κατάστασιν καθ' ἣν οὔτε ἀλγοῦμεν οὔτε ἡδόμεθα, γαλήνῃ προσεληλυθυῖαν οἶμαι.

Sext. Emp. adv. Math. VII. 191. φασὶν οὖν οἱ Κυρηναϊκοὶ κριτήρια εἶναι τὰ πάθη καὶ μόνα καταλαμβάνεσθαι καὶ ἀδιάψευστα τυγχάνειν, τῶν δὲ πεποιηκότων τὰ πάθη μηδὲν εἶναι καταληπτὸν μηδὲ ἀδιάψευστον. ὅτι μὲν γὰρ λευκαινόμεθα, φασί, καὶ γλυκαζόμεθα, δυνατὸν λέγειν ἀδιαψεύστως καὶ ἀπαραλλάκτως· ὅτι δὲ τὸ ἐμποιητικὸν τοῦ πάθους λευκόν ἐστιν ἢ γλυκύ ἐστιν, οὐχ οἷόν τ' ἀποφαίνεσθαι.

192. καθὰ γὰρ ὁ μὲν πεπονθὼς καὶ ἱκτερικὸς ὠχραντικὸς ὑπὸ πάντων κινεῖται, ὁ δὲ ὀφθαλμίαν ἐρυθαίνεται, ὁ δὲ παρατρέπων τὸν ὀφθαλμὸν ὡς ὑπὸ δυοῖν κινεῖται[1], ὁ δὲ μεμηνὼς

Plat. Theaet. p. 152. ἐκ δὴ δὴ φορᾶς τε καὶ κινήσεως καὶ κράσεως πρὸς ἄλληλα γίγνεται πάντα. p. 153. Ἔτι οὖν σοι λόγω τεκμήρια τε καὶ γε λήψεις καὶ ὅσα τοιαῦτα ὅτι αἱ μὲν ἡσυχίαι σήπουσι καὶ ἀπολλύασι, τὰ δ' ἕτερα σώζει.

See also Phileb. p. 42. μὴ πονουμένου τοῦ σώματος ἐφ' ἑκάτερα — οὔτ' ἂν ἡδονὴ γίγνοιτ' ἂν οὔτ' ἂν τι λύπη.

Plato Theaet. p. 152. Αἴσθησις ἄρα τοῦ ὄντος ἀεί ἐστι καὶ ἀψευδές, ὡς ἐπιστήμη οὖσα. 157. τὸ τοινὺν εἶναί τε καὶ τὸ πάσχειν ἂν [τῶν] δεῖ ἑνὸς ποιεῖν, ὡς φασιν, οὐκ εἶναι πεγίσει. —ἐὰν τί τις στήσῃ τῇ λόγῳ, εὐέλεγκτος ὁ ταῦτα ποιῶν. 154. ὁ δὴ καλεῖς χρῶμα λευκόν κ.τ.λ. 156. λευκότητος περιπεπλήσθη. 159. Ὅταν δὴ οἶνον πίνω ὑγιαίνων κ.τ.λ. 167. οὔτε γὰρ τὸ μὴ ὂντα δυνατὸν δοξάσαι οὔτε ἄλλα παρ' ἃ ἂν πάσχῃ· ταῦτα δὲ ἀεὶ ἀληθῆ. 178. ἔχων γὰρ αὐτὸν τὸ κριτήριον ἐν αὑτῷ, οἷα πάσχει τοιαῦτα οἰόμενος, ἀληθῆ τε αὐτὰ αὑτῷ καὶ ὄντα.

p. 157. λείπεται δὲ ἐνυπνίων τε πέρι καὶ νόσων, τῶν τε ἄλλων καὶ μανίας, ὅσα τε παρακούειν ἢ παρορᾶν ἤ τι ἄλλο παραισθάνεσθαι λέγεται. 158. δοκεῖ—πολλοὶ δέ τὸ φανέν

---
[1] This argument is met by Aristotle, when he is discussing the theories of Heraclitus and Protagoras, Met. K. 5. 1063 a: μᾶλλον γὰρ ἑκατέρα τοῦτ'

xviii   INTRODUCTION.

δισσαὶ ἰδέαι τῆς γνώμης καὶ ἡ σοφὴ φαντάζεται τῶν ἡλίων, ἐπὶ πάντων δὲ τούτων τὸ μὲν ὅτι τόδε τι πίσχουσιν, οἷον ἐχραίνονται ἢ ἐρυθαίνονται ἢ διάζονται, ἀληθίς, τὸ δὲ ὅτι ὀχρόν ἐστι τὸ ἐκτὸς αὐτοῖς ἢ ἐπερυθές ἢ διπλοῦν ψεῦδος εἶναι νενόμισται, οὔτε καὶ ἡμᾶς εὐλογώτατόν ἐστι πλέον τῶν αἰσθίων παθῶν μηδὲν λαμβάνειν δύνασθαι. 195. ἔνθεν οὐδὲ κριτήριόν φασιν εἶναι ἑκατέρων ἀνθρώπων, ἀσώματα δὲ παρὰ τίθεσθαι ταῖς κρίμασιν. 196. λευκὸν μὲν γὰρ τι καὶ γλυκὺ καλοῦσι κοινῶς πάντες, κοινὸν δέ τι λευκὸν ἢ γλυκὺ οὐκ ἔχουσιν· ἕκαστον γὰρ τοῦ ἰδίου πάθους ἀντιλαμβάνεται.

Diog. L. II. 87. ἀλλὰ μὴν οὐδὲ κατὰ μνήμην τῶν ἀγαθῶν ἢ προσδοκίαν ἡδονὴν φασιν ἀποτελεῖσθαι, ὅπερ ἤρεσκεν Ἐπικούρῳ, ἐκλύεσθαι γὰρ τῷ χρόνῳ τὸ τῆς ψυχῆς κίνημα.
Diog. L. II. 89. μηδέν τε εἶναι φύσει δίκαιον ἢ καλὸν ἢ αἰσχρόν, ἀλλὰ νόμῳ καὶ ἔθει.

μενα ἑκάστῳ ταῦτα καὶ εἶναι, ἀλλὰ τῶν τοιούτων οὐδὲν ἂν φαίνεται εἶναι. 156. δεῖ δὲ καὶ κατὰ μέρος οὕτω λέγειν καὶ περὶ πολλῶν ἀθροισθέντων, ᾧ δὴ ἀθροίσματι ἀνθρωπόν τε τίθενται καὶ λίθον καὶ καθ' ἕκαστον ζῷόν τε καὶ εἶδος. 154. τί δέ; ἄλλῳ ἀνθρώπῳ ἆρ' ὅμοιον καὶ σοὶ φαίνεται ὁτιοῦν;

Theæt. p. 166. αὐτίκα γὰρ δοκεῖς τοῦτ' ἂν ξυγχωρήσεσθαι μνήμην παρεῖναί τῳ ὧν ἔπαθε τοιοῦτόν τι αὐτῷ πάθος, οἷον ὅτε ἔπασχε, μηκέτι πάσχοντι; πολλοῦ γε δεῖ.
Theæt. 172. πολλὰ μὲν καὶ αἰσχρὰ καὶ δίκαια κ.τ.λ.

The apparent force of the above parallel must be slightly qualified by two observations. 1. Very similar language about the senses is ascribed to Democritus. Some of the expressions and illustrations, as well as the argument itself in different aspects, are thus proved to have had a wider currency. 2. In the early part of the Theætetus, motion is said to be good, and rest evil. In the Cyrenaic theory, and in the Philebus, three states are spoken of, smooth motion, which is pleasure, rough motion, which is pain, and the absence of both, which is a state of indifference, "like the sea in a calm."

But while those considerations should be allowed their full weight, it must be remembered that Aristippus and those

ἡμῶν ἢ τὰ φαινόμενα ταῖς ὑπὸ τὴν ὄψιν ὑποβάλλουσι τῶν ἄλλαλα καὶ τοαύτοις ἐν τοῖς ἐντὸς φαίνεσθαι δύο, διὰ τ' εἶναι

διὰ τὸ φαίνεσθαι ταοαῦτα καὶ τέλος ἦν. ταῖς γὰρ μὴ κινοῦσι τὴν ὄψιν ἐν φαίνεται τὸ ἕν.

who thought with him did resolve knowledge into shifting impressions of a changing world. And here the parallel of the Philebus affords a strong confirmation of the hypothesis we are considering. Nothing was more natural than that the boy Theætetus should attribute certainty to momentary impressions, and that the boy Philebus should petulantly assert that pleasure is the only good. Each in doing so presents a different aspect of a necessary phase of mind. But when they both (or rather Socrates for them) attempt to strengthen their theory by a peculiar doctrine of motion, which, however popular, must have had limits to its reception, it becomes highly probable that the two speakers drew some of their inspiration from a third, who is found to have upheld both pleasure and sensation, and to have supported them with this same doctrine of motion.

There remains therefore some ground for the hypothesis that, in the earlier part of this dialogue, Plato has these Pseudo-Socratics in his eye, together possibly with others. Whether Aristippus was really, or only by implication, a 'disciple of Protagoras,' and whether or not he consciously based his doctrine on the Heraclitean theory of the Universe, are questions which it is perhaps wisest to leave undecided.

III. More features of the personal character of Antisthenes are preserved than of Euclides and Aristippus, but fewer of his philosophy. From the way in which the grave Xenophon treats him, and from the calm epithets of Aristotle, he seems to have been the butt of the Socratic school, a sort of mixture of Ajax and Thersites. He regarded Socrates with a rude half-appreciating fondness, which was reciprocated with good-humoured pleasantry. But he boasted justly enough of a certain strength of character, which was in fact the piece of Socrates that was continued in him. He is praised for his pure and nervous Attic style, of which we have a specimen, probably genuine, in a rhetorical contest between Ajax and Ulysses. His genius, however, seems to have been opposed to abstract speculation. Hence he followed rather the form than the spirit of the Socratic teaching, both on human life and on the significance of terms. His views on the latter subject were probably influenced also by his previous intercourse with Gorgias.

There are, as might have been expected, several points of outward coincidence between his teaching and that of Euclides on the ethical side. They agree that virtue is one, that wisdom (φρόνησις) is the chief good, and so on.

But the dialectic of Antisthenes seems to have been at once more rhetorical and more sceptical: approaching much more nearly to the later Megarian subtleties, with which it finally coalesced in the teaching of the Stoics. He has been called a materialist, and no doubt the term applies to him so far as he denied ideas, but his scepticism had nothing to do with physical inquiries, which he abjured. It was a part practical, part logical nominalism. "I see a horse, equine proportion I cannot see." —"There is only one term applicable to one thing[b]." Hence controversy is impossible, and every assertion equally true. Definition is only a complex term[1], and accordingly no single thing can be defined, except in the imperfect way of comparison. You cannot say what a thing is, except by naming it, but only what it is like. Connected in some way with this theory was the saying, in which he agrees with Prodicus, that the first principle of Education is the study of names. He was thus related to Aristippus in philosophy as much as Gorgias had been to Protagoras: denying the absolute, while the other asserted the relative, or rather contending that nothing existed absolutely but facts and individual things.

1. It has been thought that the γηγενεῖς of the Sophista (p. 246 sqq.), who are manifestly identical with the 'hard and repellent' persons shut out from discussion in the Theaetetus, are meant to include Antisthenes as their chief. More than one critic has even fancied that an allusion to his name lurked in the epithet ἀνέντατοι. But (1) the abnegation of physical studies by the Cynics is inconsistent with this. The picture drawn in the Sophista especially contains several features (amongst which we may notice the repeated mention of body as

[b] Ἴσως Isocrates Ἑλένης ἐγκώμιον ad init. ἐναντιουμένους οἱ μὲν οὐ φάσκουσιν ψευδῆ λέγειν, οὐδὲ ἀντιλέγειν, οὐδὲ δύο λόγω περὶ τῶν αὐτῶν πραγμάτων ἀντειπεῖν, οἱ δὲ ὡς ἀνδρεῖα καὶ σοφία καὶ δικαιοσύνη ταὐτὸν ἐστι, καὶ φύσει μὲν οὐδὲν αὐτῶν ἔχομεν μιᾷ δ' ἐπιστήμῃ καθ' ἁπάντων ἐστίν. Socrates seems to be alluded to in the latter part of this. In the former part Protagoras and Antisthenes seem to be opposed.

[1] ἁπλοῖ λόγοι. In which there is probably the same derisive force as in Ξενοφῶν μορφὴ λόγοι. ὅπερ οὐδὲ ἡμᾶς λέγωμεν. Ar. Met. N 4.

something to be *touched* and *handled*, and the conception of δύναμις to which Plato drives them) which seem to indicate rather a physical than a logical materialism. The question thus raised will be discussed presently. (2) It is a fair inference from the tone of the passage in the Theætetus, that the 'disciples of Protagoras' would affect contempt and abhorrence of the 'uninitiated' persons in question. At all events there is a marked opposition drawn between the refined sensationalism of the one and the hard materialism of the other. But frequently (as in the Euthydemus) the saying of Antisthenes, οὐκ εἶναι ἀντιλέγειν, is represented as hardly distinguishable from the theory of Protagoras.

The hypothesis, therefore, at least of an exclusive allusion to Antisthenes here, is not altogether satisfactory[k].

2. When the disciples of Protagoras and the Heracliteans are reduced to absurdity by the negative dialectic of the Megarian Socrates, the position to which they are driven is very much that of Antisthenes, that argument is absurd, and no assertion can be considered false. (pp. 161. 183.)

3. This difficulty emerges afterwards in a more formidable shape in the question, Is false opinion possible? The statement that it is impossible to speak falsely, which Aristotle attributes to Antisthenes, by inference from his saying that controversy was absurd, appears to have been very commonly put forward (Cratyl. 429). The deeper inquiry, whether it is possible to think falsely, is seriously raised by Plato as a necessary step towards the true conception of Knowledge. It is shown to be impossible to distinguish truth from falsehood in opinion without the measure afforded by a higher light, viz. Knowledge of true ideas. The difficulty thus raised was certainly felt by others than Antisthenes, and probably by the Megarians, who perhaps disposed of it, as Plato does, to the disadvantage of Opinion in comparison with Knowledge. The arguments and images by which the discussion is conducted are certainly not borrowed from Antisthenes, and are probably Plato's own. The only argument that forcibly recalls what we know of Antisthenes

---

[k] For a different view, see a paper by Professor Thompson of Cambridge on the genuineness of the Sophista of Plato.—Cambridge Philosophical Transactions, Vol. X. Part I.

is that which proves that right opinion is not knowledge.

Compare	With
Antisthen. Aj. ad init. : Ἐβουλόμην ἂν τοὺς αὐτοὺς ἡμῖν διαλέγεσθαι οἵπερ καὶ ἐν τοῖς πράγμασι παρῆσαν· οἶδα γὰρ ὅτι ἐμὶ μὲν ἴσως συνεφη, τούτῳ δ᾽ ἂν οὐδὲν ἦν πλέον λέγοντι· νῦν δὲ οἱ μὲν παραγενόμενοι αὐτοῖς τοῖς ἔργοις ἴσασιν, ὑμεῖς δὲ οἱ οὐδὲν εἰδότες δικάζετε. καίτοι ποῖα τίς ἂν δίκῃ δικαστῶν μὴ εἰδότων γένοιτο, καὶ ταῦτα διὰ λόγων; τὸ δὲ πρᾶγμα ἐγένετο ἔργῳ.	Theaet. p. 201 : ἢ σὺ οἴει δεινοί τινες οὕτω διδασκαλοι εἶναι ὥστε οἷς μὴ παρεγένοντό τινες ἀποτεμνομένοις χρήματα ἢ τι ἄλλο βιαζομένοις, τούτοις δυνάσθαι πρὸς ὕδωρ σμικρὸν διδάξαι ἱκανῶς τῶν γενομένων τὴν ἀλήθειαν;——Οὐκοῦν ὅταν πεισθῶσι δικασταὶ περὶ ὧν ἰδόντι μόνῳ ἔστιν εἰδέναι, ἄλλως δὲ μή, ταῦτα τότε ἀκοῇ κρίνοντες, ἀληθῆ δόξαν λαβόντες, ἄνευ ἐπιστήμης ἔκριναν;——

And here, even if the argument was suggested by Antisthenes, (though it may have originated with Socrates), the application is certainly Plato's.

4. It has been commonly supposed of late that the passage which follows the above (p. 201), in which it is said that knowledge is true opinion with definition (μετὰ λόγου), and that the elements of things are known only in their combinations, contains a direct allusion to Antisthenes. The passage of Aristotle, which is quoted in support of this, is certainly a very apposite illustration of Plato's meaning.

Metaph. II. 3. 1043. b. "On inquiry then it does not appear that the complex (ἡ συλλαβή) consists of the elements (ἐκ τῶν στοιχείων) and their combination, nor is a house merely a combination of bricks. And this is right; for combination and mixture do not result from the things combined and mixed. And the like holds in the case of other processes; e. g. if the threshold is so by position, the position does not result from it, but rather it from the position. Accordingly, man does not consist of animal and biped, but, seeing these are the material part, there is required something over and above them ; and that neither an element, nor resulting from elements, but the essential part (ἡ οὐσία), leaving which out of view, they (Democritus and other physicists, see c. 2.) comprise in their definition the material only. Now seeing that this (the essential part) is that which gives being and substance, this must be

INTRODUCTION. xxiii

meant by those who speak of absolute substance. Now this must be either eternal, or perishable without perishing, and created without creation. But it has been proved and expounded elsewhere, that the Form is not made nor generated by any, but the concrete thing is made, and that which is generated results from particular elements, (γίγνεται δὲ τὸ ἐκ τούτων.) Now whether the essential part in things perishable has a separate existence, is not clear as yet, except that it cannot be so in some cases, in which there is no universal, as in a house or an implement. Perhaps indeed we should not even give the name of substances to these, nor to any other (of things perishable) that is not constituted by Nature: for in things perishable Nature alone can be conceived of as the essential part. And hence the doubt raised by the followers of Antisthenes and other narrow minds (ἀπαίδευτοι) (that the nature of a thing cannot be defined, for definition is a roundabout expression (μακρὸς λόγος), but it is possible to indicate by definition what a thing is like, e. g. Silver may be defined not in its own nature, but as being like tin)—is not wholly irrelevant, but may be applied so far as this: That of one kind of substance, viz. that which is composite, (i. e. of matter and form), whether sensible or intelligible, definition is possible: but not of its prime constituent parts: since definition is a species of predication, and this requires the presence both of matter and form."

The paradox referred to is attributed, not to Antisthenes, but to his followers, who may have extended or modified his opinion. How much is attributed to them? This will be best seen by examining the context. Aristotle is speaking of sensible substance (αἰσθητὴ οὐσία), which he has shown to be threefold, viz. matter (ὕλη), form (εἶδος), and their combination (σύνθετος οὐσία). Having determined this, he proceeds in his usual manner to the solution of difficulties. It is clear, for instance, how to settle the question whether the complex whole (ἡ συλλαβή) is the same with its elements (τῶν στοιχείων) or different from them. The elements are only the material part, and no agglomeration of them can create the form. It is this which makes them one. It is clear also, how much ground there is for the difficulty raised by some narrow minds, that real definition is impossible, because definition is only a rigmarole expression for the name. (Aristotle seems to be reminded of this by the mention of certain things which are not really substances.) As Definition implies predication, every thing, whether sensible or intelligible, may be defined, in which there is matter and form. But mere matter (e. g. the στοιχεῖα mentioned above) and simple form (e. g. καμπυλότης, cf. Met. Z. 12. 1037 b. 1.)[1] cannot be defined.—Few will doubt that the last sentence, which argues from the nature of predication and from matter and form, contains Aristotle's own opinion. If so, it means that whereas the followers of Antisthenes, improving upon their master's saying, that nothing could be expressed but in one way, said that nothing could be defined, or rather that all definitions were merely nominal, Aristotle thinks that most things can be defined, but some cannot, namely, elements and the most abstract forms. That the Antistheneans are not quoted throughout is evident from the word δυσθεύτοι. Aristotle would not have applied this epithet to persons who agreed with him.

To return to the passage of the Theætetus: It may be fairly argued, that several points in it are against a direct or exclusive allusion to Antisthenes. Is the invocation or use of the term ἐπιστητός consistent with his blunt scepticism? And if it were, which according to him would be more known, that which is named, or that which is defined?[2] Whatever faults Antisthenes had as a philosopher, mysticism or obscurity was not one of them. Would Plato, then, have spoken of any of his fellow-pupil's tenets as having been heard by Socrates " in a dream!" Then, even supposing that the logical assertions are his, must not a different origin be sought for the physical conception of the elements, of which we and other things are composed? Lastly, Antisthenes' notion of λόγος was probably a very simple one, corresponding to the first of the three meanings proposed to Theætetus, the expression of thought in language. He rather opposed it to reality, (see the passage quoted above, καὶ ταῦτα διὰ λόγων, τὸ δὲ πρᾶγμα ἐγίνετο ἔργῳ,) than identified it with knowledge. All that remains therefore in common between this passage and what we know of Antisthenes is the assertion, that that which is represented by a

[1] This appears to be the meaning of εἰ ἂν αὑτῇ τρόπον.
[2] This argument also excludes Democritus, with whom the ἄτομα were certainly more real (ἐτεῇ) than their combinations.

INTRODUCTION.

name cannot be defined. Now it is manifest that this might be held by persons who inferred from it that names do not convey knowledge, as well as by one who thought that the only knowledge was of names, and that definitions were superfluous. The further discussion of this passage may be reserved as for the present irrelevant.

5. One or two places may be referred to, in which a covert allusion to Antisthenes has been, or may be, supposed.

α. The allusion supposed to lie hid in the epithet ἀντιτύπους (p. 156) does not seem to be quite in Plato's manner, even if it were consistent with the language held in the Sophist. Contrast the playfulness of Rep. 614. οὐ μέντοι—'Αλκίνου γε ἀπόλογον ἐρῶ, ἀλλ' ἀλκίμου μὲν ἀνδρός—. It might be said with about equal plausibility that the name 'Αριστείδη (p. 150.) contained an allusion to Aristippus.

β. 'Ηρακλῆς, p. 169. Hercules was certainly a favorite hero with Antisthenes, who may be said to have resembled him as one of the physical force logicians—οἱ τὴν βίαν ἐν τοῖς λόγοις ζητοῦντες (Ar. Met. I. 1011 a.)—Still he was not singular in his choice (compare Prodicus), and probably the annotation of the Scholiast is not far from the truth of Plato's meaning. 'Ηρακλῆς τε καὶ Θησεῖς] οἱ Θρασύμαχοι, Καλλικλεῖς, Διονυσόδωροι, Εὐθύδημοι, καὶ οἱ τοιοῦτοι. That some allusion is intended appears probable if we compare the spirit of Euthyd. 297. πολὺ γάρ πού εἰμι φαυλότερος τοῦ 'Ηρακλέους, ὃς οὐχ οἷός τε ἦν τῇ τε ὕδρᾳ διαμάχεσθαι, σοφιστρίᾳ οὔσῃ—καὶ καρκίνῳ τινὶ ἑτέρῳ σοφιστῇ, ἐκ θαλάσσης ἀφιγμένῳ, νεωστί, μοι δοκεῖν, καταπεπλευκότι.

γ. Θρᾷττά τις—ἀποσκῶψαι λέγεται, p. 174. This has been thought to be pointed at Antisthenes, whose mother is said to have been a Thracian slave. The grounds for this conjecture are slight, and the epithets ἐμμελὴς καὶ χαρίεσσα (more appropriate to the rhetorician than the Cynic) must be allowed to detract from its merit.

δ. One other guess may perhaps be allowed to stand on a par with the two last mentioned. Antisthenes wrote a diatribe called 'Αρχέλαος, ἢ περὶ βασιλείας, in which he attacked Gorgias. In the Gorgias of Plato, Archelaus the Macedonian usurper is called happy by Polus. Is it possible that in the passage Εἰ βασιλεὺς εὐδαίμων κ. τ. λ. p. 175, Plato ridicules the combatants on both sides of such an argument?

d

The following slight parallels may also be mentioned:
Antisthenes, like Protagoras, is said to have written an Ἀλή-
θεια. Perhaps this may be alluded to in the Cratylus, p. 391 :
Εἰ τὴν μὲν ἀλήθειαν τὴν τοῦ Πρωταγόρου ὅλως οὐκ ἀποδέχομαι, τὰ
δὲ τῇ τοιαύτῃ ἀληθείᾳ ῥηθέντα ἀγαπῴην ὥς του ἄξια.
As Theodorus calls dialectic ψιλοὶ λόγοι (p. 164), Antisthenes
called the Ideas of Plato ψιλαὶ ἔννοιαι, 'bare notions.'
The words ἵππον ὃν οὔτε ὁρῶμεν οὔτε ἁπτόμεθα (p. 195) recall
Antisthenes' ἵππον μὲν ὁρῶ, ἱππότητα δὲ οὐχ ὁρῶ, and Plato's
retort, 'You see with your eyes but not with your mind.'
Lastly, when Theaetetus tries to define σ, by saying, 'It is *as
if* you hissed with your tongue,' we are reminded of the Antisthenean saying quoted by Aristotle, 'You cannot define
what silver is: you can only say it is like tin.'

Unless Antisthenes is wronged by Xenophon and Aristotle,
the traces of his mind are to be sought rather in the Euthydemus than in the Theaetetus, Sophista, or Philebus. It deserves to be said however, that some of the names in the list of
his works given by Diogenes Laertius are difficult to reconcile
with the general account of him. These are φυσιογνωμονικός,
περὶ δόξης καὶ ἐπιστήμης and ἐρώτημα περὶ φύσεως. But the
name of a work gives little insight into its real import, and
Diogenes is far from being always trustworthy*.

Heracli-
teans.

IV. Beyond the circle of those who had heard Socrates, the
most interesting of Plato's contemporaries in connexion with
the Theaetetus are the enthusiasts of Ephesus, with whom the
exact soul of Theodorus is vexed, who profess to be deeply
read in the wisdom of Heraclitus. They are ridiculed with less
than Plato's usual reserve, as a congeries of self-taught heads,
who support their master's principle of a flux, only by the
absence of fixity in their own thoughts. This picture, the
Oriental features of which are noticeable, may be illustrated
from the Cratylus (part of which is written in facetious imitation of the same school) where Socrates professes himself
puzzled to determine what is intended by their symbol fire.
By one it is interpreted to mean *the Sun*, by another *the principle of heat*, by another *mind*.

* As indication of the nature of these works may be sought in Cic. Tusc. I. a. 13. § 31. 'Atque etiam Anti- sthenes in eo libro, qui physicus in- scribitur, popularee deos multos, na- turalem unum esse dicens, tollit vim et naturam Deorum.'

INTRODUCTION.   xxvii

Although Heraclitus is mentioned early in the dialogue, these professed followers of his are not adverted to, until the principle of motion is being separately discussed, after the maxim of Protagoras has been dismissed. The arguments by which the same principle is upheld in the opening are almost expressly attributed to the "disciples of Protagoras" and are probably more in keeping with the refined scepticism of Cyrene than with the dark proverbs of Ephesus.

If Plato ever really followed Cratylus, as Aristotle implies (Met. I. 6. Κρατύλῳ συγγενόμενος καὶ ταῖς Ἡρακλειτείοις δόξαις), these passages acquire something of a personal interest, like those sonnets of Shakspeare that touch on theatrical life.

V. The Theætetus presents few traces of Pythagoreanism. Pythago-
The only place in which this side of Plato's teaching clearly reans.
shows itself is the mention of the region pure from evils, which is to receive the wise and righteous soul at its departure (p. 177). But a re-examination of the passage about the elements just now considered, (Theæt. p. 201.) may perhaps justify the conjecture that the person from whom Socrates heard the opinion quoted, 'as in a dream,' may have been some 'Italian or Sikelian man.' This is suggested by the following fragment of Philolaus:

"As concerning Nature and Harmony, the absolute being of things is eternal, and to know nature in its essence belongs to Gods and not to men, except so far as this. Nothing that is and that is known could have been known by us, did not Nature enter into the things, both determining and determined, of which the order of the universe is composed. And seeing that these elements were not similar nor of one kind, they could not even themselves have been reduced to order, had not Harmony arisen between them, howsoever it arose."

That is, The Absolute is not the object of knowledge, but things are known only so far as they partake of it. Without harmony, which is the participation of the absolute, the contrary elements of the universe could not even be combined.

Compare Aristot. Met. A. 5. Ἐοίκασι δ' ὡς ἐν ὕλης εἴδει τὰ στοιχεῖα τάττειν· ἐκ τούτων γὰρ ὡς ἐνυπαρχόντων συνεστάναι καὶ πεπλάσθαι φασὶ τὴν οὐσίαν. Δ. 7. Ὅσοι δὲ ὑπολαμβάνουσιν, ὥσπερ οἱ Πυθαγόρειοι καὶ Σπεύσιππος, τὸ κάλλιστον καὶ ἄριστον μὴ ἐν ἀρχῇ εἶναι, διὰ τὸ καὶ τῶν φυτῶν καὶ τῶν ζώων τὰς ἀρχὰς αἴτια μὲν εἶναι, τὸ δὲ καλὸν καὶ τέλειον ἐν τοῖς ἐκ τούτων, οὐκ

INTRODUCTION.

ὀρθῶς οἴονται. τὸ γὰρ σπέρμα ἐξ ἑτέρων ἐστὶ προτέρων τελείων, καὶ τὸ πρῶτον οὐ σπέρμα ἐστίν, ἀλλὰ τὸ τέλειον.

See also Plato Philebus p. 18. Καθορῶν δὲ (ὁ Θεὸς) ὡς οὐδεὶς ἡμῶν οὐδ' ἂν εἷς ἐν αὐτῷ καθ' αὑτὸ ἄνευ πάντων αὐτῶν μάθοι, τοῦτον τὸν θεσμὸν αὖ λογισάμενος ὡς ὄντα ἕνα καὶ πάντα ταῦτα ἦ πως ποιοῦντα μίαν ἐπ' αὐτοῖς ὡς οὖσαν γραμματικὴν τέχνην ἐπεφθέγξατο προσειπών. And compare Phæd. 92.

The presumption raised by the comparison of these passages may be strengthened by some further considerations.

In the Theætetus the relation of the elements to the whole is illustrated from number and music*, as well as from grammar. And in the passage of Aristotle already quoted (Met. II.3.), immediately after the conclusion that the elementary parts of substance cannot be defined, it is added, "And clearly, if substances are numbers, they are so in this way (as combined of matter and form), and not, as some say, of units."

The words λόγος, ἄλογος, ῥητός, in connection with the relation of parts to a whole, are not inconsistent with Pythagorean usage. The word συλλαβή is used by Philolaus, though in a narrower and technical sense.

The union of these examples and expressions with the cosmical turn of thought, has a Pythagorean air. It may be added, that in two other passages where Socrates speaks from hearsay (Phæd. 61.), or repeats what he has heard long ago, perhaps in a dream (Phil. 20.), the Pythagoreans are probably referred to.

But on the other hand, the logical phraseology, the mention of predication, the distinction between the name and the proposition, and between αἰσθητά, δοξαστά, and γνωστά, together with the term ἐπιστητός, argue a different origin.

That origin is possibly Megarian?. The Megarians, like the Eleatics, waged war against sensations and impressions, and relied solely upon reason (λόγος). It is quite conceivable that the term ἐπιστητός may have been coined by them, in common possibly with αἰσθητής, δοξαστής and τοιότης. In the Sophist it is said of the 'friends of ideas,' that they break down the 'bodily

---

* Pp. 104, 106.

? This was Schleiermacher's opinion. (Not. ed. Theæt. p. 520.) The objection of Deycks, that every follower of Socrates must have drawn a sharp line between opinion and knowledge, proves too much for those who seek here a reference to Antisthenes.

INTRODUCTION.

substance' of their opponents into little bits, and refuse to acknowledge it as 'being.' The extreme analytical tendency animadverted on in the same dialogue (τὸ πᾶν ἀπὸ παντὸς ἀποχωρίζειν) may also be detected in the words οὐδὲ τὸ αὐτὸ οὐδὲ τὸ ἐκεῖνο—προσοιστέον—ταῦτα μὲν γὰρ περιτρέχοντα πᾶσι προσφέρεσθαι, ἕτερα ὄντα ἐκείνων οἷς προστίθεται (Theæt. 202.) The distinction between ὄνομα and λόγος is not unlike Euclides; and it is worthy of a Socratic philosopher to have made capability of definition the test of the object of knowledge. Nor is it inconsistent with the general spirit of his philosophy, to have reduced 'simple ideas' to nothingness, and yet to have attached reality to 'complex' ones. It agrees with his tendency to hold unity and diversity in solution together: ἐν πολλοῖς ὀνόμασι καλούμενον.

It is true that no doctrine of elements remains amongst the fragments of Euclides, any more than a doctrine of εἴδη, which still is probably alluded to in the Sophist. Diodorus Cronus, however, a later Megarian (B. C. 300), argues from the conception of indivisible particles or monads.

But there are two points which it is difficult to reconcile with an exclusive reference to Megara; the comical expression, ἐξ ὧν ἡμεῖς τε συγκείμεθα, καὶ τἆλλα; and the distant way in which the allusion is made. Would Plato have spoken of hearing anything from his familiar friends 'as in a dream?' Contrast with this Soph. 248: Τάχ' οὖν, ὦ Θεαίτητε, αὐτῶν τὴν πρὸς ταῦτα ἀπόκρισιν σὺ μὲν σὺ κατακούεις, ἐγὼ δὲ ἴσως διὰ συνήθειαν.

These data lead to the conjecture that here, as in the beginning of the dialogue, Plato has fused together two theories, which from different starting-points appeared to him to meet in one. The more prominent is that of Euclides, which gives the key-note to the remaining argument, that knowledge is right opinion with definition (λόγος). According to this, nothing is the object of knowledge (ἐπιστητόν) but that which is expressed in a proposition. That which corresponds to a name, is the object, not of knowledge, but of sensation. From the position where the simple sensation was regarded as the only knowledge we have gradually come round to this¶. And as the hypothesis, Sense is knowledge, was supported by the

¶ See Theæt. p. 186: Ἐν μὲν ἄρα τοῖς παθήμασιν οὐκ ἔνι ἐπιστήμη ἐν δὲ τῷ περὶ ἐκείνων συλλογισμῷ

INTRODUCTION.

theory of change, so this, that definition (λόγος) is essential to knowledge, is strengthened by the Pythagorean theory of harmony. The sensible things, which can be named but not represented by a proposition, are regarded as elements, which cannot be known except as they are combined in nature. But this is merely a conjecture. There is still the alternative of falling back upon our ignorance of the time, and saying with truth, that amongst the many shades of opinion on these subjects which existed, a nearer parallel might have been discovered, if more had been preserved. And this impression is rather strengthened by the perusal of the fragments of the old Academy.—Cf. Arist. Met. Δ. 7, quoted above.

VI. Who are the 'impenetrable nay the repellent' men, with whom the 'disciples of Protagoras' will not deign to argue, as ignorant of their Heraclitean mysteries, and utterly illiterate? Who believe only in the existence of what they can clutch between their hands, and refuse to attribute Being to any action or natural process, in short to anything unseen? (p. 155.) They are more fully dealt with in the Sophist, and it has been shewn that the account of them in both dialogues taken as a whole, is unfavourable to the hypothesis that Antisthenes is meant. May they have been in any way related to Democritus? This supposition has been objected to on the ground that the Atomists (according to Aristotle, Met. I. 4.) in upholding their κενόν, asserted the existence of the μὴ ὄν. Whereas Plato (Soph. 246.) says of these men, τῶν ἄλλων εἴ τίς φησι μὴ σῶμα ἔχον εἶναι, καταφρονοῦντες τὸ παράπαν. (Here the 'bodiless' is evidently equivalent to the 'unseen' of Theaet. l. c.)

Democritus. The collection of the very numerous allusions to Democritus in Aristotle would be a valuable contribution to the History of the earlier Greek Philosophy. They would be found to present the student with this difficulty, that while occasionally, as in the passage above quoted, the Atomistic doctrine is spoken of as a kind of purely speculative dualism, it is much more frequently referred to in terms which indicate a distinctly physical theory. It is happily unnecessary to argue here at length a point which has been clearly established by Dr. Zeller in his History of Greek Philosophy (2nd edition), that the chief characteristic of the Atomistic philosophy from the first was the firm grasp with which it held the ideas (which to most contemporary schools were so unreal) of space, extension, solidity and weight.

It does not seem very hard to believe that the abstract foundation of mechanical science should thus have been laid in an age when geometry was rapidly growing to maturity: the real difficulty for us is to conceive in what manner a mechanical theory was united with, if not occasioned by, the dialectical recoil from the Eleatic Undivided Whole. Yet in the earlier stages even of modern science such a confusion of physic and metaphysic was not impossible. The 'Plenum' of Descartes has probably not been without its influence on the Interpretation of Nature.

The Absolute Being of the Eleatics, although the object of Pure Mind and identical with it, was not yet free from the associations of extension. 'Being is full of being, it is continuous, for being touches being.' Against this aspect of their doctrine the polemic of the Atomists was directed, when they asserted the existence of the non-existent. It was the non-existent, as the space in which the existent moves: and their Existence, while uncreated and unchangeable, was also that which has extension, solidity and weight. Parmenides and Democritus both sought for something absolute behind phenomena: the Eleatic found it in the Unity of Being: the Atomist resolved this into Space and body. The relations between these made it possible to conceive of motion and of primordial differences of bulk and form.—The weight of atoms of equal bulk was supposed uniform.—All else was relative and subjective (νόμῳ): depending on the impression produced on us by the Atoms in various combinations.

How far is this view of their theory consistent with the conjecture that some friends of Democritus may be alluded to in the passages already mentioned of the Theætetus and Sophist?

1. It does not seem impossible that Plato should accuse such persons of denying the existence of anything 'bodiless' or 'unseen.' For the 'bodiless existence' which they are represented as denying is the 'immaterial essence' of the εἴδων φίλοι; and the 'unseen process,' which they will not believe in, is the movement of the Heraclitean fire which annihilates all that is stable or tangible. Both these are very different from the 'void space' of the Atomist, which is only asserted as

xxxii   INTRODUCTION.

the necessary condition of matter and motion. And (except polemically) he would rather say that ἄτομον and κενόν together constitute the reality of sensible existence, than that Being exists and Not-being also exists. Aristotle speaks of the Atomistic principle as τὸ ὑποκείμενον σῶμα.

2. A presumption in favour of such an allusion is afforded by the manner in which the sense of touch and of resistance is dwelt upon. It is true that the atoms could not literally be either seen or handled; but they had all the mechanical properties of things visible and tangible, and Plato was at least as likely as Aristotle to represent them as the objects of sense. See Ar. de Sensu. c. 4: Δημόκριτος δὲ καὶ οἱ πλεῖστοι τῶν φυσιολόγων ἀτοπώτατόν τι ποιοῦσι· πάντα τὰ αἰσθητὰ ἁπτὰ ποιοῦσι.

The sense of touch and resistance (which the Ancients hardly distinguished) is naturally referred to those 'primary' qualities of body which the Atomists upheld. Now these are dwelt upon in the two passages in question more than in the whole discussion of the doctrine of sense in the Theaetetus, and in language which is much more suggestive of something *hard*. Note especially the words, Theaet. p. 155: 'Ἀτρὶξ τοῖν χεροῖν λαβέσθαι. Soph. 246: Εἰς γῆν—ἕλκουσι, ταῖς χερσὶν ἀτεχνῶς πέτρας καὶ δρῦς περιλαμβάνοντες. τῶν γὰρ τοιούτων ἐφαπτόμενοι πάντων διϊσχυρίζονται τοῦτ' εἶναι μόνον ὃ παρέχει προσβολὴν καὶ ἐπαφήν τινα. P. 247: Πότερον ὁρατὸν καὶ ἁπτόν τι αὐτῶν. Ib.: Πᾶν ὃ μὴ δυνατοὶ τοῖς χερσὶ συμπιέζειν εἰσί.

3. It may be observed further that in the Sophist the men are driven into a corner by being pressed to define (1) whether the Soul is material, which they are not afraid to admit, and (2) whether justice and wisdom are so. Might not this mode of attack be suggested to a Socratic philosopher by the apparent contradiction between the moral sayings of Democritus and his material system?

They are then imagined as retiring upon a more abstract conception of Being. 'Every thing in which there is either an active or a passive power,' i. e. they are supposed to rise from the idea of matter to that of force. The tendency thus recognised surely indicates a different materialism from that of Antisthenes, and the close sequence of the reasoning by which it is developed is not unworthy of the tenacity and penetration which seem to be justly ascribed to Democritus.

See Ar. de An. l. z. Δημόκριτος περὶ αὐτῶν τούτων γλαφυρωτέ-
ρως εἴρηκεν.

4. It may be urged against the above conjecture (1) that, although Democritus might fairly be called ὁμοίως, as the spirit of his inquiry was alien to rhetoric and poetry, and ἀμοίητος, for he is known to have written against the Protagorean maxim, yet the imputation of *coarseness* which Plato's picture conveys would seem to be unmerited.—This objection may be partly met, however, by supposing his theory to have degenerated in the hands of his followers.—(2) That the elenchus of the εἰδῶν φίλοι is described as levelled at the ἀλήθεια of those materialists, who would thus seem to be identified with the disciples of Protagoras in the Theætetus. To which it may be replied, that the account in the Sophist appears to be generalised from more schools than one, not all of whom would deserve the title of ' sprung from the ground' (σπαρτοὶ καὶ αὐτόχθονες). This last therefore alone strictly answers to the title 'hard and repellent' in the Theætetus. The difficulty must however be acknowledged, and it remains, whatever hypothesis with regard to the allusion is adopted [r].

If these passages really contain any allusion even to degenerate followers of Democritus (who might be related to him as the Ephesian enthusiasts to Heraclitus), the fact is interesting as confirming the anticipation that no Greek thought of any permanent value failed to obtain some recognition from Plato, though it might be recognized only to be rejected. We are also reminded of Aristotle's saying, that Plato's dialectical bias unfitted him for physical studies; and of Lord Bacon's, that time brings down the lighter goods of antiquity but drowns what is of solid worth, which may be thought no unfitting comment from the physical point of view.

5. Democritus would also rank with those who argued from dreams and madness that nothing which appears is real (οὐδὲν ὧν φαίνεται εἶναι).

(It is possible that the δυσχερεῖς of the Philebus, who are said to be very clever in physical science, and have an ac-

[r] Another διέξοδος is spoken of in the Cratylus, which may perhaps be that of Antisthenes, but the reference there is evidently to a logical and not a physical theory.

count to give of pleasure while they deny its reality, may have been also in some way related to the Atomistic school. Compare, for instance, the fragment Εἰδόμενοι ἄνθρωποι ἤδονται κ.τ.λ. and the minute way in which the causes of sensation are analysed by Democritus while its reality is denied: also the words τῷ τὰ συγκεκριμένα βίῃ διαχέειν ἢ τὰ διακεκριμένα συγχέειν, Phil. p. 46. ad fin.)

Semi-Protagoreans.

VII. One other distinct reference to contemporaries remains to be considered. It occurs at what may be called the turning point of the dialogue: where it is remarked that the stronghold of the doctrine—"What appears to me, is to me"—lies amongst sensible things, but that its weak point is in the answer to such questions as, What is wholesome? What is expedient? And it is added, that those who hold a partial Protagoreanism, (οἱ τὰ Πρωταγόρου μὴ παντάπασι λέγοντες,) while insisting that honour and justice are merely conventional, admit that, in regard to things expedient and good, mistake is possible, and one councillor and one state is wiser than another. These men seem to be brought forward as witnesses to the existence of something above sensation and convention, just as the "fastidious persons" are made to testify in the Philebus to the existence of mixtures of pleasure and pain. But it seems impossible to identify them with any known school. Euclides denied reality to impressions. Aristippus admitted no good beyond the present pleasure. Plato here alludes to some intermediate teachers, of whom our knowledge is a blank.

This notice of the relation of the Theætetus to contemporary theories may be concluded with a few general remarks.

General remarks.

Such an inquiry must necessarily be scanty in its positive results. Its true value, however, lies rather in the consciousness which it implies, and which it tends to strengthen, that Plato, though in advance of his contemporaries, was not isolated from them, but held living intercourse with the present as well as with the past. In studying any author, it is invigorating even to attempt to breathe the atmosphere in which he moved, and to see with his eyes the men and the ideas surrounding him. Without making this attempt, the modern reader of Plato cannot but lose much. He will be like one reading a letter without knowing to whom it is addressed. Many of the ideas and sentiments may be intelligible to him, but the living tone and expression which it would otherwise convey are lost. A few cautions however are suggested to us as the inquiry proceeds.

1. In piecing together the fragments of an ancient statue or group, a sanguine and inexperienced eye might naturally imagine some things to fit, which were really independent of each other, and some things to be incongruous which were really not so. Supposing the whole discovered, the mistaken adaptations would be displaced by more perfect symmetry, and the apparent discrepancies harmonized by the intermediate parts. The contemporary remains of Plato's time are such a fragment. The more we study them in the light of his works, the more we feel, that while distinct and opposite tendencies were at work, the various thinkers of that age (especially those who followed Socrates) had much in common; and that many shades of opinion existed besides the opposite extremes. The few names and the few sayings that have been preserved to us by no means exhaust the whole field.

2. Plato's relation to these contemporaries must not be conceived of as closer than it really was. Their theories must not be suffered to crowd in upon him so as to cramp the freedom and originality of his thoughts, of which they are not the substance, but the occasion. He views them in different lights and in different combinations as he moves amongst them, just as natural objects group themselves differently according to the point at which we stand.

For instance, the materialist and sensationalist, who in the Theætetus are opposed, in the Sophist appear to be combined as the enemies of ideas, differing only in the degree of their unregenerate hardness. And in the Cratylus, the Heraclitean and Protagorean doctrines are contrasted. Plato had certain men in his eye, but what interested him far more were the different aspects of philosophy. And these could not be narrowed to this or that individual, nor extended so as to embrace his inconsistencies. A great name in the past might so "orb into the perfect star" as to be wholly identified with one of the great streams of thought, but from the speculative height from which Plato surveyed the present, rival opinions might at one time be generalized into one view, and at another time by a change of position might be seen as wholly distinct.

xxxvi   INTRODUCTION.

3. Plato was by no means absorbed in the controversies of the hour. The grand movements of Greek thought, hidden from inferior intellects, were comprehended in one glance by him, not observed as by Aristotle, but consciously realised. Thus in the Theætetus he gathers up into a single formula one side of the alternative which philosophy had hitherto presented to the Greek mind. Looking above and beyond Aristippus, and even Protagoras, whose personal influence had hardly yet died away, he fixes his eye upon Heraclitus, who had given the highest expression to the relative side of thought. The struggle, outwardly waged between the Megarian and the Cyrenaic, is in reality a far deeper one, between Parmenides and Heraclitus, or rather between the two opposing streams of Greek Philosophy, which were seeking their unity in the mind of Plato.

§ 2.

Earlier Philosophies.

As after-ages saw amongst Plato's contemporaries distinctions which were only partially developed in his time, so in a less degree, and with the difference which his genius implies, Plato viewed the past through a generalization and an antithesis. Heraclitus and Empedocles, and from another point of view Protagoras, were the representatives of one tendency, Parmenides and his followers, of the contrary one. The opposition between them is that between rest and motion, unity and diversity, absolute and relative, universal and particular, finite and infinite, positive and negative, between knowledge and opinion, ideas or conceptions and impressions.

In endeavouring to conceive what Parmenides, Heraclitus and Protagoras really were, it would be necessary to divest our minds of this contrasted form under which we are led to think of them in reading Plato. But, although not always brought into prominence, it is of the essence of what they were to him.

This is not the place for a detailed account of the earlier stage of Greek Philosophy. But a brief sketch of it is necessary in order to make Plato's position clear.

It would only be an approximation towards a true estimate, to say that Parmenides represents the idea of unity, being, or rest, Heraclitus that of dualism, of a process, or motion, and Pythagoras that of harmony and order, or definite proportions, as intermediate between the other two.

INTRODUCTION. xxxvii

Philosophy was yet too near its origin for its streams to have diverged very far. As we come nearer to those early thinkers, we find that they had more in common than we supposed. They have a common mythological element, the atmosphere in which their thoughts move, and which they strive to pierce, although it veils their meaning partly from themselves; inhaled by some in the Greek and Sicilian valleys, by some, perhaps in earlier purity, on the Eastern plains, but in all finding its highest sensuous embodiment in the Sun or Fire. The notion of Δίκη is common to Heraclitus and Parmenides, the εἱμαρμένη of the one is paralleled by the ἀνάγκη of the other.

The endeavour to pierce this veil of language* is accompanied in all of them by a melancholy scepticism and contempt for the common opinions of men. The words of Plato in the Phædo, οἱ πολλοὶ ψηλαφῶντες ὥσπερ ἐν σκότῳ, might have been applied by any of the earlier philosophers to the condition of men, who believe the testimony of their senses before that of reason, and cling to their own narrow thoughts instead of being conformed to the law of Nature or Being.

With this scepticism is combined in all of them what may be termed an ideal Pantheism: the speculative and religious intellect filling the void of observation with the intensity of its own early thought. [τὸ γὰρ πλέον ἐστὶ νόημα. Parm.] All that is particular owes its being to Wrong, in the universal alone is harmony and righteousness and peace. The world of opinion is a world of "nought and night;" the fulness of being is absolute, and commensurate with thought. The nature of things, says Philolaus, belongs to Divine, and not to human knowledge.

Such being the ground colours more or less discernible throughout the philosophy of that age, what were the distinguishing features by which they were relieved? It is now proposed to consider this in the case of Heraclitus and (more briefly) of Parmenides; and it may be remarked in passing, that, historically speaking, it does not seem very probable that either of these philosophers pursued his reflections with direct reference to the other. The idea of the History of Philosophy is a little apt to intercept our view of the History itself. As a

* Cf. Parm. ἀνόμματα ἐρατύρατα ἀπὸ χερσὶ πολύπειρας.

Platonist sees in the Ionian and Eleatic two opposite poles, so the Hegelian is tempted to trace the progress of thought from Parmenides to Heraclitus, while a Kantian may view the Eleatic transcendentalism as the higher. Such thoughts may supply a valuable theory, but they are not strictly historical. Parmenides and Heraclitus were nearly contemporary, Heraclitus being the earlier of the two: they lived far apart, and were subject to different influences.

Heraclitus. I. Heraclitus of Ephesus (B. C. 500) was an Eastern Greek, and it is not merely fanciful to find an analogy between his thoughts and the more dreamy speculations of the remoter East. But they have a greater interest for the student of philosophy, not only as having contributed primarily to the speculative impulse of the Greek mind, but as permanently valuable in themselves, and anticipating some of the most fruitful of modern ideas. Bacon drew from them some of his happiest expressions; and Hegel professed to have embodied in his own Logic every principle which they contained. "The voice of the Sibyl," says Heraclitus, "although its notes be harsh and rude, yet penetrates to a thousand years." This pregnant saying may be well applied to the obscure utterances of Heraclitus himself. Half understood even by his own followers, imperfectly appreciated by Plato and Aristotle, he exercised a wide-spread influence, second only to that of Parmenides in its intensity. Caught up afresh by the Stoics and Neo-platonists, and by the Fathers of the Christian Church, and read by them in the light of deeper wants, his words received a new interest from their sublime spirit of awe and sadness. And thus many of them have been preserved to us; and reveal in dim and broken outline the proportions of a most noble and far-seeing intellect.

It is the common fate of great thinkers in an early time, that for the most part only the negative side of their teaching 'lives after them.' One reason is, that it is the most distinct and intelligible to themselves and their contemporaries. Deep intuitions, but unsubstantial, though clothed in palpable imagery; anticipations, vague and unsupported by proof, of the human mind, dreaming on thoughts to come, partly become engulfed by time, partly remain dead and fruitless and unknown, until their meaning is revealed by the development of cognate thoughts in distant ages, and a late sympathy detects what is hidden there in germ. So the doctrine of Heraclitus, which undoubtedly contained an element of order and unity, if not of rest, and had been as ideal as any, was degraded to be the support of the doctrine of sense, although it again enters to restore the balance of philosophy when in danger of being bound fast in the Eleatic One[1].

Heraclitus himself had followed in the wake of previous thinkers. As the emigrant Xenophanes had "looked up to the vault of heaven and said that the One was God," so Thales had looked forth on the expanse of the Ægean and said that water was the All, with a vague sense that Nature must be simple and all-pervading. The tendency of his successors had been towards the idea of an homogeneous Infinite. Heraclitus rose to the conception of Nature as a universal ever-acting Law.

He felt deeply the falseness and contradictoriness of sensation and opinion, not because he contrasted their objects with that of knowledge, but because he felt that these are presented as being something in themselves,—'not fluctuating but fixed,' —and not as moments in the Universal Process. This is itself unseen, but is symbolised in several ways. "The Order that embraces all things is an everliving Fire, Eternal, Uncreated, kindling itself by measures and extinguishing itself by measures;" i. e. The Idea of the universe implies at once absolute activity and perfect law. This Idea is also represented as "the invisible harmony" which is "better than the visible," as the "Thought which guides all through all," as the "Universal Word" or "Reason," as the "One Wisdom," as "Time," as "Righteousness," as "Fate," as the "Name of Zeus." This Eternal process, which is at the same time a law or harmony, is inseparable in the mind of Heraclitus from the notion of dualism. The process is from This to That and back again, the harmony is between opposites, which do not cease to be opposites, although the one passes into the other. This was not lost upon Plato, "The universe is ever drawn asunder and together at once, says the muse of firmer tone," viz. the Ionian: Plat. Soph. 242. It is implied in the blunt words, "War is the Father of all things;" and in a saying of more doubtful

[1] Thus the dialectic of Rep. B. VI. is a sort of *** *** *** pla. See also the Sophist and Parmenides.

INTRODUCTION.

meaning, Παλίντονος ἁρμονία κόσμου, ὥσπερ τόξου καὶ λύρας. Different interpretations of this have been suggested. Perhaps it might be paraphrased, "As the arrow leaves the string, the hands are pulling opposite ways to each other, and to the different parts of the bow (cf. Plato Rep. IV. p. 439), and the sweet note of the lyre is due to a similar tension and retention; the secret of the Universe is the same"." Thus Homer is blamed for praying that strife may be no more, since without strife there can be no harmony. "The Deity is Day and Night in one, winter and summer, war and peace, fulness and hunger." Each thing is ever producing or passing into its opposite—evil into good, and good into evil: light into darkness and darkness into light. This Eternal process is the world: "All coming out of one, and one arising out of all." Its nature is to reveal itself in contradictions: Συνάψιας οὖλα καὶ οὐχὶ οὖλα κ. τ. λ. "Ἓν τὸ σοφὸν γιγνώσκεσθαι ἐθέλει τε καὶ οὐκ ἐθέλει, Ζηνὸς ὄνομα.

But it is more particularly described as the way upwards and downwards, which is the same. In every thing there is contrariety, and the action of the all-embracing, all-dividing fire. But there is a more general contrariety between the fire itself and its grosser forms, i. e. between the absolute process itself and the elements which are at once the subjects and the products of its Law. Fire is becoming all things, and all things are becoming fire;—the things are typified as air and water and earth. Here it is more difficult to separate the symbol from the thought. There is an effort made to give greater outward reality to the process, and the language becomes more sensuous accordingly. The way upwards is the way from earth through water and air to fire[s], the way downwards is from fire through air and water to earth. Both processes are ever moving on together; and each element has its own harmony or law. There is then not only contrariety and harmony in the world, but also a lower and a higher. This is more simply expressed by the distinction between the moist and dry exhalations; e. g. the clouds and the sun: the one dark, the other light; the one tending downwards, the other

---

[a] Hor. Epist. I. 12. 'Quid velit et possit rerum concordia discors.'
[s] Compare Shakespeare, Antony and Cleopatra. 'I am fire and air, my other elements I give to baser life.'

upwards. These are, as it were, the body and soul of the world. The death of either is the other's life. The Universal Process is perpetually circling between them. At this point we return to the world of sensible things. They exist only by perpetual strife, life and death work together in them; their birth is a death, their death or absorption into the higher region is the true life; the only harmony amongst them is due to war. But is there war in heaven? Is there no escape from this region of conflicting elements? Is the fire itself, the origin and goal of the struggle of existence, torn asunder by a similar struggle? We may possibly imagine the primordial activity and its law (πῦρ, μέτρα) as two coexistent and opposite principles, the balance of which is order (κοσμός); but it is probably nearer the truth to say, that the fire is inseparable from the world, and therefore from the conflict of things: as these in their war are ever coming into existence and absorbed again, so the fire is ever parted asunder so as to become all things, and at the same time united out of them ᶠ, quenched into the lower forms and kindled into itself again. But then this process is all-embracing; not isolated like the war of particular things: and for each thing to rise from earth to fire, that is, from particular existence to the Universal Process, is to attain to peace. This seems to be implied in the notice of Diog. L. (IX. 8.): Τῶν δὲ ἐναντίων τὸ μὲν εἰς γένεσιν ἄγον καλεῖσθαι πόλεμον καὶ ἔριν, τὸ δ' ἐπὶ τὴν ἐκπύρωσιν ὁμολογίαν καὶ εἰρήνην ᵍ. On the other hand, that which is wearied with the "Eternal process moving on," is carried downwards by a weak desire of rest and of particular being; and to this is attributed the origin of the individual soul. (See Lassalle, Her. vol. I. pp. 123 sqq.)

What is the bearing of this theory on the mind, on human knowledge, and on human life?

1. The universal law or process may be conceived of as a continued act or utterance of mind (γνώμη ἣ κυβερνήσει πάντα, τὸ ἓν σοφόν, θεῖος λόγος). This, though more or less personified (as Ζεύς, Δίκη, Θεόν) is nowhere distinctly personal. The act or utterance itself is the soul of the World, not exactly "immanent," but ever moving throughout all, passing into everything and returning into itself again. Yet while thus pervading

---

ᶠ διαφερόμενον ἀεὶ συμφέρεται.   ἑκούσιον ἦθὸς καὶ ἀγαθόν.—εἴμαρτο δεδομένον.
ᵍ Cf. too the words τούτων ὑπείχειν

all things, it essentially holds the upper etherial region, and embraces all, being opposed to the things beneath it as universal to particular.

2. Knowledge therefore is the acquaintance and union with this universal and pervading mind or law. That human mind is the best, which most partakes of it; that which lives in its own world of particular impressions and notions, is "nearer earth and less in light." This idea finds a symbolical and also an abstract expression. "A dry soul is the wisest and the best, flashing through the body as lightning through a cloud" (cf. ξηρὰ ἀναθυμίασις). "The moist soul (e.g. with wine) 'embodies' itself like a gathering cloud" (cf. ὑγρὰ ἀναθυμίασις). "The Law of things is a law of universal Reason, but most men live as if they had a wisdom of their own." "To live in the light of the universal Order is to be awake, to turn aside into our own microcosm is to go to sleep." "Most men even when they hear are as though they heard not, their speech betrays that though present they are absent mentally." It is an obscure question, and one which Heraclitus probably did not distinctly ask himself, by what path, according to this theory, the mind passes from sense to knowledge, from the darkness of the particular into the light of the universal. The answer would probably be little more than that the eye of the soul is opened. As the faculty of sight is quenched in sleep, so the mind is quenched while it is concerned only with the things surrounding it. But if a man awake, the fire within him finds its kindred fire, and flashes through the clouds of the sensible world. Thus living in the universal order he becomes a partaker of the mind which follows all through all. Sensation is not annihilated, but is absorbed into the grander movement of the mind, and becomes the transparent medium of true vision. (See the expression κατὰ φύσιν ἰταλίω, where the transition from sensible to mental perception is not marked.) While the mind is thus acquainted with the universal law, it must also follow the swiftness of the universal motion (Plat. Cratyl. p. 412. διὰ τοῦ ἰόντος ἰέναι παντός) distinguishing all things into their true elements (κατὰ φύσιν διαιρέων ἕκαστα ὅκως ἔχει), perceiving their transformations, comprehending their unseen harmony (πάντα τὸ πῦρ ἐπελθὸν κρινεῖ καὶ καταλήψεται). Heraclitus could not be unconscious that this was an ideal state for

man, who "lights a taper for himself in the night," and "is but an ape to compare with God." The subtilty of Nature far exceeds the subtilty of the human intellect, and her energy far exceeds his power to grapple with it. Hence as in his Heaven there is no rest, so even in his philosophy there is occasionally a despairing tone. This however never occurs in speaking of the Eternal process, but of its revelation to and comprehension by man.

3. For in comparison with the grandeur of the Universal Law, human life becomes a very little thing, if it be not more fitly called a death. Indeed, as in all things else, so in man, life and death are ever working together. His body is ever absorbed into his soul, his soul is ever dying into his body; his birth into the world is the entombment of a higher life, the death of what is earthly in him is the awaking of the God. As the Reason is but a small part in any man, so the good amongst men are few, and misunderstood (for dogs also bark at him they know not). Even the philosopher is like the gold-digger, who toils much and finds little, [cf. Plat. Rep. 450 b.], and often his truest wisdom is to know himself, and to feel the nothingness of his individual Being in the presence of the Universal Order. Yet public law is to be zealously maintained, as more general than the private will, the excesses of which are to be quenched as a dangerous fire.

Such is the bare outline of a thought the grandeur of which was far beyond the comprehension of that time. The Λόγος or Law of Heraclitus was not exactly a law of progress, for his elements are ever circling in one round, yet it is as near an approach to that Idea as is to be found in Ancient Philosophy. A still nearer approach is made to the conception of the infinity and simplicity of Nature. And while we feel that the metaphysical systems of Plato and Aristotle owe much of their strength and reality and perfection to the One Being of Parmenides, and in part also to the Pythagoreans, in whose philosophy finite and infinite were already combined, it is impossible not to recognise in Plato a nearer kindred to Heraclitus than to any other of his predecessors. The union of Imagination and Reason, the plasticity of mind, the tendency at once to soar and to roam, may be mentioned as some of the points of communion between them. Many scattered thoughts,

INTRODUCTION.

as well as the spirit pervading whole passages, might be quoted in confirmation of this. It is not surprising therefore if Plato grasped the thought of Heraclitus more firmly than his own followers had done[a].

The fate of Heraclitus' teaching at Ephesus[b] reminds us of his own picture of the soul that is too weak to follow the Universal motion, and falls away from it to take an individual shape. The very multiplicity of his symbolism seems to have contributed to this result; each disciple interpreting the whole theory by the figure which was most intelligible to himself: one fastening on the Fire, another on the Sun, another on the dry exhalation, another on the more abstract Righteousness, or the ruling Mind, while some appear to have seized upon his habit of teaching by strange outward signs, if there be any truth in what Aristotle gravely asserts, that Cratylus at length only moved his finger. These divided members of Heraclitus continued after him a partial and spasmodic life, and the system ended consistently in a kind of war.

---

[a] Perhaps the two passages in which this appreciation appears most distinctly are, Sophist. 242: ἀσφαλέστερον γὰρ (sc. τὸ ὂν) δεῖ συραίνειν, φασὶν οἱ συντονώτεροι τῶν Μουσῶν, (with which contrast Sympos. 187, where the saying is explained away,) and Cratyl. 411: ἔστι γὰρ ἡγουμένοις τὸ τῶν ὄντων ἰέναι πάντα, τὸ μὲν πολὺ αὐτοῦ ὑπολαμβάνουσι τοιοῦτόν τι εἶναι, οἷον οὐδὲν ἄλλο ἢ χωρεῖν, διὰ δὲ τούτου παντὸς εἶναί τι διϊόν, δι' οὗ πάντα τὰ γιγνόμενα γίγνεσθαι. εἶναι δὲ τάχιστον τοῦτο καὶ λεπτότατον· οὐ γὰρ ἂν δύνασθαι ἄλλως διὰ τοῦ ὄντος ἰέναι παντός, εἰ μὴ λεπτότατόν τε ἦν, ὥστε αὐτὸ μηδὲν στέγειν, καὶ τάχιστον, ὥστε χρῆσθαι ὥσπερ ἑστῶσι τοῖς ἄλλοις. ἐπεὶ δ' οὖν ἐπιτροπεύει τὰ ἄλλα πάντα διαϊόν κ.τ.λ.

[b] This may be illustrated by the continuation of the passage of the Cratylus just quoted, λέγει μὲν οὖν ἴσως, ὦ γε δὴ Ἑλλήνων, παρὰ πολλὰ ἐμολογοῦται τοῦτο εἶναι τὸ δίκαιον. ἐγὼ δὲ, ὦ Ἐρμόγενες, ἅτε λιπαρὴς ὢν περὶ αὐτοῦ, ταῦτα μὲν πάντα διαπέπυσμαι ἐν ἀπορρήτοις. ὅτι τοῦτ' ἐστὶ τὸ δίκαιον καὶ τὸ αἴτιον—ὃ γὰρ γίγνεται, τοῦτ' ἐστὶ τὸ αἴτιον—καὶ Δία δὲ καλεῖν ἔφη τις τοῦτο ὀρθῶς ἔχειν διὰ ταῦτα. ἐπειδὰν δ' ἠρέμα αὐτοὺς ἐπανερωτῶ ἀτρέμα· Τί οὖν ποτ' ἔστιν, ὦ γαθὲ, δίκαιον, εἰ τοῦτο οὕτως ἔχει; δοκῶ τε ἤδη περαιτέρω τοῦ προσήκοντος ἐρωτᾶν καὶ ὑπὲρ τὰ ἐσκαμμένα ἅλλεσθαι. ἱκανῶς γάρ μέ φασι πεπύσθαι καὶ ἀκηκοέναι καὶ ἐπιχειροῦντες δὴ πληροῦν με ἄλλος ἄλλα λέγει, καὶ οὐκέτι συμφωνοῦσιν. ὁ μὲν γάρ τις φησιν τοῦτο εἶναι δίκαιον, τὸν ἥλιον· τοῦτον γὰρ μόνον διαϊόντα καὶ κάοντα ἐπιτροπεύειν τὰ ὄντα. ἐπειδὰν οὖν τῳ λέγω αὐτὸ ἅσμενος ὡς καλόν τι ἀκηκοώς, καταγελᾷ μου οὗτος ἀκούσας καὶ ἐρωτᾷ, εἰ οὐδὲν δίκαιον οἶμαι εἶναι ἐν τοῖς ἀνθρώποις, ἐπειδὰν ὁ ἥλιος δύῃ. λιπαροῦντος οὖν ἐμοῦ ὅ τι αὖ ἐκεῖνος λέγει, οὐδὲν τὸ πῦρ φησὶ· τοῦτο δὲ οὐ ῥᾴδιόν ἐστιν εἰδέναι. ὁ δὲ οὐκ αὐτὸ τὸ πῦρ φησὶν, ἀλλ' αὐτὸ τὸ θερμὸν τὸ ἐν τῷ πυρὶ ἐνόν. ὁ δὲ τούτων μὲν πάντων καταγελᾶν φησὶν, εἶναι δὲ τὸ δίκαιον ὃ λέγει Ἀναξαγόρας, νοῦν εἶναι τοῦτο. αὐτοκράτορα γὰρ αὐτὸν ὄντα καὶ οὐδενὶ μεμιγμένον πάντα φησὶν αὐτὸν κοσμεῖν τὰ πράγματα διὰ πάντων ἰόντα. ἐνταῦθα δὴ ἐγώ, ὦ φίλε, πολὺ ἐν πλείονι ἀπορίᾳ εἰμὶ ἢ πρὶν ἐπιχειρῆσαι μανθάνειν περὶ τοῦ δικαίου, ὅ τί ποτ' ἔστιν.

INTRODUCTION.   xlv

But its influence on the other side of the Ægean was far greater, and by warring with other ideas it renowed its vitality. As was fitting, however, before finding its true place in the Platonic Philosophy (see especially the Parmenides), it was bound again in the prison of sense, and made to fight the battle of Opinion against the reigning ideal system. Whether or not Protagoras, and after him the Cyrenaics, openly made the Heraclitean dogma the basis of their scepticism, it is certain that Plato, and probable that Euclides also, regarded this as its only real philosophical support[c].

The peculiarity of the traces of Heraclitus in the Theætetus is, that his doctrine is there brought forward in support of a subjective theory; that its influence is partly direct, partly derived through his Ephesian followers, and (possibly) through Aristippus; and that it is carried to its remotest consequences by being subjected to the Socratic or Megarian logic. He thus becomes merely the representative of the principle of the perpetual flux of all things, and their absolute diversity, in opposition to the perfect rest and unity of the Eleatic Being:—the notion that, as it is put in the Phædo, like the tides in the Euripus, all things are ever coming and going, and swaying up and down and to and fro. Nothing *is*, everything is ever *becoming*. That this was a faithful representation of the theory in its later stages, appears from what Aristotle tells of Cratylus, that he found fault with Heraclitus' maxim: δὶς εἰς τὸν αὐτὸν ποταμὸν οὐκ ἂν ἐμβαίης· αὐτὸς γὰρ ᾤετο οὐδ' ἅπαξ.

The passage which most distinctly recalls Heraclitus himself, is that in which this doctrine of 'becoming' (γένεσις) is first stated and confirmed by proofs, though even this is perhaps coloured by the 'disciples of Protagoras.'

The quotations from the poets (whom the early philosophers despised [παλαιά τις διαφορὰ φιλοσοφίᾳ τε καὶ ποιητικῇ]) and the subtile illustrations from natural and mental phenomena (contrast Heraclitus' "The drunkard has a wet soul") belong rather to the refined philosophers whom Plato is quoting (or to his own invention) than to the prophet of Ephesus. But the mention of the fire which begets and rules all else, and is itself created by motion, is thoroughly Heraclitean, and the

[c] Τὴν λεγομένην αὐτῶν ἀλήθειαν γένεσιν ἀπ' οὐσίας ὑπεστηριγμένοι φερομένην τινά. Plat. Soph.

xlvi   INTRODUCTION.

word περιφορά (which occurs again p. 181) is perhaps used, together with the symbol of the Sun, not without reference to the circling process of the elements[d], the ὁδὸς ἄνω κάτω μία, which would be reversed if the diurnal motion were interrupted, καὶ γίνοιτ᾽ ἂν τὸ λεγόμενον ἄνω κάτω πάντα. Cf. Simpl. in Arist. Categ. p. 105 b. Bas.: Εἰ γὰρ τὸ ἕτερον τῶν ἐναντίων ἐπιλείποι, οἴχοιτο ἂν πάντα ἀφανισθέντα. διὸ καὶ μέμφεται Ὁμήρῳ Ἡράκλειτος, εἰπόντι,

ὡς ἔρις ἔκ τε θεῶν ἔκ τ᾽ ἀνθρώπων ἀπόλοιτο,

οἰχήσεσθαι γάρ, φησι πάντα[e].

In the fuller statement of the doctrine of sense, p. 156, the obscure words (rendered more obscure by the interpolation of Cornarius) regarding the comparative swiftness and slowness of the different motions, are probably to be explained in connection with Heraclitus. Sensation is a process between opposites (ποιοῦν and πάσχον). If we imagine it under the image of the ὁδὸς ἄνω κάτω, the process is higher, and therefore swifter than the things between which it moves[f]; they may be contrasted as fire and earth, as the sun and the cloud, as mind and body. (In this case the process itself has an objective and subjective element). E. g. man and stone are slow motions and of the nature of earth, but vision and whiteness are swifter and more of the nature of fire. In modern language, they have a higher power or law[g]. There is probably some intermediate

[d] See Lassalle, II. 114 n. j. 119.
[e] The image of the 'golden chain' is differently applied by Milton, Par. L. B. II. l. 1004 (Chaos loq.)

Another World
Hung o'er my realm, linked in a golden chain
To that side Heaven from whence your legions fell.

Ib. l. 1051:—
And fast by, hanging in a golden chain,
This pendant world.

[f] Cf. Hensel. fr.: Ἐφαπτοί νόοι καὶ ψυχολογικὴ application of the idea παρχόντων. of 'quicker' and 'slower' elements,
[g] Shakespeare has made a fanciful in Sonnets 44, 45.

But ah! thought kills me that I am not thought
To leap large lengths of miles when thou art gone,
But that, so much of earth and water wrought,
I must attend time's leisure with my moan;
Receiving nought by elements so slow,
But heavy tears, badges of either's woe.

The other two, slight air and purging fire,
Are both with thee, wherever I abide;
The first my thought, the other my desire,

INTRODUCTION.

refinement upon Heraclitus which would more completely illustrate the words of Plato. But their interpretation is certainly assisted by a nearer acquaintance with the Heraclitean theory.

In p. 157 the following words forcibly recal Heraclitus: ἀλλὰ κατὰ φύσιν φθέγγεσθαι γιγνόμενα καὶ ποιούμενα καὶ ἀπολλύμενα καὶ ἀλλοιούμενα.

And in p. 158 the doubt raised about waking and dreaming reminds us of one of his favourite reflections: τοὺς δ᾽ ἄλλους ἀνθρώπους λανθάνει ὅκοσα ἐγερθέντες ποιοῦσιν ὅκωσπερ ὅκοσα εὕδοντες ἐπιλανθάνονται.

θάνατός ἐστιν ὅκοσα εὕδοντες ὁρέομεν ὅσα δὲ ἐγερθέντες, ὕπνος.

In one other passage, where there is no direct allusion to him, an expression occurs which is eminently descriptive of his mind: p. 173.

τὸ σῶμα μόνον ἐν τῇ πόλει κεῖται αὐτοῦ καὶ ἐπιδημεῖ, ἡ δὲ διάνοια, ταῦτα πάντα ἡγησαμένη σμικρὰ καὶ οὐδέν, ἀτιμάσασα πανταχῇ φέρεται κατὰ Πίνδαρον, [τᾶς] τε γᾶς ὑπένερθε, καὶ τὰ ἐπίπεδα γεωμετροῦσα, οὐρανοῦ τε ὕπερ ἀστρονομοῦσα, καὶ πᾶσαν πάντη φύσιν ἐρευνωμένη τῶν ὄντων ἑκάστου ὅλου, εἰς τῶν ἐγγὺς οὐδὲν αὑτὴν συγκαθιεῖσα [b].

When the doctrine of motion is again taken up and criticised in pp. 180 sqq. the more immediate reference is to the Ephesian followers of Heraclitus, the humorous account of whom has been already noticed. They are compelled to state more distinctly what is meant by motion, and to acknowledge that it comprises not only locomotion (which has hitherto been spoken of, though in a vague sense), but also change. This agrees with what Aristotle says, that the Heracliteans had nowhere defined their principle of motion[1]. The *elenchus* is therefore

> These present-absent with swift motion slide.
> For when these quicker elements are gone
> In tender embassy of love to thee,
> My life being made of four, with two alone,
> Sinks down to death, oppressed with melancholy;
> Until life's composition be recured
> By those swift messengers returned from thee,
> Who even but now come back again, assured
> Of thy fair health, recounting it to me:
> This told, I joy; but then no longer glad,
> I send them back again, and straight grow sad.

[b] Cf. Rep. 496: Ἦ ἐν σμικρῷ πολιτείᾳ ὅταν μεγάλης ψυχῆς φυῂ καὶ ἀτιμάσασα τὰ τῆς πόλεως θεωρίᾳ.

[1] Phys. Auscult. VIII. 3 § 3: Πρὸς οὖν, καίπερ οὐ διορίζονται ποίαν κίνησιν λέγουσιν ἢ πάσας, οὐ χαλεπὸν ἀπαντῆσαι.

here applied to them, and their doctrine is exploded by being precisely stated.

Lastly, it should be noticed that the conception of λόγος, with which the Theætetus closes, has no connexion with the technical and objective use of the word in the Heraclitean system; it is rather employed in a Megarian, i. e. a semi-Eleatic sense, not without a trace of the definitions of Socrates. This appears from the opening of the Sophista. With Heraclitus, ὄνομα and λόγος were symbolical expressions for the same thing.

Parmenides.

II. The sublime thought of the Eternal movement of an infinite law was not, however, destined to be the final conception of the Greek mind. While life and death and the succession of phenomena were thus idealized on the Eastern shores of the Ægean, a different, though parallel impulse was preparing elsewhere, it is said at Elea in Magna Græcia: an impulse equally if not more sublime, yet by itself no less incapable of giving rise to such a philosophy as Plato's. Xenophanes had already said—

"There is one God above all in heaven or earth, not like to mortals either in form or mind." "He is all sight, all thought, all hearing." "He even abides immoveable in one stay: nor does it become him to waver to and fro."

Inspired with this thought Parmenides rose at once into an ideal world of mind and being, not seeking there an explanation of the sensible universe, nor endeavouring to grasp its law, or idealize its continual process, but dwelling solely on the all-sufficient object of Absolute and Perfect Being. From the world in which his thought reposed, growth and decay were exiled far, into a region which Pure Being did not enter, a world of nothingness, which yet seemed to satisfy the minds of ordinary men, who trusted in the blindness of opinion and sense, and lived amongst contradictions. For in this lower world of opinion, opposite principles ever strove, light and darkness, heat and cold. But Pure Being is one, a rounded whole, perfect and full, identical with the Absolute Mind. The only symbol of Parmenides is the Perfect Sphere.

The main effort of Plato's dialectic, as is well known, is to bring these opposite poles of thought, the Eleatic and Ionian, into organic and well-balanced harmony. In its most abstract

INTRODUCTION. xlix

conception it is the problem of the one and the many (τῶν λόγων ἀγῶνας πάθος παρ' ἡμῖν), or of motion and rest. In this effort he was assisted by the Pythagoreans, who had already found a sort of middle term in number.

The doctrine of Parmenides does not enter directly into the Theaetetus, from which the discussion of it is expressly excluded: but his influence is notwithstanding present in the Megarian method, which was in part derived from Zeno (see above), in whose hands the One had acquired a negative power, and was used rather to distinguish than to comprehend, so becoming rather the form than the sole object of thought. This Eleatic influence appears chiefly (1) in the relentless way in which sensation and motion are reduced to nothingness, and because they have no unity are shown to present no object to the mind: (2) in the crowning point of the dialogue, where it is admitted that there are universal perceptions of pure mind, and that Being is the principal of these: (3) in the paradox about false opinion, which is similar to that of Zeno about motion,—not 'it is impossible for a thing to be in two places at once,' but 'it is impossible to know and not to know at the same time,'—and is solved in the same way by reverting to the conception of degrees: (4) in the form of argument with which this paradox is enforced, ὁ ἕν γέ τι ὁρῶν ὄν τι ὁρᾷ: (5) in the question about the whole and its parts, pp. 203, 204.

But it is rather in the objective side of Plato's teaching that the doctrine of Parmenides and Zeno is examined and brought to bear.

III. Protagoras, who gives to the inquiry in the Theaetetus its subjective turn, and some part of its dramatic interest, had died at the age of seventy, some ten or twelve years before the trial of Socrates, which is the supposed date of the conversation. The real share borne by him in the dialogue is less than appears at first sight. It is to his "disciples" that the doctrine of sense based on that of motion is attributed, and though he is made to bear the brunt of the attack, because the guardians whom he has left will not defend his "orphan" theory, yet when challenged to meet him upon his own ground, Socrates falls back upon the saying quoted at first, "Man is the measure of all things," and the explanation of it, "Things are to

Protagoras.

g

INTRODUCTION.

me as they appear to me, and to you as they appear to you." The same words occur also in the Cratylus. This, then, is all that we can with any certainty point to in this dialogue as Protagorean, except the name of his treatise 'Αλήθεια, the sceptical fragment about the existence of the gods, and perhaps one or two rhetorical words, such as μεγαλειοτέρως, πολυδρατος. For it is evident that the doctrine of motion and becoming, which he is said to have entrusted to his disciples "in a mystery," (cf. Cratyl. p. 413. quoted above, p. xliv. n. b), cannot have been extant in his writings. It is therefore surprising to find Sextus Empiricus representing the tenets of Protagoras in language closely resembling that used in the Theætetus. The wonder is abated, however, if we reflect that there was really a very close affinity between Protagoras and the Cyrenaics, and that of this affinity Plato is in this dialogue the interpreter. Aristotle follows Plato in identifying the theories of Protagoras and Horaclitus. And there are thus three sources, independent of Protagoras, from which the account of Sextus may have been derived: the Cyrenaics, the Theætetus, and Aristotle. The similarity of the language in which different sensationalist theories are described in later times may possibly indicate the influence of this very dialogue in fixing the terminology of that section of thought.

It is therefore the more interesting to examine the one saying of Protagoras which is here preserved: πάντων χρημάτων μέτρον ἄνθρωπον εἶναι, τῶν μὲν ὄντων ὡς ἔστι, τῶν δὲ μὴ ὄντων ὡς οὐκ ἔστι. Might not this seem at first sight to imply something less than the absolute relativeness of knowledge? Might it not even be interpreted to mean, "quod semper, quod ubique, quod ab omnibus?" In answer to this it may be remarked, first, that Protagoras appears so far at least to have interpreted his own saying, ὡς οἷα μὲν ἐμοὶ φαίνεται, τοιαῦτα μὲν ἔστιν ἐμοί, οἷα δὲ σοί, τοιαῦτα δὲ σοί. But it may be added, secondly, that the distinction between the race and the individual, between the general term "man," and the singular term "this man," was probably not distinctly present to his mind. When we reflect on the absence of any abiding consciousness of the universal and of the distinction between abstract and concrete, exhibited, for instance, in the first answer of Theætetus, or in the attempt of Meno to define virtue, it

INTRODUCTION.

becomes evident that the term *man*, thus barely used by a popular teacher, would naturally call up the idea, not of human nature or of the human mind, nor of the race collectively, but of "a man," "this or that man," an individual, "you or me," not however conceived of as an individual, nor consciously distinguished from any abstract or generic notion of man, but simply present to the imagination. [Cf. τοῦ ἀνθρώπου, Thuc. I. 140, which does not correspond to the modern generic use of the word.]

Protagoras saw that men were weary of systems which had no reference to human life, and seemed to make knowledge unattainable. He saw persons teaching astronomy and the nature of Being to those who wanted to learn how to become able and successful citizens. Like other popular teachers, he had a keener eye for the immediate wants of those who came to him than for the truth, of which, however, he is not to be supposed a careless lover. The theory of Parmenides, which had its warm advocates at Athens, was one purely objective; although beginning and ending in the mind, it was wholly independent of any human standard: the highest aim for man was to rise by pure thought into the world of being.

Protagoras felt, like Socrates, that the truth which man requires is relative to man, but, unlike Socrates, he made this the end and not the starting-point of his inquiry, and instead of searching by reflection for that one truth by which man ought to live, he was contented with inferring that truth was variable, according to the common notion, "many men, many minds."

From the pit of scepticism into which Philosophy was thus in danger of being lowered, the impulse given by Socrates to speculative inquiry rescued it, and by vindicating the unity of truth, and the importance of the search for it to human life, gave to the old philosophies their true weight and significance through the Dialectic of Plato.

As embodied in the Theætetus, however, the above doctrine receives some fresh characteristics, first as being made the type of a contemporary theory, and being interwoven with that of Heraclitus; secondly, as holding one side of an antithesis, which gives a sharpness and precision to the term ἄνθρωπος, as equivalent to ἕκαστος ἡμῶν, which it probably had not when first used; and, thirdly, by being pushed to its minutest results, according to the Megarian method,—not only 'man' but 'each man,' not only so, but 'every creature,' and even the same person at different times.

Gorgias. The name of Gorgias (of Leontini, who flourished B. C. 480, and is said to have been alive at the death of Socrates) does not appear in the Theætetus, and there is no distinct allusion to him. But his denial of absolute Knowledge and Being[1], in which he was followed by Antisthenes, finds a place in the indirect refutation of Protagoras' assertion of relative truth. The passages in which this appears most distinctly have been already noticed (Theæt. pp. 161, 183.) He would also be included amongst the professors of rhetoric who busied themselves about such questions as, Is a King happy?

Other names which might be enlarged upon are those of Euthydemus (who seems to have been a still more worthy predecessor of Antisthenes) and Prodicus.

§ 4.

Socrates. But the person of Socrates is more interesting than any further scraps of theory. It is this which almost equally with the spirit of the author himself gives life and depth to what might otherwise be a barren conflict of opinion and method. From behind the ironical mask of the Elenchus, as preserved by Euclides, there peep forth characteristics of the man Socrates, which awake the reader's imagination, and rouse in him a kindred spirit of inquiry. The way in which this negative method is represented as a preparatory exercise, ridding the mind of the lumber of its crude notions, the humorous form in which this is expressed, the courteous, but relentless manner in which the method itself is followed, the eager interest shown in the development of a young mind, the kindly sympathy mixed with playful irony with which Theætetus is treated throughout: above all, the enthusiastic joy with which the acknowledgment is welcomed in one so young, that there is something which the mind itself perceives without the senses, belong to Socrates alone. The very soul of the representation is a part of him. Beneath the negative and destructive seeming

---

[1] οὐδὲν ἔστιν—εἰ καὶ ἔστιν, ἀκατάληπτον ἀνθρώπῳ—εἰ καὶ καταληπτόν, ἀλλὰ τοί γε ἀνέξοιστον καὶ ἀνερμήνευτον τῷ πέλας.—Sext. Emp. adv. Mathem. VII. 65.

INTRODUCTION.   liii

there is a sober earnestness of belief, which breaks out in such passages as that about the Divine life, a belief in the existence of truth somewhere, and in the all-importance of the search for it, which we feel to be due above all other men to Socrates. The very form of this inquiry, as consisting in self-questioning, which we associate with Socrates, is adverted to more than once (οὐ δυσκολαίνοντες, ἀλλὰ τῷ ὄντι ἡμᾶς αὐτοὺς ἐξετάζοντες— βασανίζωμεν δὴ αὐτὰ ἀναλαμβάνοντες, μᾶλλον δὲ ἡμᾶς αὐτούς.) The conception of a definition at once simple and exhaustive as the end to be attained by every inquiry, also belongs to him. Cf. Ar. Met. M. 1079 a. δύο γάρ ἐστιν ἅ τις ἂν ἀποδοίη Σωκράτει δικαίως, τούς τ' ἐπακτικοὺς λόγους καὶ τὸ ὁρίζεσθαι καθόλου. ταῦτα γάρ ἐστιν ἄμφω περὶ ἀρχὴν ἐπιστήμης.

It deserves to be noticed here that critics have found in the picture of the dwarfed, shrewd, practical spirit, an allusion to Lycon, or to some other of the enemies of Socrates, as they have seen in the contrasted image of the philosophic life, partly a praise of Socrates, partly a trace of Plato's residence at Megara.

The person of Theætetus is also an important element. *Theætetus.* Whether or not, as seems probable, the dialogue contains a tribute of affection to a friend and pupil who was no more, the reader is certainly intended to dwell with admiring interest upon his character. His dangerous state is the subject of the most anxious solicitude to the persons who meet us on the threshold: they say of him that he has fulfilled the promise of Socrates, who augured most nobly of his future; and presently we are invited to view his portrait as a youth by the hand of his own master Theodorus, who ascribes to him the very combination of qualities described by Plato in his Republic as the ideal of the philosophic nature. We find Socrates in love with his mind at first sight, and still more delighted with him as the argument proceeds.—Theætetus is described by later writers as a great mathematician, who taught at Heraclea, after the times of the Peloponnesian war, and as the author of the first treatise on the five regular solids; and is said to have heard Socrates and to have been the companion of Plato. The latter fact may possibly have been derived from this dialogue, but it is at least natural to identify the persons, especially from the aptness for mathematics shown by the youth at the opening of the inquiry. If we are right in doing so, a passage in the Republic (p. 518.) acquires a fresh interest from the fact mentioned above, that Theætetus wrote the first treatise on the regular solids. When Plato says that the geometry of solids is yet in its infancy, but that he does not despair of its being discovered, we are tempted to suspect an allusion to the labours of his friend [u].

What have we then in Theætetus? A youth, whom, as the Eleatic Stranger in the Sophist afterwards remarks, no corruption of sophistry could long withhold from the belief in true ideas and the endeavour to grasp them, but full of perplexity and wonder (a proof of this very impulse) at the conflict between common sense, sceptical difficulties, and speculative enquiry, which he heard waged around him, and which found an echo within his mind. Yet until encouraged and helped by Socrates, he is unable to state his opinion on an abstract question, except in a subject which he has systematically studied, viz. geometry, in which he and his fellow-pupil have lately with some labour arrived at a generalised expression. But in this and in the other special studies which he has pursued, his master Theodorus has found in him qualities which are rarely combined, acuteness and gravity, gentleness and courage, a mind unruffled, rapid and unerringly successful in its application to learning and inquiry; and a spirit of generosity unaffected by reverses of fortune.

Theætetus, though a mere boy, is the most desirable of pupils for Philosophy, both as possessing all the requirements of the philosophic nature, and because without being yet irrevocably devoted to any special pursuit, he amply fulfils the condition, μηδεὶς ἀγεωμέτρητος εἰσίτω. (See Rep. B. vii.)

Theodorus. The choice of Theodorus as an interlocutor (not to dwell upon the tradition that Plato had studied under him) connects itself with the same belief in the importance of geometry as an introduction to dialectic, though in Theodorus it had not led to this result. Theodorus is also (as already noticed) of Cyrene, the town of Aristippus, and professes himself a friend of Protagoras.

§ 3.

Such appear to be the external elements of the Theætetus;

[u] Although there may be also an allusion to the Conic Sections, which were discovered in Athens about this time.

INTRODUCTION.

possessing also a more general interest because they supply us with indications of the influences which had surrounded Plato himself, the phases of thought by which his mind had been attracted or repelled, and with some of which it had been perhaps almost identified; but to each of which he could now assign its due place and value in the progress of the mind towards true ideas, or, to use his own image, in its conversion out of the dark cave and prison of sense to mount upwards towards the world of Being.

It is not enough to have taken a work like this to pieces. That is only a step towards viewing it as a whole.

1. After a preface in which the Megarian tendency of the dialogue is indicated, a youth of philosophic genius is brought into contact with the prophet of Greek thought. The mind of the youth is not "a sheet of blank paper," for besides the ordinary μουσική and γυμναστική, he has been instructed by Theodorus in geometry and other sciences, and has been stimulated to inquiry by hearing the report of questions raised by Socrates, while he is dizzy with wonder at the contradictions in common language and ideas pointed out by other teachers (compare the state of Glaucon in the Republic). But though anxious he is wholly unable to give a simple and comprehensive (i. e. abstract and general) definition of knowledge.

The Argument.

Socrates, therefore, approaches him in his character of man-midwife, professing no wisdom of his own, but only the power of bringing to the birth the minds of young men labouring with new thoughts, and of determining afterwards whether the birth be real or imaginary. Under this curious symbol there is expressed not only Plato's theory of education, which recurs in the figure of the cave and elsewhere, but also the consciousness of that which distinguishes this dialogue, and in a less degree other parts of Plato. Although it would be too much to say that he possessed the idea of the History of Philosophy in the modern sense, he approaches more nearly to it than any ancient writer except Aristotle. No one but Plato could have conceived and executed the design of showing the relation of different theories to each other, and the order of their succession, by representing them as gradually developed in an individual mind. Each theory, though negatived, is not annihilated, it has a real importance assigned to it as a stage in the progress of the human intellect. This power of tracing the evolution of thought Plato preserved from Socrates, while he retained the negative elenchus in common with Euclides. The union of both is expressed in the above metaphor, and characterises all that follows.

2. Theætetus' first real answer, "Knowledge is Sensation," though spontaneous at the moment, is the expression of a current theory, (that of the men called here "disciples of Protagoras," probably including Aristippus.)

Socrates finds in it the doctrine of Protagoras, "A man the measure of what is," which comes to this, Appearing is reality: for what appears to me, is to me.

But this is shown to have been only the popular side of a deeper doctrine, which is appealed to by the current theory, viz. that nothing exists, but all things are ever passing into their opposites, or in other words, Motion is the world. This is supported by all but universal consent, and by the testimony of Nature, (according to Heraclitean interpretation.)

The union of these two principles enables us to conceive of Sensation as a relative process. Each sensation or perception arises relatively both to the individual and to other sensations or perceptions.

Unless we admit that 'more' and 'less,' 'greater' and 'smaller,' are wholly relative, and are therefore subject to continual change, we shall contradict the self-evident axiom, that nothing can become more while it is equal to itself.

Theætetus' curiosity is now fully awakened, and he is prepared to receive a more complete statement of the doctrine, care being first taken not to let any of those 'profane' ones hear who believe only in things bodily, and not in the invisible process.

The motion which is the world is active and passive, and both kinds are infinite. From the perpetual conjunction of these there arise perpetually sensations and sensible things. The active and passive elements are slower, the twin births are swifter, for they flit to and fro between them. Not that the active and passive elements *are* anything, except as producing that which thus arises from them; nay, active may become passive, and *vice versâ*. Being therefore disappears, and all things become, and perish, and change. This applies to sorts

INTRODUCTION.   lvii

as well as to individual things. "Borne by the gale" of the argument, we even merge the Good and Noble in the universal flux.

Theætetus, however, does not rebel, and some further difficulties, occasioned by the phenomena of dreams, disease and madness, are triumphantly solved. Every such illusion is real to the subject of it at the moment. This appears most evidently in the case of the sick man's palate. At the same time the theory of a process between subject and object is more distinctly worked out. And the birth of Theætetus' first-born is pronounced complete.

3. To the surprise of Theodorus, Socrates now begins to criticise it.

The saying of Protagoras levels all distinctions as to wisdom, and makes argument absurd.

Theodorus is in vain challenged to reply to this, and Theætetus confesses himself staggered.

But Socrates again changes sides, and finds fault with the objection, as begging the question and daring to appeal to common sense.

The theory is, therefore, again examined in the form, Sensation is Knowledge.

After touching on the difficulty of sounds and characters heard and seen but not understood, Socrates dwells on the case of an object of sight remembered but not seen.

(As Theodorus still hangs back, Socrates acts the part of assailant and respondent in one.)

The advocate of sense is driven to admit that it is possible to know and not to know the same thing. He might be reduced many times even to worse extremities (and that on the ground he has himself chosen) by a merciless Eristic adversary.

Still a defence of Protagoras is possible. He is not bound to commit himself to the answers of Theætetus. Memory, he might say, is far inferior in vividness to the present impression. And it is by no means certain that he would have been afraid to admit that the same man may know and be ignorant of the same thing. Or rather he would deny that an individual viewed in different relations, or under different conditions, is the same man. But he would challenge us to prove directly either that sensation is not relative to the individual, or that, if it is relative to him, it does not follow that the object of it is real to him and to him only.

h

Differences of wisdom there assuredly are both in individuals and states, and in plants also, but they are differences not in the reality, but in the excellence of impressions, customs, or conditions. To alter these from worse to better is the work of the wise teacher or statesman or husbandman. In conclusion Protagoras would demand fair treatment, as the contrary leads only to the hatred of inquiry.

4. That his demand may be complied with, Theodorus is at length 'compelled' to engage, and Protagoras' own words are selected for criticism, no advantage being taken even of the admission, that there are degrees of wisdom, which was made in his name.

'What seems to each is true for him.' It seems to all men that some think truly and some falsely. This was the drift of our appeal to common sense. It follows that whether Protagoras is right or wrong, some think truly and some falsely.

Further, if Protagoras' saying is true for him, it is false for all men besides. But he confirms their judgment who say that he himself thinks falsely and they truly. His saying then is true for nobody.

5. The weight of his authority still makes us pause. But one thing is clear, that the strength of the theory we are considering lies in the region of sense, and, as regards the state, in the sphere of law and custom;—if it gives way at any point, it is in the decision of such questions as, What is wholesome? What is expedient? A partial Protagoreanism, relinquishing the latter ground, but still maintaining the former, seems to have been held by some.

—— The magnitude of the question that is thus stirred up reminds us of the blessedness of the life which has leisure for such inquiries. The digression which follows at once affords a rest, and by the elevation of its tone prepares the mind for the higher thoughts which are in reserve. It is of itself a sufficient answer to those who restrict the idea of Truth to particular impressions,—pointing upwards to the pattern in the Heavens and onwards to the life beyond the grave.—We proceed to apply the test indicated above. Even those who assert that what is Lawful is purely conventional dare not seriously assert this of what is Good.

To put the same admission more generally. In every judgment which, like the calculation of expediency, regards the Future, there is the possibility of error. Even if we make the impression of the moment the test of what is true, that impression, when the moment comes, proves one man to have been right in his anticipation and another wrong. This is practically admitted by Protagoras himself, whenever he gives advice to a young speaker.

6. An inroad is thus made into the enemy's territory, but his last stronghold is not yet taken. We have found something independent of sensation, but the "truth" of sensation itself is not yet overthrown. The Heraclitean principle of motion is therefore grappled with. For its Ephesian supporters give us no hold. Theodorus describes the wavering mysticism of these modern Heracliteans, "no friends of his." And Socrates resumes what was said at first of the antiquity of the doctrine, adding that there have been a few who, like Parmenides, have stood out against it, and that our present position is the dangerous middle-ground between two armies. Before closing with the slippery "movement party" we arm ourselves by distinguishing two kinds of motion: locomotion and change. They must admit that all things move in both these ways, or else there would be a way in which they stood still. In the former statement of the theory, sensation and quality were described as flitting between object and subject. But now at the same time that they flit, they must also change. Therefore in the very moment when we are naming them they have become different. Every name is therefore false as well as true: e. g. When I say sensation is Knowledge, it is equally true to say Not-sensation, i. e. according to the theory, Not-Knowledge. Thus the boasted Infinity of Motion becomes the indeterminateness, i. e. the nothingness of Sense. Every thing is nothing in particular.

7. We are now wholly free from Protagoras and from the doctrine of motion. But instead of advancing at once to examine Parmenides, Socrates proceeds with the main argument, and Theodorus is accordingly released. The truth is, there is still some intermediate ground to travel. We have risen above sensation, but the problems connected with Opinion as such (δόξα, as independent of αἴσθησις) remain to be solved.

Theætetus must first be made conscious of the existence of pure acts of thought. To this consciousness he rises easily,

INTRODUCTION.

when, reverting to sensation for a moment, Socrates proves to him that the eye and ear are only the instruments of the mind. There are some ideas common to the objects of different senses, which are perceived concerning them without any such instrument. These the mind itself, reviewing the impressions of sense, immediately contemplates. 'Being' is the most general of them, and is found in company with all the rest. They include also that perception of what is good, to which reference has been already made.

The enthusiasm with which this acknowledgment is welcomed marks it as the highest point actually gained in the dialogue. It is with this that the more advanced teaching of the Sophists immediately connects itself.

The contrast between the contemplation of these ideas by the mind, and the particular impressions of the senses, throws the latter still further into the shade, and we no longer cast our glances backwards, but advance eagerly as into a new-found world.

We examine opinion, not now as it is bound up with sense, but as the pure act of the mind.

8. But all our efforts to grasp the idea of knowledge here only tend to show that Opinion like sensation is indeterminate.

Protagoras said that all men think rightly. This we interpreted to mean that sense is knowledge, and disposed of it rather summarily by a 'reductio ad absurdum.' But the same difficulty now returns upon us in a more abstract form. How is false opinion possible? Considered quite in the abstract, it seems impossible. For whenever we think, our thought is known to us, and real. Or, if thinking be a silent proposition, it seems impossible that we should join two ideas wrongly when both are clearly present to the mind.

We must descend again from this region of pure thought, and have recourse to the conception of degrees of knowledge and of a process between the mind and sensible things. [For otherwise (as Aristotle says) Thought is like a straight line passing over things, not like a curve embracing them.] False opinion will thus be the failure of the mind in bringing together the impressions of sensation and memory. But it is shown by an example that it is possible to mistake between two things, both of which are laid up in the mind. Therefore we must conceive of a more subtle process between the mind and its own ideas, which it may possess without actually grasping them at any particular time. But when we look steadily at the image we have called up we find that the same difficulty returns. The mind is ignorant of that which is present to it. For, if I have grasped the wrong idea, how do I not know it for what it is? or if an unreal one, how, when I have grasped it, do I not know it to be unreal? The succession of such images must be continued to infinity.

The lesson drawn from this is, that we cannot define false opinion until we have defined knowledge. I. e. Opinion in its own nature is wholly Indeterminate. This is evident at once, if we examine true opinion. An opinion without any real grounds may yet happen to be true.

9. This leads the way to the last unsuccessful effort to define knowledge from the subjective side. Something more than true opinion is required to constitute knowledge. What is that 'something more?' The answer is ready. Knowledge is true opinion with an account of its object ($\mu\epsilon\tau\grave{a}$ $\lambda\acute{o}\gamma o\nu$). The mind surveying its impressions (see above) cannot give an account of the individual objects of sense; it can only name them; but the complex ideas of the various relations of those are expressed in propositions. These therefore alone are the objects of knowledge. Or, more physically, the elements of all things cannot be known, but the combination of these in Nature is the object of Knowledge.

This theory is first tested in the case of letters and syllables, from which it seems to have been derived. The elementary sounds certainly cannot be analysed, but are they therefore unknown? If separately unknown how are they known together? Is the complex independent of its elements? Can a whole be thus conceived of without its parts? If, as appears probable, the expressions, for instance, 'all the six,' 'all of the six,' and 'the whole of the six,' ($\tau\grave{a}$ $\pi\acute{a}\nu\tau a$, $\tau\grave{o}$ $\pi\tilde{a}\nu$, $\tau\grave{o}$ ὅλον,) are synonymous, and the whole cannot be considered as separable from its parts, then, if the syllable is known, so are its constituent sounds. The simple is equally known with the complex. But if the whole differs from the all, and is separable from its parts, then it is one and uncompounded, that is, a new element. The complex is equally unknown with the simple. Experience points to the former alternative. In learning grammar or music, we did not know the combinations until after we had learned the letters or notes.

lxii   INTRODUCTION.

[In this conclusion a kind of reality seems to be again awarded to the objects of sense, not as they give rise to ever varying impressions, but as they are perceived by the mind, which imparts to each of them its own stamp of unity. At the same time ideas of relation are shown to have as much and as little reality as simple ideas, and in the μία ἰδέα ἀμέριστος a glimpse is afforded of the transcendent ideal world. If we compare the Sophist, Philebus and Republic, Plato's doctrine appears here in a rudimentary form. He wavers between abstract and concrete, the one and the many. The necessity is not yet felt of finding an expression for the relation between the ideal and actual.]

10. But, though this theory is rejected, the above definition of knowledge may still be true. What is the 'account' (λόγος) required in it? It cannot be the mere reflexion of thought in language. For this power is possessed by all men. Nor is it the analysis of the complex by the enumeration of its elements. For this may be done rightly in one case and wrongly in another where the elements are the same. But knowledge is infallible. Nor, lastly, is it, what seems plausible at first sight, the comprehension of the distinctive difference. For this is essential to right opinion. And if it is meant that we must have knowledge, and not opinion merely, of the distinctive difference, the term knowledge still remains to be defined.

What then is the result of the inquiry? The answer is simply that given by Socrates, The mind of Theætetus is prepared for better things. Difficulties have been undoubtedly raised, such as Plato really felt, and which were silenced rather than solved by the contemplation of the Idea of Good; (e. g. the difficulty about false opinion.) Hypotheses have been advanced which he knew to be really valuable, and the equivalents of which have frequently satisfied the human mind, (e. g. the hypothesis expressed in the figure of the waxen block.) But Plato does not rest in these uncertainties, and is by no means satisfied. Nor is it by any means his intention to point out the hopelessness of the attempt to define Knowledge. What he does point out is the impossibility of conceiving Knowledge apart from its object. The perception of the existence of Ideas of Being and Goodness, of sameness and difference, likeness and unlikeness, and of number, which is just touched upon, is the first step towards the construction of that transcendental

INTRODUCTION. lxiii

world, the contemplation of which, in the light of the Idea of Good, is Knowledge according to Plato's highest conception of it (ἐν τῷ γνωστῷ τελευταία ἡ τοῦ ἀγαθοῦ ἰδέα). Whether or not he had attained to this when the Theætetus was written, (he had probably advanced some way towards it), the fact is certain that he was not satisfied with any lower or less triumphant view. The meaning and the merits of that final theory do not fall under discussion here.

§ 6.

The genuineness of the Theætetus has never been seriously questioned. To put its authenticity in the strongest possible light, it stands or falls with the Republic. No difficulty that may arise in assigning to it its chronological position, or in reconciling special points of teaching or method, can countervail the inward harmony, the manifold coincidences of thought and style, the incommunicable grace and beauty, the intensity of inquiry relieved with ever present humour, which bind this and the other greater dialogues to the greatest, making them one living individual whole. Genuineness.

§ 7.

The comparative study of Plato's dialogues is of importance not so much as leading to a chronological arrangement, towards which little progress has been made, but rather as throwing light upon his manner of dealing with a subject and his mode of composition generally. There are fallacies incidental to the study of one dialogue, which the comparison of others will remove: extreme views are thus corrected, assertions modified, the unevenness of the whole surface becomes more evident, as well as the inherent unity, and we become more cautious in speaking of 'Plato's view' of this or that point; and also in taking literally his development of the tenets of this or that school. It becomes apparent too, on a wider survey, that more varieties of thought existed around Plato than we have names for, or than can be easily summed up in one or two formulæ. And at every step we become more convinced that no limit can be assigned to his fertility either of imagination or thought. Such a comparison is the natural and necessary test of every hypothesis regarding any single dialogue. Relation to other dialogues.

Schleiermacher linked the Theætetus and Gorgias as companion treatises: but when read without the bias of his peculiar scheme, they do not present features of very close relationship. The interest of the Gorgias is less philosophical and more dramatic, approaching even to comedy. In the Theætetus we breathe the serene atmosphere of friendship and peace; in the Gorgias, Socrates is engaged in his ironical warfare. The Gorgias annihilates rhetoric and the vulgar belief in success which was its food; the Theætetus is a criticism of scientific theories, preparing the way for serious philosophical inquiry. The Gorgias is written in the strain of the Euthydemus, Protagoras and Meno, and of the first and second books of the Republic; the tone of the Theætetus is nearer to that of the Philebus and Sophista, and of the sixth and seventh books of the Republic. The points of coincidence, and there are several, between the two dialogues, have as much of contrast as of resemblance. The vulgar notion of the philosopher, which in the Theætetus is treated with lofty scorn, in the Gorgias is represented with humourous zest. The same may be said of the weakness of rhetoric in philosophy; and the common incentives to action, which in the Theætetus are contemptuously dismissed, in the Gorgias are stated at length with ironical gravity. Much nearer points of comparison may be found in the Philebus, Cratylus, and Meno.

The Philebus presents the other aspect of the controversy between Euclides and Aristippus, the opposition namely between pleasure and wisdom taking the place of that between sensation and knowledge. But the combatants are viewed from an independent height, and the instruments by which decision is made and the question solved, are neither Cyrenaic nor Megarian, but chiefly Platonic, and partly Pythagorean. A detailed parallel and contrast would extend this essay to undue length, but would be useful in illustrating the difference between Plato's earlier and later method, and the growth of his psychology. Some light is also thrown by the Philebus on the manner in which Plato treats contemporaries as witnesses to a truth, for which he has himself found a fuller expression.

In the Cratylus Socrates is seen moderating between the modern Heraclitean and the Sophistical or conventional view of language: thus a point of opposition is found between the doctrines which are blended in the Theætetus.

The Heraclitean or 'natural' theory is ironically set forth at great length; and etymology is tortured so as to bear witness to the flux of all things. The account given in the Cratylus of the earlier and later Heraclitean dogmas has been already quoted. The Cratylus, after acknowledging that there is a conventional element in language, and that it may possibly have no better foundation than the theory of a flux, ends, like the Theætetus, with a sort of 'dream' of the Ideas.

The Meno opens with the difficulty which haunts us in the Theætetus, How can one inquire about what he does not know? It is there solved by the half-mythical hypothesis of Recollection, to which the slave is made to bear unconscious testimony. This seems to throw some light upon the words of the Theætetus (which appear to be partly set aside as the dialogue proceeds), "I leave out of sight the intermediate processes of learning and forgetting, as beside our present purpose." (p. 188.) The image of the waxen block, which seems to take up what is thus reserved, makes it appear doubtful whether these words are meant to hint at any further theory. But a Megarian philosopher would probably know how to distinguish between μανθάνειν and μαθεῖν, ἐπιλανθάνεσθαι and ἐπιλελῆσθαι. (p. 191.)

It is of more importance, however, to examine the nature of the connexion hinted by Plato himself between the Theætetus, Sophista and Politicus. There is much substantial correspondence between the Theætetus and Sophista, which may be regarded as complementary to each other. In the Theætetus Knowledge is reduced to its elements; the aim of the Sophista is to point out the inadequacy of analysis as a method of Knowledge, and to harmonize opposite ideas, Being and Not-Being, Rest and Motion. The one dialogue is the basis of Plato's subjective, the other of his objective teaching. Heraclitus and Protagoras are examined in the one, Parmenides is brought to the test in the other. The Theætetus dwells chiefly on mental processes, the Sophista chiefly on ideas. The one is concerned with Knowledge, the other with Being. The possibility of false opinion is the cardinal difficulty of the one: the existence of the non-existent is the corresponding source of perplexity in the other. The highest point touched in the former dialogue is that there are ideas which the mind

lxvi   INTRODUCTION.

itself contemplates unaided by sense, and which, it is hinted afterwards, have each of them an indivisible unity. These ideas or nobler elements are the foundation of the chief speculations in the latter. And the Megarian method of criticism which reigns almost unquestioned in the Theætetus, in the Sophista becomes criticised in its turn.

There is also an obvious bond of connexion between the Sophista and Politicus. The one is to the intellectual what the other is to the social and moral world. As the Sophist is to the Philosopher, so is the earthly Statesman to the true King.

But is there a common link, by which the three dialogues are bound in one? There is: and it is one which, though subtle, was probably regarded by Plato as of great importance. This is the gradual development in them of a dialectical method. Indeed, in the Politicus this is expressly spoken of as the chief thing, p. 286: νῦν ἡμῖν ἡ περὶ τοῦ πολιτικοῦ ζήτησις ἕνεκα αὐτοῦ τούτου προβέβληται μᾶλλον ἢ τοῦ περὶ πάντα διαλεκτικωτέρους γίγνεσθαι; A similar reason is given for the earnestness with which minute distinctions are pursued in the Sophist, p. 227: ἀλλὰ γὰρ τῇ τῶν λόγων μεθόδῳ σπογγιστικῆς ἢ φαρμακοποσίας οὐδὲν ἧττον οὐδέ τι μᾶλλον τυγχάνει μέλον, εἰ τὸ μὲν σμικρά, τὸ δὲ μεγάλα ἡμᾶς ὠφελεῖ καθαῖρον. τοῦ κτήσασθαι γὰρ ἕνεκα νοῦν πασῶν τεχνῶν τὸ ξυγγενὲς καὶ τὸ μὴ ξυγγενὲς κατανοεῖν πειρωμένη τιμᾷ πρὸς τοῦτο ἐξ ἴσου πάσας, καὶ θάτερα τῶν ἑτέρων κατὰ τὴν ὁμοιότητα οὐδὲν ἡγεῖται γελοιότερα, σεμνότερον δέ τι τὸν διὰ στρατηγικῆς ἢ φθειριστικῆς δηλοῦντα θηρευτικὴν οὐδὲν νενόμικεν, ἀλλ' ὡς τὸ πολὺ χαυνότερον. The same spirit of ironical disregard of the subject-matter in comparison of the method appears in the Theætetus, p. 174 (mingled with a deeper irony), where it is said that the philosopher regards a king as a species of herdsman. In the Theætetus also the Socratic element of this method is described under the image of μαιευτική.

It is easier to perceive the existence of such a dialectical growth in the three dialogues than to trace the exact steps by which it is developed.

The mere outline of it is perhaps the following. First, the consciousness arises that the aim of all inquiry is to find a simple and comprehensive conception of the thing in question, (ἓν, ἁπλοῦν—ἐπὶ εἶδος περιλαβεῖν—ἐπὶ λόγῳ προσειπεῖν.) As a means to this the Socratic questioning is set forth as the art of 'delivering' the mind. Then after the analysis of sensation, the mind is seen reviewing its sensations so as to arrive at general notions concerning them (ἀναλογίζεσθαι—συλλογισμός.) Further on, thought is described as a sort of question and answer within the mind (mental dialectic).

Again, the object of Knowledge appears first as a combination of unknown elements, then as a simple unity, then as a combination of which the elements are known, and lastly as a whole parted off from others by a distinguishing mark. With this conception of λόγος the Theaetetus ends. With the same assumption that Definition implies Division, the Sophistes opens. But presently it appears that these unities which are the objects of Knowledge (elementary ideas) are not fully known, until not only the differences but also the relations between them are perceived. I do not know This, until I acknowledge the existence of all that is Not-this. The existence even of that which is not must be acknowledged, as the condition of all existence. But in the Politicus it appears that this is not enough, but that the Other things from which the object of inquiry is distinguished, must not only be acknowledged as 'something different,' but must each be known in themselves, p. 281: πότερον οὖν ἡμῖν ὁ περὶ τῆς ὑφαντικῆς λόγος—ἱκανῶς ἔσται διωρισμένος, ἐὰν ἄρ' αὐτὴν τῶν ἐπιμελειῶν, ὁπόσαι περὶ τὴν ἐρεᾶν ἐσθῆτα εἰσί, τὴν καλλίστην καὶ μεγίστην πασῶν τιθῶμεν; (cf. Theaet. 208: ἥλιον πέρι ἱκανῶς οἴμαί σοι εἶναι ἀποδέξασθαι ὅτι τὸ λαμπρότατόν ἐστι τῶν κατὰ τὸν οὐρανὸν ἰόντων περὶ γῆν.) ἢ λέγωμεν μὲν ἄν τι ἀληθές, οὐ μὴν σαφές γε οὐδὲ τέλεον, πρὶν ἂν καὶ ταύτας αὐτῆς πάσας περιέλωμεν; This seems to be in advance of the method of dichotomy, and may be described as a sort of return to the concrete. Compare Philebus 16: μέχρι περ ἂν τὸ κατ' ἀρχὰς ἓν μὴ ὅτι καὶ πολλὰ καὶ ἄπειρά ἐστι μόνον ἴδῃ τις, ἀλλὰ καὶ ὁπόσα.

And while fulness of conception as well as logical exactness is thus shown to be essential to Knowledge, Plato also points out the usefulness of the argument from analogy in proceeding from the more known to the less known, and from the lower to the higher, p. 277: Χαλεπὸν ὦ δαιμόνιε, μὴ παραδείγμασι χρώμενον ἱκανῶς ἐνδείκνυσθαί τι τῶν μειζόνων. κινδυνεύει γὰρ ἡμῶν ἕκαστος οἷον ὄναρ εἰδὼς ἅπαντα πάντ' αὖ πάλιν ὥσπερ ὕπαρ ἀγνοεῖν. The method of comparison, which was rejected as insufficient in the simpler and lower sphere, is embraced as the means of entrance to the higher: and it is shewn to be the part of inquiry not only to separate between things near together, but also to detect resemblances in what is remote. A more minute investigation of the connexion thus briefly sketched would probably repay the student. A slightly different aspect of it has been seized by Professor Thomson. Camb. Phil. Tr. vol. X. pt. 1.

It remains under the present head to consider the relation of the Theaetetus to the account of knowledge which Plato gives in the Republic.

It has been common to speak of the Ideas of Plato as if they were the beginning and end of his philosophy; not only its consummation, but its foundation. But to see them as they were presented to him, we must learn to place ourselves behind them, and to regard them as a goal aimed at, but hardly reached. In the Theaetetus he traces some of the steps by which he had arrived so far. He leads us upwards from the dark valley of sense, into which however some light from the upper region is allowed to penetrate, and makes us feel the difficulty of the ascent. We are not lifted at once to an ideal height, from which we can look down upon the world (Sophist, p. 216, καθορῶντες ὑψόθεν τὸν τῶν κάτω βίον): every inch of advance is disputed, and we have the firm ground of experience beneath our feet.

Once, indeed, in the conversation with Theodorus, we are permitted to breathe the more serene air of the higher life, and mention is made of a Divine Pattern of goodness, to which the wise and righteous man becomes conformed. Compare Rep. B. IX. ad fin. 'Ἀλλ', ἦν δ' ἐγώ, ἐν οὐρανῷ ἴσως παράδειγμα ἀνάκειται τῷ βουλομένῳ ὁρᾶν καὶ ὁρῶντι ἑαυτὸν κατοικίζειν. The passage in which this occurs, in which mention is also made of the region of pure souls, is such as vividly to recal the Phaedo.

But in the argumentative part, we are led by slow and painful steps out of the limitations of sense, and to the last no attempt is made to extricate us from its conditions.

At first we are only permitted to distinguish each individual sensation from every other: though binding them together in bundles for the convenience of naming them. Presently perception and memory are shewn to be separable from sensation, but they are still occasioned by it. The "bonds" are further loosened by the observation that in judging of what is expedient for the future, the present impression of sense is worthless in comparison with reflection: but still the future is relative to the present and the past, and the test of past wisdom is the impression of the moment when it arrives. Theætetus now seizes the great truth that the mind does perceive some things, without the instrumentality of the senses; but still it perceives them as attributes of the objects of sense. Further inquiry is made into this process of the mind itself. It can think truly and also falsely. What difference is implied in this? An attempt is made to conceive this by reasoning from an abstract alternative (knowledge or ignorance, being or not being), but we are compelled to fall back upon the conception of a process between sensation and the recollection of former sensations, or between different abstractions of the world of sense laid up in the memory.

Lastly, there is allowed to float before the mind the thought of an abstract whole; first as consisting of the conbination of the indefinite elements of sensible things, then as an indivisible elementary unit arising out of them. But we are reminded that if the combination is known, then its elements must be known also. Yet the power of analysis is an inadequate test of knowledge. It is further requisite that the complete whole, which is the object of thought, be distinguished, by its characteristic difference, from every other.

The nearest approach that is made, in this gradual progress, to the doctrine of Ideas, consists in the acknowledgment that the mind in contemplating Being and Goodness is its own instrument, and in the conception raised for a moment and then relinquished, of the abstract whole ($\mu\dot{\eta}$ $\tau\dot{\alpha}$ $\sigma\tau o\iota\chi\epsilon\tilde{\iota}\alpha$, $\dot{\alpha}\lambda\lambda'$ $\dot{\eta}$ $\dot{\epsilon}\kappa\epsilon\dot{\iota}\nu\omega\nu$ $\dot{\epsilon}\nu$ $\tau\iota$ $\gamma\epsilon\gamma o\nu\dot{o}s$ $\epsilon\tilde{\iota}\delta os$, $\dot{\iota}\delta\dot{\epsilon}\alpha\nu$ $\mu\dot{\iota}\alpha\nu$ $\alpha\dot{\upsilon}\tau\dot{o}$ $\alpha\dot{\upsilon}\tau o\tilde{\upsilon}$ $\ddot{\epsilon}\chi o\nu$). These form the double summit of this ascent, 'rugged and steep,' through experience and reflection towards the ideal world, and upon these the etherial structure of Plato's transcendental philosophy reposes. In this dialogue the subjective height alone is fully reached. Being and Goodness are still seen as relative, and the mists of doubt soon close over the momentary glimpse of the purely abstract whole as the object of knowledge.

INTRODUCTION.

Yet the consciousness, clearly brought to light, of the indeterminateness, the changes and contradictions of sense and opinion (see Rep. pp. 476, 479, 524), the endeavour to find a resting-place from the merely relative view by the Socratic method of definition, the reflection upon different processes of geometry and arithmetic, the Megarian notion suggested by Zeno and Socrates of Being as the Good, the conception of a pure act of the mind, and the questions raised about the elements, are so many distinct movements in the direction of the Ideas.

The approach is only a partial one, however. Socrates, in the Theætetus, speaks of Being as the universal attribute, and of goodness and beauty as perceptible by the comparison of the present with the past and future. In the Republic, Being is invested with a sort of Divinity, and the Form of Goodness is seen like the Sun in Heaven, giving light and colour and shape and nutriment to the supra-sensual world. The Ideas are no longer seen from beneath, but have lifted us into their own atmosphere. And yet they clothe themselves in imagery derived from the exploded doctrine of sensation. The sun was the favourite symbol of those who made motion their first principle: it is still used in a figure to typify that which is above motion. As the one principle was imagined to be the cause both of perception and life, so the other is conceived of as the Author both of Knowledge and Being. The Heraclitean element appears once again as the fire by whose glimmering light the shadows of borrowed forms are cast upon the wall of the cave or dungeon in which men lie bound. The combination of agent and patient in sensation, according to the earlier theory, resulted in the twin birth, ever recurring, of sensation and sensible thing. The consummation of the Soul's desires in the Ideal World is the Eternal Union of Mind and Being, the twin immortal offspring of which are Reason and Truth.

In the Republic, knowledge is shown to be inseparable from the reality of its object. And there are two conditions of this reality. The object of true Knowledge is, (1) above sense, (2) conformable to the Idea of Good. Knowledge is also divided into Absolute (or Transcendental) and Scientific[a].

[a] Two slight discrepancies between the Theætetus and the Republic deserve to be noticed. (1.) In the Theætetus the word δόξα is applied to

INTRODUCTION.

It is unnecessary in this brief sketch to carry our thoughts onward to the latest and most complicated stage of Plato's philosophy. But we may allude in taking leave of this subject to the wide interval which separates the vague and simple notion of the diurnal revolution of the sun and of the sky, from the elaborate astronomy of the Timæus, and on the other hand to the close parallel which subsists between the doctrine of sense which is here rejected as a theory of knowledge, and the final theory of sensation as such, in which Pythagorean and other elements are blended with the Heracleitean. (Tim. 43. sqq.)

§. 7.

It is manifest that the dialogue in its present form cannot have existed earlier than the date of the battle in which Theætetus is said to have been wounded; and the preface, at least, must probably have been written a few years later than this.

The destruction of the Spartan Mora by Iphicrates and his peltasts, an event which Mr. Grote, apparently with good reason, has placed as late as 390 B.C., seems on the whole to be most probably the occasion meant. As the Corinthian war continued three years after this, it is possible that some engagement may have taken place as late as the year 387. But if we are driven to suppose a still later date for the scene with which the Theætetus opens, the earliest assignable year is 369 B.C., when the combined forces of the Athenians and Lacedæmonians and their allies tried to dispute the passage of the Isthmus with Epaminondas.

So far as any arguments can be raised from the dialogue taken by itself, the hypothesis that it was written a few years later than 390 B.C. is quite satisfactory. It allows sufficient time for Plato's residence at Megara to have become the subject of reflection with him, and for his mind to have advanced considerably towards its final conceptions. If he was 30 at the death of Socrates, he would now be a little over 40. The bitterness caused by that event would not yet be mellowed

---

mental operations not immediately connected with sensation. In the Republic τὸ αἰσθητικὸν and τὸ δοξαστικόν are identified. (7.) δοξή life, which in the Republic is applied only to practical actions, is used in the Theætetus indifferently of the juror's verdict and of the conclusions of the arithmetician.

down, or 'rubbed off by travel;' and the unwillingness to descend 'into the cave,' would naturally still give some harshness to the contrast between philosophy and Athenian life.

And even should it be necessary to place the Sophista and Politicus much later, the conception of a trilogy or tetralogy, though most important (in this case where it is suggested by Plato himself) as indicating connexion of thought, does not necessitate continuity of composition. No one supposes that the Œdipus Tyrannus of Sophocles immediately preceded the Colonens in point of date. (οὐδὲ θεατὴν ὥσπερ ποιηταῖς, ἐπισημήσων καὶ ἀρξων ἐπιστατεῖ παρ' ἡμῖν.)

On the other hand, even the year 369 B.C. (though some time must surely be allowed for the composition of the dialogue, and we read of no *battle* till the year 368 B.C.) would seem from internal evidence considerably too late. Plato would then be upwards of 60 years old. He is said to have died in 347 B.C. at the age of 81 or 82. It seems hardly probable that at a time when he must have been putting his thoughts into their most perfect shape in the Republic, he should make an elaborate return to the 'elements' of a rejected philosophy, or that the perplexities he had encountered in his sojourn with the Megarian philosophers should 'trouble' him as they once had done, or present themselves to him with the same vividness and reality. The slight way in which the two theories 'that wisdom is the good,' and 'that pleasure is the good,' are touched upon in Rep. p. 505, 509, contrasts forcibly with the earnestness with which in the Theætetus the Cyrenaic theory of knowledge is treated as an open question, and the strong Megarian influence which is throughout perceptible. And while it is most probable that the Theætetus is written from a point of view more advanced than any which is allowed to appear in the dialogue itself, it is very difficult to conceive that (e. g.) the passage in which the existence and goodness, sameness and difference *of things*, are shown to be immediately perceived by the mind, was written nearly at the same period with the account of the Idea of Good in the Republic. (See the beginning of B. VII. where the sameness and difference (e. g.) of the fingers is spoken of as one of the first perceptions of the awakening intellect.) The freshness and individuality of the person of Socrates, and the close identification of the method with his teaching are also features which consist better with the earlier date.

The chief difficulty in the way of the above hypothesis is connected with the person of Theaetetus; who in the conversation with Socrates is represented as a boy of about 16 (μειράκιον) while Euclides and Terpsion speak of him in the preface in terms which imply that he was already a distinguished and valued citizen and had justified the prophetic words of Socrates. (Οἷον ἄνδρα λέγεις ἐν νεότητι εἶναι—τοῦτον ἐλλόγιμον γενέσθαι—ἀληθῆ εἶπεν.) If the date of the battle in question were earlier than 390 B.C. Theaetetus could hardly have had time to fulfil the prophecy of Socrates even in the eyes of his personal friends. But an interval of 9 years does seem sufficient for this. The youth of 16 would have become a man of 25, and might well have earned distinction in light-armed combat, and in other ways. Some touches in the conversation would then acquire additional point. Terpsion has no doubt of the prowess of his friend, yet Euclides mentions with some pride that men had praised him for his conduct in the battle. This praise is also the more natural, if the kind of fighting was one comparatively untried, and the occasion one in which the national honour of Athens and Sparta was nearly concerned. The words, too, εἴπερ εἰς ἡλικίαν ἔλθοι, have a more touching significance, if they apply to one who seems likely to be cut off in his prime.

The difficulty is greater, however, when the notices of later writers are taken into account. If Theaetetus is supposed to recover from his illness and his wounds, the dialogue seems to be robbed of a great ornament. And yet Theaetetus (the same Theaetetus who had heard Socrates and followed Plato) is spoken of by Suidas as a distinguished mathematician who taught at Heraclea and was the author of the first treatise on the five regular solids. That he should be a distinguished mathematician before 25, and even a discoverer in geometry, is not impossible (for, as Aristotle says, μαθητικὸς μὲν ταῖς γένοιτ' ἄν) but that he should have become a teacher of it in a foreign city is less probable, even if he is supposed to live to the age of 28. And the complaint of Plato in the Republic, that the science of solid geometry was in its infancy, would seem hardly

k

INTRODUCTION.

justifiable, if the treatise on the regular solids had been in existence so long.

But (1.) it is not *impossible* that Theætetus may have so far recovered of his wounds as to be able to be a teacher of mathematics. (2.) The point of the difficulty lies in a late testimony, a cross-examination of which, if it were possible, might place the facts in a different light.

Still it becomes worth while to examine the hypothesis of a later date (368 B. C.), the reasons against which have been already mentioned. It may be said in favour of it; (1.) that it allows ample time for all Theætetus' distinctions; (2.) that a disciple of Plato would fight more willingly with the Lacedæmonians on his side; (3.) that Megara was at this time in alliance with Athens, and hence it would be natural to expect him to put up there. (On the former occasion, however, she seems to have been neutral.)

The preface may be of this date, and yet the chief part of the dialogue may be earlier. It may have been sketched during Plato's residence at Megara (ἐγραψάμην μὲν τότ' εὐθὺς—ὑπομνήματα) and filled up and retouched at intervals (ὕστερον δὲ κατὰ σχολὴν ἀναμιμνησκόμενος ἔγραφον); and long afterwards the preface may have been added to indicate the Megarian character of the dialogue.

Some such conjecture (which in any case is not improbable) would seem to be the natural resort, if it became necessary to suppose the preface written after 368 B. C.

§ 9.

The Theætetus and Aristotle.

One chief source of difficulty in the Theætetus to the modern reader is the imperfect development which it presents of the conception of the Proposition[1]. In the earlier part, the ever-varying succession of phænomena, bound up with the ever-varying impressions of sense, are only dimly felt to belong to any Subject. Indeed as the argument proceeds the unity of that which is the subject of different impressions or qualities is expressly denied. At a further stage, where the question arises, How is false opinion possible, there appears indeed a

[1] Συλλογισμός in the Theæt. (p. 186) is nearly equivalent to "abstraction and generalization."

sort of consciousness that every act of thought implies a subject (p. 188. οὔτε περὶ τῶν ὄντων οὔτε αὐτὸ καθ᾽ αὑτό), and that to think is to say to oneself, "This is that;"—which first shows itself in the example, "I think Theætetus is Socrates," and is afterwards more distinctly expressed where it is said that thought is the mind's silent discourse.[a] But that which remains unnoticed is the relation of subject to predicate in any proposition. Thus it is assumed that when one predicate is substituted for another, (as when, in the propositions, "Yonder man is Socrates," or Thersites was handsome," the terms "Socrates" and "handsome" have been substituted by mistake for "Theætetus" and "ugly;") this is the same thing as if the terms so confounded were predicated of each other: (thus, "Theætetus is Socrates," "What is ugly is handsome.")

The relation between the terms of a proposition where the subject is something immediately perceived by sense, is brought out afterwards by the image of the waxen block, but the same indistinctness still hangs about abstract propositions. The line is not clearly drawn between saying, "the sum of 7 and 5 is 11," and saying "11 is 12."

Lastly, when it is asserted that the combination of names in speech corresponds to the combination of elements in the object of knowledge, we are still left in the dark as to the exact relation between words or things which is implied in either combination.

This confusion between subject and predicate is, in other words, to use Aristotelian language, the confusion of matter with form, and of δύναμις with ἐνέργεια. The subject is all its predicates δυνάμει, and is that which, together with the opposite quality, becomes τόδε τι. Thus Καλλίας ἄμουσος becomes μουσικός: hence Callias is in one sense the material part.

It may be said therefore, that in the earlier philosophy, when the matter changes from one form to its opposite, or from a privative to a positive state, it is lost sight of that the form cannot properly be said to change, and that the matter or

---

[a] A close study of this passage (pp. 189, 190) will afford convincing proof of the indeterminate state of the science of logic at this time, and the necessity of getting behind Aristotle (if the expression may be permitted) in order to understand Plato.

subject, as such, remains unchanged, while assuming different forms.

1. It is this aspect of the questions raised in the Theætetus which is taken up by Aristotle, who follows Plato in pointing out that the views of Heraclitus and Protagoras meet in one. Their views are thus identified and criticised at length in two very similar passages of the Metaphysics (Γ. 1005 b.—1012 b., K. 1061 b.—1063 b.), in both of which Aristotle is engaged in defending the principle of contradiction.

The theory of Heraclitus is stated in its most abstract and logical form, "Every thing at once is and is not." This is at first put forward with the qualification, "Some (i. e. Plato?) think that Heraclitus means this:" but afterwards it is made to figure as the Heraclitean theory, "adopted by many physical philosophers." The theory of Protagoras is shown to come to the same thing; for if every man's impression is true, then contradictories are true (and not true) together.

Aristotle does not profess to use direct proof in defence of what he assumes to be self-evident and the basis of all reasoning, but he brings forward a number of indirect arguments, which throw considerable light upon the nature of the question. These are intended for such persons as really feel the difficulty: there are others for whom a more summary method is required (οἱ μὲν γὰρ πειθοῦς δέονται, οἱ δὲ βίας [a]). Amongst these arguments there are two which deserve especial notice here, as being of a different kind from any which are to be met with in the dialogue. (1.) "We will not say that the act of predication must either be or *not be* something, lest they should accuse us of begging the question; but we will say, that every predicate *means* something, and that its meaning is one, and not indefinitely various; otherwise language and even thought is destroyed. And to predicate it in this one meaning of a particular subject is either true or false. Hence, man and not man cannot be truly predicated together of the same subject."

(2.) "The difference between the same man's impressions

---

[a] Cf. Plato. II. B. II. 188, 19B. "Οτιοι μὲν βασιλῆα καὶ ἔξοχον ἄνδρα κιχείη, τὸν δ' ἀγανοῖς ἐπέεσσιν ἐρητύ- σασκε παραστάς.——"Ον δ' αὖ δήμου τ' ἄνδρα ἴδοι βοόωντά τ' ἐφεύροι, τὸν σκήπτρῳ ἐλάσασκεν, ὁμοκλήσασκέ τε μύθῳ.

INTRODUCTION.

at different times regards not the quality, but the subject of it. Sweet and bitter are the same to the sick as to the healthy man: it is the wine that appears to him at one time sweet and at another bitter. The idea of sweet is the same to him in the past, present, and future."

There are other points in which the discussion is characteristic of Aristotle (as where it is said that the principle of motion rests on a too narrow induction; or that if all creatures having sensation were destroyed, the universe would still exist; or where he points out that the admission of degrees, e. g. "nearer and farther from the truth," necessitates a standard of truth to which the approach is made); but the influence of this dialogue, and of the discussions (Megarian and Platonic) which preceded and followed it, is also very apparent. The following points of coincidence are worth mentioning:

(1.) It is assumed as part of the theory, that everything is thus and not-thus (οὕτως καὶ οὐχ οὕτως.) But this is nearly the last point to which the principle of motion is reduced in the Theætetus (p. 183). Aristotle proceeds to infer that everything must be infinite; and this in two ways: first, as "not-this" means "everything but this," it follows that everything must be everything else[a]; and, secondly, (with Plato Theæt. loc. cit.) if οὕτως καὶ οὐχ οὕτως is true, then its contradictory (οὐδ᾽ οὕτως οὔτε οὐχ οὕτως) must also be true; and this, he adds, must go on to infinity. The theory gives an indefinite, that is, a purely negative account of Being (τὸ μὴ ὄν λέγει).

(2.) Further, in reference to Protagoras it is shown, that in making all impressions true, he makes them also false, and his own theory amongst the rest.

(3.) The Heraclitean or Protagorean philosopher is seen to avoid tumbling into a ditch. It is evident therefore that he acknowledges the distinction between good and bad. Every thing then is not equally indifferent. And if there are impressions to which the theory does not apply, so much has been conceded. Or, "as Plato puts it," with regard to the future, the physician is a better judge of what will prove wholesome, than a chance person.

---

[a] καὶ γίγνεται δὴ τὸ 'Αναξαγόρου, ὁμοῦ πάντα χρήματα. Aristotle thinks that if this argument had been put to Heraclitus himself, he would have been compelled to acknowledge its force.

Aristotle further points out the absolute relativeness of the doctrine. They cannot say, "What appears, is," but "What appears to me, is to me."

The following scattered touches may be quoted without comment.

"The theory of Protagoras is called ἡ περὶ τὰ φαινόμενα δόξα."

"My eyes may each receive a different impression from the same thing."

"The doubt about the criterion of knowledge is like the question whether the waking or the dreaming life is real."

"Socrates is not a different person for every different attribute."

"When a thing appears bitter, this is in consequence of a manifest defect, viz. disease. The one state then, (i. e. the healthy one) and not the other, is to be held the measure of things."

"Language is made impossible."

"The man thinks thus and not thus: i. e. it is equally true that he is not thinking as that he thinks. He is reduced to the condition of a vegetable."

Lastly, Aristotle, like Theodorus, remarks upon the difficulty of reasoning with the men, because they will not lay down any thing to start with, and allow it to remain firm. Other points of comparison will be mentioned in the notes. In brief, Aristotle meets the indefiniteness of the physical and sophistic theories by asserting the distinction between form and matter and the eternity of form.

2. But he does not deny that a continual process takes place between them, and there is a world in which growth and decay, generation and corruption, are ever going on, viz. the world of sensible things, which in Aristotle reasserts its reality, as being inseparable from the natural forms, and perhaps even from the relations expressed in mathematics.

This is not the place for the discussion of Aristotle's theory of becoming. It is enough to notice (1) that he adopts from the early philosophers, whom he classes together as upholding the material cause, on the one hand the dualism, and on the other the indeterminateness of matter (Phys. Ausc. I.) and points out that therefore it can only be the object of knowledge, "by analogy," with reference to the form. And (2) his conception of sensation as a realization of mental life, is very similar to that expressed in the Theætetus. The ἐνέργεια αἰσθήσεως, which is inseparable from the ἐνέργεια αἰσθητοῦ, is the meeting point of active and passive elements in motion. (In modern language it is a process between object and subject.) But the φαντασία or mental image, which accompanies sensation but is separable from it in thought, in the Theætetus is merged in sensation, although the term is simply the noun of φαίνεσθαι (φαντασία ἄρα καὶ αἴσθησις ταὐτόν), but is clearly distinguished from it by Aristotle. The distinction is made the ground of an argument for the possibility of error [p].

3. The same distinction between matter and form is also applied to the solution of the doubt, whether the complex whole is one or many, e. g. whether the syllable is all the letters combined, or something above and beyond them. Aristotle shows that neither the parts nor their arrangement can create the form of the whole: much rather it is this mould which determines the arrangement of the parts. It is prior to them, and is eternal and uncreated. They affect the nature of the compound thing only by being capable of receiving a certain form.

At this point Plato (in the Theætetus) and Aristotle seem almost to touch one another, except that in Aristotle the conception of the *end* (τὸ οὗ ἕνεκα) is bound up with that of the form.

As the tendency in the Theætetus is to rise from the ordinary notion of an element to that of elementary Ideas, so Aristotle points out that the universal is in one sense an element: (i. e. logically.) (Met. Δ. 1014 b.)

4. Among the germs which the Theætetus (like most of

---

[p] (Met. I. 1010 b: Οὐδ' ἡ αἴσθησις ψευδὴς τοῦ ἰδίου ἐστίν ἀλλ' ἡ φαντασία οὐ ταὐτὸν τῇ αἰσθήσει.) Again, even where the φαντασία is false the δόξα may be true. De Somn. 3. Cf. de An. III. 3.

The difference between Aristotle and Plato (in this dialogue) on this point of psychology, may be illustrated by the following tabular view:

Aristotle thus traces the gradual ascent of the human mind from sense to knowledge:

7. σοφία.
6. ἐπιστήμη.
5. τέχνη.
4. ἐμπειρία.
3. μνήμη.
2. φαντασία.
1. αἴσθησις.

These two are in some cases inseparable.

Plato distinguishes
ἐπιστήμη
from
{ μνήμη
  δόξα
  αἴσθησις } each of which is accompanied by φαντασία.

Plato's dialogues) contains of Aristotelian formulæ, the most remarkable is the distinction between possessing and having Knowledge, which obviously corresponds to Aristotle's distinction between Knowing and Contemplating (ἐπίστασθαι, θεωρεῖν), —his favourite illustration of the difference between possession and use, or between a potential and an actual state. No such general application is made of it by Plato. The notion enters into the Theætetus only as a last ineffectual attempt to reconcile the existence of Knowledge with the possibility of error, and it is expressed through an imaginary symbol. But the distinction latent in the image between the potential and the actual, is the same by which Aristotle afterwards solved this and other difficulties, if not finally, yet with admirable completeness.

While Aristotle, in adding the corner stone to the fabric of Greek philosophy, could not but draw largely from Plato, either immediately or through the discussions of his followers, yet the presence in him must be admitted of a wholly distinct element, which gives a different value to his speculations, even when in substance they coincide. This may be briefly described as the determination to be at once logical and matter of fact, the conviction that philosophy must be consistent on the one hand with itself, and on the other with experience. This return to common sense, so valuable in restoring the balance of philosophy, and this subordination of all things to logic, may be viewed partly as the natural advance or recoil from the dialectic of Plato, but they are partly the culmination of a separate tendency of the Greek mind.

§ 10.

Modern aspects.

It has been already noticed, that the completeness with which the doctrine of sense is developed in the Theætetus, probably influenced the expression of cognate ideas in the later period of Ancient Philosophy. Passing with this slight remark from the Ancient world, we proceed finally to notice in a few words the bearing of the Theætetus upon modern metaphysical inquiry.

And first it is right to observe the importance of the transition. The comparison of Ancient and Modern Philosophy is very different from the study of the relations between two schools or two periods in either. The links by which they are historically connected are comparatively slender: the external similarity, though sometimes obvious, is generally superficial; but there is also a deeper analogy, like what may be observed between separate kingdoms of nature.

Modern Philosophy starts from a more inward experience of the mind, from a wider and more varied observation of the external world, than was possible in the days of Thales or even of Parmenides. Ancient Philosophy had contributed to this, but indirectly. Descartes did not start from the Platonic Idea, but from the consciousness of his own highly-wrought mind. Bacon rebelled against the authority of Aristotle, and sought for natural and not logical 'forms' in the Interpretation of Nature. And yet it is not merely fanciful to see a kind of parallel between the resting-place from doubt, 'Cogito, ergo sum,' and the resting-place from what is particular and changeable— "The mind contemplating Being and Goodness in its own instrument;" or between Bacon's 'natural form' and the Platonic or Aristotelian εἶδος. Indeed in the latter case, the mode of expression is adapted from the Greek Philosophy.

That which gives the Theaetetus a peculiarly modern interest is its comparatively subjective character. This is partly inherent in the nature of the question, but is also partly due to the human reference of Protagoras and the self-inquiry of Socrates. An approach only is made to the consideration of abstract Being; the mind is in vain endeavouring to find the determining law of truth within itself. Thus it fails at one time to find any firm standing-ground, at another to conceive the possibility of error. In like manner Descartes, starting from within, is obliged to postulate the existence of God, almost before he can establish his first principle, certainly before he can determine whether the waking or the sleeping life is real, and feels almost as keenly as a Greek Philosopher could have done, the difficulty of conceiving error as possible [q].

Every metaphysical work, ancient or modern, is sure to

[q] E. g. Medit. III. p. 18: Jam quod ad ideas attinet, si solae in se spectentur, nec ad aliud quid illas referam, falsae propriae esse non possunt; nam sive capram sive chimaeram imaginer, non minus verum est me unam imaginari quam alteram. Nulla etiam in ipsa voluntate vel affectibus falsitas est timenda, nam quamvis prava, quamvis etiam ea quae nusquam sunt possim optare, non tamen ideo non verum est illa me optare, ac proinde sola supersunt judicia in quibus mihi cavendum est ne fallar.

1

possess some points of affinity and contrast to the Theætetus. All that will be attempted here is to indicate very briefly the points in the dialogue itself which seem capable of illustrating more recent phases of reflection. These are, (1) The analysis of sensation or perception. (2) The semi-physical theory of 'motion.' (3) The 'subjective' doctrine of Protagoras and the Cyrenaics. (4) The Theætetus as a psychology. (5) Logical difficulties.

1. The Theætetus contains a theory of sensation; or rather a doctrine of impressions of sense, in each of which there is shown to be an active and a passive—in modern language, an objective and a subjective—element. No attempt is made, however, at least in the earlier part of the dialogues, to distinguish the physical from the mental in the act of sense, the recipient from the active state of the Subject, sensation from perception. Warmth, whiteness, even comparative size and number, are viewed, so far as the Subject is concerned, (in common with pleasures, desires, hopes, fears,) simply as phenomena, experiences or impressions. And when presently it appears that there is something more in each of us than a bundle of divers faculties of sense, and that the mind, which receives and judges all, is one; the distinction is drawn, not between the mind's sensation and perception, e. g. of a white object, but between its own perceptions and the impressions which it receives through the body: e. g. the eye informs me that this ball is white, that that ball is red; the mind, reviewing these sensations, perceives that each of them *is*, that it *is one*, that it is the same with itself, different from the other, that they are together two: also that the redness and the whiteness *are*, and that they are different, and that this difference *is* a real thing.

But towards the end of the dialogue, where it is said that the simplest elements, for instance, of speech and music, may be the objects of knowledge, this may be regarded as an admission that simultaneous with every impression of sense there is, or may be, a perception of the mind.

This reasoning is not without its bearing on modern theories of sensation and perception: (and it probably implies an observation of inward facts not less complete;) but it is not to be confounded with them.

It stands in a closer and more concrete relation to the mind's experience of itself; it is far simpler, and, though less distinct, is more luminous, expressing a fresh and vivid consciousness, and an intensity of inquiry, which has not yet assumed a set form, or attained to definite results, but is neither overclouded and paralysed by subjective uncertainty, nor lost in the abstractions of logic, nor perplexed by the distracting influences of physical science.

2. For although this theory of sensation is united with a doctrine of motion, and Plato's argument may thus seem to touch upon modern physiological inquiries, or even upon the theories of light and heat and sound, the sense in which the word *motion* is used is vague in the extreme. So far as it is used with a physical meaning, it is not distinguished from force, nor from matter, for this is lost out of view. It is moreover the symbol of relation and change. And the term thus metaphorically used is not accurately defined, for while the object and subject are said to suffer change, sensations and qualities are said to be in locomotion (p. 156). It is not easy for us, with our more definite conceptions, to assign any very intelligible meaning to this. But it may be conceded that there is here an anticipation of the fact, that sensation is in every case occasioned by motion. A nearer approach to scientific truth may be found in the notion of the absolute relativeness of phenomena. Studying the world of experiences from within the mind, 'ex analogia hominis,' Plato regards the objects of sensation as wholly indeterminate, and can find no true 'measure of things' but in the contemplation of abstract Ideas. I am conscious of my own sensation, but I cannot compare it with that of any other being, still less with any universal standard. Therefore I must not look for truth here, but in the world of Ideas. Modern Experimental Science is equally distrustful of individual impressions of sense, but has found means of measuring the 'motions' by which they are caused, through the effect of the same motions upon other things besides our senses. 'When the same wind is blowing' (Theaet. p. 152) 'one of us feels it warm, another cold,'—but the mercury of the thermometer tells the same tale to all. And though the individual consciousness remains the sole judge of the exact impression momentarily received by each person, yet we are certain that

the sensation of heat and cold, like the expansion and contraction of the mercury, is in every case dependent on a universal law.

3. The philosophy of Protagoras may be described in modern language as a rhetorical scepticism, that of the Cyrenaics as a sensational idealism.

An interesting parallel might be drawn (for instance) between Protagoras and Hume. But it must be kept in mind that scepticism is a relative term, and that while that of Protagoras was directed probably as much against astronomical and mathematical speculation, as against the Eleatic Absolute Being, that of Hume was aimed at the popular belief in supernatural causes, and those a priori notions or innate ideas, which modern metaphysicians had in part elaborated and in part inherited from Greek philosophy. Both poured contempt upon the popular religion of their day; both pointed to the limited and relative nature of human knowledge; and both were content to rest within the clearly defined boundary of a 'certain uncertainty,' without even an aspiration after Absolute or Ideal Truth. Both (if Plato's representation in the Protagoras may be trusted) eminently possessed the faculty of lucid and persuasive exposition, which is sometimes found accompanying a kind of narrowness in speculation. But here the resemblance probably ends. Protagoras may however with justice be regarded as the type of a class,—the utilitarian or common sense sceptics,—of which Hume is in modern times perhaps the most brilliant example.

On the other hand the Cyrenaic dogma may be compared with the destructive or negative side of Berkeley. But their refined contempt for the materialists, who 'believe only in what they can clutch between their hands,' is of a different order from Berkeley's endeavour to resolve concrete existence into ideas of the mind. His denial of material substance as a metaphysical abstraction, was consistent on the one hand with the most searching physical inquiry, and on the other with his belief in the reality of universals, as thoughts of the Eternal mind. But the Cyrenaic could not be said to analyse phenomena: he merely dwelt upon the consciousness of the instant, and limited his view to that. True, he sought a ground of objective reality in a movement from without, corresponding to the impression within, and embraced both, the active and the passive movement, in the formula of universal change, but universal change is at each instant a mere negation. Hence, to dwell in thought for a moment on this theory was to reduce it to nothingness. And, to speak more generally, modern controversies about the 'reality of the external world' would have little meaning for any of the Ancient Philosophers, who knew so little of the laws of the material universe, although the *spirit* (for instance) of Parmenides and of Democritus may be viewed as typical of all subsequent ideal and material theories.

4. As an inquiry into the nature of Knowledge and Opinion, and the boundary which divides them, the Theætetus may be compared with Locke's Essay on the Human Understanding. Such a comparison would be interesting for many reasons. Besides the sort of kindred which often exists between minds of genuine originality even in distant ages, there is in some respects a similarity of position. Both inquiries commence from within, in both Knowledge is reduced to its elements (simple ideas of sensation), both occupy the middle ground between Material and Ideal systems, both rest upon experience, both rise by gradual steps from sense to reason; in both reflection and imagination are engaged in bodying forth the mind's modes of thinking, (with perfect originality in both, yet with the most curious coincidences in the kind of images employed: compare Locke's sandstone and marble impressions, and his dark room or cabinet, with Plato's waxen block and aviary;) in both the office of the Reason is represented to be the combination (or comparison) of the impressions of sense. Both in short present us with a psychology, clear and simple, based upon experience, and in a certain way complete.

But, not to mention the difference of style, the comparative absence in Locke of the poetical element, and the influence which Natural Philosophy exercised upon his method, there is this radical distinction between the attitude of Plato in the Theætetus, and that of the English philosopher, that while Plato's chief endeavour is to rise from the elements of sense to higher things, the first effort of Locke is to recal the human mind from a spurious Platonism to its experience of itself; and while the highest point reached in the Theætetus (that the mind reviewing its impressions and determining of their Being,

Unity, or Beauty, is its own instrument) is but the 'topmost round' of 'young ambition's ladder,' Locke rests contentedly within the subjective limits which he believed to be imposed by Providence on the human mind.

5. Lastly, the modified Eleaticism of Euclides, whom Socrates once described as 'capable of arguing with Sophists but not with men,' is not without its counterpart in modern philosophy. It may be described in modern language as the tendency to extreme logical analysis: to rest, that is, in the abstractions of logic, refusing to approciate the subtlety of Nature and the complexity of the world, and to endeavour to conceive of things as they really are.

(a.) Euclides does not stand alone in his method of following a theory to its logical conclusions, instead of inquiring into the reasonableness of the grounds on which it is based.

(b.) Nor is the 'victim of a mercenary logic,' ἐν φρέατι συνεχόμενος (caught in a pit-fall), who is compelled to admit that he sees and does not see, in a much worse plight than the student who finds himself bound hand and foot, by victorious subjective analysis, within the limits of his own organism.

(c.) The paradoxical difficulty, 'Is it possible to know and not to know?'—'How can you inquire about that which you do not know,'—has a still nearer resemblance to metaphysical paradoxes among ourselves: e. g. How is it possible that Knowledge (or Inquiry) should transcend the limits of experience? In both cases the idea of a tentative and partial Knowledge, of a sort of faith of the Intellect, is left out of view, and the result of both is equally fatal to the spirit of inquiry.

(d.) In the Theætetus the Megarian tendency to divide every thing from every thing (τὸ πᾶν ἀπὸ παντὸς ἀποχωρίζειν) is met by the conception of the blending of diverse elements in a higher unity. This thought is further developed in the Sophista, and, as we have seen, is taken up by Aristotle. Though expressed by the Greek philosophers in a dialectical form, this assertion of the presence of a higher unity in every complex whole,—of the inadequacy of analysis as a method of knowledge,—is of permanent value. For it is directed against a confusion to which many others are parallel. Such, for instance, in modern times would be the confusion between facts or phenomena, and their principles or laws, or between organism and life, or between experience and reason, or between the forms of language or imagination, and the creative mind. We may doubt, with Plato in the Theætetus, whether the higher can even be known apart from the lower, but this difficulty ought not to lead to their identification in thought.

(e.) The barren sophistry into which the method degenerated in the hands of the followers of Euclides affords a useful warning to 'intellectualism' in every time.

The mind of Plato in the Theætetus is keenly alive to the presence of logical difficulties, but is neither irritated nor deterred by them. He unravels them with the utmost patience, but at the same time treats them with a kind of compassionate irony, as if he refused to be bound within the framework of contemporary thought.

In an age when so much yearns for reconcilement, when, Conclusion. for instance, the paths of natural and mental science, after swerving far asunder, promise to converge again, when the abstractions of the intellect begin to stand in a new relation to the forms of the imagination, from which they had seemed to be finally severed, it is an interesting and suggestive labour, to turn again the earlier pages of the book of human Inquiry: to find there 'anticipations of Nature' indissolubly woven together with the reflections of the mind upon itself: to see a fast-ripening philosophy labouring with an imperfect logic; and language, and poetical imagination, with mixed modes of sense, casting their many-coloured veil over the irregularities of mental growth, and giving form and life and substance to dialectical and speculative thought. This Attic prime of intellectual manhood is beautiful to contemplate, even if philosophy may not hope from such fountains to renew her youth.

ΘΕΑΙΤΗΤΟΣ.

ΤΑ ΤΟΥ ΔΙΑΛΟΓΟΥ ΠΡΟΣΩΠΑ

ΕΥΚΛΕΙΔΗΣ, ΤΕΡΨΙΩΝ, ΣΩΚΡΑΤΗΣ,
ΘΕΟΔΩΡΟΣ, ΘΕΑΙΤΗΤΟΣ.

Ἄρτι, ὦ Τερψίων, ἢ πάλαι ἐξ ἀγροῦ;

ΤΕΡ. Ἐπιεικῶς πάλαι. καὶ σέ γε ἐζήτουν κατ' ἀγορὰν καὶ ἐθαύμαζον, ὅτι οὐχ οἷός τ' ἦ εὑρεῖν.

ΕΥ. Οὐ γὰρ ἦ κατὰ πόλιν.

ΤΕΡ. Ποῦ μήν;

ΕΥ. Εἰς λιμένα καταβαίνων Θεαιτήτῳ ἐνέτυχον φερομένῳ ἐκ Κορίνθου ἀπὸ τοῦ στρατοπέδου Ἀθήναζε.

ΤΕΡ. Ζῶντι ἢ τετελευτηκότι;

ΕΥ. Ζῶντι καὶ μάλα μόλις· χαλεπῶς μὲν γὰρ

The Preface. Terpsion and Euclides meet before Euclides' house in Megara. They converse about the dangerous state of Theaetetus, of whom Socrates had truly prophesied

3. ΕΥΚΛΕΙΔΗΣ, ΤΕΡΨΙΩΝ] Euclides and Terpsion appear also in the Phaedo as the Megarians who were present at the death of Socrates, p. 59: Καὶ Μεγαρόθεν Εὐκλείδης τε καὶ Τερψίων. Compare with the preservation of this dialogue by Euclides, and the introduction of Theodorus of Cyrene, the preservation of the Pythagorean dialogue by Phaedo, and the introduction in it of Simmias and Cebes (Φιλολάῳ συγγεγονότε).

6. καὶ σέ γε] With some emphasis. I have been looking for you.

7. καὶ ἐθαύμαζον] It is perhaps intimated that Euclides, like his master Socrates, was to be found daily in the market-place.

9. μήν expresses surprise.

11. ἐκ Κορίνθου ἀπὸ τοῦ στρατοπέδου] For the expression compare Charm. p. 25: Ἐκ Ποτιδαίας ἀπὸ τοῦ στρατοπέδου. The date is either earlier than B. C. 387, or later than B. C. 369. Either supposition presents some difficulty. See Introduction.

13. Ζῶντι ἢ τετελευτηκότι] Spoken not, as Stallbaum says, in jest, but in serious alarm, occasioned by the word φερομένῳ.

14. Ζῶντι καὶ μάλα μόλις] 'Indeed, hardly alive.' 'Only just alive.'

2 ΠΛΑΤΩΝΟΣ

ἔχει καὶ ὑπὸ τραυμάτων τινῶν, μᾶλλον μὴν αὐτὸν p.142.
αἱρεῖ τὸ γεγονὸς νόσημα ἐν τῷ στρατεύματι.

ΤΕΡ. Μῶν ἡ δυσεντερία;

ΕΥ. Ναί.

ΤΕΡ. Οἶον ἄνδρα λέγεις ἐν κινδύνῳ εἶναι.

ΕΥ. Καλόν τε καὶ ἀγαθόν, ὦ Τερψίων, ἐπεί τοι καὶ νῦν ἤκουόν τινων μάλα ἐγκωμιαζόντων αὐτὸν περὶ τὴν μάχην.

ΤΕΡ. Καὶ οὐδέν γ' ἄτοπον, ἀλλὰ πολὺ θαυμαστότερον εἰ μὴ τοιοῦτος ἦν. ἀτὰρ πῶς οὐκ αὐτοῦ c Μεγαροῖ κατέλυεν;

ΕΥ. Ἠπείγετο οἴκαδε· ἐπεὶ ἔγωγ' ἐδεόμην καὶ συνεβούλευον, ἀλλ' οὐκ ἤθελε. καὶ δῆτα προπέμψας αὐτόν, ἀπιὼν πάλιν ἀνεμνήσθην καὶ ἐθαύμασα Σωκράτους, ὡς μαντικῶς ἄλλα τε δὴ εἶπε καὶ περὶ τούτου. δοκεῖ γάρ μοι ὀλίγον πρὸ τοῦ θανάτου ἐντυχεῖν αὐτῷ μειρακίῳ ὄντι, καὶ συγγενόμενός τε καὶ διαλεχθεὶς πάνυ ἀγασθῆναι αὐτοῦ τὴν φύσιν. καί μοι ἐλθόντι Ἀθήναζε τούς τε λόγους οὓς διελέχθη αὐτῷ διηγήσατο, καὶ μάλα ἀξίους ἀκοῆς, εἶπέ τε ὅτι πᾶσα d ἀνάγκη εἴη τοῦτον ἐλλόγιμον γενέσθαι, εἴπερ εἰς ἡλικίαν ἔλθοι.

ΘΕΑΙΤΗΤΟΣ.

p.142.   ΤΕΡ. Καὶ ἀληθῆ γε, ὡς ἔοικεν, εἶπεν. ἀτὰρ τίνες ἦσαν οἱ λόγοι; ἔχοις ἂν διηγήσασθαι;

ΕΥ. Οὐ μὰ τὸν Δία, οὔκουν οὕτω γε ἀπὸ στό-
p.143. ματος· ἀλλ' ἐγραψάμην μὲν τότ' εὐθὺς οἴκαδ' ἐλθὼν ὑπομνήματα, ὕστερον δὲ κατὰ σχολὴν ἀναμιμνησκό- 5 μενος ἔγραφον, καὶ ὁσάκις Ἀθήναζε ἀφικοίμην, ἐπανηρώτων τὸν Σωκράτη ὃ μὴ ἐμεμνήμην, καὶ δεῦρο ἐλθὼν ἐπηνωρθούμην· ὥστε μοι σχεδόν τι πᾶς ὁ λόγος γέγραπται.

b   ΤΕΡ. Ἀληθῆ· ἤκουσά σου καὶ πρότερον, καὶ μέν- 10 τοι ἀεὶ μέλλων κελεύσειν ἐπιδεῖξαι διατέτριφα δεῦρο.

1. Καὶ ἀληθῆ γε — εἶπεν] In the editions before Heindorf these words were given to ΕΥ. But in the Bodleian MS. (in which the initials of the interlocutors are generally omitted) a small capital T has been inserted over καί. [Bekk. — : καὶ Δ. vulgo enim : ἀτάρ.]

3. αἴσουν—γε] Not, at least, in the way you seem to expect.
οὕτω] as we are, on the spot. Comp. the use of νῦν αὔτως.

4. ἐγραψάμην — ἔγραφον] I wrote for my own use—I went on writing.

5. ὑπομνήματα] 'notes.' See Phaedr. 275, where letters are called ὑπομνήσεως φάρμακον.

7. ὃ μὴ ἐμεμνήμην] = εἴ τι μὴ ἐμεμνήμην. μή gives indefiniteness to ὅ. Is it possible that we have here an indication of the mode in which the dialogue was really composed?

10. Ἀληθῆ· ἤκουσα] The clauses are parallel and not consequent, hence the asyndeton.

καὶ μέντοι, κ. τ. λ.] 'And now I think of it, I have always meant to ask you to shew it me, but have let opportunities slip till now.' That which is really most emphatic is expressed by the participle. It has been objected to this rendering, (a) that δεῦρο is not used as an adverb of time except with μέχρις or ἀεί, (β) that διατρίβειν, meaning 'to delay,' could not have been used here without an adverb of place. But, (a) such transference of adverbs from place to time is not unusual, and it occurs in the case of δεῦρο in Plat. Tim. 21: 'Ἣν ἤδη ἡ πόλις ἔπραξε μέν, διὰ δὲ χρόνον καὶ φθορὰν τῶν ἐργασαμένων οὐ διήρκεσε δεῦρο ὁ λόγος.' In the present passage, the deviation from common use is softened by the neighbourhood of ἀεί. Comp. Æsch. Eum. 596: Καὶ δεῦρό γ' ἀεὶ τὴν τύχην οὐ μέμφομαι. Such a refinement upon a common phrase is in the manner of Plato. And (2) there is no reason why διατρίβειν should not be used here absolutely, with a touch of blame in it, as meaning not simply 'to delay,' but 'to waste time.' See Rep. 472: λέγε, καὶ μὴ διάτριβε. Aristoph. Equ. 515: φησί

ΠΛΑΤΩΝΟΣ

ἀλλὰ τί κωλύει νῦν ἡμᾶς διελθεῖν; πάντως ἔγωγε p.143.
καὶ ἀναπαύσασθαι δέομαι, ὡς ἐξ ἀγροῦ ἥκων.

ΕΥ. Ἀλλὰ μὲν δὴ καὶ αὐτὸς μέχρι Ἐρινοῦ Θεαίτητον προὔπεμψα, ὥστε οὐκ ἂν ἀηδῶς ἀναπαυοίμην.
ἀλλ᾽ ἴωμεν, καὶ ἡμῖν ἅμα ἀναπαυομένοις ὁ παῖς ἀνα-
γνώσεται.

ΤΕΡ. Ὀρθῶς λέγεις.

ΕΥ. Τὸ μὲν δὴ βυβλίον, ὦ Τερψίων, τουτί· ἐγραψάμην δὲ δὴ οὑτωσὶ τὸν λόγον, οὐκ ἐμοὶ Σωκράτη
διηγούμενον ὡς διηγεῖτο, ἀλλὰ διαλεγόμενον οἷς ἔφη
διαλεχθῆναι. ἔφη δὲ τῷ τε γεωμέτρῃ Θεοδώρῳ καὶ
τῷ Θεαιτήτῳ. ἵνα οὖν ἐν τῇ γραφῇ μὴ παρέχοιεν
πράγματα αἱ μεταξὺ τῶν λόγων διηγήσεις περὶ αὐτοῦ τε, ὁπότε λέγοι ὁ Σωκράτης οἷον Κἀγὼ ἔφην ἢ

γὰρ ἀνὴρ οὐχ ὑπ᾽ ἀκούσας τοῦτο πε-
ποιηθὼς διατρίβειν, where it is
used with a participle as here.
Thuc. VI. 42, 43, 47.

1. πάντως ἔγωγε] This asyndeton is very frequent. Infr.
162: Πάντως καὶ νῦν δὴ μάλ᾽
ἐμμελῶς σοι ἐφαίνετο ὑπακούειν.
Polit. 269: Πάντων οὐ πολλὰ δι-
αφεύγειν ποιοῦσιν ἔτη.

2. καὶ ἀναπαύσασθαι δέομαι]
'Besides, as I have walked in
from the country, I should any
how be glad of the rest.'

3. Ἐρινοῦ] A spot on the Ce-
phisus, close to Eleusis, where
it was fabled that Pluto had descended with Proserpine. Paus.
I. 92. There were other places
of the name.

5. ὁ παῖς] Euclides' servant.

9. οὐκ ἐμοὶ Σωκράτη διηγούμενον
κ.τ.λ.] These words are parallel
to οὑτωσὶ τὸν λόγον, depending
on ἐγραψάμην. Compare Apol.
19: Ταῦτα—ἑώρατε——Σωκράτη
—περιφερόμενον.

11. τῷ τε γεωμέτρῃ Θεοδώρῳ]
Theodorus the mathematician
of Cyrene, with whom, according to a tradition, Plato once
studied. Two points in him
are of importance as regards
this dialogue: he is a geometrician, and stands thus on the
threshold of philosophy; and
he is of Cyrene, the city of
Aristippus, with whom he is
also connected as being one of
the friends of Protagoras. See
infr. 164: Οἱ ἑταῖροι οἱ Πρωταγόρου κατέλιπον—ἐν Θεοδώρου
οἷς ἄδε.

12. ἵνα οὖν ἐν τῇ γραφῇ, κ.τ.λ.]
Imitated by Cicero, de Amic.
c. 1: Quasi enim ipsos induxi
loquentes, ne inquam et inquit
saepius interponerentur.

13. αἱ μεταξὺ] The bits of
narration in the interstices of
the dialogue.

περὶ αὐτοῦ τε] This is the
reading of the Bodleian MS.
If it is adopted, περὶ αὐτοῦ de-

p. 143. Καὶ ἐγὼ εἶπον, ἦ αὖ περὶ τοῦ ἀποκρινομένου, ὅτι Συνέφη ἢ Οὐχ ὡμολόγει, τούτων ἕνεκα ὡς αὐτὸν αὐτοῖς διαλεγόμενον ἔγραψα, ἐξελὼν τὰ τοιαῦτα.

ΤΕΡ. Καὶ οὐδέν γε ἀπὸ τρόπου, ὦ Εὐκλείδη.

ΕΥ. Ἀλλά, παῖ, λαβὲ τὸ βιβλίον καὶ λέγε. 5

ΣΩ. Εἰ μὲν τῶν ἐν Κυρήνῃ μᾶλλον ἐκηδόμην, ὦ

The Dialogue.
Socrates, meeting

pends immediately on διηγήσεις, and ὁπότε λέγοι is epexegetic.

1. ᾖ αὖ περὶ τοῦ ἀποκρινομένου] sc. λέγοι. ἦ κ.τ.λ. referring to ὁπότε λέγοι is introduced instead of the regular καὶ κ.τ.λ. answering to περὶ αὐτοῦ τε. The interruptions both concerning Socrates himself, when he told me, (e. g.) 'said I,' or 'I replied;' or again, when he told of the respondent, that 'he assented,' or 'he did not agree.'

4. οὐδέν γε ἀπὸ τρόπου] Comp. Rep. 470: Καὶ οὐδέν γε, ἔφη, ἄπο τρόπου λέγεις—Ὅρα δὴ καὶ τόδε εἰ πρὸς τρόπον λέγω. See also Shakespeare's Julius Cæsar (Act. II. sc. 3.): 'Why bird and beast from (i. e. contrary to) quality and kind.' (ἄπο is the Bodleian reading.) It is not necessary to suppose any allusion to the form of the Megarian dialogue, but it adds point to this expression if we suppose that it was cast in this dramatic mould. There is then a touch of nature in the approbation of Terpsion. This is at any rate better, if a reason must be found for everything, than to suppose with Schleiermacher, that Plato is acknowledging an error in his own earlier style. But perhaps it is enough to say that the form is adopted for the sake of clearness, which was of

great importance in this and the two following dialogues. And it is equally natural that Euclides should omit Κἀγὼ ἔφην, &c. in a written report, and that vivâ voce reporters in other dialogues should insert them. In this Preface we have been introduced to Theætetus as a distinguished citizen. In what follows we are to see the promise of his youth. We are told of Theætetus by later writers (besides the fact that he heard Socrates and followed Plato) that he taught mathematics at Heracleia, and that he was the author of the first treatise on the five regular solids. The interval which this seems to require between the trial of Socrates and the death of Theætetus (to which it is difficult not to suppose an allusion here) increases the uncertainty of the date. See Introduction.

6. Εἰ μὲν—] 'If my heart were in Cyrene.' There is an imperfect sequence of clauses, arising out of the interposition of the clause ἧττον γὰρ—ἀνευνίᾳ, the last words of which form a transition to the main thought, to which Socrates gradually returns. The opening is characteristic of Socrates. He starts from an analogous instance, in which the person addressed is interested.

6 ΠΛΑΤΩΝΟΣ

p. 143. d

Θεόδωρε, τὰ ἐκεῖ ἄν σε καὶ περὶ ἐκείνων ἂν ἠρώτων, εἴ τινες αὐτόθι περὶ γεωμετρίαν ἤ τινα ἄλλην φιλοσοφίαν εἰσὶ τῶν νέων ἐπιμέλειαν ποιούμενοι· νῦν δέ —ἧττον γὰρ ἐκείνους ἢ τούσδε φιλῶ, καὶ μᾶλλον ἐπιθυμῶ εἰδέναι τίνες ἡμῖν τῶν νέων ἐπίδοξοι γενέσθαι ἐπιεικεῖς· ταῦτα δὴ αὐτός τε σκοπῶ καθ' ὅσον δύναμαι, καὶ τοὺς ἄλλους ἐρωτῶ οἷς ἂν ὁρῶ τοὺς νέους ἐθέλοντας ξυγγίγνεσθαι. σοὶ δὴ οὐκ ὀλίγιστοι πλησιάζουσι, καὶ δικαίως· ἄξιος γὰρ τά τε ἄλλα καὶ e 10 γεωμετρίας ἕνεκα. εἰ δὴ οὖν τινι ἐνέτυχες ἀξίῳ λόγου, ἡδέως ἂν πυθοίμην.

ΘΕΟ. Καὶ μὴν, ὦ Σώκρατες, ἐμοί τε εἰπεῖν καὶ

1. τὰ ἐκεῖ ἄν—περὶ ἐκείνων ἄν] 'Ἐκείνων is masc. 'Ἀμφότων, the reading of several MSS., is inappropriate here, and is perhaps due to the parallel passage of the Charmides, p. 153: Λίθι ἐγὼ αὐτοὺς ἀπηρώτων τά τῇδε, περὶ φιλοσοφίας ὅπως ἔχοι τὰ νῦν, περί τε τῶν νέων εἴ τινες ἐν αὐτοῖς διαφέρουσιν ἢ σοφίᾳ ἢ κάλλει ἢ ἀμφοτέροις ἐγγεγονότες εἶεν. The only difficulty of the reading ἂν ἠρώτων is the repetition of ἄν after the pronoun. It may be accounted for by the emphasis which the antithesis gives to τὰ ἐκεῖ and ἐκείνων, and also to ἐκείνων being an afterthought: cf. Rep. 526: Οὐκ ἂν ῥᾳδίως αὐτὶ πολλὰ ἂν εὕροις. In both cases we may avoid the reduplication of ἄν, which would be difficult to explain, by supposing a repetition of the verb understood.

2. ἤ τινα ἄλλην φιλοσοφίαν] 'or other liberal pursuit.' Comp. Tim. 88: Μουσικῇ καὶ πάσῃ φιλοσοφίᾳ προσχρώμενοι.

5. τίνες ἡμῖν τῶν νέων] ἡμῖν is not emphatic. The emphasis is anticipated in τούσδε.

5. ἡμῖν τῶν νέων—(7.) ἐ. ὑμῶν τῶν πολιτῶν] Comp. Thuc. I. 6: Οἱ πρεσβύτεροι αὐτοῖς τῶν εὐδαιμόνων.

γενέσθαι ἐπιεικεῖς] 'to make a good figure.' Ἐπιεικὴς in Plato seems frequently to mean simply 'excellent' (laudabilis, Ast. Lex.) cf. Legg. 957: "Εστ' ἐν πόλεσιν οὐκ ἀσχήμονα ἐπιεικέσιν ἀνδρῶν οὐκ ὀλίγα κομοθετήματα. Symp. 210: "Ὥστε καὶ ἐὰν ἐπιεικὴς ἂν τὴν ψυχὴν καὶ ἐὰν σμικρὸν ἄνθος ἔχῃ, ἐξαρκεῖν αὐτῷ κ. τ. λ. Rep. 398: "Ἀχρηστοι γὰρ καὶ γυναιξὶν δὲ δεῖ ἐπιεικεῖς εἶναι, μὴ ὅτι ἀνδράσιν. (Cf. 387: Γυναιξὶ δὲ ἀποδιδῶμεν, καὶ οὐδὲ ταύταις σπουδαίαις.)

9. ἄξιος γάρ] The adjective receives greater emphasis by the omission of the substantive verb. Comp. Soph. Œd. Col. 758: Τήνδε τὴν πόλιν φίλοις εἰπών, ἐπαξία γάρ. Also Rep. 500: Περὶ τούτων ἐνοῶμεν (sc. ἐσμέν) τῷ λόγῳ διαρρήδην.

10. εἰ] interrogative; 'whether.' Cf. infra p. 207.

ΘΕΑΙΤΗΤΟΣ. 7

p. 143. σοὶ ἀκοῦσαι πάνυ ἄξιον, οἵῳ ὑμῖν τῶν πολιτῶν μει- intelligent, a rare com-
ρακίῳ ἐντετύχηκα. καὶ εἰ μὲν ἦν καλός, ἐφοβούμην bination! Like a
ἂν σφόδρα λέγειν, μὴ καί τῳ δόξω ἐν ἐπιθυμίᾳ αὐτοῦ stream of oil, flowing
εἶναι· νῦν δέ, καὶ μή μοι ἄχθου, οὐκ ἔστι καλός, smoothly
προσέοικε δὲ σοὶ τήν τε σιμότητα καὶ τὸ ἔξω τῶν and swiftly
ὀμμάτων· ἧττον δὲ ἢ σὺ ταῦτ' ἔχει. ἀδεῶς δὲ λέγω. without a
p. 144. εὖ γὰρ ἴσθι ὅτι ὧν δὴ πώποτε ἐνέτυχον, καὶ πάνυ murmur.

3. μὴ καί τῳ δόξω] The ex- that each thing is beautiful in
pression is softened by the im- relation to its use, and then
personal τῳ. ' Lest it might asks: 'Ὀφθαλμῶν τίνος ἕνεκα δεό-
be thought'—' Lest I should μεθα; Δῆλον ἔφη ὅτι τοῦ ὁρᾶν.
give the impression.' This in- Οὕτω μὲν τοίνυν ἤδη οἱ ἐμοὶ ὀφθαλ-
direct reference to persons is μοὶ καλλίονες ἂν τῶν σῶν εἶησαν.
more common in Plato than Πῶς δή; Ὅτι οἱ μὲν σοὶ τὸ κατ'
appears at first sight. Cf. (in εὐθὺ μόνον ὁρῶσιν, οἱ δὲ ἐμοὶ καὶ
this dialogue) p. 175: "Ὅπως δή γέ τὸ ἐπὶ πλαγίον διὰ τὸ ἐπιπόλαια
τῳ — Πλινῦν ἄν, viz. τῶν δικαστῶν εἶναι. Λέγεις σὺ ἔφη καρκίνον
ἐκείνων. Phaed. 63: Ἀεὶ ὁ Κέβης εὐοφθαλμότατον εἶναι τῶν ζῴων.
λόγους τινὰς ἀνερευνᾷ, &c. ἐμοῦς. Πάντος δήπου, ἔφη· ἐπεὶ καὶ πρὸς
4. μοι ἄχθου] καὶ introduces ἰσχὺν τοὺς ὀφθαλμοὺς ἄριστα πε-
what is suddenly interposed. φράκτους ἔχει. Εἶεν. Ἔφη· τῶν δὲ
Comp. Gorg. 486: Καίτοι, ὦ ῥινῶν ποτέρα καλλίων, ἡ σὴ ἢ ἡ
φίλε Σώκρατες — καί μοι μηδὲν ἐμή; Ἐγὼ μέν, ἔφη, οἶμαι τὴν
ἀχθεσθῇς εὐνοίᾳ γὰρ ἐρῶ τῇ σῇ ἐμήν, εἴπερ γε ταῖς εὐοσφραισθαι
— οὐκ ἀποχρῶν δοκεῖ σοι, κ. τ. λ. ἕνεκεν ἐποίησαν ἡμῖν θεοὶ οἱ θεοί.
The outline of the sentence is Οἱ μὲν γὰρ σοὶ μυκτῆρες εἰς γῆν
εἰ μὲν ἦν—, ἐφοβούμην ἂν—· νῦν ὁρῶσιν· οἱ δὲ ἐμοὶ ἀναπέπτανται,
δὲ — οὐκ ἔστι—· ἀδεῶς δὴ λέγω. ὥστε τὰς πάντοθεν ὀσμὰς προσδέ-
Δή has something of an illative χεσθαι. Τὸ δὲ σιμὸν τῆς ῥινὸς πῶς
force. Cf. Euthyphr. 11: καί τοῦ ὀρθοῦ καλλίων; Ὅτι, ἔφη, οὐκ
εἰ μέν—σώφροντος. ἀντιφράττει, ἀλλ' εὐθὺς ᾖ τὰς
5. τήν τε σιμότητα καὶ τὸ ὄψεις ὁρᾶν ἃ ἂν βούλωνται. ἡ δὲ
ἔξω τῶν ὀμμάτων] This passage ὑψηλὴ ῥὶς ὥσπερ ἐπηρεάζουσα διὰ-
and the speech of Alcibiades τετείχικε τὰ ὄμματα. Τοῦ γε μὴν
in the Symposium (p. 215: "Ὅτι στόματος, ἔφη ὁ Κριτόβουλος, ὑφί-
μὲν τὸ εἶδος ὅμοιος εἶ τούτοις (τοῖς εμαι. Εἰ γὰρ τοῦ ἀποδάκνειν ἕνεκα
Σιληνοῖς——καὶ τῷ Μαρσύᾳ) οὐδ' πεποίηται, πολὺ ἂν σὺ μεῖζον ἢ ἐγὼ
αὐτὸς δή που ἀμφισβητήσεις.) are ἀποδάκοις. Διὰ δὲ τὸ παχέα ἔχειν
the chief allusions to Socrates' τὰ χείλη οὐκ οἴει καὶ μαλακώτερον
personal appearance in Plato. ἔχειν τὸ φίλημα; "Ἔοικα, ἔφη, κατά
See below, p. 209: Τὸν σιμόν γε τὸν σὸν λόγον, καὶ ἄσχιον ἔχειν τὸ
τε καὶ ἐξόφθαλμον. Comp. Xen. στόμα ἔχειν. Ἐκεῖνο δὲ οὐδὲν νε-
Symp. V. 5, where Critobulus, νόμηκεν λογίζῃ, ὡς ἐγὼ σοῦ καλλίων
who has been boasting of beauty, εἰμί, ὅτι καὶ Ναϊάδες θεαὶ οὖσαι τοὺς
is challenged to compete with Σιληνοὺς ἐμοὶ ὁμοιοτέρους γίγνων-
Socrates. Socrates first shews σιν ἢ σοί;

ΠΛΑΤΩΝΟΣ

πολλοῖς πεπλησίακα, οὐδένα πω ᾐσθόμην οὕτω p. 144.
θαυμαστῶς εὖ πεφυκότα. τὸ γὰρ εὐμαθῆ ὄντα, ὡς
ἄλλῳ χαλεπόν, πρᾷον αὖ εἶναι διαφερόντως, καὶ ἐπὶ
τούτοις ἀνδρεῖον παρ᾽ ὁντινοῦν, ἐγὼ μὲν οὔτ᾽ ἂν
5 ᾠόμην γενέσθαι οὔτε ὁρῶ γιγνομένους· ἀλλ᾽ οἵ τε

2. τὸ γὰρ εὐμαθῆ ὄντα—γιγνομένους] The anacoluthon adds to the expression of surprise. Comp. Protag. 317: Τὸ οὖν διαπράσσοντα μὴ δύνασθαι ἀνασῶσαι, ἀλλὰ ἀσταφανῆ εἶναι, πολλὴ μωρία καὶ τοῦ ἐπιχειρήματος. Parm. 128: Τὸ αὖ—οὕτως ἑαυτῷ ρην λέγεις ὥστε μηδὲν τῶν αὐτῶν εἰρημένα δοκεῖν σχεδόν τι λέγοντες ταὐτά, ὑπὲρ ἡμᾶς τοὺς ἄλλους φαίνεται ὑμῶν τὰ εἰρημένα εἰρῆσθαι.

ὡς ἄλλῳ χαλεπόν] The simple and obvious meaning of these words, 'as it were hard for another to be,' i. e. 'in a degree hardly to be equalled,' has been rejected by critics because it was thought that χαλεπόν could not be applied to qualities that are not acquired. But the word is not tied down to this predicament of meaning. It has passed out of it even in Homer. Od. XI. 156: Χαλεπὸν δὲ τάδε ζωοῖσιν ὁρᾶσθαι. So elsewhere in Plato it is used where human agency is not in question to signify 'next to impossible.' See Rep. 502: Χαλεπὸν γενέσθαι, οὐ μέντοι ἀδύνατόν γε—viz. that philosophers should be kings, one of the conditions of which is the existence of this very combination of qualities. What Plato would think of this refinement may be inferred from his caricature of it in the Protagoras, p. 344: Σὺ δὲ φῄς, ὦ Πιττακέ, χαλεπὸν ἐσθλὸν ἔμμεναι· τὸ δὲ—ἀδύνατον. The rendering

which it has been proposed to substitute—'so as to be ill-tempered with another,' or (with ἄλλως) 'so as in another case to be ill-tempered'—is objectionable, (a) as awkward in itself, (β) as breaking harmony (ὡς ἄλλῳ χαλεπόν, διαφερόντως, παρ᾽ ὁντινοῦν), (γ) as anticipating what is afterwards stated as a fresh thought (οἵ τε ὀξεῖς, κ. τ. λ.)

5. γενέσθαι (τοιούτόν τινα) 'I should not have thought there could have been an instance of this combination, nor do I find it usual.'

γιγνομένους] sc. τοιούτους. Cf. Rep. 492: Οὔτε γὰρ γίγνεται οὔτε γέγονεν οὐδ᾽ οὖν μὴ γένηται ἀλλοῖον ἦθος, κ. τ. λ.

οὔτε ὁρῶ γιγνομένους, κ. τ. λ.] The thought is exactly paralleled in the Republic, where the same combination of qualities is described as essential to the philosophic nature, and its rarity is dwelt upon in almost the same words. Rep. 503: Εὐμαθεῖς καὶ μνήμονες καὶ ἀγχίνοι καὶ ὀξεῖς αἰσθ᾽ ὅτι οὐκ ἐθέλουσιν ἅμα φύεσθαι καὶ νεανικοί τε καὶ μεγαλοπρεπεῖς τὰς διανοίας, οἷοι μετρίως μετὰ ἡσυχίας καὶ βεβαιότητος ἐθέλειν (ζῆν, ἀλλ᾽ οἱ τοιοῦτοι ὑπ᾽ ὀξύτητος φέρονται ὅπῃ ἂν τύχωσι, καὶ τὸ βέβαιον ἅπαν αὐτῶν ἐξοίχεται. Ἀληθῆ, ἔφη, λέγεις. Οὐκοῦν τὸ βέβαια αὖ ταῦτα ἤθη καὶ οὐκ εὐμετάβολα, οἷς τις μᾶλλον ἂν πιστεύσει χρήσαιτο, καὶ ἐν τῷ πολέμῳ πρὸς τοὺς φόβους δυσκίνητα ὄντα,

ΘΕΑΙΤΗΤΟΣ. 9

p. 144. ὀξεῖς ὥσπερ οὗτος καὶ ἀγχίνοι καὶ μνήμονες ὡς τὰ πολλὰ καὶ πρὸς τὰς ὀργὰς ὀξύρροποί εἰσι, καὶ ἄττον- b τες φέρονται ὥσπερ τὰ ἀνερμάτιστα πλοῖα, καὶ μανι- κώτεροι ἢ ἀνδρειότεροι φύονται, οἵ τε αὖ ἐμβριθέστε- ροι νωθροί πως ἀπαντῶσι πρὸς τὰς μαθήσεις καὶ λή- 5 θης γέμοντες. ὁ δὲ οὕτω λείως τε καὶ ἀπταίστως καὶ ἀνυσίμως ἔρχεται ἐπὶ τὰς μαθήσεις τε καὶ ζητήσεις μετὰ πολλῆς πραότητος, οἷον ἐλαίου ῥεῦμα ἀψοφητὶ ῥέοντος, ὥστε θαυμάσαι τὸ τηλικοῦτον ὄντα οὕτω ταῦτα διαπράττεσθαι. 10

ΣΩ. Εὖ ἀγγέλλεις. τίνος δὲ καὶ ἔστι τῶν πολι- τῶν;

ΘΕΟ. Ἀκήκοα μὲν τοὔνομα, μνημονεύω δὲ οὔ. ο ἀλλὰ γάρ ἐστι τῶνδε τῶν προσιόντων ὁ ἐν τῷ μέσῳ.

Theaetetus (son of Euphronius of

πρὸς τὰς μαθήσεις αὖ ποιεῖ ταὐτόν, δυσκινήτως ἔχει καὶ δυσμαθῶς, καὶ ὕπνου τε καὶ χάσμης ἐμπέπλασται, ὅταν τι δέῃ τοιοῦτον διαπονεῖν; So the difficulty of combining bravery with gentleness is dwelt upon, ib. 375, 6. See also Polit. p. 309, 310. The essentials of the philosophic nature enume- rated in the 6th Book of the Republic are, love of truth, quickness in learning, good memory, liberality, justice and gentleness, temperance, cou- rage. Theaetetus is the em- bodiment of this nature.

1. ὀξεῖς] This seems the ge- neric word for quickness of intellect. Rep. l. c.: Εὐμαθεῖς καὶ μνήμονες καὶ ἀγχίνοι καὶ ὀξεῖς.

2. πρὸς τὰς ὀργὰς ὀξύρροποι] 'Impetuous.' 'Of a quick tem- per.'

5. λήθης γέμοντες] Rep. 486: Εἰ μηδὲν ἂν μάθοι σώζειν δύναιτο, λήθης ἂν πλέως, ἆρ' ἂν οἷός τ' εἴη ἐπιστήμης μὴ κενὸς εἶναι.

7. ἀνυσίμως] 'Successfully'— 'Making rapid progress.'

9. ὥστε θαυμάσαι] Soph. El. 394: Καλὸν γὰρ οὐδὲν βίοτει, ὥστε θαυμάσαι. Aristoph. Plut. 810: Τὰ σκισπάρνια πλήρη 'στίν, ὥστε θαυμάσαι. By a refine- ment of language, the particu- lar cause of wonder is here expressed and made to depend on θαυμάσαι.

13. Ἀκήκοα μὲν τοὔνομα, μνημο- νεύω δὲ οὔ] Theodorus takes the interest of a teacher in the youth himself: Socrates that of a fellow-citizen in his father.

14. ἀλλὰ γάρ ἐστι—ἀλλὰ σκό- πει] This double ἀλλὰ is fre- quent in Plato. Comp. Soph. Phil. 520: Ἀλλ' αἰσχρὰ μέντοι σοῦ γ' ἐμ' ἐνδεέστερον ξείνῳ φανῆναι πρὸς τὸ καίριον πονεῖν· ἀλλ' εἰ δο- κεῖ, πλέωμεν. The second ἀλλὰ puts definitely forward the pro- position for which the first ἀλλὰ has cleared the way.

10 ΠΛΑΤΩΝΟΣ

Nunium) now refers the gymnasium between two companions. Theodorus adds that, though impoverished, he is most liberal. He is made to sit by Socrates. They converse.

ἄρτι γὰρ ἐν τῷ ἔξω δρόμῳ ἠλείφοντο ἑταῖροί τέ τινες p. 144.
οὗτοι αὐτοῦ καὶ αὐτός, νῦν δέ μοι δοκοῦσιν ἀλειψάμενοι δεῦρο ἰέναι. ἀλλὰ σκόπει εἰ γιγνώσκεις αὐτόν.

ΣΩ. Γιγνώσκω· ὁ τοῦ Σουνιέως Εὐφρονίου ἐστί, 5 καὶ πάνυ γε, ὦ φίλε, ἀνδρὸς οἷον καὶ σὺ τοῦτον διηγεῖ, καὶ ἄλλως εὐδοκίμου, καὶ μέντοι καὶ οὐσίαν μάλα πολλὴν κατέλιπε. τὸ δ᾽ ὄνομα οὐκ οἶδα τοῦ μειρακίου.

ΘΕΟ. Θεαίτητος, ὦ Σώκρατες, τό γε ὄνομα· τὴν d μέντοι οὐσίαν δοκοῦσί μοι ἐπίτροποί τινες διεφθαρκέ-
10 ναι· ἀλλ᾽ ὅμως καὶ πρὸς τὴν τῶν χρημάτων ἐλευθεριότητα θαυμαστός, ὦ Σώκρατες.

ΣΩ. Γεννικὸν λέγεις τὸν ἄνδρα. καί μοι κέλευε αὐτὸν ἐνθάδε παρακαθίζεσθαι.

ΘΕΟ. Ἔσται ταῦτα. Θεαίτητε, δεῦρο παρὰ Σω-
15 κράτη.

If Theodorus were a draughtsman, he would be an authority on the subject of

ΣΩ. Πάνυ μὲν οὖν, ὦ Θεαίτητε, ἵνα κἀγὼ ἐμαυτὸν ἀνασκέψωμαι, ποῖόν τι ἔχω τὸ πρόσωπον. φησὶ γὰρ Θεόδωρος ἔχειν με σοὶ ὅμοιον. ἀτὰρ εἰ νῷν ἐχόντοιν e

1. ἐν τῷ ἔξω δρόμῳ] The scene then is a gymnasium, perhaps the Lyceum. Compare Euthyphr. 2: Ἐν ταῖς ἐν Λυκείῳ ἀπαλαίστροις διατριβαῖς ἐνθάδε νῦν διατρίβεις περὶ τὴν τοῦ βασιλέως στοάν; taken in connection with Theæt. below, p. 210: Νῦν ἀπαντητέον μοι εἰς τὴν τοῦ βασιλέως στοάν. Theodorus had seen the young men in the portico as he entered. The word δρόμος seems to have been applied to several parts of the gymnasium. Euthyd. 273: Ἐν τῷ κατασκέπῳ δρόμῳ. (See the whole passage.) Aristias ap. Pollue. IX. 43: Ἡν μοι παλαίστρα καὶ δρόμοι ξυστοὶ φίλοι.

ἑταῖροί τέ τινες] Evidently two from the words ὁ ἐν τῷ μέσῳ. One, Νέων Σωκράτης, is named in this dialogue, and is an interlocutor in the Politicus. The other remains mute. Such κωφὰ πρόσωπα occur in many dialogues; e. g. Lysias, Charmantides, etc., in the Republic. The scene is natural and not merely dramatic. In Plato's "School of Athens" there are spectators as well as actors.

5. καὶ πάνυ] καὶ is intensive.
6. καὶ μέντοι] 'And, now I think of it.'
10. ἐλευθεριότητα] Rep. 485, 6: Καὶ μὴν που καὶ τόδε δεῖ σκοπεῖν, ὅταν κρίνειν μέλλῃς ψυχὴν φιλόσοφόν τε καὶ μή. Τὸ ποῖον; Μή σε λάθῃ μετέχουσα ἀνελευθερίας.
12. τὸν ἄνδρα] not μειράκιον. 'He must be a noble fellow.'
16. κἀγὼ] καί is to be taken closely with ἵνα. Cf. Soph. Antig. 280: Παῦσαι, πρὶν ὀργῆς καὶ μὲ μεστῶσαι λέγων.

ΘΕΑΙΤΗΤΟΣ. 11

p. 144. *ἑκατέρου λύραν ἔφη αὐτὰς ἡρμόσθαι ὁμοίως, πότερον εὐθὺς ἂν ἐπιστεύομεν ἢ ἐπεσκεψάμεθ᾽ ἂν εἰ μουσικὸς ὢν λέγει;*

ΘΕΑΙ. *Ἐπεσκεψάμεθ᾽ ἄν.*

ΣΩ. *Οὐκοῦν τοιοῦτον μὲν εὑρόντες ἐπειθόμεθ᾽ ἄν, ἄμουσον δέ, ἠπιστοῦμεν;*

ΘΕΑΙ. *Ἀληθῆ.*

ΣΩ. *Νῦν δέ γ᾽ οἶμαι, εἴ τι μέλει ἡμῖν τῆς τῶν*
p. 145. *προσώπων ὁμοιότητος, σκεπτέον εἰ γραφικὸς ὢν λέγει ἢ οὔ.*

ΘΕΑΙ. *Δοκεῖ μοι.*

ΣΩ. *Ἦ οὖν ζωγραφικὸς Θεόδωρος;*

ΘΕΑΙ. *Οὔχ, ὅσον γέ με εἰδέναι.*

ΣΩ. *Ἆρ᾽ οὐδὲ γεωμετρικός;*

ΘΕΑΙ. *Πάντως δή που, ὦ Σώκρατες.*

ΣΩ. *Ἦ καὶ ἀστρονομικὸς καὶ λογιστικός τε καὶ μουσικὸς καὶ ὅσα παιδείας ἔχεται;*

ΘΕΑΙ. *Ἔμοιγε δοκεῖ.*

ΣΩ. *Εἰ μὲν ἄρα ἡμᾶς τοῦ σώματός τι ὁμοίους φησὶν εἶναι ἐπαινῶν πῃ ἢ ψέγων, οὐ πάνυ αὐτῷ ἄξιον τὸν νοῦν προσέχειν.*

ΘΕΑΙ. *Ἴσως οὔ.*

b ΣΩ. *Τί δ᾽, εἰ ποτέρου τὴν ψυχὴν ἐπαινοῖ πρὸς*

our personal appearances. As he is a cultivated man, we must respect his judgment of our mental endowments.

2. *εἰ μουσικὸς ὢν λέγει*] The man then is not the measure of the likeness of musical sounds? Yet afterwards Theætetus is wholly unconscious of contradicting this his first admission.

4. *Ἐπεσκεψάμεθ᾽ ἄν*] Cf. Crit. p. 47: Γνοὺς(ὁμοίως ἀνὴρ καὶ τοῦτο κράττων πότερον σαυτὸν ἀνδρὸς ἐπαίῳ καὶ ψόγῳ καὶ δόξῃ τῶν ποῶν προσέχει, ἢ ἑνὸς μόνου ἐκείνου, ὅς ἂν τυγχάνῃ ἰατρὸς ἢ παιδοτρίβης ὤν;

13. *Οὔχ, ὅσον γέ με εἰδέναι*] Bekker has received γ᾽ ἡμί from a few MSS., the greatest number (including the Bodl.) reading γέ με. ἐμέ seems more pointed, 'not that *I* know of,' but με is possibly right. Cf. Aristoph. Nub. 1264: Οὐκ ἔσθ᾽ ὅ γέ μ᾽ εἰδέναι.

14. *Ἆρ᾽ οὐδὲ γεωμετρικός;*] 'Nor a geometrician, eh?' There is an archness in the expression, making doubtful what is a matter of notoriety.

16. *Ἦ καὶ ἀστρονομικός*] 'I wonder if he is also an astronomer.'

23. *εἰ ποτέρου*] 'The mind of

C 2

12   ΠΛΑΤΩΝΟΣ

ἀρετήν τε καὶ σοφίαν; ἆρ' οὐκ ἄξιον τῷ μὲν ἀκού- p. 145.
σαντι προθυμεῖσθαι ἀνασκέψασθαι τὸν ἐπαινεθέντα,
τῷ δὲ προθύμως ἑαυτὸν ἐπιδεικνύναι;

ΘΕΑΙ. Πάνυ μὲν οὖν, ὦ Σώκρατες.

Therefore, Theaetetus, you must be catechised by me, for he has praised you to me very highly.

ΣΩ. Ὥρα τοίνυν, ὦ φίλε Θεαίτητε, σοὶ μὲν ἐπιδεικνύναι, ἐμοὶ δὲ σκοπεῖσθαι· ὡς εὖ ἴσθι ὅτι Θεόδωρος πολλοὺς δὴ πρός με ἐπαινέσας ξένους τε καὶ ἀστοὺς οὐδένα πω ἐπῄνεσεν ὡς σὲ νῦν δή.

ΘΕΑΙ. Εὖ ἂν ἔχοι, ὦ Σώκρατες· ἀλλ' ὅρα μὴ παίζων ἔλεγεν.   c

ΣΩ. Οὐχ οὗτος ὁ τρόπος Θεοδώρου· ἀλλὰ μὴ ἀναδύου τὰ ὡμολογημένα σκηπτόμενος παίζοντα λέγειν τόνδε, ἵνα μὴ καὶ ἀναγκασθῇ μαρτυρεῖν· πάντως γὰρ οὐδεὶς ἐπισκήψει αὐτῷ. ἀλλὰ θαρρῶν ἔμμενε τῇ ὁμολογίᾳ.

ΘΕΑΙ. Ἀλλὰ χρὴ ταῦτα ποιεῖν, εἴ σοι δοκεῖ.

---

one of us.' The indefinite πότερος occurs several times in Plato.—E. g. Soph. 252: Ἔστιν ὁπότερον αὐτῶν, οἱοίσέ μὴ προσεπινεύωσιν; Though not common in other writers, it is precisely analogous to the indefinite use of τις, ποῦ, ποθέν, etc.

9. Εὖ ἂν ἔχοι] 'That is good!'—'I am glad to hear it.' Or perhaps more hypothetically, 'It is well, if it is so.' Compare Menex. 249: Χάριν ἕξω τῷ εἰπόντι. Σ. Εὖ ἂν ἔχοι. ἀλλ' ὅπως μου μὴ κατερεῖς. Polit. 277: Κινδυνεύει τελέως ἂν ἡμῖν ἔχειν. Σ. Καλῶς ἂν, ὦ Σ., ἡμῖν ἔχοι. Δεῖ δὲ μὴ σοὶ μόνῳ ταῦτα, ἀλλὰ κἀμοὶ—ξυνδοκεῖν.

11. μὴ ἀναδύου τὰ ὡμολ.] 'Do not shrink from what you have agreed to.' Comp. Hom. Il. XIII. 225: Οὔτε τις ἑκὼν εἶναι ἀναδύεται πολέμου κακοῦ. Xen. Symp. V. 5, where Critobulus says, when his challenge is taken, οὐκ ἀναδύομαι. Euthyd. 302: Οὐκ ἔστι γάρ μοι ἀνάδυσις.

14. ἐπισκήψει] The verb ἐπισκήπτειν, to accuse of murder or false witness (φόνον, ψευδομαρτυρίων) is more commonly found in the middle voice, because the accuser in such cases is generally an interested party. But comp. Aesch. c. Timarch. p. 142: Ἥν(sc. τὴν πόλιν) οὐδὲ ψευδομαρτυριῶν δίμως ἐστὶν ἐπισκῆψαι; and for the passive, Legg. 937: Ἐὰν ἐπισκηφθῇ τὰ ψευδῆ μαρτυρῆσαι. Soph. Ant. 1313: Ὡς αἰτίαν γε τῶνδε κἀκείνων ἔχων πρὸς τῆς θανούσης τῆσδ' ἐπεσκήπτου μόρων. The ellipsis of ψευδομαρτυριῶν is easily borne with μαρτυρεῖν preceding.

ΘΕΑΙΤΗΤΟΣ.   18

p. 145. ΣΩ. Λέγε δή μοι· μανθάνεις που παρὰ Θεοδώρου γεωμετρίας ἄττα;

ΘΕΑΙ. Ἔγωγε.

d   ΣΩ. Καὶ τῶν περὶ ἀστρονομίαν τε καὶ ἁρμονίας καὶ λογισμούς;

ΘΕΑΙ. Προθυμοῦμαί γε δή.

ΣΩ. Καὶ γὰρ ἐγώ, ὦ παῖ, παρά γε τούτου καὶ παρ' ἄλλων, οὓς ἂν οἴωμαί τι τούτων ἐπαΐειν. ἀλλ' ὅμως, τὰ μὲν ἄλλα ἔχω περὶ αὐτὰ μετρίως, σμικρὸν δέ τι ἀπορῶ, ὃ μετὰ σοῦ τε καὶ τῶνδε σκεπτέον. καί μοι λέγε· ἆρ' οὐ τὸ μανθάνειν ἐστὶ τὸ σοφώτερον γίγνεσθαι περὶ ὃ μανθάνει τις;

ΘΕΑΙ. Πῶς γὰρ οὔ;

ΣΩ. Σοφίᾳ δέ γ' οἶμαι σοφοὶ οἱ σοφοί.

ΘΕΑΙ. Ναί.

e   ΣΩ. Τοῦτο δὲ μῶν διαφέρει τι ἐπιστήμης;

ΘΕΑΙ. Τὸ ποῖον;

ΣΩ. Ἡ σοφία. ἢ οὐχ ἅπερ ἐπιστήμονες, ταῦτα καὶ σοφοί;

ΘΕΑΙ. Τί μήν;

You learn from Theodorus several things.
To learn is to become wiser.
To be wise is to know.

---

1. μανθάνεις] There is a stress upon the word.

4. τῶν περὶ ἀστρονομίαν] 'Astronomy, and what relates to it.'

6. Προθυμοῦμαί γε δή] 'I certainly do my endeavour.' He is more modest about these higher subjects.

7. παρά γε τούτου] γε (the MS. reading) may be defended: 'from such a master,' referring to προθυμοῦμαι: although τε, which is supported by the version of Ficinus, reads more harmoniously; and the change is slight. The Zurich editors, in their last edition, omit the particle.

8. ἀλλ' ὅμως, τὸ μὲν ἄλλα—σμικρὸν δέ τι ἀπορῶ] Comp. Rep. 367: Καὶ ἐγὼ ἀκούσας, ἀεὶ μὲν δὴ τὴν φύσιν τοῦ τε Γλαύκωνος καὶ τοῦ Ἀδειμάντου ἠγάμην, ἀτὰρ οὖν καὶ τότε πάνυ γε ἥσθην.

18. ἅπερ ἐπιστήμονες, ταῦτα καὶ σοφοί] For the indefinite plural comp. Gorg. 457: Οὐ δήλον δήπουτι—διωρισάμεθα πρὸς ἀλλήλους—οὕτω διαλύεσθαι τὰς συνουσίας. Cf. Xen. Mem. IV. 6, 7: Ὁ ἄρα ἐπιστάμενος ἕκαστα ταῦτα καὶ σοφός ἐστιν.

14   ΠΛΑΤΩΝΟΣ

What, then, is knowledge?

ΣΩ. Ταὐτὸν ἄρα ἐπιστήμη καὶ σοφία;   p. 145.
ΘΕΑΙ. Ναί.
ΣΩ. Τοῦτ' αὐτὸ τοίνυν ἐστὶν ὃ ἀπορῶ καὶ οὐ δύναμαι λαβεῖν ἱκανῶς παρ' ἐμαυτῷ, ἐπιστήμη ὅ τί ποτε τυγχάνει ὄν. ἆρ' οὖν δὴ ἔχομεν λέγειν αὐτό; τί p. 146. φατέ; τίς ἂν ἡμῶν πρῶτος εἴποι; ὁ δὲ ἁμαρτών, καὶ ὃς ἂν ἀεὶ ἁμαρτάνῃ, καθεδεῖται, ὥσπερ φασὶν οἱ παῖδες οἱ σφαιρίζοντες, ὄνος. ὃς δ' ἂν περιγένηται ἀναμάρτητος, βασιλεύσει ἡμῶν καὶ ἐπιτάξει ὅ τι ἂν

A passa. βούληται ἀποκρίνεσθαι. Τί σιγᾶτε; οὔ τί που, ὦ Θεόδωρε, ἐγὼ ὑπὸ φιλολογίας ἀγροικίζομαι, προθυμούμενος ἡμᾶς ποιῆσαι διαλέγεσθαι καὶ φίλους τε καὶ προσηγόρους ἀλλήλοις γίγνεσθαι;

ΘΕΟ. Ἥκιστα μέν, ὦ Σώκρατες, τὸ τοιοῦτον ἂν b εἴη ἄγροικον, ἀλλὰ τῶν μειρακίων τι κέλευέ σοι ἀποκρίνεσθαι. ἐγὼ μὲν γὰρ ἀήθης τῆς τοιαύτης διαλέκτου, καὶ οὐδ' αὖ συνεθίζεσθαι ἡλικίαν ἔχω· τοῖσδε

4. λαβεῖν ἱκανῶς] 'To grasp thoroughly.' To get a clear conception of.
λαβεῖν ἱκανῶς παρ' ἐμαυτῷ] Phileb. 50: λαβόντα δὲ τοῦτο παρὰ σαυτῷ ἀφεῖσαι με, κ.τ.λ.
6. ὁ δὲ ἁμαρτών] 'but he who makes a blunder, or whoever is in error from time to time.'
7. καθεδεῖται — ὄνος] Schol. Τῶν οὖν παιζόντων ταῦτα τοὺς μὲν νικῶντας βασιλεῖς ἐκάλουν, καὶ ὅ τι ἂν προστάττωσι τοῖς ἄλλοις ὑπήκουον, τοὺς δὲ ἡττωμένους ὄνους. Comp. Hor. Ep. I. i. 59: At pueri ludentes, Rex eris, aiunt, si recte facies.
13. προσηγόρους] The active and passive meanings are combined. 'Mutually conversible.' Compare Republic 546: Πάντα προσήγορα καὶ ῥητὰ πρὸς ἄλληλα

ἀπέφηναν. There is possibly an allusion to the mathematical meaning here: 'to make you friends, and bring you into relations with one another.' 'To create a little friendly intercourse.' Compare Rep. 534: Ἀλόγους ὄντας ὥσπερ γραμμάς, and the phrases σύμφωνα καὶ σύναγορα,—Ὅμοια καὶ συνάγορα, in later Pythagorean writings.

15. τῶν μειρακίων τι] Steph. conj. τινά, but cf. Euthyd. 277: Γνῶθι βαστιζόμενον τὸ μειράκιον. βουλόμενος ἀποπαῦσαι αὐτά. And see below, p. 169: Τάδε πάντα πλήν σοῦ σπουδῇ ἐστί.

16. διαλέκτου] 'conversation,' with a tinge, perhaps, of the more technical meaning. Compare Rep. 454: Ἐριδι, οὐ διαλέκτῳ, πρὸς ἀλλήλους χρώμενοι.

ΘΕΑΙΤΗΤΟΣ. 15

p. 146. δὴ πρέπαι τε ἂν τοῦτο καὶ πολὺ πλείων ἐπιδιδοῖεν·
τῷ γὰρ ὄντι ἡ νεότης εἰς πᾶν ἐπίδοσιν ἔχει. ἀλλ᾽,
ὥσπερ ἤρξω, μὴ ἀφίεσο τοῦ Θεαιτήτου, ἀλλ᾽ ἐρώτα.

ΣΩ. Ἀκούεις δή, ὦ Θεαίτητε, ἃ λέγει Θεόδωρος,
ᾧ ἀπιστεῖν, ὡς ἐγὼ οἶμαι, οὔτε σὺ ἐθελήσεις, οὔτε
θέμις περὶ τὰ τοιαῦτα ἀνδρὶ σοφῷ ἐπιτάττοντι νεώ-
τερον ἀπειθεῖν. ἀλλ᾽ εὖ καὶ γενναίως εἰπέ· τί σοι δοκεῖ εἶναι ἐπιστήμη;

ΘΕΑΙ. Ἀλλὰ χρή, ὦ Σώκρατες, ἐπειδήπερ ὑμεῖς
κελεύετε. πάντως γάρ, ἄν τι καὶ ἁμάρτω, ἐπανορ- 10
θώσετε.

ΣΩ. Πάνυ μὲν οὖν, ἄν πέρ γε οἷοί τε ὦμεν.

ΘΕΑΙ. Δοκεῖ τοίνυν μοι καὶ ἃ παρὰ Θεοδώρου ἄν
τις μάθοι ἐπιστῆμαι εἶναι, γεωμετρία τε καὶ ἃς νῦν δὴ
d σὺ διῆλθες, καὶ αὖ σκυτοτομική τε καὶ αἱ τῶν ἄλλων 15
δημιουργῶν τέχναι, πᾶσαί τε καὶ ἑκάστη τούτων, οὐκ
ἄλλο τι ἢ ἐπιστήμη εἶναι.

ΣΩ. Γενναίως γε καὶ φιλοδώρως, ὦ φίλε, ἓν αἰτη-
θεὶς πολλὰ δίδως καὶ ποικίλα ἀνθ᾽ ἁπλοῦ.

Theætetus is at length encouraged to attempt an answer. 'Geometry and the like, shoemaking and other useful arts, all and each of them is knowledge.' But these are many and various; knowledge

2. ἐπίδοσιν ἔχει] Rep. 536: Σόλων γάρ οὐ πιστεύει, ὡς γηράσκων τις πολλὰ δυνατὸς μανθάνειν, ἀλλ᾽ ἧττον ἢ τρέχειν, νέων δὲ πάντες οἱ μεγάλοι καὶ οἱ πολλοὶ πόνοι.

3. μὴ ἀφίεσο τ. Θ. ἀλλ᾽ ἐρώτα] Compare Lach. 186: Μὴ ἀφίεσθαι σε ἐμοῦ διακελεύετο, ἀλλ᾽ ἐρωτᾶν. Rep. 449.

5. οὔτε θέμις — πότερον ἀπειθεῖν] Instead of making ἀπιστεῖν depend on θέμις, a new clause is introduced expressing the particular points in this disobedience which make it unlawful. The like change occurs often in Plato, and is part of the fulness of his style. See above, p. 145: Ὥστε θαυμάσαι, κ.τ.λ. and note.

10. πάντως γάρ, κ.τ.λ.] Theætetus is not yet alive to the difficulty of the subject.

17. ἐπιστῆμαι] Not 'a science,' but 'science.' Theætetus does not make the distinction. The sentence is, however, humoured by the introduction of the singular ἑκάστη.

18. Γενναίως γε] Referring to εὖ καὶ γενναίως above.

19. ποικίλα] Either 'a rich variety of things,' or 'many complex notions for one simple one.' The analysis of terms which follows points rather to the latter meaning; but the former is more natural, and is supported by comparing Phile-

16   ΠΛΑΤΩΝΟΣ

in one and simple. This is illustrated.

ΘΕΑΙ. Πῶς τί τοῦτο λέγεις, ὦ Σώκρατες;   p. 146.

ΣΩ. Ἴσως μὲν οὐδέν· ὁ μέντοι οἶμαι, φράσω. ὅταν λέγῃς σκυτικήν, μή τι ἄλλο φράζεις ἢ ἐπιστήμην ὑποδημάτων ἐργασίας;

5 ΘΕΑΙ. Οὐδέν.

ΣΩ. Τί δ, ὅταν τεκτονικήν; μή τι ἄλλο ἢ ἐπι- c στήμην τῆς τῶν ξυλίνων σκευῶν ἐργασίας;

ΘΕΑΙ. Οὐδὲ τοῦτο.

ΣΩ. Οὐκοῦν ἐν ἀμφοῖν, οὗ ἑκατέρα ἐπιστήμη,
10 τοῦτο ὁρίζεις;

ΘΕΑΙ. Ναί.

ΣΩ. Τὸ δ' ἐπερωτηθέν, ὦ Θεαίτητε, οὐ τοῦτο ἦν, τίνων ἡ ἐπιστήμη, οὐδὲ ὁπόσαι τινές. οὐ γὰρ ἀριθμῆ-

bus, p. 12 (at the opening of the dialogue): Τὴν δὲ ἡδονὴν αὐδὲ ἔστι παιδίον.——ἔστι γὰρ ἁπάντων μὲν οὕτως καλὼς ὅτι τι, μορφὰς δὲ δήπου παντοίας εἴληφε καὶ τινα τρόπον ἐναντίας ἀλλήλων. The two objections (πολλὰ, πανίλα) are discussed in the reverse order. See below: Τίνων—ὁπόσαι, Πρῶτόν γέ που—Ἔπειτά γέ που, κ.τ.λ.

1. Πῶς τί] What (τί), and with what meaning (πῶς). Compare Soph. 262: Πῶς τί τοῦτ' εἴπες; ὅπερ φήσω. κ.τ.λ.

2. Ἴσως μὲν οὐδέν] sc. λέγω, 'perhaps I am talking nonsense.'

ὁ μέντοι οἶμαι] sc. λέγω.

3. σκυτικήν] This is said to have differed from σκυτοτομικῇ (above); and the change of word is an instance of Plato's love of variety. Perhaps the one was a generic, the other a specific term. At least they do not exclude each other in Plato. See Rep. 374: Ἡ σκυτικὴ δεῖ μᾶλλον αὔξεσθαι ἢ γε-

λοιωτής; Οὐδαμῶς. Ἀλλ' ἄρα τὸν σκυτοτόμον, κ.τ.λ.—Ib 601: Ποιήσει δέ γε σκυτοτόμος καὶ χαλκεύς;—αὐδ' ὁ ποιήσας ὅ τε χαλινὸς καὶ ὁ σκυτεύς;

ἄπω—φράζεις] You express by the term 'shoe-making.'

12. Τὸ δ' ἐν.] 'What I went on to ask you.' v. supr. μὴ ἀφίεσο κ. τ. λ.

13. τίνων ἡ ἐπιστήμη, οὐδὲ ὁπόσαι τινές] The first answer of Meno to the question, 'What is virtue?' is exactly analogous to this of Theætetus about knowledge. Instead of attempting to generalize, he enumerates the several kinds of virtue. Men. 71: Ἀνδρὸς ἀρετήν——γυναικὸς ἀρετήν—— παιδὸς ἀρετή, κ.τ.λ. Socrates replies (Men. 72): Πολλῇ γέ τινι εὐτυχίᾳ ἔοικα κεχρῆσθαι, ὦ Μένων, εἰ μίαν ζητῶν ἀρετὴν σμῆνός τι ἀνεύρηκα ἀρετῶν παρὰ σοὶ κειμένων. κ.τ.λ. The whole passage should be compared with this. See also Lach. 191, 192, where Socrates finds a similar difficulty in lead-

ΘΕΑΙΤΗΤΟΣ. 17

p. 146. σαι αὐτὰς βουλόμενοι ἠρόμεθα, ἀλλὰ γνῶναι ἐπιστήμην αὐτὸ ὅ τί ποτ' ἐστίν. ἦ οὐδὲν λέγω;
ΘΕΑΙ. Πάνυ μὲν οὖν ὀρθῶς.

p. 147. ΣΩ. Σκέψαι δὴ καὶ τόδε. εἴ τις ἡμᾶς τῶν φαύλων τι καὶ προχείρων ἔροιτο, οἶον περὶ πηλοῦ, ὅ τί ποτ' ἐστίν, εἰ ἀποκριναίμεθα αὐτῷ πηλὸς ὁ τῶν χυτρέων καὶ πηλὸς ὁ τῶν ἰπνοπλαθῶν καὶ πηλὸς ὁ τῶν πλινθουργῶν, οὐκ ἂν γελοῖοι εἶμεν;
ΘΕΑΙ. Ἴσως.

ΣΩ. Πρῶτον μέν γέ που οἰόμενοι συνιέναι ἐκ τῆς ἡμετέρας ἀποκρίσεως τὸν ἐρωτῶντα, ὅταν εἴπωμεν b πηλός, εἴτε ὁ τῶν κοροπλαθῶν προσθέντες εἴτε ἄλλων ὡντινωνοῦν δημιουργῶν. ἢ οἴει, τίς τι συνίησί τινος ὄνομα, ὁ μὴ οἶδε τί ἐστιν;

ing the respondent to the conception of a general notion,—and Soph. 240, where Theaetetus is again entrapped into a similar mistake in defining the word *θηλον*.

1. *ἐπιστήμην αὐτὸ*] Rep. 472: 'Ἐζητοῦμεν αὐτό τε δικαιοσύνην οἷόν ἐστι.

4. *εἴ τις ἡμᾶς—εἰ ἀποκριναίμεθα*] For the double *εἰ* comp. Rep. 331: Εἰ τις λάβοι παρὰ φίλου ἀνδρὸς σωφρονοῦντος ὅπλα, εἰ μανεὶς ἀπαιτοῖ, κ.τ.λ.

τῶν φαύλων τι καὶ προχείρων] Some trivial and obvious matter.

7. *ἰπνοπλαθῶν*] For this, the reading of all the MSS., *κοροπλαθῶν* has been substituted in the margin of some MSS, for the sake of the uniformity which Plato avoided. See below, note on *κοροπλαθῶν*, l. 12.

10. *οἰόμενοι συνιέναι*] Comp. Rep. 505: Εἰ ὀνειδίζοντές γε ὅτι οὐκ ἴσμεν τὸ ἀγαθόν, λέγουσι πάλιν ὡς εἰδόσιν· φραίνεσθαι γὰρ αὐτό φασιν

εἶναι ἀγαθοῦ, ὡς αὖ συνιέντων ἡμῶν ὅ τι λέγουσιν, ἐπειδὰν τὸ τοῦ ἀγαθοῦ φθέγξωνται ὄνομα. Soph. 244: Τί ποτε βούλεσθε σημαίνειν ὁπόταν ὂν φθέγγησθε. We find ourselves involved in a further stage of the same absurdity at the end of the dialogue, p. 210: Καὶ συντείνασί γε εὔηθες, ζητούντων ἡμῶν ἐπιστήμην, δόξαν φάναι ὀρθὴν εἶναι μετ' ἐπιστήμης εἴτε διαφορότητος εἴτε ὁτουοῦν.

12. *εἴτε ὁ τῶν κοροπλαθῶν προσθέντες*] It is in Plato's manner to surprise us with a fresh example at each step of the argument, instead of dwelling upon one already adduced. Rep. 333: 'Ὥσπερ ὁ κιθαριστικός, κ.τ.λ. —Prot. 312: 'Ὥσπερ ὁ κιθαριστής, κ.τ.λ.—and in this dialogue, p. 161: Βατράχου γυρίνου.— 169: Σὺ δὲ κατ' Ἀνταῖον, κ.τ.λ.— 178: Οὐχ ἡ τοῦ εὐθαριστοῦ.— 190: Ὑγιαίνοντι ἢ μαινόμενον.

13. *ἢ οἴει, τίς τι*] οἴει is parenthetical, and therefore does

D

ΘΕΑΙ. Οὐδαμῶς.

ΣΩ. Οὐδ' ἄρα ἐπιστήμην ὑποδημάτων συνίησιν ὁ ἐπιστήμην μὴ εἰδώς.

ΘΕΑΙ. Οὐ γάρ.

ΣΩ. Σκυτικὴν ἄρα οὐ συνίησιν ὃς ἂν ἐπιστήμην ἀγνοῇ, οὐδέ τινα ἄλλην τέχνην.

ΘΕΑΙ. Ἔστιν οὕτως.

ΣΩ. Γελοία ἄρα ἡ ἀπόκρισις τῷ ἐρωτηθέντι ἐπιστήμη τί ἐστιν, ὅταν ἀποκρίνηται τέχνης τινὸς ὄνομα. τινὸς γὰρ ἐπιστήμην ἀποκρίνεται, οὐ τοῦτ' ἐρωτηθείς.

ΘΕΑΙ. Ἔοικεν.

ΣΩ. Ἔπειτά γέ που ἐξὸν φαύλως καὶ βραχέως ἀποκρίνασθαι περιέρχεται ἀπέραντον ὁδόν. οἷον καὶ ἐν τῇ τοῦ πηλοῦ ἐρωτήσει φαῦλόν που καὶ ἁπλοῦν εἰπεῖν ὅτι γῆ ὑγρῷ φυραθεῖσα πηλὸς ἂν εἴη, τὸ δ' ὅτου ἐᾶν χαίρειν.

Theaetetus perceives

ΘΕΑΙ. Ῥᾴδιον, ὦ Σώκρατες, νῦν γε οὕτω φαίνε-

not affect the position of the enclitic. For the sense, comp. Men. 80: Καὶ τίνα τρόπον ζητήσεις, ὦ Σ., τοῦτο, ὃ μὴ οἶσθα τὸ παράπαν ὅ τι ἐστι.

12. *Ἔπειτά γέ που*] This ought strictly to refer to the illustration: which however is brought up again immediately. But we had reverted to the main subject meantime.

13. *περιέρχεται ἀπέραντον ὁδόν*] Ar. Met. 3. 1007 a: 'Ἀδύνατον ἄπειρά γ' ἐστι τὰ συμβεβηκότα διελθεῖν ἢ οὖν ἅπαντα διελθόντα ἢ μηθέν.

14. *ἐν τῇ τοῦ πηλοῦ ἐρωτήσει*] For the form of reference with ἐν, cf. Thucyd. I, 9: 'Ἐν τοῦ σκήπτρου τῇ παραδόσει. Phileb. 33: 'Ἐν τῇ συμβολῇ τῶν βίων. The frequency of this idiom perhaps

assists the genitive πηλοῦ, which is descriptive rather than objective. 'In the question of the clay.'

15. *πηλὸς ἂν εἴη*] Either, 'earth, if moistened, will be (ἂν εἴη) mud,' or 'moistened earth would seem to be (ἂν εἴη) the definition of mud.' The latter is probably right.

17. *νῦν γ' οὕτω*] 'Now as you put it.' So far Theaetetus has appeared wholly unfamiliar with the conception of a universal notion. But Socrates' illustration reminds him of the comprehensive simplicity of geometrical expressions. And thus he finds a clue in what he knows to the new labyrinth of inquiry into which Socrates invites him. Mathematical ideas,

ΘΕΑΙΤΗΤΟΣ. 19

p. 147. ται· ἀτὰρ κινδυνεύεις ἐρωτᾶν οἷον καὶ αὐτοῖς ἡμῖν ἔναγχος εἰσῆλθε διαλεγομένοις, ἐμοί τε καὶ τῷ σῷ d ὁμωνύμῳ τούτῳ Σωκράτει.

ΣΩ. Τὸ ποῖον δή, ὦ Θεαίτητε;

ΘΕΑΙ. Περὶ δυνάμεών τι ἡμῖν Θεόδωρος ὅδε 5

that the answer required is analogous to a geometrical expression; i.e. simple and comprehensive.

being the first pure abstractions which the mind arrives at, are peculiarly fitted to guide it to the contemplation of abstractions generally. So at least thought Plato, Rep. VII. 522–531. We find here the same difficulty which meets us often in Plato. We have to think of that as in process of elaboration, which is already familiar to ourselves. See Hegel, Gesch. d. Phil. p. 197: "A number of Plato's dialogues are intended merely to produce the consciousness of a general notion, which we possess without the trouble of acquiring it. Hence his discursiveness has often the effect of tediousness to us."

In reading what follows, it must be borne in mind that, by the ancients, arithmetic was studied through geometry. If a number was regarded as simple, it was a line. If as composite, it was a rectangular figure. To multiply was to construct a rectangle, to divide was to find one of its sides. Traces of this still remain in such terms as square, cube, common measure, but the method itself is obsolete. Hence it requires an effort to conceive of the square root, not as that which multiplied into itself produces a given number, but as the side of a square, which either is the number, or is equal to the rectangle which is the number. The use of the Arabic notation and of algebra has greatly assisted in expressing and conceiving the properties of numbers without reference to form.

5. Περὶ δυνάμεων τι κ. τ. λ.] See Eucl. B. X. Deff. 3–11: Εὐθεῖαι δυνάμει σύμμετροί εἰσιν, ὅταν τὰ ἀπ' αὐτῶν τετράγωνα τῷ αὐτῷ χωρίῳ μετρῆται. Ἀσύμμετροι δέ, ὅταν τοῖς ἀπ' αὐτῶν τετραγώνοις μηδὲν ἐνδέχηται χωρίον κοινὸν μέτρον γενέσθαι. Τούτων ὑποκειμένων δείκνυται ὅτι τῇ προτεθείσῃ εὐθείᾳ ὑπάρχουσιν εὐθεῖαι πλῆθει ἄπειροι ἀσύμμετροι, αἱ μὲν μήκει μόνον, αἱ δὲ καὶ δυνάμει, (v. l. σύμμετροι καὶ ἀσύμμετροι, αἱ μὲν μήκει καὶ δυνάμει, αἱ δὲ δυνάμει μόνον.) Καλείσθω οὖν ἡ μὲν προτεθεῖσα εὐθεῖα ῥητή. Καὶ αἱ ταύτῃ σύμμετροι, εἴτε μήκει καὶ δυνάμει, εἴτε δυνάμει μόνον, ῥηταί. Αἱ δὲ ταύτῃ ἀσύμμετροι, ἄλογοι καλείσθωσαν. Καὶ τὸ μὲν ἀπὸ τῆς προτεθείσης εὐθείας τετράγωνον, ῥητόν. Καὶ τὰ τούτῳ σύμμετρα, ῥητά. Τὰ δὲ τούτῳ ἀσύμμετρα, ἄλογα καλείσθω. Καὶ αἱ δυνάμεναι αὐτά, ἄλογοι· αἱ μὲν τετράγωνα εἶεν, αὐταὶ αἱ πλευραί, αἱ δὲ ἕτερά τινα εὐθύγραμμα, αἱ ἴσα αὐτοῖς τετράγωνα ἀναγράφουσαι. B. VII. 17, 19. Τετράγωνος ἀριθμός ἐστιν ὁ ἰσάκις ἴσος, ἢ ὁ ὑπὸ δύο ἴσων ἀριθμῶν περιεχόμενος. Ὅταν δὲ δύο ἀριθμοὶ πολλαπλασιάσαντες ἀλλήλους ποιῶσί τινα, ὁ γενόμενος ἐπίπεδος καλεῖται· πλευραὶ δὲ αὐτοῦ οἱ πολλαπλασιάσαντες ἀλλήλους ἀριθμοί.

5. δυνάμεων] 'Roots,' i. e. here, 'square roots,' although cube

20 ΠΛΑΤΩΝΟΣ

He relates the discovery of the integral and potential root.

ἔγραφε, τῆς τε τρίποδος πέρι καὶ πεντέποδος, ἀποφαίνων ὅτι μήκει οὐ ξύμμετροι τῇ ποδιαίᾳ, καὶ οὕτω κατὰ μίαν ἑκάστην προαιρούμενος μέχρι τῆς ἑπτακαιδεκάποδος· ἐν δὲ ταύτῃ πως ἐνέσχετο· ἡμῖν οὖν εἰσῆλθέ τι τοιοῦτον, ἐπειδὴ ἄπειροι τὸ πλῆθος αἱ δυνάμεις ἐφαίνοντο, πειραθῆναι ξυλλαβεῖν εἰς ἕν, ὅτῳ πάσας ταύτας προσαγορεύσομεν τὰς δυνάμεις.

ΣΩ. Ἦ καὶ εὑρετέ τι τοιοῦτον;

ΘΕΑΙ. Ἔμοιγε δοκοῦμεν. σκόπει δὲ καὶ σύ.

10 ΣΩ. Λέγε.

ΘΕΑΙ. Τὸν ἀριθμὸν πάντα δίχα διελάβομεν. τὸν μὲν δυνάμενον ἴσον ἰσάκις γίγνεσθαι τῷ τετραγώνῳ τὸ σχῆμα ἀπεικάσαντες τετράγωνόν τε καὶ ἰσόπλευρον προσείπομεν.

quantity is afterwards spoken of. Δύναμις is an abbreviated expression for ἡ δυναμένη εὐθεῖα. So ἡ τρίπους (δύναμις) = εὐθεῖα ἡ δυνάμει τρίπους, i. e. (a foot being the unit) √3. Cf. Polit. 266: Διάμετρος ἡ δυνάμει δίπους. Similar abbreviations occur below in the terms μήκος and δύναμις. Cf. Eucl. X. Prop. 91: Τὸ ὑπὸ ῥητῶν δυνάμει μόνον συμμέτρων εὐθειῶν περιεχόμενον ὀρθογώνιον Παρόν ἐστι. καὶ ἡ δυναμένη αὐτὸ Παρόν ἐστι. Καλείσθω δὲ μέση. Ibid. infr. Deff.: Ἐκ δύο ὀνομάτων πρώτη, δευτέρα, &c. ἀποτομὴ πρώτη, δευτέρα &c.

2. μήκει] In linear measurement. They are δυνάμει σύμμετροι, i. e. their squares are commensurable, viz. by the unit.

3. κατὰ μίαν ἑκάστην] Why did he not begin with √2? Was it because the ἄρτιος δύναμις is less than the unit, viz. 1 ft.? The ending with ἑπτακαιδεκάποδος is a mere accident, as shown by

the words, ἐν δὲ ταύτῃ πως ἐνέσχετο.

6. ξυλλαβεῖν εἰς ἕν, ὅτῳ] ὅτῳ is not the antecedent to ὅτῳ; the construction is, πρὸς τὸ σημαινόμενον, as if it were εὑρεῖν, ὅτῳ, κ.τ.λ. ' By generalizing, to find an expression that should embrace them all.' Cf. Soph. Philoct. 341: Τεκμηροῦν τὸ σὸν φράσον αὐθις πᾶλιν μοι πρᾶγμ', ὅτῳ σ' ἀνέβρισαν. Charm. 166: Ἔσθ' αὕτη τις ἐρωννύων, ὅτῳ διαφέρει πασῶν τῶν ἐπιστημῶν ἡ σωφροσύνη.

11. Τὸν ἀριθμὸν πάντα] Comp. Phaed. 104: Ἡ τριὰς καὶ ἡ πεμπτὰς καὶ ὁ ἥμισυς τοῦ ἀριθμοῦ ἅπας.
Soph. 238: Ἀριθμὸν δὴ τὸν ξύμπαντα.

12. δυνάμενον] Used here in its ordinary sense, without any reference to δυνάμεις above. ἴσον ἰσάκις γίγνεσθαι] i. e. to be made as a square number, which, as Euclid says, is ὁ ἰσάκις ἴσος, ἢ ὁ ὑπὸ δυοῖν ἴσων ἀριθμῶν περιεχόμενος. 'To arise by the

ΘΕΑΙΤΗΤΟΣ. 21

p. 147.   ΣΩ. Καὶ εὖ γε.
        ΘΕΑΙ. Τὸν τοίνυν μεταξὺ τούτου, ὧν καὶ τὰ
p. 148. τρία καὶ τὰ πέντε καὶ πᾶς ὃς ἀδύνατος ἴσος ἰσάκις
        γενέσθαι, ἀλλ' ἢ πλείων ἐλαττονάκις ἢ ἐλάττων
        πλεονάκις γίγνεται, μείζων δὲ καὶ ἐλάττων ἀεὶ πλευρὰ 5
        αὐτὸν περιλαμβάνει, τῷ προμήκει αὖ σχήματι ἀπεικά-
        σαντες προμήκη ἀριθμὸν ἐκαλέσαμεν.
        ΣΩ. Κάλλιστα. ἀλλὰ τί τὸ μετὰ τοῦτο;
        ΘΕΑΙ. Ὅσαι μὲν γραμμαὶ τὸν ἰσόπλευρον καὶ
        ἐπίπεδον ἀριθμὸν τετραγωνίζουσι, μῆκος ὡρισάμεθα, 10
        ὅσαι δὲ τὸν ἑτερομήκη, δυνάμεις, ὡς μήκει μὲν οὐ

multiplication of equal numbers.'.

7. *προμήκει — ἑτερομήκη*] These terms were distinguished by the later Pythagoreans. Nicomachus says that ἑτερομήκης ἀριθμός has one factor greater than the other by 1, προμήκης by more than 1.

10. τετραγωνίζουσι] Form as their squares.

11. ὅσαι δὲ τὸν ἑτερομήκη] sc. τετραγωνίζουσι. See Eucl. II. 14.

ὡς μήκει μὲν οὐ ξυμμέτρους ἐκείναις, τοῖς δ' ἐπιπέδοις ἃ δύνανται] Translate either, ' not commensurable with the former in linear measurement, but in the surfaces (composite numbers, see Def.) of which they are the roots,' or ' not commensurable with them in linear measurement, while they are mutually commensurable in the surfaces of which they are severally roots.' I. e. the lines which are (or stand for) the irrational roots are not commensurable with the integral roots or with unity (τῇ μονάδι), but their squares, being integers, have a common measure of unity. They are commensurable not in themselves, but in their squares, that is, they are potentially commensurable (δυνάμει μόνον σύμμετροι). For the constr. ἃ δύνανται, comp. αἱ δυνάμεναι αὐτά in the Def. above; also, Eucl. X. 22: 'Η δυναμένη αὐτά. It remains doubtful whether the one set of roots (δυνάμεις) or both are the nominative to δύνανται, and consequently, whether ταῖς ἐκείναις refers only to oblong number, or to both oblong and square number. The former alternative may be adopted as the simpler; although the latter would be the more accurate expression. Instead of enumerating all the irrational roots, which seemed infinite, they conceived the idea of finding an expression which should embrace them all. They first went for assistance from arithmetic to the less abstract forms of geometry (Ar. Met. I. 2: αἱ γὰρ ἐξ ἐλαττόνων ἀκριβέστεραι τῶν ἐκ προσθέσεως λεγομένων, οἷον ἀριθμητικὴ γεωμετρίας). Here they at once found a generalization. All numbers

22   ΠΛΑΤΩΝΟΣ

ξυμμέτρους ἐκείναις, τοῖς δ' ἐπιπέδοις ἃ δύνανται· καὶ p. 148.
περὶ τὰ στερεὰ ἄλλο τοιοῦτον.

ΣΩ. Ἀριστά γ' ἀνθρώπων, ὦ παῖδες· ὥστε μοι
δοκεῖ ὁ Θεόδωρος οὐκ ἔνοχος τοῖς ψευδομαρτυρίοις
5 ἔσεσθαι.

ΘΕΑΙ. Καὶ μήν, ὦ Σώκρατες, ὅ γε ἐρωτᾷς περὶ
ἐπιστήμης, οὐκ ἂν δυναίμην ἀποκρίνασθαι, ὥσπερ
περὶ τοῦ μήκους καὶ τῆς δυνάμεως· καίτοι σύ γέ μοι
δοκεῖς τοιοῦτόν τι ζητεῖν· ὥστε πάλιν αὖ φαίνεται
10 ψευδὴς ὁ Θεόδωρος.

ΣΩ. Τί δαί ; εἴ σε πρὸς δρόμον ἐπαινῶν μηδενὶ c

which can be produced by equal integers they called square numbers. The rest, formed of unequal factors, they called oblong. The roots of the former can be measured by unity, the roots of the latter cannot, though the numbers themselves can. Hence a general distinction, and a simple nomenclature. The roots of square numbers they called μήκη, i. e. μήκει σύμμετροι, commensurable in whole numbers, the roots of oblong numbers, δυνάμεις, i. e. δυνάμει μόνον συμμέτρους. And similarly, in regard to solid quantity, i. e. the cube roots of numbers.

In other words, $\sqrt{16} = 4$ or $16 = 4 \cdot 4$;

and $4 = \underline{2 \cdot 2} = $ the line forming one of its sides.

On the other hand

$\sqrt{12} = 3.464$ or $12 = $ □, and □ = □ ;

and $3.464 = \underline{\ldots}$, which is not commensurable with the side of the former square, although its square is commensurable, because it can be measured by unity. The boys ended with the term with which they started; and yet they had gained much: they saw now as one, what they had seen as many; as a whole, what they had seen as infinite; and this by limiting the application of the term, and distinguishing the thing from that with which they had confused it. So a real advance is made towards a true conception of knowledge, when we have distinguished it from sense and from true opinion, although we fail to define it as it is in itself.

4. οὐκ ἔνοχ. τ. ψ. ἔσεσθαι] 'Will not be found guilty of perjury.' See above, οὐδεὶς ἐπιστήψει, and note. The article refers to what has been already mentioned.

ΘΕΑΙΤΗΤΟΣ.

p. 148. οὕτω δρομικῷ ἔφη τῶν νέων ἐντετυχηκέναι, εἶτα διαθέων τοῦ ἀκμάζοντος καὶ ταχίστου ἡττήθης, ἧττόν τι ἂν οἴει ἀληθῆ τόνδ᾽ ἐπαινέσαι;

ΘΕΑΙ. Οὐκ ἔγωγε.

ΣΩ. Ἀλλὰ τὴν ἐπιστήμην, ὥσπερ νῦν δὴ ἐγὼ ἔλεγον, σμικρόν τι οἴει εἶναι ἐξευρεῖν καὶ οὐ τῶν πάντῃ ἄκρων;

ΘΕΑΙ. Νὴ τὸν Δί᾽ ἔγωγε καὶ μάλα γε τῶν ἀκροτάτων.

ΣΩ. Θάρρει τοίνυν περὶ σαυτῷ καί τι οἴου Θεόδωρον λέγειν, προθυμήθητι δὲ παντὶ τρόπῳ τῶν τε ἄλλων πέρι καὶ ἐπιστήμης λαβεῖν λόγον, τί ποτε τυγχάνει ὄν.

ΘΕΑΙ. Προθυμίας μὲν ἕνεκεν, ὦ Σώκρατες, φανεῖται.

ΣΩ. Ἴθι δή· καλῶς γὰρ ἄρτι ὑφηγήσω· πειρῶ μιμούμενος τὴν περὶ τῶν δυνάμεων ἀπόκρισιν, ὥσπερ

But he fears that the question about knowledge is not so easy.

Socrates still urges him.

He answers that he has tried ineffectually before; but is still anxious.

---

1. διαθέων] Running a course. Comp. Prot. 335: νῦν δ᾽ ἐστὶν ὥσπερ ἂν εἰ δίκαὶ μου ἐρίσειεν τῷ Ἰμεραίῳ δρομεῖ ἀκμάζοντι ἕπεσθαι, ἢ τῶν δολιχοδρόμων τῳ ἢ τῶν ἡμεροδρόμων διαθεῖν τε καὶ ἕπεσθαι. Where Socrates speaks of himself as past the δρόμων ἀκμή, (Rep. 460.) which Theaetetus here has not reached.

5. ὥσπερ νῦν δὴ] See above, σμικρὸν δέ τι ἀκορᾶ.

6. τῶν πάντῃ ἄκρων] The Bodl. MS. has ἀκριβῶν, with an accent over the α, and a dot over each of the letters ι, β. ἄκρων is required by the words which follow. Cf. Lach. 193: Τῶν πάνυ καλῶν πραγμάτων ἡμεῖ σὺ ἀνδρῶν εἶναι; Εἰ μὲν οὖν ἐσθ᾽ ὅτι τῶν μαλλίστων. The mistake perhaps originated in not perceiving that ἄκρων is masc. " Knowledge is no trifling matter to find out, but it belongs to men every way complete;" i. e. not, like the runner, in one way only.

8. τῶν ἀκροτάτων] The superlative might seem unnecessary; but cf. Legg. 906: Τῶν πανταπασιν ἀκροτάτων θεωρῶν.

12. ἐπιστήμης is governed partly by πέρι, but chiefly by λόγον.

14. προθυμ. — ἕνεκεν — φαν.] Comp. Phædr. 272: Πειρῶ λέγειν—Ἔνεκα μὲν — πείρας ἔχοιμ᾽ ἄν. Polit. 304: Πείραν μὲν τοίνυν ἕνεκα.

16. καλῶς γὰρ ἄρτι ὑφηγήσω] Comp. Gorg. 455: Αὐτὸς δεδήλωκας ὑφηγήσω.

24 ΠΛΑΤΩΝΟΣ

This is a sign, dear lad, that there is something in you, and that you ought to be made to feel the power of my art. You have heard that I am a strange fellow, but you were not aware that I practised my mother's trade. Consider the midwives; they have once had children, but are now past the age. They have thus experience

ταύτας πολλὰς οὔσας ἐνὶ εἴδει περιέλαβες, οὕτω καὶ p. 148.
τὰς πολλὰς ἐπιστήμας ἐνὶ λόγῳ προσειπεῖν.

ΘΕΑΙ. Ἀλλ' εὖ ἴσθι, ὦ Σώκρατες, πολλάκις δὴ
αὐτὸ ἐπεχείρησα σκέψασθαι, ἀκούων τὰς παρὰ σοῦ
5 ἀποφερομένας ἐρωτήσεις· ἀλλὰ γὰρ οὔτ' αὐτὸς δύναμαι πεῖσαι ἐμαυτὸν ὡς ἱκανῶς τι λέγω, οὔτ' ἄλλου
ἀκοῦσαι λέγοντος οὕτως ὡς σὺ διακελεύει· οὐ μὲν δὴ
αὖ οὐδ' ἀπαλλαγῆναι τοῦ μέλειν.

ΣΩ. Ὠδίνεις γάρ, ὦ φίλε Θεαίτητε, διὰ τὸ μὴ
10 κενὸς ἀλλ' ἐγκύμων εἶναι.

ΘΕΑΙ. Οὐκ οἶδα, ὦ Σώκρατες· ὃ μέντοι πέπονθα
λέγω.

ΣΩ. Εἶτα, ὦ καταγέλαστε, οὐκ ἀκήκοας, ὡς ἐγώ p. 149.
εἰμι υἱὸς μαίας μάλα γενναίας τε καὶ βλοσυρᾶς, Φαι-
15 ναρέτης;

ΘΕΑΙ. Ἤδη τοῦτό γε ἤκουσα.

ΣΩ. Ἄρα καί, ὅτι ἐπιτηδεύω τὴν αὐτὴν τέχνην,
ἀκήκοας;

1. ἐνὶ εἴδει περιέλαβες—ἐνὶ λόγῳ προσειπεῖν] To classify and to name (as above, συλλαβεῖν εἰς ἕν—ἑνὶ τῳ προσαγορεύσμεν) are considered as different aspects of the same thing.

2. μέλειν] The reading is doubtful. μέλειν has on the whole the best authority; but the reading of the Scholiast, εὑρεῖν, which is found on the margin of several MSS., supposing it to have been originally a gloss, agrees better with μέλειν, though it might have been suggested by either. There is an idea of uneasiness in μέλειν which suits well with the context. On the other hand, αὖθ' ἀπαλλαγῆναι τοῦ μέλειν (sc.

ἱκανῶς τι λέγω) is a thoroughly Greek expression. For μέλειν used personally, comp. Aesch. Ag. 370: θεοὺς βροτῶν ἀξιοῦσθαι μέλειν. Soph. Electr. 342: Καίτοι λαβίσθαι τῆς δὲ γιστούσης μέλειν (where it may be impersonal, as perhaps here). Eur. H. F. 772: θεοὶ θεοὶ τῶν ἀδίκων μέλουσι.

9. ὠδίνεις γάρ] Rep. 490: Καὶ οὔτω λήγοι ἄδινος, πρὶν δ' οὔ.

14. μάλα γενναίας τε καὶ βλοσυρᾶς] 'Truly noble and valiant,' or 'commanding,' 'of no common or feeble mould.'
γενναίας] 'Of the right sort.' βλοσυρᾶς, 'barly.' Comp. Rep. 535: Γενναίους τε καὶ βλοσυροὺς τὰ ἤθη.

ΘΕΑΙΤΗΤΟΣ. 25

p. 149. ΘΕΑΙ. Οὐδαμῶς.

ΣΩ. Ἀλλ' εὖ ἴσθ' ὅτι· μὴ μέντοι μου κατείπῃς πρὸς τοὺς ἄλλους· λέληθα γάρ, ὦ ἑταῖρε, ταύτην ἔχων τὴν τέχνην· οἱ δέ, ἅτε οὐκ εἰδότες, τοῦτο μὲν οὐ λέγουσι περὶ ἐμοῦ, ὅτι δὲ ἀτοπώτατός εἰμι καὶ 5 ποιῶ τοὺς ἀνθρώπους ἀπορεῖν ἢ καὶ τοῦτο ἀκήκοας ;

b ΘΕΑΙ. Ἔγωγε.

ΣΩ. Εἴπω οὖν σοι τὸ αἴτιον ;

ΘΕΑΙ. Πάνυ μὲν οὖν.

ΣΩ. Ἐννόησον δὴ τὸ περὶ τὰς μαίας ἅπαν ὡς 10 ἔχει, καὶ ῥᾷον μαθήσει ὃ βούλομαι. οἶσθα γάρ που ὡς οὐδεμία αὐτῶν ἔτι αὐτὴ κυϊσκομένη τε καὶ τίκτουσα ἄλλας μαιεύεται, ἀλλ' αἱ ἤδη ἀδύνατοι τίκτειν.

ΘΕΑΙ. Πάνυ μὲν οὖν.

ΣΩ. Αἰτίαν δέ γε τούτου φασὶν εἶναι τὴν Ἄρτε- 15 μιν, ὅτι ἄλοχος οὖσα τὴν λοχείαν εἴληχε. στερίφαις c μὲν οὖν ἄρα οὐκ ἔδωκε μαιεύεσθαι, ὅτι ἡ ἀνθρωπίνη φύσις ἀσθενεστέρα ἢ λαβεῖν τέχνην ὧν ἂν ᾖ ἄπειρος· ταῖς δὲ δι' ἡλικίαν ἀτόκοις προσέταξε, τιμῶσα τὴν αὑτῆς ὁμοιότητα. 20

of child-birth, and are also much as the virgin Goddess prefers. They perceive the state of those they meet with. They can arouse or allay the travail of a patient: and cause abortion when they think it most. They are also naturally the best matchmakers. They are slow, indeed, to acknowledge the pride they take in this, though they bring people together lawfully.

5. ἀτοπώτατος κ.τ.λ.] 'That I am the strangest of mortals, and bring men to their wit's end.' ἀτοπώτατος is the very word to express Socrates' idea of himself,—αὐτός τε καὶ τοὺς λόγους. Sympp. 215 : Οὐ γάρ τι ῥᾴδιον τὴν σὴν ἀτοπίαν ἔσθ' ὅτῳ εἰκάσομεν καὶ ἐφεξῆς καταριθμῆσαι.

ἀτοπώτατός εἰμι καὶ ποιῶ τοὺς ἀνθρώπους ἀπορεῖν] Comp. Men. 79, 80 : Ἴκανος μέν ἔγωγε καὶ πρὶν συγγενέσθαι σοι ὅτι σὺ οὐδὲν ἄλλο ἢ αὐτός τε ἀπορεῖς καὶ τοὺς ἄλλους ποιεῖς ἀπορεῖν.———καὶ δοκεῖς μοι παντελῶς, εἰ δεῖ τι καὶ σκῶψαι, ὁμοιότατος εἶναι τό τε εἶδος καὶ τἄλλα ταύτῃ τῇ πλατείᾳ νάρκῃ τῇ θαλαττίᾳ. This whole passage is at least as much in favour of the MS. reading ἀτοπώτατος, as of Stallbaum's conjecture, ἀπορώτατος, which was suggested by the former part of it.

15. Αἰτίαν] An adj. agreeing as predicate with Ἄρτεμιν. 'Artemis is responsible for this.'

16. Ἄλοχοι] Used etymologically, as if from ἀ priv., and λόχος or λοχεία.

17. ἄρα] According to this tale.

ἡ ἀνθρωπίνη φύσις ἀσθ.] 'It is not in human nature to become skilful where it is not experienced.'

19. ἀτόκοις] Bodl. p. m. ἀτόκοις. τιμῶσα τὴν αὑτῆς ὁμοιότητα] 'In

ΠΛΑΤΩΝΟΣ

fully, and not unlawfully.

ΘΕΑΙ. Εἰκός.

ΣΩ. Οὐκοῦν καὶ τόδε εἰκός τε καὶ ἀναγκαῖον, τὰς κυούσας καὶ μὴ γιγνώσκεσθαι μᾶλλον ὑπὸ τῶν μαιῶν ἢ τῶν ἄλλων;

ΘΕΑΙ. Πάνυ γε.

ΣΩ. Καὶ μὴν καὶ διδοῦσαί γε αἱ μαῖαι φαρμάκια καὶ ἐπᾴδουσαι δύνανται ἐγείρειν τε τὰς ὠδῖνας καὶ μαλθακωτέρας, ἂν βούλωνται, ποιεῖν, καὶ τίκτειν τε δὴ τὰς δυστοκούσας, καὶ ἐὰν νέον ὂν δόξῃ ἀμβλίσκειν, ἀμβλίσκουσιν;

ΘΕΑΙ. Ἔστι ταῦτα.

ΣΩ. Ἆρ' οὖν ἔτι καὶ τόδε αὐτῶν ᾔσθησαι, ὅτι καὶ προμνήστριαί εἰσι δεινόταται, ὡς πάσσοφοι οὖσαι περὶ τοῦ γνῶναι ποίαν χρὴ ποίῳ ἀνδρὶ συνοῦσαν ὡς ἀρίστους παῖδας τίκτειν;

ΘΕΑΙ. Οὐ πάνυ τοῦτο οἶδα.

ΣΩ. Ἀλλ' ἴσθ' ὅτι ἐπὶ τούτῳ μεῖζον φρονοῦσιν ἢ ἐπὶ τῇ ὀμφαλητομίᾳ. ἐννόει γάρ· τῆς αὐτῆς ἢ ἄλλης οἴει τέχνης εἶναι θεραπείαν τε καὶ ξυγκομιδὴν τῶν ἐκ γῆς καρπῶν καὶ αὖ τὸ γιγνώσκειν εἰς ποίαν γῆν ποῖον φυτόν τε καὶ σπέρμα καταβλητέον;

ΘΕΑΙ. Οὔκ, ἀλλὰ τῆς αὐτῆς.

p. 149.

honour of their resemblance to herself,' τιμῶσα, 'prizing.' Cf. Symp. 208 : Τὸ αὑτοῦ ἀναβλάστημα φύσει πᾶν τιμᾷ.

6. φαρμάκια] The Diminutive is noticeable. 'Gentle remedies.'

8. τίκτειν τε δὴ] Sc. ποιεῖν.

9. νέον ὂν] Sc. τὸ βρέφος. Said here of the embryo, 'At an early stage,' i. e. before it is dangerous to do so. Cf. Hipp. de Morb. Mul. § 3, 97: Ἢν γυναῖκον φθείρῃ τὸ παιδίον, where the same thing is spoken of. For the ellipse, which is a little difficult, v. infr. p. 161. τὸ γε οὖν, sc. κύημα. Διάνοια is lost sight of as the sentence proceeds. Such a transition to the indicative mood is not unfrequent. Cf. Rep. 465: Γῆρα διάγουσαι, ξωτίς τι, καὶ τελευτήσαντες ταφῆς ἀξίας μετέχουσι.

14. ποίαν χρή] 'What woman should be married to what man, to produce the noblest offspring.'

ΘΕΑΙΤΗΤΟΣ. 27

p. 149. ΣΩ. Εἰς γυναῖκα δέ, ὦ φίλε, ἄλλην μὲν οἴει τοῦ τοιούτου, ἄλλην δὲ ξυγκομιδῆς;

ΘΕΑΙ. Οὔκουν εἰκός γε.

p. 150. ΣΩ. Οὐ γάρ. ἀλλὰ διὰ τὴν ἄδικόν τε καὶ ἄτεχνον ξυναγωγὴν ἀνδρὸς καὶ γυναικός, ᾗ δὴ προαγωγία ὄνομα, φεύγουσι καὶ τὴν προμνηστικὴν ἅτε σεμναὶ οὖσαι αἱ μαῖαι, φοβούμεναι μὴ εἰς ἐκείνην τὴν αἰτίαν διὰ ταύτην ἐμπέσωσιν. ἐπεὶ ταῖς γε ὄντως μαίαις μόναις που προσήκει καὶ προμνήσασθαι ὀρθῶς.

ΘΕΑΙ. Φαίνεται.

ΣΩ. Τὸ μὲν τοίνυν τῶν μαιῶν τοσοῦτον, ἔλαττον δὲ τοῦ ἐμοῦ δράματος. οὐ γὰρ πρόσεστι γυναιξὶν b ἐνίοτε μὲν εἴδωλα τίκτειν, ἔστι δ᾽ ὅτε ἀληθινά, τοῦτο δὲ μὴ ῥᾴδιον εἶναι διαγνῶναι. εἰ γὰρ προσῆν, μέγιστόν τε καὶ κάλλιστον ἔργον ἦν ἂν ταῖς μαίαις τὸ κρίνειν τὸ ἀληθές τε καὶ μή. ἢ οὐκ οἴει;

ΘΕΑΙ. Ἔγωγε.

ΣΩ. Τῇ δέ γ᾽ ἐμῇ τέχνῃ τῆς μαιεύσεως τὰ μὲν

My art is greater still

1. τοῦ τοιούτου] Sic. τοῦ τοιούτου συνέρμα καταβλητέον. There is MS. authority for τούτου, but τοῦ τοιούτου is more natural in the connexion. It avoids tautology; and besides the processes are analogous, rather than similar.

4. ἄδικόν τε καὶ ἄτεχνον] 'unlawful and skill-less:' contrary to morality and nature.

6. ἅτε σεμναὶ οὖσαι αἱ μαῖαι] Socrates himself however is not so particular. Xen. Symp. III. 10: Σὺ δὲ δή, ἔφη ὁ Καλλίας, ἐπὶ τίνι μέγα φρονεῖς, ὦ Σώκρατες; καὶ ὃς μάλα σεμνῶς ἀνασπάσας τὸ πρόσωπον, Ἐπὶ μαστροπείᾳ, εἶπεν. Ἐπεὶ δὲ ἐγέλασαν ἐπ᾽ αὐτῷ, Ὑμεῖς μὲν γελᾶτε, ἔφη· ἐγὼ δὲ οἶδ᾽ ὅτι καὶ πάνυ ἂν πολλὰ χρήματα λαμ-

βάνοιμι, εἰ βουλοίμην χρῆσθαι τῇ τέχνῃ.

11. πλαττον δὲ] There is a slight irregularity in the antithesis, occasioned by the stress on τοσοῦτον. The balance of clauses is, however, completed with τῇ δέ γ᾽ ἐμῇ α. τ. λ.

18. Τῇ δέ γ᾽ ἐμῇ τέχνῃ τῆς μαιεύσεως] For the well-known metaphor, which is nowhere else so completely elaborated, compare Symp. p. 206, sqq. (where Diotima proceeds to explain the mystical expression τόκος ἐν καλῷ) κυοῦσι γάρ, ἔφη, ὦ Σώκρατες, πάντες ἄνθρωποι καὶ κατὰ τὸ σῶμα καὶ κατὰ τὴν ψυχήν, καὶ ἐπειδὰν ἔν τινι ἡλικίᾳ γένωνται, τίκτειν ἐπιθυμεῖ ἡμῶν ἡ φύσις. τίκτειν δὲ ἐν μὲν αἰσχρῷ οὐ δύναται, ἐν δὲ τῷ καλῷ.

E 2

28 ΠΛΑΤΩΝΟΣ

than theirs, for it is exercised upon the minds of men, and I can also discern the false birth

ἀλλὰ ὑπάρχει ὅσα ἐκείναις, διαφέρει δὲ τῷ τε ἄνδρας p. 150. ἀλλὰ μὴ γυναῖκας μαιεύεσθαι καὶ τῷ τὰς ψυχὰς αὐτῶν τικτούσας ἐπισκοπεῖν ἀλλὰ μὴ τὰ σώματα. μέγιστον δὲ τοῦτ' ἔνι τῇ ἡμετέρᾳ τέχνῃ, βασανίζειν 5 δυνατὸν εἶναι παντὶ τρόπῳ, πότερον εἴδωλον καὶ 5

ἔστι δὲ τοῦτο θεῖον τὸ πρᾶγμα καὶ τοῦτο ἐν θνητῷ ἐστι τῷ ζῴῳ ἀθάνατόν ἐστιν, ἡ αἴσθησις καὶ ἡ γέννησις.
——ὅθεν δὴ τῷ ἀνιόντι τε καὶ ἤδη ἀνεωγμένῳ πολλὴ ἡ ἀπορία· γέγονε περὶ τὸ καλὸν διὰ τὸ μεγάλης ἀδίκως ἀπολύειν τὸν ἔχοντα. ib. 209. τούτων αὖ ὅταν τις ἐκ νέου ἐγκύμων ᾖ τὴν ψυχὴν θεῖος ὤν, κ. τ. λ. to the end of the speech. Repub. p. 490: Οὐκ ἀμβλύνοιτο οὐδ' ἀπολήγοι τοῦ ἔρωτος, πρὶν αὐτοῦ ὃ ἔστιν ἑκάστου τῆς φύσεως ἅψασθαι ᾧ προσήκει ψυχῆς ἐφάπτεσθαι τοῦ τοιούτου· πελάσας δὲ καὶ μιγεὶς τῷ ὄντι ὄντως, γεννήσας νοῦν καὶ ἀλήθειαν, γνοίη τε καὶ ἀληθῶς ζῴη καὶ τρέφοιτο καὶ οὕτω λήγοι ὠδῖνος, πρὶν δ' οὔ. So far of the relation of the mind to knowledge. For the relation of the teacher and the taught see Phaedr. 276, 278: Πολὺ δ', οἶμαι, καλλίων σπουδὴ περὶ αὐτὰ γίγνεται, ὅταν τις τῇ διαλεκτικῇ τέχνῃ χρώμενος, λαβὼν ψυχὴν προσήκουσαν, φυτεύῃ τε καὶ σπείρῃ μετ' ἐπιστήμης λόγους, οἳ ἑαυτοῖς τῷ τε φυτεύσαντι βοηθεῖν ἱκανοί, καὶ οὐχὶ ἄκαρποι ἀλλὰ ἔχοντες σπέρμα. — ἐὰν δὲ τοῖς τοιούτοις λόγοις αὐτοῦ λέγεσθαι οἷον υἱέσι γνησίοις εἶναι, πρῶτον μὲν τῷ ἐν ἑαυτῷ, ἐὰν εὑρεθεὶς ἐνῇ, ἔπειτα εἴ τινες τούτου ἔκγονοί τε καὶ ἀδελφοὶ ἅμα ἐν ἄλλαισιν ἄλλων ψυχαῖς κατ' ἀξίαν ἐνέφυσαν. For the theory of teaching and learning thus illustrated see Rep. 518: δεῖ δή, ἔφην, ἡμᾶς τοιόνδε νομίσαι περὶ αὐτῶν, εἰ τοῦτ' ἀληθές, τὴν παιδείαν, οὐχ οἵαν τινες ἐπαγγελλό-

μενοί φασιν εἶναι τοιαύτην καὶ εἶναι. φασὶ δέ που οὐκ ἐνούσης ἐν τῇ ψυχῇ ἐπιστήμης σφεῖς ἐντιθέναι, οἷον τυφλοῖς ὀφθαλμοῖς ὄψιν ἐντιθέντες, κ. τ. λ. Where it occurs under a different metaphor, that of the cave.

It is always difficult to separate the Platonic from the real Socrates. In the present passage they are indissolubly blended. That men thought Socrates the strangest being, and that he brought them to their wit's end, is matter of fact. The quaint humour, perhaps even the name 'Son of a Midwife,' is Socrates' own. But it is impossible to determine how far the theory based upon his practice, that to teach is not to put something into the mind but to evolve something out of it, or to turn the mind from darkness to light, was consciously held by Socrates himself, and how far it is Plato's theory of the method Socrates pursued. It receives its full development in the VIIth book of the Republic.

3. μέγιστον δὲ τοῦτ' ἔνι] 'But as its greatest triumph my art comprises this.' δὲ answers to μὲν above, the former δὲ being parenthetical.

5. δυνατὸν] Sc. τὸν ἔχοντα αὐτήν.

εἴδωλον] Comp. Rep. 520. (From whence Bacon probably took his Idola.) Soph. 240, 264, 266.

ΘΕΑΙΤΗΤΟΣ. 29

p. 150. ψεῦδος ἀποτίκτει τοῦ νέου ἡ διάνοια ἡ γόνιμόν τε καὶ
ἀληθές. ἐπεὶ τόδε γε καὶ ἐμοὶ ὑπάρχει, ὅπερ ταῖς
μαίαις· ἄγονός εἰμι σοφίας, καὶ ὅπερ ἤδη πολλοί μοι
ὠνείδισαν, ὡς τοὺς μὲν ἄλλους ἐρωτῶ, αὐτὸς δὲ οὐδὲν
ἀποκρίνομαι περὶ οὐδενὸς διὰ τὸ μηδὲν ἔχειν σοφόν, 5
ἀληθὲς ὀνειδίζουσι. τὸ δὲ αἴτιον τούτου τόδε· μαιεύ-
εσθαί με ὁ θεὸς ἀναγκάζει, γεννᾶν δὲ ἀπεκώλυσεν.
εἰμὶ δὴ οὖν αὐτὸς μὲν οὐ πάνυ τις σοφός, οὐδέ τί μοι
d ἔστιν εὕρημα τοιοῦτο γεγονός, τῆς ἐμῆς ψυχῆς ἔκ-
γονον· οἱ δ᾽ ἐμοὶ ξυγγιγνόμενοι τὸ μὲν πρῶτον φαί- 10
νονται ἔνιοι μὲν καὶ πάνυ ἀμαθεῖς, πάντες δὲ προϊού-
σης τῆς ξυνουσίας, οἷσπερ ἂν ὁ θεὸς παρείκῃ, θαυμαστὸν ὅσον ἐπιδιδόντες, ὡς αὑτοῖς τε καὶ τοῖς ἄλλοις
δοκοῦσι· καὶ τοῦτο ἐναργὲς ὅτι παρ᾽ ἐμοῦ οὐδὲν πώποτε μαθόντες, ἀλλ᾽ αὐτοὶ παρ᾽ αὑτῶν πολλὰ καὶ 15

1. ἀποτίκτει] 'Is delivered of.'

2. ἐπεὶ τόδε γε] 'For I have the same previous condition which the midwives have, in being barren of wisdom.'

7. ὁ θεὸς] Who presides over my art as Artemis does over that of the midwives. This must not be identified with τὸ δαιμόνιον, though they are probably connected (see below, and cf. Apol. 40: τὸ τοῦ θεοῦ σημεῖον), but belongs rather to the belief expressed in Apol. 21, 23, where he speaks of his cross-questioning as a Divine service, because occasioned by the oracle at Delphi; and Phaed. 85: Ἐγὼ δὲ καὶ αὐτὸς ἡγοῦμαι ὁμόδουλός εἰμι τῶν κύκνων καὶ ἱερὸς τοῦ αὐτοῦ θεοῦ, viz. of Apollo the god of the true μουσική (Phaed. 61: Ὡς φιλοσοφίας οὔσης μεγίστης μουσικῆς): but here, as in one or two places of the Apology, the feeling is generalized.

8. τις] Bodl. Vat. Ven. Π.

οὐδέ τί μοι] 'Nor have I had such a prize of my invention born to me, the offspring of my own mind.' Perhaps there is a slight play upon the word εὕρημα. Compare Soph. Œd. Tyr. 1107: Εἴθ᾽ ὁ Βακχεῖος θεὸς εὕρημα δέξατ᾽ ἔκ του Νυμφᾶν Ἑλικωνίδων, αἷς πλεῖστα συμπαίζει; but the primary meaning is 'invention,' cf. Phaedr. 278: Υἱεῖς γνησίους — ἑαυτοῦ, ἐὰν εὑρεθεὶς ἐνῇ, and εὑρόντες below.

9. ἔστιν—γεγονός] This differs from γέγονεν as ἔχω with aor. or perf. partic. differs from the perf. act.

13. ἐπιδιδόντες] Sc. φαίνονται.

14. καὶ τοῦτο ἐναργὲς ὅτι] 'And that manifestly.' τοῦτο sc. συνοῦσιν, viz. ἐπιδιδόασιν.

ἐναργὲς ὅτι] A strengthened form of δῆλον ὅτι. 'As clear as day.' Plato frequently thus extends an idiom.

If I am permitted to receive them, they again improve.

καλὰ εὑρόντες τε καὶ κατέχοντες. τῆς μέντοι μαιείας p. 150.
ὁ θεός τε καὶ ἐγὼ αἴτιος. ὧδε δὲ δῆλον· πολλοὶ ἤδη
τοῦτο ἀγνοήσαντες καὶ ἑαυτοὺς αἰτιασάμενοι, ἐμοῦ
δὲ καταφρονήσαντες, ἢ αὐτοὶ ὑπ' ἄλλων πεισθέντες,
5 ἀπῆλθον πρωιαίτερον τοῦ δέοντος, ἀπελθόντες δὲ τά
τε λοιπὰ ἐξήμβλωσαν διὰ πονηρὰν ξυνουσίαν καὶ τὰ
ὑπ' ἐμοῦ μαιευθέντα κακῶς τρέφοντες ἀπώλεσαν,
ψευδῆ καὶ εἴδωλα περὶ πλείονος ποιησάμενοι τοῦ
ἀληθοῦς, τελευτῶντες δ' αὑτοῖς τε καὶ τοῖς ἄλλοις
10 ἔδοξαν ἀμαθεῖς εἶναι. ὧν εἷς γέγονεν Ἀριστείδης ὁ p. 151.
Λυσιμάχου καὶ ἄλλοι πάνυ πολλοί. οἵς, ὅταν πάλιν
ἔλθωσιν δεόμενοι τῆς ἐμῆς ξυνουσίας καὶ θαυμαστὰ
δρῶντες, ἐνίοις μὲν τὸ γιγνόμενόν μοι δαιμόνιον ἀπο-
κωλύει ξυνεῖναι, ἐνίοις δὲ ἐᾷ, καὶ πάλιν αὐτοὶ ἐπι-

4. ἢ αὐτοὶ ὑπ'] 'They left me, whether it was that they despised me, or were themselves won over by some one else.' The minuteness of the antithesis need not throw suspicion on the reading. πεισθέντες, 'attracted,' 'captivated.' v. Thucyd. VI. 54. (One MS. however has αὐτοὶ ἢ ὑπ'.)

6. ἐξήμβλωσαν] Cf. Aristoph. Nub. 137. φροντίδ' ἐξήμβλωκας ἐξηυρημένην.

διὰ πονηρὰν ξυνουσίαν] Symp. l. c.: Τίκτειν δ' ἐν μὲν αἰσχρῷ οὐ δύναται, ἐν δὲ τῷ καλῷ.

10. Ἀριστείδης ὁ Λυσιμάχου] We read of the introduction of this youth to Socrates in the Laches, p. 179: Λυσίμ. Ἡμῖν εἰσιν υἱεῖς οὑτοιί, ὅδε μὲν τοῦδε—ἐμὸς δὲ αὖ ὅδε πατέρος δὲ καὶ οὗτος ὄνομα ἔχει τοὐμοῦ σατράπα. Ἀριστείδην γὰρ αὐτὸν καλοῦμεν. Lysimachus and Melesias are consulting Nicias and Laches, in the presence of Socrates, about their sons, Aristides and Thucydides.

12. θαυμαστὰ δρῶντες] 'Showing extraordinary solicitude.' 'Going on their knees to me.' Cf. Apol. 35: Ἑόρακά τινας—θαυμάσια ἐργαζομένους, ἐν δαιμόν τι αἰσομένους τείσεσθαι εἰ ἀποθανοῦνται.

13. τὸ δαιμόνιον] Here, as always, not commanding, but forbidding; and, as generally, neuter and impersonal. This is not the place to discuss the subject. It suits well with the intensely self-reflective nature of Socrates (lost sometimes for whole days in thought) that he should pause suddenly on the eve of doing something, without being able (at the time) to explain to himself and others the motives of reason or feeling which checked him.

14. αὐτοὶ] v. l. οὕτοι. αὐτοὶ has the best authority, and is perhaps also preferable as the more difficult reading. It is certainly admissible. 'In some cases I am permitted to do so, and the men themselves improve.' Not unfrequently the

ΘΕΑΙΤΗΤΟΣ. 31

p. 151. διδόασι. πάσχουσι δὲ δὴ οἱ ἐμοὶ ξυγγιγνόμενοι καὶ
τοῦτο ταὐτὸν ταῖς τικτούσαις· ὠδίνουσι γὰρ καὶ ἀπορίας ἐμπίπλανται νύκτας τε καὶ ἡμέρας πολὺ μᾶλλον
ἢ ἐκεῖναι. ταύτην δὲ τὴν ὠδῖνα ἐγείρειν τε καὶ ἀπο-
b παύειν ἡ ἐμὴ τέχνη δύναται. καὶ οὗτοι μὲν δὴ οὕτως. 5
ἐνίοτε δέ, ὦ Θεαίτητε, οἳ ἄν μοι μὴ δόξωσί πως ἐγ-
κύμονες εἶναι, γνοὺς ὅτι οὐδὲν ἐμοῦ δέονται, πάνυ
εὐμενῶς προμνῶμαι, καὶ ξὺν θεῷ εἰπεῖν, πάνυ ἱκανῶς
τοπάζω οἷς ἂν ξυγγενόμενοι ὄναιντο. ὧν πολλοὺς μὲν
δὴ ἐξέδωκα Προδίκῳ, πολλοὺς δὲ ἄλλοις σοφοῖς τε 10
καὶ θεσπεσίοις ἀνδράσι. Ταῦτα δή σοι, ὦ ἄριστε,
ἕνεκα τοῦδε ἐμήνυσα, ὑποπτεύων σε, ὥσπερ καὶ αὐτὸς
οἴει, ὠδίνειν τι κυοῦντα ἔνδον. προσφέρου οὖν πρός
c με ὡς πρὸς μαίας υἱὸν καὶ αὐτὸν μαιευτικόν, καὶ ἃ ἂν
ἐρωτῶ, προθυμοῦ ὅπως οἷός τ' εἶ, οὕτως ἀποκρίνασθαι. 15
καὶ ἐὰν ἄρα σκοπούμενός τι ὧν ἂν λέγῃς, ἡγήσωμαι
εἴδωλον καὶ μὴ ἀληθές, εἶτα ὑπεξαιρῶμαι καὶ ἀπο-
βάλλω, μὴ ἀγρίαινε ὥσπερ αἱ πρωτοτόκοι περὶ τὰ
παιδία. πολλοὶ γὰρ ἤδη, ὦ θαυμάσιε, πρός με οὕτω
διετέθησαν, ὥστε ἀτεχνῶς δάκνειν ἕτοιμοι εἶναι, ἐπει- 20
δάν τινα λῆρον αὐτῶν ἀφαιρῶμαι, καὶ οὐκ οἴονται

My patience is also sore in travail, and my art can rouse or allay this pain. And if some come to me whom I perceive not to need my skill, I give them away to Prodicus or to some other: and in this department too I seldom fail. Take courage then, and be not angry if I put aside your first-born as not worth rearing. I am guided in this also by the Deity, who desires your good.

more subtle and minute antithesis is preferred to the broader and more obvious one. Thus often the reader is puzzled for a moment by finding a negative reply where he expected an affirmative, or vice versa: that which is negatived or affirmed being contained not in the whole of the previous sentence, but in the last word of it. But it must be admitted that the argument is more perfect with αὐτοῦ.

6. πως] Qualifying μὴ δόξωσι. 'Whom, somehow, I perceive not' etc.

10. ἐξέδωκα] For the word, cf. Soph. 242: Διὸ δὴ ἕτερον εἰπεῖν (τὸ ὄντα). Ὑγρὸν καὶ ξηρὸν ἢ θερμὸν καὶ ψυχρόν, στοιχειώζει τε αὐτὰ καὶ ἐκδίδωσι. For the thing, see Lach. 200: Νικ. τὸν Νικηρατον τούτῳ ἥκιστα ἐπιτετράμμαι, εἰ ἐθέλοι αὐτὸν ἄλλα γὰρ ἄλλοντ' μοι ἑκάστοτε συνιστάναι.

12. ὥσπερ καὶ αὐτὸς οἴει] Cf. supr. p. 148: 'Ἀλλ' τὸ ἐσθ—ταπασθα λέγω.

13. προσφέρου] Charm. 165: Σὺ μὲν δέ φάσκοντι ἐμοὶ εἰδέναι περὶ ὧν ἐρωτῷ προσφέρει κρὶν μι.

17. ὑπεξαιρῶμαι] Bekk. corr. The MSS. have ὑπεξαίρωμαι. See below, ἀφαιρῶμαι.

ἀποβάλλω] Bodl. ὑποβάλλω.

32   ΠΛΑΤΩΝΟΣ

εὐνοίᾳ τοῦτο ποιεῖν, πόρρω ὄντες τοῦ εἰδέναι ὅτι οὐδεὶς p. 151.
θεὸς δύσνους ἀνθρώποις, οὐδ᾽ ἐγὼ δυσνοίᾳ τοιοῦτον d
οὐδὲν δρῶ, ἀλλά μοι ψεῦδός τε ξυγχωρῆσαι καὶ ἀληθὲς ἀφανίσαι οὐδαμῶς θέμις. Πάλιν δὴ οὖν ἐξ ἀρχῆς,
ὦ Θεαίτητε, ὅ τί ποτ᾽ ἐστὶν ἐπιστήμη, πειρῶ λέγειν·
ὡς δ᾽ οὐχ οἷός τ᾽ εἶ, μηδέποτ᾽ εἴπῃς. ἐὰν γὰρ θεὸς
ἐθέλῃ καὶ ἀνδρίζῃ, οἷός τ᾽ ἔσει.

Theaetetus now ventures to answer.

ΘΕΑΙ. Ἀλλὰ μέντοι, ὦ Σώκρατες, σοῦ γε οὕτω
παρακελευομένου αἰσχρὸν μὴ οὐ παντὶ τρόπῳ προθυ-

I. Knowledge is Sensation.

μεῖσθαι ὅ τί τις ἔχει λέγειν. δοκεῖ οὖν μοι ὁ ἐπιστά- e
μενός τι αἰσθάνεσθαι τοῦτο ὃ ἐπίσταται, καὶ ὥς γε

1. 'Why Protagoras meant this

νυνὶ φαίνεται, οὐκ ἄλλο τί ἐστιν ἐπιστήμη ἢ αἴσθησις.

(21.) τοῦ λέγειν] Some 'barren aim.'

αἰσυναι] Plutarch in quoting this passage reads αἰσυναί με.

1. εἰδὼς θεόν] 'And therefore not the presiding genius of my Art.'

8. σοῦ γε] I. e. 'You, whom I respect so highly.'

9. μὴ οὐ] See Appendix B.

12. ἐπιστήμη — αἴσθησις] The term αἴσθησις is more simple and more extensive than any one by which it could be rendered in English. See below, 156: Αἱ μὲν οὖν αἰσθήσεις τὰ τοιάδε ἡμῖν ἔχουσιν ὀνόματα, ὄψεις τε καὶ ἀκοαὶ καὶ ὀσφρήσεις καὶ ψύξεις καὶ καύσεις καὶ ἡδοναί γε δὴ καὶ λῦπαι καὶ ἐπιθυμίαι καὶ φόβοι κ.τ.λ. Perhaps 'to see and feel is to know,' is the nearest equivalent to what Theaetetus means. But 'feeling' has ethical associations which must be excluded here. The German word 'Sinn' presents a nearer parallel.

Before reflection begins, our individual impressions are those of which we are most conscious and most certain. And subjective certainty is the primitive meaning of τὸ ἐπίστασθαι Hence αἴσθησις seems at first sight identical with ἐπιστήμη. Vid. Phaed. 83: Ὅτι ψυχὴ παντὸς ἀνθρώπου ἀναγκάζεται ἅμα τε ἡσθῆναι ἢ λυπηθῆναι σφόδρα ἐπί τῳ καὶ ἡγεῖσθαι, περὶ ὃ ἂν μάλιστα τοῦτο πάσχῃ, τοῦτο ἐναργέστατόν τε καὶ ἀληθέστατον, οὐχ οὕτως ὄν. Aristotle Metaph. III. 1009 b: 'Ἡ περὶ τὰ φαινόμενα ἀλήθεια ἐνίοις ἐκ τῶν αἰσθητῶν ἐλήλυθεν.—Ὅπως δὲ διὰ τὸ ὑπολαμβάνειν φρόνησιν μὲν τὴν αἴσθησιν, ταύτην δ᾽ εἶναι ἀλλοίωσιν, τὸ φαινόμενον κατὰ τὴν αἴσθησιν ἐξ ἀνάγκης ἀληθὲς εἶναί φασιν. The saying of Theaetetus is shown to be the meeting point of two lines of speculation; the one of which may be termed in modern language, subjective, the other objective: the one regarding all knowledge as relative and apparent to man: the other regarding things without reference to man as in a state of transience or

ΘΕΑΙΤΗΤΟΣ. 33

p. 151. ΣΩ. Εὖ γε καὶ γενναίως, ὦ παῖ· χρὴ γὰρ οὕτως ἀποφαινόμενον λέγειν. ἀλλὰ φέρε δὴ αὐτὸ κοινῇ σκεψώμεθα, γόνιμον ἢ ἀνεμαῖον τυγχάνει ὄν. αἴσθησις, φῄς, ἐπιστήμη;

ΘΕΑΙ. Ναί.

ΣΩ. Κινδυνεύεις μέντοι λόγον οὐ φαῦλον εἰρη-
p. 152. κέναι περὶ ἐπιστήμης, ἀλλ' ὃν ἔλεγε καὶ Πρωταγόρας. τρόπον δέ τινα ἄλλον εἴρηκε τὰ αὐτὰ ταῦτα. φησὶ γάρ που πάντων χρημάτων μέτρον ἄνθρωπον εἶναι, τῶν μὲν ὄντων, ὡς ἔστι, τῶν δὲ μὴ ὄντων, ὡς οὐκ ἔστιν. ἀνέγνωκας γάρ που;

ΘΕΑΙ. Ἀνέγνωκα καὶ πολλάκις.

ΣΩ. Οὐκοῦν οὕτω πως λέγει, ὡς οἷα μὲν ἕκαστα ἐμοὶ φαίνεται, τοιαῦτα μέν ἐστιν ἐμοί, οἷα δὲ σοί, τοιαῦτα δὲ αὖ σοί· ἄνθρωπος δὲ σύ τε κἀγώ;

ΘΕΑΙ. Λέγει γὰρ οὖν οὕτως.

when he said, 'The man the measure of what is.' i. e. What appears to me, is real to me.

relation; thus sense cannot be knowledge, unless knowledge is relative, and being is change. This leads to an analysis of Sensation. We are made aware of its real nature, and so taught to distinguish Knowledge from it. See Aristot. de An. III. 3: δοκεῖ δὲ τὸ νοεῖν καὶ τὸ φρονεῖν ὥσπερ αἰσθάνεσθαί τι εἶναι· ἐν ἀμφοτέροις γὰρ τούτοις ἡ ψυχὴ κρίνει τι καὶ γνωρίζει τῶν ὄντων· καὶ οἵ γε ἀρχαῖοι τὸ φρονεῖν καὶ τὸ αἰσθάνεσθαι ταὐτόν εἶναί φασιν. ὥσπερ καὶ Ἐμπεδοκλῆς εἴρηκε, Πρὸς παρεὸν γὰρ μῆτις ἀέξεται ἀνθρώποισιν, καὶ ἐν ἄλλοις—Ὅθεν σφίσιν αἰεὶ καὶ τὸ φρονεῖν ἀλλοῖα παρίσταται. Τὸ δ' αὐτὸ βούλεται τούτοις καὶ τὸ τοῦ Ὁμήρου, Τοῖος γὰρ νόος ἐστὶν ἐπιχθονίων ἀνθρώπων, οἷον ἐπ' ἦμαρ ἄγῃσι πατὴρ ἀνδρῶν τε θεῶν τε.

9. ἄνθρωπος] Not 'Man,' i. e. collective human nature; nor yet exactly 'Each man.' As we have seen, p. 147, Theætetus is little conscious of the universal. Hence ἄνθρωπος signifies to him not humanity, nor yet the individual, as opposed to it, but this or that man, 'any man you choose.' And whether or not it was so intended by Protagoras, it certainly appears to have been so understood by his 'disciples,' who are here referred to.

6. Κινδυνεύεις μέντοι] 'Well, after all, I should not wonder if'——

13. ἐν οἷα μὲν, κ. τ. λ.] Cf. Cratyl. 385, 6: Ὥσπερ Πρωταγόρας ἔλεγε, λέγων πάντων χρημάτων μέτρον εἶναι ἄνθρωπον, ὡς ἄρα οἷα μὲν ἂν ἐμοὶ φαίνηται τὰ πράγματα εἶναι, τοιαῦτα μέν ἐστιν ἐμοί, οἷα δ' ἂν σοί, τοιαῦτα δ' αὖ σοί.

84   ΠΛΑΤΩΝΟΣ

p. 152.

e. g. When it is asked, Is the wind cold? Protagoras would say it is cold to him who feels cold. Appearance in this case is sensation. The wind is to me as I sensibly perceive it. i. e. Sensation discovers that which is.

ΣΩ. Εἰκὸς μέντοι σοφὸν ἄνδρα μὴ ληρεῖν ἐπα- b
κολουθήσωμεν οὖν αὐτῷ. ἆρ᾽ οὐκ ἐνίοτε πνέοντος
ἀνέμου τοῦ αὐτοῦ ὁ μὲν ἡμῶν ῥιγοῖ, ὁ δ᾽ οὔ; καὶ ὁ
μὲν ἠρέμα, ὁ δὲ σφόδρα;

5 ΘΕΑΙ. Καὶ μάλα.

ΣΩ. Πότερον οὖν τότε αὐτὸ ἐφ᾽ ἑαυτὸ τὸ πνεῦμα
ψυχρὸν ἢ οὐ ψυχρὸν φήσομεν; ἢ πεισόμεθα τῷ
Πρωταγόρᾳ ὅτι τῷ μὲν ῥιγοῦντι ψυχρόν, τῷ δὲ
μὴ οὔ;

10 ΘΕΑΙ. Ἔοικεν.

ΣΩ. Οὐκοῦν καὶ φαίνεται οὕτως ἑκατέρῳ;

ΘΕΑΙ. Ναί.

ΣΩ. Τὸ δέ γε φαίνεται αἰσθάνεσθαί ἐστιν;

ΘΕΑΙ. Ἔστι γάρ.

15 ΣΩ. Φαντασία ἄρα καὶ αἴσθησις ταὐτόν ἔν τε c

1. μέντοι] 'Well, at all events.' εἰκὸς μέντοι σοφὸν ἄνδρα μὴ λ.] Phaedr. 260: Οὐκ ἀπόβλητον ἔπος εἶπα δεῖ—ὃ ἂν εἴπωσι σοφοί, ἀλλὰ σκοπεῖν μή τι λέγωσι. καὶ δὴ καὶ τὸ σὸν ληκθὲν οὐκ ἀφετέον.

6. ἐφ᾽ ἑαυτὸ] The accusative may be defended from Thucyd. I. 141: Τὸ ἐφ᾽ ἑαυτὸν ἕκαστος συνίδῃ. IV. 28: Τὸ ἐπὶ σφᾶς εἶπα. The prep. is used in a slightly pregnant sense, = ἡμαστατικῶς, 'As far as to itself, and no further.' v. infr. p. 160: Οὐδὶ — ἱαυτὸ—ἑαυτῷ ταὐτόν γενήσεται. (Perhaps the accus. is also partly due to the action of φήσομεν, or to the idea of motion in πνεῦμα.) For the use of the reflexive pronoun cf. Rep. 419: Καὶ ταῦτα δι᾽ ἑαυτόν. Compare with this passage Locke Hum. Underst. II. 8. § 21: "The same water may produce the sensation of cold in the one hand and heat in the other."

13. Τὸ δέ γε φαίνεται αἰσθάνεσθαί ἐστιν] 'When you say "appears," it is that he has a sensation.' The example is kept in view throughout. There is MS. authority for αἰσθάνεται. (Cf. inf. 164: Τὸ δέ γε οὐχ ὁρᾷ οὐκ ἐνίοταται λέγει, εἴπερ καὶ τὸ ὁρᾷ ἐπίσταται.) But the change of subject makes αἰσθάνεσθαι preferable. Cf. inf. 187. Τί οὖν δὴ ἐκεῖνο ἀποδίδως ὄνομα, κ.τ.λ. Αἰσθάνεσθαι ἔγωγε. Crat. 411: Τὸ γὰρ γεγάασι γεγεννῆσθαι λέγει. And the repetition of the termination is a more probable corruption than the recurrence of σθ in the same word. Φαίνεσθαι appears as a correction for φαίνεται in two MSS.

15. φαντασία ἄρα] i. e. 'In regard to heat and cold and the like your theory and that of Protagoras agree.' Φαντασία occurs here simply as the noun of φαίνεσθαι, = 'appearing,' rather than 'appearance,' and must be

p. 152. θερμοῖς καὶ πᾶσι τοῖς τοιούτοις. οἷα γὰρ αἰσθάνεται ἕκαστος, τοιαῦτα ἑκάστῳ καὶ κινδυνεύει εἶναι.

ΘΕΑΙ. Ἔοικεν.

ΣΩ. Αἴσθησις ἄρα τοῦ ὄντος ἀεί ἐστι καὶ ἀψευδές, ὡς ἐπιστήμη οὖσα.

ΘΕΑΙ. Φαίνεται.

ΣΩ. Ἆρ᾽ οὖν πρὸς Χαρίτων πάσσοφός τις ἦν ὁ Πρωταγόρας, καὶ τοῦτο ἡμῖν μὲν ᾐνίξατο τῷ πολλῷ συρφετῷ, τοῖς δὲ μαθηταῖς ἐν ἀπορρήτῳ τὴν ἀλήθειαν ἔλεγεν;

This theory of Knowledge, then, depends upon a theory of Being, which Protagoras reserved for his disciples.

kept clear from the notion of *faculty*, and the associations due to Aristotle, (see de An. III. 3, where he defines it, αἴσθησις ὑπὸ τῆς αἰσθήσεως τῆς κατ᾽ ἐνέργειαν γεγενημένη.) Appearance (or relative being) becomes a middle term between sensation and being, so that all is merged in sensation. Thus, while the answer of Theaetetus is shown to coincide with the saying of Protagoras, the reader is gently led to acquiesce in their common point of view.

1. ἔν τε θερμοῖς] Cf. infr. p. 205: Ἐν γε τοῖς ἴσοις ἐξ ἀριθμοῦ ἐστιν. They are instances of Plato's tentative method.

οἶα γὰρ αἰσθάνεται]sc. αὐτά, which however is purposely omitted; viz., τὰ θερμά, κ.τ.λ. Or, while τὰ θερμά, κ.τ.λ. are subj. of αἰσθ. οἷα may be conj. acc. "For they would seem to be to each according to his sensation." As we dwell upon the above example in support of the identification of appearance and sense, ὅτι τῷ μὲν ῥηγοῦντι ψυχρόν, τῷ δὲ μὴ οὔ, (where, however, ἐστί was carefully excluded,) we are led insensibly to substitute "relative being" for appearance, by a play of words, which may be preserved in English, "What appears to me, is to me." And from relative being (δοκοῦν εἶναι) we argue at once to 'being' (Αἴσθησις ἄρα τοῦ ὄντος). For a similar recapitulation, in which the argument is really carried a step further, (with γάρ) cf. p. 191: Οὔτε γὰρ ταύτῃ αὔτε κατὰ τὰ πρότερα φαίνεται ψευδὴς ἐν ἡμῖν οὖσα δόξα.

4. Αἴσθησις ἄρα] Sensation then is of being, and, as being knowledge, (in accordance with your theory,) is infallible. Compare with ὡς ἐπιστήμη οὖσα. infr. p. 160: Κατὰ τὸν Πρωταγόραν.

7. Ἆρ᾽ οὖν—] If sensation is of being, then being is not being but change.

9. τοῖς δὲ μαθηταῖς ἐν ἀπορρήτῳ] He told the real *truth*, not in his book which is so entitled, but privately to his disciples. Cf. Crat. 413: Ἐγὼ δέ, ὦ Ἑρμόγενες, ἅτε λιπαρὴς ὢν περὶ αὐτοῦ, ταῦτα μὲν πάντα διεσκέπτομαι ἐν ἀπορρήτοις. (He had just given a derivation of the word δικαιοσύνη, which he then ironically attributes to the disciples of Heraclitus as an esoteric doctrine.) By a similar irony, he

ΘΕΑΙ. Πῶς δή, ὦ Σώκρατες, τοῦτο λέγεις;

ΣΩ. Ἐγὼ ἐρῶ καὶ μάλ' οὐ φαῦλον λόγον· ὡς ἄρα ἓν μὲν αὐτὸ καθ' αὑτὸ οὐδέν ἐστιν, οὐδ' ἄν τι προσείπαις ὀρθῶς οὐδ' ὁποιονοῦν τι, ἀλλ', ἐὰν ὡς μέγα προσαγορεύῃς, καὶ σμικρὸν φανεῖται, καὶ ἐὰν βαρύ, κοῦφον, ξύμπαντά τε οὕτως, ὡς μηδενὸς ὄντος ἑνὸς μήτε τινὸς μήτε ὁποιουοῦν· ἐκ δὲ δὴ φορᾶς τε καὶ κινήσεως καὶ κράσεως πρὸς ἄλληλα γίγνεται πάντα, ἃ δή φαμεν εἶναι, οὐκ ὀρθῶς προσαγορεύοντες· ἔστι μὲν γὰρ οὐδέποτ' οὐδέν, ἀεὶ δὲ γίγνεται. καὶ περὶ τούτου πάντες ἑξῆς οἱ σοφοὶ πλὴν Παρμενίδου ξυμ-

pim, to whom he told the real truth 'in a mystery.'

2. If sensation is knowledge, being is change. Things are not, but become. Heraclitus, Empedocles, Homer, Epicharmus, all agree in this.

says here that the 'friends of Protagoras' have learnt their doctrine from their master 'in a mystery.' Clearly then the doctrine which Socrates proceeds to develop, was not to be found in the written teaching of Protagoras, but in the interpretations of his followers. The question, how far the Cyrenaics are indicated by the phrase, 'disciples of Protagoras,' has been discussed in the introduction.

(9.) τὴν ἀλήθειαν] There is probably a slight allusion here to the work of Protagoras of this name, which is more distinctly referred to afterwards.

2. καὶ μάλ' οὐ φαῦλον λόγον] 'I will tell you, and it is indeed a high argument.' He had spoken of a λόγος οὐ φαῦλος above.

3. οὐδ' ἄν τι προσείπαις] 'Nor can you call any thing rightly by any name.' Whoever the contemporaries were to whom Plato refers as the disciples of Protagoras, he aims beyond them at the whole relative side of Greek thought, of which Heraclitus was the most prominent exponent.

8. καὶ κράσεως πρὸς ἄλληλα] These words are introduced in order to include Empedocles, whose elements, however, were not subject to growth and decay, and who was probably not independent of an Eleatic influence. His Muse is called in the Sophist φιλαρωτέρα, because his friendship and strife do not possess the world together, but alternately.

11. ξυμφερέσθω] MS. authority preponderates (numerically) in favour of ξυμφέρεσθω, which, however, gives no meaning. Stallbaum fails to defend it, by quoting ξανθῇ τε καὶ σὺ Πάδεργε κ.τ.λ.; because we can hardly argue from Homer's use of the dual to Plato's, and because philosophers do not run in couples. Stobaeus, who quotes this passage, has ξυμφέρονται. In the Bodleian MS. there is an erasure to the left of the omicron, which seems originally to have been ω. An accent on the penultimate has also been

ΘΕΑΙΤΗΤΟΣ.

p. 152. φερέσθων, Πρωταγόρας τε καὶ Ἡράκλειτος καὶ Ἐμπεδοκλῆς, καὶ τῶν ποιητῶν οἱ ἄκροι τῆς ποιήσεως ἑκατέρας· κωμῳδίας μέν, Ἐπίχαρμος, τραγῳδίας δέ, Ὅμηρος, εἰπὼν

Ὠκεανόν τε θεῶν γένεσιν καὶ μητέρα Τηθύν,

πάντα εἴρηκεν ἔκγονα ῥοῆς τε καὶ κινήσεως. ἢ οὐ δοκεῖ τοῦτο λέγειν ;

ΘΕΑΙ. Ἔμοιγε.

p. 153. ΣΩ. Τίς οὖν ἂν ἔτι πρός γε τοσοῦτον στρατόπεδον καὶ στρατηγὸν Ὅμηρον δύναιτο ἀμφισβητήσας μὴ καταγέλαστος γενέσθαι ;

---

ernard. Thus ξυμφερέσθων is supported by the Bodleian p. m., besides three other MSS. 'Let it be assumed (since we cannot ask them) that the philosophers of all ages speak with one voice concerning this.' For the imperative, cf. Soph. 244: Τόδε τοίνυν ἐπισκεπτέον. Possibly the word ξυμφ. retains here something of its literal meaning, ' are gathered together,' ' move all one way.' The boldness of the language, especially the word στρατόπεδον, is in favour of this.

3. Ἐπίχαρμος] Epicharmus ed. Krüsemann fr. 95 : — ἀνεκρίθη, καὶ διεκρίθη, καὶ ἀπῆνθεν ὅθεν ἦνθε πάλιν τὰ μὲν εἰς γᾶν, πνεῦμα δ' ἄνω. Ib. fr. 90 : φύσιν ἀνθρώπων ἀυτοὶ σεφυσιγμένα. The passage quoted by Diog. Laert. III. 10. (who says that Plato borrowed from Epicharmus) though interesting, is authentic, is too long for quotation here. (V. Mullach. Fragment. Phil. Gr. Epicharm. vv. 177—194.) Epicharmus (circ. 490 B.C.) is called a Pythagorean. One or two of his γνῶμαι remind us of Heraclitus.

3. τραγῳδίας δέ, Ὅμηρος] Where the form is in question, ἔπη are distinguished from τραγῳδία : as in Rep. 394. Where this is not the case, they are combined as tragedy, this being another name for σπουδαία μιμητική : e. g. Rep. 605 : 'λεγώμενος Ὁμήρου ἢ ἄλλου τινὸς τῶν τραγῳδοποιῶν.

4. εἰπὼν] γὰρ add. C. H. et re B. (Bekk.) Flor. a. b. c. (Stallb.) So in the similar passage, p. 175. (Ὠγγνῶν τε κ.τ.λ.) γὰρ is added in one MS. (Ven. Π.) The Zurich editors give δὲ εἰπών, without MS. authority. But the reading in the text is possibly right. See Appendix A.

5. Ὠκ. θ. γ. κ. μ. Τ.] Il. ξ, 201, 302.

11. μὴ αὐτοῦ.] A few MSS. have μὴ οὐ, which has been adopted by most editors. See Appendix B. Compare with the whole passage, Cratyl. 401, 402, where, after proposing first Ἑστία (fire) and then ὠσία (successive motion), as derivations for οὐσία, Socrates says: 'Ω 'γαθέ, ἐννενόηκά τι σμῆνος σοφίας. Πῶς δὴ τοῦτο ; Γελοῖον μὲν πάνυ εἰπεῖν, οἶμαι μέντοι τινὰ πιθανότητα ἔχειν. Τίνα ταύτην ;

ΠΛΑΤΩΝΟΣ

ΘΕΑΙ. Οὐ ῥᾴδιον, ὦ Σώκρατες.

ΣΩ. Οὐ γάρ, ὦ Θεαίτητε. ἐπεὶ καὶ τάδε τῷ λόγῳ σημεῖα ἱκανά, ὅτι τὸ μὲν εἶναι δοκοῦν καὶ τὸ γίγνεσθαι κίνησις παρέχει, τὸ δὲ μὴ εἶναι καὶ ἀπόλλυσθαι ἡσυχία· τὸ γὰρ θερμόν τε καὶ πῦρ, ὃ δὴ καὶ τἆλλα

Motion is the principle of growth, rest of decay. Fire, the providing element, is

p. 153.

Τὸν Ἡράκλειτόν μοι δοκῶ καθορᾶν παλαί᾽ ἄττα σοφὰ λέγοντα, ἀτεχνῶς τὰ ἐπὶ Κρόνου καὶ Ῥέας, ἃ καὶ Ὅμηρος ἔλεγεν. πῶς τοῦτο λέγεις; λέγει που Ἡράκλειτος ὅτι πάντα χωρεῖ καὶ οὐδὲν μένει, καὶ ποταμοῦ ῥοῇ ἀπεικάζων τὰ ὄντα λέγει ὡς δὶς ἐς τὸν αὐτὸν ποταμὸν οὐκ ἂν ἐμβαίης κ. τ. λ. Two Orphic lines are quoted besides this of Homer and Hesiod: 'Ὠκεανός πρῶτος καλλίρροος ἦρξε γάμοιο, Ὅς ῥα κασιγνήτην ὁμομήτορα Τηθὺν ὄπυιεν.' fl. adds, ταὐτὸν οὖν σαίνει ὅτι καὶ ἄλληλα συμφωνεῖ καὶ πρὸς τὰ τοῦ Ἡρακλείτου πάντα τείνει. The last words are a good commentary on ξυμφερέσθαι.

The theory of knowledge, 'All impressions are true,' is shown to require the theory of being, 'All things come and go.' And thus of the Protagorean and Heraclitean traditions there is woven a doctrine of sense, similar to that which was held by the Cyrenaics and perhaps others at this time. As a doctrine of sense it is received, as a doctrine of knowledge and being it is negatived. And yet some such relative view will return upon us after every effort to bind things in an abstract unity. Compare the way in which δόξα is treated in the Republic, p. 429: Τῶν πολλῶν καλῶν μῶν τι ἔστιν, ὃ οὐκ αἰσχρὸν φανήσεται; καὶ τῶν δικαίων, ὃ οὐκ ἄδικον; καὶ τῶν ὁσίων, ὃ οὐκ ἀνόσιον; κ. τ. λ. τί δέ; τὰ

πολλὰ διπλάσια ἦττόν τι ἡμίσεα ἢ διπλάσια φαίνεται; Οὐδέν. Καὶ μεγάλα δὴ καὶ σμικρὰ καὶ κοῦφα καὶ βαρέα μή τι μᾶλλον ἃ ἂν φήσωμεν ταῦτα προσρηθήσεται ἢ τἀναντία;

2. ἐπεὶ καὶ τάδε] Cf. Thuc. I. 2: Καὶ παράδειγμα τόδε τοῦ λόγου οὐκ ἐλάχιστόν ἐστι, διὰ τὰς μεταοικίας ἐς τὰ ἄλλα μὴ ὁμοίως αὐξηθῆναι· ἐκ γὰρ κ. τ. λ.

3. δοκοῦν] The expression is a little harsh; and Badham proposes to read ἐνεόν. But cf. 152: Ἃ δὴ φαίνεν εἶναι. 154: Καὶ ὁ δὴ ἕκαστον εἶναί φαμεν χρῶμα. Cf. also p. 176: Δικαιότητί τε δοκοῦσι. 'Being so called.'

5. πῦρ, ὃ δὴ τἆλλα γεννᾷ] Which is assumed to produce all other things. The symbol of fire as the primal element, is elsewhere associated with the theory of a flux. See Cratyl. l. c. (401.) ib. 413. (speaking of the Heracliteans): Ὁ μὲν γάρ τίς φησιν τοῦτο εἶναι δίκαιον, τὸν ἥλιον· τοῦτον γὰρ μόνον διαϊόντα καὶ κάοντα ἐπιτροπεύειν τὰ ὄντα. ἐπειδὰν οὖν τῳ λέγω αὐτὸ ἄσμενος ὡς καλόν τι ἀκηκοώς, καταγελᾷ μου οὗτος ἀκούσας καὶ ἐρωτᾷ, εἰ οὐδὲν δίκαιον οἶμαι εἶναι ἐν τοῖς ἀνθρώποις, ἐπειδὰν ὁ ἥλιος δύῃ. λιπαροῦντος οὖν ἐμοῦ ὅ τι αὖ ἐκεῖνος λέγει, αὐτὸ τὸ πῦρ φησί· τοῦτο δὲ οὐ ῥᾴδιόν ἐστιν εἰδέναι. ὁ δὲ οὐκ αὐτὸ τὸ πῦρ φησίν, ἀλλ᾽ αὐτὸ τὸ θερμὸν τὸ ἐν τῷ πυρὶ ἐνόν. ὁ δὲ τούτων μὲν πάντων καταγελᾶν φησίν, εἶναι δὲ τὸ δίκαιον ὃ λέγει Ἀναξαγόρας, νοῦν εἶναι τοῦτο κ.τ.λ.

ΘΕΑΙΤΗΤΟΣ. 39

p. 153. γεννᾷ καὶ ἐπιτροπεύει, αὐτὸ γεννᾶται ἐκ φορᾶς καὶ τρίψεως· †τούτω δὲ κινήσεις.† ἡ οὐχ αὗται γενέσεις πυρός;

b ΘΕΑΙ. Αὗται μὲν οὖν.

ΣΩ. Καὶ μὴν τό γε τῶν ζώων γένος ἐκ τῶν αὐτῶν τούτων φύεται.

ΘΕΑΙ. Πῶς δ᾽ οὔ;

ΣΩ. Τί δέ; ἡ τῶν σωμάτων ἕξις οὐχ ὑπὸ ἡσυχίας μὲν καὶ ἀργίας διόλλυται, ὑπὸ γυμνασίων δὲ καὶ κινήσεων ἐπὶ πολὺ σώζεται;

ΘΕΑΙ. Ναί.

ΣΩ. Ἡ δ᾽ ἐν τῇ ψυχῇ ἕξις, οὐχ ὑπὸ μαθήσεως

generated by friction, that is, by motion.

Living creatures owe their origin to a similar cause.

Exercise is essential to the preservation and improvement of body and mind.

Thus the mythology of the doctrine was rationalized by its adherents. In this dialogue every feature of it is presented, from the most sensuous symbolism (φλοξ, χρυσῆ σειρά) to the most abstract principle (τὸ πᾶν κίνησις ἦν, p. 156), and its most remote application. See also the famous saying of Heraclitus: (fr. 27. Mullach.) κάσμον τὸν αὐτὸν ἁπάντων, οὔτε θεῶν τις οὔτε ἀνθρώπων ἐποίησεν, ἀλλ᾽ ἔστιν ἦν τε ἀεὶ καὶ ἔσται πῦρ ἀείζωον ἁπτόμενον μέτρα καὶ σβεννύμενον μέτρα. But the symbol fire was by no means confined to Heraclitus, (—the Atomists, Pythagoreans, etc.) Cf. Rep. B. VI, where the sun appears as the chief of the sensible world, and the symbol of the idea of good.

2. τούτῳ δὲ κινήσεις] The Bodl. marg. (rather indistinctly) with several MSS. has τοῦτο δὲ κίνησις, which is perhaps right. τοῦτο will then refer to τρίψεως. It seems unnecessary to assert that φορά is κίνησις. The ο of τούτῳ in the Bodleian MS. is partially erased. But the note Δικαίως in the margin is in the ancient hand.

10. ἐπὶ πολύ] 'To a great extent;' or 'for a long time.' So the Bodleian MS. The others vary between ἐν ἐπὶ πολύ, and ἐπὶ τὸ πολύ, from which ἐν ἐπὶ τὸ πολύ has been conjectured.

12. Ἡ δὲ ἐν τῇ ψυχῇ ἕξις] Ἕξις in Plato, like φαντασία, is less technical than in Aristotle. It is simply the noun of ἔχω, and wavers between the active and neuter meanings of the word. The body is said ἔχειν πως, the mind is rather said ἔχειν τὰ μαθήματα; hence ἡ τοῦ σώματος ἕξις, the condition of the body; but ἡ ἐν τῇ ψυχῇ ἕξις, the having in the mind. Cf. Rep. 591: Ἡ ψυχὴ τιμιωτέραν ἕξιν λαμβάνει σῶμα· ε. δικαίως. μετὰ φρον. ετοιμίης. Ar. Met. Δ. 1022, 6: Ἕξις δὲ λέγεται ἕνα μὲν τρόπον οἷον ἐνέργειά τις τοῦ ἔχοντος καὶ ἐχομένου—ἄλλον δὲ τρόπον διάθεσις, κ. τ. λ.

For a similar transition from one sense of a word to another, cf. p. 158: τὸ δεῖ δοκοῦντα τῷ δοκοῦντι εἶναι ἀληθῆ.

'But with regard to the having the mind, is it not through learning and practice, which are motions, that it gains and pro-

ΠΛΑΤΩΝΟΣ

μὲν καὶ μελέτης, κινήσεων ὄντων, κτᾶταί τε μαθήματα p. 153.
καὶ σώζεται καὶ γίγνεται βελτίων, ὑπὸ δ' ἡσυχίας,
ἀμελετησίας τε καὶ ἀμαθίας οὔσης, οὔτε τι μανθάνει
ἅ τε ἂν μάθῃ ἐπιλανθάνεται;   c

ΘΕΑΙ. Καὶ μάλα.

ΣΩ. Τὸ μὲν ἄρα ἀγαθόν, κίνησις, κατά τε ψυχὴν
καὶ κατὰ σῶμα, τὸ δὲ τοὐναντίον;

ΘΕΑΙ. Ἔοικεν.

ΣΩ. Ἔτι οὖν σοι λέγω νηνεμίας τε καὶ γαλήνας

Motion, then, is good, and rest is evil.

serves what it learns, (or gains what it learns and is preserved,) and becomes better?' The sentence proceeds as if ψυχὴ were the subject, at all events of the latter part. Cf. Rep. 532: 'Ἡ δέ γε, ἦν δ' ἐγώ, λύσις τε ἀπὸ τῶν δεσμῶν κ.τ.λ., where there is a similar 'nominativus pendens.'

1. κινήσεων ὄντων] Cf. Prot. 329: ὅτι ἑνὸς ὄντος τῆς ἀρετῆς μόριά ἐστιν ἡ ἐρωτῆς. Οὖτως is neuter; 'things which are of the nature of motion,' like ταῦτα δὲ κινήσεις above.

2. σώζεται] 'Retains' (middle), or 'is preserved' (passive). Ἕξις, as above interpreted, the preceding κτᾶται τε — και, and ἐπιλανθάνεται in the corresponding clause, are in favour of the former: for which cf. p. 163: "Ἔτι ἐχωντα; μήπερ τοῦτο καὶ σωζόμενον. Rep. 455: Μηδ' ὁ ῥᾷον σώζοντα. But when it is rendered as passive, there is a more natural progress in the thought, 'gets knowledge, is preserved, improves,' while ἐπιλανθάνεται may be as justly opposed to improvement as to retention. And we avoid the difficulty of supposing that the word is used differently here, and a few lines above and below: cf. Symp. 208: Μελέτη —— σώζει τὴν ἐπιστήμην. See the whole passage. In the indeterminate state of grammar, may there not be a real, though not unconscious, ambiguity?

6. τὸ μὲν ἄρα] 'The one, then, viz. motion, is good.'

There seems no reason to suspect a gloss. There would be a want of Plato's usual explicitness without κίνησις; and the variety of genders presents no difficulty. Cf. Rep. 434: Ἔνι μᾶλλον ἄρα—ἡ δύναμις; inf. p. 156: Τὸ δὲ αἴσθησις.

9. Ἔτι οὖν σοι λέγω ——ὅτι]
'Must I go on to mention still weather and calms, and the like, showing how quietness in every case corrupts and destroys, while its opposite preserves: and for my crowning instance, pressing it into the service, shall I insist upon it that by his golden chain Homer means the sun?' For the meaning here given to προσβιβάζων, 'making it yield to my theory,' cf. Phaedr. 229: Ἀλλ' εἰ τε ἀπιστῶν προσβιβῇ κατὰ τὸ εἰκὸς ἕκαστον.—'If one is to force each of them (the mythoi) to harmonize with probability.' Cratyl. 427: Καὶ πόλλ' οὕτω φαίνεται προσβιβάζειν — ὁ νομοθέτης, viz. 'the sound of words to square with the sense.' Mythology, poetry, nature, body, mind, the elements, had already been 'pressed

ΘΕΑΙΤΗΤΟΣ. 41

p. 153. καὶ ὅσα τοιαῦτα, ὅτι αἱ μὲν ἡσυχίαι σήπουσι καὶ ἀπολλύασι, τὰ δ᾽ ἕτερα σώζει; καὶ ἐπὶ τούτοις τὸν κολοφῶνα ἀναγκάζω προσβιβάζων τὴν χρυσῆν σειρὰν

Water and air are preserved by motion. The argu-

into the service.' But this final instance requires still greater force. The position of the accusative τὴν χρυσῆν σειρὰν is possibly due to the attraction of the active προσβιβάζων, and the previous acc. τ. κολοφῶνα. For the transitive clause with ἀναγκάζω. cf. Symp. 202: Μὴ ταύτῃ ἀνάγκαζε, ὃ μὴ καλὸν ἐστιν, αἰσχρὸν εἶναι. Parm. 133: Ὁ ἔγνωστα ἀναγκάζων αὐτὰ ἰέναι. Rep. 611: Ὅτι—ἀδύνατον ψυχῇ καὶ ὁ ἄρτι λόγος καὶ οἱ ἄλλοι ἀναγκάσειαν ἂν (where, however, the word has a different meaning). The construction is assisted by λέγω in what precedes. τὸν κολοφῶνα (to which ἐπὶ τούτοις closely adheres) is accusative in apposition to τὴν χρυσῆν σειρὰν ἐπὶ κ.τ.λ. Schol.: ἐἰ ποτε ἴσας οἱ ψῆφοι ἡγέμοντο, οἱ Κολοφώνιοι ἐπιρρεπὴν ἐτίθεντο τὴν μετὰ σφῶν Σμυρναίων γὰρ ἐλθόντες εἶχον σύνοικον, ὑπὲρ ἂν καὶ τρίτον τὴν ψῆφον ἐτίθεντο.

Three alternatives to the above rendering may be proposed:

(a.) ἀναγκάζω may be used absolutely, and προσβιβάζων may be the governing word.

'Shall I clinch my argument, making this to yield to my theory as its crowning instance, how that, &c. !'

The obscurity of this construction would be a little softened by the position of τὴν χρυσῆν σειρὰν.

(b.) ἀναγκάζω προσβιβάζων might mean, 'convince you, bringing you to terms,' i.e. forcing your assent. In this case σε must be repeated from σου. (This is somewhat remote.) Ὅτι κ.τ.λ. depends on ἀναγκάζω, πρὸς τὸ σημαινόμενον, as a sort of cognate accusative, (for it contains the final argument, and not the thing convincingly proved,) and τὸν κολοφῶνα is accusative in apposition to all that follows. Both τὸν κολοφῶνα and ὡς κ.τ.λ. are softened by the influence of λέγω, for which ἀναγκάζω is substituted.

Or (c.), This construction might be a little modified by taking ἀναγκάζω absolutely. 'Shall I clinch or complete my argument, forcing your assent !' But the two latter interpretations are perhaps a little violent.

2. αἱ μὲν ἡσυχίαι] There is a slight redundancy of expression in order to bring the instance in question under the general theory.

3. τὴν χρ. σειρὰν] Il. VIII. 18, sqq. At this point Socrates has entered fully into the Heraclitean vein; as when he says of himself in the Cratylus, 407: Ὄφρα ᾖσι οἷαι Εὐθύφρονος ἴπποι, or in the Phædrus, 238: Οὐκέτι πόρρω Διθυραμβων φθέγγομαι. This is the crowning argument, because it adduces the capital fact of nature witnessed to by the oldest and gravest authority (στρατηγὸν Ὁμηρον). The lines chiefly adverted to are 23—26: Ἀλλ᾽ ὅτε δὴ κεν ἐγὼ πρόφρων ἐθέλοιμι ἐρύσσαι, αὐτῇ κεν γαίῃ ἐρύσαιμ᾽ αὐτῇ τε θαλάσσῃ σειρὴν μέν κεν ἔπειτα περὶ ῥίον Οὐλύμποιο δησαίμην, τὰ δέ κ᾽ αὖτε μετήορα πάντα γένοιτο. Cf. Heracl. fr. 36: (Mullach) Εἰ μὴ ἥλιος ἦν.

42   ΠΛΑΤΩΝΟΣ

moon is clinched with Homer's golden chain. If the revolution of

ὡς οὐδὲν ἄλλο ἢ τὸν ἥλιον Ὅμηρος λέγει, καὶ δηλοῖ p. 153.
ὅτι ἕως μὲν ἂν ἡ περιφορὰ ᾖ κινουμένη καὶ ὁ ἥλιος, d
πάντα ἔστι καὶ σώζεται τὰ ἐν θεοῖς τε καὶ ἀνθρώποις·
εἰ δὲ σταίη τοῦτο ὥσπερ δεθέν, πάντα χρήματ' ἂν

εὐφράνῃ ἂν ἦν. Fr. 34: φλὸς οὐχ ὑπερβήσεται μέτρα, εἰ δὲ μή, Ἐρινύες μιν Δίκης ἐπίκουροι ἐξευρήσουσι. As fire was the symbol of motion, so the sun was the still more concrete symbol of fire. See Πέρι p. 508, where the sun is allowed to be paramount in the region of sense; being essential to vision and to life. For the way in which the authority of Homer and the poets is used, ironically by Plato, but seriously by those whom he imitates, cf. Cratyl. 391, where an argument is based upon the line ὃν Ξάνθον καλέουσι θεοί, ἄνδρες δὲ Σκάμανδρον, and infr. p. 194: Ὅταν τοίνυν λέγῃς σὺ τὸ εἶαρ ᾖ, ὁ δὴ ἐπῄνεσεν ὁ πάντα σοφὸς ποιητήν. See also Xen. Symp. III. 6. (Antisth. loq.): Οἷσθά τι ὧν ἔθνος, ἔφη, ἠλιθιώτερον ῥαψῳδῶν; Οὐ μὰ τὸν Δί', ἔφη ὁ Νικήρατος, οὔκουν ἔμοιγε δοκεῖ. Δῆλον γάρ, ἔφη ὁ Σωκράτης, ὅτι τὰς ὑπονοίας οὐκ ἐπίστανται.

2. ἡ περιφορὰ ἢ κιν.—καὶ ὁ ἥλιος] The motion of the whole universe, and the perpetual interchange of the different elements, was symbolized in the Heraclitean theory by the revolution of the sun, who not only rose and descended, traversing the sky, but was also quenched and rekindled daily, Νέος ἐφ' ἡμέρῃ. See Lassalle II. 119. sqq., who compares Aristot. Meteor. I. 9: Ἢ μὲν οὖν ἐκ κινοῦσα καὶ κυρία καὶ πρώτη τῶν ἀρχῶν ὁ κύκλος ἐστίν· ἐν ᾧ φανερῶς ἡ τοῦ ἡλίου φορὰ διακρίνουσα καὶ συγκρίνουσα τῷ γίγνεσθαι

πλησίον ἢ πορρώτερον, αἰτία τῆς γενέσεως καὶ τῆς φθορᾶς ἐστι——Ἔστι δ' ἡ μὲν ἐξ ὕδατος ἀναθυμίασις, ἀτμίς· ἡ δ' ἐξ ἀέρος εἰς ὕδωρ, νέφος.—Γίνεται δὲ κύκλος οὗτος μιμούμενος τὸν τοῦ ἡλίου κύκλον, ἅμα γὰρ ἐκεῖνος εἰς τὰ πλάγια μεταβάλλει, καὶ οὗτος ἄνω καὶ κάτω. Δεῖ δὲ νοῆσαι τοῦτον ὥσπερ ποταμὸν ῥέοντα κύκλῳ ἄνω καὶ κάτω, κοινὸν ἀέρος καὶ ὕδατος.—Ὥστ' εἴπερ ἡ γίνεται τὸν ὠκεανὸν οἱ πρότεροι, τάχ' ἂν τοῦτον τὸν ποταμὸν λέγοιεν τὸν κύκλῳ ῥέοντα περὶ τὴν γῆν. Cf. infr. p. 181. τὴν δὲ περιφοράν.

4. εἰ δὲ σταίη] (f. Phædr. 245. (where the point of view is nearly Plato's own.) Τὸ δὲ κινοῦντα ἀθάνατον, τὸ δ' ἄλλο κινοῦν καὶ ὑπ' ἄλλου κινούμενον, παῦλαν ἔχον κινήσεως, παῦλαν ἔχει ζωῆς——οὕτω δὴ κινήσεως μὲν ἀρχὴ τὸ αὐτὸ αὑτὸ κινοῦν. τοῦτο δ' οὔτ' ἀπόλλυσθαι οὔτε γίγνεσθαι δυνατόν, ἢ πᾶσάν τε οὐρανὸν πᾶσάν τε γένεσιν συμπεσοῦσαν στῆναι καὶ μήποτε αὖθις ἔχειν ὅθεν κινηθέντα γενέσθαι. In the text all is made to depend on change; in the above passage all change depends on that which is self-moving, but in both, motion is essential to being. See Ar. Met. a. 994 A: Τῶν μὲν ἀνθρώπων ὑπὸ τοῦ ἀέρος κινηθῆναι, τοῦτον δ' ὑπὸ τοῦ ἡλίου, τὸν δὲ ἥλιον ὑπὸ τοῦ νείκους, καὶ τούτου μηδὲν εἶναι πέρας. Cf. Simpl. in Aristot. Cat. p. 1056. Bas. (quoted by Lassalle) Εἰ γάρ τὸ ἕτερον τῶν ἐναντίων ἐκλείπει, οἴχεται ἂν πάντα ἀφανισθέντα· διὸ καὶ μέμφεται Ὁμήρῳ Ἡράκλειτος εἰπόντι, Ὡς ἔρις κ.τ.λ. Οἰχήσεσθαι,

ΘΕΑΙΤΗΤΟΣ.

p. 153. διαφθαρείη καὶ γένοιτ᾽ ἂν τὸ λεγόμενον ἄνω κάτω πάντα;

ΘΕΑΙ. Ἀλλ᾽ ἔμοιγε δοκεῖ, ὦ Σώκρατες, ταῦτα δηλοῦν, ἅπερ λέγεις.

ΣΩ. Ὑπόλαβε τοίνυν, ὦ ἄριστε, οὑτωσί. κατὰ τὰ ὄμματα πρῶτον, ὃ δὴ καλεῖς χρῶμα λευκόν, μὴ εἶναι αὐτὸ ἕτερόν τι ἔξω τῶν σῶν ὀμμάτων μηδ᾽ ἐν τοῖς ὄμμασι· μηδέ τιν᾽ αὐτῷ χώραν ἀποτάξῃς· ἤδη γὰρ ἂν εἴη τε [ὄν] που ἐν τάξει καὶ μένοι καὶ οὐκ ἂν ἐν γενέσει γίγνοιτο.

ΘΕΑΙ. Ἀλλὰ πῶς;

ΣΩ. Ἑπώμεθα τῷ ἄρτι λόγῳ, μηδὲν αὐτὸ καθ᾽ αὑτὸ ἓν ὂν τιθέντες· καὶ ἡμῖν οὕτω μέλαν τε καὶ λευκὸν καὶ ὁτιοῦν ἄλλο χρῶμα ἐκ τῆς προσβολῆς τῶν ὀμμάτων πρὸς τὴν προσήκουσαν φορὰν φανεῖται

the sun and of the heaven were stopped, the order of the universe would be overthrown.

3. The theory is now applied. (1) Color is not something without, nor in the eye, it arises between, when the eye encounters a particular motion. Hence it is different to

γάρ, φησι, κινεῖται. Schol. Ven. ad Iliad. XVIII. 107 : (Ὃς ἔρις ἔκ τε θεῶν ἔκ τ᾽ ἀνθρώπων ἀπόλοιτο) 'Ἡράκλειτος τὴν τῶν ὄντων φύσιν κατ᾽ ἔριν συνιστάναι νομίζων μέμφεται Ὁμήρῳ, σύγχυσιν κόσμου δοκῶν αὐτὸν εὔχεσθαι. In the words ἄνω κάτω there is perhaps an allusion to Heraclitus' ὁδὸς ἄνω κάτω μία.

Some of the latest guesses at truth have sometimes had a real or fanciful resemblance to the earlier ones. See Comte in Miss Martineau's abridgment, Vol. I. p. 439. 'Amidst the confusion and obscurity which exist on this subject, I think we may conclude that no organism, even the simplest, could live in a state of complete immobility. The double movement of the earth, and especially its rotation, may probably be as necessary to the development of life as to the periodical distribution of heat and light.'

5. Ὑπόλαβε] If being then is motion, how are we to conceive of knowledge, i. e. of sensible perception? This is now evolved, a fresh appeal to experience being made at every step. Each sensation is the result of a double movement from within and from without. Hence they are, 1. relative to the individual (ἑκάστῳ ἡμῶν γενομένη); 2. relative to each other. 1. is proved chiefly of the sensations of colour, warmth, &c.: 2. of the perceptions of size and number.

κατὰ τὰ ὄμματα] 'In the sphere of vision.'

9. &c] MSS. ἄν.

15. πρὸς τὴν προσήκουσαν φοράν] The theory does not consider the origin of this motion. The instinctive belief in

44   ΠΛΑΤΩΝΟΣ

man and other animals, to different men, and to the same man in different states.

γεγενημένον, καὶ ὃ δὴ ἕκαστον εἶναί φαμεν χρῶμα, οὔτε τὸ προσβάλλον οὔτε τὸ προσβαλλόμενον ἔσται, p. 154 ἀλλὰ μεταξύ τι ἑκάστῳ ἴδιον γεγονός· ἢ σὺ διϊσχυρίσαιο ἂν ὡς οἷον σοὶ φαίνεται ἕκαστον χρῶμα, τοιοῦτον 5 καὶ κυνὶ καὶ ὁτῳοῦν ζῴῳ;

ΘΕΑΙ. Μὰ Δί᾽ οὐκ ἔγωγε.

ΣΩ. Τί δέ; ἄλλῳ ἀνθρώπῳ ἆρ᾽ ὅμοιον καὶ σοὶ φαίνεται ὁτιοῦν; ἔχεις τοῦτο ἰσχυρῶς, ἢ πολὺ μᾶλλον, ὅτι οὐδὲ σοὶ αὐτῷ ταὐτὸν διὰ τὸ μηδέποτε ὁμοίως 10 αὐτὸν σεαυτῷ ἔχειν;

ΘΕΑΙ. Τοῦτο μᾶλλόν μοι δοκεῖ ἢ ἐκεῖνο.

(11) *Warmth is like*

ΣΩ. Οὐκοῦν εἰ μὲν ᾧ παραμετρούμεθα ἢ οὗ ἐφα-

the reality of external things is already dissolved.

1. ὃ δὴ ἕκαστον εἶναί φαμεν] Cf. p. 153: ἃ δή φαμεν εἶναι τὸ προσβάλλον, sc. ἡ φορά. τὸ προσβαλλόμενον, sc. τὸ ὄμματα. Cf. inf. ἄλλῳ τῳ προσπεσόν—ἄλλον προσελθόντος.

2. οὔτε τὸ προσβάλλον οὔτε τὸ προσβαλλόμενον] Neither that which gives, nor that which receives, the impulse.

12. ᾧ παραμετρούμεθα] Cornar. (followed by most editors), read *á*. Ficin. id, quod mensuramus. Their difficulty was created by not observing that there is a tacit reference to the example adduced below—ἢ ὅταν φῶμεν ἐμὲ ὑψηλότερον ὄντα κ.τ.λ. If this is borne in mind, the text of the MSS reads smoothly enough, the middle voice is accounted for, and παρα retains its full meaning. ' If that, with which we compare ourselves in size, were large,' &c., (ᾧ is emphatic.) We are introduced to a new class of objects, and advance a step in the argument at the same time. All that I see, hear, feel,&c., is seen, heard, felt, &c. by me alone, and arises solely in relation to me. Again I view the size of other bodies in relation to my own, or I compare different quantities. I cannot think of any magnitude or number as great or small, except in relation to some other magnitude or number. For the use of παρα. cf. Lucian I. 198: Οὕτω γὰρ ἂν τὸ μέγα δειχθείη ἂν μέγα εἰ τῷ μικρῷ παραμετροῖτο. For a similar anticipation of an illustration, see Rep. 495: Ὥσπερ οἱ ἐκ τῶν εἰργμῶν εἰς τὰ ἱερὰ ἀποδιδράσκοντες — Νεωστὶ μὲν ἐκ δεσμῶν λελυμένων, where Plato seems to have the allegory of the cave in his mind. Cf. also Thucyd. I. 7: Αἱ δὲ παλαιαί–ἀπὸ θαλάσσης μᾶλλον ᾠκίσθησαν, αἵ τε ἐν ταῖς νήσοις καὶ ἐν ταῖς ἠπείροις (ἔφερον γὰρ ἀλλήλους τε καὶ τῶν ἄλλων ὅσοι ὄντες οὐ θαλάσσιοι κάτω ᾤκουν), where the fact that the islanders were the chief pirates, which is mentioned in the next chapter, is assumed.

ΘΕΑΙΤΗΤΟΣ. 45

p. 154. πτόμεθα, μέγα ἢ λευκὸν ἢ θερμὸν ἦν, οὐκ ἄν ποτε
b ἄλλῳ προσπεσὸν ἄλλο ἂν ἐγεγόνει, αὐτό γε μηδὲν
μεταβάλλον· εἰ δὲ αὖ τὸ παραμετρούμενον ἢ ἐφαπτόμενον
ἕκαστον ἦν τούτων, οὐκ ἂν αὖ ἄλλου προσελθόντος
ἤ τι παθόντος αὐτὸ μηδὲν παθὸν ἄλλο ἂν 5
ἐγένετο. ἐπεὶ νῦν γε, ὦ φίλε, θαυμαστά τε καὶ γελοῖα
εὐχερῶς πως ἀναγκαζόμεθα λέγειν, ὡς φαίη ἂν Πρωταγόρας
τε καὶ πᾶς ὁ τὰ αὐτὰ ἐκείνῳ ἐπιχειρῶν
λέγειν.
ΘΕΑΙ. Πῶς δὴ καὶ ποῖα λέγεις ; 10
c ΣΩ. Σμικρὸν λαβὲ παράδειγμα, καὶ πάντα εἴσει ἃ
βούλομαι. ἀστραγάλους γάρ που ἕξ, ἂν μὲν τέτταρας
αὐτοῖς προσενέγκῃς, πλείους φαμὲν εἶναι τῶν τεττάρων
καὶ ἡμιολίους, ἐὰν δὲ δώδεκα, ἐλάττους καὶ ἡμίσεις·
καὶ οὐδὲ ἀνεκτὸν ἄλλως λέγειν. ἢ σὺ ἀνέξει ; 15
ΘΕΑΙ. Οὐκ ἔγωγε.
ΣΩ. Τί οὖν ; 'ἄν σε Πρωταγόρας ἔρηται ἤ τις
ἄλλος, 'Ω Θεαίτητε, ἔσθ' ὅπως τι μεῖζον ἢ πλέον
γίγνεται ἄλλως ἢ αὐξηθέν ; τί ἀποκρινεῖ ;
ΘΕΑΙ. Ἐὰν μέν, ὦ Σώκρατες, τὸ δοκοῦν πρὸς τὴν 20
d νῦν ἐρώτησιν ἀποκρίνωμαι, ὅτι οὐκ ἔστιν· ἐὰν δὲ πρὸς
τὴν προτέραν, φυλάττων μὴ ἐναντία εἴπω, ὅτι ἔστιν.

manner is relative to the touch, and size and number are wholly relative. For want of observing this, we allow ourselves to fall into contradictions. e. g. We say that six dice are more and fewer ; more than four, fewer than twelve. Can anything be some more unless increased ?

3. τὸ παραμετρούμενον ἢ ἐφαπτόμενον] I. e. 'I, the subject.' Cf. p. 182, τὸ πάσχον. Ar. Eth. N. X. 4: λέγω δὲ (τὴν αἴσθησιν) λέγειν ἐνεργεῖν ἢ ἐν ᾧ ἐστὶ μηδὲν διαφέροντα.

7. εὐχερῶς πως ἀναγκαζόμεθα] 'We allow ourselves to be driven to use strange and contradictory expressions.' Protagoras would not find fault with us for calling the six dice more than the four, but for using the verb εἶναι to express the relation.

12. ἀστραγάλους γάρ που ἕξ] The difficulty has been stated with regard to size, it is now illustrated with regard to number.

20. τὸ δοκοῦν] Cf. p. 157: Ἀποκρίνεσθαι ὅτι.

22. φυλάττων] Not exactly 'avoiding' (φυλαττόμενος), but 'being careful :' keeping watch on one point only. Cf. Gorg. 461: Ἐὰν μοι ἓν μόνον φυλάττῃς. Τί τοῦτο λέγεις ; Τὴν μακρολογίαν —ᾖ ἀφόρίξῃ. Infr. p. 180 : Εὖ οὖν φυλάττουσι τὸ μηδὲν βέβαιον ᾖν εἶναι. So too, p. 169. τῶν τῇ τε τὸ τοιόνδε, μὴ κ. τ. λ.

46   ΠΛΑΤΩΝΟΣ

ΣΩ. Εὖ γε νὴ τὴν Ἥραν, ὦ φίλε, καὶ θείως. ἀτάρ, p. 154.
ὡς ἔοικεν, ἐὰν ἀποκρίνῃ ὅτι ἐστιν, Εὐριπίδειόν τι ξυμ-
βήσεται· ἡ μὲν γὰρ γλῶττα ἀνέλεγκτος ἡμῖν ἔσται,
ἡ δὲ φρὴν οὐκ ἀνέλεγκτος.

ΘΕΑΙ. Ἀληθῆ.

Let us consider this, not in the spirit of controversy, but of calm inquiry.

ΣΩ. Οὐκοῦν εἰ μὲν δεινοὶ καὶ σοφοὶ ἐγώ τε καὶ σὺ
ἦμεν, πάντα τὰ τῶν φρενῶν ἐξητακότες, ἤδη ἂν τὸ
λοιπὸν ἐκ περιουσίας ἀλλήλων ἀποπειρώμενοι, ξυνελ-
θόντες σοφιστικῶς εἰς μάχην τοιαύτην, ἀλλήλων τοὺς
λόγους τοῖς λόγοις ἐκρούομεν· νῦν δὲ ἅτε ἰδιῶται
πρῶτον βουλησόμεθα θεάσασθαι αὐτὰ πρὸς αὑτά, τί
ποτ' ἐστὶν ἃ διανοούμεθα, πότερον ἡμῖν ἀλλήλοις
ξυμφωνεῖ ἢ οὐδ' ὁπωστιοῦν.

ΘΕΑΙ. Πάνυ μὲν οὖν ἔγωγε τοῦτ' ἂν βουλοίμην.

What are these apparitions

ΣΩ. Καὶ μὴν ἔγωγε. ὅτε δ' οὕτως ἔχει, ἄλλο τι ἢ
ἠρέμα, ὡς πάνυ πολλὴν σχολὴν ἄγοντες, πάλιν ἐπανα-

1. Εὖ γε—καὶ θείως] Theætetus' answer showed great dialectical aptitude. He perceives the contradiction, and yet will not answer παρὰ τὸ δοκοῦν.

3. ἡ μὲν γὰρ γλῶττα] 'Our tongue will be unconvinced, but not our mind.' Eur. Hipp. 612: Ἡ γλῶσσ' ὀμώμοχ', ἡ δὲ φρὴν ἀνώμοτος.

7. πάντα τὰ τῶν φρενῶν] Having ransacked every mental problem.

8. ἐκ περιουσίας] 'Out of our superfluity,' 'for mere pastime.' Dem. de Cor. 226: Οὗτοι δ' ἐκ περιουσίας ἐμοῦ κατηγοροῦσι.

9. εἰς μάχην τοιαύτην] Sc. σοφιστικήν. Cf. Symp. 210: "Ωστε καὶ ἐὰν ἐπιεικὴς ὢν τὴν ψυχήν τις καὶ σμικρὸν ἄνθος ἔχῃ, ἐξαρκεῖν αὐτῷ καὶ ἐρᾶν καὶ κήδεσθαι καὶ τίκτειν λόγους τοιούτους, viz. ἐρωτικῆς.

τοὺς λόγοις ταῖς λόγοις ἐκρού-
ομεν] Ar. Nub. 321: Καὶ γνωμιδίῳ γνώμην νύξασ', ἑτέρῳ λόγῳ ἀν-
τιλογήσω.

10. ἐκρούομεν] 'Would have knocked our arguments together,' like swords in a sham fight; 'would have bandied arguments.'

11. αὐτὰ πρὸς αὑτά] Compared with one another. The reading of the old edd. αὐτὰ πρὸς αὑτά, might be defended; but αὐτά is the Bodleian reading.

15. Καὶ μὴν ἔγωγε] The abruptness of ἐγὼ without γε might be defended from Rep. 500: Καὶ ἐγώ, ἀμέλει, ἔφη, συνοίομαι. Eur. Med. 1375: Καὶ μὴν ἐγὼ σήν. Alcest. 369: Καὶ μὴν ἐγώ σε τῇδε—συνοίσω. But the correction of the Bodleian MS. is in the ancient hand. In either case καὶ belongs to the pronoun.

ΘΕΑΙΤΗΤΟΣ. 47

p. 155. σκεψώμεθα, οὐ δυσκολαίνοντες, ἀλλὰ τῷ ὄντι ἡμᾶς αὐτοὺς ἐξετάζοντες, ἄττα ποτ' ἐστὶ ταῦτα τὰ φάσματα ἐν ἡμῖν· ὧν πρῶτον ἐπισκοποῦντες φήσομεν, ὡς ἐγὼ οἶμαι, μηδέποτε μηδὲν ἂν μεῖζον μηδὲ ἔλαττον γενέσθαι μήτε ὄγκῳ μήτε ἀριθμῷ, ἕως ἴσον εἴη αὐτὸ ἑαυτῷ. οὐχ οὕτως;

ΘΕΑΙ. Ναί.

ΣΩ. Δεύτερον δέ γε, ᾧ μήτε προστίθοιτο μήτε ἀφαιροῖτο, τοῦτο μήτε αὐξάνεσθαί ποτε μήτε φθίνειν, ἀεὶ δὲ ἴσον εἶναι.

ΘΕΑΙ. Κομιδῇ μὲν οὖν.

b ΣΩ. Ἆρ' οὖν οὐ καὶ τρίτον, ὃ μὴ πρότερον ἦν, ἀλλὰ ὕστερον τοῦτο εἶναι ἄνευ τοῦ γενέσθαι καὶ γίγνεσθαι ἀδύνατον;

ΘΕΑΙ. Δοκεῖ γε δή.

ΣΩ. Ταῦτα δή, οἶμαι, ὁμολογήματα τρία μάχεται

that have been raised within us? One voice says, Nothing can become more or less, greater or less, while it is equal to itself. Another: That to which nothing is added, and from which nothing is taken, remains equal to itself. A third: Nothing can be, what it was not, without becoming.

1. οὐ δυσκολαίνοντες] 'With no feeling of irritation.' Cf. Men. 75: Εἰ μὲν γε τῶν σοφῶν τις εἴη καὶ ἐριστικῶν ὁ ἐρόμενος, εἴποιμ' ἂν αὐτῷ, ὅτι Ἐμοὶ μὲν εἴρηται· εἰ δὲ μὴ ὀρθῶς λέγω, σὸν ἔργον λαμβάνειν λόγον καὶ ἐλέγχειν· εἰ δὲ ὥσπερ ἐγώ τε καὶ σὺ νυνὶ φίλοι ὄντες βουλόμεθα ἀλλήλοις διαλέγεσθαι, δεῖ δὴ πρᾳότερόν πως καὶ διαλεκτικώτερον ἀποκρίνεσθαι.

2. φάσματα] These mental phenomena (that have started up before us). Cf. Polit. 268: Τὸ περὶ τὴν Ἀτρέως τε καὶ Θυέστου λεχθεῖσαν ἔριν φάσμα. Cf. Meno 85: "Ὥσπερ ὄναρ ἄρτι ἀνακεκίνηνται αἱ δόξαι αὗται κ. τ. λ. For the thought, comp. p. 203: Βασανίζομεν δὴ αὐτὰ ἀναλαβόντες, μᾶλλον δὲ ἡμᾶς αὐτούς. Prot. 331: Οὐδὲν γὰρ δέομαι τὸ εἰ βούλει τοῦτο καὶ εἰ σοι δοκεῖ ἐλέγχεσθαι ἀλλ' ἐμέ τε καὶ σέ.

5. ὄγκῳ] Cf. Phaed. 102. 'Simmias is at once taller and shorter, taller than Socrates, shorter than Phaedo.' Where the difficulty is met in a different spirit.

12. ὃ μὴ πρότερον ἦν] This may be construed in two ways. 1. What existed not before, but afterwards, this cannot be, without production and a process of becoming. 2. What was not before, neither can that be afterwards, without production, &c.

The latter is the more subtle, but is probably right. Schol.: Ὁ Πρόκλος τὸ ἀλλὰ παρέλκειν λέγει. Pronusque ita Latine dixeris quod non prius erat ad postea id esse. Heind. 'Nay but, if it was not before, it cannot be afterwards.' Cf. Soph. 265: Ἦ τις ἂν αἰτία γίγνηται ταῖς μὴ πρότερον οὔσαις ὕστερον γίγνεσθαι.

48   ΠΛΑΤΩΝΟΣ

These seem to jar, when we say that the dice which were fewer are now more without being increased; or that I, that was taller than you, am now shorter, without becoming so. Theaetetus is full of

αὐτὰ αὑτοῖς ἐν τῇ ἡμετέρᾳ ψυχῇ, ὅταν τὰ περὶ τῶν p. 155.
ἀστραγάλων λέγωμεν, ἢ ὅταν φῶμεν ἐμὲ τηλικόνδε
ὄντα, μήτε αὐξηθέντα μήτε τοὐναντίον παθόντα, ἐν
ἐνιαυτῷ σοῦ τοῦ νέου νῦν μὲν μείζω εἶναι, ὕστερον δὲ
5 ἐλάττω, μηδὲν τοῦ ἐμοῦ ὄγκου ἀφαιρεθέντος ἀλλὰ
σοῦ αὐξηθέντος. εἰμὶ γὰρ δὴ ὕστερον ὁ πρότερον οὐκ c
ἤ, οὐ γενόμενος· ἄνευ γὰρ τοῦ γίγνεσθαι γενέσθαι
ἀδύνατον, μηδὲν δὲ ἀπολλὺς τοῦ ὄγκου οὐκ ἄν ποτε
ἐγιγνόμην ἐλάττων. καὶ ἄλλα δὴ μυρία ἐπὶ μυρίοις
10 οὕτως ἔχει, εἴπερ καὶ ταῦτα παραδεξόμεθα. [ἔπει] γάρ

1. τηλικόνδε] Of the height you see me.

5. μηδὲν τοῦ ἐμοῦ ὄγκου ἀφαιρεθέντος] 'My size having been stripped of nothing,' i.e. 'Without anything being taken from my height.' Badham conjectures μηδὲν ἐμοῦ τοῦ ὄγκου ἀφαιρεθέντος. But this is unnecessary.

7. ἄνευ γὰρ τοῦ γίγνεσθαι γενέσθαι ἀδύνατον) This axiom is supplementary to the 3 former. In the first, the aorist was used (γενέσθαι), the present in the second (οὐξάνεσθαι, φθίνειν). Both (γενέσθαι καὶ γίγνεσθαι) are accordingly combined in the third, by means of which the two former are applied. It is now shown that the aorist implies the present. To us such refinements are difficult, because unnecessary. The subtlety is carried still further in the Parmenides, until it is reduced to the formula, ' That which is, is.' Parm. 156: Ἔστι τι πρότερον ὕστερον κινεῖσθαι καὶ πρότερον κινούμενον ὕστερον ἑστάναι, ἄνευ μὲν τοῦ μεταβάλλειν οὐχ οἷόν τε ἔσται ταῦτα σχεῖν;—Ἀλλ' οὐδὲ μὴν μεταβάλλει ἄνευ τοῦ μεταβάλλειν.

9. καί, which implies a subtle connexion between ταῦτα and ἄλλα μυρία, can only be expressed in English by the emphasis on ' these.' Cf. Soph. OEd. Col. 376: ὥσπερ με κινοστήσεις, ὧδε σώζειν.

10. παραδεξόμεθα] Sc. παρὰ τοῦ Πρωταγόρου. ' If we are to take this at his hands ;' i.e. not only accept, but adopt this as our own difficulty. Cf. Charm. 162: εἰ οὖν ξυγχωρεῖς τοῦτ' εἶναι σωφρ. ὥσπερ οὑτοσὶ λέγει, καὶ παραδέχει τὸν λόγον, ἔγωγε πολὺ ἂν ἥδιον μετὰ σοῦ σκοποίμην—. 'Ἀλλὰ πάνυ ξυγχωρῶ, ἔφη, καὶ παραδέχομαι.

[ἔπει] γάρ που] 'I assume this (δή), for I suppose I take you with me.' Cf. Euthyph. 12: Ἐπεὶ γάρ που νῦν γε ; Euth. νῦν γε. The MSS. have εἶεν, but there can be little doubt about the emendation. The six dice are more when compared with four. They were fewer when compared with twelve. They cannot be more without having become more, and they cannot have become more without increase. Protagoras would say; It is true the same thing cannot be more without addition, but the dice in the two cases are not the same thing, for they are in

ΘΕΑΙΤΗΤΟΣ. 49

p. 155. του, ὦ Θεαίτητε· δοκεῖς γοῦν μοι οὐκ ἄπειρος τῶν τοιούτων εἶναι.

ΘΕΑΙ. Καὶ νὴ τοὺς θεούς γε, ὦ Σώκρατες, ὑπερφυῶς ὡς θαυμάζω τί ποτ' ἐστὶ ταῦτα, καὶ ἐνίοτε ὡς ἀληθῶς βλέπων εἰς αὐτὰ σκοτοδινιῶ.

d ΣΩ. Θεόδωρος γάρ, ὦ φίλε, φαίνεται οὐ κακῶς τοπάζειν περὶ τῆς φύσεώς σου. μάλα γὰρ φιλοσόφου τοῦτο τὸ πάθος, τὸ θαυμάζειν· οὐ γὰρ ἄλλη ἀρχὴ φιλοσοφίας ἢ αὕτη, καὶ ἔοικεν ὁ τὴν Ἶριν Θαύμαντος ἔκγονον φήσας οὐ κακῶς γενεαλογεῖν. ἀλλὰ πότερον μανθάνεις ἤδη δι' ὃ ταῦτα τοιαῦτ' ἐστὶν ἐξ ὧν τὸν Πρωταγόραν φαμὲν λέγειν, ἢ οὔπω;

ΘΕΑΙ. Οὔπω μοι δοκῶ.

ΣΩ. Χάριν οὖν μοι εἴσει, ἐάν σοι ἀνδρός, μᾶλλον

wonder and bewilderment at this: a sign of his philosophic nature.

a different relation. The distinction between relative and absolute quantity is so familiar to us, that this is apt to appear a mere verbal quibble. But the solution of such difficulties was one of the steps by which the Greeks arrived at that distinction.

6. οὐ κακῶς τοπάζειν] 'Theodorus is evidently right in his conception of you. For this Wonder is a true symptom of the philosophic nature.'

8. οὐ γὰρ ἄλλη ἀρχὴ φιλοσοφίας ἢ αὕτη] Arist. Metaph. I. 2: Διὰ τὸ θαυμάζειν οἱ ἄνθρωποι καὶ νῦν καὶ τὸ πρῶτον ἤρξαντο φιλοσοφεῖν, κ.τ.λ.

9. τὴν Ἶριν Θαύμαντος ἔκγονον] Hes. Theog. 265. Θαύμας δ' Ὠκεανοῖο βαθυρρείταο θυγάτρα ἠγάγετ' Ἠλέκτρην· ἡ δ' ὠκεῖαν τέκεν Ἶριν, cf. v. 780.

10. πότερον μανθάνεις ἤδη] 'Do you begin to perceive what is

the reason of this, according to the theory we attribute to Protagoras?'

Aristotle, Met. K. 1063 A, points out that the Protagorean doctrine rests very much on the relativeness of quantity. Φαίνονται γὰρ οὐχ ἧττον τὰ κατὰ τὰς ἀντιφάσεις τούτου συνηγορεῖν ἐκ τοῦ τὰ πολλὰ ὑπειληφέναι μὴ μόνον ἐπὶ τῶν σωμάτων ἀλλὰ τὸ καὶ εἶναι τετράπηχυ τὸ αὐτὸ καὶ οὐκ εἶναι. ἡ δ' οὐσία κατὰ τὸ ποσὸν, τοῦτο δὲ τῆς ἀριζομένης φύσεως, τὸ δὲ ποσὸν τῆς ἀορίστου.

14. Χάριν, κ.τ.λ.] 'Shall I then earn your gratitude, if in regard to a man, or rather men, of high renown, I help you to elicit the *truth* of their meaning from its hidingplace in their minds?'

μᾶλλον δὲ ἀνδρῶν] viz. Heraclitus, Homer, and the rest mentioned above, p. 152.

50 ΠΛΑΤΩΝΟΣ

δὲ ἀνδρῶν ὀνομαστῶν τῆς διανοίας τὴν ἀλήθειαν ἀποκεκρυμμένην συνεξερευνήσωμαι αὐτῶν;

ΘΕΑΙ. Πῶς γὰρ οὐκ εἴσομαι, καὶ πάνυ γε πολλήν;

ΣΩ. Ἄθρει δὴ περισκοπῶν, μή τις τῶν ἀμυήτων ἐπακούῃ. εἰσὶ δὲ οὗτοι οἱ οὐδὲν ἄλλο οἰόμενοι εἶναι ἢ οὗ ἂν δύνωνται ἀπρὶξ τοῖν χεροῖν λαβέσθαι, πράξεις δὲ καὶ γενέσεις καὶ πᾶν τὸ ἀόρατον οὐκ ἀποδεχόμενοι ὡς ἐν οὐσίας μέρει.

ΘΕΑΙ. Καὶ μὲν δή, ὦ Σώκρατες, σκληρούς γε λέγεις καὶ ἀντιτύπους ἀνθρώπους.

ΣΩ. Εἰσὶ γάρ, ὦ παῖ, μάλ' εὖ ἄμουσοι. ἄλλοι δὲ

ΘΕΑΙΤΗΤΟΣ. 51

p. 156. πολὺ κομψότεροι, ὧν μέλλω σοι τὰ μυστήρια λέγειν. ἀρχὴ δέ, ἐξ ἧς καὶ ἃ νῦν δὴ ἐλέγομεν πάντα ἤρτηται, ἥδε αὐτῶν, ὡς τὸ πᾶν κίνησις ἦν καὶ ἄλλο παρὰ τοῦτο οὐδέν, τῆς δὲ κινήσεως δύο εἴδη, πλήθει μὲν ἄπειρον ἑκάτερον, δύναμιν δὲ τὸ μὲν ποιεῖν ἔχον, τὸ δὲ πά- 5 σχειν. ἐκ δὲ τῆς τούτων ὁμιλίας τε καὶ τρίψεως πρὸς ὐ ἄλληλα γίγνεται ἔκγονα πλήθει μὲν ἄπειρα, δίδυμα δέ, τὸ μὲν αἰσθητόν, τὸ δὲ αἴσθησις, ἀεὶ συνεκπίπτουσα καὶ γεννωμένη μετὰ τοῦ αἰσθητοῦ. αἱ μὲν οὖν αἰσθήσεις τὰ τοιάδε ἡμῖν ἔχουσιν ὀνόματα, ὄψεις 10 τε καὶ ἀκοαὶ καὶ ὀσφρήσεις καὶ ψύξεις τε καὶ καύσεις καὶ ἡδοναί γε δὴ καὶ λῦπαι καὶ ἐπιθυμίαι καὶ φόβοι

The men whom mysteries we teach, are more refined. Their first principle, upon which the whole depends, is that All is motion. Motion is active and passive, and each kind is infinite. These meet and produce in-

Protagoras is almost an idealist. His disciples believe not indeed in a world of πρῶτα εἴδη, but in a hidden process underlying appearances, cf. Rep. 477: δυνάμεως γὰρ ἐγὼ οὔτε τινὶ χρόαν ὁρῶ οὔτε σχῆμα, κ. τ. λ.

(11.) ἄλλοι δέ] viz. the μαθηταὶ Πρωταγόρου, to whom he communicated his doctrine ἐν ἀπορρήτῳ, p. 152. Schleiermacher conjectured ἀλλ' οἵδε ; but they would then be liable to be confused with the ἄνδρες ὀνομαστοὶ above. The 'disciples of Protagoras,' are evidently contemporaries of Plato. Aristippus is probably included. (Κομψός and σοφιστικός are opposed, Hippias Maj. 288 : Οὐ σμικρὸν ἀλλὰ συμφανές.) The word κομψός is used similarly of certain nameless philosophers (who are clearly the Pythagoreans) Polit. 285 Πολλοὶ τῶν σοφῶν λέγουσιν ὅτι ἅμα μετρητικὴ περὶ πάντ' ἐστὶ τὰ γιγνόμενα. Cf. Phil. 53 : κομψοὶ γὰρ δή τινες αὖ τούτων τὸν λόγον ἐπιχειροῦσι μηνύειν ἡμῖν ὡς ἀεὶ χάριν ἔχειν. (Megarians?)

3. ἦν] 'really is,' according to the well-known idiom, which becomes more frequent in Aristotle. What a thing proves to be when an inquiry is finished, that it was before the inquiry began. It is a transference of the reality of history to a general statement. Soph. Œd. Col. 117 : Τίς ἄρ' ἦν ; The doctrine asserted above is now more minutely developed.

8. συνεκπίπτουσα] 'Tumbling forth to light at the same moment.' Compare the lively expression in Rep 432, when justice is discovered, πάλαι ὁ μακάριος φαίνεται πρὸ ποδῶν ἡμῖν ἐξ ἀρχῆς κυλινδεῖσθαι. For the insertion of καὶ γεννωμένη, cf. Soph. Ant. 533 : Καὶ ξυμμετίσχε καὶ φέρει τῆς αἰτίας. Aesch. Prom. 339. Πάντων μετασχὼν καὶ τετολμηκὼς ἐμοί.

10. τὰ τοιάδε—ἔχουσιν ὀνόματα, ὄψεις—τελευταῖα] The slight redundancy helps to connect the sentence.

12. ἡδοναί γε δὴ] The particles mark the transition to a class of things less familiarly known by the name αἴσθησις.

52   ΠΛΑΤΩΝΟΣ

κεκλημέναι καὶ ἄλλαι, ἀπέραντοι μὲν αἱ ἀνώνυμοι, p. 156.
παμπληθεῖς δὲ αἱ ὠνομασμέναι· τὸ δ' αὖ αἰσθητὸν
γένος τούτων ἑκάσταις ὁμόγονον, ὄψεσι μὲν χρώματα
παντοδαπαῖς παντοδαπά, ἀκοαῖς δὲ ὡσαύτως φωναί, b
5 καὶ ταῖς ἄλλαις αἰσθήσεσι τὰ ἄλλα αἰσθητὰ ξυγγενῆ
γιγνόμενα. Τί δὴ οὖν ἡμῖν βούλεται οὗτος ὁ μῦθος,
ὦ Θεαίτητε, πρὸς τὰ πρότερα ; ἆρα ἐννοεῖς ;
ΘΕΑΙ. Οὐ πάνυ, ὦ Σώκρατες.
ΣΩ. Ἀλλ' ἄθρει ἐάν πως ἀποτελεσθῇ. βούλεται
10 γὰρ δὴ λέγειν ὡς ταῦτα πάντα μέν, ὥσπερ λέγομεν,
κινεῖται, τάχος δὲ καὶ βραδυτὴς ἔνι τῇ κινήσει αὐτῶν.
ὅσον μὲν οὖν βραδύ, ἐν τῷ αὐτῷ καὶ πρὸς τὰ πλησιά-
ζοντα τὴν κίνησιν ἴσχει καὶ οὕτω δὴ γεννᾷ, τὰ δὲ d

innumerable twin births: amounting and sensible thing coming forth together. Nameables include pleasures, pains, desires and fears, and there are many without a name. Nameable things are colours, sounds, and the like. All the things now spoken of

1. αἱ ἀνώνυμοι] See Locke, Hum. Und. B. II. c. 3. I think it will be needless to enumerate all the particular simple ideas belonging to each sense, nor indeed is it possible if we would, there being a great many more of them belonging to most of the senses than we have names for.

3. The Bodleian with nine other MSS. has ἑκάστης.

6. οὗτος ὁ μῦθος] Cf. Soph. 242 : Μῦθόν τινα ἕκαστος φαίνεταί μοι διηγεῖσθαι παισὶν ὡς οὖσιν ἡμῖν κ.τ.λ. For the spirit with which all this is done, compare Rep. p. 545 : Φῶμεν αὐτὰς τραγικῶς, ὡς πρὸς παῖδας ἡμᾶς παιζούσας καὶ ἐρεσχηλούσας, ὡς δὴ σπουδῇ λεγούσας, ὑψηλολογουμένας λέγειν ;

7. πρὸς τὰ πρότερα] 'In reference to what preceded,' viz. from p. 153. Ὑπέλαβε — to p. 155. παραδεξώμεθα.

9. Ἀλλ' ἄθρει ἐάν] 'Well, look attentively, perhaps we shall be able to finish it.' (Cf. infr. p.

192 : Ἰδὶ δή, ἐάν τι μᾶλλον νῦν ἐπισπῇ ἰδεῖν = in the hope that.

10. ταῦτα] ποιοῦντα, πάσχοντα, αἰσθητά, αἰσθήσεις.

τόντα—κινεῖται] Comp. Locke. ' The next thing to be considered is, how bodies produce ideas in us, and that is manifestly by impulse, the only way which we can conceive bodies operate in.'

12. ὅσον μὲν οὖν βραδύ] 'The slower have their motion in one spot, and in relation to what is in contact with them, and are thus the producing elements ; but those which are thus produced are swifter ; for they are carried along, and their motion is from place to place.'

13. τὰ — γεννώμενα οὕτω δή] Schol. Εἰς τὸ δὴ ὑποστικτέον. The (probably conjectural) interpolation of Cornarius after οὕτω δὴ [βραδύτερά ἐστιν· ὅσον δὲ αὖ ταχύ, πρὸς τὰ πόρρωθεν τὴν κίνησιν ἴσχει, καὶ οὕτω γεννᾷ, τὰ δὲ γεννώμενα οὕτω δή] is quite un-

ΘΕΑΙΤΗΤΟΣ. 53

p. 156. γεννώμενα οὕτω δὴ θάττω ἐστί· φέρεται γὰρ καὶ ἐν φορᾷ αὐτῶν ἡ κίνησις πέφυκεν. ἐπειδὰν οὖν ὄμμα καὶ ἄλλο τι τῶν τούτῳ ξυμμέτρων πλησιάσαν γεννήσῃ τὴν λευκότητά τε καὶ αἴσθησιν αὐτῇ ξύμφυτον, ἃ οὐκ ἄν ποτε ἐγένετο ἑκατέρου ἐκείνων πρὸς ἄλλο ἐλθόντος, τότε δὴ μεταξὺ φερομένων τῆς μὲν ὄψεως πρὸς τῶν ὀφθαλμῶν, τῆς δὲ λευκότητος πρὸς τοῦ συναποτίκτοντος τὸ χρῶμα, ὁ μὲν ὀφθαλμὸς ἄρα ὄψεως ἔμπλεως ἐγένετο καὶ ὁρᾷ δὴ τότε καὶ ἐγένετο

are in motion. But the motion of some is swift and of others slow. Those which produce are slow, and they move only when in contact. The things produced are swifter,

necessary, and confuses the real sense. The slower motions are the ποιοῦντα and πάσχοντα, which, when in contact, produce (without changing place) the αἰσθητὰ and αἰσθήσεις (i. e. qualities and sensations) which are the 'quicker motions,' and pass to and fro between the ποιοῦν and πάσχον. Cf. inf. p. 159: 'Εγέννησεν γὰρ δὴ ἐκ τῶν προωμολογημένων τό τε ποιοῦν καὶ τὸ πάσχον γλυκύτητά τε καὶ αἴσθησιν, ἅμα φερόμενα ἀμφότερα. It is not quite clear what is intended by the qualities and sensations being in locomotion. Perhaps nothing more is distinctly meant than that they flow from subject to object, and from object to subject. But when it is said that they are the swifter motions, the idea is vaguely connected with the Heraclitean doctrine. Sensations and qualities are drops in the ever-flowing river of succession. The man or the tree is like the dull weed that clogs it, itself to be carried down in time. Subject and object are more of the nature of Earth, sensation and quality are sparks of the everliving Fire. This is not, however, brought out consciously here. It is shown afterwards, p. 182, that while sensation and qua-

lity are flowing between subject and object, they have also changed. The above interpretation was first suggested by Voegelinus, quoted by the Zurich editors in the preface to their last edition. He seems however, by a curious error, to make ποιοῦν and γεννώμενον equivalent to ποιοῦν and πάσχον. That the ποιοῦν and πάσχον are both γεννῶντα, appears from p. 159: Ἐγέννησεν γὰρ δὴ — τό τε ποιοῦν καὶ τὸ πάσχον, quoted above.

3. τῶν τούτῳ ξυμμέτρων] Men. 76: Ἔστι γὰρ χρόα ἀπορροὴ σχημάτων ὄψει σύμμετρος καὶ αἰσθητός. This definition is said to be "κατὰ Γοργίαν." In Tim. 67 colour is called, φλόγα τῶν σωμάτων ἑκάστων ἀπορρέουσαν, ὄψει ξύμμετρα μόρια ἔχουσαν πρὸς αἴσθησιν. Cf. ib. 45, 6.

6. τότε δή, κ. τ. λ.] Then it is that while these are issuing in the midst, sight from the eyes, whiteness from that which helps to create the colour, the eye is filled with seeing, and sees now, and becomes not sight indeed, but a seeing eye, and that which helps to give the colour birth is covered with whiteness, and it too becomes not whiteness but white, whether stick or stone, or whatever it is that

54   ΠΛΑΤΩΝΟΣ

for their motion is from place to place, e. g. The eye and its appropriate active motion come in contact. Then sight begins to flit from the eye and

οὔ τι ὄψις ἀλλὰ ὀφθαλμὸς ὁρῶν, τὸ δὲ ξυγγεννῆσαν p. 156.
τὸ χρῶμα λευκότητος περιεπλήσθη καὶ ἐγίνετο οὐ
λευκότης αὖ ἀλλὰ λευκόν, εἴτε ξύλον εἴτε λίθος εἴτε
ὁτουοῦν ξυνέβη †χρῶμα† χρωσθῆναι τῷ τοιούτῳ
χρώματι. καὶ τἆλλα δὴ οὕτω, σκληρὸν καὶ θερμὸν
καὶ πάντα τὸν αὐτὸν τρόπον ὑποληπτέον, αὐτὸ μὲν
καθ᾽ αὑτὸ μηδὲν εἶναι, ὃ δὴ καὶ τότε ἐλέγομεν, ἐν δὲ p. 157.
τῇ πρὸς ἄλληλα ὁμιλίᾳ πάντα γίγνεσθαι καὶ παντοῖα

happens to have been coloured with this hue.

(6.) μεταξὺ φερομένων] It is doubtful whether this means "whilst they are moving," or "as they are moving in the midst." The former is excellent Greek, but the latter seems preferable if we turn to p. 154 : Μεταξύ τι (αἴστηρ ἔλαν γεγονός, and infr. p. 182 : φέρεσθαι ἑκαστον τούτων ἅμα αἰσθήσει, μεταξὺ τοῦ ποιοῦντος τε καὶ τοῦ πάσχοντος.

3. εἴτε ὁτουοῦν, κ. τ. λ.] Heind. who receives ὁπωοῦν χρῶμα, (Cornarius' emendation,) adds, "ne ipso quidem χρῶμα opus fuerit, h. l." It has not been sufficiently remarked that ὁπωοῦν has scarcely more authority than χρῶμα. This is sacrificing too much for a weak reading. One MS. (Par. II.) has σῶμα on the margin, but ὁπωοῦν — σῶμα, though it has thus some slight authority, would introduce a distinction between organic and inorganic matter scarcely known to Plato, and at all events too novel to be so slightly hinted at. The real text is perhaps restored by dropping χρῶμα, and reading ὁτωοῦν, (ὁπωοῦν Par. F.) ἀπωοῦν, εἴτε ξύλον εἴτε λίθος εἴτε ὁτωοῦν ξυνέβη χρωσθῆναι τῷ τοιούτῳ χρώματι. 'White, whether stick or stone, or whatsoever happens to be coloured with that colour.' The repetition of similar consonants is a frequent form of corruption, cf. esp. p. 158: ὅτῳ χρή, κ. τ. λ.: where three MSS. (Bodl. Vat. Ven. Π.) read ὅτῳ χρώτῃ χρή, κ.τ.λ. (Χρώτω, χρώσων, χρώντων, χρώτων, occurring within the next few lines.) Also, p. 149, ὁτόσως for ὁπόσως Vat. pr. Bodl pr. Ven. Π. with ἀποπάντων a few lines above.

(Yet the reading ὁπωοῦν—χρῶμα, in which most MSS. agree, may possibly be right. For our theory has reduced us to narrow limits in the use of language. We have already been within a very little of saying 'motions move.' Cf. also, Rep. 601 : τὸν τοιοῦτοδε φήσομεν χρώματ' ἄντα-πιχρωματίζειν.) For εἴτε ξύλον εἴτε λίθος, cf. infr. ἀνθρωπός τε καὶ λίθος καὶ ἕκαστον (φῶν τε καὶ εἶδος. Hipp. Maj. 292 : Καὶ λίθος καὶ ξύλον καὶ ἄνθρωπος καὶ θεός, κ. τ. λ. The sentence is turned like Phaedr. 237 : Εἴτε δι᾽ ἔρῳς εἶδος λεγοίαν, εἴτε διὰ γένος μονουσίαν τὸ λεγόμενον τούτῳ ἔσχατε τὴν ἐπωνυμίαν. Rep. 612 : Εἴτε πολυειδὴς εἴτε μονοειδὴς εἴτε ὅπῃ ἔχει καὶ ὅπως. The aorists give a sort of picturesqueness to the expression, referring, as in the Homeric similes, to an imaginary case.

ΘΕΑΙΤΗΤΟΣ.   55

p. 157. ἀπὸ τῆς κινήσεως· ἐπεὶ καὶ τὸ ποιοῦν εἶναί τι καὶ τὸ πάσχον αὐτῶν ἐπὶ ἑνὸς νοῆσαι, ὥς φασιν, οὐκ εἶναι παγίως· οὔτε γὰρ ποιοῦν ἐστί τι, πρὶν ἂν τῷ πάσχοντι ξυνέλθῃ, οὔτε πάσχον, πρὶν ἂν τῷ ποιοῦντι· τό τέ τινι ξυνελθὸν καὶ ποιοῦν ἄλλῳ αὖ προσπεσὸν πάσχον ἀνεφάνη. ὥστε ἐξ ἁπάντων τούτων, ὅπερ ἐξ ἀρχῆς ἐλέγομεν, οὐδὲν εἶναι ἓν αὐτὸ καθ᾽ αὐτό, ἀλλά
b τινι ἀεὶ γίγνεσθαι, τὸ δ᾽ εἶναι πανταχόθεν ἐξαιρετέον, οὐχ ὅτι ἡμεῖς πολλὰ καὶ ἄρτι ἠναγκάσμεθα ὑπὸ συνηθείας καὶ ἀνεπιστημοσύνης χρῆσθαι αὐτῷ. τὸ δ᾽ οὐ δεῖ, ὡς ὁ τῶν σοφῶν λόγος, οὔτε τι ξυγχωρεῖν οὔτε του οὔτ᾽ ἐμοῦ οὔτε τόδε οὔτ᾽ ἐκεῖνο οὔτε ἄλλο οὐδὲν ὄνομα ὅ τι ἂν ἱστῇ, ἀλλὰ κατὰ φύσιν φθέγγεσθαι

colours from the object of sight; the eye becomes a seeing eye, and the object becomes coloured. Neither seeing eye nor coloured object can be thought of as existing independently of this mutual process. We must not speak of anything as existing.

1. *ἐπεὶ καὶ τὸ ποιοῦν*] 'For it is impossible to have a firm notion (they say) even of the active and passive elements as existing separately in the case of any single thing.' αὐτῶν sc. τῶν συνεργούντων, 'To distinguish amongst them the active or passive element as existing in any single case.' Or ἐπὶ ἑνὸς may be taken differently : 'To conceive steadily of agent and patient, as each existing separately in one ;' i. e. 'as a single thing.' Cf. Soph. 259 : Ἓν ἐπὶ ξυμμένων, and the common expression ἐφ᾽ ἑαυτοῦ. But the former rendering is more probable. Cf. Arist. Met. V. 20 : Μεγέθη ἀξιῶν λέγεσθαι πλὴν τῇ αἰσίῳ λόγῳ ἓν ἐφ᾽ ἑνός. For αὐτῶν Cornarius suggested αὖ τι. If a change were necessary, αὖ τῶν would seem more probable. τῶν ἐπὶ ἑνός, 'of things taken singly,' might then be compared with τῶν ἐν ἑκάστῳ, Phil. 16.

2. *ταῦτα—παγίως*] Rep. 479 : Καὶ γὰρ ταῦτα ἐπαμφοτερίζει, καὶ οὔτ᾽ εἶναι, οὔτε μὴ εἶναι οὐδὲν αὐτῶν δύναται παγίως νοῆσαι, οὔτ᾽ ἀμφότερα οὔτε οὐδέτερον. The word is used by Aristotle.

9. *οὐχ ὅτι ἡμεῖς*] The irony of this appears very clearly, if we compare p. 197 : Εἰ μέντοι ἦν ἀντιλογικός κ.τ.λ.

10. *τὸ δ᾽ οὐ δεῖ*] This may be regarded as a sentence of which τό is the subject, and all that follows the predicate. The idiom occurs frequently in Plato, Apol. 23. Πεπ. 340. De Legg. 803. Soph. 244. Its growth may be traced in the following passages, Rep. 357 : Τὸ δὲ γε ἦν ἄρα, ὡς ἔοικε, τρισσόμεν. 443 : Τὸ δέ γε ἦν ἄρα κ.τ.λ. Τὸ δέ γε ἀληθὲς κ.τ.λ., 489. τὸ δὲ ἀληθὲς πέφυκεν κ.τ.λ. See also Thuc. II. 44 : Τὸ δ᾽ εὐτυχές κ.τ.λ.

11. *οὔτε του*] The genitive is a point of transition to ἐμοῦ.

13. *φθέγγεσθαι—*] 'To use the expression.'

56   ΠΛΑΤΩΝΟΣ

but only as becoming this or that, arising, perishing, or changing. This applies not only to single things, but to those bundles of things, which men call sorts.

γιγνόμενα καὶ ποιούμενα καὶ ἀπολλύμενα καὶ ἄλλοι- p. 157.
σύμενα· ὡς ἐάν τί τις στήσῃ τῷ λόγῳ, εὐέλεγκτος ὁ
τοῦτο ποιῶν. δεῖ δὲ καὶ κατὰ μέρος οὕτω λέγειν καὶ
περὶ πολλῶν ἀθροισθέντων, ᾧ δὴ ἀθροίσματι ἄνθρω-
5 πόν τε τίθενται καὶ λίθον καὶ ἕκαστον ζῷόν τε καὶ c
εἶδος. Ταῦτα δή, ὦ Θεαίτητε, ἆρ᾽ ἡδέα δοκεῖ σοι
εἶναι, καὶ γεύαιο ἂν αὐτῶν ὡς ἀρεσκόντων;

ΘΕΑΙ. Οὐκ οἶδα ἔγωγε, ὦ Σώκρατες· καὶ γὰρ
οὐδὲ περὶ σοῦ δύναμαι κατανοῆσαι, πότερα δοκοῦντά
10 σοι λέγεις αὐτὰ ἢ ἐμοῦ ἀποπειρᾷ.

ΣΩ. Οὐ μνημονεύεις, ὦ φίλε, ὅτι ἐγὼ μὲν οὔτ᾽
οἶδα οὔτε ποιοῦμαι τῶν τοιούτων οὐδὲν ἐμόν, ἀλλ᾽
εἰμὶ αὐτῶν ἄγονος, σὲ δὲ μαιεύομαι καὶ τούτου ἕνεκα
ἐπᾴδω τε καὶ παρατίθημι ἑκάστων τῶν σοφῶν ἀπο-
15 γεύσασθαι, ἕως ἂν εἰς φῶς τὸ σὸν δόγμα ξυνεξαγάγω· d
ἐξαχθέντος δέ, τότ᾽ ἤδη σκέψομαι εἴτ᾽ ἀνεμιαῖον εἴτε
γόνιμον ἀναφανήσεται. ἀλλὰ θαρρῶν καὶ καρτερῶν
εὖ καὶ ἀνδρείως ἀποκρίνου ἃ ἂν φαίνηταί σοι περὶ ὧν
ἂν ἐρωτῶ.

Theaetetus is invited to acknowledge the theory as far devel-

2. ὁ τοῦτο ποιῶν] For the redundancy, cf. Rep. 506: Δίκαια καὶ καλὰ ἀγνοούμενα ὅπῃ ποτὲ ἀγαθά ἐστιν, οὐ πολλοῦ τινος ἄξιον φύλακα κεκτῆσθαι τὸν ταῦτα ἀγνοοῦντα.

4. ᾧ δὴ ἀθροίσματι—τίθενται] Sc. ἄνομα. The subject of τίθενται is indefinite. From our Protagorean point of view, that which answers to a common name is not ἐν ἐπὶ πολλῶν, nor ἓν παρὰ τὰ πολλά, but an arbitrary or conventional aggregate of phenomena. Cf. Parm. 165, where the word ὅπως answers to ἄθροισμα here, but implies something even more vague and formless.

12. σύμενα] 'Tanquam proprium mihi vindico,' velut dicitur παιεῖσθαί τως υἱόν. Heind. Is it not rather, 'give birth to'? Cf. Rep. 372: Ποιούμενα τοὺς παῖδας. Crit. 45: Ἦ γὰρ οὐ χρὴ παιεῖσθαι παῖδας.

14. παρατίθημι] P. 149; διδόασί γε αἱ μαῖαι φαρμάκια καὶ ἐπᾴδουσαι. See the description of the education of a Greek youth in the Protagoras, 325: Παρατιθέασιν αὐτοῖς ἐπὶ τῶν βάθρων ἀναγιγνώσκειν ποιητῶν ἀγαθῶν ποιήματα. The genitive is perhaps partitive, but more probably governed by ἀπογεύσασθαι.

17. καὶ καρτερῶν] 'And with perseverance.' Boldness was all he required at first. p. 148. θάρρει. 151 ἑὰν ἀνδρίζῃ.

ΘΕΑΙΤΗΤΟΣ. 57

ΘΕΑΙ. Ἐρώτα δή.

ΣΩ. Λέγε τοίνυν πάλιν, εἴ σοι ἀρέσκει τὸ μή τι εἶναι ἀλλὰ γίγνεσθαι ἀεὶ ἀγαθὸν καὶ καλὸν καὶ πάντα ἃ ἄρτι διῇμεν.

ΘΕΑΙ. Ἀλλ' ἔμοιγε, ἐπειδὴ σοῦ ἀκούω οὕτω διεξιόντος, θαυμασίως φαίνεται ὡς ἔχειν λόγον καὶ ὑποληπτέον ᾗπερ διελήλυθας.

ΣΩ. Μὴ τοίνυν ἀπολίπωμεν ὅσον ἐλλεῖπον αὐτοῦ. λείπεται δὲ ἐνυπνίων τε πέρι καὶ νόσων, τῶν τε ἄλλων καὶ μανίας ὅσα τε παρακούειν ἢ παρορᾶν ἤ τι ἄλλο παραισθάνεσθαι λέγεται. οἶσθα γάρ που ὅτι ἐν πᾶσι τούτοις ὁμολογουμένως ἐλέγχεσθαι δοκεῖ ὃν ἄρτι διῇμεν λόγον, ὡς παντὸς μᾶλλον ἡμῖν ψευδεῖς αἰσθήσεις

*opnd. Socrates disclaims having any share in it, except that he has helped to bring it to the birth. The Good and Noble must be thought of with other things, as not existing, but arising occasionally.
3. A formidable*

2. εἰ σοι ἀρέσκει] 'Whether you are pleased with the idea that nothing is, but is ever becoming, good and noble, as well as what we have just enumerated.'

3. ἀγαθὸν καὶ καλὸν] As, above, αἰσθήσεις is made to include desire, fear, &c., so by the subtle introduction of these words, the doctrine is pushed to its farthest limits, and thus its chief fallacy is hinted at—that of arguing from sense to higher things. So afterwards Protagoras is made to assume that the doctrine applies to states as well as individuals. It is a good example of the irony of dialectic.

8. Μὴ τοίνυν] The doctrine is now so far developed, that we have only to notice an objection, and it will be complete. As false opinion is our stumbling-block afterwards, so now false impressions have to be accounted for. The solution is a simple one—they are not false to him who is the subject of them. The position, Sense is knowledge, was at first made equivalent to its having a real object (p. 152). But are dreams real? Are the illusions of madness true? Is that really bitter which tastes so to the diseased palate?—If truth is wholly relative, if nothing is but what becomes, it must be so. (In fact, such impressions are not contrary to sense, but to reason.)

9. καὶ νόσων, τῶν τε ἄλλων καὶ] And disease, especially madness and its delusions. μανίας is the subject of λέγεται, and ὅσα is cogn. accus. Cf. Soph. Trach. 406, λώσσαν μάνια. alib.

ὅσα — τί ἄλλο] The double cognate accusative is noticeable. 'The cases in which it is said—to have any other illusory impression.'

I

58   ΠΛΑΤΩΝΟΣ

class of objections is now disposed of. It is commonly said that in dreams and madness nothing of what appears is real. Protagoras says, All that appears to me is real to me. What account does he then give of these phenomena?

ἐν αὑτοῖς γιγνομένας, καὶ πολλοῦ δεῖ τὰ φαινόμενα p. 158. ἑκάστῳ ταῦτα καὶ εἶναι, ἀλλὰ πᾶν τοὐναντίον οὐδὲν ὧν φαίνεται εἶναι.

ΘΕΑΙ. Ἀληθέστατα λέγεις, ὦ Σώκρατες.

ΣΩ. Τίς δὴ οὖν, ὦ παῖ, λείπεται λόγος τῷ τὴν αἴσθησιν ἐπιστήμην τιθεμένῳ καὶ τὰ φαινόμενα ἑκάστῳ ταῦτα καὶ εἶναι τούτῳ ᾧ φαίνεται;

ΘΕΑΙ. Ἐγὼ μέν, ὦ Σώκρατες, ὀκνῶ εἰπεῖν ὅτι οὐκ ἔχω τί λέγω, διότι μοι νῦν δὴ ἐπέπληξας εἰπόντι αὐτό. ἐπεὶ ὡς ἀληθῶς γε οὐκ ἂν δυναίμην ἀμφισβητῆσαι ὡς οἱ μαινόμενοι ἢ οἱ ὀνειρώττοντες οὐ ψευδῆ δοξάζουσιν, ὅταν οἱ μὲν θεοὶ αὐτῶν οἴωνται εἶναι, οἱ δὲ πτηνοί τε, καὶ ὡς πετόμενοι ἐν τῷ ὕπνῳ διανοῶνται.

There is a doubt which is often felt about them: e. g. when it is asked, Can we prove that we are not dreaming now?

ΣΩ. Ἆρ᾽ οὖν οὐδὲ τὸ τοιόνδε ἀμφισβήτημα ἐννοεῖς περὶ αὐτῶν, μάλιστα δὲ περὶ τοῦ ὄναρ τε καὶ ὕπαρ;

ΘΕΑΙ. Τὸ ποῖον;

ΣΩ. Ὃ πολλάκις σε οἶμαι ἀκηκοέναι ἐρωτώντων τί ἄν τις ἔχοι τεκμήριον ἀποδεῖξαι, εἴ τις ἔροιτο νῦν οὕτως ἐν τῷ παρόντι, πότερον καθεύδομεν καὶ πάντα ἃ διανοούμεθα ὀνειρώττομεν, ἢ ἐγρηγόραμέν τε καὶ ὁ ὕπαρ ἀλλήλοις διαλεγόμεθα.

1. πολλοῦ δεῖ] These words are adverbial.

2. ἀλλὰ πᾶν τοὐναντίον οὐδὲν ὧν φαίνεται εἶναι] E. g. Democritus (who is believed to have written against Protagoras) said of all sensations except hardness and weight : Σημεῖον δ᾽ ὡς οὐκ εἰσὶ φύσει τὸ μὴ ταὐτὰ πᾶσι φαίνεσθαι τοῖς ζώοις, ἀλλ᾽ ἃ ἡμῖν γλυκύ, τοῦτ᾽ ἄλλοις πικρὸν καὶ ἑτέροις ὀξὺ καὶ ἄλλοις δριμύ, τοῖς δὲ στρυφνὸν καὶ τὰ ἄλλα δὲ ὡσαύτως.

12. οἱ μὲν — αὐτῶν] i. e. the madmen.

13. πτηνοί τε] sc. αἴωνται εἶναι.

18. Ὃ πολλάκις] ὃ is not exactly governed by ἀκηκοέναι ἐρωτώντων, but it is cognate accusative in apposition with the whole sentence that follows. ' What question do you allude to? This I dare say you have often heard it asked, &c.' Cf. p. 165: 'Ἀ φιλόχορος ἂν τελευταῖός ἀνὴρ μισθοφόρος ἐν λόγοις ἐρόμενος κ. τ. λ. Rep. 443: Τὸ ἐνύπνιον, ὃ ἔφαμεν ἱσταντύεσθαι, κ. τ. λ.

Arist. Met. Γ, 6, 1011 A: Τὸ δὴ τοιαῦτα ἀπορήματα ὅμοιά ἐστι τῷ ἀπορεῖν πότερον καθεύδομεν νῦν ἢ ἐγρηγόραμεν.

ΘΕΑΙΤΗΤΟΣ.

p. 158. ΘΕΑΙ. Καὶ μήν, ὦ Σώκρατες, ἀπορῶν γε ὅτῳ χρὴ ἐπιδείξαι τεκμηρίῳ. πάντα γὰρ ὥσπερ ἀντίστροφα τὰ αὐτὰ παρακολουθεῖ. ἅ τε γὰρ νυνὶ διειλέγμεθα, οὐδὲν κωλύει καὶ ἐν τῷ ὕπνῳ δοκεῖν ἀλλήλοις διαλέγεσθαι· καὶ ὅταν δὴ ὄναρ ὀνείρατα δοκῶμεν διηγεῖσθαι,—ἄτοπος ἡ ὁμοιότης τούτων ἐκείνοις.

ΣΩ. Ὁρᾷς οὖν ὅτι τό γε ἀμφισβητῆσαι οὐ χαλεπόν, ὅτε καὶ πότερόν ἐστιν ὕπαρ ἢ ὄναρ ἀμφισβητεῖται, καὶ δὴ ἴσου ὄντος τοῦ χρόνου ὃν καθεύδομεν ᾧ ἐγρηγόραμεν, ἐν ἑκατέρῳ διαμάχεται ἡμῶν ἡ ψυχὴ τὰ ἀεὶ παρόντα δόγματα παντὸς μᾶλλον εἶναι ἀληθῆ, ὥστε ἴσον μὲν χρόνον τάδε φαμὲν ὄντα εἶναι, ἴσον δὲ ἐκεῖνα, καὶ ὁμοίως ἐφ᾽ ἑκατέροις διϊσχυριζόμεθα.

ΘΕΑΙ. Παντάπασι μὲν οὖν.

Dreams have as much reality to the dreaming mind, as daylight impressions have to the waking mind. And half our life is spent in dreaming. The impressions

1. ἀπορῶν γε ὅτῳ χρὴ ἐπιδείξαι] Descartes de la Méthode, p. 164 (Cousin.): Et que les meilleurs esprits y étudient tant qu'il leur plaira, je ne crois pas qu'ils puissent donner aucune raison, qu'il soit suffisante pour ôter cette doute, s'ils ne présupposent l'existence de Dieu. Descartes however would not say ὁμοίως ἐφ᾽ ἑκατέροις διϊσχυριζόμεθα. As early as the age of Homer, attention had been attracted by the phenomena of dreams. Il. XXII. 199: 'Ὡς δ᾽ ἐν ὀνείρῳ οὐ δύναται φεύγοντα διώκειν. (Bodl. ὅτῳ χρήσῃ χρῇ.)

2. πάντα γὰρ ὥσπερ ἀντίστροφα τὰ αὐτὰ παρακολουθεῖ] 'For everything corresponds in each exactly, as if one was the counterpart of the other.'

4. ἐν τῷ ὕπνῳ] This is the reading of the best MSS. though ἐνυπνίῳ is supported by the greater number. But the article with ἐνυπνίῳ is out of place, and the indefinite τῳ is not used adjectively.

5. καὶ ὅταν δή] 'And when in a dream we do seem to be telling thoughts which are dreams, —it is strange, the resemblance of this state to that.'

ὀνείρατα—διηγεῖσθαι] Not 'to tell dreams,' but 'to give utterance to thoughts which are only dreams.' Cf. supr. πάντα ἃ διανοούμεθα ἀνειρώτωμεν. 'Ὀνείρατα is a sort of cognate accusative, or rather, is in apposition to the suppressed object of διηγεῖσθαι. Ὄναρ is adverbial to δοκῶμεν. (Meno 85: Ὥσπερ ὄναρ ἄρτι ἀνακεκίνηνται αἱ δόξαι αὐτῷ.) Τούτων refers to the waking, ἐκείνοις to the sleeping state, like τῳδὶδε, ἐπεὶ of the visible and invisible world. There is probably a slight break in the sentence before ἄτοπος, κ.τ.λ. The collocation ὄναρ ὀνείρατα is like καλὸν κακὸν p. 177, and adds intensity to the expression.

60 ΠΛΑΤΩΝΟΣ

of madness, too, though more short-lived, are real at the time to him who experiences them. In both cases it is impossible to demonstrate which is the real world.

ΣΩ. Οὐκοῦν καὶ περὶ νόσων τε καὶ μανιῶν ὁ αὐτὸς p. 158. λόγος, πλὴν τοῦ χρόνου, ὅτι οὐχὶ ἴσος;

ΘΕΑΙ. Ὀρθῶς.

ΣΩ. Τί οὖν; πλήθει χρόνου καὶ ὀλιγότητι τὸ ἀληθὲς ὁρισθήσεται;

ΘΕΑΙ. Γελοῖον μέντ' ἂν εἴη πολλαχῇ.

ΣΩ. Ἀλλά τι ἄλλο ἔχεις σαφὲς ἐνδείξασθαι, ὁποῖα τούτων τῶν δοξασμάτων ἀληθῆ;

ΘΕΑΙ. Οὔ μοι δοκῶ.

Our theory resolves this doubt as follows:

ΣΩ. Ἐμοῦ τοίνυν ἄκουε οἷα περὶ αὐτῶν ἂν λέγοιεν οἱ τὰ ἀεὶ δοκοῦντα ὁριζόμενοι τῷ δοκοῦντι εἶναι ἀληθῆ. λέγουσι δέ, ὡς ἐγὼ οἶμαι, οὕτως ἐρωτῶντες, Ὦ Θεαίτητε, ὃ ἂν ἕτερον ᾖ παντάπασι, μή πῃ τινα δύναμιν τὴν αὐτὴν ἕξει τῷ ἑτέρῳ; καὶ μὴ ὑπολάβωμεν τῇ μὲν ταὐτὸν εἶναι ὃ ἐρωτῶμεν, τῇ δὲ ἕτερον, ἀλλ' ὅλως ἕτερον. p. 159.

That which is different has a different power,

ΘΕΑΙ. Ἀδύνατον τοίνυν ταὐτόν τι ἔχειν ἢ ἐν δυνάμει ἢ ἐν ἄλλῳ ὁτῳοῦν, ὅταν ᾖ κομιδῇ ἕτερον.

Whether this be

ΣΩ. Ἆρ' οὖν οὐ καὶ ἀνόμοιον ἀναγκαῖον τὸ τοιοῦτον ὁμολογεῖν;

4. πλήθει χρόνου καὶ ὀλιγότητι] The supporters of the same doctrine as quoted by Aristotle extended this argument to meet that from general consent. Met. Γ. 5. 1009 B: Τὸ μὲν γὰρ ἀληθὲς οὐ πλήθει κρίνεσθαι οἴονται προσήκειν οὐδὲ ὀλιγότητι.

7. τι ἄλλο—σαφές] 'Any other certain test.'

11. ὁριζόμενοι] 'Who determine.' Perhaps there is a touch of irony in the application of the word to them.

14. μὴ ὑπολάβωμεν τῇ μὲν ταὐτόν] Megarian subtilty is here ironically brought to the help of Protagoras. The language of logic is applied to the sensible world: the language of ideas to things that admit of degrees. And throughout, the idea dwelt upon is that of difference. The language is humoured accordingly. Socrates ill can hardly be said to be, ὅλως ἕτερον, wholly different, from Socrates well, but they differ when taken each as a whole, ὅλως τοῦτο ὅλῳ ἐκείνῳ. For the application of this logic in the mouth of a Sophist see Euthyd. 283. 'Kleinias is not wise. You wish him to be made what he is not: i.e. no longer to be what he is. You wish him to be annihilated.' Cf.

ΘΕΑΙΤΗΤΟΣ. 61

p. 159. ΘΕΑΙ. Ἔμοιγε δοκεῖ.

active or passive.

ΣΩ. Εἰ ἄρα τι ξυμβαίνει ὅμοιόν τῳ γίγνεσθαι ἢ ἀνόμοιον, εἴτε ἑαυτῷ εἴτε ἄλλῳ, ὁμοιούμενον μὲν ταὐτὸν φήσομεν γίγνεσθαι, ἀνομοιούμενον δὲ ἕτερον;

ΘΕΑΙ. Ἀνάγκη. 5

ΣΩ. Οὐκοῦν πρόσθεν ἐλέγομεν ὡς πολλὰ μὲν εἴη τὰ ποιοῦντα καὶ ἄπειρα, ὡσαύτως δέ γε τὰ πάσχοντα;

ΘΕΑΙ. Ναί.

ΣΩ. Καὶ μὴν ὅτι γε ἄλλο ἄλλῳ συμμιγνύμενον 10 καὶ ἄλλῳ οὐ ταὐτὰ ἀλλ᾽ ἕτερα γεννήσει;

And the same thing in combination with different things has different products.

b ΘΕΑΙ. Πάνυ μὲν οὖν.

ΣΩ. Λέγωμεν δὴ ἐμέ τε καὶ σὲ καὶ τἄλλ᾽ ἤδη κατὰ τὸν αὐτὸν λόγον· Σωκράτη ὑγιαίνοντα καὶ Σωκράτη αὖ ἀσθενοῦντα· πότερον ὅμοιον τοῦτ᾽ ἐκείνῳ ἢ 15 ἀνόμοιον φήσομεν;

Socrates ill, is a different man from Socrates well;

ΘΕΑΙ. Ἆρα τὸν ἀσθενοῦντα Σωκράτη, ὅλον τοῦτο λέγεις ὅλῳ ἐκείνῳ, τῷ ὑγιαίνοντι Σωκράτει;

Democritus ap. Ar. de Gen. et Corr. I. 2: Καὶ ὅλως ἕτερον φαίνεσθαι ἐνὸς μεταπεσόντος· ἐκ τῶν αὐτῶν γὰρ τραγῳδία καὶ κωμῳδία γίγνεται γραμμάτων.

2. Εἰ ἄρα] 'What is the same is like, therefore what is like is the same.' This is one of many examples of the imperfect state of logic, which puts Socrates' respondent at his mercy. He does not always escape unchecked, however, see Prot. 350: Ἔγωγε ἐρωτηθεὶς ὑπὸ σοῦ εἰ οἱ ἀνδρεῖοι θαρραλέοι εἰσίν, ὡμολόγησα· εἰ δὲ καὶ οἱ θαρραλέοι ἀνδρεῖοι, οὐκ ἠρωτήθην· εἰ γάρ με τότε ἤρου, εἶπον ἂν ὅτι οὐ πάντες.

6. πρόσθεν ἐλέγομεν] Soph. 259: Ὃ καὶ πρόσθεν εἴρηται.

10. Ἄλλο ἄλλῳ—καὶ ἄλλῳ] Cf. Rep. p. 369: Παραλαμβάνων ἄλλος ἄλλον ἐπ᾽ ἄλλου, τὸν δ᾽ ἐπ᾽ ἄλλου χρείᾳ. The combination of one element with this and another with that, and again with another different from all. Compare with what follows, Ar. Met. E. 2. 1026 B: εἰσὶ γὰρ οἱ τῶν σοφιστῶν λόγοι περὶ τὸ συμβεβηκὸς ὡς εἰπεῖν μάλιστα πάντων, πότερον ἕτερον ἢ ταὐτὸν ——μουσικὸς Κορίσκος καὶ Κορίσκος, κ. τ. λ.

13. Λέγωμεν δή] Phaed. 100: Καὶ πάντα δὴ οὕτω λέγω. Σωκράτη is governed partly by λέγωμεν, partly by φήσομεν.

ἤδη] i. e. having laid down these premises.

ΠΛΑΤΩΝΟΣ

ΣΩ. Κάλλιστα ὑπέλαβες· αὐτὸ τοῦτο λέγω. p. 159.
ΘΕΑΙ. Ἀνόμοιον δή που.
ΣΩ. Καὶ ἕτερον ἄρα οὕτως ὥσπερ ἀνόμοιον;
ΘΕΑΙ. Ἀνάγκη.

Socrates sleeping from Socrates waking, and so on.

ΣΩ. Καὶ καθεύδοντα δὴ καὶ πάντα ἃ νῦν διήλ- c
θομεν, ὡσαύτως φήσεις;
ΘΕΑΙ. Ἔγωγε.

Therefore in combination with the same active motion they will produce different results.

ΣΩ. Ἕκαστον δὴ τῶν πεφυκότων τι ποιεῖν, ἄλλο
τι, ὅταν μὲν λάβῃ ὑγιαίνοντα Σωκράτη, ὡς ἑτέρῳ μοι
χρήσεται, ὅταν δὲ ἀσθενοῦντα, ὡς ἑτέρῳ;
ΘΕΑΙ. Τί δ᾽ οὐ μέλλει;
ΣΩ. Καὶ ἕτερα δὴ ἐφ᾽ ἑκατέρου γεννήσομεν ἐγώ
τε ὁ πάσχων καὶ ἐκεῖνο τὸ ποιοῦν;
ΘΕΑΙ. Τί μήν;
ΣΩ. Ὅταν δὴ οἶνον πίνω ὑγιαίνων, ἡδύς μοι φαίνεται καὶ γλυκύς;
ΘΕΑΙ. Ναί.

Accordingly, wine both seems and really is pleasant to me when well.

ΣΩ. Ἐγέννησε γὰρ δὴ ἐκ τῶν προωμολογημένων
τό τε ποιοῦν καὶ τὸ πάσχον γλυκύτητά τε καὶ αἴσθη- d
σιν, ἅμα φερόμενα ἀμφότερα, καὶ ἡ μὲν αἴσθησις
πρὸς τοῦ πάσχοντος οὖσα αἰσθανομένην τὴν γλῶσσαν ἀπειργάσατο, ἡ δὲ γλυκύτης πρὸς τοῦ οἴνου περὶ
αὐτὸν φερομένη γλυκὺν τὸν οἶνον τῇ ὑγιαινούσῃ
γλώττῃ ἐποίησε καὶ εἶναι καὶ φαίνεσθαι.

ΘΕΑΙ. Πάνυ μὲν οὖν τὰ πρότερα ἡμῖν οὕτως
ὡμολόγητο.

5. καθεύδοντα] Par. F. marg. add. καὶ ἐγρηγορότα. Bodl. καθεύδοντι. Is it possible that καθεύδοντα δὴ ἐγρηγορότι may be the true reading?

6. ὡσαύτως φήσεις] Sc. διάφορον καὶ ἕτερον εἶναι τοῦ ἐγρηγορότος, κ. τ. λ.

8. τι ποιεῖν] To act upon something; to be agents. So τὸ ποιοῦν ipsi, below. Soph. 247: Εἴτε εἰς τὸ ποιεῖν ἕτερον ὁτιοῦν.

12. ἐφ᾽ ἑκατέρου] In either case. Cf. Parm. 130: Λέγοντος δὴ τοῦ Σωκράτους — ἐφ᾽ ἑκάστου ἄχθεσθαι τόν τε Παρμενίδην καὶ τὸν Ζήνωνα.

22. ἀπειργάσατο] 'The sensation arising on the side of the subject renders the tongue percipient.'

ΘΕΑΙΤΗΤΟΣ. 63

p. 159. ΣΩ. Ὅταν δὲ ἀσθενοῦντα, ἄλλο τι πρῶτον μὲν τῇ ἀληθείᾳ οὐ τὸν αὐτὸν ἔλαβεν; ἀνομοίῳ γὰρ δὴ προσῆλθεν.

ΘΕΑΙ. Ναί.

e ΣΩ. Ἕτερα δὴ αὖ ἐγεννησάτην ὅ τε τοιοῦτος Σω- 5 κράτης καὶ ἡ τοῦ οἴνου πόσις, περὶ μὲν τὴν γλῶτταν αἴσθησιν πικρότητος, περὶ δὲ τὸν οἶνον γιγνομένην καὶ φερομένην πικρότητα, καὶ τὸν μὲν οὐ πικρότητα ἀλλὰ πικρόν, ἐμὲ δὲ οὐκ αἴσθησιν ἀλλ' αἰσθανόμενον;

ΘΕΑΙ. Κομιδῇ μὲν οὖν. 10

ΣΩ. Οὔκουν ἐγώ τε οὐδὲν ἄλλο ποτὲ γενήσομαι οὕτως αἰσθανόμενος· τοῦ γὰρ ἄλλου ἄλλη αἴσθησις,
p. 160. καὶ ἀλλοῖον καὶ ἄλλον ποιεῖ τὸν αἰσθανόμενον· οὔτ' ἐκεῖνο τὸ ποιοῦν ἐμὲ μήποτ' ἄλλῳ συνελθὸν ταὐτὸν γεννῆσαν τοιοῦτον γένηται· ἀπὸ γὰρ ἄλλου ἄλλο 15 γεννῆσαν ἀλλοῖον γενήσεται.

ΘΕΑΙ. Ἔστι ταῦτα.

ΣΩ. Οὐδὲ μὴν ἔγωγε ἐμαυτῷ τοιοῦτος, ἐκεῖνό τε ἑαυτῷ τοιοῦτον γενήσεται.

But the same wine both seems and really is distasteful to me when ill. For I am then a different man.

I should never receive the same impression from anything else. And it would never produce the same impression upon another person. Nor could

1. ἀσθενοῦντα] The constr. is resumed from ὅταν—λάβῃ above.

5. ἐγεννησάτην] The use of the 3ᵈ pers. helps to support the notion of 'Socrates being a different man.' Observe, too, the accuracy with which not the wine, but the drinking of the wine is spoken of as the 'active motion.' The dual is expressive. 'They produce when paired.'

11. οὐδὲν ἄλλο—γενήσομαι οὕτως αἰσθανόμενος] 'There is nothing else from which I can receive the same sensation.' That ἄλλο is the object of αἰσθανόμενος seems required by what follows. For the accusative, see p. 185: 'Ἃ δι' ἑτέρας δυνάμεως αἰσθάνει, ἀδύνατον εἶναι δι' ἄλλης ταῦτ' αἰσθέσθαι, and elsewhere. There is a stress on οὕτως. For γενήσομαι—αἰσθανόμενος, see a few lines below, ὅταν αἰσθανόμενος γίγνωμαι. The words γίγνεσθαι, αἰσθανόμενος, have become in a manner technical; cf. p. 182. γιγ. αἰσθ. answers to ἐγεννησάτην—αἰσθανόμενον above. The point insisted on is not the identity of the subject while in the same combination, but the difference which arises with every new combination. For Ἄλλου τινί, (the Bodleian reading) cf. supr. οὐ τὸν αὐτόν ἔλ. (γενήσομαι Bodl. Vat. Δ.) 'For a different object implies a different sensation, and makes him who perceives it a different man,' i.e. I and my sensation become different, with every change in the object of sense.

64 ΠΛΑΤΩΝΟΣ

ΘΕΑΙ. Οὐ γὰρ οὖν.

ΣΩ. Ἀνάγκη δέ γε ἐμέ τε τινὸς γίγνεσθαι, ὅταν p. 160.
αἰσθανόμενος γίγνωμαι· αἰσθανόμενον γάρ, μηδενὸς δὲ
αἰσθανόμενον ἀδύνατον γίγνεσθαι· ἐκεῖνό τε τινὶ γί- b
γνεσθαι, ὅταν γλυκὺ ἢ πικρὸν ᾖ τι τοιοῦτον γίγνηται·
γλυκὺ γάρ, μηδενὶ δὲ γλυκύ, ἀδύνατον γενέσθαι.

ΘΕΑΙ. Παντάπασι μὲν οὖν.

ΣΩ. Λείπεται δή, οἶμαι, ἡμῖν ἀλλήλοις, εἴτ᾽ ἐσμέν,
εἶναι, εἴτε γιγνόμεθα, γίγνεσθαι, ἐπείπερ ἡμῶν ἡ
ἀνάγκη τὴν οὐσίαν συνδεῖ μέν, συνδεῖ δὲ οὐδενὶ τῶν
ἄλλων, οὐδ᾽ αὖ ἡμῶν αὐτοῖς. ἀλλήλοις δὴ λείπεται
συνδεδέσθαι. ὥστε εἴτε τις εἶναί τι ὀνομάζει, τινὶ εἶναι
ἢ τινὸς ἢ πρός τι ῥητέον αὐτῷ, εἴτε γίγνεσθαι· αὐτὸ
δὲ ἐφ᾽ αὑτοῦ τι ἢ ὂν ἢ γιγνόμενον οὔτε αὐτῷ λεκτέον c
οὔτ᾽ ἄλλου λέγοντος ἀποδεκτέον, ὡς ὁ λόγος ὃν διελη-
λύθαμεν σημαίνει.

ΘΕΑΙ. Παντάπασι μὲν οὖν, ὦ Σώκρατες.

ΣΩ. Οὐκοῦν ὅτε δὴ τὸ ἐμὲ ποιοῦν ἐμοί ἐστι καὶ
οὐκ ἄλλῳ, ἐγὼ καὶ αἰσθάνομαι αὐτοῦ, ἄλλος δ᾽ οὔ;

ΘΕΑΙ. Πῶς γὰρ οὔ;

ΣΩ. Ἀληθὴς ἄρα ἐμοὶ ἡ ἐμὴ αἴσθησις· τῆς γὰρ
ἐμῆς οὐσίας ἀεί ἐστι. καὶ ἐγὼ κριτὴς κατὰ τὸν Πρωταγόραν τῶν τε ὄντων ἐμοί, ὡς ἔστι, καὶ τῶν μὴ
ὄντων, ὡς οὐκ ἔστιν.

ΘΕΑΙ. Ἔοικεν.

ΣΩ. Πῶς ἂν οὖν ἀψευδὴς ὢν καὶ μὴ πταίων τῇ διανοίᾳ περὶ τὰ ὄντα ἢ γιγνόμενα οὐκ ἐπιστήμων ἂν εἴην ὧνπερ αἰσθητής;

ΘΕΑΙ. Οὐδαμῶς ὅπως οὔ.

ΣΩ. Παγκάλως ἄρα σοι εἴρηται ὅτι ἐπιστήμη οὐκ ἄλλο τί ἐστιν ἢ αἴσθησις, καὶ εἰς ταὐτὸν συμπέπτωκε, κατὰ μὲν Ὅμηρον καὶ Ἡράκλειτον καὶ πᾶν τὸ τοιοῦτον φῦλον οἷον ῥεύματα κινεῖσθαι τὰ πάντα, κατὰ δὲ Πρωταγόραν τὸν σοφώτατον πάντων χρημάτων ἄνθρωπον μέτρον εἶναι, κατὰ δὲ Θεαίτητον τούτων οὕτως ἐχόντων αἴσθησιν ἐπιστήμην γίγνεσθαι. ἢ γάρ, ὦ Θεαίτητε; φῶμεν τοῦτο σὸν μὲν εἶναι οἷον νεογενὲς παιδίον, ἐμὸν δὲ μαίευμα; ἢ πῶς λέγεις;

ΘΕΑΙ. Οὕτως ἀνάγκη, ὦ Σώκρατες.

ΣΩ. Τοῦτο μὲν δή, ὡς ἔοικε, μόλις ποτὲ ἐγεννήσα-

66   ΠΛΑΤΩΝΟΣ

the doctrine of sense.

μεν, ὅ τι δή ποτε καὶ τυγχάνει ὄν. μετὰ δὲ τὸν τόκον p. 160.
τὰ ἀμφιδρόμια αὐτοῦ ὡς ἀληθῶς ἐν κύκλῳ περιθρεκτέον τῷ λόγῳ, σκοπουμένους μὴ λάθῃ ἡμᾶς οὐκ
ἄξιον ὂν τροφῆς τὸ γιγνόμενον, ἀλλὰ ἀνεμιαῖόν τε p. 161.
5 καὶ ψεῦδος. ἢ σὺ οἴει πάντως δεῖν τό γε σὸν τρέφειν
καὶ μὴ ἀποτιθέναι; ἢ καὶ ἀνέξει ἐλεγχόμενον ὁρῶν,
καὶ οὐ σφόδρα χαλεπανεῖς, ἐάν τις σοῦ ὡς πρωτοτό-
κου αὐτὸ ὑφαιρῇ;

ΘΕΟ. Ἀνέξεται, ὦ Σώκρατες, Θεαίτητος· οὐδαμῶς
10 γὰρ δύσκολος. ἀλλὰ πρὸς θεῶν εἰπέ, ἢ αὖ οὐχ οὕτως
ἔχει;

ΣΩ. Φιλόλογος γ' εἶ ἀτεχνῶς καὶ χρηστός, ὦ

distinctness, and boldness, and apparent certainty. At first only warmth, colour, and the like were spoken of; gradually our eyes were opened to the relativeness of size and number. By and by it was assumed that the term αἴσθησις includes pleasure, pain, hope, fear, &c. Then we are quietly asked to concede that things good and beautiful have only a relative existence. And, being now fairly at the mercy of the argument, we cannot resist the admission that the illusions of dreams and madness are as real as our waking and sane impressions. They are real to us at the time when we experience them; which is all the reality any thing is permitted to claim.

2. τὰ ἀμφιδρόμια αὐτοῦ] Cogn. acc. in somewhat vague connection with what follows: like τὸν παλαμναῖον, supr. p. 153. Schol.: Ἡμέρα πέμπτη ταῖς θρίψεσιν ἐν γενέσθαι αὐτὰ ἐληθεῖσα παρ' ὅσον ἐν ταύτῃ καθαίρονσι τὰς χεῖρας αἱ συνεφαψάμεναι τῆς μαιώσεως, καὶ τὸ βρέφος περὶ τὴν ἑστίαν φέρουσι τρέχουσαι κύκλῳ, καὶ τοὔνομα τί-

θενται τούτῳ, δῶρά τε πέμπουσι τῷ παιδίῳ, ὡς ἐπὶ πλεῖστον πολύποδας καὶ σηπίας, οἵ τε φίλοι καὶ οἰκεῖοι καὶ ἀπλῶς οἱ προσήκοντες.

ἐν κύκλῳ περιθρεκτέον] 'All round;' i. e. leaving out no point of view. There is an allusion to the etymology of ἀμφιδρ., as the words ὡς ἀληθῶς indicate.

3. τῷ λόγῳ] In our argument.

4. τὸ γιγνόμενον] In this and in some other cases where the reading has been questioned, the present or imperfect tense really gives additional vividness. 'That which is now born to us.'

7. τις σοῦ] Bodl. p. m. τίσσον?

10. γὰρ δύσκολος] Γ. 145: Μετὰ πάσης πρᾳότητος. p. 155: Οὐ δυσκολαίνοντε κ.τ.λ.

12. Φιλόλογος γ' εἶ ἀτεχνῶς καὶ χρηστός, ὦ Θ.] Phaedr. 235: Φιλότατε εἶ καὶ ὡς ἀληθῶς χρυσοῦς, ὦ Φαῖδρε. Π. 264. χρηστὸς εἶ, ὅτι κ.τ.λ.

Φιλόλογος] 'You are truly a patient inquirer and an ingenuous person, Theodorus, if you take me for a sack full of different theories; and expect me without any difficulty to

p. 161. Θεόδωρε, ὅτι με οἴει λόγων τινὰ εἶναι θύλακον καὶ
ῥᾳδίως ἐξελόντα ἐρεῖν ὡς οὐκ αὖ ἔχει οὕτω ταῦτα· τὸ
b δὲ γιγνόμενον οὐκ ἐννοεῖς, ὅτι οὐδεὶς τῶν λόγων ἐξέρ-
χεται παρ' ἐμοῦ ἀλλ' ἀεὶ παρὰ τοῦ ἐμοὶ προσδιαλεγο-
μένου, ἐγὼ δὲ οὐδὲν ἐπίσταμαι πλέον πλὴν βραχέος, 5
ὅσον λόγον παρ' ἑτέρου σοφοῦ λαβεῖν καὶ ἀποδέξασθαι μετρίως. καὶ νῦν τοῦτο παρὰ τοῦδε πειράσομαι, οὔ τι αὐτὸς εἰπεῖν.

ΘΕΟ. Σὺ κάλλιον, ὦ Σώκρατες, λέγεις· καὶ ποίει
οὕτως.   10

ΣΩ. Οἶσθ' οὖν, ὦ Θεόδωρε, ὃ θαυμάζω τοῦ ἑταίρου
σου Πρωταγόρου;

c ΘΕΟ. Τὸ ποῖον;

ΣΩ. Τὰ μὲν ἄλλα μοι πάνυ ἡδέως εἴρηκεν, ὡς τὸ
δοκοῦν ἑκάστῳ τοῦτο καὶ ἔστι· τὴν δ' ἀρχὴν τοῦ 15
λόγου τεθαύμακα, ὅτι οὐκ εἶπεν ἀρχόμενος τῆς ἀληθείας ὅτι πάντων χρημάτων μέτρον ἐστὶν ὗς ἢ κυνο-

I. Why did not Protagoras say that a pig or a tadpole was the mea.

pull out the refutation of what has been now stated. But you do not perceive what is really taking place.'

5. ἐγὼ δὲ οὐδὲν] 'But I have no advantage in wisdom beyond this simple skill, to receive a theory from some wise person, and admit it on fair conditions.'

7. μετρίως] In a spirit of fairness. P. 179: Μετρίως ἄρα πρὸς τὸν ἀδ. εἰρήσεται.

παρὰ τοῦδε] Viz. Theætetus. Or is Protagoras meant?

11. ὁ θαυμάζω] A courteous way of expressing strong dissent. Prot. 329: Εἴπερ ἄλλῳ τῳ ἀνθρώ-πων συνεθείμην ἄν, καὶ σοὶ συνεθεί-μην· ὃ δ' ἐθαύμασα σοῦ λέγοντος—. Gorg. 458: "Ακουε δή, ὦ Γοργία, ἃ θαυμάζω ἐν τοῖς λεγομένοις ὑπὸ σοῦ. No fault is found with

the arguments of Protagoras, only if we follow his doctrine to its results, all creatures that have sense must be equally infallible. Hence there can be no teaching and no discussion.

14. Τὰ — ἄλλα — εἴρηκεν, ὡς] Cf. supr. p. 153: Ἔτι οὖν σοι λέγω—γαλήνας,—ὅτι κ. τ. λ.

16. τῆς ἀληθείας] The title of Protagoras' work. It is often covertly alluded to in this and other dialogues. The most pointed instance is in Cratyl. 391: Εἰ τὴν μὲν ἀλήθειαν τὴν Πρω-ταγόρου οὐκ ἀποδέχομαι, τὰ δὲ τῇ τοιαύτῃ ἀληθείᾳ ῥηθέντα ἀγαπῴην ὥς του ἄξια.

17. ὗς] The type of stupidity. Lach. 196: Κατὰ τὴν παροιμίαν οὐδ' ἂν ὗς ὃς γνοίη.

κυνοκέφαλοι] Something more remote even than the Μυσῶν

68 ΠΛΑΤΩΝΟΣ

sure of things? His principle clearly includes all creatures that have sense: and destroys his own pretension to superior wisdom. Not to say that it cuts at the root of dialectic and of all discussion.

κέφαλος ἤ τι ἄλλο ἀσπώτερον τῶν ἐχόντων αἴσθη- p. 161.
σιν, ἵνα μεγαλοπρεπῶς καὶ πάνυ καταφρονητικῶς
ἤρξατο ἡμῖν λέγειν, ἐνδεικνύμενος ὅτι ἡμεῖς μὲν αὐτὸν
ὥσπερ θεὸν ἐθαυμάζομεν ἐπὶ σοφίᾳ, ὁ δ᾽ ἄρα ἐτύγ-
5 χανεν ὢν εἰς φρόνησιν οὐδὲν βελτίων βατράχου γυρί- d
νου, μὴ ὅτι ἄλλου του ἀνθρώπων. ἢ πῶς λέγωμεν,
ὦ Θεόδωρε; εἰ γὰρ δὴ ἑκάστῳ ἀληθὲς ἔσται ὃ ἂν δι᾽
αἰσθήσεως δοξάζῃ, καὶ μήτε τὸ ἄλλου πάθος ἄλλος
βέλτιον διακρινεῖ, μήτε τὴν δόξαν κυριώτερος ἔσται
10 ἐπισκέψασθαι ἕτερος τὴν ἑτέρου, ὀρθὴ ἢ ψευδής, ἀλλ᾽
ὃ πολλάκις εἴρηται, αὐτὸς τὰ αὑτοῦ ἕκαστος μόνος
δοξάσει, ταῦτα δὲ πάντα ὀρθὰ καὶ ἀληθῆ, τί δή ποτε,
ὦ ἑταῖρε, Πρωταγόρας μὲν σοφός, ὥστε καὶ ἄλλων
διδάσκαλος ἀξιοῦσθαι δικαίως μετὰ μεγάλων μισθῶν, e
15 ἡμεῖς δὲ ἀμαθέστεροί τε καὶ φοιτητέον ἡμῖν ἦν παρ᾽
ἐκεῖνον, μέτρῳ ὄντι αὐτῷ ἑκάστῳ τῆς αὑτοῦ σοφίας;
ταῦτα πῶς μὴ φῶμεν δημούμενον λέγειν τὸν Πρωταγόραν; τὸ δὲ δὴ ἐμόν τε καὶ τῆς ἐμῆς τέχνης τῆς
μαιευτικῆς σιγῶ, ὅσον γέλωτα ὀφλισκάνομεν· οἶμαι

ἔσχατοι, infr. p. 209. As we might say, Why not the African apes?

2. τῶν καταφρονητικῶς] 'Showing a magnificent contempt for our opinion of him.'

3. ἤρξατο) The use of the aor. ind. with ἵνα, ὅπως &c., as with εἰ, though not frequent, is wellknown. Euthyd. 304: καὶ μήν, ἔφη, ἐξιὸν γ᾽ ἦν ἀκοῦσαι. Τί δὴ; ἦν δ᾽ ἐγώ. Ἵνα ἠκούσατε ἀνδρῶν διαλεγομένων, οἳ νῦν σοφώτατοί εἰσιν. Aesch. Prom. 749: Ὅπως πτῆμα σαυτῆσαι τῶν πάντων πόνων ἀπηλλάχθης &c.

6. λέγωμεν] λέγωμεν, Bodl. Ven. Π. λέγωμεν, Vat.

13. ὥστε καὶ ἄλλων διδάσκαλος] The negative form of the same saying, viz., 'Οὐκ εἶπαι ἀντιλέγειν,' is in like manner turned against itself, Euthyd. 287: εἰ γὰρ μὴ ἀμαρτάνομεν μήτε πράττοντες μήτε λέγοντες μήτε διανοούμενοι, ὑμεῖς, ὦ πρὸς Διός, εἰ αὐτὸν ἔχει, τίνος διδάσκαλοι ἥκετε;

15. ἦν] Viz. In his life-time.

17. ταῦτα] So the Bodleian with the greater number of MSS. C. F. Hermann quotes its authority for καὶ ταῦτα, the reading formerly received; judging, probably, from the silence of Gaisford.

19. οἶμαι δὲ καὶ ξυμπάντα] Locke, Hum. Und. 13, § 88: But if it should so happen that two thinking men have different ideas, I do not see how they

ΘΕΑΙΤΗΤΟΣ. 69

δὲ καὶ ξύμπασα ἡ τοῦ διαλέγεσθαι πραγματεία. τὸ
p. 162. γὰρ ἐπισκοπεῖν καὶ ἐλέγχειν τὰς ἀλλήλων φαντασίας
τε καὶ δόξας, ὀρθὰς ἑκάστου οὔσας, οὐ μακρὰ μὲν καὶ
διωλύγιος φλυαρία, εἰ ἀληθὴς ἡ ἀλήθεια Πρωταγόρου,
ἀλλὰ μὴ παίζουσα ἐκ τοῦ ἀδύτου τῆς βύβλου ἐφθέγ- 5
ξατο;

could argue or discourse with one another.

1. ἡ τοῦ διαλέγεσθαι πραγματεία] Ar. Met. Γ, 4, 1006: Τὸ γὰρ μὴ ἕν τι σημαίνειν οὐθὲν σημαίνειν ἐστίν, μὴ σημαινόντων δὲ τῶν ὀνομάτων ἀνῄρηται τὸ διαλέγεσθαι πρὸς ἀλλήλους, κατὰ δὲ τὴν ἀλήθειαν καὶ πρὸς αὑτόν· οὐθὲν γὰρ ἐνδέχεται νοεῖν μὴ νοοῦντα ἕν. Euthyd. 286: Τοῦτόν γε τὸν λόγον πολλῶν δὴ καὶ πολλάκις ἀκηκοὼς ἀεὶ θαυμάζω. καὶ γὰρ οἱ ἀμφὶ Πρωταγόραν σφόδρα ἐχρῶντο αὐτῷ καὶ οἱ ἔτι παλαιότεροι· ἐμοὶ δὲ ἀεὶ θαυμαστός τις δοκεῖ εἶναι καὶ τούς τε ἄλλους ἀνατρέπων καὶ αὐτὸς αὑτόν. οἶμαι δὲ αὐτοῦ τὴν ἀλήθειαν παρὰ σοῦ κάλλιστα πεύσεσθαι. Ἄλλο τι ἢ ψευδῆ λέγειν οὐκ ἔστι; τοῦτο γὰρ δύναται ὁ λόγος. Gorg. 481: Εἰ μή τι ἦν ταῖς ἀνθρώποις πάθος, ταῖς μὲν ἄλλο, τοῖς δ' ἄλλο τι, τὸ αὐτό, ἀλλά τις ἡμῶν ἴδιόν τι ἔπασχε πάθος ἢ οἱ ἄλλοι, οὐκ ἂν ἦν ῥᾴδιον ἐνδείξασθαι τῷ ἑτέρῳ τὸ ἑαυτοῦ πάθημα.

3. μακρὰ μὲν καὶ διωλύγιος] 'Great, nay enormous.' μὲν points forwards to the alternative implied in ἀλλὰ μὴ παίζουσα κ. τ. λ. 'But then perhaps he was in jest.' Διωλύγιος, lich.: Μεγάλη, ἡ ἐπὶ πολὺ διήκουσα. ἀντὶ τοῦ περιβόητου—σημαίνει δ' ἔσθ' ὅτε καὶ τὸ συντενὲς καὶ τὸ πιστερινόν. The meaning, 'loud' (if it really existed, but it is perhaps due to a fanciful derivation from διαλύ(ω)) must have

been derived from the meaning 'long.' Cf. Μακρὰν ἀνύειν, φωνὴ οὐρανομήκης. The idea of vast size, or length, may again have arisen from the idea of gloom. If so, the word is possibly related to ἠλυγή, λυγή. Compare μέξ, μάξ· πτύσσω πτύσσω, &c. 'Vast in extent,' is the only meaning admissible here, and in de Legg. 890: Τί δ' αὖ χαλεπά τε ἐστὶ ξυνακολουθεῖν λόγοις οὕτως εἰς πλῆθη λεγόμενα, μήκη τε αὖ πέπτηται διωλύγια. This, too, is the meaning in which it is used by the Neoplatonists. For the climax, compare p. 156: Σκληρούς τι— καὶ ἀντιτύπους. P. 174: Σμικρὰ καὶ οὐδέν. Rep. 449: Μέγα καὶ θεῖον.

5. ἐκ τοῦ ἀδύτου τῆς βύβλου] 'If the Truth of Protagoras is sincere, and was not laughing when she uttered this from behind her impenetrable screen of written words.' There is an allusion to the etymology of ἄδυτον (βύβλου, Rodl.: πέπλου, Vat. et pr. Ven. II.)

Cf. the celebrated passage in the Phaedrus, about written teaching, without dialectic, 275: Δεινὸν γάρ που ὦ Φαῖδρε, τοῦτ' ἔχει γραφή, καὶ ὡς ἀληθῶς ὅμοιον ζωγραφίᾳ· καὶ γὰρ τὰ ἐκείνης ἔκγονα ἕστηκε μὲν ὡς ζῶντα, ἐὰν δ' ἀνέρῃ τι, σεμνῶς πάνυ σιγᾷ κ. τ. λ. For the imagery which is here resumed, see above, p. 152: Τού-

70   ΠΛΑΤΩΝΟΣ

ΘΕΟ. Ὦ Σώκρατες, φίλος ἀνήρ, ὥσπερ σὺ νῦν p. 162.
δὴ εἶπες. οὐκ ἂν οὖν δεξαίμην δι' ἐμοῦ ὁμολογοῦντος
ἐλέγχεσθαι Πρωταγόραν, οὐδ' αὖ σοὶ παρὰ δόξαν
ἀντιτείνειν. τὸν οὖν Θεαίτητον πάλιν λαβέ· πάντως
καὶ νῦν δὴ μάλ' ἐμμελῶς σοι ἐφαίνετο ὑπακούειν.

ΣΩ. Ἆρα κἂν εἰς Λακεδαίμονα ἐλθών, ὦ Θεόδωρε, πρὸς τὰς παλαίστρας ἀξιοῖς ἂν ἄλλους θεώμενος b γυμνούς, ἐνίους φαύλους, αὐτὸς μὴ ἀντεπιδεικνύναι τὸ εἶδος παραποδυόμενος;

ΘΕΟ. Ἀλλὰ τί μὴν δοκεῖς, εἴπερ μέλλοιέν μοι ἐπιτρέψειν καὶ πείσεσθαι; ὥσπερ νῦν οἶμαι ὑμᾶς

ΘΕΑΙΤΗΤΟΣ. 71

p. 162. κείσειν ἐμὲ μὲν ἐᾶν θεᾶσθαι καὶ μὴ ἕλκειν πρὸς τὸ γυμνάσιον σκληρὸν ἤδη ὄντα, τῷ δὲ δὴ νεωτέρῳ τε καὶ ὑγροτέρῳ ὄντι προσπαλαίειν.

ΣΩ. Ἀλλ' εἰ οὕτως, ὦ Θεόδωρε, σοὶ φίλον, οὐδ' ἐμοὶ ἐχθρόν, φασὶν οἱ παροιμιαζόμενοι. πάλιν δὴ οὖν 5 ἐπὶ τὸν σοφὸν Θεαίτητον ἰτέον. Λέγε δή, ὦ Θεαίτητε, πρῶτον μὲν ἃ νῦν διήλθομεν, ἆρα οὐ συνθαυμάζεις εἰ ἐξαίφνης οὕτως ἀναφανήσει μηδὲν χείρων εἰς σοφίαν ὁτουοῦν ἀνθρώπων ἢ καὶ θεῶν; ἢ ἧττόν τι οἴει τὸ Πρωταγόρειον μέτρον εἰς θεοὺς ἢ εἰς ἀνθρώ- 10 πους λέγεσθαι;

ΘΕΑΙ. Μὰ Δί' οὐκ ἔγωγε. καὶ ὅπερ γε ἐρωτᾷς, πάνυ θαυμάζω. ἡνίκα γὰρ διῇμεν ὃν τρόπον λέγοιεν τὸ δοκοῦν ἑκάστῳ τοῦτο καὶ εἶναι τῷ δοκοῦντι, πάνυ μοι εὖ ἐφαίνετο λέγεσθαι· νῦν δὲ τοὐναντίον τάχα 15 μεταπέπτωκεν.

ΣΩ. Νέος γὰρ εἶ, ὦ φίλε παῖ· τῆς οὖν δημηγορίας ὀξέως ὑπακούεις καὶ πείθει. πρὸς γὰρ ταῦτα ἐρεῖ Πρωταγόρας ἤ τις ἄλλος ὑπὲρ αὐτοῦ, Ὦ γενναῖοι

Sidenote: According to this theory, Theætetus is no wiser than any God. The confidence of the youth is shaken by these objections, but they are dismissed by Socrates, who points out that argument should be met with argument and not with ridicule.

2. σκληρὸν] 'Stiff,' opposed to ὑγροτέρῳ, 'more supple.' Symp. 196: Ὑγρὸν τὸ εἶδος (ὁ Ἔρως) οὗ γὰρ ἂν οἷός τ' ἦν πάντῃ περιπτύσσεσθαι —— οἱ σκληροὶ ἦν. Cf. Rep. 410, where σκλ. is metaphorically applied to character: Ἀγριωθέντος τε καὶ σκληρότητος καὶ μαλακίας τε καὶ ἡμερότητος. See too Hor. Od. IV. 1: Desine—Sectere mollibus jam durum imperiis.

3. προσπαλαίειν] Sc. σε.

6. σοφόν] Qui scientiam aἰσθήσεως esse ponendo repente sapiens evasit. Heind.

7. συνθαυμ.] Cf. supr. ὁ θαυμάζω.

10. εἰς θεοὺς] Contrast with this de Legg. 716: Ὁ δὴ θεὸς ἡμῖν πάντων χρημάτων μέτρον ἂν εἴη μάλιστα, καὶ πολὺ μᾶλλον ἤ πού τις ὥς φασιν ἄνθρωπος.

15. τοὐναντίον] viz., οὐκ εὖ φαίνεσθαι λέγεσθαι. This word is not the subject of μεταπέπτωκεν, but in apposition with the subject, forming part of the predicate. Nunc autem res subito in contrarium vertit. Ut Menon, p. 70 C. Εὐθὺδὲ διὰ τὸ ἐναντίον περιέστηκεν. Heind.

τάχα] So the Bodleian MS. with Vat. Ven. Π.

17. Νέος γὰρ εἶ] Parm. 130: Νέος γὰρ εἶ ἔτι, φάναι τὸν Παρμενίδην, ὦ Σώκρατες, καὶ οὔπω σου ἀντείληπται φιλοσοφία ὡς ἔτι ἀντιλήψεται.

τῆς δημηγορίας ὀξέως ὑπακούεις καὶ πείθει] 'Your ear is quickly caught, and your mind influenced, by popular arguments.'

72 ΠΛΑΤΩΝΟΣ

παῖδές τε καὶ γέροντες, δημηγορεῖτε ξυγκαθεζόμενοι, p. 162.
θεούς τε εἰς τὸ μέσον ἄγοντες, οὓς ἐγὼ ἔκ τε τοῦ
λέγειν καὶ τοῦ γράφειν περὶ αὐτῶν, ὡς εἰσὶν ἢ ὡς
οὐκ εἰσίν, ἐξαιρῶ, καὶ ἃ οἱ πολλοὶ ἂν ἀποδέχοιντο
5 ἀκούοντες, λέγετε ταῦτα, ὡς δεινὸν εἰ μηδὲν διοίσει
εἰς σοφίαν ἕκαστος τῶν ἀνθρώπων βοσκήματος ὁτουοῦν·
ἀπόδειξιν δὲ καὶ ἀνάγκην οὐδ᾽ ἡντινοῦν λέγετε,

1. δημηγορεῖτε] 'You talk clap-trap.'

2. ἄγοντες] Hipp. Maj. 298: Μηδὲν τὸ τῶν νόμων εἰς μέσον παράγοντες. Phædr. 267: Τὸν δ'—Εὔηνον εἰς μέσον οὐκ ἄγομεν. The Bodl. MS. with its two followers, Vat. and Ven. Π., gives λέγοντες. But the tendency to the repetition of consonants, already noticed, weakens its testimony in this instance with λέγειν and λέγετε following. Compare, besides the instances adduced in the note on p. 156, p. 160: Οὔτ᾽ αὐτῷ λεκτέον, οὔτ᾽ ἄλλον λέγοντος ἀνεκτέον, Bodl. Vat. ἀνεκτέον, p. 169. ἀντιλέγω, ἀλλ᾽ ἄγε, Bodl. Vat. Ven. Π. ἄν. ἀλλὰ λέγε. As regards the sense there would be a slight awkwardness in the repetition of the same common word, which it is in Plato's manner to avoid, though, on the other hand, the expression ἔκ τε τοῦ λέγειν καὶ τοῦ γράφειν, is made more pointed at first sight. But the general sense with δημηγορεῖν is enough to occasion this, without the introduction of λέγοντες. And if we look closely at the expression ἐς τὸ μέσον λέγειν θεούς, it is hardly supported by comparing Herod. VI. 129: Ἔρων εἶχον ἀμφὶ μουσικῇ καὶ τῷ λεγομένῳ ἐς τὸ μέσον;

de Legg. 817: (the poets are addressed) Μὴ δὴ δόξητε ἡμᾶς—ἐπιτρέψειν ὑμᾶς δημηγορεῖν πρὶν κρῖναι τὰς ἀρχὰς εἴτε ῥητὰ καὶ ἐπιτήδεια ποιήσαντες λέγειν εἰς τὸ μέσον εἴτε μή. Here λέγειν εἰς τὸ μέσον is not equivalent to δημηγορεῖν, but means rather to 'recite in public.' Cf. ib. 664: Εἰς τὸ μέσον φθέγγειν. The passages already quoted show that ἄγειν εἰς τὸ μέσον, meaning 'to adduce in illustration or argument,' is quite Platonic. See also Phil. 57: Οὐ δ᾽ ἵνεκα ταῦτα προηνεγκάμεθα εἰς τὸ μέσον. There is a slight expression of violence in διακόπτοντες which suits the context well.

οὓς ἐγώ] Here, as p. 152, Protagoras' opinion is quoted in his own words. Diog. Laert. IX: Περὶ θεῶν οὐκ ἔχω εἰδέναι, οὔθ᾽ ὡς εἰσὶν οὔθ᾽ ὡς οὐκ εἰσίν. πολλὰ γὰρ τὰ κωλύοντα εἰδέναι, ἥ τε ἀδηλότης, καὶ βραχὺς ὢν ὁ βίος ὁ τοῦ ἀνθρώπου.

4. ἐξαιρῶ] Rep. 492: Θεῶν μέντοι κατὰ τὴν παροιμίαν ἐξαιρῶμεν λόγον.

7. ἀπόδειξιν δὲ καὶ ἀνάγκην] In dealing with a metaphysical theory it is not enough to have shown its inconsistency with common sense. It must be met upon its own ground, and the truth which it contains, as well as the sources of falsehood,

ΘΕΑΙΤΗΤΟΣ. 73

p. 162. ἀλλὰ τῷ εἰκότι χρῆσθε· ᾧ εἰ ἐθέλοι Θεόδωρος ἢ ἄλλος τις τῶν γεωμετρῶν χρώμενος γεωμετρεῖν, ἄξιος οὐδ' ἑνὸς μόνου ἂν εἴη. σκοπεῖτε οὖν σύ τε καὶ Θεό-
p. 163. δωρος εἰ ἀποδέξεσθε πιθανολογίαις τε καὶ εἰκόσι περὶ τούτων λεγομένους λόγους.

ΘΕΑΙ. Ἀλλ' οὐ δίκαιον, ὦ Σώκρατες, οὔτε σὺ οὔτε ἂν ἡμεῖς φαῖμεν.

ΣΩ. Ἄλλῃ δὴ σκεπτέον, ὡς ἔοικεν, ὥς ὅ τε σὸς καὶ ὁ Θεοδώρου λόγος.

ΘΕΑΙ. Πάνυ μὲν οὖν ἄλλῃ.

ΣΩ. Τῇδε δὴ σκοπῶμεν, εἰ ἄρα ἐστὶν ἐπιστήμη τε καὶ αἴσθησις ταὐτὸν ἢ ἕτερον. εἰς γὰρ τοῦτό που πᾶς ὁ λόγος ἡμῖν ἔτεινε, καὶ τούτου χάριν τὰ πολλὰ καὶ ἄτοπα ταῦτα ἐκινήσαμεν. οὐ γάρ;

ΘΕΑΙ. Παντάπασι μὲν οὖν.

b ΣΩ. Ἦ οὖν ὁμολογήσομεν, ἃ τῷ ὁρᾶν αἰσθανό-

2. The doctrine is therefore examined in the shape in which it first appeared; viz. Sense is knowledge. If to see and hear is to know, when a person

clearly distinguished. This, and not merely, as the Scholiast says, that he may draw out Theætetus further, is Socrates' motive in relinquishing the ground he has just taken.

3. αὐθ' ἑνὸς μόνου] Sch. ἐν τῆς τῶν καθιστώσαν συνηθείας Πλάβε τὸ οὐδενὸς μόνου, ὅπου ἐπὶ πίση ἐν τῷ παίζειν ἐν τῷ Πλάχωντος.

'Not worth an ace.' Or, if, as Stallbaum conjectures, the phrase originated in the line of Homer, Il. VIII. 234, Νῦν δ' οὐδ' ἑνὸς ἄξιοί εἰμεν Ἕκτορος, 'No better than a single man,' whereas he is now ἑτέρων πολλῶν ἀντάξιος. Cf. Polit. 297: Τῶν ἑτέρων πολλῶν ἀντάξιοι ἰατροί. See above, p. 144: 'Ἄξιος γὰρ — γεωμετρεῖν εἶναι, and below, p. 167: 'Ὁ σοφιστής — ἄξιος πολλῶν χρημάτων τοῖς παιδευθεῖσιν.

4. πιθανολογίαις τε καὶ εἰκόσι]

The Bodleian reading is the ancient hand. Cf. Ar. Eth. N. I. 2: Παραπλήσιον γὰρ φαίνεται μαθηματικοῦ τε πιθανολογοῦντος ἀποδέχεσθαι καὶ ῥητορικοῦ ἀποδείξεις ἀπαιτεῖν.

5. τούτων] Several MSS. have τηλικούτων.

8. ὅ τε σὸς καὶ] Theæt. has answered for both. See above, σύ τε καὶ Θεαί.

14. ἐκινήσαμεν] Rep. 450: Ὅσον λόγον πάλιν, ὥσπερ ἐξ ἀρχῆς, κινεῖτε περὶ τῆς πολιτείας!

16.] The argument is in brief the following: 'If sensation is knowledge, we can know and not know the same thing; since (1.) we have perfect sensible perception of things we do not know thoroughly; and (2.) we remember (i. e. know) things which we do not sensibly perceive.'

L

74   ΠΛΑΤΩΝΟΣ

hears a strange language, or some characters which he has never learnt, does he know or not know what is said and written?

μεθα ἢ τῷ ἀκούειν, πάντα ταῦτα ἅμα καὶ ἐπίστασθαι ; p. 163.
οἷον τῶν βαρβάρων πρὶν μαθεῖν τὴν φωνὴν πότερον
οὐ φήσομεν ἀκούειν, ὅταν φθέγγωνται, ἢ ἀκούειν τε
καὶ ἐπίστασθαι ἃ λέγουσι ; καὶ αὖ γράμματα μὴ
ἐπιστάμενοι βλέποντες εἰς αὐτὰ πότερον οὐχ ὁρᾶν, ἢ
ἐπίστασθαι, εἴπερ ὁρῶμεν, διϊσχυριούμεθα ;

ΘΕΑΙ. Αὐτό γε, ὦ Σώκρατες, τοῦτο αὐτῶν, ὅπερ
ὁρῶμέν τε καὶ ἀκούομεν, ἐπίστασθαι φήσομεν· τῶν
μὲν γὰρ τὸ σχῆμα καὶ τὸ χρῶμα ὁρᾶν τε καὶ ἐπί- c
στασθαι, τῶν δὲ τὴν ὀξύτητα καὶ βαρύτητα ἀκούειν
τε ἅμα καὶ εἰδέναι· ἃ δὲ οἵ τε γραμματισταὶ περὶ
αὐτῶν καὶ οἱ ἑρμηνεῖς διδάσκουσιν, οὔτε αἰσθάνεσθαι
τῷ ὁρᾶν ἢ ἀκούειν οὔτε ἐπίστασθαι.

Allowing this to pass,

ΣΩ. Ἄριστά γ', ὦ Θεαίτητε, καὶ οὐκ ἄξιόν σοι
πρὸς ταῦτα ἀμφισβητῆσαι, ἵνα καὶ αὐξάνῃ. ἀλλ' ὅρα
δὴ καὶ τόδε ἄλλο προσιόν, καὶ σκόπει πῇ αὐτὸ διω-
σόμεθα.

15. ἵνα καὶ αὐξάνῃ] 'That I may leave you room to grow,' 'That I may not be always stunting and stopping you.' Lys. 206: Οἱ καλοὶ, ἐπειδάν τις αὐτῶν ἐπαινῇ καὶ αὔξῃ. Phædr. 246: Ταύτας δὲ τρέφεταί τε καὶ αὔξεται μάλιστά γε τὸ τῆς ψυχῆς πτέρωμα. Rep. p. 497: Ἐν γὰρ προσηκούσῃ αὐτός τε μᾶλλον αὐξήσεται. The expression in Aristoph. Vesp. 638, Ηὐξάνθην ἀκούων, though more humorous, also affords an illustration.

We may naturally ask what objection Socrates would have raised, had he not feared to check Theætetus' growing intelligence. This may perhaps be gathered from below, where he ventures to puzzle him a little further, p. 166 : 'ἴσως δὴ γ' ἂν θαυμάσαις πλείω ἂν τοιαῦτ' ἔτε-

θιε κ. τ. λ. Socrates might have asked, Does every one who sees the forms and colours, or who hears the sounds, possess the science of them ((ζωγραφική, μουσική, p. 145)? Could he give an account e. g. of the ὀξύτης and βαρύτης of what he hears? Cf. Rep. 524 : Μέγα μὲν καὶ ὄψις καὶ σμικρὸν ἑώρα ἀλλ' οὐ κεχωρισμένον ἀλλὰ συγκεχυμένον τι. Not even the objects of sense are known by sense, but by a higher faculty.

16. τόδε ἄλλο προσιόν, κ. τ. λ.] The implied metaphor is probably that of the wave. It is continued below, p. 161 : Λέγοι δὲ ἡμᾶς—ἵνα λέγων μείζων ἐξ ἐλάττονος ἀπολαμβάνοι : and is slightly varied, p. 177 : Πλείω δεῖ ἀνηρότητα ἐσπευκόσιν ὑμῖν τὸν ἐξ ἀρχῆς λόγον.

ΘΕΑΙΤΗΤΟΣ. 75

p. 163. ΘΕΑΙ. Τὸ ποῖον δή;
d ΣΩ. Τὸ τοιόνδε· εἴ τις ἔροιτο, ἆρα δυνατόν, ὅτου τις ἐπιστήμων γένοιτό ποτε, ἔτι ἔχοντα μνήμην αὐτοῦ ταύτου καὶ σωζόμενον, τότε ὅτε μέμνηται μὴ ἐπίστασθαι αὐτὸ τοῦτο ὃ μέμνηται, μακρολογῶ δέ, ὡς ἔοικε, βουλόμενος ἐρέσθαι, εἰ μαθών τίς τι μεμνημένος μὴ οἶδεν.
ΘΕΑΙ. Καὶ πῶς, ὦ Σώκρατες; τέρας γὰρ ἂν εἴη ὁ λέγεις.
ΣΩ. Μὴ οὖν ἐγὼ ληρῶ; σκόπει δέ. ἆρα τὸ ὁρᾶν οὐκ αἰσθάνεσθαι λέγεις καὶ τὴν ὄψιν αἴσθησιν;
ΘΕΑΙ. Ἔγωγε.
ΣΩ. Οὐκοῦν ὁ ἰδών τι ἐπιστήμων ἐκείνου γέγονεν
e ὃ εἶδε κατὰ τὸν ἄρτι λόγον;
ΘΕΑΙ. Ναί.
ΣΩ. Τί δέ; μνήμην οὐ λέγεις μέντοι τι;
ΘΕΑΙ. Ναί.
ΣΩ. Πότερον οὐδενὸς ἢ τινός;
ΘΕΑΙ. Τινὸς δή που.
ΣΩ. Οὐκοῦν ὧν ἔμαθε καὶ ὧν ᾔσθετο, τοιουτωνί τινων;
ΘΕΑΙ Τί μήν;
ΣΩ. Ὁ δὴ ἰδὼν τις, μέμνηταί που ἐνίοτε;
ΘΕΑΙ. Μέμνηται.
ΣΩ. Ἦ καὶ μύσας; ἢ τοῦτο δράσας ἐπελάθετο;
ΘΕΑΙ. Ἀλλὰ δεινόν, ὦ Σώκρατες, τοῦτό γε φάναι.
p. 164. ΣΩ. Δεῖ γε μέντοι, εἰ σώσοιμεν τὸν πρόσθε λόγον· εἰ δὲ μή, οἴχεται.

76   ΠΛΑΤΩΝΟΣ

ΘΕΑΙ. Καὶ ἐγώ, νὴ τὸν Δία, ὑποπτεύω, οὐ μὴν p. 164. ἱκανῶς γε συννοῶ· ἀλλ' εἰπὲ πῇ.

ΣΩ. Τῇδε· ὁ μὲν ὁρῶν ἐπιστήμων, φαμέν, τούτου γέγονεν οὗπερ ὁρῶν· ὄψις γὰρ καὶ αἴσθησις καὶ ἐπιστήμη ταὐτὸν ὡμολόγηται.

ΘΕΑΙ. Πάνυ γε.

I remember it and do not see it.

ΣΩ. Ὁ δέ γε ὁρῶν καὶ ἐπιστήμων γεγονὼς οὗ ἑώρα, ἐὰν μύσῃ, μέμνηται μέν, οὐχ ὁρᾷ δὲ αὐτό· ἢ γάρ;

ΘΕΑΙ. Ναί.

i.e., If to see is to know,

ΣΩ. Τὸ δέ γε οὐχ ὁρᾷ οὐκ ἐπίσταταί ἐστιν, εἴπερ b καὶ τὸ ὁρᾷ ἐπίσταται.

ΘΕΑΙ. Ἀληθῆ.

I remember it and do not know it.

ΣΩ. Συμβαίνει ἄρα, οὗ τις ἐπιστήμων ἐγένετο, ἔτι μεμνημένον αὐτὸν μὴ ἐπίστασθαι, ἐπειδὴ οὐχ ὁρᾷ· ὃ τέρας ἔφαμεν ἂν εἶναι εἰ γίγνοιτο.

ΘΕΑΙ. Ἀληθέστατα λέγεις.

But this seemed to us a monstrous supposition; Therefore, sense is not knowledge.

ΣΩ. Τῶν ἀδυνάτων δή τι ξυμβαίνειν φαίνεται, ἐάν τις ἐπιστήμην καὶ αἴσθησιν ταὐτὸν φῇ εἶναι.

ΘΕΑΙ. Ἔοικεν.

ΣΩ. Ἄλλο ἄρα ἑκάτερον φατέον.

ΘΕΑΙ. Κινδυνεύει.

—We are in too great a hurry.

ΣΩ. Τί οὖν δῆτ' ἂν εἴη ἐπιστήμη, πάλιν ἐξ ἀρχῆς, ὡς ἔοικε, λεκτέον. Καίτοι τί ποτε μέλλομεν, ὦ Θεαί- c τητε, δρᾷν;

ΘΕΑΙ. Τίνος πέρι;

ΣΩ. Φαινόμεθά μοι ἀλεκτρυόνος ἀγεννοῦς δίκην,

---

1. οὐ μὴν ἱκανῶς γε συννοῶ] 'But I do not quite comprehend why it is so.'

4. οὗπερ ὁρῶν] So Bodl. Vat. Ven. Π. ὁρῶν sc. ἐστὶν or γέγονεν. Compare the technical use of αἰσθανόμενος, noticed above, pp. 159, 160. Also p. 157: 'Ἐγένετο οὔτε ὄψις ἀλλ' ὀφθαλμοὶ ὁρῶν. See also p. 160. ἐπιστήμων—οὗπερ αἰσθητής.

10. Τὸ δέ γε οὐχ ὁρᾷ] Soph. 264: Φαίνεται δ' ὁ λέγομεν.

23. πίλω] μὴ πίλω Bodl. Vat. Ven. Π. The Bodleian margin however says, ἐν ἑτέρῳ λείπει τὸ μή. If μή were right, the subjunctive ᾖ would be required to complete the sense.

ΘΕΑΙΤΗΤΟΣ. 77

p. 164. πρὶν νενικηκέναι, ἀποπηδήσαντες ἀπὸ τοῦ λόγου ᾄδειν.

ΘΕΑΙ. Πῶς δή;

ΣΩ. Ἀντιλογικῶς ἐοίκαμεν πρὸς τὰς τῶν ὀνομάτων ὁμολογίας ἀνομολογησάμενοι καὶ τοιούτῳ τινὶ
περιγενόμενοι τοῦ λόγου ἀγαπᾶν, καὶ οὐ φάσκοντες
ἀγωνισταὶ ἀλλὰ φιλόσοφοι εἶναι λανθάνομεν ταὐτὰ
ἃ ἐκείνοις τοῖς δεινοῖς ἀνδράσι ποιοῦντες.

Perhaps the contradiction is only verbal.

ΘΕΑΙ. Οὔπω μανθάνω ὅπως λέγεις.

ΣΩ. Ἀλλ' ἐγὼ πειράσομαι δηλῶσαι περὶ αὐτῶν ὅ
γε δὴ νοῶ. ἠρόμεθα γὰρ δὴ εἰ μαθὼν καὶ μεμνημένος
τίς τι μὴ ἐπίσταται, καὶ τὸν ἰδόντα καὶ μύσαντα μεμνημένον, ὁρῶντα δὲ οὔ, ἀποδείξαντες, οὐκ εἰδότα
ἀπεδείξαμεν καὶ ἅμα μεμνημένον· τοῦτο δ' εἶναι ἀδύνατον. καὶ οὕτω δὴ μῦθος ἀπώλετο ὁ Πρωταγόρειος,

---

1. ἀπὸ τοῦ λόγου] Viz. the theory of Protagoras, which we are trampling upon. v. infr. πρωτγ. λαχίζομεν.

3. Ἀντιλογικῶς ἐοίκαμεν] Rep. 453, 4: Ἤ γιγνώσκεις, ἦν δ' ἐγώ, ὦ Γλαύκων, ἡ δύναμις τῆς ἀντιλογικῆς τέχνης. Τί δή; Ὅτι, εἶπον, δοκοῦσί μοι εἰς αὐτὴν καὶ ἄκοντες πολλοὶ ἐμπίπτειν καὶ οἴεσθαι οὐκ ἐρίζειν ἀλλὰ διαλέγεσθαι, διὰ τὸ μὴ δύνασθαι κατ' εἴδη διαιρούμενοι τὸ λεγόμενον ἐπισκοπεῖν, ἀλλὰ κατ' αὐτὸ τὸ ὄνομα διώκειν τοῦ λεχθέντος τὴν ἐναντίωσιν, ἔριδι, οὐ διαλέκτῳ, πρὸς ἀλλήλους χρώμενοι.

πρὸς τὰς τῶν ὀνομάτων ὁμολογίας] 'With a view to mere verbal consistency.' Lys. 216: Καὶ ἡμῖν εὐθὺς ἄσμενοι ἐπιπηδήσαντες οὕτω οἱ πάνσοφοι ἄνδρες, οἱ ἀντιλογικοί, καὶ ἐρήσονται εἰ οὐκ ἐναντιώτατον ἔχθρᾳ φιλία; The tendencies of Ἀντιλογική are, int. al. to argue from contradictions of language, leading in the last resort to scepticism. Phaed. 90: Καὶ μάλιστα δὴ οἱ περὶ τοὺς ἀντιλογικοὺς λόγους διατρί-ψαντες οἶσθ' ὅτι τελευτῶντες οἴονται σοφώτατοι γεγονέναι τε καὶ κατανενοηκέναι ὅτι τῶν πραγμάτων οὐδενὸς οὐδὲν ὑγιὲς οὐδὲ βέβαιον τῶν λόγων. 2nd, to confuse ideas or principles with facts or results. Ib. p. 101: Ἅμα δὲ οὐκ ἂν φύροιο ὥσπερ οἱ ἀντιλογικοὶ περί τε τῆς ἀρχῆς διαλεγόμενος καὶ τῶν ἐξ ἐκείνης ὡρμημένων, εἴπερ βούλοιό τι τῶν ὄντων εὑρεῖν.

5. οὐ φάσκοντες] Viz. p. 154: Οὐκοῦν εἰ μὲν δεινοὶ καὶ σοφοὶ κ.τ.λ.

14. μῦθος ἀπώλετο] Schol: Παροιμία ἐπὶ τῶν τὴν διήγησιν μὴ ἐπὶ πέρας ἀγόντων. Hence probably the absence of the article. Cf. Rep. 621: Καὶ οὕτως, ὦ Γλαύκων, μῦθος ἐσώθη καὶ οὐκ ἀπώλετο. See also Phil. 14: Ὁ λόγος, ὥσπερ μῦθος, ἀπολόμενος οἴχεται.

μῦθος ὁ Πρωταγόρειος] P. 157: Οὗτος ὁ μῦθος. Soph. 242: Μῦθόν τινα ἕκαστος φαίνεταί μοι διηγεῖσθαι παισὶν ὡς οὖσιν ἡμῖν. Arist. Met. Α 10. 993 A. (cf. (Iorg. 485): ψελλιζομένη γὰρ ἔοικεν ἡ πρώτη φιλοσοφία.

78 ΠΛΑΤΩΝΟΣ

καὶ ὁ σὸς ἅμα ὁ τῆς ἐπιστήμης καὶ αἰσθήσεως, ὅτι p. 164.
ταὐτόν ἐστιν.

ΘΕΑΙ. Φαίνεται.

ΣΩ. Οὔ τι ἄν, οἶμαι, ὦ φίλε, εἴπερ γε ὁ πατὴρ
τοῦ ἑτέρου μύθου ἔζη, ἀλλὰ πολλὰ ἂν ἤμυνε· νῦν δὲ
ὀρφανὸν αὐτὸν ἡμεῖς προπηλακίζομεν. καὶ γὰρ οὐδ᾽
οἱ ἐπίτροποι οὓς Πρωταγόρας κατέλιπε, βοηθεῖν ἐθέλουσιν, ὧν Θεόδωρος εἷς ὅδε. ἀλλὰ δὴ αὐτοὶ κινδυ-
νεύσομεν τοῦ δικαίου ἕνεκ᾽ αὐτῷ βοηθεῖν.

ΘΕΟ. Οὐ γὰρ ἐγώ, ὦ Σώκρατες, ἀλλὰ μᾶλλον
Καλλίας ὁ Ἱππονίκου τῶν ἐκείνου ἐπίτροπος· ἡμεῖς p. 165.
δέ πως θᾶττον ἐκ τῶν ψιλῶν λόγων πρὸς τὴν γεωμετρίαν ἀπενεύσαμεν. χάριν γε μέντοι ἕξομεν, ἐὰν
αὐτῷ βοηθῇς.

Protagoras would still have much to say.

4. εἴπερ ὁ πατήρ] See the passage of the Phaedrus already quoted, p. 275: Πλημμελούμενος δὲ ὁ λόγος καὶ οὐκ ἐν δίκῃ λοιδορηθεὶς τοῦ πατρὸς ἀεὶ δεῖται βοηθοῦ κ.τ.λ. Cf. Soph. 241: Μή με οἷον πατραλοίαν ὑπολάβῃς γίγνεσθαί τινα. Τί δή; Τὸν τοῦ πατρὸς Παρμενίδου λόγον ἀναγκαῖον ἡμῖν ἀμυνομένοις ἔσται βασανίζειν.

8. κινδυνεύσομεν] Not, 'I will undertake the risk,' but = κινδυνεύσω βοηθήσειν, 'It seems I shall have to take his part myself.' Cf. Cratyl 399: Καὶ κινδυνεύσω ἔγωγε μὴ εὐλαβεῖσθαι, ὅτι τήμερον σοφώτερος τοῦ δέοντος γενέσθαι. Symp. 174: Ἴσως μέντοι κινδυνεύσω καὶ ἐγὼ οὐχ ὃν σὺ λέγεις, ὦ Σώκρατες, ἀλλὰ καθ᾽ Ὅμηρον φαῦλος ὢν ἐπὶ σοφοῦ ἀνδρὸς ἰέναι θοίνην ἀέκλητος.

11. Καλλίας ὁ Ἱππονίκου] With whom Protagoras stayed when he came to Athens. Apol. p. 20: 'Ἀνδρί, ὃς τετέλεκε χρήματα σοφισταῖς πλείω ἢ ξύμπαντες οἱ ἄλλοι, Καλλίᾳ τῷ Ἱππονίκου. Prot. 311, 315: Xen. Symp. I. 5.

12. ἐκ τῶν ψιλῶν λόγων] 'From the mere abstractions of dialectic.' We are accustomed to speak of Geometry as a purely abstract science, but see Arist. Met. I. 2: Αἱ γὰρ ἐκ ἐλαττόνων ἀκριβέστεραι τῶν ἐκ προστιθέντων λεγομένων, οἷον ἀριθμητικὴ γεωμετρίας. The expression ψιλοὶ λόγοι is used differently in Symp. 215: ψιλοῖς λόγοις ἄνευ ὀργάνων, but cf. Phaedr. 262: Νῦν γὰρ ψιλῶς πως λέγομεν οὐκ ἔχοντες ἱκανὰ παραδείγματα. Antisthenes is said to have called the Ideas of Plato ψιλαὶ ἔννοιαι. For λόγοι = διαλεκτική, cf. Phaed. 99: Ἔδοξε δή μοι χρῆναι εἰς τοὺς λόγους καταφυγόντα ἐν ἐκείνοις σκοπεῖν τὴν ἀλήθειαν. See also Arist. de An. I. 1, where a distinction is drawn between φιλοσοφίας, μαθηματικῆς and φυσικῆς.

13. μέντοι] οὖν is added in the MSS. except Bodl. Vat. Ven. Π.

ΘΕΑΙΤΗΤΟΣ. 79

p. 165. ΣΩ. Καλῶς λέγεις, ὦ Θεόδωρε. σκέψαι οὖν τὴν γ' ἐμὴν βοήθειαν. τῶν γὰρ ἄρτι δεινότερα ἄν τις ὁμολογήσειε μὴ προσέχων τοῖς ῥήμασι τὸν νοῦν, ᾗ τὸ πολὺ εἰθίσμεθα φάναι τε καὶ ἀπαρνεῖσθαι. σοὶ λέγω ὅπῃ, ἢ Θεαιτήτῳ;

ΘΕΟ. Εἰς τὸ κοινὸν μὲν οὖν, ἀποκρινέσθω δὲ ὁ νεώτερος· σφαλεὶς γὰρ ἧττον ἀσχημονήσει.

ΣΩ. Λέγω δὴ τὸ δεινότατον ἐρώτημα. ἔστι δὲ οἶμαι τοιόνδε τι· ἆρα οἷόν τε τὸν αὐτὸν εἰδότα τι τοῦτο ὃ οἶδε μὴ εἰδέναι;

ΘΕΟ. Τί δὴ οὖν ἀποκρινούμεθα, ὦ Θεαίτητε;

ΘΕΑΙ. Ἀδύνατόν που, οἶμαι ἔγωγε.

ΣΩ. Οὔκ, εἰ τὸ ὁρᾶν γε ἐπίστασθαι θήσεις. τί γὰρ χρήσει ἀφύκτῳ ἐρωτήματι, τὸ λεγόμενον ἐν φρέατι συνεχόμενος, ὅταν ἐρωτᾷ ἀνέκπληκτος ἀνήρ, καταλαβὼν τῇ χειρὶ σοῦ τὸν ἕτερον ὀφθαλμόν, εἰ ὁρᾷς τὸ ἱμάτιον τῷ κατειλημμένῳ;

The 'crucial' question is this,

Is it possible for the same person to know and not to know the same thing?

You are bound to say it is, if sight be knowledge. Nay, you may be driven to it without

(13.) *ἕξομεν*] Theod. speaks on behalf of the *ἀνέτρωπω Πρωταγόρου*.

3. *μὴ προσέχων τοῖς ῥήμασι τὸν νοῦν, ᾗ τὸ πολὺ εἰθίσμεθα*] By freeing ourselves from the habitual oppositions of words, we are sometimes reconciled to what at first appears a pure contradiction. Spinoza (Cog. Met. I.) shows a still loftier indifference to common language: 'At vero si rem accuratius examinare vellemus, possemus forte ostendere Deum non nisi improprie unum et unicum vocari; sed res non est tanti imo nullius momenti iis qui de rebus non vero de nominibus sunt solliciti.' Many of the difficulties in Greek philosophy arose, as Plato himself points out in the Sophist, from the too great stress laid upon logical alternatives; while the complexity and variety of things as they exist was lost sight of.

ᾗ τὸ πολὺ εἰθίσμεθα] 'According to our common mode of affirming and denying :' viz. with a view to words.

8. *λέγω δὴ τὸ δεινότατον ἐρώτημα*] Compare Rep. 473: 'Ἐπ' αὐτὸ δή, ἦν δ' ἐγώ, εἶμι ὃ τῷ μεγίστῳ προσεικάζομεν κύματι. Where Socrates assumes the same tragic tone as here.

14. *ἐν φρέατι συνεχόμενος*] 'Caught in a pit,' i.e. unable to stir hand or foot.

16. *καταλαβὼν τὸν ὀφθαλμὸν — εἰ ὁρᾷς τὸ ἱμάτιον*) Perhaps there is here a trace of the spirit which was afterwards de-

80 ΠΛΑΤΩΝΟΣ

reference to memory, within the sphere of sense itself. A relentless adversary will pin you down, covering one eye with his mantle, to confess that you see and do not see, and therefore know and do not know. And thus you will be proved to know both vividly and dimly, near but not far off, softly and violently.

ΘΕΑΙ. Οὐ φήσω, οἶμαι, τούτῳ γε, τῷ μέντοι p. 165. ἑτέρῳ.

ΣΩ. Οὐκοῦν ὁρᾷς τε καὶ οὐχ ὁρᾷς ἅμα ταὐτόν;

ΘΕΑΙ. Οὕτω γέ πως.

5 ΣΩ. Οὐδὲν ἐγώ, φήσει, τοῦτο οὔτε τάττω οὔτ' ἠρόμην, τὸ ὅπως, ἀλλ' εἰ, ὃ ἐπίστασαι, τοῦτο καὶ οὐκ ἐπίστασαι. νῦν δ' ὃ οὐχ ὁρᾷς, ὁρῶν φαίνει. ὡμολόγηκας δὲ τυγχάνεις τὸ ὁρᾶν ἐπίστασθαι καὶ τὸ μὴ ὁρᾶν μὴ ἐπίστασθαι. ἐξ οὖν τούτων λογίζου τί σοι 10 συμβαίνει.

ΘΕΑΙ. Ἀλλὰ λογίζομαι ὅτι τἀναντία οἷς ὑπε- d θέμην.

ΣΩ. Ἴσως δέ γ', ὦ θαυμάσιε, πλείω ἂν τοιαῦτ' ἔπαθες, εἴ τίς σε προσηρώτα εἰ ἐπίστασθαι ἔστι μὲν 15 ὀξύ, ἔστι δὲ ἀμβλύ, καὶ ἐγγύθεν μὲν ἐπίστασθαι, πόρρωθεν δὲ μή, καὶ σφόδρα καὶ ἠρέμα τὸ αὐτό, καὶ ἄλλα μυρία, ἃ ἐλλοχῶν ἂν πελταστικὸς ἀνὴρ μισθο-

veloped in the sophisms of Eubulides.

5. οὐδὲν—τοῦτο, κ. τ. λ.] Τάττω sc. ἀνερωτήσαι. Cf. Rep. 473: Ἐξευρημένων δὲ δυνατὰ ταῦτα γενέσθαι ἃ σὺ ἐπιτάττεις (sc. ἐξευρεῖν). For the sense cf. supr. p. 159: Μὴ ὑπολάβωμεν τῇ μὲν ταὐτὸν εἶναι, κ.τ.λ. Cf. Euthyd. 295: Πάντων ἐπίστασαί τῳ ἃ ἐπίστασαι, ἢ οὔ; Ἔγωγε, ἔφην, τῇ γε ψυχῇ. Οὗτος αὖ, ἔφη, προσκαταμιαίνεται τοῖς ἐρωτωμένοις. αὖ γὰρ ἔγωγε ἐρωτῶ ὅτῳ, ἀλλ' εἰ ἐπίστασαί τῳ, κ.τ.λ. For the intentional abruptness of the expression, cf. Phil. 28: Οὐδὲν τῶν αὑτῶν. 'None of that! I never asked you for it.'

τοῦτο—τὸ ὅπως] This, viz. the manner.

13. ὦ θαυμάσιε] Such addresses interposed give a tone of increased earnestness to the conversation. See Appendix D.

15. ὀξύ—ἀμβλύ) These terms are properly applicable to vision.

ἐγγύθεν μὲν — πόρρωθεν δὲ μή] This probably refers to the sense of smell, v. τὸ ὀσφραίνεσθαι below.

16. σφόδρα καὶ ἠρέμα τὸ αὐτό] To have an intense and slight knowledge of the same thing: e. g. Τὸ ψυχρόν, p. 152, μέγα—ὁ μὲν ἠρέμα, ὁ δὲ σφόδρα; but the reference here is probably to sound, v. τὸ ἀκούειν below. (Cf. Phil. p. 14: Βαρὺν καὶ κοῦφον τὸν αὐτόν, καὶ ἄλλα μυρία.) Aristotle does not feel the difficulty. Met. Z. 1029 B: Τὰ δ' ἴσως γνώριμα καὶ πρῶτα πολλάκις ἠρέμα ἐστὶ γνώριμα. Plato would not allow that anything is known, except what, in Aristotle's language, are ἁπλῶς γνώριμα.

17. ἃ] An accusative depend-

ΘΕΑΙΤΗΤΟΣ. 81

p. 165. φόρος ἐν λόγοις ἐρόμενος, ἡνίκ' ἐπιστήμην καὶ αἴσθησιν
ταὐτὸν ἔθου, ἐμβαλὼν ἂν εἰς τὸ ἀκούειν καὶ ὀσφραίνεσθαι καὶ τὰς τοιαύτας αἰσθήσεις, ἤλεγχεν ἂν ἐπέχων
καὶ οὐκ ἀνιείς, πρὶν θαυμάσας τὴν πολυάρατον σοφίαν
ξυνεποδίσθης ὑπ' αὐτοῦ, οὗ δὴ σε χειρωσάμενός τε
καὶ ξυνδήσας ἤδη ἂν τότε ἐλύτρου χρημάτων ὅσων
σοί τε κἀκείνῳ ἐδόκει. Τῷ' οὖν δὴ ὁ Πρωταγόρας,
φαίης ἂν ἴσως, λόγον ἐπίκουρον τοῖς αὑτοῦ ἐρεῖ;
ἄλλο τι πειρώμεθα λέγειν;

ΘΕΑΙ. Πάνυ μὲν οὖν.

ΣΩ. Ταῦτά τε δὴ πάντα ὅσα ἡμεῖς ἐπαμύνοντες
αὐτῷ λέγομεν, καὶ ὁμόσε, οἶμαι, χωρήσεται, καταφρονῶν ἡμῶν καὶ λέγων, Οὗτος δὴ ὁ Σωκράτης ὁ

How would Protagoras defend his own against the attacks of such a light-armed mercenary?

ing chiefly on ἐρόμενος, but vaguely also on all that follows.

1. μισθοφόρος ἐν λόγοις] A logical mercenary.

2. ἐμβαλὼν] 'Making his assault.'

3. ἐπέχων καὶ οὐκ ἀνιείς] Rep. 411: ὅταν δ' ἐπέχων μὴ ἀνιῇ ἀλλὰ κηλῇ. 'Keeping up the attack.'

4. πολυάρατον] Buttmann conjectures πολυάρουτον, 'cunning,' which occurs as a v. l. for πολυ-ήρατον in the first line of the Odyssee. Heind. πολυήρατον, but aida, ne hoc quidem satisfacit. In Ven. Π. both a's are erased. Πολυάρητος occurs twice in the Odyssee, VI. 280; XIX. 404: "Ὅνομ' ὅττι κε μήτηρ πατὴρ παιδὶ φίλῳ πολυάρητος δέ τοί ἐστιν. Protagoras seems to have affected certain rhetorical expressions, and perhaps may have used this word. See Phaedr. 268: ὀρθοέπεια, &c. Stallbaum quotes Themist. Orat. XXII. p. 325. 19. ed. Dindorf.: Τὸν πολυάρατον πλοῦτον τί ἂν καὶ λέγωμεν ὁποίαν ἀγευνεδίτης πολέμων ἐστιν. For the sense cf. Euthyd. 272: Τὴν σοφίαν ἣν ἐγὼγε ἐπιθυμῶ, τῆς ἐριστικῆς. Ib. 273: τί δὲ νῦν ἀληθὲς ταύτη τῇ ἐπιστήμῃ ἔχε-τον, ἵλεῳ εἴπετον. ἀτεχνῶς γὰρ ἔγωγε σφὼ ἕσπερ θεὼ προσηγορεύω. Ib. 296: 'Ἀλλὰ βουληθείης, ἦν δ' ἐγώ, ὦ πολυτίμητε Εὐθύδημε. Ph. 301: "Ἤδη δὲ τοῦ ἀνδρεῖοι τὴν σοφίαν ἐπεχείρουν μιμεῖσθαι, ὅτι ἐπιθυμιῶ αὐτῆς.

6. χρημάτων ὅσων] Protag. 328: Καὶ τὸν τρόπον τῆς πράξεως τοῦ μισθοῦ τοιοῦτον πεποίημαι. ἐπει-δὰν γάρ τις παρ' ἐμοῦ μάθῃ, ἐὰν μὲν βούληται, ἀποδέδωκεν ὃ ἐγὼ πράττομαι ἀργύριον· ἐὰν δὲ μή, ἐλθὼν εἰς ἱερόν, ὀμόσας, ὅσου ἂν φῇ ἄξια εἶναι τὰ μαθήματα, τοσοῦτον κατέθηκεν.

12. καὶ ὁμόσε ο. χ.] 'He will grapple with us.' There is a change of construction similar to that in p. 149: Καὶ πέττειν τε δὴ τὰς δυστοκούσας, καὶ—ἀμβλί-σκουσι.

ΠΛΑΤΩΝΟΣ

3: He would say that he is not refuted, because not fairly represented by you. He would urge that memory is far less vivid than sensation. And, while not fearing to admit that it is possible to know and not to know the same thing, he would assert that the man knowing

χρηστός, ἐπειδὴ αὐτῷ παιδίον τι ἐρωτηθὲν ἔδεισεν, εἰ p. 167.
οἷόν τε τὸν αὐτὸν τὸ αὐτὸ μεμνῆσθαι ἅμα καὶ μὴ
εἰδέναι, καὶ δείσαν ἀπέφησε διὰ τὸ μὴ δύνασθαι
προορᾶν, γέλωτα δὴ τὸν ἐμὲ ἐν τοῖς λόγοις ἀπέδειξε.
5 τὸ δέ, ὦ ῥᾳθυμότατε Σώκρατες, τῇδ᾽ ἔχει. ὅταν τι
τῶν ἐμῶν δι᾽ ἐρωτήσεως σκοπῇς, ἐὰν μὲν ὁ ἐρωτηθεὶς
οἷάπερ ἂν ἐγὼ ἀποκριναίμην ἀποκρινάμενος σφάλλη-
ται, ἐγὼ ἐλέγχομαι, εἰ δὲ ἀλλοῖα, αὐτὸς ὁ ἐρωτηθείς. b
αὐτίκα γὰρ δοκεῖς τινά σοι ξυγχωρήσεσθαι μνήμην
10 παρεῖναί τῳ ὧν ἔπαθε τοιοῦτόν τι οὖσαν πάθος, οἷον
ὅτε ἔπασχε, μηκέτι πάσχοντι; πολλοῦ γε δεῖ. ἢ αὖ
ἀποκνήσειν ὁμολογεῖν οἷόν τ᾽ εἶναι εἰδέναι καὶ μὴ εἰδέναι τὸν αὐτὸν τὸ αὐτό; ἢ ἐάνπερ τοῦτο δείσῃ, δώ-
σειν ποτὲ τὸν αὐτὸν εἶναι τὸν ἀνομοιούμενον τῷ πρὶν
15 ἀνομοιοῦσθαι ὄντι; μᾶλλον δὲ τὸν εἶναί τινα, ἀλλ᾽

4. τὸν ἐμέ] Cf. Soph. 239: Τὸν μὲν ταίνυν ἐμέ γε ἔτι τί τις ἂν λέγοι; Phaedr. 258: Τὸν αὐτόν. Phil. 14: Τοὺς ἐμέ (see below). Ib. 20: Τὸν ἐμέ. Ib. 59: Τοῦτ μὲν δὴ σὺ καὶ ἐμὲ καὶ Γοργίαν καὶ Φίληβον.

5. ὦ ῥᾳθυμότατε Σώκρατες] 'Slovenly Socrates!'

9. αὐτίκα] 'To begin with.'
τινά σοι ξυγχ.] i. e. ἐμέ. 'Do you think a man would admit!'

μνήμην] 'That the memory a man has of an impression when it is past, is anything like what he experienced at the time.'

10. τοιοῦτόν τι οὖσαν πάθος] Hume, Inquiry Conc. Human Understanding: 'Every one will readily allow that there is a considerable difference between the perceptions of the mind, when a man feels the pain of excessive heat, or the pleasure of moderate warmth, and when he afterwards recalls to his memory this sensation, or anticipates it by his imagination.'— 'We may observe a like distinction to run through all the other perceptions of the mind.' — 'When we reflect on our past sentiments and affections, our thought is a faithful mirror, and copies its objects truly; but the colours which it employs are faint and dull, in comparison of those in which our original perceptions were clothed.'

15. τὸν εἶναί τινα] τινα is subj. τὸν pred. Cf. Phil. 14: 'Ἀρ᾽ οὖν λέγεις, ὅταν τις ἐμὲ φῇ Πρώταρχον ἕνα γεγονότα φύσει πολλοὺς εἶναι πάλιν, τοὺς ἐμὲ καὶ ἐναντίους ἀλλήλοις μέγαν καὶ σμικρὸν τιθέμενον, καὶ βαρὺν καὶ κοῦφον τὸν αὐτὸν καὶ ἄλλα μυρία. Compare a strange fancy of Comte's: Catéchisme Posit. p. 2: 'For each man differs from himself successively as much as he differs simultaneously from other men.'

ΘΕΑΙΤΗΤΟΣ. 85

p. 166. οὐχὶ τούς, καὶ τούτους γιγνομένους ἀπείρους, ἐάνπερ ὁ ἀνομοίωσις γίγνηται, εἰ δὴ ὀνομάτων γε δεήσει θηρεύσεις διευλαβεῖσθαι ἀλλήλων; ἀλλ᾽, ὦ μακάριε, φήσει, γενναιοτέρως ἐπ᾽ αὐτὸ ἐλθὼν ὃ λέγω, εἰ δύνασαι, ἐξέλεγξον ὡς οὐχὶ ἴδιαι αἰσθήσεις ἑκάστῳ ἡμῶν γίγνονται, ἢ ὡς ἰδίων γιγνομένων οὐδέν τι ἂν μᾶλλον τὸ φαινόμενον μόνῳ ἐκείνῳ γίγνοιτο, ἢ εἰ εἶναι δεῖ ὀνομάζειν, εἴη, ᾧπερ φαίνεται. ὃς δὲ δὴ καὶ κυνοκεφάλους λέγων οὐ μόνον αὐτὸς ὑηνεῖς, ἀλλὰ καὶ τοὺς ἀκούοντας τοῦτο δρᾶν εἰς τὰ συγγράμματά μου ἀναπείθεις, οὐ καλῶς ποιῶν. ἐγὼ γὰρ φημὶ μὲν τὴν ἀλήθειαν ἔχειν ὡς γέγραφα· μέτρον γὰρ ἕκαστον ἡμῶν εἶναι τῶν τε ὄντων καὶ μή· μυρίον μέντοι διαφέρειν ἕτερον ἑτέρου αὐτῷ τούτῳ, ὅτι τῷ μὲν ἄλλα ἔστι τε καὶ φαίνεται, τῷ δὲ ἄλλα. καὶ σοφίαν καὶ σοφὸν ἄνδρα πολλοῦ δέω τὸ μὴ φάναι εἶναι, ἀλλ᾽ αὐτὸν τοῦτον καὶ λέγω σοφόν, ὃς ἄν τινα ἡμῶν ᾧ φαίνεται καὶ ἔστι κακά, μεταβάλλων ποιήσῃ ἀγαθὰ φαίνεσθαί τε καὶ εἶναι. τὸν δὲ λόγον αὖ μὴ τῷ ῥήματί μου δίωκε, ἀλλ᾽ ὧδε ἔτι σαφέστερον μάθε τί λέγω. οἷον γὰρ ἐν τοῖς πρόσθεν ἐλέγετο ἀναμνήσθητι, ὅτι τῷ μὲν ἀσθενοῦντι πικρὰ φαίνεται ἃ ἐσθίει,

is different from the man ignorant, and that every man becomes as many as the changes he undergoes. More seriously, he would challenge us to prove either that sensations are not peculiar to him, or that it does not follow from this, that what appears to each man, is to him.

1. καὶ τούτους γιγνομένους ἀπείρους] 'Becoming multiplied to infinity, if only alteration take place.'

2. ἀνομοίως γίγν. the reading of Bodl. Vat. admits of a possible rendering, 'If only the man becomes in a different way:' i. e. when he is the subject of a different process. But the reading of the other MSS. is more probable.

ὀνομάτων——θηρεύσεις] 'Entanglements of words.' The genitive is not objective but descriptive. Cf. Euthyd. 295: Βουλόμεθά με θηρεύσαι τὰ ὀνόματα εὐρυστήσει. 'If we must really be on our guard against being entangled by each other with words.'

10. μου) To be taken with λόγον.

22. φαίνεται——καὶ ἔστι ἔστι καὶ φαίνεται) What is to the healthy man, also appears to him. Protagoras asserts that what appears to the sick man also is to him.

M 2

84   ΠΛΑΤΩΝΟΣ

καὶ ἔστι, τῷ δὲ ὑγιαίνοντι τἀναντία ἔστι καὶ φαίνεται· p. 167.
σοφώτερον μὲν οὖν τούτων οὐδέτερον δεῖ ποιῆσαι·
οὐδὲ γὰρ δυνατόν. οὐδὲ κατηγορητέον ὡς ὁ μὲν κάμ-
νων ἀμαθής, ὅτι τοιαῦτα δοξάζει, ὁ δὲ ὑγιαίνων σοφός,
5 ὅτι ἀλλοῖα· μεταβλητέον δ' ἐπὶ θάτερα· ἀμείνων γὰρ
ἡ ἑτέρα ἕξις. οὕτω δὲ καὶ ἐν τῇ παιδείᾳ ἀπὸ ἑτέρας
ἕξεως ἐπὶ τὴν ἀμείνω μεταβλητέον. ἀλλ' ὁ μὲν ἰατρὸς
φαρμάκοις μεταβάλλει, ὁ δὲ σοφιστὴς λόγοις. ἐπεὶ
οὔ τί γε ψευδῆ δοξάζοντά τίς τινα ὕστερον ἀληθῆ
10 ἐποίησε δοξάζειν. οὔτε γὰρ τὰ μὴ ὄντα δυνατὸν
δοξάσαι, οὔτε ἄλλα παρ' ἃ ἂν πάσχῃ· ταῦτα δὲ ἀεὶ
ἀληθῆ. ἀλλ' οἶμαι, πονηρᾶς ψυχῆς ἕξει δοξάζοντας b

He would tell us that he is far from disparaging the wisdom of the wise; but he would define wisdom as the power of bringing men over, not from false ideas to true ones, but from a

12. πονηρᾶς ψυχῆς ἕξει δοξάζοντας συγγενῆ ἑαυτῆς] Πονηρᾶς is the
reading of all the MSS. δοξάζοντας of Bodl. Vat. Ven. Π. ἑαυτῆς is
found in all the MSS. but one.
(Flor. h. αὐτῆς). Πονηρᾶς ψυχῆς
ἕξει, 'through having a bad or
vicious soul.' Ἕξις, like φαντασία, is not with Plato, as with Aristotle, a term of art, it is simply
the noun of the verb ἔχειν, and
accordingly has two meanings,
'condition,' ἀπὸ τοῦ ἔχειν πως,
and 'having'; and, like πρᾶξις, it
sometimes wavers between both.
For instances of the active sense,
cf. Rep. 433: Ἡ τοῦ οἰκείου τε καὶ
ἑαυτοῦ ἕξις καὶ πρᾶξις. Soph. 247:
Δικαιοσύνης ἕξις καὶ παρουσία, and
infr. p. 197: Ἐπιστήμης τῶν ἕξιν
φασὶν εἶναι. Also Crat. 414. d.
Legg. 625. Tim. 73, 74, 87.
For an instance where it seems
to waver, cf. Rep. 509: Ἔτι μει-
ζόνως τιμητέον τὴν τοῦ ἀγαθοῦ ἕξιν.
Ib. 591: Ἡ ψυχὴ τιμιωτέραν
ἕξιν λαμβάνει, σωφροσύνης κτωμέ-
νη. Gorg. 524: Ἔχει τὴν ἕξιν
τὴν αὑτοῦ. And above, p. 153:
Ἡ τοῦ σώματος ἕξις —— ἡ δ' ἐν τῇ
ψυχῇ ἕξις, we seem to pass from
one meaning to the other within

a few lines, as here. Comp. also
Gorg. 523: Ψυχὴν πονηρὰς ἔχοντες. Ἑαυτῆς presents more difficulty, but it may still be genuine.
The transition is easy and not
unfrequent from the person
thinking to the mind thinking.
Cf. Phaedr. 82, where the change
from the masculine to the feminine, i. e. from the persons to
the souls, occurs several times
together. Gorg. 526, ταυτότε
τινα — ἰδόντα δ' ἄλλην. inf. 173:
σμικροὶ δὲ καὶ οὐκ ὀρθοὶ τὰς ψυχάς.
τὴν γὰρ αὔξην καὶ τὸ εὐθύ —— ἡ ἐκ
νέων δουλεία ἀφῄρηται ——
—— ἔτι ἀπαλαῖς ψυχαῖς ἐπιβάλλουσα, οὔτε οὗ δυνάμενοι, κ. τ. λ.
Supr. 153: Ἡ δὲ ἐν τῇ ψυχῇ ἕξις,
and note. See also, for an instance of a like change of subject, Rep. 442: Μουσικῇ καὶ γυμ-
ναστικῇ κραθεῖσι —— ἐμμετρότερον.
(That such a change of subject
does occur here, is evident
from the nominative χρηστή.)
The reflexive pronoun is also
facilitated by συγγενῆ, being a
correlative word. Cf. Phaed. 84:
Εἰς τὸ ξυγγενὲς καὶ τὸ τοιοῦτο
ἀφικομένη. Phaedr. 238: Τῶν ἑαυτῆς συγγενῶν ἐπιθυμιῶν. Compare

p. 167. συγγενῆ ἑαυτῆς χρηστὰ ἐποίησε δοξάσαι ἕτερα τοιαῦτα, ἅ δή τινες τὰ φαντάσματα ὑπὸ ἀπειρίας ἀληθῆ καλοῦσιν, ἐγὼ δὲ βελτίω μὲν τὰ ἕτερα τῶν ἑτέρων, ἀληθέστερα δὲ οὐδέν. καὶ τοὺς σοφούς, ὦ φίλε Σώκρατες, πολλοῦ δέω βατράχους λέγειν, ἀλλὰ κατὰ μὲν σώματα ἰατροὺς λέγω, κατὰ δὲ φυτὰ γεωργούς. φημὶ

worse to a better state : and would argue that until this is disproved, Socrates man be content to be a "measure of things."

also for the use of the reflexive pronoun, where it cannot be strictly referred to the subject of the sentence, Rep. p. 419: 'Ἐὰν τίς σε φῇ μὴ πάνυ εὐδαίμονας ποιεῖν τούτους τοὺς ἄνδρας, καὶ ταῦτα δι' ἑαυτούς. Supr. p. 152: ἕτερον — ἐφ' ἑαυτὸ τὸ πνεῦμα ψυχρὸν ᾗ οὐ ψυχρὸν φήσομεν.

(12.) δοξάζοντες is preferable as the reading of the best MS, as the harder reading, and because the change to δοξάζοντα was so easy with the same word occurring a few lines above. For the change from the singular τινὰ, to the indefinite plural, cf. Rep. 344: 'Ἐπειδὰν δὲ τυραννικοὺς—βουλήσηται—ἀντὶ τούτων τῶν αἰσχρῶν ὀνομάτων—μακάριοι καλοῦνται, οὐ μόνον ὑπὸ τῶν πολιτῶν ἀλλὰ καὶ ὑπὸ τῶν ἄλλων, ὅσοι ἂν πύθωνται αὐτὸν τὴν ὅλην ἀδικίαν ἠδικηκότα: et passim.

'For it is not to be supposed that any one ever makes one, who thinks falsely, afterwards think truly. For it is impossible either to think what is not, or to think any thing beyond the present impression, which is always real. But, I suppose, whereas men, through having an inferior mind, entertain thoughts of a kindred nature; a good mind causes them to have good thoughts, those, namely, which the inexperienced call true.'

If any change of reading were required, the most probable would be the transposition of ξυγγενῆ ἑαυτῆς and ἕτερα τοιαῦτα.

1. χρηστά] Sc. ψυχή.

ἕτερα τοιαῦτα] Sc. χρηστά. 'Whereas inferior minds have opinions kindred to themselves, a superior mind creates in them opinions which resemble it.'

2. φαντάσματα] This word here contains no association of falsehood, seeing that φαίνεσθαι and εἶναι are identified ; but neither does it imply truth.

4. ἀληθέστερα δ' οὐδέν] I. e. 'all are equally real.'

6. κατὰ δὲ φυτὰ γεωργούς] The theory is exposed by being gravely carried to the farthest point. Man is reduced to a level not only with brutes but with vegetables. Cf. Ar. Met. 1008 B: Εἰ δὲ μηδὲν ὑπολαμβάνει, ἀλλ' ὁμοίως οἴεταί τε καὶ οὐκ οἴεται, τί ἂν διαφερόντως ἔχοι τῶν φυτῶν ; This however is only remotely hinted at. At present we are to receive this as an additional proof of Protagoras' boldness. For a more serious use of the analogy between human nature and the vegetable world, see Rep. 492: Σπέρματος πέρι ἢ φυτοῦ εἴτε ἐγγείων εἴτε τῶν ζώων κ.τ.λ. Heind. quotes Aristot. de Plant. I. 1, where after mentioning the opinions of Anaxagoras and Empedocles on the question, 'Do plants feel?' he adds, 'Ἀναξίνος καὶ ὁ Πλάτων ἐπιθυμεῖν μόνον αὐτὰ

ΠΛΑΤΩΝΟΣ

γὰρ καὶ τούτους τοῖς φυτοῖς ἀντὶ πονηρῶν αἰσθήσεων, p. 167.
ὅταν τι αὐτῶν ἀσθενῇ, χρηστὰς καὶ ὑγιεινὰς αἰσθήσεις c
τε καὶ ἀληθεῖς ἐμποιεῖν, τοὺς δέ γε σοφούς τε καὶ
ἀγαθοὺς ῥήτορας ταῖς πόλεσι τὰ χρηστὰ ἀντὶ τῶν
πονηρῶν δίκαια δοκεῖν εἶναι ποιεῖν. ἐπεὶ οἷά γ᾽ ἂν
ἑκάστῃ πόλει δίκαια καὶ καλὰ δοκῇ, ταῦτα καὶ εἶναι
αὐτῇ, ἕως ἂν αὐτὰ νομίζῃ· ἀλλ᾽ ὁ σοφὸς ἀντὶ πονηρῶν
ὄντων αὐτοῖς ἑκάστων χρηστὰ ἐποίησεν εἶναι καὶ
δοκεῖν. κατὰ δὲ τὸν αὐτὸν λόγον καὶ ὁ σοφιστὴς
τοὺς παιδευομένους οὕτω δυνάμενος παιδαγωγεῖν
σοφός τε καὶ ἄξιος πολλῶν χρημάτων τοῖς παιδευ- d
θεῖσι· καὶ οὕτω σοφώτεροί τέ εἰσιν ἕτεροι ἑτέρων καὶ
οὐδεὶς ψευδῆ δοξάζει, καὶ σοί, ἐάν τε βούλῃ ἐάν τε μή,

διὰ τὴν σφοδρὰν τῆς θρεπτικῆς δυνάμεως ἀνάγκην ἔφησεν, ὁ ἐὰν συσταίη, ἥδεσθαι ὄντων αὐτὰ καὶ λυπεῖσθαι αἰσθάνεσθαί τι σύμφωνον ἔσται. Cf. Æsch. Eumen. 911:
Λθ. στέργω γάρ, ἀνδρὸς φιτυποιμένοε δίκην, τὸ τῶν δικαίων τῶνδ᾽ ἀπένθητον γένος.

3. χρηστὰς καὶ ὑγιεινὰς αἰσθήσεις τε] 'Impart to them good and healthy sensations, and real ones too;' i. e. not only real (which they all are), but also good and healthy. The difference of idiom by which in Greek what is most emphatic is put first, though well-known, is often a source of difficulty. E. g. Soph. Œd. Col. 308: 'Ἀλλ᾽ εὐτυχὴς ἵκοιτο τῇ θ᾽ αὑτοῦ πόλει ἐμοί τε· τίς γὰρ ἐσθλὸς οὐχ αὑτῷ φίλος; 'May he come, a blessing to his own city, as well as to me. For who by kindness does not befriend himself?' where the second clause refers to τῇ αὑτοῦ πόλει as the emphatic words.
Cf. supr. p. 150: Αὐτοῖς τε καὶ τοῖς ἄλλοις ἴδοξαν ἀμαθεῖς εἶναι.

Schleiermacher's conjecture, ἀληθείας, has been generally received, but ἀληθεῖς is very possibly right. For the difficult position of τε, comp. Rep. 466:
Καὶ γάρ ἐστι δίκαιον παρὰ τῆς αὑτῶν πόλεως (ζωντές τε καὶ τελευτήσαντι ταφῆς ἀξίας μετέχουσιν. Ib. 472:
Εἰκότων ἄρα δεόντων τε καὶ ἰδαλαίων οὕτω παράδοξον λέγειν λόγον τε καὶ ἐπιχειρῶν διασκοπεῖν. The objection drawn from supr. d δὴ τινες—ὑπὸ ἀπειρίας ἀληθῆ καλοῦσιν, is cancelled by the preceding ταῦτα δὲ δεῖ ἀληθῆ. The state of plants has as much reality as that of the wise man: and the latter has no advantage in point of truth.

4. ταῖς πόλεσι] A further step is thus made in advance. Having already included the good and noble amongst the things of which each man is judge for himself, it is natural to apply the same theory to the state, and to law and justice.

ΘΕΑΙΤΗΤΟΣ. 87

p. 167. ἀνεκτέον ὄντι μέτρῳ· σώζεται γὰρ ἐν τούτοις ὁ λόγος
οὗτος· ᾧ σὺ εἰ μὲν ἔχεις ἐξ ἀρχῆς ἀμφισβητεῖν,
ἀμφισβήτει, λόγῳ ἀντιδιεξελθών, εἰ δὲ δι' ἐρωτήσεων
βούλει, δι' ἐρωτήσεων. οὐδὲ γὰρ τοῦτο φευκτέον ἀλλὰ
πάντων μάλιστα διωκτέον τῷ νοῦν ἔχοντι. ποίει 5
μέντοι οὑτωσί· μὴ ἀδίκει ἐν τῷ ἐρωτᾷν. καὶ γὰρ
πολλὴ ἀλογία ἀρετῆς φάσκοντα ἐπιμελεῖσθαι μηδὲν
ἀλλ' ἢ ἀδικοῦντα ἐν λόγοις διατελεῖν. ἀδικεῖν δ' ἐστὶν
ἐν τῷ τοιούτῳ, ὅταν τις μὴ χωρὶς μὲν ὡς ἀγωνι-
ζόμενος τὰς διατριβὰς ποιῆται, χωρὶς δὲ διαλεγό- 10
μενος, καὶ ἐν μὲν τῷ παίζῃ τε καὶ σφάλλῃ καθ' ὅσον
ἂν δύνηται, ἐν δὲ τῷ διαλέγεσθαι σπουδάζῃ τε καὶ
ἐπανορθοῖ τὸν προσδιαλεγόμενον, ἐκεῖνα μόνα αὐτῷ
ἐνδεικνύμενος τὰ σφάλματα, ἃ αὐτὸς ὑφ' ἑαυτοῦ καὶ

p. 168. τῶν προτέρων συνουσιῶν παρεκέκρουστο. ἂν μὲν γὰρ 15
οὕτω ποιῇς, ἑαυτοὺς αἰτιάσονται οἱ προσδιατρίβοντές
σοι τῆς αὑτῶν ταραχῆς καὶ ἀπορίας, ἀλλ' οὐ σέ, καὶ
σὲ μὲν διώξονται καὶ φιλήσουσιν, αὑτοὺς δὲ μισή-
σουσι, καὶ φεύξονται ἀφ' ἑαυτῶν εἰς φιλοσοφίαν, ἵν'
ἄλλοι γενόμενοι ἀπαλλαγῶσι τῶν οἳ πρότερον ἦσαν· 20
ἐὰν δὲ τἀναντία τούτων δρᾷς ὥσπερ οἱ πολλοί, τἀναν-

He would
be willing
to proceed
by question
and answer,
only he
would de-
mand fair
treatment.
For Dia-
lectic, if
fairly used,
leads to
sincere in-
quiry: if
controver-
sially, to
the hatred
of inquiry.

3. λόγῳ ἀντιδιεξελθών κ. τ. λ.] Protagoras himself is represented as master of both styles (Prot. 329: 'ἱκανὸς μὲν μακροὺς
λόγους—εἰπεῖν—ἱκανὸς δὲ καὶ ἐρω-
τηθεὶς ἀποκρίνασθαι κατὰ βραχύ'), and in the Phaedrus Socrates
himself adopts both, of course to the implied disadvantage of
the rhetorical, which is more openly ridiculed in the Gorgias.
Cf. also Soph. 217: Πότερον εἴ-
ωθας μακρῷ λόγῳ διεξιέναι—ἢ δι' ἐρωτήσεων;

9. ἐν τῷ τοιούτῳ] Sc. ἐν τῷ ἐρω-
τᾷν, ἐν λόγοις, supr. Probably this passage contains a covert censure of the eristic method that pervades this dialogue. Cf. Rep.
487, where perhaps Socrates himself is gently criticized:
'Ἡγοῦνται—ὑπὸ τοῦ λόγου παρ'
ἕκαστον τὸ ἐρώτημα σμικρὸν παρα-
γόμενοι,—ἐπὶ τελευτῆς τῶν λόγων
μέγα τὸ σφάλμα καὶ ἐναντίον τοῖς
πρώτοις ἀναφαίνεσθαι.

13. ἐκεῖνα—τὰ σφάλματα] These slips and deflections
which are due to himself and to the company he has previously
kept. παρακρούειν is said to have been a wrestler's term.

ΠΛΑΤΩΝΟΣ

τία ξυμβήσεταί σοι καὶ τοὺς ξυνόντας ἀντὶ φιλο- p. 168.
σόφων μισοῦντας τοῦτο τὸ πρᾶγμα ἀποφανεῖς, ἐπει- b
δὰν πρεσβύτεροι γένωνται. ἐὰν οὖν ἐμοὶ πείθῃ, ὃ καὶ
πρότερον ἐρρήθη, οὐ δυσμενῶς οὐδὲ μαχητικῶς, ἀλλ'
ἵλεῳ τῇ διανοίᾳ συγκαθεὶς ὡς ἀληθῶς σκέψει τί ποτε
λέγομεν, κινεῖσθαί τε ἀποφαινόμενοι τὰ πάντα τό τε
δοκοῦν ἑκάστῳ τοῦτο καὶ εἶναι ἰδιώτῃ τε καὶ πόλει.
καὶ ἐκ τούτων ἐπισκέψει εἴτε ταὐτὸν εἴτε καὶ ἄλλο
ἐπιστήμη καὶ αἴσθησις, ἀλλ' οὐχ, ὥσπερ ἄρτι, ἐκ
συνηθείας ῥημάτων τε καὶ ὀνομάτων, ἃ οἱ πολλοὶ ὅπῃ
ἂν τύχωσιν ἕλκοντες ἀπορίας ἀλλήλοις παντοδαπὰς
παρέχουσι. Ταῦτα, ὦ Θεόδωρε, τῷ ἑταίρῳ σου εἰς
βοήθειαν †προσηρξάμην† κατ' ἐμὴν δύναμιν, σμικρὰ
ἀπὸ σμικρῶν· εἰ δ' αὐτὸς ἔζη, μεγαλειότερον ἂν τοῖς
αὑτοῦ ἐβοήθησεν.

ΘΕΟ. Παίζεις, ὦ Σώκρατες· πάνυ γὰρ νεανικῶς
τῷ ἀνδρὶ βεβοήθηκας.

He would invite us to examine the meaning of his own saying, and of the principle of motion, and thus to meet the doctrine of sense on its own ground, avoiding the captiousness of verbal criticism.

2. μισοῦντας τοῦτο τὸ πρᾶγμα] Viz. Τὴν φιλοσοφίαν, i. e. μισολόγους γεγονότας. See the remarkable passage in the Phædo on this subject, p. 89, 90; where a parallel is drawn between the growth of misanthropy and scepticism.

3. ὃ καὶ πρότερον ἐρρήθη] Viz. supr. 167: Γενναιοτέραν ἐπ' αὐτὸ ἴλθω ὁ λόγος. The unusual form ἐρρήθη was perhaps adopted in imitation of Protagoras.

5. ἵλεῳ τῇ διανοίᾳ συγκαθεὶς] Sc. σεαυτόν. Cf. infr. 174: λόγῳ συγκαθιεὶς. 'Meeting us without reserve, in a candid and good-humoured spirit.'

10. ὅπῃ ἂν τύχωσιν ἕλκοντες] Soph. 259: Τότε μὲν ἐπὶ θάτερα τότε δ' ἐπὶ θάτερα τοὺς λόγους ἕλκων. Phil. 57: Τοὺς δεινοὺς περὶ λόγους ὀλίγον.

14. προσηρξάμην] Notwithstanding Buttmann's ingenious defence of this word, Lexil. I. p. 103, it is difficult not to incline to the conjecture of Cornius, προσήρεισα μέν. Cf. Soph. (Ed. Col. 73: Ὡς ἂν προσερείσω σμικρά, περθάνῃ μέγα. See however p. 171: Ὑπογράψωμεν βοηθοῦντες.

15. μεγαλειότερον] A rhetorical word, used probably in ironical imitation of Protagoras' style. See notes on πολυάρατον, ἐρρήθη, supr. Cf. Xen. Mem. III. 1: Οὕτω πῶς διέκειτο Πρόδικος τὴν ὑπ' Ἀρετῆς Ἡρακλέους παίδευσιν, ἐνδέησεν μέντοι τὰν γνῶμας ἔτι μεγαλειοτέροις ῥήμασιν ἢ ἐγὼ νῦν.

17. πάνυ γὰρ νεανικῶς τῷ ἀνδρὶ βεβοήθηκας] 'Your defence of our friend has been most vigorous.'

p. 168. ΣΩ. Εὖ λέγεις, ὦ ἑταῖρε. καί μοι εἰπέ ἐνενόησάς που λέγοντος ἄρτι τοῦ Πρωταγόρου καὶ ὀνειδίζοντος ἡμῖν ὅτι πρὸς παιδίον τοὺς λόγους ποιούμενοι τῷ τοῦ παιδὸς φόβῳ ἀγωνιζοίμεθα εἰς τὰ ἑαυτοῦ, καὶ χαριεντισμόν τινα ἀποκαλῶν, ἀποσεμνύνων δὲ τὸ πάντων μέτρον, σπουδάσαι ἡμᾶς διεκελεύσατο περὶ τὸν αὑτοῦ λόγον;

ΘΕΟ. Πῶς γὰρ οὐκ ἐνενόησα, ὦ Σώκρατες;

ΣΩ. Τί οὖν; κελεύεις πείθεσθαι αὐτῷ;

ΘΕΟ. Σφόδρα γε.

ΣΩ. Ὁρᾷς οὖν ὅτι τάδε πάντα πλὴν σοῦ παιδία ἐστίν· εἰ οὖν πεισόμεθα τῷ ἀνδρί, ἐμὲ καὶ σὲ δεῖ ἐρωτῶντάς τε καὶ ἀποκρινομένους ἀλλήλοις σπουδάσαι αὐτοῦ περὶ τὸν λόγον, ἵνα μή τοι τοῦτό γ' ἔχῃ ἐγκαλεῖν, ὡς παίζοντες πρὸς μειράκια διεσκεψάμεθ' αὖ τοῦτον τὸν λόγον.

ΘΕΟ. Τί δ'; οὐ πολλῶν τοι Θεαίτητος μεγάλους πώγωνας ἐχόντων ἄμεινον ἂν ἐπακολουθήσειε λόγῳ διερευνωμένῳ;

ΣΩ. Ἀλλ' οὔ τι σοῦ γε, ὦ Θεόδωρε, ἄμεινον. μὴ οὖν οἴου ἐμὲ μὲν τῷ σῷ ἑταίρῳ τετελευτηκότι δεῖν p. 169. παντὶ τρόπῳ ἐπαμύνειν, σὲ δὲ μηδενί, ἀλλ' ἴθι, ὦ ἄριστε, ὀλίγον ἐπίσπου, μέχρι τούτου αὐτοῦ ἕως ἂν εἰδῶμεν, εἴτε ἄρα σὲ δεῖ διαγραμμάτων πέρι μέτρον

That Protagoras may be treated with due gravity, Theodorus is at last compelled to join in the discussion.

4. χαριεντισμόν τινα ἀποκαλῶν, ἀποσεμνύνων δὲ τὸ πάντων μέτρον] 'Abusing us for a certain quibbling vein, and exalting the respect due to his maxim, he bade us be in earnest when we are dealing with his theory.'

15. αὖ τοῦτον τὸν λόγον] Coisl. p. m. Αὑτοῦ τὸν λόγον. The Bodl. p. m. had αὑτοῦ τὸν τὸν λόγον. Cf. p. 167: Τὸν δὲ λόγον αὖ μὴ τῷ ῥήματί μου δίωκε. τοῦτον τὸν λόγον, if correct, refers to the fresh arguments which Protagoras had assumed in his defence, and the discussion founded on them.

22. σὲ δὲ μηδενί] The pronoun is simply used to strengthen the negative.

24. διαγραμμάτων—ἀστρονομίαν] Note the variety.

N

90   ΠΛΑΤΩΝΟΣ

εἶναι, εἴτε πάντες ὁμοίως σοὶ ἱκανοὶ ἑαυτοῖς εἴς τε p. 169.
ἀστρονομίαν καὶ τἆλλα ὧν δὴ σὺ πέρι αἰτίαν ἔχεις
διαφέρειν.

ΘΕΟ. Οὐ ῥᾴδιον, ὦ Σώκρατες, σοὶ παρακαθήμενον
μὴ διδόναι λόγον, ἀλλ' ἐγὼ ἄρτι παρελήρησα φάσκων
σε ἐπιτρέψειν μοι μὴ ἀποδύεσθαι, καὶ οὐχὶ ἀναγκάσειν
καθάπερ Λακεδαιμόνιοι· σὺ δέ μοι δοκεῖς πρὸς τὸν
Σκίρρωνα μᾶλλον τείνειν. Λακεδαιμόνιοι μὲν γὰρ b
ἀπιέναι ἢ ἀποδύεσθαι κελεύουσι, σὺ δὲ κατ' Ἀνταῖον
τί μοι μᾶλλον δοκεῖς τὸ δρᾶμα δρᾶν· τὸν γὰρ προσ-
ελθόντα οὐκ ἀνίης πρὶν ἀναγκάσῃς ἀποδύσας ἐν τοῖς
λόγοις προσπαλαῖσαι.

ΣΩ. Ἄριστά γε, ὦ Θεόδωρε, τὴν νόσον μου ἀπεί-
κασας· ἰσχυρικώτερος μέντοι ἐγὼ ἐκείνων. μυρίοι
γὰρ ἤδη μοι μοι Ἡρακλέες τε καὶ Θησέες ἐντυγχά-
νοντες καρτεροὶ πρὸς τὸ λέγειν μάλ' εὖ ξυγκεκόφασιν,
ἀλλ' ἐγὼ οὐδέν τι μᾶλλον ἀφίσταμαι· οὕτω τις ἔρως

2. αἰτίαν ἔχεις] 'You are reputed.' Rep. 435: Οἱ δὴ καὶ ἔχουσι ταύτην τὴν αἰτίαν (τοῦ θυμοειδεῖς εἶναι).

8. τείνειν] Cf. Phaed. 65 : Ἐγγύς τι τείνει τοῦ τεθνάναι. 'You come nearer to the analogy of Sciron.'

9. κατ' Ἀνταῖον] The allusion to the Lacedaemonian custom is repeated, but, as usual, with fresh imagery, and additional point. The Lacedaemonians tell one to strip or go away. But you, like Sciron, strip all you meet with, and, like Antaeus, force them to wrestle with you.

10. τὸ δρᾶμα δρᾶν] 'To go about your work.' Supr. 150: Ἐλάττων δὲ τοῦ ἐμοῦ δράματος.

11. ἀποδύσας] 'Having stript him of every excuse.'

14. ἰσχυρικώτερος μέντοι ἐγὼ ἐκεί-

νων] 'But I have more of the athlete in me than they had.'

15. Ἡρακλέες τε καὶ Θησέες] Schol. Οἱ Θρασυμάχου, Καλλικλεῖς, Διονυσοδώρου, Εὐθυδήμου καὶ οἱ τοιοῦτοι. Winkelmann (Fr. Antisthenis) suspects an allusion to Antisthenes here. But the Scholiast is probably nearer the mark. See Introduction; and cf. Euthyd. 297.

16. καρτ. πρ. τ. λ.) 'Men of valour in the art of controversy.'
μάλ' εὖ ξυγκ.] 'Have bruised me well.'

17. οὕτω τις ἔρως δεινὸς ἐνδέδυκεν] Sc. με implied in ἐγὼ supr. It is left doubtful whether οὕτω is to be joined with δεινὸς or ἐνδέδυκεν. 'So strong a passion for this kind of exercise has taken possession of me.'

p. 169. δεινὸς ἐνδέδυκε τῆς περὶ ταῦτα γυμνασίας. μὴ οὖν μηδὲ σὺ φθονήσῃς προσανατριψάμενος σαυτόν τε ἅμα καὶ ἐμὲ ὀνῆσαι.

ΘΕΟ. Οὐδὲν ἔτι ἀντιλέγω, ἀλλ' ἄγε ὅπῃ ἐθέλεις· πάντως τὴν περὶ ταῦτα εἱμαρμένην, ἣν ἄν σὺ ἐπικλώσῃς, δεῖ ἀνατλῆναι ἐλεγχόμενον. οὐ μέντοι περαιτέρω γε ὧν προτίθεσαι οἷός τ' ἔσομαι παρασχεῖν ἐμαυτόν σοι.

ΣΩ. Ἀλλ' ἀρκεῖ καὶ μέχρι τούτων. καί μοι πάνυ τήρει τὸ τοιόνδε, μή που παιδικόν τι λάθωμεν εἶδος τῶν λόγων ποιούμενοι, καί τις πάλιν ἡμῖν αὐτὸ ὀνειδίσῃ.

ΘΕΟ. Ἀλλὰ δὴ πειράσομαί γε καθ' ὅσον ἂν δύνωμαι.

ΣΩ. Τοῦδε τοίνυν πρῶτον πάλιν ἀντιλαβώμεθα οὗπερ τὸ πρότερον, καὶ ἴδωμεν, ὀρθῶς ἢ οὐκ ὀρθῶς ἐδυσχεραίνομεν ἐπιτιμῶντες τῷ λόγῳ, ὅτι αὐτάρκη ἕκαστον εἰς φρόνησιν ἐποίει, καὶ ἡμῖν ξυνεχώρησεν ὁ Πρωταγόρας, περί τε τοῦ ἀμείνονος καὶ χείρονος διαφέρειν τινάς, οὓς δὴ καὶ εἶναι σοφούς. οὐχί;

ΘΕΟ. Ναί.

2. προσανατριψάμενος] 'Giving me a grip,' 'trying one fall with me.'

7. ὧν προτίθεσαι] Viz. διαγραμμάτων πέρι, supr.

11. τις] Somebody; i.e. Protagoras.

15. ἀντιλαβώμεθα] 'Let us attack the question from the same point as before.' Cf. Rep. 544: Πάλιν—ὥσπερ παλαιστὴς τὴν αὐτὴν λαβὴν πάρεχε.

18. καὶ ἡμῖν ξυνεχώρησεν] The sentence breaks and reverts to the direct form. Cf. Rep. 489: Οὓς δὴ σὺ φῂς κ. τ. λ. ἐγὼ ξυνεχώρησα ἀληθῆ σε λέγειν. In conceding for Protagoras that some men are wise, we went beyond his own words. We must try to prove it out of his own mouth. He says, What appears to each man, is to him. Now it certainly appears to every man that some are wiser than himself, and some less wise; that some think truly, others falsely. Therefore, whether he be right or wrong, it is the case that some think truly, and some falsely.

ΠΛΑΤΩΝΟΣ

1. 8. Prologue of section is criticised.

ΣΩ. Εἰ μὲν τοίνυν αὐτὸς παρὼν ὡμολόγει, ἀλλὰ p. 169. μὴ ἡμεῖς βοηθοῦντες ὑπὲρ αὐτοῦ ξυνεχωρήσαμεν, οὐδὲν ἂν πάλιν ἔδει ἐπαναλαβόντας βεβαιοῦσθαι· νῦν δὲ τάχ᾿ ἄν τις ἡμᾶς ἀκύρους τιθείη τῆς ὑπὲρ ἐκείνου ὁμολογίας. διὸ καλλιόνως ἔχει σαφέστερον περὶ τούτου αὐτοῦ διομολογήσασθαι· οὐ γάρ τι σμικρὸν παραλλάττει οὕτως ἔχον ἢ ἄλλως.

ΘΕΟ. Λέγεις ἀληθῆ.

ΣΩ. Μὴ τοίνυν δι᾿ ἄλλων, ἀλλ᾿ ἐκ τοῦ ἐκείνου λόγου ὡς διὰ βραχυτάτων λάβωμεν τὴν ὁμολογίαν. p. 170.

ΘΕΟ. Πῶς;

'What appears to each man, is to him.' And does it not, then, appear to every man that some know more than he does and some less: so that in the greatest dangers, they look up to the wise man as to a God, submitting to be taught and ruled by him? And they account wisdom to be true

ΣΩ. Οὑτωσί. Τὸ δοκοῦν ἑκάστῳ τοῦτο καὶ εἶναί φησί που ᾧ δοκεῖ;

ΘΕΟ. Φησὶ γὰρ οὖν.

ΣΩ. Οὐκοῦν, ὦ Πρωταγόρα, καὶ ἡμεῖς ἀνθρώπου, μᾶλλον δὲ πάντων ἀνθρώπων δόξας λέγομεν, καὶ φαμὲν οὐδένα ὅν τινα οὐ τὰ μὲν αὐτὸν ἡγεῖσθαι τῶν ἄλλων σοφώτερον, τὰ δὲ ἄλλους ἑαυτοῦ, καὶ ἔν γε τοῖς μεγίστοις κινδύνοις, ὅταν ἐν στρατείαις ἢ νόσοις ἢ ἐν θαλάττῃ χειμάζωνται, ὥσπερ πρὸς θεοὺς ἔχειν τοὺς ἐν ἑκάστοις ἄρχοντας, σωτῆρας σφῶν προσδοκῶντας, οὐκ ἄλλῳ τῳ διαφέροντας ἢ τῷ εἰδέναι. καὶ πάντα που μεστὰ τἀνθρώπινα ζητούντων διδασκάλους τε καὶ ἄρχοντας ἑαυτῶν τε καὶ τῶν ἄλλων ζῴων τῶν τε ἐργασιῶν, οἰομένων τε αὖ ἱκανῶν μὲν διδάσκειν, ἱκανῶν δὲ ἄρχειν εἶναι. καὶ ἐν τούτοις ἅπασι τί ἄλλο

---

5. καλλιόνως ἔχει] 'It would seem the less exceptionable course.'

6. οὐ γάρ τι σμικρὸν παραλλάττει] It is of no small importance to the question at issue.

10. ὥσπερ πρὸς θεοὺς ἔχειν] Cf.

Rep. 489: Τὸ δ᾿ ἀληθὲς πέφυκεν, ἐάν τε πλούσιος ἐάν τε πένης κάμνῃ, ἀναγκαῖον εἶναι ἐπὶ ἰατρῶν θύρας ἰέναι, καὶ πάντα τὸν ἄρχεσθαι δεόμενον ἐπὶ τὰς τοῦ ἄρχειν δυναμένου.

33. μεστά] So Bodl. with Ven. Π. Par. F.

ΘΕΑΙΤΗΤΟΣ. 93

p. 170. φήσομεν ἢ αὐτοὺς τοὺς ἀνθρώπους ἡγεῖσθαι σοφίαν καὶ ἀμαθίαν εἶναι παρὰ σφίσιν; *thought; and folly to be false opinion.*

ΘΕΟ. Οὐδὲν ἄλλο.

ΣΩ. Οὐκοῦν τὴν μὲν σοφίαν ἀληθῆ διάνοιαν ἡγοῦνται, τὴν δὲ ἀμαθίαν ψευδῆ δόξαν;

c ΘΕΟ. Τί μήν;

ΣΩ. Τί οὖν, ὦ Πρωταγόρα, χρησόμεθα τῷ λόγῳ; πότερον ἀληθῆ φῶμεν ἀεὶ τοὺς ἀνθρώπους δοξάζειν, ἢ ποτὲ μὲν ἀληθῆ, ποτὲ δὲ ψευδῆ; ἐξ ἀμφοτέρων γάρ που ξυμβαίνει μὴ ἀεὶ ἀληθῆ ἀλλ' ἀμφότερα αὐτοὺς δοξάζειν. σκόπει γάρ, ὦ Θεόδωρε, εἰ ἐθέλοι ἄν τις τῶν ἀμφὶ Πρωταγόραν ἢ σὺ αὐτὸς διαμάχεσθαι ὡς οὐδεὶς ἡγεῖται ἕτερος ἕτερον ἀμαθῆ τε εἶναι καὶ ψευδῆ δοξάζειν. *It follows that, if all men think truly, some men think falsely.*

ΘΕΟ. Ἄλλ' ἄπιστον, ὦ Σώκρατες.

ΣΩ. Καὶ μὴν εἰς τοῦτό γε ἀνάγκης ὁ λόγος ἥκει ὁ d πάντων χρημάτων μέτρον ἄνθρωπον λέγων.

ΘΕΟ. Πῶς δή;

ΣΩ. Ὅταν σὺ κρίνας τι παρὰ σαυτῷ πρός με ἀποφαίνῃ περί τινος δόξαν, σοὶ μὲν δὴ τοῦτο κατὰ τὸν ἐκείνου λόγον ἀληθὲς ἔστω, ἡμῖν δὲ δὴ τοῖς ἄλλοις περὶ τῆς σῆς κρίσεως πότερον οὐκ ἔστι κριταῖς γενέσθαι, ἢ ἀεί σε κρίνομεν ἀληθῆ δοξάζειν; ἢ μυρίοι ἑκάστοτέ σοι μάχονται ἀντιδοξάζοντες, ἡγούμενοι ψευδῆ κρίνειν τε καὶ οἴεσθαι; *As a matter of fact men do become judges of each other's impressions.*

ΘΕΟ. Νὴ τὸν Δία, ὦ Σώκρατες, μάλα μυρίοι e δῆτα, φησὶν Ὅμηρος, οἵ γέ μοι τὰ ἐξ ἀνθρώπων πράγματα παρέχουσιν.

7. ὁ Π.] Bodl. Vat. pr. Ven. Π. τῷ Πρωταγόρᾳ.

15. εἰς τοῦτο—ἀνάγκης—ἥκει] 'Is driven to this.'

35. Νὴ τὸν Δία, ὦ Σώκ.] 'Yes, truly, Socrates, I have opponents more than I can tell, as

Homer says, and they give me worlds of trouble.'

26. φησὶν Ὅμηρος] Od. Π. 121: τῷ νῦν δυσμενέες μάλα μυρίοι εἰσ' ἐνὶ οἴκῳ.

τὰ ἐξ ἀνθρώπων πράγματα] 'A world of annoyance,' lit.

ΠΛΑΤΩΝΟΣ

ΣΩ. Τί οὖν; βούλει λέγωμεν ὡς σὺ τότε σαυτῷ μὲν ἀληθῆ δοξάζεις, τοῖς δὲ μυρίοις ψευδῆ; p. 170.

ΘΕΟ. Ἔοικεν ἔκ γε τοῦ λόγου ἀνάγκη εἶναι.

ΣΩ. Τί δὲ αὐτῷ Πρωταγόρᾳ; ἆρ' οὐχὶ ἀνάγκη, εἰ μὲν μηδὲ αὐτὸς ᾤετο μέτρον εἶναι ἄνθρωπον μηδὲ οἱ πολλοί, ὥσπερ οὐδὲ οἴονται, μηδενὶ δὴ εἶναι ταύτην τὴν ἀλήθειαν ἣν ἐκεῖνος ἔγραψεν; εἰ δὲ αὐτὸς μὲν ᾤετο, τὸ δὲ πλῆθος μὴ συνοίεται, οἶσθ' ὅτι πρῶτον μὲν ὅσῳ πλείους οἷς μὴ δοκεῖ ἢ οἷς δοκεῖ, τοσούτῳ μᾶλλον οὐκ ἔστιν ἢ ἔστιν. p. 171.

ΘΕΟ. Ἀνάγκη, εἴπερ γε καθ' ἑκάστην δόξαν ἔσται καὶ οὐκ ἔσται.

ΣΩ. Ἔπειτά γε τοῦτ' ἔχει κομψότατον· ἐκεῖνος μὲν περὶ τῆς αὑτοῦ οἰήσεως τὴν τῶν ἀντιδοξαζόντων οἴησιν, ᾗ ἐκεῖνον ἡγοῦνται ψεύδεσθαι, ξυγχωρεῖ που ἀληθῆ εἶναι ὁμολογῶν τὰ ὄντα δοξάζειν ἅπαντας.

ΘΕΟ. Πάνυ μὲν οὖν.

ΣΩ. Οὐκοῦν τὴν αὑτοῦ ἂν ψευδῆ ξυγχωροῖ, εἰ τὴν τῶν ἡγουμένων αὑτὸν ψεύδεσθαι ὁμολογεῖ ἀληθῆ εἶναι; b

ΘΕΟ. Ἀνάγκη.

ΘΕΑΙΤΗΤΟΣ. 95

p. 171. ΣΩ. Οἱ δέ γ' ἄλλοι οὐ ξυγχωροῦσιν ἑαυτοὺς ψεύδεσθαι;

ΘΕΟ. Οὐ γὰρ οὖν.

ΣΩ. Ὁ δέ γ' αὖ ὁμολογεῖ καὶ ταύτην ἀληθῆ τὴν δόξαν ἐξ ὧν γέγραφεν.

ΘΕΟ. Φαίνεται.

ΣΩ. Ἐξ ἁπάντων ἄρα ἀπὸ Πρωταγόρου ἀρξαμένων ἀμφισβητήσεται, μᾶλλον δὲ ὑπό γε ἐκείνου ὁμολογήσεται, ὅταν τῷ τἀναντία λέγοντι ξυγχωρῇ ἀληθῆ αὐτὸν δοξάζειν, τότε καὶ ὁ Πρωταγόρας αὐτὸς ξυγχωρήσεται μήτε κύνα μήτε τὸν ἐπιτυχόντα ἄνθρωπον μέτρον εἶναι μηδὲ περὶ ἑνὸς οὗ ἂν μὴ μάθῃ. οὐχ οὕτως;

ΘΕΟ. Οὕτως.

ΣΩ. Οὐκοῦν ἐπειδὴ ἀμφισβητεῖται ὑπὸ πάντων, οὐδενὶ ἂν εἴη ἡ Πρωταγόρου ἀλήθεια ἀληθής, οὔτε τινὶ ἄλλῳ οὔτ' αὐτῷ ἐκείνῳ.

ΘΕΟ. Ἄγαν, ὦ Σώκρατες, τὸν ἑταῖρόν μου καταθέομεν.

uncertainty of discussit is not broken even by Protagoras himself.

The saying of Protagoras is true for nobody.

7. Ἐξ ἁπάντων ἄρα] 'So then, what we get from all is this.' Cf. Soph. 245: Τοὺς δὲ ἄλλους λέγοντας αὖ θεατέον, ἵν' ἐκ πάντων εἰδῶμεν ὅτι τὸ δν τοῦ μὴ ὄντος οὐδὲν εὐπορώτερόν ἐστιν ὅ τί ποτ' ἔστιν. Ar. Met. 988 A: Τοσοῦτόν γ' ἔχομεν ἐξ αὐτῶν, ὅτι, κ.τ.λ. The preposition is probably suggested by ἐξ ὧν immediately preceding. 'On all hands, then, including Protagoras, it is disputed, or rather on his part it is admitted.'

9. ὅταν—ξυγχωρήσεται] These words are explanatory of ὑπὸ ἐκείνου ὁμολογήσεται, and what follows, from μήτε onwards, depends immediately on ξυγχωρήσεται, but really also on all that precedes. The construction of a sentence is frequently thus disturbed by the introduction of an explanatory or appositional clause. Cf. Rep. p. 529: Οὐ δόκιμον ἄλλο τι νομίσαι ἄνω ποιεῖν ψυχὴν βλέπειν μάθημα ἢ ἐκεῖνο, ὃ ἂν περὶ τὸ ὂν τε ᾖ καὶ τὸ ἀόρατον, ἐάν τέ τις ἄνω κεχηνὼς ἢ κάτω συμμεμυκὼς τῶν αἰσθητῶν τι ἐπιχειρῇ μανθάνειν, οὔτε μαθεῖν ποτέ φημι αὐτόν, οὔτε ἄνω ἀλλὰ κάτω αὐτοῦ βλέπειν τὴν ψυχήν, κἂν ἐξ ὑπτίας νέων ἐν γῇ ἢ ἐν θαλάττῃ μανθάνῃ.

18. Ἄγαν] 'We are urging my friend too vehemently.' 'running him very hard.'

καταθέομεν] De Legg. 806:

96   ΠΛΑΤΩΝΟΣ

Could he put his head above the ground, no doubt he might convince us of much folly. But we have done our best. No one will deny that one man is wiser, and another less wise, than his neighbour. It is clear, too, that

ΣΩ. Ἀλλά τοι, ὦ φίλε, ἄδηλον εἰ καὶ παραθέομεν p. 171.
τὸ ὀρθόν. εἰκός γε ἄρα ἐκεῖνον πρεσβύτερον ὄντα σοφώτερον ἡμῶν εἶναι· καὶ εἰ αὐτίκα ἐντεῦθεν ἀνακύψειε d
μέχρι τοῦ αὐχένος, πολλὰ ἂν ἐμέ τε ἐλέγξας ληροῦντα,
5 ὡς τὸ εἰκός, καὶ σὲ ὁμολογοῦντα, καταδὺς ἂν οἴχοιτο
ἀποτρέχων. ἀλλ' ἡμῖν ἀνάγκη, οἶμαι, χρῆσθαι ἡμῖν
αὐτοῖς, ὁποῖοί τινές ἐσμεν, καὶ τὰ δοκοῦντα ἀεὶ ταῦτα
λέγειν. καὶ δῆτα καὶ νῦν ἄλλο τι φῶμεν ὁμολογεῖν
ἂν τοῦτό γε ὁντινοῦν, τὸ εἶναι σοφώτερον ἕτερον ἑτέ-
10 ρου, εἶναι δὲ καὶ ἀμαθέστερον;

ΘΕΟ. Ἐμοὶ γοῦν δοκεῖ.

ΣΩ. Ἡ καὶ ταύτῃ ἂν μάλιστα ἵστασθαι τὸν λόγον,

Τί δράσωμεν, ὦ Κλεινία; τὸν ξένον ἐάσωμεν τὸν ἕτερον ἡμῖν οὕτω καταδραμεῖν;

1. Ἀλλά—ἄδηλον] 'But it does not appear that we are out-running what is right,' i. e. I do not see that we are transgressing any rule of truth or fairness. Τὸ ὀρθόν means simply (as in Rep. 540: Τὸ ὀρθὸν περὶ πλεῖστον ποιησάμενοι) 'What is just and true.' There is no necessity therefore for making παραθεῖν (with the accus.) mean 'to swerve from.'

2. εἰκός γε ἄρα] Socrates admits that there is some ground for Theodorus' remonstrance. 'It is reasonable, I grant, to presume that as he is older so he is wiser than we are.' Ἄρα refers partly to what Theodorus has suggested, but chiefly gives emphasis to εἰκός and the words that follow, and perhaps marks the illative connexion between them (πρεσβύτερον ὄντα, σοφώτερον ἄρα εἶναι) 'Indeed, when we come to think of it, Protagoras, being older, must be wiser than we are.'

5. καὶ σὲ ὁμολογοῦντα] Sc. ληροῦντα.

6. ἀλλ' ἡμῖν] Socrates returns to the charge with the second ἀλλά.

7. τὰ δοκοῦντα] P. 154: Ἐὰν μέν τῷ δοκῶν, κ.τ.λ. Men. 83: Ἔμοιγε δοκεῖ οὕτως. Κ. Καλῶς· τὸ γάρ σοι δοκοῦν τοῦτο ἀποκρίνου.

12. ταύτῃ ἂν μάλιστα ἵστασθαι] 'Will by preference take its stand (or will take its stand most resolutely) in this position, which we sketched out for it in our defence of Protagoras.' Or μάλιστα may be taken closely with ταύτῃ, 'Hereabouts, as near as we can guess.' Cf. Parm. 130: ὅπως ταύτῃ στῇ. 'The argument' is more or less personified, as so often in Plato, (cf. Rep. 484: Δεῖ μακροῦ τινος διεξελθόντος λόγου. Ib. 503: Τοιαῦτ' ἄττα ἦν τὰ λεγόμενα συμβαίνοντα καὶ παρακεκαλυμμένα τοῦ λόγου,) and is the subject of ξυγχωρεῖσθαι, ἐθελήσειν, ὁμολογήσειν, and τολμήσειν, in what follows. Ἵστασθαι depends immediately on φῶμεν. May there also be a slight play upon the word !

p. 171. ᾗ ἡμεῖς ὑπεγράψαμεν βοηθοῦντες Πρωταγόρᾳ, ὡς τὰ
μὲν πολλὰ ᾗ δοκεῖ ταύτῃ καὶ ἔστιν ἑκάστῳ, θερμά,
ξηρά, γλυκέα, πάντα ὅσα τοῦ τύπου τούτου· εἰ δέ
που ἔν τισι ξυγχωρήσεται διαφέρειν ἄλλον ἄλλου,
περὶ τὰ ὑγιεινὰ καὶ νοσώδη ἐθελήσαι ἂν φάναι μὴ πᾶν 5
γύναιον καὶ παιδίον καὶ θηρίον δὲ ἱκανὸν εἶναι ἰᾶσθαι
αὑτὸ γιγνῶσκον ἑαυτῷ τὸ ὑγιεινόν, ἀλλὰ ἐνταῦθα δὴ
ἄλλον ἄλλου διαφέρειν, εἴπερ που ;
ΘΕΟ. Ἔμοιγε δοκεῖ οὕτως.

p. 172. ΣΩ. Οὐκοῦν καὶ περὶ πολιτικῶν, καλὰ μὲν καὶ αἰ- 10
σχρὰ καὶ δίκαια καὶ ἄδικα καὶ ὅσια καὶ μή, οἷα ἂν
ἑκάστη πόλις οἰηθεῖσα θῆται νόμιμα ἑαυτῇ, ταῦτα καὶ
εἶναι τῇ ἀληθείᾳ ἑκάστῃ, καὶ ἐν τούτοις μὲν οὐδὲν
σοφώτερον οὔτε ἰδιώτην ἰδιώτου οὔτε πόλιν πόλεως
εἶναι· ἐν δὲ τῷ ξυμφέροντα ἑαυτῇ ἢ μὴ ξυμφέροντα 15
τίθεσθαι, ἐνταῦθ᾽, εἴπερ που, αὖ ὁμολογήσει ξύμβουλόν
τε ξυμβούλου διαφέρειν καὶ πόλεως δόξαν ἑτέραν
ἑτέρας πρὸς ἀλήθειαν, καὶ οὐκ ἂν πάνυ τολμήσειε
b φῆσαι, ἃ ἂν θῆται πόλις ξυμφέροντα οἰηθεῖσα αὑτῇ,
παντὸς μᾶλλον ταῦτα καὶ ξυνοίσειν. ἀλλ᾽ ἐκεῖ οὔ 20

'This unstable theory will make a stand hereabouts if anywhere.' See also Thuc. VI. 34 : Πρὸς τὰ λεγόμενα καὶ αἱ γνῶμαι ἴστανται.

1. ᾗ ἡμεῖς ὑπεγράψαμεν βοηθοῦντες Πρωταγόρᾳ] This 'new wave' of discussion rises upon the last, pp. 167, 168: Κατὰ μὲν σώματα ἰατροὺς λέγω, κατὰ δὲ φυτὰ γεωργούς——ταῖς πόλεσι τὰ χρηστὰ ἀντὶ τῶν πονηρῶν δίκαια δοκεῖν εἶναι ποιεῖν. ἐπεὶ ἀεὶ γ᾽ ἂν ἑκάστῃ πόλει δίκαια καὶ καλὰ δοκῇ, ταῦτα καὶ εἶναι αὐτῇ, ἕως ἂν αὐτὰ νομίζῃ. The argument is beginning to relax a little under the influence of the ἀγαθὸν καὶ κακὸν thrown carelessly in, p. 157.

6. καὶ θηρίον δέ] 'Nay, even every inferior animal.'

10. Οὐκοῦν——περὶ πολιτικῶν] The distinction in the case of sensible things between the impressions of sense, and the knowledge of what is good, is evident enough. The analogous distinction in the case of things moral and social is less obvious. See, amongst other passages, Rep. 505 : Τί δέ ; τόδε οὐ φανερόν, ὡς δίκαια μὲν καὶ καλὰ πολλοὶ ἂν ἕλοιντο τὰ δοκοῦντα κἂν μὴ ᾖ ὅμως ταῦτα πράττειν καὶ κεκτῆσθαι καὶ δοκεῖν, ἀγαθὰ δὲ οὐδενὶ ἔτι ἀρκεῖ τὰ δοκοῦντα κτᾶσθαι, ἀλλὰ τὰ ὄντα ζητοῦσιν, τὴν δὲ δόξαν ἐνταῦθα ἤδη πᾶς ἀτιμάζει ;

ΠΛΑΤΩΝΟΣ

justice are matters of convention merely, yet in deciding what is expedient, mistake is possible both to individuals and states. This is the attitude of some who have partially relinquished the Protagorean doctrine. They offer us a new and important handle for discussion.

λέγω, ἐν τοῖς δικαίοις καὶ ἀδίκοις καὶ ὁσίοις καὶ ἀνο- p. 172.
σίοις, ἐθέλουσιν ἰσχυρίζεσθαι ὡς οὐκ ἔστι φύσει
αὐτῶν οὐδὲν οὐσίαν ἑαυτοῦ ἔχον, ἀλλὰ τὸ κοινῇ δόξαν
τοῦτο γίγνεται ἀληθὲς τότε ὅταν δόξῃ καὶ ὅσον ἂν
5 δοκῇ χρόνον. καὶ ὅσοι γε δὴ μὴ παντάπασι τὸν Πρωταγόρου λόγον λέγουσιν, ὧδέ πως τὴν σοφίαν ἄγουσι.
λόγος δὲ ἡμᾶς, ὦ Θεόδωρε, ἐκ λόγου, μείζων ἐξ ἐλάττονος, καταλαμβάνει.   c

ΘΕΟ. Οὐκοῦν σχολὴν ἄγομεν, ὦ Σώκρατες;

10 ΣΩ. Φαινόμεθα. καὶ πολλάκις μέν γε δή, ὦ δαιμόνιε, καὶ ἄλλοτε κατενόησα, ἀτὰρ καὶ νῦν, ὡς εἰκότως
οἱ ἐν ταῖς φιλοσοφίαις πολὺν χρόνον διατρίψαντες εἰς
τὰ δικαστήρια ἰόντες γελοῖοι φαίνονται ῥήτορες.

ΘΕΟ. Πῶς δὴ οὖν λέγεις;

2. ἐθέλουσιν ἰσχυρίζεσθαι] He drops the figure, and passes from what the 'argument' would naturally say, to what certain persons, who are presently defined, actually do say. For a somewhat similar transition to an indefinite plural, cf. Gorg. 457: Οἶμαι, ὦ Γοργία, καὶ σὲ ἔμ- πειρον εἶναι πολλῶν λόγων καὶ καθ- εωρακέναι ἐν αὐτοῖς τὸ τοιόνδε, ὅτι οὐ ῥᾳδίως δύνανται περὶ ὧν ἂν ἐπι- χειρήσωσι διαλέγεσθαι διορισάμε- νοι πρὸς ἀλλήλους καὶ μαθόντες καὶ διδάξαντες ἑαυτοὺς οὕτω διαλύεσθαι τὰς συνουσίας—καὶ ἐμοί γε τελευ- τῶντες (cf. καὶ ὅσοι γε in the present passage) κ.τ.λ.

6. τὴν σοφίαν ἄγουσι] Cf. Men. p. 80: 'Ορᾷς τοῦτον ὃν ἐρωτικὸν λόγον κατάγεις;
Aristotle (Met. 1008 A), uses the expression, τοῖς τὸν Πρωταγό- ρου λέγουσι λόγον. The digression which follows is not merely an ornament. As in the Sophistes the philosopher and the sophist are the counterpart of being and not-being respectively, so here the man of the world and the philosopher represent the contrast between the life of sense and the life of knowledge. There are similar digressions in the Phaedrus and Protagoras.

9. Οὐκοῦν σχολὴν ἄγομεν] Compare the opening of the digression in the Phaedrus, σχολὴ μὲν δὴ ὡς ἔοικε—, and Cic. de Am. V: Et sumus, ut dixit Fannius, otiosi.

12. ἐν ταῖς φιλοσοφίαις] 'In scientific pursuits.' Supr. p. 144: Γεωμετρίας ἤ τινος ἄλλης φιλοσο- φίας. Tim. 88: Μουσικῇ καὶ πά- σῃ φιλοσοφίᾳ. He takes common ground with Theodorus. Cf. Infr. p. 173: Τά τε γὰρ ὑπὲρ γῆς καὶ τὰ ἐπίπεδα γεωμετροῦντα, οὐρανοῦ τε ὕπερ ἀστρονομοῦντα. Compare with the whole passage the opening words of the Apology.

ΘΕΑΙΤΗΤΟΣ. 99

p. 172. ΣΩ. Κινδυνεύουσιν οἱ ἐν δικαστηρίοις καὶ τοῖς τοιούτοις ἐκ νέων κυλινδούμενοι πρὸς τοὺς ἐν φιλοσοφίᾳ
d καὶ τῇ τοιᾷδε διατριβῇ τεθραμμένους ὡς οἰκέται πρὸς
ἐλευθέρους τεθράφθαι.

ΘΕΟ. Πῇ δή; 5

ΣΩ. Ἧι τοῖς μέν, τοῦτο ὃ σὺ εἶπες, ἀεὶ πάρεστι
σχολὴ καὶ τοὺς λόγους ἐν εἰρήνῃ ἐπὶ σχολῆς ποιοῦνται, ὥσπερ ἡμεῖς νυνὶ τρίτον ἤδη λόγον ἐκ λόγου
μεταλαμβάνομεν, οὕτω κἀκεῖνοι, ἐὰν αὐτοὺς ὁ ἐπελθὼν
τοῦ προκειμένου μᾶλλον, καθάπερ ἡμᾶς, ἀρέσῃ· καὶ 10

(Digression.) Before entering upon this, however, we pause to reflect upon the happiness and freedom of the philosophic life, which has leisure to take up fresh topics or to lay them down at will. Not so the

2. *ἐκ νέων κυλινδούμενοι*] 'Who have been jostled about from their youth.' Compare Aristophanes' περίτριμμα δικῶν. (Nub. 447): cf. Dem. de Cor. 269.

κυλινδούμενοι] The word expresses contempt. Cf. Rep. 479: Μεταξύ που κυλινδεῖται.

3. *πρὸς ἐλευθέρους*] Soph. 253 (referring to this): Ἡ πρὸς Δία διάβρωσις εἰς τὴν τῶν ἐλευθέρων ἐμπεσόντες ἐπιστήμην, καὶ κινδυνεύομεν ζητοῦντες τὸν σοφιστὴν πρότερον ἀνηυρηκέναι τὸν φιλόσοφον; Rep. 499: Οὐδέ γε οὖν λόγους, ὦ μακάριε, καλῶν τε καὶ ἐλευθέρων ἱκανῶς ἐπήκοοι γεγόνασιν, οἷων ζητεῖν μὲν τὸ ἀληθὲς κ.τ.λ. 536: Οὐδὲν μάθημα μετὰ δουλείας τὸν ἐλεύθερον χρὴ μανθάνειν—and the whole image of the cave with its captives and their liberation. See also Aristot. Met. I. 2 : Δῆλον οὖν ὡς δι' οὐδεμίαν αὐτὸ ζητοῦμεν χρείαν ἑτέραν, ἀλλ' ὡς ἄνθρωπος φαμὲν ἐλεύθερος ὁ αὑτοῦ ἕνεκα καὶ μὴ ἄλλου ὤν, οὕτω καὶ αὕτη μόνη ἐλευθέρα οὖσα τῶν ἐπιστημῶν.

8. *τρίτον ἤδη λόγον ἐκ λόγου*] 'We are for the third time beginning a fresh argument.' The first fresh λόγος was the criticism of Protagoras and his defence; the second begins where Theodorus is induced to accept Socrates' challenge (see the words, p. 168, αὖ τοῦτον τὸν λόγον); the third arises with the mention of the wholesome and expedient, and the partial supporters of Protagoras.

9. *οὕτω κἀκεῖνοι*] Sc. μεταλαμβάνουσιν. This part of the sentence (from ἐὰν αὐτοὺς—) is in apposition with what precedes. Cf. supr. 171: Τότε καὶ ὁ Πρωτ., and note; also Rep. 557: Κινδυνεύει ἦν δ' ἐγώ, καλλίστη αὕτη τῶν πολιτειῶν εἶναι· ὥσπερ ἱμάτιον ποικίλον πᾶσιν ἄνθεσι πεποικιλμένον οὕτω καὶ αὕτη πᾶσιν ἤθεσι πεποικιλμένη καλλίστη ἂν φαίνοιτο. Also ib. p. 533: Οὕτω καὶ ὅταν τις τῷ διαλέγεσθαι ἐπιχειρῇ, ἄνευ πασῶν τῶν αἰσθήσεων διὰ τοῦ λόγου ἐπ' αὐτὸ ὃ ἔστιν ὁρμᾷ, καὶ μὴ ἀποστῇ πρὶν ἂν αὐτὸ ὃ ἔστιν ἀγαθὸν αὐτῇ νοήσει λάβῃ, ἐπ' αὐτοῦ γίγνεται τῷ τοῦ νοητοῦ τέλει, ὥσπερ ἐκεῖνος ἐπὶ τῷ τοῦ ὁρατοῦ.

10. *καθάπερ ἡμᾶς*] Such slight redundancies are natural in conversation.

ἀρέσειν seems to govern the accusative with the meaning to *satisfy*. The whole sentence is in construction with ἧι.

O 2

100   ΠΛΑΤΩΝΟΣ

mind which is exercised in the courts of law. The one is the training of a freeman, the other of a slave—

διὰ μακρῶν ἢ βραχέων μέλει οὐδὲν λέγειν, ἂν μόνον p. 172.
τύχωσι τοῦ ὄντος. οἱ δὲ ἐν ἀσχολίᾳ τε ἀεὶ λέγουσι·
κατεπείγει γὰρ ὕδωρ ῥέον, καὶ οὐκ ἐγχωρεῖ περὶ οὗ ἂν ε
ἐπιθυμήσωσι τοὺς λόγους ποιεῖσθαι, ἀλλ᾽ ἀνάγκην
5 ἔχων ὁ ἀντίδικος ἐφέστηκε καὶ ὑπογραφὴν παραναγι-
γνωσκομένην, ὧν ἐκτὸς οὐ ῥητέον· (ἣν ἀντωμοσίαν
καλοῦσιν·) οἱ δὲ λόγοι ἀεὶ περὶ ὁμοδούλου πρὸς δεσπότην καθήμενον, ἐν χειρί τινα δίκην ἔχοντα, καὶ οἱ
ἀγῶνες οὐδέποτε τὴν ἄλλως ἀλλ᾽ ἀεὶ τὴν περὶ αὐτοῦ·
10 πολλάκις δὲ καὶ περὶ ψυχῆς ὁ δρόμος· ὥστ᾽ ἐξ ἁπάν- p. 173.

1. *διὰ μακρῶν ἢ βραχέων*] See Polit. 286.

4. *ἀνάγκην*] Pesych.: 'Ἀνάγκη' ἡ δικαστικὴ ἐλευθέρα. Pollux VIII. 17: "Ἐποι δ᾽ οἴονται καὶ ἀνάγκην ταύτην εἶναι δικαστικήν. The latter quotation expresses doubt. May not the notion mentioned by the grammarian have arisen from the present passage? The structure of the sentence (τε—καί) forbids our identifying ἀνάγκη here with the clepsydra, which has been already alluded to. It is rather 'the strong arm of the law,' which the adversary would bring to bear, if the speaker wandered from the indictment. 'But the other sort are always pressed for time: for the ebbing water hurries on the speaker: and he has no liberty to follow whither fancy leads him, but the adversary is at hand to wield over him the resistless logic of coercion, holding a written outline of the points to which he must confine himself, which forms a running commentary to his oration.'

6. *ὧν ἐκτὸς οὐ ῥ.*] ὑπογραφήν retains its verbal force nearly

as if it were ὑπογεγραμμένα, but is not the antecedent to ὧν. See p. 147, note on ὅτῳ.

ἣν ἀντωμοσίαν καλοῦσιν] 'What they call their affidavits.' The affected unfamiliarity with legal terms is in good keeping. Compare Rep. 400: Καὶ, ἐν ἐγᾦμαι, λαμβάνω καὶ τοῦ ἄλλου τροχαίου ἀνάπαιστ᾽.

7. *πρὸς δεσπότην*] Not simply the δικαστής, but rather δῆμος or νόμος, which he represents. Compare the passages in the Republic in which δῆμος is spoken of as the master of the ship (488), as the great sophist (493), and as a mighty beast (493); and cf. Euthyphr. p. 2 : Ἔρχεται κατηγορήσων μου, ὥσπερ πρὸς μητέρα, πρὸς τὴν πόλιν. Also Herodotus VII. 104 (of the Spartans): "Ἔπεστι γάρ σφι δεσπότης, νόμος, τὸν ὑποδειμαίνουσι πολλῷ ἔτι μᾶλλον, ἢ οἱ σοὶ σέ. Pindar III. 38: Νόμος πάντων βασιλεύς.

8. *τινα δίκην*] So Bodl. Vat. Ven. Π. 'Some cause or other.'

καὶ οἱ ἀγῶνες] 'And the trial is never for an indifferent stake, but always immediately concerns the speaker.'

10. *περὶ ψυχῆς ὁ δρόμος*] Π.

ΘΕΑΙΤΗΤΟΣ.

p. 173. τῶν τούτων ἔντονοι καὶ δριμεῖς γίγνονται, ἐπιστάμενοι τὸν δεσπότην λόγῳ τε θωπεῦσαι καὶ ἔργῳ χαρίσασθαι, σμικροὶ δὲ καὶ οὐκ ὀρθοὶ τὰς ψυχάς. τὴν γὰρ αὔξην καὶ τὸ εὐθύ τε καὶ τὸ ἐλεύθερον ἡ ἐκ νέων δουλεία ἀφῄρηται, ἀναγκάζουσα πράττειν σκολιά, μεγάλους κινδύνους καὶ φόβους ἔτι ἁπαλαῖς ψυχαῖς ἐπιβάλλουσα, οὓς οὐ δυνάμενοι μετὰ τοῦ δικαίου καὶ ἀληθοῦς ὑποφέρειν, εὐθὺς ἐπὶ τὸ ψεῦδός τε καὶ τὸ ἀλλήλους ἀνταδικεῖν τρεπόμενοι πολλὰ κάμπτονται καὶ συγ-

Whose mind is come inevitably dwarfed and crooked and servile

XXII. 161 (of Achilles and Hector): Ἐπεὶ οὐχ ἱερήιον, οὐδὲ βοείην ἀρνύσθην, ἅ τε ποσσὶν ἀέθλια γίγνεται ἀνδρῶν· ἀλλὰ περὶ ψυχῆς θέον Ἕκτορος ἱπποδάμοιο. In Herodotus the metaphor is already softened down, VII. 57: Περὶ ἑωυτοῦ τρέχων (said of Xerxes). Aristoph. Vesp. 375: Ποιήσω δεκεῖν τὴν καρδίαν καὶ τὸν περὶ ψυχῆς δρόμον δραμεῖν. The expression τὴν περὶ αὐτοῦ, is suggested by τὴν ἄλλην. (τὴν ἄλλην Bodl. p. m.)

1. ἔντονοι καὶ δριμεῖς] 'Keen and shrewd.'

3. τὴν γὰρ αὔξην—ἐλεύθερον] 'Of all mental growth, and all honest and liberal culture;' 'of self-respect and the spirit of upright independence.' Both meanings are expressed in the Greek.

7. οὓς οὐ δυνάμενοι] 'Not being able to undergo these consistently with righteousness and truth, they betake themselves immediately to falsehood, and to avenging themselves on one another by wrong, and so are repeatedly bent and stunted; whence they pass from youth to manhood with no soundness in their mind, but supposing themselves to have become capable and accomplished men.'

Cf. Rep. 519: Ἡ οὕτω ἐννοεῖς τῶν λεγομένων πονηρῶν μέν σοφῶν δέ, ὡς δριμὺ μὲν βλέπει τὸ ψυχάριον καὶ ὀξέως διορᾷ ταῦτα ἐφ᾽ ἃ τέτραπται, ὡς οὐ φαύλην ἔχον τὴν ὄψιν, κακίᾳ δ᾽ ἠναγκασμένον ὑπηρετεῖν ὥστε ὅσῳ ἂν ὀξύτερον βλέπῃ τοσούτῳ πλείω κακὰ ἐργαζόμενον.——Ταῦτα μέντοι ἂν δ᾽ ἐγώ, τὸ τῆς τοιαύτης φύσεως εἰ ἐκ παιδὸς εὐθὺς κοπτόμενον περιεκόπη τὰς τῆς γενέσεως συγγενεῖς ὥσπερ μολυβδίδας, αἳ δὴ ἐδωδαῖς τε καὶ τῶν τοιούτων ἡδοναῖς τε καὶ λιχνείαις προσφυεῖς γιγνόμεναι, περὶ τὰ κάτω στρέφουσι τὴν τῆς ψυχῆς ὄψιν, κ. τ. λ.

9. πολλὰ κάμπτονται καὶ συγκλῶνται] 'Are continually thwarted and cramped in their growth.' Rep. 495: Ἀτελεῖς μὲν τὰς φύσεις, ὑπὸ δὲ τῶν τεχνῶν τε καὶ βαναυσιῶν ὥσπερ τὰ σώματα λελώβηνται οὕτω καὶ τὰς ψυχὰς ξυγκεκλασμένοι τε καὶ ἀποτεθρυμμένοι διὰ τὰς βαναυσίας τυγχάνουσιν. 611: Τεθεάμεθα μέντοι δεκαιούμενον αὐτό, ὥσπερ οἱ τὸν θαλάττιον Γλαῦκον ὁρῶντες οὐκ ἂν ἔτι ῥᾳδίως αὐτοῦ ἴδοιεν τὴν ἀρχαίαν φύσιν, ὑπὸ τοῦ τά τε παλαιὰ τοῦ σώματος μέρη τὰ μὲν ἐκκεκλάσθαι, τὰ δὲ συντετρῖφθαι καὶ πάντως λελωβῆσθαι ὑπὸ τῶν κυμάτων.

ΠΛΑΤΩΝΟΣ

κλῶνται, ὥσθ' ὑγιὲς οὐδὲν ἔχοντες τῆς διανοίας εἰς p. 173. ἄνδρας ἐκ μειρακίων τελευτῶσι, δεινοί τε καὶ σοφοὶ b γεγονότες, ὡς οἴονται. Καὶ οὗτοι μὲν δὴ τοιοῦτοι, ὦ Θεόδωρε· τοὺς δὲ τοῦ ἡμετέρου χοροῦ πότερον βούλει 5 διελθόντες ἢ ἐάσαντες πάλιν ἐπὶ τὸν λόγον τρεπώμεθα, ἵνα μὴ καί, ὁ νῦν δὴ ἐλέγομεν, λίαν πολὺ τῇ ἐλευθερίᾳ καὶ μεταλήψει τῶν λόγων καταχρώμεθα;

Turn we now from them; and let us still use our liberty to describe the leaders of our own band.

ΘΕΟ. Μηδαμῶς, ὦ Σώκρατες, ἀλλὰ διελθόντες. πάνυ γὰρ εὖ τοῦτο εἴρηκας, ὅτι οὐχ ἡμεῖς οἱ ἐν τῷ ο 10 τοιῷδε χορεύοντες τῶν λόγων ὑπηρέται, ἀλλ' οἱ λόγοι οἱ ἡμέτεροι ὥσπερ οἰκέται, καὶ ἕκαστος αὐτῶν περιμένει ἀποτελεσθῆναι ὅταν ἡμῖν δοκῇ· οὔτε γὰρ δικαστὴς οὔτε θεατής, ὥσπερ ποιηταῖς, ἐπιτιμήσων τε καὶ ἄρξων ἐπιστατεῖ παρ' ἡμῖν.

They know nothing of politics and

ΣΩ. Λέγωμεν δή, ὡς ἔοικεν, ἐπεὶ σοί γε δοκεῖ, περὶ 15 τῶν κορυφαίων· τί γὰρ ἂν τις τούς γε φαύλως δια-

4. τοὺς δὲ τοῦ ἡμετέρου χοροῦ] Phaedr. 247: θεῶν μὲν γὰρ ἔφη θεῖον χορὸς ἵσταται. Polit. 291: Ἡμῖν γοῦν ταύτην ἀπιδοῦσι τὸν περὶ τὰ τῶν πόλεων πράγματα χορόν. The metaphor is continued in the words οἱ ἐν τῷ τοιῷδε χορεύοντες, —οὔτε θεατὴς ὥσπερ ποιηταῖς—περὶ τῶν κορυφαίων—.

5. διελθόντες] The expression is a little confused: for the words πάλιν ἐπὶ τὸν λόγον τρεπώμεθα, as understood with διελθόντες, are unemphatic, while in the second part of the clause they are emphatic. Probably but for the attraction of the other participle, διελθόντες would have been διελθῶμεν. (Coisl. τραπόμ.)

(ἐάσαντες] Since here, as in the Sophista, we have stumbled prematurely on the philosophic life.

6. τῇ ἐλευθερίᾳ καὶ μετ.] 'Our freedom, which consists, as we have said, in the power of ranging from one topic to another.' Cf. Tim. 26: καὶ τίν' ἂν ὁ Κριτία, μᾶλλον ἀντὶ τούτου μεταλάβοιμεν; Polit. 257: Διασπευάσωμεν αὐτὸν μεταλαβόντες οἷον τοῦ νῦν συγγυμναστὴν τόνδε Σωκράτη;——Καθάπερ εἶπες, μεταλήμβανε.

11. οἱ ἡμέτεροι] οἱ is suspicious. If genuine, it still belongs to the predicate,—'our servants,' i. e. those which, as philosophers, we have.

περιμένει] 'Waits our pleasure for its completion.'

13. ἐπιτιμήσων] 'Stands over us to criticise and to compel.'

15. ὡς ἔοικεν] The sentence continues as if λέγωμεν had been λεκτέον.

16. τοὺς φαύλως διατρίβοντας ἐν φιλοσοφίᾳ λέγοι] ἐν φ. is empha-

ΘΕΑΙΤΗΤΟΣ. 103

p. 173. τρίβοντας ἐν φιλοσοφίᾳ λέγοι· Οὗτοι δέ που ἐκ νέων
d πρῶτον μὲν εἰς ἀγορὰν οὐκ ἴσασι τὴν ὁδόν, οὐδὲ ὅπου
δικαστήριον ἢ βουλευτήριον ἤ τι κοινὸν ἄλλο τῆς πόλεως συνέδριον· νόμους δὲ καὶ ψηφίσματα λεγόμενα
ἢ γεγραμμένα οὔτε ὁρῶσιν οὔτε ἀκούουσι. σπουδαὶ 5
δὲ ἑταιρειῶν ἐπ' ἀρχὰς καὶ σύνοδοι καὶ δεῖπνα καὶ σὺν
αὐλητρίσι κῶμοι, οὐδὲ ὄναρ πράττειν προσίσταται
αὐτοῖς. εὖ δὲ ἢ κακῶς τι γέγονεν ἐν πόλει, ἢ τί τῳ
κακόν ἐστιν ἐκ προγόνων γεγονὸς ἢ πρὸς ἀνδρῶν ἢ

public life, still less of revels and intrigues for power.

The philo- sopher's

tic, i. e. 'in such a pursuit.' For an account of these gentry, see Rep. 489—496., where they are called παμπόνηροι—ἅτεπερ οἱ ἐκ τῶν εἰργμῶν εἰς τὰ ἱερὰ ἀποδιδράσκοντες, κ. τ. λ.

1. Οὗτοι δέ που] Compare the less ironical description in the Republic 488 : νάυτην γὰρ τοιοῦ- τους γενόμενον, κ. τ. λ. The con- tradiction between philosophy and common life is here stated in its most paradoxical aspect. Nor do there appear any fea- tures of the transcendental phi- losopher. (V. infr. τῶν ὄντων ἑκάστου ὅλων.) We find a trace of him for the first time in the Sophist, as of the ideal king in the Politicus.

5. σπουδαὶ δέ, κ. τ. λ.] 'But the ambitious striving of poli- tical clubs for power, and pub- lic meetings and banquets and revellings with minstrelsy, are actions which do not occur to them even in dreams.'

For a similar 'nominativus pendens,' cf. Rep. 532: Ἡ δέ γε λύσις—ἡ πραγματεία τῶν τεχνῶν —ταύτην ἔχει τὴν δύναμιν. The irregularity is softened in the present instance by the fact that the earlier part of the sentence forms a sort of collective no-

minative to προσίσταται. With this list of 'worldly goods,' compare Rep. 491 : πάντα τὰ λεγόμενα ἀγαθά, κάλλος καὶ πλοῦ- τος καὶ ἰσχὺν σώματος καὶ ξυγγέ- νεια ἐρρωμένη ἐν πόλει καὶ πάντα τὰ τούτων οἰκεῖα.

6. ἑταιρειῶν] 'Clubs' or 'leagues.' See Rep. 365: ἐπὶ γὰρ τὸ λανθάνειν ξυνωμοσίας τε καὶ ἑταιρείας συνάξομεν—. Thucyd. VIII. 54 : καὶ ὁ μὲν Πείσανδρος τάς τε ξυνωμοσίας, αἴπερ ἐτύγχανον πρότερον ἐν τῇ πόλει οὖσαι ἐπὶ δί- καις καὶ ἀρχαῖς, ἁπάσας ἐπελθών, κ. τ. λ.: and Arnold's note.

8. τι γέγονεν] So the Bodleian and several other MSS. But Clement in quoting the passage reads τις with the majority of manuscripts. This, however, may easily have arisen out of what follows. Stallbaum says, 'Si quis alius, certe philosophus scit, quid recte, quid secus in republica fiat.' But if he is ignorant of what is passing, how can he be judge of it? See above, νόμους δὲ καὶ ψηφίσματα κ. τ. λ. The fate of Archimedes would be an illustration of what is meant. It is true that we cannot imagine Socrates to have been ignorant (e. g.) of the mutilation of the Hermae.

104 ΠΛΑΤΩΝΟΣ

Ignorance of these things, and of his neighbour's pedigree, is not ironical but real. His body is at home in the city, but his mind is traversing the earth and heaven, compassing the whole of everything.

γυναικῶν, μᾶλλον αὐτὸν λέληθεν ἢ οἱ τῆς θαλάττης p. 173. λεγόμενοι χόες. καὶ ταῦτα πάντ' οὐδ' ὅτι οὐκ οἶδεν, ε οἶδεν· οὐδὲ γὰρ αὐτῶν ἀπέχεται τοῦ εὐδοκιμεῖν χάριν, ἀλλὰ τῷ ὄντι τὸ σῶμα μόνον ἐν τῇ πόλει κεῖται αὐ-5 τοῦ καὶ ἐπιδημεῖ, ἡ δὲ διάνοια, ταῦτα πάντα ἡγησαμένη σμικρὰ καὶ οὐδέν, ἀτιμάσασα πανταχῇ φέρεται κατὰ Πίνδαρον, τά τε γᾶς ὑπένερθε καὶ τὰ ἐπίπεδα γεωμετροῦσα, οὐρανοῦ τε ὕπερ ἀστρονομοῦσα, καὶ πᾶσαν πάντῃ φύσιν ἐρευνωμένη τῶν ὄντων ἑκάστου p. 174. 10 ὅλου, εἰς τῶν ἐγγὺς οὐδὲν αὑτὴν συγκαθιεῖσα.

1. οἱ τῆς θαλάττης λεγόμενοι χόες] Aristid. Or. III. T. 1. p. 30. ed. Dind.: τὸ λέγειν περὶ τούτων καὶ ἐγχειρεῖν ἐστιν ἂν εἴ τις ἐξαριθμεῖσθαι βούλοιτο τοὺς χόας τῆς θαλάττης. (Stallb.)

3. οὐδὲ γὰρ αὐτῶν ἀπέχεται τοῦ εὐδοκιμεῖν χάριν] Cf. Ar. Eth. N. IV. 3. §§ 27, 28. (of the high-minded man)—πρὸς τὰ ἔντιμα μὴ κινεῖσθαι πρὸς τοὺς πολλούς.

6. ἀτιμάσασα] Cf. Rep. 496: ἢ ἐν σμικρᾷ πόλει ὅταν μεγάλη ψυχῇ φυῇ καὶ ἀτιμάσασα τὰ τῆς πόλεως ὑπερίδῃ· βραχὺ δέ πού τι καὶ ἀπ' ἄλλης τύχης διαπίως ἀτιμάσασα εὐφυὴς ἐπ' αὐτὴν ἂν ἔλθοι.

7. κατὰ Πίνδαρον] The fragment is thus quoted by Clem. Alex. Str. V. 707: τέτατο κατὰ Πίνδαρον τά τε γᾶς ὑπένερθεν οὐρανοῦ τε ὑπερ ἀστρονομίαν, καὶ πᾶσαν πάντῃ φύσιν ἐρευνώμενος. (v. l. ἐρευνώμενος.) He seems to have had the poet's words, as well as this passage, in his mind. Plato therefore seems to have changed τέτατο into the more prosaic φέρεται, (τέτατο occurs as a marginal reading,) and to have introduced the words καὶ τὰ ἐπίπεδα γεωμετροῦσα, (perhaps also

ἀστρονομοῦσα,) in compliment to Theodorus, adding τῶν ὄντων ἑκάστου κ.τ.λ. Plato almost always thus weaves quotation with his own language, and accommodates the poet's measures to the rhythm of prose; e. g. Rep. 365: ἐσόμεθα διὰ τείχη ὑψηλὰ ἢ σκολιαῖς ἀπάταις ἀκαβὴς καὶ ἐμαυτὸν οὕτω στρεφομένῳ διαβιῶ; ib. 364.: τῆς δ' ἀρετῆς ἱδρῶτα θεοὶ προπάροιθεν ἔθηκαν καὶ τινα ἄλλα μακρὰν τε καὶ ἀνάντη. Protag. 340: ὅταν δέ τις αὐτῆς εἰς ἄκρον ἵκηται, ῥηϊδίην δ' ἔπειτα πέλειν, χαλεπήν περ ἐοῦσαν, ἐκτῆσθαι.

τά τε γᾶς] Bodl. τότε. Is it possible that Plato wrote τάς τε, as in the quotation of Clement? This seems probable, when it is considered that τὰ ἐπίπεδα κ.τ.λ. is an afterthought, to which the transition as the words stand in the text is somewhat abrupt; and also that the term γεωμετροῦσα is more naturally applicable to the surface of the Earth.

9. τῶν ὄντων ἑκάστου ὅλου] Ὁ γὰρ συνοπτικὸς διαλεκτικός, ὁ δὲ μή, οὔ. (Rep. 537.) See the humorous illustration of this in

ΘΕΑΙΤΗΤΟΣ. 105

p. 174. ΘΕΟ. Πῶς τοῦτο λέγεις, ὦ Σώκρατες;

ΣΩ. Ὥσπερ καὶ Θαλῆν ἀστρονομοῦντα, ὦ Θεόδωρε, καὶ ἄνω βλέποντα, πεσόντα εἰς φρέαρ, Θρᾷττά τις ἐμμελὴς καὶ χαρίεσσα θεραπαινὶς ἀποσκῶψαι λέγεται, ὡς τὰ μὲν ἐν οὐρανῷ προθυμοῖτο εἰδέναι, τὰ δ᾽ ἔμπροσθεν αὐτοῦ καὶ παρὰ πόδας λανθάνοι αὐτόν. ταὐτὸν δὲ ἀρκεῖ σκῶμμα ἐπὶ πάντας ὅσοι ἐν φιλοσοφίᾳ διάγουσι. τῷ γὰρ ὄντι τὸν τοιοῦτον ὁ μὲν πλησίον καὶ ὁ γείτων λέληθεν, οὐ μόνον ὅ τι πράττει, ἀλλ᾽ ὀλίγου καὶ εἰ ἄνθρωπός ἐστιν ἤ τι ἄλλο θρέμμα· τί δέ ποτ᾽ ἐστὶν ἄνθρωπος καὶ τί τῇ τοιαύτῃ φύσει προσήκει διάφορον τῶν ἄλλων ποιεῖν ἢ πάσχειν, ζητεῖ τε καὶ πράγματ᾽ ἔχει διερευνώμενος. μανθάνεις γάρ που, ὦ Θεόδωρε. ἢ οὔ;

ΘΕΟ. Ἔγωγε· καὶ ἀληθῆ λέγεις.

ΣΩ. Τοιγάρτοι, ὦ φίλε, ἰδίᾳ τε συγγιγνόμενος ὁ

5

10

15

the Republic, 474: ὅτι ἂν ἐν φέρειν φιλοῦν τι, δεῖ φαίνεσθαι αὐτῆς, ἵνα ὀρθῶς λέγηται, οὐ τὸ μὲν φιλοῦντα ἐκείνου, τὸ δὲ μή, ἀλλὰ πᾶν στέργοντα, s. v. λ. And ib. 486: ἰσωτιάτωτω σμικρολογία ψυχῇ μελλούσῃ τοῦ ὅλου καὶ παντὸς ἀεὶ ἐπορέξεσθαι θείου τε καὶ ἀνθρωπείου.—ᾗ οὖν ὑπάρχει διανοίᾳ μεγαλοπρέπεια καὶ θεωρία παντὸς μὲν χρόνου, πάσης δὲ οὐσίας, οἷόν τε οἴει τούτῳ μέγα τι δοκεῖν εἶναι τὸν ἀνθρώπινον βίον; Φησ, 'In its universal aspect.'

(10.) εἰς τῶν ἐγγύς] 'Not lowering herself to contemplate any of the things surrounding her.'

Θρᾷττά τις] Θρᾷτταν a patria ancillam hanc dicit. *ἐμμελῆ* autem h. l. ad leporem et venustatem in jocando trahendam docuit Ruhnken. ad Longin. p. 361. Fabellam hinc forte duxit Laërt. L 34. (Heind.)

Do not the epithets rather refer to the slave's neatness in her own department? v. τορός καὶ ἀξίαν p. 175. 'A trim and dainty Thracian handmaid.'

7. ταὐτὸν δὲ ἀρκεῖ σκῶμμα] 'The same piece of raillery does not fail to apply,'—' will serve—.' For the metaphorical use of ἀρκεῖν ἐπί, cf. Soph. Ant. 611: τό τ᾽ ἔπειτα καὶ τὸ μέλλον καὶ τὸ πρὶν ἐπαρκέσει νόμος ὅδε.

For the application of the σκῶμμα in the mouth of an enemy, see the speech of Callicles in the Gorgias, 484 sqq., which presents many points of similarity to the present passage.

11. τῇ τοιαύτῃ φ.] Sc. ἀνθρωπίνῃ.

He is laughed at by ordinary people, as Thales was by the Thracian maid-servant. For knowing nothing of his neighbour, while he searches into the nature of man, he appears helpless in public and private life, having no topics for scandal, and despising the common subjects of praise and

P

106   ΠΛΑΤΩΝΟΣ

Inserting thinking of a king merely as the shepherd of a troublesome flock, who for want of leisure must be a clown: looking upon broad acres as a narrow strip of earth: and on high pedigree as but a single reach in an endless river.

τοιοῦτος ἑκάστῳ καὶ δημοσίᾳ, ὅπερ ἀρχόμενος ἔλεγον, p. 174.
ὅταν ἐν δικαστηρίῳ ᾖ που ἄλλοθι ἀναγκασθῇ περὶ
τῶν παρὰ πόδας καὶ τῶν ἐν ὀφθαλμοῖς διαλέγεσθαι,
γέλωτα παρέχει οὐ μόνον Θρᾴτταις ἀλλὰ καὶ τῷ
5 ἄλλῳ ὄχλῳ, εἰς φρέατά τε καὶ πᾶσαν ἀπορίαν ἐμπί-
πτων ὑπὸ ἀπειρίας, καὶ ἡ ἀσχημοσύνη δεινή, δόξαν
ἀβελτερίας παρεχομένη. ἔν τε γὰρ ταῖς λοιδορίαις
ἴδιον ἔχει οὐδὲν οὐδένα λοιδορεῖν, ἅτ' οὐκ εἰδὼς κακὸν
οὐδὲν οὐδενὸς ἐκ τοῦ μὴ μεμελετηκέναι· ἀπορῶν οὖν
10 γελοῖος φαίνεται· ἔν τε τοῖς ἐπαίνοις καὶ ταῖς τῶν d
ἄλλων μεγαλαυχίαις, οὐ προσποιήτως, ἀλλὰ τῷ ὄντι
γελῶν ἔνδηλος γιγνόμενος ληρώδης δοκεῖ εἶναι. τυ-
ραννικόν τε γὰρ ἢ βασιλέα ἐγκωμιαζόμενον ἕνα τῶν
νομέων, οἷον συβώτην, ἢ ποιμένα, ἤ τινα βουκόλον

1. ὅπερ ἀρχόμενος ἔλεγον] These words refer only to δημοσίᾳ.

5. εἰς φρέατα] 'Into pitfalls and all manner of perplexity.' Supr. 165. τὸ λεγόμενον ἐν φρέατι συνέχεσθαι.

6. ἡ ἀσχημοσύνη] 'And the awkwardness of the position is terrible, and makes him seem no better than a fool.'

8. ἅτε] 'He cannot use personality in invective.'

12. τύραννον—ἐγκωμιαζόμενον] Governed by δοκεῖν, implied in δοκεῖν below.

13. ἕνα τῶν νομέων] Comp. the Politicus, p. 266, where this is regarded as the most universal conception of the kingly office. Regarding ποιμενική as a whole, the philosopher thinks of βασι-λική only as a part of it. ὅτι τῇ τοιᾷδε μεθόδῳ τῶν λόγων οὔτε σε-μνοτέραν μᾶλλον ἐμέλησεν ἢ μή, τῶν τε σμικροτέρων οὐδὲν ἠτίμασε πρὸ τοῦ μείζονος, ἀεὶ δὲ καθ' αὑτὸν περαίνει τἀληθέστατον. Soph. 227.

τῇ τῶν λόγων μεθόδῳ συγγραμματικῆ ἢ φαρμακοποσίας οὐδὲν ἧττον οὐδέ τι μᾶλλον τυγχάνει μέλον, εἰ τὸ μὲν σμικρὰ τὸ δὲ μεγάλα ὠφελεῖ ἡμᾶς καθαῖρον. τοῦ γὰρ κτήσασθαι ἕνεκα νοῦν πασῶν τεχνῶν τὸ ξυγγενὲς καὶ τὸ μὴ ξυγγενὲς κατανοεῖν πει-ρωμένη τιμᾷ πρὸς τοῦτο ἐξ ἴσου πάσας, καὶ θάτερα τῶν ἑτέρων κατὰ τὴν ὁμοιότητα οὐδὲν ἡγεῖται γελοι-ότερα, σεμνότερον δέ τι τὸν διὰ στρατηγικῆς ἢ φθειριστικῆς δη-λοῦντα θηρευτικὴν οὐδὲν νενόμικεν ἀλλ' ὡς τὸ πολὺ χαυνότερον.—The latter passage has also a slight tinge of the irony of the text. The figure probably originated in some saying of Socrates. Compare Xen. Mem. l. 2. § 32: ὅτι θαυμαστὸν οἱ δοκοίη εἶναι, εἴ τις γενόμενος βοῶν ἀγέλης ἐπιμελητὴς καὶ τὰς βοῦς ἐλάττους τε καὶ χείρους ποιῶν μὴ ὁμολογοίη ἑαυτὸν βουκόλον εἶναι. Ib. § 38: Ὁ δὲ Κριτίας· Ἀλλὰ τωνδί τοί σε ἀπέχεσθαι δεήσει, τῶν σκυτέων καὶ τῶν τεκτόνων καὶ

ΘΕΑΙΤΗΤΟΣ. 107

p. 174. ἡγεῖται ἀκούειν εὐδαιμονιζόμενον πολὺ βδάλλοντα· δυσκολώτερον δὲ ἐκείνων ζῶον καὶ ἐπιβουλότερον ποιμαίνειν τε καὶ βδάλλειν νομίζει αὐτούς· ἄγροικον δὲ καὶ ἀπαίδευτον ὑπὸ ἀσχολίας οὐδὲν ἧττον τῶν νομέων τὸν τοιοῦτον ἀναγκαῖον γίγνεσθαι, σηκὸν ἐν ὄρει τὸ τεῖχος περιβεβλημένον. γῆς δὲ ὅταν μυρία πλέθρα ἢ ἔτι πλείω ἀκούσῃ ὥς τις ἄρα κεκτημένος θαυμαστὰ πλήθει κέκτηται, πάνσμικρα δοκεῖ ἀκούειν εἰς ἅπασαν εἰωθὼς τὴν γῆν βλέπειν. τὰ δὲ δὴ γένη ὑμνούντων, ὡς γενναῖός τις ἑπτὰ πάππους πλουσίους ἔχων ἀποφῆναι, παντάπασιν ἀμβλὺ καὶ ἐπὶ σμικρὸν
p. 175. ὁρώντων ἡγεῖται τὸν ἔπαινον, ὑπὸ ἀπαιδευσίας οὐ δυναμένων εἰς τὸ πᾶν ἀεὶ βλέπειν οὐδὲ λογίζεσθαι ὅτι πάππων καὶ προγόνων μυριάδες ἑκάστῳ γεγόνασιν ἀναρίθμητοι, ἐν αἷς πλούσιοι καὶ πτωχοὶ καὶ βασιλεῖς καὶ δοῦλοι βάρβαροί τε καὶ Ἕλληνες πολ-

τῶν χαλεπῶν.—Ναὶ μὰ Δί᾿, ἔφη ὁ Σωκράτης, καὶ τῶν βουκολίων γε· εἰ δὲ μὴ φυλάττοιτο, ὅσοι μὴ καὶ σὺ ἐλάττους τὰς βοῦς ταύτης.

1. πολὺ βδάλλοντα] Lit., As being rich in milk, i. e. sucking out no small advantage. Compare the speeches of Thrasymachus in Rep. B. 1.

2. ἐκείνων] masculine.

3. ποιμαίνειν τε καὶ βδάλλειν] 'Only he thinks the creature whom they tend, and out of whom they squeeze their wealth, to be of a less tractable and more insidious nature.'

ἄγροικον δὲ) 'rough and uncivilized from stress of work'—

10. ὑμνούντων] 'And when they cant of pedigree'—

11. πανταπασιν ἀμβλὺ—ὁρώντων] 'Betraying a dull and contracted vision'—

14. ὅτι πάππων καὶ προγόνων] Compare the comic fragment ascribed to Epicharmus or Menander. (Krüsemann's Epicharmus, 119.)

Ἀπολεῖ με τὸ γένος μή λέγ᾽, εἰ φιλεῖς ἐμέ,
Μήτερ, ἐφ᾽ ἑκάστῳ τὸ γένος οἷς ἂν τῇ φύσει
Ἀγαθὸν ὑπάρχῃ μηδὲν οἰκεῖον κρατόν,
Ἐκείνοι καταφεύγουσιν εἰς τὰ μνήματα,
Καὶ τὸ γένος, ἀριθμοῦσίν τε τοὺς πάππους ὅσοι.
Οὐδ᾽ ἔστι δ᾽ ἔχεις ἰδεῖν ἄν, οὐδ᾽ εἰπεῖν, ὅτῳ
Οὐκ εἰσὶ πάππου· πῶς γὰρ ἠγνόουν ἂν εἰσί; κ. τ. λ.

μυριάδες ἀναρίθμητοι] This expression recurs frequently in later Greek authors.

16. βάρβαροί τε καὶ Ἕλληνες] These words belong to all the preceding nouns.

108 ΠΛΑΤΩΝΟΣ

λάκις μυρίοι γεγόνασιν ότφοῦν, ἀλλ' ἐπὶ πέντε καὶ p. 175.
εἴκοσι καταλόγῳ προγόνων σεμνυνομένων καὶ ἀναφερόντων εἰς Ἡρακλέα τὸν Ἀμφιτρύωνος ἄτοπα αὐτῷ
καταφαίνεται τῆς σμικρολογίας, ὅτι δὲ ὁ ἀπ' Ἀμφι-
5 τρύωνος εἰς τὸ ἄνω πεντεκαιεικοστὸς τοιοῦτος ἦν, οἷα b
συνέβαινεν αὐτῷ τύχη, καὶ ὁ πεντηκοστὸς ἀπ' αὐτοῦ,
γελᾷ οὐ δυναμένων λογίζεσθαί τε καὶ χαυνότητα
ἀνοήτου ψυχῆς ἀπαλλάττειν. ἐν ἅπασι δὴ τούτοις ὁ
τοιοῦτος ὑπὸ τῶν πολλῶν καταγελᾶται, τὰ μὲν ὑπερ-
10 ηφάνως ἔχων, ὡς δοκεῖ, τὰ δ' ἐν ποσὶν ἀγνοῶν τε καὶ
ἐν ἑκάστοις ἀπορῶν.

ΘΕΟ. Παντάπασι τὰ γιγνόμενα λέγεις, ὦ Σώκρατες.

1. *ἐπὶ πέντε καὶ εἴκοσι*) The order is ἐπὶ καταλόγῳ πέντε καὶ εἴκοσι προγόνων.

2. *ἀναφερόντων*) Sc. τὸ γένος. The genitives depend upon σμικρολογίας, or rather, more vaguely, upon the sense of the words ἀν. ε. αυτ. τ. σμικρ., as δυναμένων upon γελᾷ below,—ταῦτα in καταφαίνεται being probably used in its condemnatory sense.

3. ἄτοπα—τῆς σμικρολογίας] The genitive is not quite analogous to ἀμήχανον εὐδαιμονίας, Ap. 41., which is rather quantitative: nor is it exactly equivalent to ἄτοπος ἡ σμικρολογία, (like ἀσημα—βοῆς,—φώτων ἀθλίων ἰστόρια, in Sophocles), though as in these last cases the adjective is isolated for the sake of emphasis, but the genitive has the additional meaning, 'in respect of,' as after interjections and epithets. Cf. Protagor. 317 : πολλὴ μωρία καὶ τῶν ἐπιχειρημάτων. Rep. 328. χαλεπῶν τοῦ βίου (for its way of life !) Rep. 532 : νέφαντλο ἔργων λέγεις. τοῦ προσωμίου, ἦν δ' ἐγώ ; Phaed. 99 : πολλὴ ἄν καὶ μακρὰ ῥᾳθυμία ἄν εἴη τοῦ λόγου.

The whole sense lies somewhere between συνυνομένων καὶ ἀναφέροντες—ἄτοπα φαίνονται τῆς σμικρ. and σεμνυνομένων καὶ ἀναφέροντων—ἄτοπα φαίνεται ἡ σμικρολογία.

5. *οἷα συνέβ.*] The Bodl. reads οἷα συνέβαινεν αὐτῷ τύχῃ. Perhaps rightly. The meaning in both cases is the same. 'He was,—what Fortune made him.'

6. *ἀπ' αὐτοῦ*] Sc. τοῦ πεντεκαιεικοστοῦ. Compare Rep. 515, 6 : Εἰ δ', ἦν δ' ἐγώ, ἐντεῦθεν ἧκοι τις αὐτὸν βίᾳ διὰ τραχείας τῆς ἀναβάσεως καὶ ἀνάντους, καὶ μὴ ἀνείη πρὶν ἐξελκύσειε πρὸς τὸ τοῦ ἡλίου φῶς, ἆρα οὐχὶ ὀδυνᾶσθαί τε ἂν καὶ ἀγανακτεῖν ἑλκόμενον, καὶ ἐπειδὴ πρὸς τὸ φῶς ἔλθοι, αὐγῆς ἂν ἔχοντα τὰ ὄμματα μεστὰ ὁρᾶν αὐτ' ἂν ἓν δύνασθαι τῶν νῦν λεγομένων ἀληθῶν.

ΘΕΑΙΤΗΤΟΣ. 109

p. 175. ΣΩ. Ὅταν δέ γέ τινα αὐτός, ὦ φίλε, ἑλκύσῃ ἄνω, ο καὶ ἐθελήσῃ τις αὐτῷ ἐκβῆναι ἐκ τοῦ Τί ἐγώ σὲ ἀδικῶ ἢ σὺ ἐμέ; εἰς σκέψιν αὐτῆς δικαιοσύνης τε καὶ ἀδικίας, τί τε ἑκάτερον αὐτοῖν καὶ τί τῶν πάντων ἢ ἀλλήλων διαφέρετον; ἢ ἐκ τοῦ Εἰ βασιλεὺς εὐδαίμων 5 κεκτημένος τ' αὖ πολὺ χρυσίον, βασιλείας πέρι καὶ ἀνθρωπίνης ὅλως εὐδαιμονίας καὶ ἀθλιότητος ἐπὶ σκέψιν, ποίω τέ τινε ἐστὸν καὶ τίνα τρόπον ἀνθρώπου φύσει προσήκει τὸ μὲν κτήσασθαι αὐτοῖν, τὸ δὲ ἀποφυγεῖν,—περὶ τούτων ἁπάντων ὅταν αὖ δέῃ λόγον 10
d διδόναι τὸν σμικρὸν ἐκεῖνον τὴν ψυχὴν καὶ δριμὺν

1. τινα—τινι] The indefinites are used with an indirect reference to the philosopher and to τὸν σμικρὸν ἐκεῖνον καὶ δριμὺν καὶ δικανικόν below.

5. Εἰ βασιλεὺς εὐδαίμων] See the passage of the Gorgias (p. 471.), in which Polus contends that Archelaus is happy. (Diog. mentions a diatribe of Antisthenes, called 'Αρχέλαος, ἢ περὶ βασιλείας, in which Gorgias was assailed.)

Buttmann thus defends εἰ, which three MSS. omit:— "Quamvis certum exploratumque haberent vulgares illi oratores, regem propter divitias suas unice beatum putandum esse, tamen rem ita in encomiis tractabant, ut, quasi dubia ea videri posset, multis cum exemplis argumentisque probarent. Quidni igitur v. c. encomii alicujus in Croesum argumentum his verbis indicari potuerit; εἰ Κροῖσος εὐδαίμων;" It may be questioned, however, whether ἢ βασ. might not give a better meaning.

In the words which follow, τι seems to impede the sense, and αὖ is superfluous. If Plato is really quoting from a rhetorician, this is possibly not a fatal objection, though the conjectures πάσιν πολύ, πάμπολυ, (Heind. Hirschig. Badh.) would seem probable. Possibly, however, the words βασιλείας—χρυσίον are adapted from some poet. (Cf. Theogn. εὐδαίμων εἴην, καὶ θεοῖς φίλος ἀθανάτοισιν, Κύρν', ἀρετῆς δ' ἄλλης οὐδεμιᾶς ἔραμαι.) In which case γὰρ συλλύχνευον is perhaps the true reading. For κεκτημένος in such an adaptation, cf. (besides Protag. 340., quoted above), the quotation of Tyrtaeus in the Laws, p. 629: οὔτ' ἂν μνησαίμην οὔτ' ἐν λόγῳ ἄνδρα τιθείμην, οὔτ' εἰ πλουσιώτατος ἀνθρώπων εἴη, φησίν, οὔτ' εἰ πολλὰ ἀγαθὰ κεκτημένος, εἰπὼν σχεδὸν ἅπαντα, κ. τ. λ.

There is a close parallel between the present passage and page 174. τοιγάροντι κ. τ. λ.

Cf. τί ἐγὼ σὲ ἀδικῶ, with ἐν δικαστηρίῳ—διαγκασθῇ λέγειν: ἢ σὺ ἐμέ, with ἐν ταῖς λοιδορίαις: εἰ (or ἢ) βασιλεύς—with τύραννόν τε γάρ—.

7. ἐπὶ σκέψιν] MSS. ἐπίσκεψιν.

110   ΠΛΑΤΩΝΟΣ

καὶ δικανικόν, πάλιν αὖ τὰ ἀντίστροφα ἀποδίδωσιν. p. 175.
ἰλιγγιῶν τε ἀφ' ὑψηλοῦ κρεμασθεὶς καὶ βλέπων μετέωρος ἄνωθεν ὑπὸ ἀηθείας, ἀδημονῶν τε καὶ ἀπορῶν
καὶ βαρβαρίζων, γέλωτα Θρᾴτταις μὲν οὐ παρέχει οὐδ᾽
5 ἄλλῳ ἀπαιδεύτῳ οὐδενί, οὐ γὰρ αἰσθάνονται, τοῖς δ᾽
ἐναντίως ἢ ὡς ἀνδραπόδοις τραφεῖσιν ἅπασιν. Οὗτος
δὴ ἑκατέρου τρόπος, ὦ Θεόδωρε, ὁ μὲν τῷ ὄντι ἐν
ἐλευθερίᾳ τε καὶ σχολῇ τεθραμμένου, ὃν δὴ φιλόσο- c
φον καλεῖς, ᾧ ἀνεμέσητον εὐήθει δοκεῖν καὶ οὐδενὶ
10 εἶναι, ὅταν εἰς δουλικὰ ἐμπέσῃ διακονήματα, οἷον
στρωματόδεσμον μὴ ἐπισταμένου συσκευάσασθαι
μηδὲ ὄψον ἡδῦναι ἢ θῶπας λόγους· ὁ δ᾽ αὖ τὰ μὲν
τοιαῦτα πάντα δυναμένου τορῶς τε καὶ ὀξέως διακονεῖν, ἀναβάλλεσθαι δὲ οὐκ ἐπισταμένου ἐπιδέξια

Those that dwarfed shrewd legal mind is puzzled in its turn, and becomes a laughing-stock not to the uneducated, but to the wise and free. The philosopher may be well con-

2. Ἰλιγγιῶν τε] 'He gives the philosopher his revenge; (for) dizzied by the height where he finds himself hanging by a thread, and from which he looks downwards into space, (a strange experience to him), and being dismayed and lost, and broken in his utterance, he is laughed at, not by Thracian handmaids, nor by any other of the uneducated, for they do not perceive his plight; but by all whose nurture has been the reverse of servile.'

The sentence probably divides after ἀηθείας, and ἀδημονῶν τε answers to ἰλιγγιῶν τε. (ἰλιγγιῶν τε. γάρ add. Ven. Σ. This is quite unnecessary.)

9. ᾧ ἀνεμέσητον] 'Who may, without our surprise or censure, appear simple and a mere cipher, when some menial service is required of him, if he has no skill, for instance, in tying up bed-clothes with the proper knot, nor in flavouring a sauce, or a fawning speech :— the other character is that of the man who is able to do all such service with smartness and dispatch, but has not the skill to throw his cloak over his right shoulder with a gentlemanly grace; no, nor to celebrate aright with the music of discourse, in his turn, that life which is lived in truth by the immortals and by heaven-favoured men.'

11. ἐπισταμένου] So Bodl. Vat. Ven. Π. ἐπιστάμενος cett.

13. τορῶς] 'Smartly.' ἄτε δραμὼν ἂν.

14. ἀναβάλλεσθαι—ἐπιδέξια]'Probably,' to wear his garment over his right shoulder in a gentlemanly fashion.' Aristoph. Av. 1566: οὗτος, τί δρᾷς; ἐπ᾽ ἀριστέρ᾽ οὕτως ἀμπέχει; οὐ μεταβαλεῖς θοἰμάτιον ὧδ᾽ ἐπὶ δεξιά; Cf. Hor.

ΘΕΑΙΤΗΤΟΣ. 111

p. 176. ἐλευθέρως οὐδέ γ' ἁρμονίαν λόγων λαβόντος ὀρθῶς ὑμνῆσαι θεῶν τε καὶ ἀνδρῶν εὐδαιμόνων βίον ἀληθῆ.

ΘΕΟ. Εἰ πάντας, ὦ Σώκρατες, πείθοις ἃ λέγεις ὥσπερ ἐμέ, πλείων ἂν εἰρήνη καὶ κακὰ ἐλάττω κατ' ἀνθρώπους εἴη.

ΣΩ. 'Αλλ' οὔτ' ἀπολέσθαι τὰ κακὰ δυνατόν, ὦ Θεόδωρε· ὑπεναντίον γάρ τι τῷ ἀγαθῷ ἀεὶ εἶναι ἀνάγκη· οὔτ' ἐν θεοῖς αὐτὰ ἱδρῦσθαι, τὴν δὲ θνητὴν

best known unskilled in servile arts, in comparison with those who are dumb in the highest music of the soul.

Ep. I. § 96. si toga dissidet impar, Rides. Quid, mea cum pugnat sententia secum? A possible rendering at first sight is, 'to strike up the song in his turn.' Vid. οὐδέ γ' ἁρμονίαν λαβόντα, and cf. Rep. 420: κατακλίναντες ἐπὶ δεξιὰ πρὸς τὸ πῦρ διαπίνουσιν. Symp. 177: εἰπεῖν ἕκαστον Ἔρωτος ἐπὶ δεξιά. But one person could hardly be said to sing ἐπὶ δεξιά, and the antithesis requires the other rendering. The slave can tuck in bed-clothes, the freeman wears his garment with a grace. The slaves' contribution to the banquet is literally ἄγειν ᾠδῶν, figuratively θῶνται λόγοισι ᾠδ. (Cf. Gorg. 465: τὴν ῥητορικὴν—ἀντίστροφον ὀψοποιίας ἐν ψυχῇ ὡς ἐκείνη ἐν σώματι.) The 'freeman's' is literally the lyre and song; in a higher sense, discourse of philosophy and virtue. This is his proper ἔργον. Cf. Symp. 177., where the minstrel is dismissed, and Eryximachus proposes that they should discourse of the praises of love. δοκεῖ γάρ μοι χρῆναι ἕκαστον ἡμῶν λόγον εἰπεῖν ἕκαστον Ἔρωτος ἐπὶ δεξιὰ ὡς ἂν δύνηται κάλλιστον. v. Prot. 347. There is a further 'harmony'

between the discourse and life of the philosopher. Lach. 188: καὶ κομιδῇ μοι δοκεῖ μουσικὸς ὁ τοιοῦτος εἶναι, ἁρμονίαν κάλλιστην ἡρμοσμένος οὐ λύραν οὐδὲ παιδιᾶς ὄργανα, ἀλλὰ τῷ ὄντι ζῆν ἡρμοσμένος αὐτὸς αὑτοῦ τὸν βίον ξύμφωνον τοῖς λόγοις πρὸς τὰ ἔργα, ἀτεχνῶς δωριστὶ ἀλλ' οὐκ ἰαστί, οἴομαι δὲ οὐδὲ φρυγιστὶ οὐδὲ λυδιστί, ἀλλ' ἥπερ μόνη Ἑλληνική ἐστιν ἁρμονία.

There is an allusion to the well-known custom of taking the lyre in turn. θείους λόγους is perhaps rightly supposed by Ruhnk. ad Tim. p. 146. to be a poetical expression, quoted probably from Euripides or Epicharmus.

2. θεῶν τε καὶ ἀνδρῶν εὐδαιμόνων βίον ἀληθῆ] There is a rhythmical cadence in the words, cf. Phaedr. 261: πάρετε δή, θρέμματα γενναῖα, καλλίπαιδά τε Φαίδρον πείθετε. Rep. 617: Λαχέσεως θυγατρὸς κόρης Λαχέσεως λόγος κ. τ. λ. Symp. 197. the end of Agathon's speech.

7. ὑπεναντίον γάρ] Compare the saying of Heraclitus, παλίντονος ἁρμονία κόσμου ὥσπερ τόξου καὶ λύρας. The prep. conveys the idea of 'bearing up against.'

ΠΛΑΤΩΝΟΣ

φύσιν καὶ τόνδε τὸν τόπον περιπολεῖ ἐξ ἀνάγκης. p. 176.
διὸ καὶ πειρᾶσθαι χρὴ ἐνθένδε ἐκεῖσε φεύγειν ὅ τι
τάχιστα. φυγὴ δὲ ὁμοίωσις θεῷ κατὰ τὸ δυνατόν· b
ὁμοίωσις δὲ δίκαιον καὶ ὅσιον μετὰ φρονήσεως γενέ-

Men will not hear

1. τόνδε τὸν τόπον] viz. τὸν σωματοειδῆ τε καὶ ὁρατὸν τόπον. Rep. 532. The imagery of place in which Plato's philosophy is enfolded appears most prominently in the Phædo, the Phædrus, and Rep. B. VI. and VII.

The notion that evil must exist in everything but the Divine Nature reappears in a curious mythical form in the Politicus, p. 270. and is implied Tim. 87: τὰ δὲ περὶ ψυχήν (sc. νοσήματα) διὰ σώματος ἕξιν κ.τ.λ. Ib. 69: ξυγκερασάμενοί τ' αὐτὰ ἀναγκαίως τὸ θνητὸν γένος ξυνέθεσαν. In the Phædo evil is almost identified with the bodily principle. Our ignorance on the subject is, however, confessed in the Lysis, p. 220, 1: νέμεσαν, ἦν δ' ἐγώ, ἕως τὸ κακὸν ἀπέλυμεν, οὐδὲ εἰσορᾶν ἔτι ἔσται οὐδὲ διψῆν οὐδ' ἄλλο οὐδὲν τῶν τοιούτων;—ἢ γελοῖον τὸ ἐρώτημα, ὅ τί ποτ' ἔσται τότε ἢ μὴ ἔσται; τίς γὰρ οἶδεν;

3. φυγὴ δὲ ὁμοίωσις θεῷ] Phædr. 252, 3: ἰχνεύοντες δὲ παρ' ἑαυτῶν ἀνευρίσκειν τὴν τοῦ σφετέρου θεοῦ φύσιν, εὐποροῦσι διὰ τὸ συντόνως ἠναγκάσθαι πρὸς τὸν θεὸν βλέπειν, καὶ ἐφαπτόμενοι αὐτοῦ τῇ μνήμῃ, ἐνθουσιῶντες, ἐξ ἐκείνου λαμβάνουσι τὰ ἔθη καὶ τὰ ἐπιτηδεύματα, καθ' ὅσον δυνατὸν θεοῦ ἀνθρώπῳ μετασχεῖν.

Rep. 613: οὐ γὰρ δὴ ὑπό γε θεῶν ποτὲ ἀμελεῖται, ὃς ἂν προθυμεῖσθαι ἐθέλῃ δίκαιος γίγνεσθαι καὶ ἐπιτηδεύων ἀρετὴν εἰς ὅσον δυνατὸν ἀνθρώπῳ ὁμοιοῦσθαι θεῷ. Ibid. 500: Οὐδὲ γάρ που, ὦ Ἀδείμαντε, σχολὴ τῷ γε ὡς ἀληθῶς πρὸς τοῖς οὖσι τὴν διάνοιαν ἔχοντι κάτω βλέπειν εἰς ἀνθρώπων πραγματείας καὶ μαχόμενον αὐτοῖς φθόνου τε καὶ δυσμενείας ἐμπίπλασθαι, ἀλλ' εἰς τεταγμένα ἄττα καὶ κατὰ ταὐτὰ ἀεὶ ἔχοντα ὁρῶντας καὶ θεωμένους οὔτ' ἀδικοῦντα οὔτ' ἀδικούμενα ὑπ' ἀλλήλων, κόσμῳ δὲ πάντα καὶ κατὰ λόγον ἔχοντα, ταῦτα μιμεῖσθαί τε καὶ ὅ τι μάλιστα ἀφομοιοῦσθαι. Phæd. 107: νῦν δὲ ἐπειδὴ ἀθάνατος φαίνεται οὖσα, οὐδεμία ἂν εἴη αὐτῇ ἄλλη ἀποφυγὴ κακῶν οὐδὲ σωτηρία πλὴν τοῦ ὡς βελτίστην τε καὶ φρονιμωτάτην γενέσθαι. Tim. 90: τῷ δὲ περὶ φιλομαθίαν καὶ περὶ τὰς ἀληθεῖς φρονήσεις ἐσπουδακότι καὶ ταῦτα μάλιστα τῶν αὑτοῦ γεγυμνασμένῳ φρονεῖν μὲν ἀθάνατα καὶ θεῖα, ἄνπερ ἀληθείας ἐφάπτηται, πᾶσα ἀνάγκη που, καθ' ὅσον δ' αὖ μετασχεῖν ἀνθρωπίνῃ φύσις ἀθανασίας ἐνδέχεται, τούτου μηδὲν μέρος ἀπολείπειν—διὰ τὸ ἀεὶ θεραπεύοντα τὸ θεῖον ἔχοντά τε εὖ κεκοσμημένον τὸν δαίμονα σύνοικον ἑαυτῷ διαφερόντως εὐδαίμονα εἶναι.

4. ὁμοίωσις δὲ] 'And to be made like to Him is to become righteous and holy, not without wisdom.'

μετὰ φρονήσεως] Is virtue possible apart from knowledge? This question is discussed in the Protagoras and the Meno. The answer given is, that practically it would appear so, but that virtue can be

ΘΕΑΙΤΗΤΟΣ. 113

p. 176. σθαι. ἀλλὰ γάρ, ὦ ἄριστε, οὐ πάνυ ῥᾴδιον πεῖσαι ὡς ἄρα οὐχ ὧν ἕνεκα οἱ πολλοί φασι δεῖν πονηρίαν μὲν φεύγειν, ἀρετὴν δὲ διώκειν, τούτων χάριν τὸ μὲν ἐπιτηδευτέον, τὸ δ' οὔ, ἵνα δὴ μὴ κακὸς καὶ ἵνα ἀγαθὸς δοκῇ εἶναι. ταῦτα γάρ ἐστιν ὁ λεγόμενος γραῶν ὕθλος, ὡς ἐμοὶ φαίνεται. τὸ δὲ ἀληθὲς ὧδε λέγωμεν.
e θεὸς οὐδαμῇ οὐδαμῶς ἄδικος, ἀλλ' ὡς οἷόν τε δικαιότατος, καὶ οὐκ ἔστιν αὐτῷ ὁμοιότερον οὐδὲν ἢ ὃς ἂν

this for there must be some evil to resist the good, and this cannot be in heaven, but in this lower world. Our wisdom therefore is to escape heaven.

proved to be inseparable from knowledge. And in the Meno the paradox is solved by saying that practical virtue is a Divine gift, θείᾳ μοίρᾳ παραγιγνομένη ἄνευ νοῦ, but that if there should be a virtuous man who could teach virtue, he would be like Tiresias amongst the shades; ὥσπερ παρὰ σκιὰς ἀληθὲς ἂν πρᾶγμα εἴη πρὸς ἀρετήν. In the more dialectical dialogues one side of the contradiction disappears, and it is assumed that philosophy is essential to real virtue. Phaed. 69: ὦ μακάριε Σιμμία, μὴ γὰρ οὐχ αὕτη ᾖ ἡ ὀρθὴ πρὸς ἀρετὴν ἀλλαγή, ἡδονὰς πρὸς ἡδονὰς καὶ λύπας πρὸς λύπας καὶ φόβον πρὸς φόβον καταλλάττεσθαι——ἀλλ' ᾖ ἐκεῖνο τὸ νόμισμα ὀρθόν,——φρόνησις,——καὶ ξυλλαβδὴν ἀληθὴς ἀρετὴ ᾖ μετὰ φρονήσεως.——χωριζόμενα δὲ φρονήσεως καὶ ἀλλαττόμενα ἀντὶ ἀλλήλων, μὴ σκιαγραφία τις ᾖ ἡ τοιαύτη ἀρετή, κ.τ.λ. In the Republic it is again acknowledged that it is possible to partake of virtue without philosophy, but in an imperfect way; e. g. in the case of the soul which laments its choice of another life. P. 619: εἶπας δὲ αὐτὸν τῶν ἐκ τοῦ οὐρανοῦ ἡκόντων, ἐν τεταγμένῃ πολιτείᾳ ἐν τῷ προτέρῳ βίῳ βεβιω-

κότα, ἔθει ἄνευ φιλοσοφίας ἀρετῆς μετειληφότα. And the education of the φύλακες generally (not of the rulers) is independent of reason, though in harmony with it. Rep. 401, 2. (In the Philebus also the perfect life contains the knowledge of practical things. The philosopher must know his way home.) Thus the contradiction felt at first is reconciled by acknowledging the existence of different parts of our nature, which, though connected, and indispensable to each other's perfection, are not identical. There is a slight emphasis on μετὰ φρονήσεως in opposition to what follows.

4. ἵνα——δοκῇ εἶναι——ἀγνοοῦσι γὰρ [ζημίαν ἀδικίας] The whole of this passage is parallel to the speeches of Glaucon and Adimantus in the 2nd book of the Republic, and the same thought is differently worked out in the Gorgias.

5. ὁ λεγόμενος γραῶν ὕθλος] 'This is what men commonly repeat, an old wives' fable, it appears to me.' The meaning of λεγόμενος here (not as 'as the saying is') seems determined by λέγωμεν following.

Q

114   ΠΛΑΤΩΝΟΣ

wink, by becoming just and pure with wisdom, in becoming like to God.

ἡμῶν αὖ γένηται ὅ τι δικαιότατος. περὶ τούτου καὶ ἡ p.176. ὡς ἀληθῶς δεινότης ἀνδρὸς καὶ οὐδενία τε καὶ ἀναυ- δρία. ἡ ·μὲν γὰρ τούτου γνῶσις σοφία καὶ ἀρετὴ ἀληθινή, ἡ δὲ ἄγνοια ἀμαθία καὶ κακία ἐναργής· αἱ
5 δ' ἄλλαι δεινότητές τε δοκοῦσαι καὶ σοφίαι ἐν μὲν πολιτικαῖς δυναστείαις γιγνόμεναι φορτικαί, ἐν δὲ τέχναις βάναυσοι. τῷ οὖν ἀδικοῦντι καὶ ἀνόσια λέ-

This is a man's true 'cleverness' and proof of virtue. And the real penalty of vice is one which cannot be escaped by clever shifts. For to act wrongly is to be removed from the Divine pattern, and to be brought nearer to the likeness of the Evil.

γοντι ἢ πράττοντι μακρῷ ἄριστ' ἔχει τὸ μὴ συγχω- d ρεῖν δεινῷ ὑπὸ πανουργίας εἶναι. ἀγάλλονται γὰρ
10 τῷ ὀνείδει, καὶ οἴονται ἀκούειν ὅτι οὐ ληροί εἰσι, γῆς ἄλλως ἄχθη, ἀλλ' ἄνδρες οἵους δεῖ ἐν πόλει τοὺς σωθησομένους. λεκτέον οὖν τἀληθές, ὅτι τοσούτῳ μᾶλλόν εἰσιν οἷοι οὐκ οἴονται, ὅτι οὐχὶ οἴονται· ἀγνο- οῦσι γὰρ ζημίαν ἀδικίας, ὃ δεῖ ἥκιστα ἀγνοεῖν. οὐ
15 γάρ ἐστιν ἣν δοκοῦσι, πληγαί τε καὶ θάνατοι, ὧν ἐνίοτε πάσχουσιν οὐδὲν ἀδικοῦντες, ἀλλὰ ἣν ἀδύνατον ἐκφυγεῖν.

ΘΕΟ. Τίνα δὴ λέγεις ;
ΣΩ. Παραδειγμάτων, ὦ φίλε, ἐν τῷ ὄντι ἑστώτων,

1. περὶ τούτου] 'Moreover a man's real ability, or else his nothingness and want of manhood, is concerned with this.' The genitive is accounted for by the vagueness of the relation expressed. ἀναυδρία is suggested by ἀνδρός.

6. φορτικαί—βάναυσοι] 'vulgar'—'mechanical,' or 'mean.'

7. τῷ οὖν ἀδικοῦντι, κ. τ. λ.] This very favourite thought is developed in the Gorgias.

9. ὑπὸ πανουργίας] 'Not to admit that villany constitutes him a clever man.'

10. οὐ ληροί] 'that they are not mere absurdities, cumbering the ground ;'—' not sole-

cisms,' as Carlyle might say.

γῆς ἄλλως ἄχθη] ἐτώσιον ἄχθος ἀρούρης (Il. XVIII. 104., quoted Διοl. p. 28.) Aristoph. Nub. 1203: περίβοστ' ἄλλως.—Milton, Areopag. : 'Many a man lives a burden to the Earth.'

ληροι] Charm. 176. ἐμὶ μὲν ληροῖν ἡγεῖσθαι εἶναι καὶ ἀδύνατον λόγῳ ὁτιοῦν ζητεῖν. Phaed. 72 : τελευτῶντα πάντα ληροῦ τὸν Ἐνδυμίωνα ἀποδείξειε καὶ οὐδαμοῦ ἂν φαίνοιτο.

11. τοὺς σωθησομένους] Who deserve to live in it, i. e. for whose interest the laws are to be made. Cf. Soph. Ant. 189 : ἧδ' ἐστὶν ἡ σώζουσα.

19. παραδειγμάτων] Cf. Rep.

ΘΕΑΙΤΗΤΟΣ.

p. 176. τοῦ μὲν θείου εὐδαιμονεστάτου, τοῦ δὲ ἀθέου ἀθλιωτάτου, οὐχ ὁρῶντες ὅτι οὕτως ἔχει, ὑπὸ ἠλιθιότητός τε καὶ τῆς ἐσχάτης ἀνοίας λανθάνουσι τῷ μὲν ὁμοι-
p. 177. ούμενοι διὰ τὰς ἀδίκους πράξεις, τῷ δὲ ἀνομοιούμενοι. οὗ δὴ τίνουσι δίκην ζῶντες τὸν εἰκότα βίον ᾧ ὁμοιοῦνται. ἐὰν δ' εἴπωμεν ὅτι, ἂν μὴ ἀπαλλαγῶσι τῆς δεινότητος, καὶ τελευτήσαντας αὐτοὺς ἐκεῖνος μὲν ὁ τῶν κακῶν καθαρὸς τόπος οὐ δέξεται, ἐνθάδε δὲ τὴν αὑτοῖς ὁμοιότητα τῆς διαγωγῆς ἀεὶ ἕξουσι, κακοὶ κακοῖς συνόντες, ταῦτα δὴ καὶ παντάπασιν ὡς δεινοὶ καὶ 10 πανοῦργοι ἀνοήτων τινῶν ἀκούσονται.

ΘΕΟ. Καὶ μάλα δή, ὦ Σώκρατες.

b ΣΩ. Οἶδά τοι, ὦ ἑταῖρε. ἐν μέντοι τι αὐτοῖς συμ-

The soul that does so will not be received at death into the region pure from evils.—They will laugh at this, and call us simpletons. But if they would consent to remain with us, they would ere long become confused and silent, and their fluent rhetoric would fade away, leav-

592 : 'Ἀλλ', ἦν δ' ἐγώ, ἐν οὐρανῷ ἴσως παράδειγμα ἀνάκειται τῷ βουλομένῳ ὁρᾶν καὶ ὁρῶντι ἑαυτὸν κατοικίζειν.

1. τοῦ ἀθέου] 'From which the Divine has fled.'

6. τῆς δεινότητος] 'From this cleverness which is their boast.'

8. τῶν κακῶν καθαρὸν] Vid. πλάνης καὶ ἀνοίας καὶ φόβων καὶ ἀγρίων ἐρώτων καὶ τῶν ἄλλων κακῶν τῶν ἀνθρωπείων. Phaed. 81.

καθαρόν) Phaed. 83. ἐν γὰρ τοῦ ὁμοδοξεῖν τῷ σώματι καὶ τοῖς αὑτοῖς χαίρειν ἀναγκάζεται, οἶμαι, ὁμότροπός τε καὶ ὁμότροφος γίγνεσθαι καὶ οἵα μηδέποτε καθαρῶς εἰς Ἅιδου ἀφίκεσθαι ἀλλ' ἀεὶ τοῦ σώματος ἀναπλέα ἐξιέναι, ὥστε ταχὺ πάλιν πίπτειν εἰς ἄλλο σῶμα καὶ ὥσπερ σπειρομένη ἐμφύεσθαι, καὶ ἐκ τούτων ἄμοιρον εἶναι τῆς τοῦ θείου τε καὶ καθαροῦ καὶ μονοειδοῦς συνουσίας.

Ibid. 69 : καὶ ἡ σωφροσύνη κ. τ. λ. καὶ αὐτή ἡ φρόνησις μὴ καθαρμός τις ᾖ, καὶ αὐδυνώσεων καὶ αἱ τὰς τελετὰς—καταστήσαντες—

ἕνεκα αἰνίττεσθαι ὅτι ὃς ἂν ἀμύητος καὶ ἀτέλεστος εἰς Ἅιδου ἀφίκηται, ἐν βορβόρῳ κείσεται, ὁ δὲ κεκαθαρμένος τε καὶ τετελεσμένος ἐκεῖσε ἀφικόμενος μετὰ θεῶν οἰκήσει.

τὴν αὑτοῖς ὁμοιότητα τῆς διαγωγῆς] 'They will always retain their way of life like to themselves—evil as they are, associating with evil things'. κακοῖς is neut. Compare the well-known passage of the Phaedo, p. 81. 'Ἀλλὰ διειλημμένην γε, οἶμαι, ὑπὸ τοῦ σωματοειδοῦς κ. τ. λ. imitated by Milton, Comus, circ. v. 460 :

'The soul grows clotted by contagion,
Imbodies, and imbrutes, till she quite lose
The divine property of her first being.'

See especially the words κατὰ τὴν αὑτῶν ὁμοιότητα τῆς μελέτης.

10. καὶ τοσούτοις γε δεινοί] i. e. their feeling of superiority will only be confirmed.

13. Οἶδά τοι, ὦ ἑταῖρε] 'I am

Q 2

116   ΠΛΑΤΩΝΟΣ

ing them as helpless as a child. But we must return, and take up the broken thread of discussion

βέβηκεν, ὅτι ἂν ἰδίᾳ λόγον δέῃ δοῦναί τε καὶ δέξα- p.177. σθαι περὶ ὧν ψέγουσι, καὶ ἐθελήσωσιν ἀνδρικῶς πολὺν χρόνον ὑπομεῖναι καὶ μὴ ἀνάνδρως φεύγειν, τότε ἀτόπως, ὦ δαιμόνιε, τελευτῶντες οὐκ ἀρέσκουσιν
5 αὐτοὶ αὐτοῖς περὶ ὧν λέγουσι, καὶ ἡ ῥητορικὴ ἐκείνη πως ἀπομαραίνεται, ὥστε παίδων μηδὲν δοκεῖν διαφέρειν. Περὶ μὲν οὖν τούτων, ἐπειδὴ καὶ πάρεργα τυγχάνει λεγόμενα, ἀποστῶμεν· εἰ δὲ μή, πλείω ἀεὶ ἐπιρρέοντα καταχώσει ἡμῶν τὸν ἐξ ἀρχῆς λόγον· ἐπὶ c
10 δὲ τὰ ἔμπροσθεν ἴωμεν, εἰ καὶ σοὶ δοκεῖ.

ΘΕΟ. Ἐμοὶ μὲν τὰ τοιαῦτα, ὦ Σώκρατες, οὐκ ἀηδέστερα ἀκούειν· ῥᾷω γὰρ τηλικῷδε ὄντι ἐπακολουθεῖν· εἰ μέντοι δοκεῖ, πάλιν ἐπανίωμεν.

l. 7. Third criticism of the doctrine. What appears to me, is to me. We found that even

ΣΩ. Οὐκοῦν ἐνταῦθά που ἦμεν τοῦ λόγου, ἐν ᾧ
15 ἔφαμεν τοὺς τὴν φερομένην οὐσίαν λέγοντας, καὶ τὸ ἀεὶ δοκοῦν ἑκάστῳ τοῦτο καὶ εἶναι τούτῳ ᾧ δοκεῖ, ἐν μὲν τοῖς ἄλλοις ἐθέλειν διϊσχυρίζεσθαι, καὶ οὐχ ἥκιστα περὶ τὰ δίκαια, ὡς παντὸς μᾶλλον, ἃ ἂν θῆται d

quite aware of it, my friend!' i. e. 'I know the full extent of the ridicule that they will pour on us.' He refers to the emphatic answer of Theodorus.

3. καὶ μὴ ἀνάνδρως φεύγειν] Cf. Rep. 518: οὐκ ἂν ἀλογίστως μελῷ.

5. ἡ ῥητορικὴ ἐκείνη πως ἀπομαραίνεται] 'That brilliant rhetoric of theirs fades utterly, leaving them to appear no better than children.'

6. παίδων μηδὲν δοκεῖν διαφέρειν] Crit. 49: ἐλάθομεν ἡμᾶς αὐτοὺς παίδων οὐδὲν διαφέροντες.

8. πλείω ἀεὶ ἐπιρρέοντα καταχώσει ἡμῶν τὸν ἐξ ἀρχῆς λόγον] 'They will bury us under the discussion to be commenced afresh, i. e. the arrears of discussion, which will gather against us with an ever-increasing stream.' He means, that if the main stream of the inquiry is dammed up any longer, it will come in upon us with overwhelming force. Cf. Rep. p. 450: ὅσων λόγων σμῆνος ὥσπερ ἐξ ἀρχῆς κινεῖτε περὶ πολιτείας. Polit. p. 302: τοῦ νῦν ἐπικεχυμένου λόγου ἀπ' ἀρχάς.

11. τὰ τοιαῦτα] Quam spinosiora ista. Cic. Tuscul. I.

18. περὶ τὰ δίκαια ... περὶ τὰ γαθοῦ] 'In regard to what is just—concerning what is good'

p.177. πόλις δόξαντα αὐτῇ, ταῦτα καὶ ἔστι δίκαια τῇ θεμένῃ, ἕωσπερ ἂν κέηται· περὶ δὲ τἀγαθοῦ οὐδένα ἀνδρεῖον ἔθ᾽ οὕτως εἶναι, ὥστε τολμᾶν διαμάχεσθαι ὅτι καὶ ἃ ἂν ὠφέλιμα οἰηθεῖσα πόλις ἑαυτῇ θῆται, καὶ ἔστι τοσοῦτον χρόνον ὅσον ἂν κέηται ὠφέλιμα, πλὴν εἴ τις τὸ ὄνομα λέγοι· τοῦτο δέ πού σκῶμμ᾽ ἂν εἴη πρὸς ὃ λέγομεν. οὐχί;

ΘΕΟ. Πάνυ γε.

ΣΩ. Μὴ γὰρ λεγέτω τὸ ὄνομα, ἀλλὰ τὸ πρᾶγμα ὃ ὀνομαζόμενον θεωρεῖται.

1. *τῇ θεμένῃ*] So Bodl. with Vat. Ven. Π.

2. *περὶ δὲ τἀγαθοῦ*] Rep. 505: ὃ δὴ διώκει μὲν ἅπασα ψυχὴ καὶ τούτου ἕνεκα πάντα πράττει, ἀπομαντευομένη τι εἶναι, ἀποροῦσα δέ— What is good cannot be apparent merely. (Compare the saying of Des Cartes and Spinoza: The idea of God implies His existence.) This was not, however, universally admitted. Ar. Eth. N. 1, 2: τοιούτῳ δέ τινα πλάνην ἔχει καὶ τἀγαθά, κ. τ. λ.

τἀγαθοῦ—ὠφέλιμα] Rep. 457, 458: κάλλιστα γὰρ τοῦτο καὶ λέγεται καὶ λελέξεται ὅτι τὸ μὲν ὠφέλιμον καλὸν τὸ δὲ βλαβερὸν αἰσχρόν. —γάμους—συνάψομεν ἱερούς· εἰς δύναμιν ὅτι μάλιστα· εἶεν δ᾽ ἂν ἱεροὶ οἱ ὠφελιμώτατοι.

We have not yet risen to the conception of the ideal good ἐπέκεινα τῆς οὐσίας: good is still a relative term, though knowledge begins to find a resting-place there. In the concrete the good and expedient are identical. See Spinoza, Cog. Met. I. c. 6. § 7. § 11. Res sola considerata neque bona dicitur, neque mala, sed tantum respective ad aliam, cui conducit ad id quod amat acquirendum, vel contra; ideoque unaquaeque res diverso respectu eodemque tempore bona et mala potest dici—Deus vero dicitur summe bonus, quia omnibus conducit, nempe uniuscujusque esse quo nihil magis amabile, suo concursu conservando. Malum autem absolutum nullum datur, ut per se est manifestum. Porro uti bonum et malum non dicitur nisi respective, sic etiam perfectio, nisi quando perfectionem sumimus pro ipsa rei essentia, quo sensu antea diximus, Deum Infinitam perfectionem habere, hoc est Infinitam essentiam, seu Infinitum esse.

5. *πλὴν εἴ τις—λέγομεν*] Rep. 533: ἔστι δ᾽, ὡς ἐμοὶ δοκεῖ, οὐ περὶ ὀνόματος ἀμφισβήτησις, οἷς τοσούτων πέρι σκέψις ὅσων ἡμῖν πρόκειται.

7. *πρὸς ὃ λέγομεν*] In respect of that which we mean.

9. *Μὴ γὰρ λεγέτω τὸ ὄνομα*] Let him not intend the name but the thing which is contemplated under it. (γὰρ add. Bodl. Vat. Ven. Π.) Dr. Badham con-

ΘΕΟ. Μὴ γάρ.

ΣΩ. Ἀλλ' ὃ ἂν τοῦτο ὀνομάζῃ, τούτου δή που στοχάζεται νομοθετουμένη, καὶ πάντας τοὺς νόμους, καθ' ὅσον οἴεταί τε καὶ δύναται, ὡς ὠφελιμωτάτους ἑαυτῇ τίθεται. ἢ πρὸς ἄλλο τι βλέπουσα νομοθετεῖται;

ΘΕΟ. Οὐδαμῶς.

ΣΩ. Ἦ οὖν καὶ τυγχάνει ἀεί, ἢ πολλὰ καὶ διαμαρτάνει ἑκάστη;

ΘΕΟ. Οἶμαι ἔγωγε καὶ διαμαρτάνειν.

ΣΩ. Ἔτι τοίνυν ἐνθένδε ἂν μᾶλλον πᾶς τις ὁμολογήσειε ταὐτὰ ταῦτα, εἰ περὶ παντός τις τοῦ εἴδους ἐρωτῴη, ἐν ᾧ καὶ τὸ ὠφέλιμον τυγχάνει ὄν. ἔστι δέ που καὶ περὶ τὸν μέλλοντα χρόνον. ὅταν γὰρ νομοθετώμεθα, ὡς ἐσομένους ὠφελίμους τοὺς νόμους τιθέμεθα εἰς τὸν ἔπειτα χρόνον. τοῦτο δὲ [μέλλον] ὀρθῶς ἂν λέγοιμεν.

ΘΕΟ. Πάνυ γε.

ΣΩ. Ἴθι δή, οὑτωσὶ ἐρωτῶμεν Πρωταγόραν ἢ ἄλλον τινὰ τῶν ἐκείνῳ τὰ αὐτὰ λεγόντων, Πάντων μέτρον ἄνθρωπός ἐστιν, ὡς φατέ, ὦ Πρωταγόρα,

ΘΕΑΙΤΗΤΟΣ. 119

p. 178. λευκῶν, βαρέων, κούφων, οὐδενὸς ὅτου οὐ τῶν τοιούτων. ἔχων γὰρ αὐτῶν τὸ κριτήριον ἐν αὑτῷ, οἷα πάσχει τοιαῦτα οἰόμενος, ἀληθῆ τε οἴεται αὑτῷ καὶ ὄντα. οὐχ οὕτως;

ΘΕΟ. Οὕτως.

ΣΩ. Ἦ καὶ τῶν μελλόντων ἔσεσθαι, φήσομεν, ὦ Πρωταγόρα, ἔχει τὸ κριτήριον ἐν αὑτῷ, καὶ οἷα ἂν οἰηθῇ ἔσεσθαι, ταῦτα καὶ γίγνεται ἐκείνῳ τῷ οἰηθέντι; οἷον θερμά, ἆρ᾽ ὅταν τις οἰηθῇ ἰδιώτης αὑτὸν πυρετὸν λήψεσθαι καὶ ἔσεσθαι ταύτην τὴν θερμότητα, καὶ ἕτερος, ἰατρὸς δέ, ἀντοιηθῇ, κατὰ τὴν ποτέρου δόξαν φῶμεν τὸ μέλλον ἀποβήσεσθαι, ἢ κατὰ τὴν ἀμφοτέρων, καὶ τῷ μὲν ἰατρῷ οὐ θερμὸς οὐδὲ πυρέττων γενήσεται, ἑαυτῷ δὲ ἀμφότερα;

1. λευκῶν βαρέων κούφων οὐδενὸς ὅτου οὔ] Cf. supr. 172 : τὸ μὲν πολλὰ ᾗ ἑαυτῷ ταύτῃ καὶ ἔστιν ἑκάστῳ, θερμά, ξηρά, γλυκέα, πάντα ὅσα τοῦ γένους τούτου.

2. τὸ κριτήριον] The word is formed from κριτήρ, on the analogy of δικαστήριον. Cf. Legg. 767 : δύο δὴ τῶν λεχθὲν ἔστω κριτήρια. The present is probably one of the earliest instances of its use.

οἷα πάσχει τοιαῦτα οἰόμενος] sc. εἶναι. Or rather the accusatives are cognate. Vid. supr. p. 152. Οἷα γὰρ αἰσθάνεται—.

4. ὄντα] There is a slight stress on the present tense in opposition to μελλόντων ἔσεσθαι.

5. Ἦ καὶ τῶν μελλόντων ἔσεσθαι φήσομεν] As here knowledge seems to emerge with the mention of future time, so in the Protagoras, p. 357, virtue is shown to be knowledge, because it implies the power of comparing the future with the present. (Cf. the line of Homer, Οὐδέ τι οἶδε νοῆσαι ἅμα πρόσσω καὶ ὀπίσσω.)

7. ἔχει τὸ κριτήριον ἐν αὑτῷ] 'The tribunal for deciding these things is within him.' 'The decision rests with him.'

9. οἷον θερμά] The word is placed absolutely. Heind. compares Crat. 393 : οἷον τὸ βῆτα ὁρᾷς ὅτι τοῦ η καὶ τοῦ τ καὶ τοῦ α προστεθέντων οὐδὲν λυπήσει κ.τ.λ.

ἅμα—κατὰ τὴν ποτέρου δόξαν] 'Surely we must suppose (must we not?) that the result will be according to the opinion of one of them, or shall we say that it will be in accordance with both?' It is implied in what follows, which opinion is probably right.

14. ἑαυτῷ δὲ ἀμφότερα.—ὁ καὶ ἔσεσθαι αὐτῷ τῷ ὑπολπιβῇ δόξει ἑτέρμαστον εἶναι—τὸ μέλλον—καὶ δόξειν καὶ ἔσεσθαι] These words contain the point of the argument.

ἑαυτῷ δὲ ἀμφότερα) Viz. καὶ

henry, and the like, for he has the standard of them in himself. Has he also the standard in himself of future things? If he thinks he is going to have a fever, and the physician tells him No, which opinion will prove true for him in the sequel?

120   ΠΛΑΤΩΝΟΣ

ΘΕΟ. Γελοῖον μέν τ' ἂν εἴη.   p.178.

ΣΩ. Ἀλλ', οἶμαι, περὶ οἴνου γλυκύτητος καὶ αὐ- d
στηρότητος μελλούσης ἔσεσθαι ἡ τοῦ γεωργοῦ δόξα,
ἀλλ' οὐχ ἡ τοῦ κιθαριστοῦ, κυρία.

ΘΕΟ. Τί μήν;

ΣΩ. Οὐδ' ἂν αὖ περὶ ἀναρμόστου τε καὶ εὐαρ-
μόστου ἐσομένου παιδοτρίβης ἂν βέλτιον δοξάσειε
μουσικοῦ, ὃ καὶ ἔπειτα αὐτῷ τῷ παιδοτρίβῃ δόξει
εὐάρμοστον εἶναι.

ΘΕΟ. Οὐδαμῶς.

ΣΩ. Οὐκοῦν καὶ τοῦ μέλλοντος ἑστιάσεσθαι μὴ
μαγειρικοῦ ὄντος, σκευαζομένης θοίνης, ἀκυροτέρα ἡ
κρίσις τῆς τοῦ ὀψοποιοῦ περὶ τῆς ἐσομένης ἡδονῆς.
περὶ μὲν γὰρ τοῦ ἤδη ὄντος ἑκάστῳ ἡδέος ἢ γεγονό- e
τος μηδέν πω τῷ λόγῳ διαμαχώμεθα, ἀλλὰ περὶ τοῦ
μέλλοντος ἑκάστῳ καὶ δόξειν καὶ ἔσεσθαι πότερον
αὐτὸς αὑτῷ ἄριστος κριτής, ἢ σύ, ὦ Πρωταγόρα, τό
γε περὶ λόγους πιθανὸν ἑκάστῳ ἡμῶν ἐσόμενον εἰς
δικαστήριον βέλτιον ἂν προδοξάσαις ἢ τῶν ἰδιωτῶν
ὁστισοῦν;

ΘΕΟ. Καὶ μάλα, ὦ Σώκρατες, τοῦτό γε σφόδρα
ὑπισχνεῖτο πάντων διαφέρειν αὐτός.

The musician is a better judge of future harmony than the gymnast, as the latter will himself confess when he hears the sounds.

Surely Protagoras himself professed to be a better prophet than those he taught, of the probable effect of a rhetor-

---

θερμὸς καὶ πυρέττων. The repetition of the word is curious. Aristotle, Met. I. 5. 1010 b.: "Ἔτι δὲ περὶ τοῦ μέλλοντος, ὥσπερ καὶ Πλάτων λέγει, οὐ δήπου ὁμοίως κυρία ἡ τοῦ ἰατροῦ δόξα καὶ ἡ τοῦ ἀγνοοῦντος, οἷον περὶ τοῦ μέλλοντος ἔσεσθαι ὑγιοῦς ἢ μὴ μέλλοντος.

15. μηδέν πω τῷ λόγῳ διαμαχώμεθα] The certainty of present impressions is swept away together with the doctrine of motion, infr. p. 182. The relation of present to past impressions is further discussed under the guise of a new inquiry, pp. 191, sq. (See espec. the word μνημεῖον.)

17. τό γε περὶ λόγους πιθανὸν] A farther home-thrust at Protagoras.

18. ἑκάστῳ ἡμῶν ἐσόμενον εἰς δικαστήριον] 'That which each of us will find persuasive to be spoken in court.'

ΘΕΑΙΤΗΤΟΣ. 121

ΣΩ. Νὴ Δία, ὦ μέλε· ἢ οὐδείς γ' ἂν αὐτῷ διε- p. 179. λέγετο διδοὺς πολὺ ἀργύριον, εἰ †μὴ† τοὺς συνόντας ἔπειθεν ὅτι καὶ τὸ μέλλον ἔσεσθαί τε καὶ δόξειν οὔτε μάντις οὔτε τις ἄλλος ἄμεινον κρίνειεν ἂν ἢ αὐτὸς αὑτῷ.

ΘΕΟ. Ἀληθέστατα.

2. εἰ †μὴ†] εἰ μὴ τοὺς συνόντας —Profecto in futurarum quoque rerum cognitione omnibus praecellere se Protagoras profitebatur, aut nemo ipsi magnam doctrinae mercedem solvisset, si quo malo persuasisset discipulis, etiam de futuris rebus neque vatem neque alium quemquam melius posse judicare, quam ipsum sibi unumquemque. V. ad Clarg. § 75, p. 47. Platonis autem sententiam restituimus unius litterulae mutatione. Quippe vulgo scriptum εἰ μὴ τοὺς συν., aude contrarium prorsus et absurdus sensus efficitur. Quam scripturam nequis tuendam arbitretur verbo αὐτὸν ad Protagoram trabendo et αὐτῷ nutando in αὐτῷ (sc. τῷ συνόντι), manifesta h. l. est superiorum verborum πότερον αὐτὸς αὑτῷ ἄριστος κριτής repetitio, neque tum ferri posset hoc αὐτῷ; adeo id molesto redundaret. Idem vitium insedit Philel. p. 34 α. ὅταν μὴ τὴν ψυχὴν ἡδονῆς χωρὶς σώματος ὅτι μάλιστα καὶ ἐνεργέστατα λάβωμεν. Corr. ἕως συν. et Protag. p. 331 d. καὶ γὰρ δικαίον δικαίου ἀμήγηπη προσίεται. τὸ γὰρ λευκὸν τῷ μέλανι ἔστιν ὃ μὴ (l. ὅτι) προσίεται καὶ τὸ σκληρὸν τῷ μαλακῷ. Helnd.

This reasoning is probably correct. But δή, which is the received correction of Phil. l. c. seems more forcible here than

συν, which has no particular aptness in this passage. ' If he had really persuaded them of that which has been now suggested.' Cf. p. 166. εἰ δὴ ἀσαμάτων γε—: alib. The corruption probably originated in the slightly obscure reference of αὐτὸς αὑτῷ, or perhaps simply from the neighbourhood of μή, (i. e. Nỹ.)

Schleiermacher solved the difficulty by omitting αὐτῷ, and referring αὐτὸν to Protagoram. But this destroys the force of καὶ, and the question is not between one oracle and another, but between the opinion of the master and of the common individual. For αὐτῷ referring to an indefinite subject, cf. Apol. 39: οὐ γάρ ἐσθ' αὕτη ἡ ἀπαλλαγὴ οὔτε πάνυ δυνατὴ οὔτε καλή, ἀλλ' ἐκείνη καὶ καλλίστη καὶ ῥᾴστη, μὴ τοὺς ἄλλους κολούειν, ἀλλ' ἑαυτὸν παρασκευάζειν ὅπως ἔσται ὡς βέλτιστος. The change from plural to singular has been elsewhere illustrated.

The μάντις is introduced as being ἐπιστήμων of the future generally, just as the physician is of future health or sickness, the musician of future harmony, &c. τις ἄλλος points distantly at Protagoras himself, and his position as the prophet of his school is hinted at. Cf. supr. 162. ἐκ τοῦ ἀδύτου τῆς βίβλου ἐφθέγξατο.

K

122 ΠΛΑΤΩΝΟΣ

And it is acknowledged that a state must often fail in its legislation, which regards the future. Therefore one man is wiser than another, and not every man, but the wise man, is the measure of things.

ΣΩ. Οὐκοῦν καὶ αἱ νομοθεσίαι καὶ τὸ ὠφέλιμον p. 179. περὶ τὸ μέλλον ἐστί, καὶ πᾶς ἂν ὁμολογοῖ νομοθετουμένην πόλιν πολλάκις ἀνάγκην εἶναι τοῦ ὠφελιμωτάτου ἀποτυγχάνειν;

ΘΕΟ. Μάλα γε.

ΣΩ. Μετρίως ἄρα ἡμῖν πρὸς τὸν διδάσκαλόν σου εἰρήσεται, ὅτι ἀνάγκη αὐτῷ ὁμολογεῖν σοφώτερόν τε b ἄλλον ἄλλου εἶναι καὶ τὸν μὲν τοιοῦτον μέτρον εἶναι, ἐμοὶ δὲ τῷ ἀνεπιστήμονι μηδὲ ὁπωστιοῦν ἀνάγκην εἶναι μέτρῳ γίγνεσθαι, ὡς ἄρτι με ἠνάγκαζεν ὁ ὑπὲρ ἐκείνου λόγος, εἴτ' ἐβουλόμην εἴτε μή, τοιοῦτον εἶναι.

ΘΕΟ. Ἐκείνῃ μοι δοκεῖ, ὦ Σώκρατες, μάλιστα ἁλίσκεσθαι ὁ λόγος, ἁλισκόμενος καὶ ταύτῃ, ᾗ τὰς τῶν ἄλλων δόξας κυρίας ποιεῖ, αὗται δὲ ἐφάνησαν τοὺς ἐκείνου λόγους οὐδαμῇ ἀληθεῖς ἡγούμεναι.

On this ground, then, the theory cannot stand. And there are other points where it is easily assailable. But it is more diffi-

ΣΩ. Πολλαχῇ, ὦ Θεόδωρε, καὶ ἄλλῃ ἂν τό γε c τοιοῦτον ἁλοίη, μὴ πᾶσαν παντὸς ἀληθῆ δόξαν εἶναι. περὶ δὲ τὸ παρὸν ἑκάστῳ πάθος, ἐξ ὧν αἱ αἰσθήσεις καὶ αἱ κατὰ ταύτας δόξαι γίγνονται, χαλεπώτερον ἑλεῖν ὡς οὐκ ἀληθεῖς. ἴσως δὲ οὐδὲν λέγω· ἀνάλωτοι γάρ, εἰ ἔτυχον, εἰσί, καὶ οἱ φάσκοντες αὐτὰς ἐναργεῖς τε εἶναι καὶ ἐπιστήμας τάχα ἂν ὄντα λέγοιεν, καὶ

2. πᾶς ἂν ὁμολογοῖ] Both from experience and from the analogies just adduced. We pass from the individual to the state, as in p. 172.
Arist. Met. K. 1063 a. ταύτου δ' ἐστὶ τοιούτων, τοὺς ἑτέρους μὲν ὑπολήψεσιν μέτρων εἶναι, τοὺς δ' ἑτέρους οὐχ ὑπολήψεσιν.
16. Πολλαχῇ δὲ] We revert from the general saying of Protagoras to the particular interpretation of it given above, viz. in its application to the doctrine of sense. This has not been disproved by the above argument, as it has nothing to do with the future.
18. ἐξ ὧν] 'The momentary effect produced on each man, from which arise the sensations, and the beliefs which are in accordance with them.' Vid. p. 156; and note the incipient distinction between αἴσθησις and δόξα.
22. ὄντα] Art. conj. τὰ ὄντα, but see above. p. 178. ἀληθῆ τε οὖσαν αὑτῷ καὶ ὄντα.

ΘΕΑΙΤΗΤΟΣ. 123

p. 179. Θεαίτητος ὅδε οὐκ ἀπὸ σκοποῦ εἴρηκεν αἴσθησιν καὶ ἐπιστήμην ταὐτὸν θέμενος. προσιτέον οὖν ἐγγυτέρω, d ὡς ὁ ὑπὲρ Πρωταγόρου λόγος ἐπέταττε, καὶ σκεπτέον τὴν φερομένην ταύτην οὐσίαν διακρούοντα, εἴτε ὑγιὲς εἴτε σαθρὸν φθέγγεται. μάχη δ' οὖν περὶ αὐτῆς οὐ 5 φαύλη οὐδ' ὀλίγοις γέγονεν.

ΘΕΟ. Πολλοῦ καὶ δεῖ φαύλη εἶναι, ἀλλὰ περὶ μὲν τὴν Ἰωνίαν καὶ ἐπιδίδωσι πάμπολυ. οἱ γὰρ τοῦ Ἡρακλείτου ἑταῖροι χορηγοῦσι τούτου τοῦ λόγου μάλα ἐρρωμένως. 10

ΣΩ. Τῷ τοι, ὦ φίλε Θεόδωρε, μᾶλλον σκεπτέον· καὶ ἐξ ἀρχῆς, ὥσπερ αὐτοὶ ὑποτείνονται.

cult to attach the main position, viz. that the present sensible impression is true. Perhaps this is impregnable, but let us approach, and try whether its foundation in the doctrine of motion is secure.

I. 2. Criticism of the

1. οὐκ ἀπὸ σκοποῦ εἴρηκεν] Hom. Odyss. Λ. 343: Ὢ φίλοι, οὐ μὰν ὕμμιν ἀπὸ σκοποῦ οὐδ' ἀπὸ δόξης Μυθοῦμαι βασίλεια περίφρων. Xen. Symp. II. 11: καὶ οὗτος δὴ ὁ λόγος οὐκ ἀπὸ τοῦ σκοποῦ ἴδοξέν εἰρῆσθαι.

3. σκεπτέον—διακρούοντα] Soph. 246: Ταγηροῦν οἱ πρὸς αὐτοὺς ἀμφισβητοῦντες μάλα εὐλαβῶς ἄνωθεν ἐξ ἀοράτου ποθὲν ἀμύνονται, νοητὰ ἄττα καὶ ἀσώματα εἴδη βιαζόμενοι τὴν ἀληθινὴν οὐσίαν εἶναι· τὰ δὲ ἐκείνων σώματα καὶ τὴν λεγομένην ὑπ' αὐτῶν ἀλήθειαν κατὰ σμικρὰ διαθραύοντες ἐν τοῖς λόγοις γένεσιν ἀντ' οὐσίας φερομένην τινὰ προσαγορεύουσιν. ἐν μέσῳ δὲ περὶ ταῦτα ἀπλέτως ἀμφοτέρων μάχη τις ὦ Θεαίτητε, ἀεὶ ξυνέστηκεν. This combat is somewhat differently described in the present passage.

4. τὴν φερομένην — οὐσίαν] This is the ground on which the 'semi-Protagoreans' take their stand, the last stronghold of the doctrine, as it was the first point it occupied.

διακρούοντα] Schol.: ἐκ μεταφορᾶς τῶν διακρουόντων τὸ περίσμα, εἰ ἀκραιᾶ εἴσιν. Cf. Phileb. p. 55: γεννάδας δέ, εἰ τῇ σαθρὸν ἔχει, τῶν παρεπομένων. Compare the English expression, 'As sound as a bell.'

8. ἐπιδίδωσι πάμπολυ] 'Makes rapid strides,' 'gains in importance,' 'is waged with increasing energy.'

9. χορηγοῦσι] Vid. Demetr. Byz. ap. Athen. p. 295. ed. Schw.: ἐκάλουν δὲ καὶ χορηγούς, ὥς φησιν ὁ Βυζάντιος Δημήτριος, οὐχ ὥσπερ νῦν τοὺς μισθουμένους τοὺς χορούς, ἀλλὰ τοὺς καθηγουμένους τοῦ χοροῦ, καθάπερ τοὔνομα σημαίνει.

τούτου τοῦ λόγου] λόγος is here almost equivalent to "school of thought." Cf. supr. τοὺς τοῦ ἡμετέρου χοροῦ κ. τ. λ. infr. τῶν ἐπινευσμαζόντων λόγων.

11. Τῷ τοι] 'We are the more bound to consider the question, and that in the light of its first principle, even as they present it to us in the discussion.' Gorg.

principle,
All is motion.

Final rejection of the doctrine of sense.

Orest has been the conflict

ΘΕΟ. Παντάπασι μὲν οὖν. καὶ γάρ, ὦ Σώκρατες, p. 179. περὶ τούτων τῶν Ἡρακλειτείων, ἡ ὥσπερ σὺ λέγεις ͨ Ὁμηρείων, καὶ ἔτι παλαιοτέρων, αὐτοῖς μὲν τοῖς περὶ τὴν Ἔφεσον, ὅσοι προσποιοῦνται ἔμπειροι [εἶναι,] 5 οὐδὲν μᾶλλον οἷόν τε διαλεχθῆναι ἢ τοῖς οἰστρῶσιν. ἀτεχνῶς γὰρ κατὰ τὰ συγγράμματα φέρονται, τὸ δ'

448: ὥσπερ σου τὸ ἔμπροσθεν ὑπετείνατο Χαιρεφῶν. (καὶ add. Bodl.)
(12.) ὥσπερ αὐτοὶ ὑποτείνονται] Viz. in referring every thing to a first principle, whether of fire or motion.

2. τῶν Ἡρακλειτείων] Sc. δογμάτων. περὶ τούτων κ. τ. λ. depends verbally partly on διαλεχθῆναι, partly on ἔμπειροι, really upon the notion " there is no discussion possible." (Cf. infr. ὅπερ 30 εἴπω. If the genitives were masculine, and out of construction, the use of ἔμπειροι without an object would be too abrupt. Compare, however, παρὸ μὲν τούτων, below.

ὥσπερ σὺ λέγεις] p. 152. Cf. Cratyl. 439: φαίνονται γὰρ καὶ ἔμοιγε αὐτὸ δασυνθῆναι.

3. Ὁμηρείων] Cf. p. 152.

ἔτι παλαιοτέρων] Orpheum intelligit: conf. Cratyl. § 41. (p. 402.) Heind.

4. εἶναι] Om. Bodl. with seven other MSS.

5. τοῖς οἰστρῶσιν] ' with men in frenzy.'

6. ἀτεχνῶς γάρ] " For, in true accordance with their master's writings they are ever in motion; but as for dwelling upon an argument or question, and quietly asking and answering in turn, they are absolutely without the power of doing so; or rather they possess in a sur-

passing degree the most perfect absence of all quietness, even in the minutest respect."

The weak point in this rendering of the last words is πρὸς τὸ μηδὲ σμικρόν = ' in respect of what is less than little.' For πρὸς, compare Soph. p. 248: ὅταν τῷ παρῇ ἢ τοῦ πάσχειν ἢ δρᾶν καὶ πρὸς τὸ σμικρότατον δύναμις. And for μηδὲ σμικρόν, cf. Philebus, p. 60 e. φρόνησιν — ἡδονῆς μηδὲ τὸ σμικρότατον ἴσχουσαν. But the article still presents some difficulty. We can only suppose that in the accumulation of negatives μηδὲ σμικρὸν has taken the place of σμικρότατον.

Another possible rendering is: ' Or rather the utter negation of it (τὸ οὐδ' οὐδὲν) surpasses every thing, in regard to the absence of all quietness in the men.' But it is difficult to find a parallel for this use of τὸ οὐδ' οὐδέν.

In either case ὑπερβάλλει is probably used absolutely, and not with reference to μηδέν. The point is, not that οὐδ' οὐδὲν is a stronger expression than μηδέν, (it should be compared w'th ἧττον—ἢ τὸ μηδέν), but (1) the negation is put more strongly by being affirmed; (2) ὑπερβάλλει assists the climax, as being a stronger word than any in the former clause; and,

ΘΕΑΙΤΗΤΟΣ.

ἐπιμεῖναι ἐπὶ λόγῳ καὶ ἐρωτήματι καὶ ἡσυχίας ἐν
p. 180. μέρει ἀποκρίνασθαι καὶ ἐρέσθαι ἧττον αὐτοῖς ἔνι ἢ τὸ
μηδέν· μᾶλλον δὲ ὑπερβάλλει τὸ οὐδ' οὐδὲν πρὸς τὸ
μηδὲ σμικρὸν ἐνεῖναι τοῖς ἀνδράσιν ἡσυχίας· ἀλλ' ἄν
τινά τι ἔρῃ, ὥσπερ ἐκ φαρέτρας ῥηματίσκια αἰνιγματώδη ἀνασπῶντες ἀποτοξεύουσι, κἂν τούτου ζητῇς
λόγον λαβεῖν, τί εἴρηκεν, ἑτέρῳ πεπλήξει καινῶς
μετωνομασμένῳ, περανεῖς δὲ οὐδέποτε οὐδὲν πρὸς
οὐδένα αὐτῶν· οὐδέ γε ἐκεῖνοι αὐτοὶ πρὸς ἀλλήλους,
ἀλλ' εὖ πάνυ φυλάττουσι τὸ μηδὲν βέβαιον ἐᾶν εἶναι
μήτ' ἐν λόγῳ μήτ' ἐν ταῖς αὐτῶν ψυχαῖς, ἡγούμενοι,
ὡς ἐμοὶ δοκεῖ, αὐτὸ στάσιμον εἶναι· τούτῳ δὲ πάνυ
πολεμοῦσι, καὶ καθ' ὅσον δύνανται πανταχόθεν ἐκ-
βάλλουσιν.

ΣΩ. Ἴσως, ὦ Θεόδωρε, τοὺς ἄνδρας μαχομένους
ἑώρακας, εἰρηνεύουσι δὲ οὐ συγγέγονας. οὐ γάρ σοι
ἑταῖροί εἰσιν. ἀλλ', οἶμαι, τὰ τοιαῦτα τοῖς μαθηταῖς
ἐπὶ σχολῆς φράζουσιν, οὓς ἂν βούλωνται ὁμοίους αὑτοῖς ποιῆσαι.

and many the com-
batants on either side.
The friends of Heracli-
tus in Ionia defend the
doctrine of motion with all their might. But we must take their theory into our own hands to test it. For the men are in a fix, and offer us no hold for argument.

(3) if the former rendering is correct, what was at first spoken of only with reference to argu-
ment, is now asserted generally. Cf. infr. μήτ' ἐν λόγῳ μήτ' ἐν ταῖς αὐτῶν ψυχαῖς. Compare with ὑπερβάλλει τὸ οὐδ' οὐδὲν—ἐνεῖναι, Arist. Eth. N. IV. 1. § 39. ὑπερ-
βολὴ τοῦ μηδενὸς ἂν εἰδέναι.

5. ὥσπερ ἐκ φαρέτρας κ. τ. λ.] Cf. Protag. 342. (of the Spartans) τὸ μὲν πολλὰ ἐν τοῖς λόγοις εὑρήσεις φαῦλόν τινα φαινόμενον, ἔπειτα, ὅπου ἂν τύχῃ τῶν λεγομένων, ἐνέ-
βαλε ῥῆμα βραχὺ καὶ συνεστραμ-
μένον, ὥσπερ δεινὸς ἀκοντιστήν.

ῥηματίσκια αἰνιγμ.] 'Plucking up as from a quiver sayings brief and dark, they let them

fly at you.'
6. ἀνασπῶντες] Cf. Soph. Aj. 302. λόγους ἀνίσους.
τούτου] Sc. τοῦ ῥηματισκίου.
7. τί εἴρηκεν] Sc. τὰ ῥηματίσκια.
καινῶς μετωνομασμένῳ] 'Of words new-fangled ill,' 'of terms strangely twisted to an unheard-of sense.'
10. βέβαιον—στάσιμον] 'Fix-
ed or settled—stationary.'
εἶναι] γενέσθαι is purposely avoided.
16. οὐ γάρ σοι ἑταῖροί εἰσιν] The dislike of a geometrician to the Heraclitean method is not unnatural.
17. τὰ τοιαῦτα] Sc. εἰρηνικά s. τὸ βέβαιον ἐν τοῖς λόγοις.

126   ΠΛΑΤΩΝΟΣ

ΘΕΟ. Ποίοις μαθηταῖς, ὦ δαιμόνιε; οὐδὲ γίγνεται p. 180.
τῶν τοιούτων ἕτερος ἑτέρου μαθητής, ἀλλ' αὐτόματοι c
ἀναφύονται, ὁπόθεν ἂν τύχῃ ἕκαστος αὐτῶν ἐνθουσιάσας, καὶ τὸν ἕτερον ὁ ἕτερος οὐδὲν ἡγεῖται εἰδέναι.
παρὰ μὲν οὖν τούτων, ὅπερ ᾖα ἐρῶν, οὐκ ἄν ποτε
λάβοις λόγον οὔτε ἑκόντων οὔτε ἀκόντων· αὐτοὺς δὲ
δεῖ παραλαβόντας ὥσπερ πρόβλημα ἐπισκοπεῖσθαι.

ΣΩ. Καὶ μετρίως γε λέγεις. τό γε δὴ πρόβλημα
ἄλλο τι παρειλήφαμεν παρὰ μὲν τῶν ἀρχαίων, μετὰ
ποιήσεως ἐπικρυπτομένων τοὺς πολλούς, ὡς ἡ γένεσις d
τῶν ἄλλων πάντων Ὠκεανός τε καὶ Τηθὺς ῥεύματα

The problem now before us has come down from ancient times.

1. Ποίοις μαθηταῖς] Rep. 330. Παῖ' ἐπιεστραμμην, ὦ Σ.; et alib.

2. αὐτόματοι ἀναφύονται) 'They spring up unbidden, wherever each happens to have caught the *afflatus*.'

3. ὁπόθεν ἂν τύχῃ—ἐνθουσιάσας] Contrast with this Hegel, G. d. Ph. p. 55. 'It is the very spirit of this whole recital, that the more developed Philosophy of a later age, is really the product of the previous labours of the thinking mind: that it is required and determined by these earlier views, and has not sprung of itself independently from the ground.' (Nicht isolirt für sich aus dem Boden gewachsen ist.) For the expression αὐτόματα ἀναφύονται, cf. Rep. 520: αὐτόματα γὰρ ἐμφύονται ἀκούσης τῆς ἐν ἑκάστῃ πολιτείᾳ. As in pp. 172 sqq. we had a description of the man corresponding to Protagoras' theory, so here we have the men of Heraclitus. The wildness and the enthusiasm, at once speculative and irrational, are Oriental rather than Greek, and

are probably due rather to the soil than to the germ. Comparatively little of this is to be found in Heraclitus himself, although for their abrupt quaintness his sayings might be called βηματίσαι αἰνιγματώδη.

5. οὐκ ἄν ποτε λάβοις λόγον] Ar. Met. Γ. 4. 1006. a. γελοῖον τὸ ζητεῖν λόγον πρὸς τὸν μηθενὸς ἔχοντα λόγον, ᾖ μὴ ἔχει· ὅμοιος γὰρ φυτῷ ὁ τοιοῦτος ᾖ τοιοῦτος ἤδη. K. 1063 a : μηδὲν γὰρ τιθέντες ἀναιροῦσι τὸ διαλέγεσθαι καὶ ὅλως λόγον, ὥστε πρὸς μὲν τοὺς τοιούτους οὐκ ἔστι λόγος.

6. αὐτοὺς δὲ δεῖ παραλαβόντας] 'But we must take the doctrine out of their hands, and con it over by ourselves like a geometrical theorem.' The object of παραλαβόντας is vague; neither λόγον in the sense just used, nor ἀρχήν; but τὰ Ἡρακλείτεια ταῦτα, ἤ τι τοιοῦτον.

8. τό γε δὴ πρόβλημα] 'Well, the theorem, as you call it.' Compare with the repetition of γε the double use of γάρ, ἀλλά, κ. τ. λ.

11. ῥεύματα τυγχάνει] Sc. ὄντα.

ΘΕΑΙΤΗΤΟΣ.

p. 180. τυγχάνει καὶ οὐδὲν ἕστηκε, παρὰ δὲ τῶν ὑστέρων, ἅτε σοφωτέρων, ἀναφανδὸν ἀποδεικνυμένων, ἵνα καὶ οἱ σκυτοτόμοι αὐτῶν τὴν σοφίαν μάθωσιν ἀκούσαντες καὶ παύσωνται ἠλιθίως οἰόμενοι τὰ μὲν ἑστάναι, τὰ δὲ κινεῖσθαι τῶν ὄντων, μαθόντες δ᾽ ὅτι πάντα κινεῖ- 5 ται τιμῶσιν αὐταύς ; ὀλίγου δὲ ἐπελαθόμην, ὦ Θεόδωρε, ὅτι ἄλλοι αὖ τἀναντία τούτοις ἀπεφήναντο, Οἷον ἀκίνητον †τελέθει, τῷ παντί† ὄνομ᾽ εἶναι, καὶ ἄλλα ὅσα Μέλισσοί τε καὶ Παρμενίδαι ἐναντιούμενοι πᾶσι τούτοις διϊσχυρίζονται, ὥς ἕν τε πάντα ἐστὶ καὶ ἕστηκεν 10 αὐτὸ ἐν αὑτῷ, οὐκ ἔχον χώραν ἐν ᾗ κινεῖται. Τούτοις

But wise men formerly veiled their meaning from the multitude in poetry, not as these now, who make no secret of their views, and seek to win universal suffrage for them, and to convert men from the foolishness of common sense.

which is purposely (or instinctively) omitted. Ἀκινονός τε καὶ Τηθὺν are in apposition with ἡ γένεσις, and ῥεύματα is predicate. ὄν, &c. express not what the poets said, but what they meant, depending partly on παρεμφῆ.

3. σκυτοτόμοι] I.e. ' The meanest artificers.' Cf. Prot. 324.: ὡς μέν — εἰδότων ἀποδέχονται — καὶ χαλκέως καὶ σκυτοτόμων συμβουλεύοντος τὰ πολιτικά: alib. They do not inquire whether they are understood or not.

7. Οἷον] MSS. οἵον. But the words of Simplicius in Aristot. Phys. f. 7. a. are decisive : δείκνυσιν αὐτὸ ἀνώνυμόν καὶ μόνον ὃν πάντων ἐξῃρημένον.

8. τελέθει, τῷ παντί] So all the MSS. Buttm. conj. γ᾽ ἔμπεσεν, τῷ πάν᾽. This is gathered from the quotations of Simplicius, and is probably right.

10. ἕστηκεν αὐτὸ ἐν αὑτῷ] ' All Being is One, and standeth self-contained, not having any space in which it moves.' The nearest approach to this latter assertion in the fragments of Parmenides is in the lines—

(78—85 Mull.) Οὐδὲ διαιρετόν ἐστιν, ἐπεὶ πᾶν ἐστιν ὁμοῖον, οὐδέ τι τῇ μᾶλλον τό κεν εἴργοι μιν ξυνέχεσθαι, οὐδέ τι χειρότερον· πᾶν δὲ πλέον ἐστὶν ἐόντος τῷ ξυνεχὲς πᾶν ἐστίν, ἐὸν γὰρ ἐόντι πελάζει. Αὐτὰρ ἀκίνητον μεγάλων ἐν πείρασι δεσμῶν ἐστιν, ἄναρχον, ἄπαυστον, ἐπεὶ γένεσις καὶ ὄλεθρος τῆλε μάλ᾽ ἐπλάγχθησαν, ἀπῶσε δὲ πίστις ἀληθής. ταὐτό δ᾽ ἐν ταὐτῷ τε μίμνον καθ᾽ ἑαυτό τε κεῖται.

He asserts, however, that Being is not without boundaries, else it would be imperfect. Zeno appears to have said, that being was neither with nor without boundaries. Cf. Arist. de Xenoph. Gorg. et Melisso, c. 3: Λίθως δὲ ἔστιν καὶ ἵνα καὶ σφαιροειδῆ, οὔτ᾽ ἄπειρον, οὔτε πεπεράνθαι· Ἄπειρον γὰρ τὸ μὴ εἶναι ──── τὸ δὲ ἐν οὔτε τῷ οὐκ ἔστι οὔτε ταῖς πολλοῖς ὁμοιοῦσθαι. 'Ἐν γὰρ οὐκ ἔχει πρὸς ὅτι περαίνει.

The Eleatics did not abstract the idea of Being from that of extension, although its falness destroyed the idea of space. It was here that the Atomists joined issue with them. To

128 ΠΛΑΤΩΝΟΣ

οὖν, ὦ ἑταῖρε, πᾶσι τί χρησόμεθα; κατὰ σμικρὸν p. 180.
γὰρ προϊόντες λελήθαμεν ἀμφοτέρων εἰς τὸ μέσον
πεπτωκότες, καὶ ἂν μὴ πῃ ἀμυνόμενοι διαφύγωμεν,
δίκην δώσομεν ὥσπερ οἱ ἐν ταῖς παλαίστραις διὰ p.181.
γραμμῆς παίζοντες, ὅταν ὑπ' ἀμφοτέρων ληφθέντες
ἕλκωνται εἰς τἀναντία. δοκεῖ οὖν μοι τοὺς ἑτέρους
πρότερον σκεπτέον, ἐφ' οὕσπερ ὡρμήσαμεν, τοὺς
ῥέοντας, καὶ ἐὰν μέν τι φαίνωνται λέγοντες, συνέλ-
ξομεν μετ' αὐτῶν ἡμᾶς αὐτούς, τοὺς ἑτέρους ἐκφυγεῖν
10 πειρώμενοι. ἐὰν δὲ οἱ τοῦ ὅλου στασιῶται ἀληθέστερα λέγειν δοκῶσι, φευξόμεθα παρ' αὐτοὺς ἀπ' αὖ
τῶν τὰ ἀκίνητα κινούντων. ἀμφότεροι δ' ἂν φανῶσι b

Leucippus and Democritus the relations of body were not symbolical but real. They felt that they must account for motion. Hence their assertion of the existence of empty space, τὸ κενόν, or, in other words, τὸ μὴ ὂν in the material sense.

2. εἰς τὸ μέσον] Viz. by having partly discarded and partly retained the principle, ἐπιστήμη αἴσθησις,—τὸν Πρωταγόραν λόγον μὴ παντάπασι λέγοντες.

4. δίκην δώσομεν] For the humour, cf. Rep. 474: τῷ ἀντι νωθαιζόμενος δώσεις δίκην.

διὰ γραμμῆς παίζοντες] A game, like our French and English, was called διελκυστίνδα.

6. δοκεῖ οὖν μοι] "I think therefore we ought first to examine the one faction, in the direction of whom we started, these wavering movers of unrest; and if we find any truth in them, we will join our efforts with theirs to pull us to them, endeavouring to shake the others off. But if those who stand for the unbroken Whole of Being seem to speak more reasonably, we will desert to these again from the revolutionary violence of the movement party."

7. τοὺς ῥέοντας] They are humorously identified with their principle. Vid. supr. ἀνεχνῶς γὰρ κατὰ τὰ συγγράμματα φέρονται.

For a similar reference to a set of persons by an epithet, cf. Phileb. 46: οἱ εἰσομεν δυσχερεῖς. Soph. 248: τὸ νῦν δὴ ῥηθὲν πρὸς τοὺς γηγενεῖς. Ilep. p. 488: τὸ πάθος τῶν ἑταιρει- στικῶν.

11. ἀπ' αὖ τῶν] (ἀπ' αὐτῶν τῶν παρ' αὐτοὺς ἀπ' αὐτῶν octt. ἀπ' αὖ τῶν Bekk.) We pass from the image of the game to that of a civil war, in which the Heracliteans are the 'movement,' or revolutionary, party. There is probably a slight play on the word στασιῶται.

ΘΕΑΙΤΗΤΟΣ.

p. 181. μηδὲν μέτριον λέγοντες, γελοῖοι ἐσόμεθα ἡγούμενοι
ἡμᾶς μέν τι λέγειν φαύλους ὄντας, παμπαλαίους δὲ
καὶ πασσόφους ἄνδρας ἀποδεδοκιμακότες. ὅρα οὖν,
ὦ Θεόδωρε, εἰ λυσιτελεῖ εἰς τοσοῦτον προϊέναι κίν-
δυνον. 5
ΘΕΟ. Οὐδὲν μὲν οὖν ἀνεκτόν, ὦ Σώκρατες, μὴ οὐ
διασκέψασθαι τί λέγουσιν ἑκάτεροι τῶν ἀνδρῶν.
ΣΩ. Σκεπτέον ἂν εἴη σοῦ γε οὕτω προθυμουμένου.
Δοκεῖ οὖν μοι ἀρχὴ εἶναι τῆς σκέψεως κινήσεως πέρι,
c ποῖόν τί ποτε ἄρα λέγοντες φασὶ τὰ πάντα κινεῖσθαι. 10
βούλομαι δὲ λέγειν τὸ τοιόνδε· πότερον ἕν τι εἶδος
αὐτῆς λέγουσιν ἢ ὥσπερ ἐμοὶ φαίνεται, δύο; μὴ μέντοι μόνον ἐμοὶ δοκείτω, ἀλλὰ συμμέτεχε καὶ σύ, ἵνα
κοινῇ πάσχωμεν, ἄν τι καὶ δέῃ. καί μοι λέγε· ἆρα
κινεῖσθαι καλεῖς, ὅταν τι χώραν ἐκ χώρας μεταβάλλῃ 15
ἢ καὶ ἐν τῷ αὐτῷ στρέφηται.
ΘΕΟ. Ἔγωγε.
ΣΩ. Τοῦτο μὲν τοίνυν ἓν ἔστω εἶδος. ὅταν δὲ ᾖ
d μὲν ἐν τῷ αὐτῷ, γηράσκῃ δέ, ἢ μέλαν ἐκ λευκοῦ ἢ
σκληρὸν ἐκ μαλακοῦ γίγνηται, ἤ τινα ἄλλην ἀλλοίω- 20

gerous mid-
dle ground
between
them ar-
mies. With
which side
shall we go?
Shall we
declare for
the inviola-
ble consti-
tution of all
things, or
for the
movement
party? Let
us examine
the latter
first, as we
began with
them.
Motion is
their prin-
ciple. Do
they admit
that motion
is of two
kinds, loco-
motion and
change?

1. μηδὲν μέτριον] 'Nothing
worthy of our reception.'
6. Οὐδὲν μὲν οὖν ἀνεκτόν] 'No
course is to be endured that
would prevent us from determining, &c.'
8. σοῦ γε οὕτω προθυμουμένου]
'You, that were so reluctant to
begin the discussion.' Cf. supr.
p. 169: οὐ μέντοι περαιτέρω γε ἂν
προίθισαι οἷός τ' ἔσομαι παρασχεῖν
ἐμαυτόν σοι.
9. ἀρχή] This is the predicate: the subject being contained in what follows. Hence
no article is required.

12. ἢ ὥσπερ ἐμοὶ φαίνεται,
δύο] Parm. 138: κινούμενόν γε
ἢ φέροιτο ἢ ἀλλοιοῖτο ἂν αὕτη
γὰρ μόναι κινήσεις. No argument can be drawn from this
about the comparative dates of
the two dialogues: although
the passage in which the distinction is elaborated, and not
assumed, might naturally be
supposed the earlier.
Aristot. Phys. Ausc. VIII. 3.
§ 3: πρὶν οὖν, ὥσπερ οὐ διορίζον-
τες ποίας κινήσεις λέγουσιν ἢ πάσας,
οὐ χαλεπὸν ἀπαντῆσαι.

190 ΠΛΑΤΩΝΟΣ

σιν ἀλλοιῶται, ἆρα οὐκ ἄξιον ἕτερον εἶδος φάναι κι- p. 181.
νήσεως;

ΘΕΟ. Ἔμοιγε δοκεῖ.

ΣΩ. Ἀναγκαῖον μὲν οὖν. δύο δὴ λέγω τούτω εἴδη
5 κινήσεως, ἀλλοίωσιν, τὴν δὲ περιφοράν.

ΘΕΟ. Ὀρθῶς γε λέγων.

On their granting this, we ask, Do you mean that all things move in both these ways? And they must say, Yes; or else it will be as true to say that things stand still, as that they move.

ΣΩ. Τοῦτο τοίνυν οὕτω διελόμενοι διαλεγώμεθα ἤδη τοῖς τὰ πάντα φάσκουσι κινεῖσθαι καὶ ἐρωτῶμεν· πότερον πᾶν φατὲ ἀμφοτέρως κινεῖσθαι, φερόμενόν
10 τε καὶ ἀλλοιούμενον, ἢ τὸ μέν τι ἀμφοτέρως, τὸ δ' ἑτέρως;

ΘΕΟ. Ἀλλὰ μὰ Δί' ἔγωγε οὐκ ἔχω εἰπεῖν· οἶμαι δ' ἂν φάναι ἀμφοτέρως.

ΣΩ. Εἰ δέ γε μή, ὦ ἑταῖρε, κινούμενά τε [αὐτοῖς]
15 καὶ ἑστῶτα φανεῖται, καὶ οὐδὲν μᾶλλον ὀρθῶς ἕξει εἰπεῖν ὅτι κινεῖται τὰ πάντα ἢ ὅτι ἕστηκεν.

ΘΕΟ. Ἀληθέστατα λέγεις.

ΣΩ. Οὐκοῦν ἐπειδὴ κινεῖσθαι αὐτὰ δεῖ, τὸ δὲ μὴ κινεῖσθαι μὴ ἐνεῖναι μηδενί, πάντα δὴ πᾶσαν κίνησιν p. 182.
20 ἀεὶ κινεῖται.

5. ἀλλοίωσιν, τὴν δὲ περιφοράν] Coisl. τὴν μὲν ἀλλ., τὴν δὲ περιφ. —quod glossema sapit. Stallb. It may be asked why circular motion should be chosen to represent φορά. The answer probably is, that the revolution of the Heavens is conceived of as embracing all other kinds of motion. Cf. supr. ἔστι μὲν ᾗ περιφορᾷ ᾗ κινουμένη καὶ ὁ ἥλιος. Perhaps also the revolution of the Heavens (or of the Sun) is symbolical of the Heraclitean cycle of elements. (Lassalle.) For περιφορά interchanged with φορά, see Rep. p. 528: ἐν περι-

φορᾷ ἤδη ὂν στερεὸν λαβόντες—— ἀστρονομίαν ἔλεγον, φοράν οὖσαν βάθους.

7. διαλεγώμεθα ἤδη] Imagining them, for the sake of our argument, to be less impracticable. ὑποτιθέμενοι κομψοτέρους αὐτοὺς ἢ νῦν ἐθέλοντες ἂν ἀποκρίνεσθαι. (Soph. 246.)

14. κινούμενά τε [αὐτοῖς] καὶ ἑστῶτα φανεῖται] Cf. Rep. 436: εἰ αἱ γε στρόβιλοι ὅλαι ἑστᾶσί τε ἅμα καὶ κινοῦνται. MSS. ἑαυτοῖς.

19. ἐνεῖναι] Almost all the MSS. have ἐν εἶναι. But the correction of the Bodl. MS. appears to be in an ancient hand.

ΘΕΑΙΤΗΤΟΣ. 131

p. 182. ΘΕΟ. Ἀνάγκη.

ΣΩ. Σκόπει δή μοι τόδε αὐτῶν· τῆς θερμότητος ἢ λευκότητος ἢ ὁτουοῦν γένεσιν οὐχ οὕτω πως ἐλέγομεν φάναι αὐτούς, φέρεσθαι ἕκαστον τούτων ἅμα αἰσθήσει μεταξὺ τοῦ ποιοῦντός τε καὶ πάσχοντος, καὶ τὸ μὲν b πάσχον †αἰσθητὸν† ἀλλ' οὐκ αἴσθησιν ἔτι γίγνεσθαι,

Let us now recal their theory of sensations and qualities, which were said to flit between the

2. Σκόπει δή μοι τόδε αὐτῶν] Cf. p. 149: Ἀρ' οὖν ἔτι καὶ τόδε αὐτῶν βοήσεις;
3. οὕτω πως ἐλέγομεν] Supr. pp. 156. 157. 159.
5. τὸ μὲν πάσχον †αἰσθητὸν†] αἰσθητὸν is inconsistent with the context, and with the language used elsewhere in the dialogue. Huttmann conjectured αἰσθητῷ, to which Schleiermacher objected that τὸ πάσχον means the sensorium, and not the sentient subject. But the distinction between them is not clearly marked from the Protagorean point of view. Indeed the conception of a 'sensorium' nowhere appears, at least in this part of the dialogue. It is only in speaking of a particular sense that τὸ πάσχον means, for instance, the eye. (p. 157.) In p. 159 it appears doubtful whether τὸ πάσχον means the tongue or Socrates, or more indefinitely the 'recipient.' And even if τὸ πάσχον is limited to the organ of sense, there is no reason why αἰσθητὴν should not be used of this. (Cf. Xen. Mem. I. 5: ἡ γλῶσσα γυμνῶν τούτων ἐπισπωμένη.) The noun αἰσθητὴς appears to be suggested in p. 160, (if it is not coined on the spot,) by the use of ἐπιστήμων just before.

In the present place it might recur naturally, as it is in the manner of Plato to recal a train of thought by repeating some remarkable word. (Rep. 488. οἱ ἐπιστήσονται. Supr. 180. τό γε δὴ πρόχθημα.) To which it may be added, that there is a consciousness of technicality observable in the present passage. (ἴσως οὖν ἡ ποιότης ἅμα ἀλλόκοτόν τι φαίνεται ὄνομα κ. τ. λ.) Apart from these considerations, the rareness of the word, which would be a strong argument in its favour if it had MS. authority, must be allowed to weigh against it as a conjectural reading. And it may also be urged, that the masculine gender of αἰσθητῆς would impair the effect of the passage, in which every thing seems to be made, as far as possible, neuter and impersonal.

The other conjectural reading, αἰσθανόμενον, agrees perfectly with the context and with all that precedes, and it is quite possible that αἰσθητὼ may have slipped in instead of it by an unconscious logical inversion on the part of the copyist.

6. ἔτι] i. e. when we carry our analysis so far.

S 2

132   ΠΛΑΤΩΝΟΣ

subject and τὸ δὲ ποιοῦν ποιόν τι ἀλλ' οὐ ποιότητα; ἴσως οὖν ἡ p. 182.
the object.   ποιότης ἅμα ἀλλόκοτόν τε φαίνεται ὄνομα καὶ οὐ
μανθάνεις ἀθρόον λεγόμενον· κατὰ μέρη οὖν ἄκουε.
τὸ γὰρ ποιοῦν οὔτε θερμότης οὔτε λευκότης, θερμὸν b
5 δὲ καὶ λευκὸν γίγνεται, καὶ τἆλλα οὕτω. μέμνησαι
γάρ που ἐν τοῖς πρόσθεν ὅτι οὕτως ἐλέγομεν, ἓν
μηδὲν αὐτὸ καθ' αὑτὸ εἶναι, μηδ' αὖ τὸ ποιοῦν ἢ
πάσχον, ἀλλ' ἐξ ἀμφοτέρων πρὸς ἄλληλα συγγιγνο-
μένων τὰς αἰσθήσεις καὶ τὰ αἰσθητὰ ἀποτίκτοντα τὰ
10 μὲν ποιά ἄττα γίγνεσθαι, τὰ δὲ αἰσθανόμενα.

ΘΕΟ. Μέμνημαι· πῶς δ' οὔ;

ΣΩ. Τὰ μὲν τοίνυν ἄλλα χαίρειν ἐάσωμεν, εἴτε c
ἄλλως εἴτε οὕτως λέγουσιν· οὗ δ' ἕνεκα λέγομεν,
τοῦτο μόνον φυλάττωμεν, ἐρωτῶντες· Κινεῖται καὶ
15 ῥεῖ, ὥς φατέ, τὰ πάντα; ἢ γάρ;

1. ποιόν τι] MSS. ποιοῦντι. But the Bodleian margin has ποιόν τι, with marg. F, corr. E.

ἡ ποιότης] Two difficulties stand in the way of the reception of any new 'term of art;' the strangeness of the word, and the effort required to follow the generalization which it presupposes.

2. ἀλλόκοτον] 'Strange and uncouth.'

3. ἀθρόον λεγόμενον] 'The collective (i. e. general) expression.' This harmonises with the language adopted above, p. 157. δεῖ δὲ καὶ κατὰ μέρος αὐτῶ λέγειν καὶ περὶ πολλῶν ἀθροισθέντων, ᾦ δὴ ἀθροίσματι ἄνθρωπόν τε τίθενται καὶ λίθον καὶ ἕκαστον ζῶόν τε καὶ εἶδος.

The conception of quality is of later growth than that of kind or form; this being less abstract, and still retaining a tinge of metaphor.

8. ἀλλ' ἐξ ἀμφοτέρων—αἰσθανόμενα] The construction alters as the sense develops itself; at first scarcely more is intended than γίγνεσθαι ὅσα δεῖ γίγνεται: presently the genitive becomes the subject of the infinitive. 'But out of both as they come together—they become, while producing sensations and sensible things, the one of a certain kind, the other percipient.'

14. φυλάττωμεν—ἵνα μὴ ἀλῷ ταύτῃ μόνον] Cf. supr. p. 154: φυλάττου μὴ ἐναντία εἴπω. Infr. p. 183: ἵνα δὴ ἑκούσῃ ἡ ἀνθρώπινε ὀρθὴ φανῇ. And, for the argument, Cratyl. 439: 'Αρ' οὖν οἷόν τε προσειπεῖν αὐτὸ ὀρθῶς, εἰ ἀεὶ ὑπεξέρχεται, πρῶτον μὲν ὅτι ἐκεῖνό ἐστιν, ἔπειτα ὅτι τοιοῦτον. ἢ ἀνάγκη ἅμα ἡμῶν λεγόντων ἄλλο αὐτὸ εὐθὺς

ΘΕΑΙΤΗΤΟΣ. 193

p. 182. ΘΕΟ. Ναί.

ΣΩ. Οὐκοῦν ἀμφοτέρας ἃς διειλόμεθα κινήσεις, φερόμενά τε καὶ ἀλλοιούμενα;

ΘΕΟ. Πῶς δ' οὔ; εἴ πέρ γε δὴ τελέως κινήσεται.

ΣΩ. Εἰ μὲν τοίνυν ἐφέρετο μόνον, ἠλλοιοῦτο δὲ μή, εἴχομεν ἄν που εἰπεῖν, οἷα ἄττα ῥεῖ τὰ φερόμενα· ἢ πῶς λέγωμεν;

ΘΕΟ. Οὕτως.

d ΣΩ. Ἐπειδὴ δὲ οὐδὲ τοῦτο μένει, τὸ λευκὸν ῥεῖν τὸ ῥέον, ἀλλὰ μεταβάλλει, ὥστε καὶ αὐτοῦ τούτου εἶναι ῥοήν, τῆς λευκότητος, καὶ μεταβολὴν εἰς ἄλλην χρόαν, ἵνα μὴ ἁλῷ ταύτῃ μένον· ἆρά ποτε οἷόν τέ τι προσειπεῖν χρῶμα, ὥστε καὶ ὀρθῶς προσαγορεύειν;

ΘΕΟ. Καὶ τίς μηχανή, ὦ Σώκρατες; ἢ ἄλλο γέ τι τῶν τοιούτων, εἴπερ ἀεὶ λέγοντος ὑπεξέρχεται, ἅτε δὴ ῥέον;

ΣΩ. Τί δὲ περὶ αἰσθήσεως ἐροῦμεν ὁποιασοῦν, οἷον τῆς τοῦ ὁρᾶν ἢ ἀκούειν; μένειν ποτὲ ἐν αὐτῷ τῷ e ὁρᾶν ἢ ἀκούειν;

ΘΕΟ. Οὔκουν δεῖ γε, εἴπερ πάντα κινεῖται.

ΣΩ. Οὔτε ἄρα ὁρᾶν προσρητέον τι μᾶλλον ἢ μὴ ὁρᾶν, οὐδέ τιν' ἄλλην αἴσθησιν μᾶλλον ἢ μή, πάντων γε πάντως κινουμένων.

ΘΕΟ. Οὐ γὰρ οὖν.

ΣΩ. Καὶ μὴν αἴσθησίς γε ἐπιστήμη, ὡς ἔφαμεν ἐγώ τε καὶ Θεαίτητος.

ΘΕΟ. Ἦν ταῦτα.

If the qua-lity were moved without changing, we might give them names. But now, while each of them is moving between object and subject, it also changes, so that while you are naming it, it has become something else.

And the same argument applies to the sensations, and to Sensation, which we said was Knowledge. Therefore when we said Sensation was Knowledge, it would have been equally true to say, Not-knowledge.

γίγνεσθαι καὶ ἐπεξιέναι καὶ μηκέτι οὕτως ἔχειν;

14. τι προσειπεῖν χρῶμα] To give the name of any color (to an object) — To use the name of any colour so as to apply it rightly.

17. Τί δὲ περὶ αἰσθήσεως] So far of αἰσθητά, now of αἰσθήσεις.

ΠΛΑΤΩΝΟΣ

The principle of motion has proved a fallacious support, since according to it every answer, whether Yes or No, is, or rather becomes, equally true, except that both Yes and No are falsified while we are uttering them. A new dialect should be invented to carry out this theory. The only word for it

ΣΩ. Οὐδὲν ἄρα ἐπιστήμην μᾶλλον ἢ μὴ ἐπιστή- p. 182.
μην ἀπεκρινάμεθα ἐρωτώμενοι ὅ τί ἐστιν ἐπιστήμη.
ΘΕΟ. Ἐοίκατε. p. 183.
ΣΩ. Καλὸν ἂν ἡμῖν συμβαίνοι τὸ ἐπανόρθωμα
5 τῆς ἀποκρίσεως, προθυμηθεῖσιν ἀποδεῖξαι ὅτι πάντα
κινεῖται, ἵνα δὴ ἐκείνη ἡ ἀπόκρισις ὀρθὴ φανῇ. τὸ δ᾽,
ὡς ἔοικεν, ἐφάνη, εἰ πάντα κινεῖται, πᾶσα ἀπόκρισις,
περὶ ὅτου ἄν τις ἀποκρίνηται, ὁμοίως ὀρθὴ εἶναι, οὕτω
τ᾽ ἔχειν φάναι καὶ μὴ οὕτω, εἰ δὲ βούλει, γίγνεσθαι,
10 ἵνα μὴ στήσωμεν αὐτοὺς τῷ λόγῳ.
ΘΕΟ. Ὀρθῶς λέγεις.
ΣΩ. Πλήν γε, ὦ Θεόδωρε, ὅτι οὕτω τε εἶπον καὶ
οὐχ οὕτω. δεῖ δὲ οὐδὲ τοῦτο τὸ οὕτω λέγειν· οὐδὲ γὰρ
ἂν ἔτι κινοῖτο τὸ οὕτω· οὐδ᾽ αὖ μὴ οὕτω· οὐδὲ γὰρ b
15 τοῦτο κίνησις· ἀλλά τιν᾽ ἄλλην φωνὴν θετέον τοῖς

4. Καλὸν ἂν ἡμῖν] "Here is a fine result of having corrected (or completed) our first answer in our eagerness to prove that nothing is at rest, and so to make it clear that that first answer was right, whereas it would seem to be made clear that if nothing is at rest, every answer upon whatever subject is equally right, both 'it is so' and 'it is not so,' or, if you choose, 'becomes so,' that we may say nothing that would bring them to a stand-still." Heind. compares Rep. X. 602: χαρίεν ὃν εἴη κ.τ.λ.

8. οὕτω τ᾽ ἔχειν φάναι] In apposition to ἀπόκρισι. While you are naming a quality, it is altered and slips away; and while you are naming a sensation, it has given place to another. While you say the words Sense is knowledge, your theory of change compels you to utter in the same breath, Sense is not knowledge. In supporting your answer by the doctrine of motion, you have made this and every other answer alike unstable.

12. Πλήν γε, ὦ Θεόδωρε] μή is changed to οὐχ, because the words are taken out of their hypothetical connexion. Compare the language of the Parmenides, e.g. p. 158: ἕν τε ἓν καὶ πολλὰ καὶ μήτε ἓν μήτε πολλά.

13. οὐδὲ γάρ] "For when we think of 'so,' there is no motion in it: nor yet in 'not so.'"

15. ἀλλά τιν᾽ ἄλλην φωνὴν θετέον] Cf. supr. 157. Soph. 252 : τῷ τε εἶναί που περὶ πάντα ἀπηυδήκασι χρῆσθαι καὶ τῷ χωρὶς καὶ τῷ ἄλλων καὶ τῷ καθ᾽ αὑτὸ καὶ μυρίοις ἕτεροις, ἐν ἀκρατεῖς ὄντες εἰργεσθαι καὶ μὴ συνάπτειν ἐν τοῖς λόγοις οὐκ

ΘΕΑΙΤΗΤΟΣ.

p. 183. τὸν λόγον τοῦτον λέγουσιν, ὡς νῦν γε πρὸς τὴν αὑτῶν ὑπόθεσιν οὐκ ἔχουσι ῥήματα, εἰ μὴ ἄρα τὸ οὐδ᾽ ὅπως. μάλιστα δ᾽ οὕτως ἂν αὐτοῖς ἁρμόττοι, ἄπειρον λεγόμενον.

ΘΕΟ. Οἰκειοτάτη γοῦν διάλεκτος αὕτη αὐτοῖς.

ΣΩ. Οὐκοῦν, ὦ Θεόδωρε, τοῦ τε σοῦ ἑταίρου ἀπηλλάγμεθα, καὶ οὔπω συγχωροῦμεν αὐτῷ πάντ᾽ ἄνδρα πάντων χρημάτων μέτρον εἶναι, ἂν μὴ φρόνιμός τις ᾖ· ἐπιστήμην τε αἴσθησιν οὐ συγχωρησόμεθα κατά γε τὴν τοῦ πάντα κινεῖσθαι μέθοδον. εἰ μή τί πως ἄλλως Θεαίτητος ὅδε λέγει.

ἄλλων δέονται τῶν ἐξελεγχόντων, κ. τ. λ.

(15) φωνήν] "Dialect."
Arist. Met. I. 4. 1008. a: οὔτε γὰρ οὕτως οὔτ᾽ οὐχ οὕτως λέγει, ἀλλ᾽ οὕτως τε καὶ οὐχ οὕτως. καὶ πάλιν γε ταῦτα ἀπόφησιν ἄμφω ὅτι οὔθ᾽ οὕτως οὔτε οὐχ οὕτως. εἰ γὰρ μή, ἤδη ἂν εἴη τι ὡρισμένον.

Aristotle points out (1), that it does not follow, because quantity is wholly relative, that quality need be so also; (2) that it is not the quality, but the subject of it, which changes.

Sensations are wholly shifting and relative. They could not be the objects of the mind, unless we perceived resemblance and difference in them. In every act of sense, therefore, there is a universal element, and the mind gives to it its own stamp of unity.

Arist. Met. Γ. 1008. a: καὶ γίγνεται δὴ τὸ Ἀναξαγόρου, ὁμοῦ πάντα χρήματα· ὥστε μηθὲν ἀληθῶς ὑπάρχειν. τὸ ἀόριστον οὖν ἐοίκασι λέγειν, καὶ οἰόμενοι τὸ ὂν λέγειν, περὶ τοῦ μὴ ὄντος λέγουσιν· τὸ γὰρ δυνάμει ὂν καὶ μὴ ἐντελεχείᾳ τὸ

ἀόριστόν ἐστιν.

2. τὸ αὐθ᾽ ὅπως—ἄπειρον λεγόμενον] With most of the Greek philosophers the Infinite was a purely negative idea.

At this point sensation appears to be annihilated. And yet if we view the dialogue as a whole, the impression we receive from it is rather this:— Sensations are purely relative to the individual, and infinitely diverse: taken alone, therefore, they cannot be the objects of knowledge and thought: but it is not denied that they are the occasions of thought and the conditions of knowledge. (p. 186. ἐν μὲν ἄρα τοῖς παθήμασιν οὔκ ἔνι ἐπιστήμη, ἐν δὲ τῷ περὶ ἐκείνων συλλογισμῷ.)

3. οὕτως ἂν αὐτ.] Viz. οὐδ᾽ ὅπως.

6. τοῦ τε σοῦ ἑταίρου] This τε is answered to by ἐπιστήμην τε—, and is epexegetic.

Aristotle, Met. Γ. 1009. a, expresses the same sense of relief, καὶ τοῦ λόγου ἀπηλλαγμένοι ἂν εἴημεν τοῦ ἀορίστου καὶ κωλύοντός τι τῇ διανοίᾳ ὁρίσαι.

marginal note: Thus we are rid, not only of Protagoras, but also of the theory of sense, so far as it is based on motion.

136 ΠΛΑΤΩΝΟΣ

ΘΕΟ. Ἄριστ' εἴρηκας, ὦ Σώκρατες· τούτων γὰρ p. 183.
περανθέντων καὶ ἐμὲ δεῖ ἀπηλλάχθαι σοι ἀπυκρινό-
μενον κατὰ τὰς συνθήκας, ἐπειδὴ τὸ περὶ τοῦ Πρωταγόρου λόγου τέλος σχοίη.

ΘΕΑΙ. Μὴ πρίν γ' ἄν, ὦ Θεόδωρε, Σωκράτης τε
καὶ σὺ τοὺς φάσκοντας αὖ τὸ πᾶν ἑστάναι διέλθητε, d
ὥσπερ ἄρτι προύθεσθε.

ΘΕΟ. Νέος ὤν, ὦ Θεαίτητε, τοὺς πρεσβυτέρους
ἀδικεῖν διδάσκεις ὁμολογίας παραβαίνοντας; ἀλλὰ
παρασκευάζου ὅπως τῶν ἐπιλοίπων Σωκράτει δώσεις
λόγον.

ΘΕΑΙ. Ἐάνπερ γε βούληται. ἥδιστα μέντ' ἂν
ἤκουσα περὶ ὧν λέγω.

ΘΕΟ. Ἱππέας εἰς πεδίον προκαλεῖ Σωκράτη εἰς
λόγους προκαλούμενος· ἐρώτα οὖν καὶ ἀκούσει.

ΣΩ. Ἀλλά μοι δοκῶ, ὦ Θεόδωρε, περί γε ὧν κελεύει Θεαίτητος, οὐ πείσεσθαι αὐτῷ. e

ΘΕΟ. Τί δὴ οὖν οὐ πείσεσθαι;

ΣΩ. Μέλισσον μὲν καὶ τοὺς ἄλλους οἳ ἓν ἑστὸς
λέγουσι τὸ πᾶν, αἰσχυνόμενος μὴ φορτικῶς σκοπῶμεν, ἧττον αἰσχύνομαι ἢ ἕνα ὄντα Παρμενίδην. Παρ-

Theaetetus desires now to hear the opposite theory (that of rest) discussed. But Socrates declines doing so. 'Parmenides, whom I once saw in his old age, inspires me, for his glorious depth, with reverence.

4. σχοίη] The optative depends on συνθήκαις. As it was agreed I should, when the discussion of Protagoras' argument should be completed.

14. Ἱππέας εἰς πεδίον] "You challenge cavalry to an encounter in an open plain."

Schol.: Ἱππέας προκαλεῖσθαι εἰς πεδίον, ἐπὶ τῶν τοῖς ἐν τισι βελτίοσιν καὶ ἐπιστημονεστέροις αὐτῶν εἰς ἔριν προκαλουμένων. Πλάτων ἐν Θεαιτήτῳ καὶ Μένανδρος Καταψευδομένῳ. γράφεται δὲ καὶ Ἵππον εἰς πεδίον προκαλεῖσθαι ἐπὶ τῶν εἰς ἃ βούλεταί τις προκαλούντων. The latter interpretation is alone suitable here.

18. Τί δὴ οὖν] Either 'in what respect?' or 'for what reason?' The former is preferable. Comp. Rep. p. 449: Τί μάλιστα, ἔφην, ὑμεῖς οὐκ ἀφίετε; Σί, ἦ δ' ὅς. Ἔτι ἐγὼ ἑστώς, τί μάλιστα; Ἀποφράθυμεῖν ἡμῖν δοκεῖς, ἔφην.

19. ἑστὸς] So Bodl. (though rather doubtfully) with Vat. Ven, Π.

ΘΕΑΙΤΗΤΟΣ. 187

p. 183. μενίδης δέ μοι φαίνεται, τὸ τοῦ Ὁμήρου, αἰδοῖός τέ μοι ἅμα [εἶναι] δεινός τε. συμπροσέμιξα γὰρ δὴ τῷ ἀνδρὶ πάνυ νέος πάνυ πρεσβύτῃ, καί μοι ἐφάνη βάθος
p. 184. τι ἔχειν παντάπασι γενναῖον. φοβοῦμαι οὖν μὴ οὔτε τὰ λεγόμενα ξυνιῶμεν, τί τε διανοούμενος εἶπε πολὺ 5 πλέον λειπώμεθα, καὶ τὸ μέγιστον, οὗ ἕνεκα ὁ λόγος ὥρμηται, ἐπιστήμης πέρι, τί ποτ' ἐστίν, ἄσκεπτον γένηται ὑπὸ τῶν ἐπεισκωμαζόντων λόγων, εἴ τις αὐ-

1. τὸ τοῦ Ὁμήρου] Il. III. 172: αἰδοῖός τέ μοι ἐσσὶ, φίλε ἑκυρέ, δεινός τε. (Post ἅμα Zitt. Ven. Π. Par. C. εἶναι inserunt. Stallb. This is very possibly right.)

2. συμπροσέμιξα γὰρ—τῷ ἀνδρὶ πάνυ νέος πάνυ πρεσβύτῃ] In what connection do these words stand with the Parmenides? Do they imply that Plato had already written it, or that he had conceived it; or do they refer to a fact or to a supposition which was the germ from which that dialogue sprang, or which was used to ornament it, by Plato or by some one else? Or did Plato add the present passage after both dialogues had been written? Some light is thrown upon this question by comparing Soph. 217: οἶον (δ' ἐρωτήσεων) καὶ Παρμενίδῃ χρωμένῳ καὶ διεξιόντι λόγους παγκάλους παρεγενόμην ἐγὼ νέος ὤν, ἐκείνου μάλα δὴ τότε ὄντος πρεσβύτου. This passage conveys the impression that the written dialogue is referred to. At all events, the repeated reference helps to mark the Parmenides as belonging to this series of dialogues. The same conception of the time at which Parmenides lived, and the same reverence for him, is implied in the words of the Eleatic stranger,

(his professed disciple), Soph. 237: Παρμενίδῃ δὲ ὁ μέγας, ὦ παῖ, παισὶν ἡμῖν οὖσιν——διεμαρτύρατο——ἑκάστοτε λέγων,

3. βάθος τι] "A magnificent depth of mind." Schol. φαίνεται καὶ Ἀριστοτέλης συμφύνων τῷ Παρμενίδῃ.

4. οὔτε τὰ λεγόμενα] It is remarkable to find in Plato such a distinct perception of the difference between the grammatical sense and the real drift of an author.

7. ἄσκεπτον γένηται] "Should fail to be considered through the endless intrusion of alien subjects of inquiry."

8. ἐπεισκωμαζόντων λόγων] We pass from the image of a flood (sup. 177.) to that of a disorderly crowd of discussions. Compare Philebus, p. 62: βούλει δῆτα, ὥσπερ θυρωρὸς ὑπ' ὄχλου τις ὠθούμενος καὶ βιαζόμενος, ἡττηθεὶς ἀναπετάσας τὰς θύρας ἀφῶ πάσας τὰς ἐπιστήμας εἰσρεῖν καὶ μίγνυσθαι ὁμοῦ καθαρᾷ τῇ ἐνδεεστέρᾳ; See also Shakespeare, Rape of Lucrece: 'Much like a press of people at a door throng her inventions, which shall go before.' For the use of the verb, see Rep. p. 500: ἐπεισκωμαζόντας—— said of the bad philosophers.

τ

ΠΛΑΤΩΝΟΣ

water in should cause the quotation about Knowledge to be endlessly deferred.

τοῖς πείσεται· ἄλλως τε καί, ὃν νῦν ἐγείρομεν πλήθει p. 184. ἀμήχανον, εἴ τέ τις ἐν παρέργῳ σκέψεται, ἀνάξι᾽ ἂν πάθοι, εἴτε ἱκανῶς, μηκυνόμενος τὸ τῆς ἐπιστήμης ἀφανιεῖ. δεῖ δὲ οὐδέτερα, ἀλλὰ Θεαίτητον ὧν κυεῖ b
5 περὶ ἐπιστήμης πειρᾶσθαι ἡμᾶς τῇ μαιευτικῇ τέχνῃ ἀπολῦσαι.

ΘΕΟ. Ἀλλὰ χρή, εἰ δοκεῖ, οὕτω ποιεῖν.

Transition from sense to opinion. We therefore return once more upon our old track, and ask, With what do we see and hear what is white or shrill?

ΣΩ. Ἔτι τοίνυν, ὦ Θεαίτητε, τοσόνδε περὶ τῶν εἰρημένων ἐπίσκεψαι. αἴσθησιν γὰρ δὴ ἐπιστήμην
10 ἀπεκρίνω. ἦ γάρ;

ΘΕΑΙ. Ναί.

ΣΩ. Εἰ οὖν τίς σε ὧδ᾽ ἐρωτῴη· τῷ τὰ λευκὰ καὶ μέλανα ὁρᾷ ἄνθρωπος καὶ τῷ τὰ ὀξέα καὶ βαρέα ἀκούει; εἴποις ἄν, οἶμαι, ὄμμασί τε καὶ ὠσίν.

15 ΘΕΑΙ. Ἔγωγε.

Do we see and hear with our eyes and ears or through them? Not with, but through.

ΣΩ. Τὸ δὲ εὐχερὲς τῶν ὀνομάτων τε καὶ ῥημάτων c καὶ μὴ δι᾽ ἀκριβείας ἐξεταζόμενον τὰ μὲν πολλὰ οὐκ ἀγεννές, ἀλλὰ μᾶλλον τὸ τούτου ἐναντίον ἀνελεύθερον, ἔστι δὲ ὅτε ἀναγκαῖον, οἷον καὶ νῦν ἀνάγκη ἐπι-
20 λαβέσθαι τῆς ἀποκρίσεως ἣν ἀποκρίνει, ᾗ οὐκ ὀρθή.

---

2. εἴ τε τις κ.τ.λ.] The reasons given here for avoiding a criticism of Parmenides and the Eleatic doctrine are not such as would prevent its being discussed in another dialogue. It would therefore be a mistake to argue from them against the genuineness of the Sophista. Compare with the expression ὃν νῦν ἐγείρομεν πλήθει ἀμήχανον— Rep. p. 450: οὐκ ἔστε ἔσω ἰσμὲν λόγων ἐπεγείρατι.

4. ἂν κυεῖ] Bodl. Vat. Ven. Π. ὄν. Perhaps rightly.

6. ἀπολῦσαι] "To deliver."

8. Ἔτι τοίνυν] As usual, the transition to a new hypothesis is not made without reference to the last.

16. Τὸ—εὐχερὲς]'Facility about words and phrases rather than minute criticism.' Cf. Polit. 261: ἂν διαφυλάξῃς τὸ μὴ σπουδάζειν ἐπὶ τοῖς ὀνόμασιν, πλουσιώτερος εἰς τὸ γῆρας ἀναφανήσει φρονήσεως. Cf. Arist. Met. 995 a: τοῦτο δὲ λυπεῖ τὸ ἀκριβὲς ἢ διὰ τὸ μὴ δύνασθαι συνείρειν ἢ διὰ τὴν μικρολογίαν· ἔχει γάρ τι τὸ ἀκριβὲς τοιοῦτον, ὥστε καθάπερ ἐπὶ τῶν συμβολαίων, καὶ ἐπὶ τῶν λόγων ἀνελεύθερον εἶναί τισι δοκεῖ.

ΘΕΑΙΤΗΤΟΣ.

p. 184. σκόπει γάρ, ἀπόκρισις ποτέρα ὀρθοτέρα, ᾧ ὁρῶμεν, τοῦτο εἶναι ὀφθαλμούς, ἢ δι' οὗ ὁρῶμεν, καὶ ᾧ ἀκούομεν, ὦτα, ἢ δι' οὗ ἀκούομεν;

ΘΕΑΙ. Δι' ὧν ἕκαστα αἰσθανόμεθα, ἔμοιγε δοκεῖ, ὦ Σώκρατες, μᾶλλον ἢ οἷς.

d ΣΩ. Δεινὸν γάρ που, ὦ παῖ, εἰ πολλαί τινες ἐν ἡμῖν, ὥσπερ ἐν δουρείοις ἵπποις, αἰσθήσεις ἐγκάθηνται, ἀλλὰ μὴ εἰς μίαν τινὰ ἰδέαν, εἴτε ψυχὴν εἴτε ὅ τι δεῖ καλεῖν, πάντα ταῦτα ξυντείνει, ᾗ διὰ τούτων οἷον ὀργάνων αἰσθανόμεθα ὅσα αἰσθητά.

ΘΕΑΙ. Ἀλλά μοι δοκεῖ οὕτω μᾶλλον ἢ ἐκείνως.

ΣΩ. Τοῦ δέ τοι ἕνεκα αὐτά σοι διακριβοῦμαι, εἴ τινι ἡμῶν αὐτῶν τῷ αὐτῷ διὰ μὲν ὀφθαλμῶν ἐφικνούμεθα λευκῶν τε καὶ μελάνων, διὰ δὲ τῶν ἄλλων

e ἑτέρων αὖ τινῶν. καὶ ἕξεις ἐρωτώμενος πάντα τὰ τοιαῦτα εἰς τὸ σῶμα ἀναφέρειν; ἴσως δὲ βέλτιον σὲ λέγειν αὐτὰ ἀποκρινόμενον μᾶλλον ἢ ἐμὲ ὑπὲρ σοῦ πολυπραγμονεῖν. καί μοι λέγε· θερμὰ καὶ σκληρὰ καὶ κοῦφα καὶ γλυκέα δι' ὧν αἰσθάνει, ἆρα οὐ τοῦ σώματος ἕκαστα τίθης; ἢ ἄλλου τινός;

ΘΕΑΙ. Οὐδενὸς ἄλλου.

We are not each of us a sort of Trojan-horse-full of faculties. There is one pro- 10 viding na- ture, in which they all meet. It is this with which we see through our eyes and hear 15 through our ears. But we cannot see and hear through the same organ.

6. Δεινὸν γάρ που] 'Would it not be strange, if in each of us there were perched, as in a sort of Trojan horse, a number of separate perceptions, and these did not all meet in some one nature, the Mind or what you will, *with* which, *through* these as instruments, we perceive the various objects of sense?'

7. ὥσπερ ἐν δουρείοις ἵπποις] The plural is caused by ἡμῶν. As if each of us were a sort of wooden machine, like the Trojan horse.—Man cannot be regarded as a bundle of separate faculties having no higher unity: that would be too mechanical a conception of his nature. The term 'organ of sense' perhaps originates with this passage.

12. Τοῦ δέ τοι ἕνεκα] It is with a view to this that I am so exact with you, namely, to the inquiry whether, &c. τοῦδε has a double reference to εἰς μίαν τινὰ ἰδέαν—αἰσθητά and to εἴ τινι κ. τ. λ.

ΣΩ. Ἦ καὶ ἐθελήσεις ὁμολογεῖν, ἃ δι' ἑτέρας δυνάμεως αἰσθάνει, ἀδύνατον εἶναι δι' ἄλλης ταῦτ' p. 185. αἰσθέσθαι, οἷον ἃ δι' ἀκοῆς, δι' ὄψεως, ἢ ἃ δι' ὄψεως, δι' ἀκοῆς;

ΘΕΑΙ. Πῶς γὰρ οὐκ ἐθελήσω;

ΣΩ. Εἴ τι ἄρα περὶ ἀμφοτέρων διανοεῖ, οὐκ ἂν διά γε τοῦ ἑτέρου ὀργάνου, οὐδ' αὖ διὰ τοῦ ἑτέρου περὶ ἀμφοτέρων αἰσθάνοι' ἄν.

ΘΕΑΙ. Οὐ γὰρ οὖν.

ΣΩ. Περὶ δὴ φωνῆς καὶ περὶ χρόας πρῶτον μὲν αὐτὸ τοῦτο περὶ ἀμφοτέρων ἦ διανοεῖ, ὅτι ἀμφοτέρω ἐστόν;

ΘΕΑΙ. Ἔγωγε.

ΣΩ. Οὐκοῦν καὶ ὅτι ἑκάτερον ἑκατέρου μὲν ἕτερον, ἑαυτῷ δὲ ταὐτόν;

ΘΕΑΙ. Τί μήν;   b

ΣΩ. Καὶ ὅτι ἀμφοτέρω δύο, ἑκάτερον δὲ ἕν;

ΘΕΑΙ. Καὶ τοῦτο.

ΣΩ. Οὐκοῦν καὶ εἴτε ἀνομοίω εἴτε ὁμοίω ἀλλήλοιν, δυνατὸς εἰ ἐπισκέψασθαι;

ΘΕΑΙ. Ἴσως.

ΣΩ. Ταῦτα δὴ πάντα διὰ τίνος περὶ αὐτοῖν διανοεῖ; οὔτε γὰρ δι' ἀκοῆς οὔτε δι' ὄψεως οἷόν τε τὸ κοινὸν λαμβάνειν περὶ αὐτῶν. ἔτι δὲ καὶ τόδε τεκμήριον περὶ οὗ λέγομεν· εἰ γὰρ δυνατὸν εἴη· ἀμφοτέρω

There are some things which we perceive about the objects of both senses, e. g. that they are both, that they are different from each other, and each the same with itself. That both are two, and each is one. That they are like or unlike. Through what do you perceive these things? If I had asked through

1. ἃ δι' ἑτέρας δυνάμεως] The object of one sense cannot be perceived by another. Therefore if I perceive anything about the objects of two different senses, it cannot be through either of them.

23. τὸ κοινόν] That which regards them both. You can refer any particular sensation to its proper organ. Can you do so in the case of these common perceptions?

Cf. Rep. p. 523: οἷον τοῦτο τὸ ταὐτόν, ᾧ πᾶσαι προσχρῶνται—ἐπιστήμαι—τὸ ἕν τε καὶ τὰ δύο καὶ τὰ τρία διαγιγνώσκειν.

ΘΕΑΙΤΗΤΟΣ. 141

p. 185. σκέψασθαι, ἆρ' ἐστὸν ἁλμυρὰ ἢ οὔ, οἶσθ' ὅτι ἕξεις ὁ εἰπεῖν ᾧ ἐπισκέψει, καὶ τοῦτο οὔτε ὄψις οὔτε ἀκοὴ φαίνεται, ἀλλά τι ἄλλο.

ΘΕΑΙ. Τί δ' οὐ μέλλει, ἥ γε διὰ τῆς γλώττης δύναμις;

ΣΩ. Καλῶς λέγεις. ἡ δὲ δὴ διὰ τίνος δύναμις τό τ' ἐπὶ πᾶσι κοινὸν καὶ τὸ ἐπὶ τούτοις δηλοῖ σοι, ᾧ τὸ ἔστιν ἐπονομάζεις καὶ τὸ οὐκ ἔστι καὶ ἃ νῦν δὴ ἠρωτῶμεν περὶ αὐτῶν; τούτοις πᾶσι ποῖα ἀποδώσεις ὄργανα, δι' ὧν αἰσθάνεται ἡμῶν τὸ αἰσθανόμενον ἕκαστα;

ΘΕΑΙ. Οὐσίαν λέγεις καὶ τὸ μὴ εἶναι, καὶ ὁμοιότητα καὶ ἀνομοιότητα, καὶ τὸ ταὐτόν τε καὶ τὸ ἕτερον, d ἔτι δὲ ἕν τε καὶ τὸν ἄλλον ἀριθμὸν περὶ αὐτῶν. δῆλον δὲ ὅτι καὶ ἄρτιόν τε καὶ περιττὸν ἐρωτᾷς, καὶ τἆλλα ὅσα τούτοις ἕπεται, διὰ τίνος ποτὲ τῶν τοῦ σώματος τῇ ψυχῇ αἰσθανόμεθα.

ΣΩ. Ὑπέρευ, ὦ Θεαίτητε, ἀκολουθεῖς, καὶ ἔστιν ἃ ἐρωτῶ αὐτὰ ταῦτα.

ΘΕΑΙ. Ἀλλὰ μὰ Δία, ὦ Σώκρατες, ἔγωγε οὐκ ἂν ἔχοιμι εἰπεῖν, πλήν γ' ὅτι μοι δοκεῖ τὴν ἀρχὴν οὐδ' εἶναι τοιοῦτον οὐδὲν τούτοις ὄργανον ἴδιον ὥσπερ ἐκείνοις, ἀλλ' αὐτὴ δι' αὑτῆς ἡ ψυχὴ τὰ κοινά μοι φαίνεται περὶ πάντων ἐπισκοπεῖν.

ΣΩ. Καλὸς γὰρ εἶ, ὦ Θεαίτητε, καὶ οὐχ, ὡς ἔλεγε

6. τό τ' ἐπὶ πᾶσι κοινὸν καὶ τὸ ἐπὶ τούτοις] Which is common not only to all the senses, but to all things.

8. ἃ νῦν δὴ ἠρωτῶμεν] Viz. as Theætetus understands it, ὁμοιότητα καὶ ἀνομοιότητα, καὶ τὸ ταὐτόν τε καὶ τὸ ἕτερον, ἔτι δὲ ἕν τε καὶ τὸν ἄλλον ἀριθμὸν περὶ αὐτῶν, referring to what has just preceded.

9. περὶ αὐτῶν] Concerning the objects of sense.

22. ὄργανον ἴδιον] The Bodl. MS. has ὀργανίδιον.

25. Καλὸς γὰρ εἶ] The enthusiasm with which Socrates accepts Theætetus' acknowledg-

Θεόδωρος, αἰσχρός· ὁ γὰρ καλῶς λέγων καλός τε p. 185.
κἀγαθός. πρὸς δὲ τῷ καλῷ εὖ ἐποίησάς με μάλα
συχνοῦ λόγου ἀπαλλάξας, εἰ φαίνεταί σοι τὰ μὲν
αὐτὴ δι' αὑτῆς ἡ ψυχὴ ἐπισκοπεῖν, τὰ δὲ διὰ τῶν τοῦ
σώματος δυνάμεων. τοῦτο γὰρ ἦν ὃ καὶ αὐτῷ μοι
ἐδόκει, ἐβουλόμην δὲ καὶ σοὶ δόξαι.

ΘΕΑΙ. Ἀλλὰ μὴν φαίνεταί γε.   p. 186.

ΣΩ. Ποτέρων οὖν τίθης τὴν οὐσίαν; τοῦτο γὰρ
μάλιστα ἐπὶ πάντων παρέπεται.

ΘΕΑΙ. Ἐγὼ μὲν ὧν αὐτὴ ἡ ψυχὴ καθ' αὑτὴν
ἐπορέγεται.

ΣΩ. Ἦ καὶ τὸ ὅμοιον καὶ τὸ ἀνόμοιον, καὶ τὸ ταὐτὸν καὶ ἕτερον;

ΘΕΑΙ. Ναί.

p. 186. ΣΩ. Τί δέ καλὸν καὶ αἰσχρόν, καὶ ἀγαθὸν καὶ κακόν;

ΘΕΑΙ. Καὶ τούτων μοι δοκεῖ ἐν τοῖς μάλιστα πρὸς ἄλληλα σκοπεῖσθαι τὴν οὐσίαν, ἀναλογιζομένη ἐν ἑαυτῷ τὰ γεγονότα καὶ τὰ παρόντα πρὸς τὰ μέλλοντα.

ΣΩ. Ἔχε δή· ἄλλο τι τοῦ μὲν σκληροῦ τὴν σκληρότητα διὰ τῆς ἐπαφῆς αἰσθήσεται, καὶ τοῦ μαλακοῦ τὴν μαλακότητα ὡσαύτως;

ΘΕΑΙ. Ναί.

ΣΩ. Τὴν δέ γε οὐσίαν καὶ ὅ τι ἐστὸν καὶ τὴν ἐναντιότητα πρὸς ἀλλήλω καὶ τὴν οὐσίαν αὖ τῆς ἐναντιότητος αὐτὴ ἡ ψυχὴ ἐπανιοῦσα καὶ συμβάλλουσα πρὸς ἄλληλα κρίνειν πειρᾶται ἡμῖν.

ΘΕΑΙ. Πάνυ μὲν οὖν.

ΣΩ. Οὐκοῦν τὰ μὲν εὐθὺς γενομένοις πάρεστι φύσει αἰσθάνεσθαι ἀνθρώποις τε καὶ θηρίοις, ὅσα

---

3. *ἐν τοῖς μάλιστα*] In this and similar phrases the article retains its demonstrative force, as is evident where the words are separated; e. g. Euthyd. 303: *ἐν δὲ ταῖς καὶ τοῦτο μεγαλοπρεπέστερον*. Soph. (Ed. Col. 746: *ἐν δὲ τῶν μάλιστ' ἐγώ*.

4. *πρὸς ἄλληλα σκοπεῖσθαι*] Viz. as opposites. Theaetetus is probably thinking of the recent argument in which *ἀγαθόν*, *ὠφέλιμον*, *μέλλον*, were identified. Throughout this dialogue we can hardly be said to rise to the conception of an existence or a goodness above time, except almost mythically in p. 177. That goodness in its actual working is always relative, is asserted Rep. 457: *μάλιστα γὰρ δὴ τοῦτο καὶ λέγεται καὶ λελέξεται, ὅτι τὸ μὲν ὠφέλιμον καλόν, τὸ δὲ βλαβερὸν αἰσχρόν*.

ἀναλογιζομένη] 'Thinking over the past and present with a view to the future.'

11. *Τὴν δέ γε οὐσίαν*] Sc. *τοῦ σκληροῦ καὶ τοῦ μαλακοῦ*. In this and similar passages Plato may be said to be appealing to the consciousness of his reader.

13. *ἐπανιοῦσα καὶ συμβάλλουσα*] Returning upon (reviewing) the sensations, it perceives the Being of their objects, and comparing these together, perceives their opposition, and the Being of this again.

144   ΠΛΑΤΩΝΟΣ

suffices, and that this opposition is, the mind itself seeks to decide, returning over its sensations, and comparing them.

διὰ τοῦ σώματος παθήματα ἐπὶ τὴν ψυχὴν τείνει· p. 186.
τὰ δὲ περὶ τούτων ἀναλογίσματα πρός τε οὐσίαν καὶ
ὠφέλειαν μόγις καὶ ἐν χρόνῳ διὰ πολλῶν πραγμάτων
καὶ παιδείας παραγίγνεται οἷς ἂν καὶ παραγίγνηται.

5 ΘΕΑΙ. Παντάπασι μὲν οὖν.

ΣΩ. Οἷόν τε οὖν ἀληθείας τυχεῖν, ᾧ μηδὲ οὐσίας;

ΘΕΑΙ. Ἀδύνατον.

ΣΩ. Οὗ δὲ ἀληθείας τις ἀτυχήσει, ποτὲ τούτου
ἐπιστήμων ἔσται;

The one power belongs to all live creatures from their birth: the other is slowly attained, and only by some men. Sensation does not reach being, therefore

10 ΘΕΑΙ. Καὶ πῶς ἄν, ὦ Σώκρατες;   d

ΣΩ. Ἐν μὲν ἄρα τοῖς παθήμασιν οὐκ ἔνι ἐπιστήμη, ἐν δὲ τῷ περὶ ἐκείνων συλλογισμῷ· οὐσίας
γὰρ καὶ ἀληθείας ἐνταῦθα μέν, ὡς ἔοικε, δυνατὸν
ἅψασθαι, ἐκεῖ δὲ ἀδύνατον.

15 ΘΕΑΙ. Φαίνεται.

1. *ἐπὶ τὴν ψυχὴν τείνει*] 'Extend to the mind.' Cf. Tim. 64: τὸ μὲν γὰρ κατὰ φύσιν εὐκίνητον καὶ βραχὺ πάθος—διαδίδωσιν—ἐπὶ τὸ φρόνιμον—τὸ δ᾽ ἐναντίον ἑδραῖον ἀπαθέστερον παρέσχε τὸ παθός.

Phileb. 33: διὰ τῶν περὶ τὸ σῶμα ἡμῶν ἑκάστοτε παθημάτων τὸ μὲν ἐν τῷ σώματι κατασβεννύμενον πρὶν ἐπὶ τὴν ψυχὴν διεξελθεῖν, ἀπαθῆ ἐκείνην ἐάσαντα, τὸ δὲ δι᾽ ἀμφοῖν ἰόντα, καί τινα ὥσπερ σεισμὸν ἐντιθέντα ἴδιόν τε καὶ κοινὸν ἑκατέρῳ.

2. *ἀναλογίσματα*] 'But what the mind discovers by reflecting upon these.' The idea of proportion (τὸ ἀνάλογον) does not seem to enter into the verb ἀναλογίζομαι and its derivative noun.

6. *ᾧ μηδὲ οὐσίας*] Ad dat. hunc ᾧ reprehendum est οἷόν τε (potestne illud verum assequi quod ne οὐσίαν quidem assequi potest?), ut declarant illa mox: κύρωσαι ἆρ᾽ αὐτὸ καλεῖς αἴσθησιν; Ἀπέχει. Οἷόν τε, φάμεν, οὐ μέντοι ἀληθείας ἅψασθαι, οὐδὲ γὰρ οὐσίας. Heindorf.

But in the present connexion ᾧ is probably masculine. 'Is it possible for him to reach truth who misses being?' There is a transition in the next question from the subject to the object, from αἰσθανόμενος to αἴσθησις. 'But can one have knowledge of that, the truth of which he misses?'

12. *ἐν δὲ τῷ περὶ ἐκείνων συλλογισμῷ*] Something very different from syllogism is meant, and more nearly analogous to generalization. Cf. Phaedr. 249: δεῖ γὰρ ἄνθρωπον συνιέναι κατ᾽ εἶδος λεγόμενον, ἐκ πολλῶν ἰὸν αἰσθήσεων εἰς ἓν λογισμῷ συναιρούμενον.

ΘΕΑΙΤΗΤΟΣ. 145

p. 186. ΣΩ. Ἡ οὖν ταὐτὸν ἐκεῖνό τε καὶ τοῦτο καλεῖς, τοσαύτας διαφορὰς ἔχοντε;

ΘΕΑΙ. Οὔκουν δὴ δίκαιόν γε.

ΣΩ. Τί οὖν δὴ ἐκείνῳ ἀποδίδως ὄνομα, τῷ ὁρᾷν, ἀκούειν, ὀσφραίνεσθαι, ψύχεσθαι, θερμαίνεσθαι;

e ΘΕΑΙ. Αἰσθάνεσθαι ἔγωγε· τί γὰρ ἄλλο;

ΣΩ. Σύμπαν ἄρ᾽ αὐτὸ καλεῖς αἴσθησιν;

ΘΕΑΙ. Ἀνάγκη.

ΣΩ. Ὧ̣ι γε, φαμέν, οὐ μέτεστιν ἀληθείας ἅψασθαι· οὐδὲ γὰρ οὐσίας.

ΘΕΑΙ. Οὐ γὰρ οὖν.

ΣΩ. Οὐδ᾽ ἄρ᾽ ἐπιστήμης.

ΘΕΑΙ. Οὐ γάρ.

ΣΩ. Οὐκ ἄρ᾽ ἂν εἴη ποτέ, ὦ Θεαίτητε, αἴσθησίς τε καὶ ἐπιστήμη ταὐτόν.

ΘΕΑΙ. Οὐ φαίνεται, ὦ Σώκρατες. καὶ μάλιστά γε νῦν καταφανέστατον γέγονεν ἄλλο ὂν αἰσθήσεως ἐπιστήμη.

fore it falls of truth: therefore it is not knowledge. This has not in our impressions, but in that which the mind collects from them.

Sensation, therefore, has no share in knowledge. They are wholly distinct.

We have found what knowledge

12. Οὐδ᾽ ἄρ᾽ ἐπιστήμης] The gen. is governed by μέτεστιν alone. ἀληθείας and οὐσίας are governed partly by μέτεστιν, partly by ἅψασθαι.

16. μάλιστά γε νῦν καταφανέστατον] For the double superl. cf. Rep. 331: ἀλλὰ γε ἴσ ̓ ἂν δ᾽ ἴσως οὐκ ἐλάχιστον ἔγωγε θείην ἂν εἰς τοῦτο ἀσφαλῶς ἔχοντι, ὦ Σώκρατες, πλοῦτον χρησιμώτατον εἶναι.

17. καταφανέστατον γέγονεν] The criticism of sensation is now complete. We see it clearly, as relative, shifting, momentary, inseparable from physical conditions: we have placed ourselves above it, and proceed to explore the region next beyond, that of opinion.

To recapitulate the criticism of ἐπιστήμη αἴσθησις. 1. Certain presumptions are raised against the saying ἄνθρωπος μέτρον, as that it makes all beings equally wise, and that it implies that we can at once know and not know the same thing. 2. Protagoras is convicted out of his own mouth, for in confirming the opinion of other men he confutes himself. 3. There is at least one sphere of knowledge which is above sense, the foresight of consequences, the perception of what is good. 4. And within the sphere of sense, if sensation depend on motion, and motion include change, no quality can have a

146   ΠΛΑΤΩΝΟΣ

ΣΩ. Ἀλλ' οὔ τι μὲν δὴ τούτου γε ἕνεκα ἠρχόμεθα p. 187. διαλεγόμενοι, ἵνα εὕρωμεν τί ποτ' οὐκ ἔστ' ἐπιστήμη, ἀλλὰ τί ἐστιν. ὅμως δὲ τοσοῦτόν γε προβεβήκαμεν, ὥστε μὴ ζητεῖν αὐτὴν ἐν αἰσθήσει τὸ παράπαν, ἀλλ' ἐν ἐκείνῳ τῷ ὀνόματι, ὅ τί ποτ' ἔχει ἡ ψυχή, ὅταν αὐτὴ καθ' αὑτὴν πραγματεύηται περὶ τὰ ὄντα.

ΘΕΑΙ. Ἀλλὰ μὴν τοῦτό γε καλεῖται, ὦ Σώκρατες, ὡς ἐγᾦμαι, δοξάζειν.

ΣΩ. Ὀρθῶς γὰρ οἴει, ὦ φίλε. καὶ ὅρα δὴ νῦν πάλιν ἐξ ἀρχῆς, πάντα τὰ πρόσθεν ἐξαλείψας, εἴ τι b μᾶλλον καθορᾷς, ἐπειδὴ ἐνταῦθα προελήλυθας. καὶ λέγε αὖθις τί ποτ' ἐστὶν ἐπιστήμη.

ΘΕΑΙ. Δόξαν μὲν πᾶσαν εἰπεῖν, ὦ Σώκρατες, ἀδύνατον, ἐπειδὴ καὶ ψευδής ἐστι δόξα· κινδυνεύει δὲ ἡ ἀληθὴς δόξα ἐπιστήμη εἶναι, καί μοι τοῦτο ἀποκεκρίσθω. ἐὰν γὰρ μὴ φανῇ προϊοῦσιν, ὥσπερ τὸ νῦν, ἄλλο τι πειρασόμεθα λέγειν.

ΣΩ. Οὕτω μέντοι χρή, ὦ Θεαίτητε, λέγειν προθύμως μᾶλλον ἢ ὡς τὸ πρῶτον ὤκνεις ἀποκρίνεσθαι.

ΘΕΑΙΤΗΤΟΣ.

p. 187. ἐὰν γὰρ οὕτω δρῶμεν, δυοῖν θάτερα, ἢ εὑρήσομεν ἐφ᾽ ὃ ἐρχόμεθα, ἢ ἧττον οἰησόμεθα εἰδέναι ὃ μηδαμῇ ἴσμεν· καί τοι οὐκ ἂν εἴη μεμπτὸς μισθὸς ὁ τοιοῦτος. καὶ δὴ καὶ νῦν τί φῄς; δυοῖν ὄντοιν [εἰδίοιν] δόξης, τοῦ μὲν ἀληθινοῦ, ψευδοῦς δὲ τοῦ ἑτέρου, τὴν ἀληθῆ δόξαν ἐπιστήμην ὁρίζει;

ΘΕΑΙ. Ἔγωγε· τοῦτο γὰρ αὖ νῦν μοι φαίνεται.

ΣΩ. Ἆρ᾽ οὖν ἔτ᾽ ἄξιον περὶ δόξης ἀναλαβεῖν πάλιν;

ΘΕΑΙ. Τὸ ποῖον δὴ λέγεις;

d ΣΩ. Θράττει μέ πως νῦν τε καὶ ἄλλοτε δὴ πολλάκις, ὥστ᾽ ἐν ἀπορίᾳ πολλῇ πρὸς ἐμαυτὸν καὶ πρὸς ἄλλον γεγονέναι, οὐκ ἔχοντα εἰπεῖν τί ποτ᾽ ἐστὶ τοῦτο τὸ πάθος παρ᾽ ἡμῖν καὶ τίνα τρόπον ἐγγιγνόμενον.

ΘΕΑΙ. Τὸ ποῖον δή;

ΣΩ. Τὸ δοξάζειν τινὰ ψευδῆ. σκοπῶ δὴ καὶ νῦν ἔτι διστάζων, πότερον ἐάσωμεν αὐτὸ ἢ ἐπισκεψώμεθα ἄλλον τρόπον ἢ ὀλίγον πρότερον.

But, still to return upon a former track,

Is false opinion possible?

---

4. [εἰδίοιν]] MSS. ἰδίοιν.
8. ἀναλαβεῖν πάλιν] 'To take up a thread of the previous argument.'
Though we have dismissed the saying of Protagoras, so far as it is bound up with sense, τὸ δοκοῦν ἑκάστῳ τοῦτο καὶ εἶναι, (φαντασία being συμπλοκὴ δόξης καὶ αἰσθήσεως), yet the same question returns upon us in regard to opinion considered by itself. This forms a link of connexion between the present inquiry and the foregoing. Cf. Cratyl. 429: 'Ἆρ᾽ ὅτι ψευδῆ λέγειν τὸ παράπαν οὐκ ἔστιν, ἆρα τοῦτό σοι δύναται ὁ λόγος; συχνοὶ γάρ τινες οἱ λέγοντες, ὦ φίλε Κρατύλε, καὶ νῦν καὶ πάλαι.
See also Euthyd. 284, 286, where the ἀπορία (ὅτι ψεύδεσθαι, ἀντιλέγειν, οὐκ ἔστιν) is ascribed to the followers of Protagoras amongst others.
13. τοῦτο τὸ πάθος παρ᾽ ἡμῖν] 'This experience of the human mind.'
16. σκοπῶ δὴ καὶ νῦν ἔτι] Though the past discussion has been "wiped out," this still remains "to trouble the mind's eye."
18. ἄλλον τρόπον ἢ ὀλίγον πρότερον] i. e. Not with reference to sensation and motion, but in a more abstract way. The 'manner' has something in it of the Eleatic spirit. For the expression, compare Soph. 245, τοὺς δὲ ἄλλως λέγοντας αὖ θεατέον.

148   ΠΛΑΤΩΝΟΣ

ΘΕΑΙ. Τί μήν, ὦ Σώκρατες, εἴ πέρ γε καὶ ὅπῃ- p. 187.
γοῦν φαίνεται δεῖν; ἄρτι γὰρ οὐ κακῶς γε σὺ καὶ
Θεόδωρος ἐλέγετε σχολῆς πέρι, ὡς οὐδὲν ἐν τοῖς τοι-
οῖσδε κατεπείγει.

ΣΩ. Ὀρθῶς ὑπέμνησας. ἴσως γὰρ οὐκ ἀπὸ και- e
ροῦ πάλιν ὥσπερ ἴχνος μετελθεῖν. κρεῖττον γάρ που
σμικρὸν εὖ ἢ πολὺ μὴ ἱκανῶς περᾶναι.

ΘΕΑΙ. Τί μήν;

ΣΩ. Πῶς οὖν; τί δὴ καὶ λέγομεν; ψευδῆ φαμὲν
ἑκάστοτε εἶναι δόξαν, καί τινα ἡμῶν δοξάζειν ψευδῆ,
τὸν δ' αὖ ἀληθῆ, ὡς φύσει οὕτως ἐχόντων;

ΘΕΑΙ. Φαμὲν γὰρ δή.

ΣΩ. Οὐκοῦν τόδε γ' ἔσθ' ἡμῖν περὶ πάντα καὶ p. 188.
καθ' ἕκαστον, ἤτοι εἰδέναι ἢ μὴ εἰδέναι; μανθάνειν
γὰρ καὶ ἐπιλανθάνεσθαι μεταξὺ τούτων ὡς ὄντα χαίρειν λέγω ἐν τῷ παρόντι· νῦν γὰρ ἡμῖν πρὸς λόγον
ἐστὶν οὐδέν.

1. Is regard to every thing one of two alternatives is true of us. Either we know it, or do not know it.

6. πάλιν ὥσπερ [ἴχνος μετελθεῖν] We seemed to ourselves to be launching into a wholly new inquiry, but we have fallen into the same track by a different route. Cf. Aristot. Eth. I.: μεταβαίνων δὲ ὁ λόγος εἰς ταὐτὸν ἀφῖκται. Aesch. Prom. 864. ταὐτὸν μετελθεῖν τῶν πάλαι λόγων ἴχνος.

4. ἤτοι εἰδέναι ἢ μὴ εἰδέναι] This takes up the thread of reflection introduced above, p. 165: ἆρ' οὐδέν τε τὸν αὐτὸν εἰδότα τι τοῦτο ὃ οἶδε μὴ εἰδέναι; It was one weakness of the 'sensational' doctrine that it led to this contradiction. The same opposition considered in the abstract is now used to prove the impossibility of falsehood in opinion.

The discussion which follows probably bears some relation to the notions of Gorgias, and perhaps of Antisthenes. At all events it would seem to be a fragment of Eleaticism; being exactly parallel to the difficulties raised by Zeno against the possibility of motion. It runs parallel also to the subtilties of the later Megarians.

6. νῦν γὰρ ἡμῖν πρὸς λόγον ἐστὶν οὐδέν] Because we choose to dwell on the absolute alternative, knowledge or ignorance. Cf. supr. p. 158. μὴ ὑπολάβωμεν—.

Plato thus hints at the true solution of the difficulty, viz. the conception of a gradual process, which is afterwards presented under the image of the impressions on wax, &c.

The doctrine of recollection, developed in the Meno and Phaedo, is also held in reserve.

ΘΕΑΙΤΗΤΟΣ.

p. 188.   ΘΕΑΙ. Ἀλλὰ μήν, ὦ Σώκρατες, ἄλλο γ' οὐδὲν λείπεται περὶ ἕκαστον πλὴν εἰδέναι ἢ μὴ εἰδέναι.

ΣΩ. Οὐκοῦν ἤδη ἀνάγκη τὸν δοξάζοντα δοξάζειν ἢ ὧν τι οἶδεν ἢ μὴ οἶδεν;

ΘΕΑΙ. Ἀνάγκη.

ΣΩ. Καὶ μὴν εἰδότα γε μὴ εἰδέναι τὸ αὐτὸ ἢ μὴ b εἰδότα εἰδέναι ἀδύνατον.

ΘΕΑΙ. Πῶς δ' οὔ;

ΣΩ. Ἆρ' οὖν ὁ τὰ ψευδῆ δοξάζων, ἃ οἶδε, ταῦτα οἴεται οὐ ταῦτα εἶναι ἀλλὰ ἕτερα ἄττα ὧν οἶδε, καὶ ἀμφότερα εἰδὼς ἀγνοεῖ ἀμφότερα;

ΘΕΑΙ. Ἀλλ' ἀδύνατον, ὦ Σώκρατες.

ΣΩ. Ἀλλ' ἆρα, ἃ μὴ οἶδεν, ἡγεῖται αὐτὰ εἶναι ἕτερα ἄττα ὧν μὴ οἶδε, καὶ τοῦτ' ἔστι τῷ μήτε Θεαίτητον μήτε Σωκράτη εἰδότι εἰς τὴν διάνοιαν λαβεῖν ὡς ὁ Σωκράτης Θεαίτητος ἢ ὁ Θεαίτητος Σωκράτης;

c   ΘΕΑΙ. Καὶ πῶς ἄν;

ΣΩ. Ἀλλ' οὐ μήν, ἅ γέ τις οἶδεν, οἴεταί που ἃ μὴ οἶδεν αὐτὰ εἶναι, οὐδ' αὖ ἃ μὴ οἶδεν, ἃ οἶδεν.

ΘΕΑΙ. Τέρας γὰρ ἔσται.

ΣΩ. Πῶς οὖν ἄν τις ἔτι ψευδῆ δοξάσειεν; ἐκτὸς γὰρ τούτων ἀδύνατόν που δοξάζειν, ἐπείπερ πάντ' ἢ ἴσμεν ἢ οὐκ ἴσμεν, ἐν δὲ τούτοις οὐδαμοῦ φαίνεται δυνατὸν ψευδῆ δοξάσαι.

ΘΕΑΙ. Ἀληθέστατα.

ΣΩ. Ἆρ' οὖν οὐ ταύτῃ σκεπτέον ὃ ζητοῦμεν, κατὰ τὸ εἰδέναι καὶ μὴ εἰδέναι ἰόντας, ἀλλὰ κατὰ τὸ εἶναι d καὶ μή;

ΘΕΑΙ. Πῶς λέγεις;

19. αὐτὰ] Cf. Phaed. 99: ὁ δὴ γὰρ ἂν εἴη ὀλίγοις. Phaed. 101. alib. μὴ φαίνεται —— δι' αὐτοῦ αὐτὸ   23. ἐν δὴ τούτοις] 'And under προσαγορεύειν: and see p. 155 D.   this alternative.'
20. Τέρας] Supr. p. 163: τέρατ   27. εἶναι] So the Coislinian MS.

ΠΛΑΤΩΝΟΣ

my mind. Nor what I do not know to be what I know, nor what I know to be what I do not know.

And what albeit can (under the above alternative) is conceivable?

1. The path of knowledge being thus hemmed in, we try the path of being. To think that which is not, is to think falsely. Not can I think of

ΣΩ. Μὴ ἁπλοῦν ᾖ ὅτι ὁ τὰ μὴ ὄντα περὶ ὁτουοῦν p. 188. δοξάζων οὐκ ἔσθ᾽ ὡς οὐ ψευδῆ δοξάσει, κἂν ὁπωσοῦν ἄλλως τὰ τῆς διανοίας ἔχῃ.

ΘΕΑΙ. Εἰκός γ᾽ αὖ, ὦ Σώκρατες.

ΣΩ. Πῶς οὖν; τί ἐροῦμεν, ὦ Θεαίτητε, ἐάν τις ἡμᾶς ἀνακρίνῃ· Δυνατὸν δὲ ὁτῳοῦν ὃ λέγεται, καί τις ἀνθρώπων τὸ μὴ ὂν δοξάσει, εἴτε περὶ τῶν ὄντων του εἴτε αὐτὸ καθ᾽ αὑτό; Καὶ ἡμεῖς δή, ὡς ἔοικε, πρὸς ταῦτα φήσομεν Ὅταν γε μὴ ἀληθῆ οἴηται οἰόμενος. ε ἢ πῶς ἐροῦμεν;

ΘΕΑΙ. Οὕτως.

ΣΩ. Ἦ οὖν καὶ ἄλλοθί που τὸ τοιοῦτόν ἐστιν;

ΘΕΑΙ. Τὸ ποῖον;

ΣΩ. Εἴ τις ὁρᾷ μέν τι, ὁρᾷ δὲ οὐδέν.

ΘΕΑΙ. Καὶ πῶς;

ΣΩ. Ἀλλὰ μὴν εἰ ἕν γέ τι ὁρᾷ, τῶν ὄντων τι ὁρᾷ. ἢ σὺ οἴει ποτὲ τὸ ἓν ἐν τοῖς μὴ οὖσιν εἶναι;

---

1. Μὴ ἁπλοῦν ᾖ] "May it not possibly be simply thus:" μὴ expresses suspicion = "I should not wonder if." Cf. Phaed. 67. μὴ οὐ θέμις ᾖ. Ibid. 69.: γὰρ οὐχ αὕτη ᾖ ἡ ὀρθὴ ἀλλογὴ κ. τ. λ. μὴ σκωγραφία τις ᾖ ἡ τοιαύτη ἀρετή. Crit. 48 : μὴ τοῦτο σωφρόνως ᾖ; and see Ast. Lex. sub v. For ἁπλοῦν in this sense, v. supr. 147 : ἁπλοῦν εἰπεῖν. Symp. 184. Polit. 306: σύμπτωσιν οὗτος ἁπλοῦν ἐστι τοῦτο. ἢ — ἔχει διαφοράν—. Aristot. Eth. N. V. 9. 9: ἡ οὐδὲ τοῦτο ἁπλοῦν.

6. ὃ λέγεται] Which is asserted. Buttmann and Bekker conj. λέγειν, which seems probable, but not necessary. Cf. Phaed. 77, where there is a similar doubt.

14. Εἰ] Interrogative.

16. εἰ ἕν γέ τι ὁρᾷ] The converse argument is used Rep. 478, where it is asked, 'What is opinion conversant with?' ἢ οἴει τι ἂν δοξάζειν μὲν δοξάζειν δὲ μηδέν; Ἀδύνατον. Ἀλλ᾽ ἕν γε τι δοξάζει ὁ δοξάζων; Ναί. Ἀλλὰ μὴν μὴ ὂν γε οὐχ ἕν τι, ἀλλὰ μηδὲν ὀρθότατ᾽ ἂν προσαγορεύοιτο. Πάνυ γε. This close relation between the ideas of unity and being, derived from Parmenides, appears frequently. See esp. Soph. 238: ἀνάγκη τόν τι λέγοντα ἕν γέ τι λέγειν. The mind cannot recognise being except where it finds its own impress of unity.

Ar. Met. 1006. b.: οὐδὲν γὰρ ἐνδέχεται νοεῖν μὴ νοοῦντα ἕν.

ΘΕΑΙΤΗΤΟΣ. 151

p. 188. ΘΕΑΙ. Οὐκ ἔγωγε.

ΣΩ. Ὁ ἄρα ἔν γέ τι ὁρῶν ὄν τι ὁρᾷ.

ΘΕΑΙ. Φαίνεται.

p. 189. ΣΩ. Καὶ ὁ ἄρα τι ἀκούων ἔν γέ τι ἀκούει καὶ ὂν ἀκούει.

ΘΕΑΙ. Ναί.

ΣΩ. Καὶ ὁ ἁπτόμενος δή του, ἑνός γέ του ἅπτεται καὶ ὄντος, εἴπερ ἑνός;

ΘΕΑΙ. Καὶ τοῦτο.

ΣΩ. Ὁ δὲ δὴ δοξάζων οὐχ ἕν τι δοξάζει;

ΘΕΑΙ. Ἀνάγκη.

ΣΩ. Ὁ δ' ἕν τι δοξάζων οὐκ ὄν τι;

ΘΕΑΙ. Ξυγχωρῶ.

ΣΩ. Ὁ ἄρα μὴ ὂν δοξάζων οὐδὲν δοξάζει.

ΘΕΑΙ. Οὐ φαίνεται.

ΣΩ. Ἀλλὰ μὴν ὅ γε μηδὲν δοξάζων τὸ παράπαν οὐδὲ δοξάζει.

ΘΕΑΙ. Δῆλον, ὡς ἔοικεν.

b ΣΩ. Οὐκ ἄρα οἷόν τε τὸ μὴ ὂν δοξάζειν, οὔτε περὶ τῶν ὄντων οὔτε αὐτὸ καθ' αὑτό.

ΘΕΑΙ. Οὐ φαίνεται.

ΣΩ. Ἄλλο τι ἄρ' ἐστὶ τὸ ψευδῆ δοξάζειν τοῦ τὰ μὴ ὄντα δοξάζειν.

ΘΕΑΙ. Ἄλλο ἔοικεν.

ΣΩ. Οὔ [τε] γὰρ οὕτως οὔτε ὡς ὀλίγον πρότερον ἐσκοποῦμεν, ψευδής ἐστι δόξα ἐν ἡμῖν.

ΘΕΑΙ. Οὐ γὰρ οὖν δή.

ΣΩ. Ἀλλ' ἄρα ὧδε γιγνόμενον τοῦτο προσαγορεύομεν;

19. περὶ τῶν ὄντων] Arist. Met. Γ. 2, 1004: ἀνύφασιν δὲ καὶ στέρησιν μίαν ἐστι θεωρῆσαι διὰ τὸ ἀμφοτέρων θεωρεῖσθαι τὸ ἓν, οὗ ἡ ἀπόφασις ἢ ἡ στέρησις (ἢ γὰρ ἁπλῶς λέγομεν ὅτι οὐχ ὑπάρχει ἐκεῖνο ἢ τινι γένει κ. τ. λ.)

25. MSS. οὐ γάρ. τι seems required, but γάρ is right. Cf. p. 190.

28. 'Ἀλλ' ἄρα ὧδε γιγν.] 'But

152   ΠΛΑΤΩΝΟΣ

ΘΕΑΙ. Πῶς;   p. 189

ΣΩ. Ἀλλοδοξίαν τινὰ οὖσαν ψευδῆ φαμὲν εἶναι δόξαν, ὅταν τίς τι τῶν ὄντων ἄλλο αὖ τῶν ὄντων, ἀνταλλαξάμενος τῇ διανοίᾳ, φῇ εἶναι. οὕτω γὰρ ὂν μὲν ἀεὶ δοξάζει, ἕτερον δὲ ἀνθ' ἑτέρου, καὶ ἁμαρτάνων οὗ ἐσκόπει δικαίως ἂν καλοῖτο ψευδῆ δοξάζων.

ΘΕΑΙ. Ὀρθότατά μοι νῦν δοκεῖς εἰρηκέναι. ὅταν γάρ τις ἀντὶ καλοῦ αἰσχρὸν ἢ ἀντὶ αἰσχροῦ καλὸν δοξάζῃ, τότε ὡς ἀληθῶς δοξάζει ψευδῆ.

ΣΩ. Δῆλος εἶ, ὦ Θεαίτητε, καταφρονῶν μου καὶ οὐ δεδιώς.

ΘΕΑΙ. Τί μάλιστα;

ΣΩ. Οὐκ ἄν, οἶμαι, σοὶ δοκῶ τοῦ ἀληθῶς ψεύδους ἀντιλαβέσθαι, ἐρόμενος εἰ οἷόν τε ταχὺ βραδέως ἢ κοῦφον βαρέως ἢ ἄλλο τι ἐναντίον μὴ κατὰ τὴν αὑτοῦ φύσιν ἀλλὰ κατὰ τὴν τοῦ ἐναντίου γίγνεσθαι ἑαυτῷ ἐναντίως. τοῦτο μὲν οὖν, ἵνα μὴ μάτην θαρρήσῃς, ἀφίημι. ἀρέσκει δέ, ὡς φῄς, τὸ τὰ ψευδῆ δοξάζειν ἀλλοδοξεῖν εἶναι;

ΘΕΑΙ. Ἔμοιγε.

ΘΕΑΙΤΗΤΟΣ. 153

p. 189. ΣΩ. Ἔστιν ἄρα κατὰ τὴν σὴν δόξαν ἕτερόν τι ὡς ἕτερον καὶ μὴ ὡς ἐκεῖνο τῇ διανοίᾳ τίθεσθαι.

ΘΕΑΙ. Ἔστι μέντοι.

ΣΩ. Ὅταν οὖν τοῦθ' ἡ διάνοιά του δρᾷ, οὐ καὶ ἀνάγκη αὐτὴν ἤτοι ἀμφότερα ἢ τὸ ἕτερον διανοεῖσθαι;

ΘΕΑΙ. Ἀνάγκη μὲν οὖν.

ΣΩ. Ἤτοι ἅμα γε ἢ ἐν μέρει;

ΘΕΑΙ. Κάλλιστα.

ΣΩ. Τὸ δὲ διανοεῖσθαι ἆρ' ὅ περ ἐγὼ καλεῖς;

ΘΕΑΙ. Τί καλῶν;

ΣΩ. Λόγον ὃν αὐτὴ πρὸς αὑτὴν ἡ ψυχὴ διεξέρχεται περὶ ὧν ἂν σκοπῇ. ὥς γε μὴ εἰδώς σοι ἀποφαίνομαι. τοῦτο γάρ μοι ἰνδάλλεται διανοουμένη, οὐκ

p. 190. ἄλλο τι ἢ διαλέγεσθαι, αὐτὴ ἑαυτὴν ἐρωτῶσα καὶ ἀποκρινομένη, καὶ φάσκουσα καὶ οὐ φάσκουσα. ὅταν δὲ ὁρίσασα, εἴτε βραδύτερον, εἴτε καὶ ὀξύτερον ἐπαΐξασα, τὸ αὐτὸ ἤδη φῇ καὶ μὴ διστάζῃ, δόξαν ταύτην τίθεμεν αὐτῆς. ὥστ' ἔγωγε τὸ δοξάζειν λέγειν καλῶ

When I take one thing for another, I must have either one or both things in my mind, either at once or in turn.

Now thought is the mind's self-dialogue, is question and answer. When it has agreed with itself upon a final answer, we call this its opinion.

2. ὡς ἐκεῖνο] Referring to the first ἕτερον.

8. Ἤτοι ἅμα γε ἢ ἐν μέρει] The bearing of these words is not quite clear. Perhaps they are meant to introduce the analysis of thinking, in which things are present to the mind at first successively, afterwards in one view.

Compare with this account of thinking Phileb. pp. 38, 39, where the mind not only talks with itself, but has a writer and a painter within it. 'Ἆρ' οὖν ἡμῶν —— κ. τ. λ. Soph. 263: Οὐκοῦν διάνοια μὲν καὶ λόγος ταὐτόν· πλὴν ὁ μὲν ἐντὸς τῆς ψυχῆς πρὸς αὑτὴν διάλογος ἄνευ

φωνῆς γιγνόμενος κ. τ. λ.

14. τοῦτο γάρ μοι] Plato was probably thinking of Odyssee 19. 224: ἰρέω, ὥς μοι ἰνδάλλεται ἦτορ. Compare the φάσματα in the beginning of the dialogue. 'The semblance it presents to me, when it thinks, is simply that of conversing, and of being engaged in question and answer with itself.'

16. ὅταν δὲ ὁρίσασα] 'But when it has come to a determination, whether slowly, or having flown rapidly to its conclusion, and so is now at one and not divided in judgment, we call this its opinion.'

x

καὶ τὴν δόξαν λόγον εἰρημένον, οὐ μέντοι πρὸς ἄλλον p.190.
οὐδὲ φωνῇ, ἀλλὰ σιγῇ πρὸς αὑτόν. σὺ δὲ τί;
ΘΕΑΙ. Κἀγώ.
ΣΩ. Ὅταν ἄρα τις τὸ ἕτερον ἕτερον δοξάζῃ, καὶ
φησίν, ὡς ἔοικε, τὸ ἕτερον ἕτερον εἶναι πρὸς ἑαυτόν.
ΘΕΑΙ. Τί μήν;   b
ΣΩ. Ἀναμιμνήσκου δὴ εἰ πώποτ᾽ εἶπες πρὸς σεαυτὸν ὅτι παντὸς μᾶλλον τό τοι καλὸν αἰσχρόν ἐστιν
ἢ τὸ ἄδικον δίκαιον, ἢ καί, τὸ πάντων κεφάλαιον,
σκόπει εἴ ποτ᾽ ἐπεχείρησας σεαυτὸν πείθειν ὡς παντὸς μᾶλλον τὸ ἕτερον ἕτερόν ἐστιν, ἢ πᾶν τοὐναντίον
οὐδ᾽ ἐν ὕπνῳ πώποτε ἐτόλμησας εἰπεῖν πρὸς σεαυτὸν

Opinion is a silent prompting.
To think this to be that, is to say, This is that.
Now who ever said to himself, 'Surely fair is foul,' or 'wrong is right,' or 'old is even'!

8. σαυτὸν μᾶλλον—παντάπασιν ἄρα—ἀνήγες] The dramatic force of such particles is noticeable: cf. Phil. 38: αὑτόν—ἀνέροιτ᾽ ἂν ἑαυτί ποτ᾽ ἄρα ἔστι τὸ παρὰ τὴν πέτραν—
The Greek language from Homer downwards was peculiarly apt to suggest the above reflections on the nature of thought. Διαλεκτική was its proper development. The following remarks of Col. Mure (Lit. of Greece, B. II. c. xiv. § 1.) on the self-dialogue of Homer, apply in some degree to all Greek literature. "Exclusively proper to Homer is his power of dramatizing, not merely action, but thought; not merely the intercourse between man and man, but between man and himself, between his passions and his judgment. The mechanism of which the poet here chiefly avails himself is to exhibit the person under the influence of excited feelings as communing with, or, as Homer defines it, addressing his own mind; discussing the subject of his solicitude under its various aspects as a question at issue between his judgment and himself. The conflicting feelings are thus, as it were, personified; while the current of the language, often the very sound of the words, is so nicely adapted to the turns of the self-dialogue, that the breast of the man seems to be laid open before us, and in the literal sense of the term, we read his thoughts as they flit through his bosom."

12. ἐν ὕπνῳ—ὑγιαίνοντα ἢ μαινόμενον] Note the liveliness with which fresh touches are thrown in. It must be remembered here that sensible perception is excluded from consideration for the present, as well as learning and forgetting. Everything is either known or unknown: present to the mind, or not present.

ΘΕΑΙΤΗΤΟΣ. 155

p. 190. ὡς παντάπασιν ἄρα τὰ περιττὰ ἄρτιά ἐστιν ἤ τι
ἄλλο τοιοῦτον.

ΘΕΑΙ. Ἀληθῆ λέγεις.

ΣΩ. Ἄλλον δέ τινα οἴει ὑγιαίνοντα ἢ μαινόμενον *Or, 'the*
τολμῆσαι σπουδῇ πρὸς ἑαυτὸν εἰπεῖν, ἀναπείθοντα *cow must*
αὐτόν, ὡς ἀνάγκη τὸν βοῦν ἵππον εἶναι ἢ τὰ δύο ἕν; *be a horse,'*
                                                    or 'two is
ΘΕΑΙ. Μὰ Δί' οὐκ ἔγωγε.   *one.'*

ΣΩ. Οὐκοῦν εἰ τὸ λέγειν πρὸς ἑαυτὸν δοξάζειν *Therefore*
ἐστίν, οὐδεὶς ἀμφότερά γε λέγων καὶ δοξάζων καὶ *when I mis-*
ἐφαπτόμενος ἀμφοῖν τῇ ψυχῇ εἴποι ἂν καὶ δοξάσειεν *take this*
                                                   for that, I
ὡς τὸ ἕτερον ἕτερόν ἐστιν. ἐατέον δὲ καὶ σοὶ τὸ ῥῆμα *cannot*
                                                      have both
                                                      in my mind.

11. ἐατέον δὲ καί] Several of the MSS., including Bodl. and Coisl., have ἐατέον δὲ καὶ σοὶ τὸ ῥῆμα ἐπὶ τῶν ἐν μέρει, ἐπειδὴ τὸ ῥῆμα ἕτερον τῷ ἑτέρῳ κατὰ ῥῆμα ταὐτόν ἐστι περὶ τοῦ ἑτέρου, where ἐπὶ τῶν ἐν μέρει evidently refers to p. 190: ἕνα ἅμα γε ἢ ἐν μέρει. This cannot be adopted without rejecting περὶ τοῦ ἑτέρου as confusing the sentence. The drift would then be, 'You must not dwell upon the words as regards things alternately presented to the mind, seeing that the word ἕτερον, as far as the word goes, is the same as applied to both.' This would be an imperfect way of developing the distinction thrown out above, and unlike Socrates, who, especially in this dialogue, always waits for Theætetus to follow him. And it is equally necessary to 'let the word alone,' whether the objects are conceived alternately or both at once. And it may be asked, What difference is there in this respect between saying ὅτι ταυτὸν μᾶλλον τό τοι καλὸν αἰσχρῷ, and ὡς τὸ αἰσχρὸν καλόν? The words ἐπὶ τῶν ἐν μέρει must therefore be rejected as a mistaken gloss.

If the words ἐπειδή—ταὐτόν ἐστι are genuine, περὶ τοῦ ἑτέρου must either be omitted or transposed. But it is possible that this explanation has also crept in from the margin, and this suspicion is strengthened by the fact that the Bodl. p. m. wrote ἐστιν. We should thus revert to the reading of several MSS. ἐατέον δὲ καὶ σοὶ τὸ ῥῆμα περὶ τοῦ ἑτέρου. περὶ is often used rather vaguely, e.g. Περ. p. 538. καὶ περὶ δικαίου ἐσωτέρω καὶ ἀγαθοῦ. καί is a little difficult. It seems to belong to the whole sentence rather than to any particular word. Cf. Soph. Œd. Tyr. 44. ὡς ταὐτὸν ἐμπείροισι καὶ τὰς ξυμφορὰς ζώσας ὁρῶ μάλιστα τῶν βουλευμάτων. Ant. 289. παύσαι πρὶν ὀργὴν καὶ μ' ἀντᾶσαι λέγων. Œd. Col. 1582. τοῦτ' ἔστιν ἤδη κἀποθαυμάσαι πρέπον. See Ellendt's Lex. Soph. sub voce καί, C. 4.

"Now as regards the word 'this or that,' you must e'en let it alone." Or more dis-

X 2

περὶ τοῦ ἑτέρου· [ἐπειδὴ τὸ ῥῆμα ἕτερον τῷ ἑτέρῳ μ. 190.
κατὰ ῥῆμα ταὐτόν ἐστι.] λέγω γὰρ αὐτὸ τῇδε, μηδένα
δοξάζειν ὡς τὸ αἰσχρὸν καλὸν ἢ ἄλλο τι τῶν τοιούτων.

ΘΕΑΙ. Ἀλλ᾽, ὦ Σώκρατες, ἐῶ τε καί μοι δοκεῖ
ὡς λέγεις.

ΣΩ. Ἄμφω μὲν ἄρα δοξάζοντα ἀδύνατον τὸ ἕτερον ἕτερον δοξάζειν.

ΘΕΑΙ. Ἔοικεν.

ΣΩ. Ἀλλὰ μὴν τὸ ἕτερόν γε μόνον δοξάζων, τὸ δὲ ἕτερον μηδαμῇ, οὐδέποτε δοξάσει τὸ ἕτερον ἕτερον εἶναι.

ΘΕΑΙ. Ἀληθῆ λέγεις· ἀναγκάζοιτο γὰρ ἂν ἐφάπτεσθαι καὶ οὗ μὴ δοξάζει.

ΣΩ. Οὔτ᾽ ἄρ᾽ ἀμφότερα οὔτε τὸ ἕτερον δοξάζοντι ἐγχωρεῖ ἀλλαδοξεῖν. ὥστ᾽ εἴ τις ὁριεῖται δόξαν εἶναι ψευδῆ τὸ ἑτεροδοξεῖν, οὐδὲν ἂν λέγοι· οὔτε γὰρ ταύτῃ οὔτε κατὰ τὰ πρότερα φαίνεται ψευδὴς ἐν ἡμῖν οὖσα δόξα.

ΘΕΑΙ. Οὐκ ἔοικεν.

ΣΩ. Ἀλλὰ μέντοι, ὦ Θεαίτητε, εἰ τοῦτο μὴ φανήσεται ὄν, πολλὰ ἀναγκασθησόμεθα ὁμολογεῖν καὶ ἄτοπα.

ΘΕΑΙ. Τὰ ποῖα δή;

ΘΕΑΙΤΗΤΟΣ. 157

p. 190. ΣΩ. Οὐκ ἐρῶ σοι πρὶν ἂν πανταχῇ πειραθῶ σκοπῶν. αἰσχυνοίμην γὰρ ἂν ὑπὲρ ἡμῶν, ἐν ᾧ ἀπορούμεν, ἀναγκαζομένων ὁμολογεῖν οἷα λέγω. ἀλλ' ἐὰν
p. 191. εὕρωμεν καὶ ἐλεύθεροι γενώμεθα, τότ' ἤδη περὶ τῶν ἄλλων ἐροῦμεν ὡς πασχόντων, αὐτοὶ ἐκτὸς τοῦ γελοίου ἑστῶτες· ἐὰν δὲ πάντῃ ἀπορήσωμεν, ταπεινωθέντες, οἶμαι, τῷ λόγῳ παρέξομεν ὡς ναυτιῶντες πατεῖν τε καὶ χρῆσθαι ὅ τι ἂν βούληται. ᾗ οὖν ἔτι πόρον τινὰ εὑρίσκω τοῦ ζητήματος ἡμῖν, ἄκουε.

We are in great straits. But we have not lost the consequences of failure until we have turned every stone.

5. αὐτοὶ ἐκτὸς τοῦ γελοίου ἑστῶτες] 'When we are ourselves free from the absurdity,' 'exempt from the ridicule.'

7. παρέξομεν—πατεῖν] Gorg. 476: γενναῖος τῷ λόγῳ ὥσπερ ἰατρῷ παρέχων ἀποκρίνου. alib. There is probably an allusion to Soph. Aj. 1142 seqq.: Ἤδη ποτ' εἶδον ἄνδρ' ἐγὼ γλώσσῃ θρασὺν ναύτας ἐφορμήσαντα χειμῶνος τὸ πλεῖν ᾧ φθέγγ' ἂν οὐκ ἂν ηὗρες ἡνίκ' ἐν κακῷ χειμῶνος εἶχετ', ἀλλ' ὑφ' εἵματος κρυβεὶς ναύταις παρεῖχε τῷ θέλοντι ναυτίλων.

The argument from p. 187 to p. 191 may be thus condensed.

We no longer search for knowledge in sensation, which is neither true nor false, but in opinion, where the mind is engaged with its own objects by itself. But here an old difficulty meets us in another form. It seemed that sensation could not be false, because it was relative to the subject. It now seems as though opinion cannot be false, because we cannot separate a thinking subject from knowledge and being. What I do not know cannot be present in thought. Neither can I lay hold in thought on that which is not. But can I take one thing which is for another which also is? Thought being silent speech, if I lay hold of both, (i. e. if both are present to the mind,) I cannot mistake them; e. g. No one ever said to himself, Good is evil. And if only one is present to me, I cannot discourse about them, e. g. if I am thinking only of the good, I cannot say, Good is evil. We are in great straits. For the result at which we seem in danger of arriving is contradictory to most important facts.

We must not appeal to these, however, until we have extricated our minds, if possible, from this metaphysical tangle. For logical and metaphysical difficulties are not to be solved "ambulando," but by a higher criticism of the forms of thought which have occasioned them.

In what follows, we are brought gradually back from the simple to the complex, from the more abstract to the more concrete. We are compelled to image to ourselves, what was discarded at a former

158   ΠΛΑΤΩΝΟΣ

We said it was impossible that I should think what I do not know to be what I know, also I should be ignorant of what I know.

ΘΕΑΙ. Λέγε μόνον.   p. 191.

ΣΩ. Οὐ φήσω ἡμᾶς ὀρθῶς ὁμολογῆσαι, ἡνίκα ὡμολογήσαμεν, ἅ τις οἶδεν, ἀδύνατον δοξάσαι ἃ μὴ οἶδεν εἶναι αὐτά, καὶ ψευσθῆναι· ἀλλά πῃ δυνατόν. b

ΘΕΑΙ. ᾎρα λέγεις ὃ καὶ ἐγὼ τότε ὑπώπτευσα ἡνίκ' αὐτὸ ἔφαμεν, τοιοῦτον εἶναι, ὅτι ἐνίοτ' ἐγὼ γιγνώσκων Σωκράτη, πόρρωθεν δὲ ὁρῶν ἄλλον ὃν οὐ γιγνώσκω, ᾠήθην εἶναι Σωκράτη ὃν οἶδα; γίγνεται γὰρ δὴ ἐν τῷ τοιούτῳ οἷον λέγεις.

But perhaps it is possible in a certain way; e.g. Theaetetus knows Socrates, and yet may

ΣΩ. Οὐκοῦν ἀπέστημεν αὐτοῦ, ὅτι ἃ ἴσμεν, ἐποίει ἡμᾶς εἰδότας μὴ εἰδέναι;

ΘΕΑΙ. Πάνυ μὲν οὖν.

ΣΩ. Μὴ γὰρ οὕτω τιθῶμεν, ἀλλ' ὧδε· ἴσως πῃ ἡμῖν συγχωρήσεται, ἴσως δὲ ἀντιτενεῖ· ἀλλὰ γὰρ ἐν

stage of the inquiry, a process between the relativeness of sense and the absoluteness of knowledge, which, like every process, admits of degrees. Thus, it may be said, the idea of motion returns upon us in a higher form.

The mind is a storehouse of old impressions, in which we are continually looking for the types of new ones. But the old impressions fade and get confused, and we fail to bring them with precision and clearness into contact with the new. This is to think falsely.

6. τοιούτων εἶναι] sc. αὐτό.

13. ἀλλ' ὧδε·] This is the punctuation of the Bodleian MS, which seems better than that usually followed. καὶ ἴσως, the reading of the later MSS, is unnecessary. A qualifying clause is sometimes thus introduced before ἀλλά—without any particle of connexion with what precedes. Compare Soph. El. 430: σμικρὸ μέν τοὶ, ἀλλ' ὅμως ἔχω, διὰ αὐτῷ.

Œd. Col. 1615:
σελαγεῖν μέν, οἶδα, οὐδέν· ἀλλ'
    ἐν γὰρ μόνον
τὸ πάντα λύει ταῦτ' ἴσων μοχθήματα.

Eur. Alc. 353:
ψυχρὸν μέν, οἶμαι, τέρψιν· ἀλλ'
    ὅμως βάρος
ψυχῆς ἀπαντλοίην ἄν.

Soph. p. 171: εἰσὶν γε ἄρα—
ἀλλ' ἡμῖν ἀνωγαί - - - Compare also the frequent asyndeton with πάντως. For ἴσως—ἴσως δέ cf. Apol. p. 18: ἴσως μὲν γὰρ χείρων, ἴσως δὲ βελτίων ἄν εἴη—.

14. συγχωρήσεται — ἀντιτενεῖ] Cf. Repub. 354: ἐὰν ἄρα ἡμῖν τῇ παρεικάθῃ τὸ μὴ ὡς λέγουσιν ὡς ἔστω ἔστω· μὴ ὡς ἀξίᾳς ἀπαλλάττειν.

ΘΕΑΙΤΗΤΟΣ. 159

p. 191. τοιούτῳ ἐχόμεθα, ἐν ᾧ ἀνάγκη πάντα μεταστρέφοντα
c λόγον βασανίζειν. σκόπει οὖν εἴ τι λέγω. ἆρα ἔστι
μὴ εἰδότα τι πρότερον ὕστερον μαθεῖν;
  ΘΕΑΙ. Ἔστι μέντοι.
  ΣΩ. Οὐκοῦν καὶ αὖθις ἕτερον καὶ ἕτερον;
  ΘΕΑΙ. Τί δ' οὔ;
  ΣΩ. Θὲς δή μοι λόγου ἕνεκα ἐν ταῖς ψυχαῖς ἡμῶν
ἐνὸν κήρινον ἐκμαγεῖον, τῷ μὲν μεῖζον, τῷ δ' ἔλαττον,
καὶ τῷ μὲν καθαρωτέρου κηροῦ, τῷ δὲ κοπρωδεστέρου,
d καὶ σκληροτέρου, ἐνίοις δὲ ὑγροτέρου, ἔστι δ' οἷς με- 10
τρίως ἔχοντος.
  ΘΕΑΙ. Τίθημι.
  ΣΩ. Δῶρον τοίνυν αὐτὸ φῶμεν εἶναι τῆς τῶν

(14.) ἀλλὰ γάρ] 'But we must risk the chance of failure, for,' &c.

3. μαθεῖν] The tense is noticeable. Whatever difficulty may attend the conception of the process of learning and forgetting, (μανθάνειν, ἐπιλανθάνεσθαι), it is certain that things are learnt and forgotten (μαθεῖν, ἐπιλελῆσθαι.) In what follows the process itself is imagined rather than analysed.

7. Θὲς] Cf. Philcb. 34: θὲς τῶν περὶ τὸ σῶμα ἡμῶν—καθημάτων τὰ μέν. alib—. The image is not unlike Locke's illustration of the different kinds of memory. Hum. Und. B. II. 10. §§ 4, 5: 'The brain in some retains the characters drawn on it like marble, in others like freestone, and in others little better than sand.' Ib. 19. § 3. 'If the organs or faculties of perception, like wax overhardened with cold, will not

receive 'the impression of the seal from the usual impress wont to imprint it, or like wax of a temper too soft, will not hold it when well imprinted; or else, supposing the wax of a temper fit, but the seal not applied with sufficient force to make a clear impression—in any of these cases the print left by the seal will be obscure.'

8. κήρινον ἐκμαγεῖον] Plato's image is not the common one of a waxen tablet, but of a 'block of wax,' such as was used for sealing. ἐκμαγεῖον is used first of the whole mass, afterwards of those parts of it which have received the particular impressions.

13. τῆς τῶν Μουσῶν μητρός] Aesch. Prom. 461: μνήμην δ' ἁπάντων μουσομήτορ' ἐργάτιν.— Plat. Euthyd. 275: καθάπερ αἱ τραγικαὶ δεινὰ ἀρχόμενοι τῆς διηγήσεως Μοῦσάς τε καὶ Μνημοσύνην ἐπικαλεῖσθαι.

160 ΠΛΑΤΩΝΟΣ

means of the following images.

Each of us has in his mind a block of wax, on which he receives the stamp of those sensations and perceptions which he wishes to remember. That which he succeeds in stamping is remembered and known so long as the impression lasts, but that of which the impression is rubbed out, or is imperfectly made, in

Μουσῶν μητρὸς Μνημοσύνης, καὶ ἐς τοῦτο, ὅ τι ἂν p. 191.
βουληθῶμεν μνημονεῦσαι ὧν ἂν ἴδωμεν ἢ ἀκούσωμεν
ἢ αὐτοὶ ἐννοήσωμεν, ὑπέχοντας αὐτὸ ταῖς αἰσθήσεσι
καὶ ἐννοίαις, ἀποτυποῦσθαι, ὥσπερ δακτυλίων σημεῖα
5 ἐνσημαινομένους. καὶ ὃ μὲν ἂν ἐκμαγῇ, μνημονεύειν
τε καὶ ἐπίστασθαι, ἕως ἂν ἐνῇ τὸ εἴδωλον αὐτοῦ· ὅταν
δ' ἐξαλειφθῇ ἢ μὴ οἷόν τε γένηται ἐκμαγῆναι, ἐπιλε- ο
λῆσθαί τε καὶ μὴ ἐπίστασθαι.

ΘΕΑΙ. Ἔστω οὕτως.

10 ΣΩ. Ὁ τοίνυν ἐπιστάμενος μὲν αὐτά, σκοπῶν δέ
τι ὧν ὁρᾷ ἢ ἀκούει, ἄθρει εἰ ἄρα τοιῷδε τρόπῳ ψευδῆ
ἂν δοξάσαι.

ΘΕΑΙ. Ποίῳ δή τινι;

ΣΩ. Ἃ οἶδεν, οἰηθεὶς εἶναι τοτὲ μὲν ἃ οἶδε, τοτὲ δὲ
15 ἃ μή. ταῦτα γὰρ ἐν τοῖς πρόσθεν οὐ καλῶς ὡμολογήσαμεν ὁμολογοῦντες ἀδύνατα.

ΘΕΑΙ. Νῦν δὲ πῶς λέγεις;

ΣΩ. Δεῖ ὧδε λέγεσθαι περὶ αὐτῶν, ἐξ ἀρχῆς διο- p. 192.

1. ἐς τοῦτο — ἀποτυποῦσθαι] 'To stamp them upon this, as if we were taking on it the impressions of seal-rings.'

3. ὑπέχοντας αὐτό] Holding it (the wax) to receive our perceptions and thoughts, we stamp them there, as if taking the impression of a seal. The infinitives are used, because the impressions are taken from our own sensations for our own use.

4. ὥσπερ δακτυλίων σημεῖα ἐνσημαινομένους] For the image of the seal, cf. Phaed. p. 76, where it is used of the mind impressing its idea of Being upon things.

6. ὅταν δ' ἐξαλειφθῇ] Ven. Π. corr. ἂν δ' ἂν. Bodl. et Vat. δὲ omittunt. The Bodl. however, has δ' in the margin by a later hand. The common reading is sufficiently probable: the regularity of the sentence is broken by the introduction of ἕως ἂν, so that instead of ἂν δ' ἂν we have ἕως δέ. Cf. supr. p. 159. ἂν ἂν ——— ὅταν.

10. αὐτά] Viz. ἃ ἂν ἴδῃ καὶ ἀκούσῃ ἢ αὐτὸς ἐννοήσῃ. (supr.)

Although I know what is present to me in sensation, i. e. though I may have in me a previous impression of the same thing, yet I may mistake it, i. e. fail to identify it as the original of that previous impression.

18. ἐξ ἀρχῆς] A priori.

ΘΕΑΙΤΗΤΟΣ.

p. 192. ῥιζομένοις, ὅτι ὁ μέν τις οἶδε σχὼν αὐτοῦ μνημεῖον ἐν τῇ ψυχῇ, αἰσθάνεται δὲ αὐτὸ μή, τοῦτο οἰηθῆναι ἕτερόν τι ὧν οἶδεν, ἔχοντα καὶ ἐκείνου τύπον, αἰσθανόμενον δὲ μή, ἀδύνατον. καὶ ὅ γε οἶδεν αὖ, οἰηθῆναι εἶναι ὃ μὴ οἶδε μηδ᾽ ἔχει αὐτοῦ σφραγῖδα· καὶ ὃ μὴ 5 οἶδεν, ὃ μὴ οἶδεν αὖ· καὶ ὃ μὴ οἶδεν, ὃ οἶδε· καὶ ὃ αἰσθάνεταί γε, ἕτερόν τι ὧν αἰσθάνεται οἰηθῆναι εἶναι· καὶ ὃ αἰσθάνεται, ὧν τι μὴ αἰσθάνεται· καὶ ὃ μὴ αἰσθάνεται, ὧν μὴ αἰσθάνεται· καὶ ὃ μὴ αἰσθάνεται, ὧν αἰσθάνεται. καὶ ἔτι γε αὖ ὧν οἶδε καὶ αἰσθάνεται 10 καὶ ἔχει τὸ σημεῖον κατὰ τὴν αἴσθησιν, οἰηθῆναι αὖ ἕτερόν τι ὧν οἶδε καὶ αἰσθάνεται καὶ ἔχει αὖ καὶ ἐκείνου τὸ σημεῖον κατὰ τὴν αἴσθησιν, ἀδυνατώτερον ἔτι ἐκείνων, εἰ οἷόν τε. καὶ ὃ οἶδε καὶ ὃ αἰσθάνεται ἔχων τὸ μνημεῖον ὀρθῶς, ὃ οἶδεν οἰηθῆναι ἀδύνατον· καὶ ὃ 15

forgotten and not known. For what I know in this way I may mistake, sometimes what I know, sometimes what I do not know. Mistake is impossible between things both of which are thus known but not present to sense, nor indeed is it possible in any case without sensation.

4. ὃ μὴ οἶδεν] i. e. not supposing him to have a sensible perception of it.

6. καὶ ὃ αἰσθάνεταί γε] i. e. not supposing him to know it. Both the above cases are distinguished from that in which a thing is both known and perceived.

11. καὶ ἔχει τὸ σημεῖον κατὰ τὴν αἴσθησιν] He holds the stamp left by the former sensation in a line with the present sensation, so that the two impressions coincide. Vid. inf. 194. καταντικρὺ μὲν καὶ κατὰ τὸ εὐθύ.

14. ἔχων τὸ μνημεῖον ὀρθῶς] Cf. the common expressions ὀρθαῖς ἔμμασιν, ἐξ ὀρθῆς φρενός.

The above statement may be put shortly thus: Mistake is impossible—1. Between things not perceived by sense, when we know both or one or neither of them. 2. Between things not known, when we have a sensible impression of one or both or neither of them. 3. Still more impossible, if that may be, between things, (a.) both of which are known, both perceived by sense, and the knowledge of each of which is identified with its proper sensation: (b.) One of which we know and also perceive sensibly, and identify the knowledge of it with the sensation: (c.) Both or either of which we neither know nor perceive sensibly.

The only cases left in which mistake is possible are (1.) when one thing is known and another perceived sensibly; or (2.) when two things are known and also present to sense, but we fail to connect knowledge and sensation rightly.

162   ΠΛΑΤΩΝΟΣ

Still less when two things are known and present to sense, and when the sensation and the old impression coincide: or when neither is present to the mind at all. But when something, either known or unknown, is present to sense, and the mind brings the sensation over against the old impression of a different thing—then the mind mistakes.

οἶδε καὶ αἰσθάνεται ἔχων κατὰ ταὐτά, ὃ αἰσθάνεται· p. 192.
καὶ ὃ αὖ μὴ οἶδε μηδὲ αἰσθάνεται, ὃ μὴ οἶδε μηδὲ ὃ
αἰσθάνεται· καὶ ὃ μὴ οἶδε μηδὲ αἰσθάνεται, ὃ μὴ οἶδε·
καὶ ὃ μὴ οἶδε μηδὲ αἰσθάνεται, ὃ μὴ αἰσθάνεται.
5 πάντα ταῦτα ὑπερβάλλει ἀδυναμίᾳ τοῦ ἐν αὑτοῖς
ψευδῆ τινα δοξάσαι. λείπεται δὴ ἐν τοῖς τοιοῦσδε, εἴ
πέρ που ἄλλοθι, τὸ τοιοῦτον γενέσθαι.

ΘΕΑΙ. Ἐν τίσι δή; ἐὰν ἄρα ἐξ αὐτῶν τι μᾶλλον
μάθω· νῦν μὲν γὰρ οὐχ ἕπομαι.

10 ΣΩ. Ἐν οἷς οἶδεν, οἰηθῆναι αὐτὰ ἕτερ' ἄττα εἶναι
ὧν οἶδε καὶ αἰσθάνεται· ἢ ὧν μὴ οἶδεν, αἰσθάνεται
δέ· ἢ ὧν οἶδε καὶ αἰσθάνεται, ὧν οἶδεν αὖ καὶ αἰσθά- d
νεται.

ΘΕΑΙ. Νῦν πολὺ πλεῖον ἀπελείφθην ἢ τότε.

15 ΣΩ. Ὧδε δὴ ἀνάπαλιν ἄκουε. ἐγὼ εἰδὼς Θεόδωρον καὶ ἐν ἐμαυτῷ μεμνημένος οἷός ἐστι, καὶ Θεαίτητον κατὰ ταὐτά, ἄλλο τι ἐνίοτε μὲν ὁρῶ αὐτούς,
ἐνίοτε δὲ οὔ, καὶ ἅπτομαί ποτ' αὐτῶν, τοτὲ δ' οὔ, καὶ
ἀκούω ἤ τινα ἄλλην αἴσθησιν αἰσθάνομαι, τοτὲ δ'
20 αἴσθησιν μὲν οὐδεμίαν ἔχω περὶ ὑμῶν, μέμνημαι δὲ
ὑμᾶς οὐδὲν ἧττον καὶ ἐπίσταμαι αὐτὸς ἐν ἐμαυτῷ;

ΘΕΑΙ. Πάνυ μὲν οὖν.   e

2. καὶ ὃ αὖ μὴ οἶδε] In order to exhaust every conceivable case, the converse or negative of each of the foregoing cases, in which knowledge and sense were combined, must be fully stated.

5. ὑπερβάλλει ἀδυναμίᾳ] Cf. supr. ἀδυνατώτερον ὅτι ἐκείνων τι οἶδέ τι. The gen. is governed by ἀδυναμίᾳ. ὑπερβάλλει is abs. 'All these cases are beyond every thing in regard to the impossibility of any man's thinking wrongly in any of them.'

8. ἐὰν ἄρα ἐξ αὐτῶν τι μᾶλλον μάθω] 'For perhaps if you state them, I may perceive your meaning better.'

12. ἐν οἶδε καὶ αἰσθάνεται] Subaud. ὄντα.

14. ἀπελείφθην] For this use of the aorist when a person reflects on his own state, cf. Soph. Aj. 678: ἔφριξ' ἔρωτι, ἐπτοήθην δ' ἀπροσδοκήτως. alib.

ΘΕΑΙΤΗΤΟΣ.

p. 192. ΣΩ. Τοῦτο τοίνυν πρῶτον μαθὲ ὧν βούλομαι δηλῶσαι, ὡς ἔστι μὲν ἃ οἶδε μὴ αἰσθάνεσθαι, ἔστι δὲ αἰσθάνεσθαι.

ΘΕΑΙ. Ἀληθῆ.

ΣΩ. Οὐκοῦν καὶ ἃ μὴ οἶδε, πολλάκις μὲν ἔστι μηδὲ αἰσθάνεσθαι, πολλάκις δὲ αἰσθάνεσθαι μόνον;

ΘΕΑΙ. Ἔστι καὶ τοῦτο.

ΣΩ. Ἰδὲ δή, ἐάν τι μᾶλλον νῦν ἐπίσπῃ. Σωκράτης

p. 193. ἐπιγιγνώσκει Θεόδωρον καὶ Θεαίτητον, ὁρᾷ δὲ μηδέτερον, μηδὲ ἄλλη αἴσθησις αὐτῷ πάρεστι περὶ αὐτῶν· οὐκ ἄν ποτε ἐν ἑαυτῷ δοξάσειεν ὡς ὁ Θεαίτητός ἐστι Θεόδωρος. λέγω τι ἢ οὐδέν;

ΘΕΑΙ. Ναί, ἀληθῆ γε.

ΣΩ. Τοῦτο μὲν τοίνυν ἐκείνων πρῶτον ἦν ὧν ἔλεγον.

ΘΕΑΙ. Ἦν γάρ.

ΣΩ. Δεύτερον τοίνυν, ὅτι τὸν μὲν γιγνώσκων ὑμῶν, τὸν δὲ μὴ γιγνώσκων, αἰσθανόμενος δὲ μηδέτερον, οὐκ ἄν ποτε αὖ οἰηθείην, ὃν οἶδα, εἶναι ὃν μὴ οἶδα.

ΘΕΑΙ. Ὀρθῶς.

b ΣΩ. Τρίτον δέ, μηδέτερον γιγνώσκων μηδὲ αἰσθανόμενος οὐκ ἂν οἰηθείην, ὃν μὴ οἶδα, ἕτερόν τιν' εἶναι ὧν μὴ οἶδα. καὶ τἆλλα τὰ πρότερα πάνθ' ἑξῆς νόμιζε πάλιν ἀκηκοέναι, ἐν οἷς οὐδέποτ' ἐγὼ περὶ σοῦ καὶ Θεοδώρου τὰ ψευδῆ δοξάσω, οὔτε γιγνώσκων οὔτε ἀγνοῶν ἄμφω, οὔτε τὸν μέν, τὸν δ' οὐ γιγνώσκων. καὶ περὶ αἰσθήσεων κατὰ ταὐτά, εἰ ἄρα ἕπει.

ΘΕΑΙ. Ἕπομαι.

ΣΩ. Λείπεται τοίνυν τὰ ψευδῆ δοξάσαι ἐν τῷδε, ὅταν γιγνώσκων σὲ καὶ Θεόδωρον, καὶ ἔχων ἐν ἐκείνῳ ο τῷ κηρίῳ ὥσπερ δακτυλίων σφῷν ἀμφοῖν τὰ σημεῖα,

διὰ μακροῦ καὶ μὴ ἱκανῶς ὁρῶν ἄμφω προθυμηθῶ, τὸ p. 193. οἰκεῖον ἑκατέρου σημεῖον ἀποδοὺς τῇ οἰκείᾳ ὄψει, ἐμ-
βιβάσας προσαρμόσαι εἰς τὸ ἑαυτῆς ἴχνος, ἵνα γένη-
ται ἀναγνώρισις, εἶτα τούτων ἀποτυχὼν καὶ ὥσπερ
5 οἱ ἔμπαλιν ὑποδούμενοι παραλλάξας προσβάλω τὴν
ἑκατέρου ὄψιν πρὸς τὸ ἀλλότριον σημεῖον, ἢ καὶ οἷα
τὰ ἐν τοῖς κατόπτροις τῆς ὄψεως πάθη, δεξιὰ εἰς ἀρι-
στερὰ μεταρρεούσης, ταὐτὸν παθὼν διαμάρτω· τότε d
δὴ συμβαίνει ἡ ἑτεροδοξία καὶ τὸ ψευδῆ δοξάζειν.
10 ΘΕΑΙ. Ἔοικε γάρ, ὦ Σώκρατες· θαυμασίως ὡς
λέγεις τὸ τῆς δόξης πάθος.
ΣΩ. Ἔτι τοίνυν καὶ ὅταν ἀμφοτέρους γιγνώσκων

ΘΕΑΙΤΗΤΟΣ.

p. 193. τὸν μὲν πρὸς τῷ γιγνώσκειν αἰσθάνωμαι, τὸν δὲ μή, τὴν δὲ γνῶσιν τοῦ ἑτέρου μὴ κατὰ τὴν αἴσθησιν ἔχω, ὃ ἐν τοῖς πρόσθεν οὕτως ἔλεγον καί μου τότε οὐκ ἐμάνθανες.

ΘΕΑΙ. Οὐ γὰρ οὖν.

ΣΩ. Τοῦτο μὴν ἔλεγον, ὅτι γιγνώσκων τὸν ἕτερον καὶ αἰσθανόμενος, καὶ τὴν γνῶσιν κατὰ τὴν αἴσθησιν αὐτοῦ ἔχων, οὐδέποτε οἰήσεται εἶναι αὐτὸν ἕτερόν τινα ὃν γιγνώσκει τε καὶ αἰσθάνεται καὶ τὴν γνῶσιν αὖ καὶ ἐκείνου ἔχει κατὰ τὴν αἴσθησιν. ἦν γὰρ τοῦτο;

ΘΕΑΙ. Ναί.

ΣΩ. Παρελείπετο δέ γέ που τὸ νῦν λεγόμενον, ἐν ᾧ δὴ φαμὲν τὴν ψευδῆ δόξαν γίγνεσθαι τὸ ἄμφω γι-
p. 194. γνώσκοντα καὶ ἄμφω ὁρῶντα ἤ τινα ἄλλην αἴσθησιν ἔχοντα ἀμφοῖν, τὸ σημεῖον μὴ κατὰ τὴν αὑτοῦ αἴσθησιν †ἑκάτερον† ἔχειν, ἀλλ' οἷον τοξότην φαῦλον ἰέντα παραλλάξαι τοῦ σκοποῦ καὶ ἁμαρτεῖν, ὃ δὴ καὶ ψεῦδος ἄρα ὠνόμασται.

2. τοῦ ἑτέρου] Viz. of the former.

6. Heind. would insert ὁ before γιγνώσκων: but for the transition from the 1st to the 3rd person, when the nom. is indefinite, cf. inf. 196. οὐδέποτε — αἰσθήσει.

9. ἂν γιγνώσκει] This is the Bodleian reading, which seems preferable. The reference of ἐκείνου is thus made more distinct.

10. ἦν γὰρ τοῦτο;] 'We agreed to this?'

16. τὴν αὑτοῦ αἴσθησιν] Translate, adopting Stallbaum's conjecture, ἑκατέρου, 'Or having some other sensible perception of both, to fail in holding your previous impression of each person over against your present sensation of him.'

Or, retaining the common reading, τὸ σημεῖον — ἑκάτερον, 'Or having some other sensible perception of them, to fail in holding the previous impressions of both, each over against the sensation which belongs to it.' But it must be confessed that this is not so good.

17. ἀλλ' οἷον τοξότην φαῦλον] We are beginning to have a livelier conception of the movement of the mind and of the remoteness of sensible things from our notions of them.

166   ΠΛΑΤΩΝΟΣ

ΘΕΑΙ. Εἰκότως γε.   p. 194

ΣΩ. Καὶ ὅταν τοίνυν τῷ μὲν παρῇ αἴσθησις τῶν σημείων, τῷ δὲ μή, τὸ δὲ τῆς ἀπούσης αἰσθήσεως τῇ παρούσῃ προσαρμόσῃ, πάντῃ ταύτῃ ψεύδεται ἡ διά-
5 νοια. καὶ ἑνὶ λόγῳ, περὶ ὧν μὲν μὴ οἶδέ τις μηδὲ ἐπῄ-σθετο πώποτε, οὐκ ἔστιν, ὡς ἔοικεν, οὔτε ψεύδεσθαι b οὔτε ψευδὴς δόξα, εἴ τι νῦν ἡμεῖς ὑγιὲς λέγομεν. περὶ δὲ ὧν ἴσμεν τε καὶ αἰσθανόμεθα, ἐν αὐτοῖς τούτοις στρέφεται καὶ ἑλίττεται ἡ δόξα ψευδὴς καὶ ἀληθὴς
10 γιγνομένη, καταντικρὺ μὲν καὶ κατὰ τὸ εὐθὺ τὰ οἰκεῖα συνάγουσα ἀποτυπώματα καὶ τύπους ἀληθής, εἰς πλάγια δὲ καὶ σκολιὰ ψευδής.

ΘΕΑΙ. Οὐκοῦν καλῶς, ὦ Σώκρατες, λέγεται;

ΣΩ. Ἔτι τοίνυν καὶ τάδε ἀκούσας μᾶλλον αὐτὸ c
15 ἐρεῖς. τὸ μὲν γὰρ τἀληθὲς δοξάζειν καλόν, τὸ δὲ ψεύδεσθαι αἰσχρόν.

ΘΕΑΙ. Πῶς δ᾽ οὔ;

ΣΩ. Ταῦτα τοίνυν φασὶν ἐνθένδε γίγνεσθαι. ὅταν μὲν ὁ κηρός του ἐν τῇ ψυχῇ βαθύς τε καὶ πολὺς καὶ
20 λεῖος καὶ μετρίως * ὠργασμένος ᾖ, τὰ ἰόντα διὰ τῶν

The sense of this line is the nature of the whole.

3. τὸ δὲ τῆς ἀπούσης αἰσθ.] Sc. σημείου.

4. προσαρμόσῃ] Sc. ἡ διάνοια.

5. ἐπῄσθετο] The corr. of the Bodl. is in the ancient hand.

8. ἐν αὐτοῖς τούτοις] Here, and here alone, opinion turns and twirls about, becoming true and false alternately.

ἐν αὐτοῖς τούτοις στρέφεται καὶ ἑλίττεται ἡ δόξα] Cf. Rep. 479: ὅτι τὰ τῶν πολλῶν πολλὰ νόμιμα — μεταξύ που κυλινδεῖται κ. τ. λ.

11. ἀποτυπώματα καὶ τύπους] τύπος is here the present sensation, which we endeavour to fit into the former impression, (ἀποτύπωμα.) τύπος can scarcely be 'the form of the object.' This would be inconsistent with the previous use of the word, p. 192.

18. φασίν] This need not imply a reference to any contemporary doctrine. It rather indicates the half mythical tone which Socrates has assumed.

20. ὠργασμένος] 'Tempered.' This word has been restored from Timæus and Suidas, the latter of whom quotes this passage. MSS. εἰργασμένος.

τὰ ἰόντα διὰ τῶν αἰσθήσεων—

ΘΕΑΙΤΗΤΟΣ. 167

p. 194 αἰσθήσεων, ἐνσημαινόμενα εἰς τοῦτο τὸ τῆς ψυχῆς
κέαρ, ὃ ἔφη Ὅμηρος αἰνιττόμενος τὴν τοῦ κηροῦ
d ὁμοιότητα, τότε μὲν καὶ τούτοις καθαρὰ τὰ σημεῖα
ἐγγιγνόμενα καὶ ἱκανῶς τοῦ βάθους ἔχοντα πολυχρόνιά
τε γίγνεται καὶ εἰσὶν οἱ τοιοῦτοι πρῶτον μὲν εὐμαθεῖς, 5
ἔπειτα μνήμονες, εἶτα οὐ παραλλάττουσι τῶν αἰσθήσεων τὰ σημεῖα ἀλλὰ δοξάζουσιν ἀληθῆ. σαφῆ γὰρ
καὶ ἐν εὐρυχωρίᾳ ὄντα ταχὺ διανέμουσιν ἐπὶ τὰ αὑτῶν
ἕκαστα ἐκμαγεῖα, ἃ δὴ ὄντα καλεῖται. καὶ σοφοὶ δὴ
οὗτοι καλοῦνται. ἦ οὐ δοκεῖ σοι; 10

ΘΕΑΙ. Ὑπερφυῶς μὲν οὖν.

e ΣΩ. Ὅταν τοίνυν λάσιόν του τὸ κέαρ ᾖ, ὃ δὴ
ἐπῄνεσεν ὁ πάντα σοφὸς ποιητής, ἢ ὅταν κοπρῶδες
καὶ μὴ καθαροῦ τοῦ κηροῦ, ἢ ὑγρὸν σφόδρα ἢ σκληρόν, ὧν μὲν ὑγρόν, εὐμαθεῖς μέν, ἐπιλήσμονες δὲ γί- 15

block, which may be either too shallow, or too hard or too soft, or too narrow, or impure, whence the impressions are either imperfect or faint, or short-lived, or crowded, or coarse and dim, so that it is difficult for the mind to make each sensation correspond to its proper footprint.

ἐνσημαινόμενα—καθαρὰ τὰ σημεῖα ἐγγιγνόμενα] The thread of the sentence is resumed in an altered form. Cf. Polit. 295. πᾶν τὸ τοιοῦτο—ξυμβαίνει—γίλοιον ἂν—γίγνοιτο τῶν τοιούτων—. Phaed. 69. χωριζόμενα δέ.

2. κέαρ] The Homeric form is κῆρ. But Plato avoids bringing poetical words too abruptly into his prose. See above, p. 173, and n.

6. τῶν αἰσθήσεων] The gen. depends on παραλλάττουσι, like τοῦ σαυτοῦ above.

7. σαφῆ γὰρ καὶ ἐν εὐρυχωρίᾳ ὄντα—καλεῖται] There is here a similar irregularity to that just noticed. The sentence begins as though it were to be σαφῆ γὰρ—ὄντα (sc. τὰ σημεῖα) ταχὺ νέμουσιν, or something of the kind: but the thought grows as we proceed: and σαφῆ—ὄντα

is left as a sort of accusativus pendens. What follows is to be construed thus: ταχὺ διανέμουσιν (οἱ τοιοῦτοι ταῦτα) ἃ δὴ ὄντα καλεῖται, ἕκαστα ἐπὶ τὰ αὑτῶν ἐκμαγεῖα. 'Such persons quickly distribute things (as we term them) each to the place of its own former impress upon the block.'

9. ὁ δὴ ὄντα καλεῖται] The latter part of the dialogue does not forget the earlier part.

12. λάσιον—κέαρ] Il. B. 851: Πυλαιμένεα λάσιον κῆρ. Π. 554: Πατροκλῆος λάσιον κῆρ.

13. ὁ πάντα σοφὸς ποιητής] To appreciate the irony here, it is necessary to compare Soph. p. 234, where the parallel is drawn between the man who 'creates' every thing and the man who knows every thing; as well as Rep. B. X. p. 596, sqq.

168   ΠΛΑΤΩΝΟΣ

γνωνται, ὧν δὲ σκληρόν, τἀναντία. οἱ δὲ δὴ λάσιον p. 194.
καὶ τραχύ, λιθῶδές †τι† ἢ γῆς ἢ κόπρου συμμιγείσης
ἔμπλεων, ἔχοντες, ἀσαφῆ τὰ ἐκμαγεῖα ἴσχουσιν. ἀσαφῆ
δὲ καὶ οἱ τὰ σκληρά· βάθος γὰρ οὐκ ἔνι. ἀσαφῆ δὲ
καὶ οἱ τὰ ὑγρά· ὑπὸ γὰρ τοῦ συγχεῖσθαι ταχὺ γίγνε- p. 195.
ται ἀμυδρά. ἐὰν δὲ πρὸς πᾶσι τούτοις ἐπ' ἀλλήλων
συμπεπτωκότα ᾖ ὑπὸ στενοχωρίας, ἐάν του σμικρὸν
ᾖ τὸ ψυχάριον, ἔτι ἀσαφέστερα ἐκείνων. πάντες οὖν
οὗτοι γίγνονται οἷοι δοξάζειν ψευδῆ. ὅταν γάρ τι
10 ὁρῶσιν ἢ ἀκούωσιν ἢ ἐπινοῶσιν, ἕκαστα ἀπονέμειν

1. λάσιον] 'Shaggy.' Here, as in the case of βλοσυρός, we experience what is a frequent difficulty in Plato, that of determining the precise ethical meaning with which he adapts an Epic word.

2. λιθῶδές τι] The difficulty of the MS. reading is, that it presents as one case what were spoken of above as two. (λάσιον — ἢ συμπιλές), 'Those in whom it is shaggy and rugged, a gritty substance filled with an admixture either of earth or dung.' This is not an insuperable difficulty in a writer like Plato. But the correction λιθῶδές τι (Ficin. Heusd.) is extremely probable; 'In whom it is shaggy and rugged and stony, or full of the admixture of earth or dung.'

8. ψυχάριον] Cf. Περ. 519ι ὡς ὀμμὰ βλέπει τὸ ψυχάριον.

10. ἢ ἐπινοῶσιν] Cf. supr. 191. ἢ αὐτοὶ ἐννοήσωμεν. It may be asked, whether these expressions do not provide for the difficulty that is raised afterwards about 11 and 12? The answer probably is, that the difficulty, which is brought into full light afterwards, is here silently anticipated. (Compare the introduction of ἀγαθόν and καλόν in p. 157.) ἐπινοῶσιν however does not necessarily imply an abstract object of thought. As we dwell upon the image we have raised, we find that it is too simple to express more than the relations of sense and memory, and instead of multiplying κήρινα πλάσματα, a fresh image is introduced in Plato's usual manner. The touches of humour have led some critics to suppose that Plato is alluding to contemporary opinions. But may he not be laughing at himself?

The description of the act of recollecting in the Philebus, p. 34, is worth comparing with the present passage. 'Ὅταν δὲ μετὰ τοῦ σώματος ἑκάστοτε πάθῃ ἡ ψυχή, ταῦτ' ἄνευ τοῦ σώματος αὐτὴ ἐν ἑαυτῇ ὅ τι μάλιστα ἀναλαμβάνῃ, τότε ἀναμιμνήσκεσθαί που λέγομεν. ἦ γάρ; Π. μ. οὖν. Καὶ μὴν καὶ ὅταν ἀπολέσασα μνήμην εἴτε αἰσθήσεως εἴτ' αὖ μαθήματος αὖθις ταύτην ἀναπολήσῃ ἐν ἑαυτῇ, καὶ ταῦτα ξύμπαντα ἀναμνήσεις καὶ μνήμας

ΘΕΑΙΤΗΤΟΣ.

p. 195. ταχὺ ἑκάστοις οὐ δυνάμενοι βραδεῖς τέ εἰσι καὶ ἀλλοτριονομοῦντες παρορῶσί τε καὶ παρακούουσι καὶ παρανοοῦσι πλεῖστα, καὶ καλοῦνται αὖ οὗτοι ἐψευσμένοι τε δὴ τῶν ὄντων καὶ ἀμαθεῖς.

b ΘΕΑΙ. Ὀρθότατα ἀνθρώπων λέγεις, ὦ Σώκρατες.
ΣΩ. Φῶμεν ἄρα ἐν ἡμῖν ψευδεῖς δόξας εἶναι;
ΘΕΑΙ. Σφόδρα γε.
ΣΩ. Καὶ ἀληθεῖς δή;
ΘΕΑΙ. Καὶ ἀληθεῖς.
ΣΩ. Ἤδη οὖν οἰόμεθα ἱκανῶς ὡμολογῆσθαι ὅτι παντὸς μᾶλλον ἐστὸν ἀμφοτέρα τούτω τὼ δόξα;
ΘΕΑΙ. Ὑπερφυῶς μὲν οὖν.
ΣΩ. Δεινόν τε, ὦ Θεαίτητε, ὡς ἀληθῶς κινδυνεύει καὶ ἀηδὲς εἶναι ἀνὴρ ἀδολέσχης.
ΘΕΑΙ. Τί δέ; πρὸς τί τοῦτ᾽ εἶπες;

c ΣΩ. Τὴν ἐμαυτοῦ δυσμαθίαν δυσχεράνας καὶ ὡς ἀληθῶς ἀδολεσχίαν. τί γὰρ ἄν τις ἄλλο θεῖτο ὄνομα, ὅταν ἄνω κάτω τοὺς λόγους ἕλκῃ τις ὑπὸ νωθείας οὐ δυνάμενος πεισθῆναι, καὶ ᾖ δυσαπάλλακτος ἀφ᾽ ἑκάστου λόγου;
ΘΕΑΙ. Σὺ δὲ δὴ τί δυσχεραίνεις;

τον λέγομεν. The former and simpler process corresponds to the search for the impression upon the wax; the latter to the hunt in the aviary for a missing bird.]

(10.) *ἴκαντα*] Sc. τὰ ὄντα.

1. *ἰσάντων*] Sc. ταῖς ἐπιστήμαις.

ἀλλοτριονομοῦντες] 'Misappropriating,' i. e. 'Assigning wrongly.'

3. *καλοῦνται αὖ οὗτοι*] *αὖ* refers to supr. *καὶ σοφοὶ δὴ οὗτοι καλοῦνται. ἀμαθεῖς* is the opposite of *σοφοί*: *ἐψ. τ. ὄντων,* being inserted epexegetically.

13. *Δεινόν τε*] The old editions had *γε*. The abruptness of the reading in the text is better than such a meaningless connexion. Socrates breaks out, after a pause, with an expression, the relevancy of which does not at once appear.

18. *ἄνω κάτω τοὺς λόγους ἕλκῃ τις*] Compare with this expression, which frequently occurs, the still livelier image supr. p. 191. *ἐν ᾧ ἀνάγκη τόν τε μεταστρέφοντα λόγον βασανίζειν.*

170   ΠΛΑΤΩΝΟΣ

ΣΩ. Οὐ δυσχεραίνω μόνον, ἀλλὰ καὶ δέδοικα ὅ τι p. 195.
ἀποκρινοῦμαι, ἄν τις ἔρηταί με· ' Ὦ Σώκρατες, εὕρηκας
δὴ ψευδῆ δόξαν, ὅτι οὔτε ἐν ταῖς αἰσθήσεσίν ἐστι
πρὸς ἀλλήλας οὔτ' ἐν ταῖς διανοίαις, ἀλλ' ἐν τῇ συν- d
άψει αἰσθήσεως πρὸς διάνοιαν; Φήσω δὲ ἐγώ, οἶμαι,
καλλωπιζόμενος ὥς τι εὑρηκότων ἡμῶν καλόν.

ΘΕΑΙ. Ἔμοιγε δοκεῖ, ὦ Σώκρατες, οὐκ αἰσχρὸν
εἶναι τὸ νῦν ἀποδεδειγμένον.

ΣΩ. Οὐκοῦν, φήσει, λέγεις ὅτι αὖ τὸν ἄνθρωπον
ὃν διανοούμεθα μόνον, ὁρῶμεν δ' οὔ, ἵππον οὐκ ἄν
ποτε οἰηθείημεν εἶναι, ὃν αὖ οὔτε ὁρῶμεν οὔτε ἁπτόμεθα, διανοούμεθα δὲ μόνον, καὶ ἄλλ' οὐδὲν αἰσθανόμεθα περὶ αὐτοῦ; Ταῦτα, οἶμαι, φήσω λέγειν.

ΘΕΑΙ. Καὶ ὀρθῶς γε.

ΣΩ. Τί οὖν, φήσει, τὰ ἕνδεκα, ἃ μηδὲν ἄλλο ἢ e
διανοεῖταί τις, ἄλλο τι ἐκ τούτου τοῦ λόγου οὐκ ἄν
ποτε οἰηθείη δώδεκα εἶναι, ἃ μόνον αὖ διανοεῖται; Ἴθι
οὖν δή, σὺ ἀποκρίνου.

ΘΕΑΙ. Ἀλλ' ἀποκρινοῦμαι, ὅτι ὁρῶν μὲν ἄν τις ἢ
ἐφαπτόμενος οἰηθείη τὰ ἕνδεκα δώδεκα εἶναι, ἃ μέντοι
ἐν τῇ διανοίᾳ ἔχει, οὐκ ἄν ποτε περὶ αὐτῶν ταῦτα
δοξάσειεν οὕτως.

ΣΩ. Τί οὖν; οἴει τινὰ πώποτε αὐτὸν ἐν αὑτῷ
πέντε καὶ ἑπτά, λέγω δὲ μὴ ἀνθρώπους ἑπτὰ καὶ p. 196.
πέντε προθέμενον σκοπεῖν μηδ' ἄλλο τοιοῦτον, ἀλλ'

ΘΕΑΙΤΗΤΟΣ. 171

p. 196. αὐτὰ πέντε καὶ ἑπτά, ἅ φαμεν ἐπεὶ μνημεῖα ἐν τῷ ἐκμαγείῳ εἶναι καὶ ψευδῆ ἐν αὐτοῖς οὐκ εἶναι δοξάσαι, ταῦτα αὐτὰ εἴ τις ἀνθρώπων ἤδη πώποτε ἐσκέψατο λέγων πρὸς αὑτὸν καὶ ἐρωτῶν πόσα ποτ' ἐστί, καὶ ὁ μέν τις εἶπεν οἰηθεὶς ἕνδεκα αὐτὰ εἶναι, ὁ δὲ δώδεκα, ἢ πάντες λέγουσί τε καὶ οἴονται δώδεκα αὐτὰ εἶναι.

ΘΕΑΙ. Οὐ μὰ τὸν Δία, ἀλλὰ πολλοὶ δὴ καὶ ἕνδεκα· ἐὰν δέ γε ἐν πλείονι ἀριθμῷ τις σκοπῆται, b μᾶλλον σφάλλεται. οἶμαι γάρ σε περὶ παντὸς μᾶλλον ἀριθμοῦ λέγειν.

ΣΩ. Ὀρθῶς γὰρ οἴει. καὶ ἐνθυμοῦ μή τί †ποτε† γίγνεται ἄλλο ἢ αὐτὰ τὰ δώδεκα τὰ ἐν τῷ ἐκμαγείῳ ἕνδεκα οἰηθῆναι.

ΘΕΑΙ. Ἔοικέ γε.

ΣΩ. Οὐκοῦν εἰς τοὺς πρώτους πάλιν ἀνήκει λόγους; ὁ γὰρ τοῦτο παθών, ὁ οἶδεν, ἕτερον αὐτὸ οἴεται εἶναι ὧν αὖ οἶδεν. ὃ ἔφαμεν ἀδύνατον, καὶ τούτῳ αὐτῷ

had proceeded regularly, it would be followed by συνήδεσαν—εἰσίν.

1. αὐτὰ πέντε καὶ ἑπτά] The insertion of the article does not seem necessary, though it may possibly be right.

(ἐπεὶ) Sc. ἐν τῷ ἐκμαγείῳ.

μνημεῖα] 'Records.'

3. εἴ τις ἀνθρώπων] The question is resumed with εἰ, depending on λέγω, which has broken the regularity of the sentence. 'I mean to ask if ———.' The Bodleian MS. has ἦ with Heindorf and Bekker.

4. λέγων πρὸς αὐτὸν] Socrates refers to his own description of the process of thinking, supr. p. 189, 190.

8. ἐὰν δέ γε] Theaetetus is permitted to enlarge a little upon his own subject. We seek to identify the sum of 7 and 5, of which we have thought (ἐπεψάμεν) with the corresponding number in our minds; and by mistake we identify it with 11 instead of 12.

The statement of this case shews the inadequacy of the figure we have adopted. For where are the 7 and 5 and the sum of them of which we think? They are not in sensation: must they not then be in the waxen block? The former difficulty returns—we have taken one thing which we know for another thing which we know.

11. ποτε] Heind. conj. τότε.

15. Οὐκοῦν εἰς τοὺς πρώτους] 'The discussion has returned to its first stage.'

172   ΠΛΑΤΩΝΟΣ

ἠναγκάζομεν μὴ εἶναι ψευδῆ δόξαν, ἵνα μὴ τὰ αὐτὰ ὁ p. 196.
αὐτὸς ἀναγκάζοιτο εἰδὼς μὴ εἰδέναι ἅμα.   c

ΘΕΑΙ. Ἀληθέστατα.

ΣΩ. Οὐκοῦν ἄλλ' ὁτιοῦν δεῖ ἀποφαίνειν τὸ τὰ ψευδῆ δοξάζειν ἢ διανοίας πρὸς αἴσθησιν παραλλαγήν. εἰ γὰρ τοῦτ' ἦν, οὐκ ἄν ποτε ἐν αὐτοῖς τοῖς διανοήμασιν ἐψευδόμεθα. νῦν δὲ ἤτοι οὐκ ἔστι ψευδὴς δόξα, ἢ ἅ τις οἶδεν, οἷόν τε μὴ εἰδέναι. καὶ τούτων πότερα αἱρεῖ;

ΘΕΑΙ. Ἄπορον αἵρεσιν προτίθης, ὦ Σώκρατες.

ΣΩ. Ἀλλὰ μέντοι ἀμφότερά γε κινδυνεύει ὁ λόγος d οὐκ ἐάσειν. ὅμως δέ, πάντα γὰρ τολμητέον, τί εἰ ἐπιχειρήσαιμεν ἀναισχυντεῖν;

To meet this difficulty, we venture to say what it is to know, —(a daring step, as we are still seeking the definition of Knowledge.)

ΘΕΑΙ. Πῶς;

ΣΩ. Ἐθελήσαντες εἰπεῖν ποῖόν τί ποτ' ἐστὶ τὸ ἐπίστασθαι.

ΘΕΑΙ. Καὶ τί τοῦτο ἀναίσχυντον;

ΣΩ. Ἔοικας οὐκ ἐννοεῖν, ὅτι πᾶς ἡμῖν ἐξ ἀρχῆς ὁ λόγος ζήτησις γέγονεν ἐπιστήμης, ὡς οὐκ εἰδόσι τί ποτ' ἐστίν.

ΘΕΑΙ. Ἐννοῶ μὲν οὖν.

ΣΩ. Ἔπειτ' οὐκ ἀναιδὲς δοκεῖ, μὴ εἰδότας ἐπιστή-

---

1. ἠναγκάζομεν — ἀναγκάζοιτο] 'It was by this very argument we tried to make the non-existence of false opinion inevitable, because otherwise it would be inevitable that the same person should know and be ignorant at once.'

4. ἀλλ' ὁτιοῦν] 'Any thing but this.' Most MSS. give ἀλλὰ τι οὖν.

11. ἀμφότερα] Viz. τὸ εἶναι ψευδῆ δόξαν κ. ἅ τις οἶδεν οὐχ οἷόν τε εἶναι μὴ εἰδέναι. The distinction here indicated is analogous to that noticed by Aristotle between ἐπίστασθαι and θεωρεῖν; which is his favourite example of the difference between ἕξις and ἐνέργεια. Vid. Eth. N. I. 8. διαφέρει δ' οὐ μικρὸν ἐν κτήσει ἢ ἐν χρήσει τὸ ἄριστον ὑπολαμβάνειν. The tendency to this distinction appears in Sophocles Ant. 1378. ὃ δεινόν, ὡς, ἔχων τε καὶ κεκτημένος, κ. τ. λ.

p. 197. μὴν ἀποφαίνεσθαι τὸ ἐπίστασθαι οἷόν ἐστιν; ἀλλὰ γάρ, ὦ Θεαίτητε, πάλαι ἐσμὲν ἀνάπλεῳ τοῦ μὴ καθαρῶς διαλέγεσθαι. μυριάκις γὰρ εἰρήκαμεν τὸ γιγνώσκομεν καὶ οὐ γιγνώσκομεν, καὶ ἐπιστάμεθα καὶ οὐκ ἐπιστάμεθα, ὥς τι συνιέντες ἀλλήλων ἐν ᾧ ἔτι ἐπιστήμην ἀγνοοῦμεν. εἰ δὲ βούλει, καὶ νῦν ἐν τῷ παρόντι κεχρήμεθ᾽ αὖ τῷ ἀγνοεῖν τε καὶ συνιέναι, ὡς προσῆκον αὑτοῖς χρῆσθαι, εἴπερ στερόμεθα ἐπιστήμης.

ΘΕΑΙ. Ἀλλὰ τίνα τρόπον διαλέξει, ὦ Σώκρατες, τούτων ἀπεχόμενος;

2. ἀνάπλεῳ τοῦ μὴ καθαρῶς διαλέγεσθαι] 'Infected with logical imperfection.'

τοῦ μὴ καθαρῶς διαλέγεσθαι] In other words, we have felt our way hitherto, not by abstract definition and inference, but (as it is expressed Rep. 533) τὰς ὑποθέσεις ἀναιροῦντες ἐπὶ τὴν ἀρχήν. We first ventured the hypothesis αἴσθησις ἐπιστήμη. This was rejected, but the difficulties we met with pointed to a further hypothesis, ὅτι ἡ ἀληθὴς δόξα ἐπιστήμη ἐστίν. Here again we are met by fresh difficulties, but the discussion of them leads to a fresh hypothesis, that we may know, without having knowledge in hand.

3. μυριάκις γὰρ εἰρήκαμεν] We are haunted throughout by a difficulty respecting the search for knowledge akin to that respecting its first definition. Can we know it, and yet not know it? To inquire about it implies ignorance of its nature, and yet how can we use the name even in inquiry without knowing the meaning of the name? p. 147.

ᾗ αἰεὶ τίς τι συνιησί τινος ὄνομα, ὃ μὴ οἶδε τί ἐστι; 210. καὶ τοιοῦτοί γε εὔηθες ζητοῦντων ἡμῶν ἐπιστήμην δόξαν φαίει ὀρθὴν εἶναι μετ᾽ ἐπιστήμης.

10. Ἀλλὰ τίνα τρόπον διαλέξει, ὦ Σ.] Compare what was said of being, p. 156. τὸ δ᾽ εἶναι πανταχόθεν ἐξαιροῦσιν, οὐχ ὅτι καὶ ἡμεῖς πολλὰ καὶ ἄρτι ἠναγκάσμεθα ὑπὸ συνηθείας καὶ ἀνεπιστημοσύνης χρῆσθαι αὐτῷ.

That there is such a thing as absolute knowledge and absolute being is the postulate of Plato's mind. That he himself or any man had wholly grasped either, is more than he dares to say. The sacredness of this belief, which it would be impious to relinquish, appears also in Theaetetus' answer: τούτων δὲ μὴ ἀπεχομένῳ ἔστω σοι πολλὴ συγγνώμη. For a similar feeling in regard to the practice of virtue, cf. Rep. 407. ὁ δὲ δὴ πλούσιος, ὥς φαμεν, οὐδὲν ἔχει τοιοῦτον ἔργον προσκείμενον, οὗ ἀναγκαζομένῳ ἀπέχεσθαι ἀβίωτον. Apol. 38. ὁ δ᾽ ἀνεξέταστος βίος οὐ βιωτὸς ἀνθρώπῳ.

174 ΠΛΑΤΩΝΟΣ

ΣΩ. Οὐδένα ὧν γε ὃς εἰμί· εἰ μέντοι ἦν ἀντιλο- p. 197. γικός, οἷος ἀνὴρ εἰ καὶ νῦν παρῆν, τούτων τ' ἂν ἔφη ἀπέχεσθαι καὶ ἡμῖν σφόδρ' ἂν ἃ ἐγὼ λέγω ἐπέπληττεν. ἐπειδὴ οὖν ἐσμὲν φαῦλοι, βούλει τολμήσω εἰπεῖν οἷόν ἐστι τὸ ἐπίστασθαι; φαίνεται γάρ μοι προὔργου τι ἂν γενέσθαι.

ΘΕΑΙ. Τόλμα τοίνυν νὴ Δία. τούτων δὲ μὴ ἀπεχομένῳ σοι ἔσται πολλὴ συγγνώμη.

ΣΩ. Ἀκήκοας οὖν ὃ νῦν λέγουσι τὸ ἐπίστασθαι;

To know is not to have, but to possess, knowledge.

ΘΕΑΙ. Ἴσως· οὐ μέντοι ἔν γε τῷ παρόντι μνημονεύω.

ΣΩ. Ἐπιστήμης που ἕξιν φασὶν αὐτὸ εἶναι. b

ΘΕΑΙ. Ἀληθῆ.

ΣΩ. Ἡμεῖς τοίνυν σμικρὸν μεταθώμεθα καὶ εἴπωμεν ἐπιστήμης κτῆσιν.

ΘΕΑΙ. Τί οὖν δὴ φήσεις τοῦτο ἐκείνου διαφέρειν;

ΣΩ. Ἴσως μὲν οὐδέν· ὃ δ' οὖν δοκεῖ, ἀκούσας συνδοκίμαζε.

ΘΕΑΙ. Ἐάν πέρ γε οἷός τ' ὦ.

This distinction is illustrated by a new image.

ΣΩ. Οὐ τοίνυν μοι ταὐτὸν φαίνεται τῷ κεκτῆσθαι τὸ ἔχειν. οἷον ἱμάτιον πριάμενός τις καὶ ἐγκρατὴς ὢν μὴ †φοροῖ† ἔχειν μὲν οὐκ ἂν αὐτὸν αὐτό, κεκτῆσθαι δέ γε φαῖμεν.

1. ὧν γε ὃς εἰμί] Cf. Phaedr. 243. ἴσασιν ἂν γε ὃς εἰ.
εἰ μέντοι ἦν ἀντιλογικός] The apodosis is omitted, and the construction changed, because from supposing himself ἀντιλογικόν, Socrates proceeds to imagine the effect of the presence of such a man upon the discussion.
2. τούτων τ' ἂν ἔφη ἀπέχεσθαι] Not exactly with Heind. Stallb. ' abstinere nos jubeatur,' but (sub. ἄν) ' would have dwelt on the necessity of abstaining,' or, possibly, (throwing an emphasis on ἡμῖν) ' Would have professed to abstain.'

12. ἐπιστήμης —ἕξιν] Eulbyd. 277. τὸ δ' ἐπίστασθαι—ἄλλο τι ἢ ἔχειν ἐπιστήμην ἤδη ἐστίν; Phaed. 76.

21. [φέρων] Stallb. attempts to defend the optative without εἰ (which has only slight authority), from Rep. 549. ἄγρως εἴη, which is not quite parallel, (and there is MS. authority for ἄν.) The comparison of p. 193. Σωκράτης μηχανᾶσαι κ. τ. λ. suggests the conjecture φοροῖ.

ΘΕΑΙ. Ὀρθῶς γε.

ΣΩ. Ὅρα δὴ καὶ ἐπιστήμην εἰ δυνατὸν οὕτω κεκτημένον μὴ ἔχειν, ἀλλ' ὥσπερ εἴ τις ὄρνιθας ἀγρίας, περιστερὰς ἤ τι ἄλλο, θηρεύσας οἴκοι κατασκευασάμενος περιστερεῶνα τρέφοι. τρόπον μὲν γὰρ ἄν πού τινα φαῖμεν αὐτὸν αὐτὰς ἀεὶ ἔχειν, ὅτι δὴ κέκτηται. ἦ γάρ;

ΘΕΑΙ. Ναί.

ΣΩ. Τρόπον δέ γ' ἄλλον οὐδεμίαν ἔχειν, ἀλλὰ δύναμιν μὲν αὐτῷ περὶ αὐτὰς παραγεγονέναι, ἐπειδὴ ἐν οἰκείῳ περιβόλῳ ὑποχειρίους ἐποιήσατο, λαβεῖν καὶ σχεῖν, ἐπειδὰν βούληται, θηρευσαμένῳ ἣν ἂν ἀεὶ ἐθέλῃ, καὶ πάλιν ἀφιέναι· καὶ τοῦτο ἐξεῖναι ποιεῖν, ὁποσάκις ἂν δοκῇ αὐτῷ.

ΘΕΑΙ. Ἔστι ταῦτα.

ΣΩ. Πάλιν δή, ὥσπερ ἐν τοῖς πρόσθεν κήρινόν τι ἐν ταῖς ψυχαῖς κατεσκευάζομεν οὐκ οἶδ' ὅ τι πλάσμα, νῦν αὖ ἐν ἑκάστῃ ψυχῇ ποιήσωμεν περιστερεῶνά τινα παντοδαπῶν ὀρνίθων, τὰς μὲν κατ' ἀγέλας οὔσας χωρὶς τῶν ἄλλων, τὰς δὲ κατ' ὀλίγας, ἐνίας δὲ μόνας διὰ πασῶν ὅπῃ ἂν τύχωσι πετομένας.

II. 2. *Hypothesis of the cage full of birds.*

The mind is like a cage, empty at birth, which we fill by degrees with what we learn. Whatever knowledge there is caught by us, is known so long as it remains in this cage. And yet before we have it in hand, there is a further chase required.

3. μὴ ἔχειν, ἀλλ'] This opposition between minute parts of a sentence is very characteristic of the Greek idiom.

ὥσπερ] The apodosis is to be sought in Πάλιν δὴ κ. τ. λ.

16. κήρινόν τι] 'We established in the mind a sort of moulded form of wax.'

19. τὰς μὲν κατ' ἀγέλας] The distinction indicated is probably that between, 1. individuals in the aggregate (πολλὰ ἀθρόα ὄντα, p. 157.); 2. intermediate abstractions, as the virtues, numbers, &c.; 3. the highest abstractions, as Being, Goodness, resemblance, difference, &c. Little is thought, however, of any process of abstraction, as appears from the interchange of the terms μνημεῖον and διανόημα in what precedes.

20. κατ' ὀλίγας] e.g. The virtues, arts, &c.

ἐνίας δὲ μόνας διὰ πασῶν] e.g. τὴν οὐσίαν—τοῦτο γὰρ μάλιστα ἐπὶ πάντων παρέπεται, p. 186.

176 ΠΛΑΤΩΝΟΣ

ΘΕΑΙ. Πεποιήσθω δή. ἀλλὰ τί τοὐντεῦθεν; p. 197.

ΣΩ. Παιδίων μὲν ὄντων, φάναι χρή, εἶναι τοῦτο τὸ ἀγγεῖον κενόν, ἀντὶ δὲ τῶν ὀρνίθων ἐπιστήμας νοῆσαι· ἣν δ' ἂν ἐπιστήμην κτησάμενος καθείρξῃ εἰς τὸν περίβολον, φάναι αὐτὸν μεμαθηκέναι ἢ ηὑρηκέναι τὸ πρᾶγμα οὗ ἦν αὕτη ἡ ἐπιστήμη, καὶ τὸ ἐπίστασθαι τοῦτ' εἶναι.

ΘΕΑΙ. Ἔστω.

ΣΩ. Τὸ τοίνυν πάλιν ἣν ἂν βούληται τῶν ἐπιστη- p. 198.
μῶν θηρεύειν καὶ λαβόντα ἴσχειν καὶ αὖθις ἀφιέναι, σκόπει τίνων δεῖται ὀνομάτων, εἴτε τῶν αὐτῶν ὧν τὸ πρῶτον, ὅτε ἐκτᾶτο, εἴτε ἑτέρων. μαθήσει δ' ἐντεῦθεν σαφέστερον τί λέγω. ἀριθμητικὴν μὲν γὰρ λέγεις τέχνην;

To apply this to the case of number:

ΘΕΑΙ. Ναί.

ΣΩ. Ταύτην δὴ ὑπόλαβε θήραν ἐπιστημῶν ἀρτίου τε καὶ περιττοῦ παντός.

ΘΕΑΙ. Ὑπολαμβάνω.

ΣΩ. Ταύτῃ δή, οἶμαι, τῇ τέχνῃ αὐτός τε ὑποχειρίους τὰς ἐπιστήμας τῶν ἀριθμῶν ἔχει καὶ ἄλλῳ παραδίδωσιν ὁ παραδιδούς.

ΘΕΑΙ. Ναί.

ΣΩ. Καὶ καλοῦμέν γε παραδιδόντα μὲν διδάσκειν, παραλαμβάνοντα δὲ μανθάνειν, ἔχοντα δὲ δὴ τῷ κεκτῆσθαι ἐν τῷ περιστερεῶνι ἐκείνῳ ἐπίστασθαι.

ΘΕΑΙ. Πάνυ μὲν οὖν.

2. φάναι χρή, εἶναι] Although φάναι χρή is introduced parenthetically, the sentence receives an indirect turn from it.
3. ἀγγεῖον] 'Receptacle.'
12. ἐντεῦθεν] From this point of view, viz. where I am already standing.
19. ὑποχειρίους] 'Under (in the power of) his hand.' But not necessarily προχείρους, 'in hand.'

ΘΕΑΙΤΗΤΟΣ.

p. 198. ΣΩ. Τῷ δὴ ἐντεῦθεν ἤδη πρόσσχες τὸν νοῦν. ἀριθμητικὸς γὰρ ὢν τελέως ἄλλο τι πάντας ἀριθμοὺς ἐπίσταται; πάντων γὰρ ἀριθμῶν εἰσὶν αὐτῷ ἐν τῇ ψυχῇ ἐπιστῆμαι.

ΘΕΑΙ. Τί μήν;

ΣΩ. Ἦ οὖν ὁ τοιοῦτος ἀριθμοῖ ἄν ποτέ τι ἢ αὐτὸς πρὸς αὑτὸν αὐτὰ ἢ ἄλλο τι τῶν ἔξω ὅσα ἔχει ἀριθμόν;

ΘΕΑΙ. Πῶς γὰρ οὔ;

ΣΩ. Τὸ δὲ ἀριθμεῖν γε οὐκ ἄλλο τι θήσομεν τοῦ σκοπεῖσθαι πόσος τις ἀριθμός τυγχάνει ὤν.

ΘΕΑΙ. Οὕτως.

ΣΩ. Ὃ ἄρα ἐπίσταται, σκοπούμενος φαίνεται ὡς οὐκ εἰδώς, ὃν ὡμολογήκαμεν ἅπαντα ἀριθμὸν εἰδέναι. ἀκούεις γάρ που τὰς τοιαύτας ἀμφισβητήσεις.

ΘΕΑΙ. Ἔγωγε.

ΣΩ. Οὐκοῦν ἡμεῖς ἀπεικάζοντες τῇ τῶν περιστερῶν κτήσει τε καὶ θήρᾳ ἐροῦμεν, ὅτι διττὴ ἦν ἡ θήρα,

The arithmetician has knowledge of every number in his mind.

Yet in calculating he searches for what he knows, as if were putting his hand into the cage.

1. τῷ δὴ ἐντεῦθεν] δὲ δή, the reading of the Bodl. and its two companions, has probably slipped in from ἔχοντα δὲ δή above.

6. ἢ αὐτὸς πρὸς αὑτὸν αὐτά] This is the reading of the MSS. with the exception of Vat. Δ, which omits αὐτά: the reading ἑαυτὸς is a conjecture of Cornarius. The common reading is defensible. If αὐτά is omitted, the antithesis is imperfect; and if grammatical symmetry were desired, it could be restored by substituting αὐτά for αὑτά. But there is no real flaw, for τι is cogn. accusative, and ἀριθμοῖ τι = cast up a sum. The second accusative in the plural of the things which constitute the sum is therefore perfectly admissible; and it is also pointed, referring to αὐτὰ αὑτὸν καὶ ἑαυτὰ above. Might he not cast up a sum, either of abstract numbers in his head, or of the things about him?

As in the Parmenides, where unity is negatived, so here, where it has not been fully reached, the objects of Knowledge (or rather Knowledges themselves) appear in loose bundles which fly as we approach them.

11. πόσος τις ἀριθμὸς τυγχάνει ὤν] 'What such-and-such a sum amounts to.'

18. ἦν] The past tense implies 'We found it to be—'

A a

ἡ μὲν πρὶν κεκτῆσθαι τοῦ κεκτῆσθαι ἕνεκα· ἡ δὲ κε-
κτημένῳ τοῦ λαβεῖν καὶ ἔχειν ἐν ταῖς χερσὶν ἃ πάλαι
ἐκέκτητο. οὕτω δὲ καὶ ὧν πάλαι ἐπιστῆμαι ἦσαν αὐτῷ
μαθόντι καὶ ἠπίστατο αὐτά, πάλιν ἔστι καταμανθάνειν
ταὐτὰ ταῦτα ἀναλαμβάνοντα τὴν ἐπιστήμην ἑκάστου
καὶ ἴσχοντα, ἣν ἐκέκτητο μὲν πάλαι, πρόχειρον δ' οὐκ
εἶχε τῇ διανοίᾳ;

ΘΕΑΙ. Ἀληθῆ.

ΣΩ. Τοῦτο δὴ ἄρτι ἠρώτων, ὅπως χρὴ τοῖς ὀνόμασι χρώμενον λέγειν περὶ αὐτῶν, ὅταν ἀριθμήσων
ἴῃ ὁ ἀριθμητικὸς ἤ τι ἀναγνωσόμενος ὁ γραμματικός,
ὡς ἐπιστάμενος ἄρα ἐν τῷ τοιούτῳ πάλιν ἔρχεται μα-
θησόμενος παρ' ἑαυτοῦ ἃ ἐπίσταται;

ΘΕΑΙ. Ἀλλ' ἄτοπον, ὦ Σώκρατες.

ΣΩ. Ἀλλ' ἃ οὐκ ἐπίσταται φῶμεν αὐτὸν ἀναγνώ-
σεσθαι καὶ ἀριθμήσειν, δεδωκότες αὐτῷ πάντα μὲν
γράμματα, πάντα δὲ ἀριθμὸν ἐπίστασθαι;

ΘΕΑΙ. Ἀλλὰ καὶ τοῦτ' ἄλογον.

ΣΩ. Βούλει οὖν λέγωμεν ὅτι τῶν μὲν ὀνομάτων
οὐδὲν ἡμῖν μέλει, ὅπῃ τις χαίρει ἕλκων τὸ ἐπίστασθαι
καὶ μανθάνειν, ἐπειδὴ δὲ ὡρισάμεθα ἕτερον μέν τι τὸ
κεκτῆσθαι τὴν ἐπιστήμην, ἕτερον δὲ τὸ ἔχειν, ὃ μέν
τις κέκτηται μὴ κεκτῆσθαι ἀδύνατόν φαμεν εἶναι,
ὥστε οὐδέποτε συμβαίνει ὅ τις οἶδε μὴ εἰδέναι, ψευδῆ

ΘΕΑΙΤΗΤΟΣ. 179

p. 199. μέντοι δόξαν οἷόν τ' εἶναι περὶ αὐτοῦ λαβεῖν; μὴ γὰρ
b ἔχειν τὴν ἐπιστήμην τούτου οἷόν τε, ἀλλ' ἑτέραν ἀντ'
ἐκείνης, ὅταν θηρεύων τινὰ ἀπ' αὐτοῦ ἐπιστήμην δια-
πετομένων ἀνθ' ἑτέρας ἑτέραν ἁμαρτὼν λάβῃ, ὅτε ἄρα
τὰ ἕνδεκα δώδεκα ᾠήθη εἶναι, τὴν τῶν ἕνδεκα ἐπιστή- 5
μην ἀντὶ τῆς τῶν δώδεκα λαβών, τὴν ἐν ἑαυτῷ οἷον
φάτταν ἀντὶ περιστερᾶς.

but yet he
may mis-
take one
thing that
he knows
for another
that he
knows,
when, fall-
ing in this
after-
wards, he
takes the

across him; that is to say,
when he thought eleven to be
twelve, he got hold of the knowledge of eleven instead of that
of twelve,—in other words, the
rock-pigeon that was caged
within him instead of the dove.'

1. μὴ γὰρ ἔχειν] These words
are put emphatically forward
in antithesis to μὴ κεκτῆσθαι.
When hunting for some particular knowledge amongst what
he possesses and knows, he
catches one for another as they
fly about: e. g. the arithmetician makes a mistake in regard
to number when he seeks in
the tribe of numbers for that
which = 7 + 5, and takes hold
of 11 instead of 12.

The germ of the present metaphor appears in the Euthydemus, pp. 290, 291. θηρευτικοὶ
γάρ εἰσι καὶ αὐτοὶ (οἱ λογιστικοί)
κ.τ.λ. αὐτοὶ γὰρ (οἱ στρατηγοί) οὐκ
ἐπίστανται χρῆσθαι τούτοις ἃ ἐθή-
ρευσαν, ὥσπερ, οἶμαι, οἱ ὀρτυγοθή-
ραι τοῖς ὀρνιθοτρόφοις παραδιδόασιν
——ἀλλ' ὅμως πάνυ γελοῖοι, ὥσπερ τὰ παιδία τὰ τοὺς κορύδους
διώκοντα, ἀεὶ ᾠόμεθα ἑκάστην τῶν
ἐπιστημῶν αὐτίκα λήψεσθαι· αἱ δ'
ἀεὶ ὑπεκφεύγω. Compare also
Arist. Met. I. 5. 1009 b. τὸ γὰρ
τὸ συντόμως διώκειν τὸ ζητεῖν ἂν
εἴη τὴν ἀλήθειαν.

3. ἀπ' αὐτοῦ] The difficulty of

the sentence lies in these words.
They probably refer to ὁ ἐπιστάμενος—ὁ οἶδε above. For it is difficult to imagine that ἀπ' αὐτοῦ
and περὶ αὐτοῦ above do not refer to the same thing. If this
be so, the meaning is, that he
makes a mistake concerning
some general subject, e. g. concerning number in general,
when he takes one particular
thing contained in it for another. τούτου therefore means,
'of this particular thing,' viz.
which he is in search of. For
a similar use of τούτου, without
anything to which it immediately refers, cf. supr. 180. εἰν
τούτου (ζητῇ λόγον λαβεῖν), τί εἰ-
ρηκε. Infr. p. 202. τὸ μὴ δυνάμενον—ἀνεπιστήμονα εἶναι περὶ
τούτου.

4. ὅτε ἄρα—ᾠήθη εἶναι,——
λαβών] We pass from ὅταν to
ὅτε ἄρα, because reference is
now made to the actual case
supposed. The participle λαβών
is epexegetic to the verb understood in what precedes. He
has hold of something else :
that is, in the above case, taking the knowledge of eleven
for that of twelve. As if ἔχων
—οἶόν τι were τάχ' ἂν ἔχοι. Or
the nominative is due to a
kind of attraction from the in-
tervening clauses.

ΘΕΑΙ. Ἔχει γὰρ οὖν λόγον.

ΣΩ. Ὅταν δέ γε ἣν ἐπιχειρεῖ λαβεῖν λάβῃ, ἀψευδεῖν τε καὶ τὰ ὄντα δοξάζειν τότε, καὶ οὕτω δὴ εἶναι ἀληθῆ τε καὶ ψευδῆ δόξαν, καὶ ὧν ἐν τοῖς πρόσθεν ἐδυσχεραίνομεν οὐδὲν ἐμποδὼν γίγνεσθαι; ἴσως οὖν μοι συμφήσεις. ἢ πῶς ποιήσεις;

ΘΕΑΙ. Οὕτως.

ΣΩ. Καὶ γὰρ τοῦ μὲν ἃ ἐπίστανται μὴ ἐπίστασθαι ἀπηλλάγμεθα· ἃ γὰρ κεκτήμεθα μὴ κεκτῆσθαι οὐδαμοῦ ἔτι συμβαίνει, οὔτε ψευσθεῖσί τινος οὔτε μή. δεινότερον μέντοι πάθος ἄλλο παραφαίνεσθαί μοι δοκεῖ.

ΘΕΑΙ. Τὸ ποῖον;

ΣΩ. Εἰ ἡ τῶν ἐπιστημῶν μεταλλαγὴ ψευδὴς γενήσεταί ποτε δόξα.

ΘΕΑΙ. Πῶς δή;

ΣΩ. Πρῶτον μὲν τό τινος ἔχοντα ἐπιστήμην τοῦτο αὐτὸ ἀγνοεῖν, μὴ ἀγνωμοσύνῃ ἀλλὰ τῇ ἑαυτοῦ ἐπιστήμῃ· ἔπειτα ἕτερον αὖ τοῦτο δοξάζειν, τὸ δ' ἕτερον τοῦτο, πῶς οὐ πολλὴ ἀλογία, ἐπιστήμης παραγενο-

ΘΕΑΙΤΗΤΟΣ.

p. 199. μένης γνῶναι μὲν τὴν ψυχὴν μηδέν, ἀγνοῆσαι δὲ πάντα; ἐκ γὰρ τούτου τοῦ λόγου κωλύει οὐδὲν καὶ ἄγνοιαν παραγινομένην γνῶναί τι ποιῆσαι καὶ τυφλότητα ἰδεῖν, εἴπερ καὶ ἐπιστήμη ἀγνοῆσαί ποτέ τινα ποιήσει.

e ΘΕΑΙ. Ἴσως γάρ, ὦ Σώκρατες, οὐ καλῶς τὰς ὄρνιθας ἐτίθεμεν ἐπιστήμας μόνον τιθέντες, ἔδει δὲ καὶ ἀνεπιστημοσύνας τιθέναι ὁμοῦ συνδιαπετομένας ἐν τῇ ψυχῇ, καὶ τὸν θηρεύοντα τοτὲ μὲν ἐπιστήμην λαμβάνοντα, τοτὲ δ' ἀνεπιστημοσύνην τοῦ αὐτοῦ πέρι ψευδῆ μὲν δοξάζειν τῇ ἀνεπιστημοσύνῃ, ἀληθῆ δὲ τῇ ἐπιστήμῃ.

ΣΩ. Οὐ ῥᾴδιόν γε, ὦ Θεαίτητε, μὴ ἐπαινεῖν σε. ὃ μέντοι εἶπες, πάλιν ἐπίσκεψαι. ἔστω μὲν γὰρ ὡς

p. 200. λέγεις· ὁ δὲ δὴ τὴν ἀνεπιστημοσύνην λαβὼν ψευδῆ μέν, φής, δοξάσει. ἦ γάρ;

ΘΕΑΙ. Ναί.

ΣΩ. Οὐ δή που καὶ ἡγήσεταί γε ψευδῆ δοξάζειν.

ΘΕΑΙ. Πῶς γάρ;

ΣΩ. Ἀλλ' ἀληθῆ γε, καὶ ὡς εἰδὼς διακείσεται περὶ ὧν ἔψευσται.

ΘΕΑΙ. Τί μήν;

ΣΩ. Ἐπιστήμην ἄρα οἰήσεται τεθηρευκὼς ἔχειν, ἀλλ' οὐκ ἀνεπιστημοσύνην.

ΘΕΑΙ. Δῆλον.

ΣΩ. Οὐκοῦν μακρὰν περιελθόντες πάλιν ἐπὶ τὴν πρώτην πάρεσμεν ἀπορίαν. ὁ γὰρ ἐλεγκτικὸς ἐκεῖνος b γελάσας φήσει· Πότερον, ὦ βέλτιστοι, ἀμφοτέρας

182   ΠΛΑΤΩΝΟΣ

take it for knowledge? After taking a long circuit, we are again at fault.

Unless we have recourse to the image of another cage or waxen block, containing the knowledge of the knowledge and ignorances, and go on thus to infinity, "in wandering mazes lost."

τις εἰδώς, ἐπιστήμην τε καὶ ἀνεπιστημοσύνην, ἥν p. 200.
οἶδεν, ἑτέραν αὐτὴν οἴεταί τινα εἶναι ὧν οἶδεν ; ἢ οὐ-
δετέραν αὐτοῖν εἰδώς, ἣν μὴ οἶδε, δοξάζει ἑτέραν ὧν
οὐκ οἶδεν; ἢ τὴν μὲν εἰδώς, τὴν δ' οὔ, ἣν οἶδεν, ἣν μὴ
5 οἶδεν ; ἢ ἣν μὴ οἶδεν, ἣν οἶδεν ἡγεῖται ; ἢ πάλιν αὖ
μοι ἐρεῖτε ὅτι τῶν ἐπιστημῶν καὶ ἀνεπιστημοσυνῶν
εἰσὶν αὖ ἐπιστῆμαι, ἃς ὁ κεκτημένος ἐν ἑτέροις τισὶ
γελοίοις περιστερεῶσιν ἢ κηρίνοις πλάσμασι καθείρ-
ξας, ἕως περ ἂν κεκτῆται, ἐπίσταται, καὶ ἐὰν μὴ προ- c
10 χείρους ἔχῃ ἐν τῇ ψυχῇ ; καὶ οὕτω δὴ ἀναγκασθή-
σεσθε εἰς ταὐτὸν περιτρέχειν μυριάκις οὐδὲν πλέον
ποιοῦντες ; Τί πρὸς ταῦτα, ὦ Θεαίτητε, ἀποκρινούμεθα ;

ΘΕΑΙ. Ἀλλὰ μὰ Δία, ὦ Σώκρατες, ἔγωγε οὐκ
15 ἔχω τί χρὴ λέγειν.

ΣΩ. Ἆρ' οὖν ἡμῖν, ὦ παῖ, καλῶς ὁ λόγος ἐπι-
πλήττει, καὶ ἐνδείκνυται ὅτι οὐκ ὀρθῶς ψευδῆ δόξαν
προτέραν ζητοῦμεν ἐπιστήμης, ἐκείνην ἀφέντες ; τὸ
δ' ἐστὶν ἀδύνατον γνῶναι, πρὶν ἄν τις ἐπιστήμην d
20 ἱκανῶς λάβῃ τί ποτ' ἐστίν.

The truth is, we have no right to be searching for false opinion until we have

ΘΕΑΙ. Ἀνάγκη, ὦ Σώκρατες, ἐν τῷ παρόντι ὡς
λέγεις οἴεσθαι.

ΣΩ. Τί οὖν τις ἐρεῖ πάλιν ἐξ ἀρχῆς ἐπιστήμην ;
οὐ γάρ που ἀπεροῦμέν γέ πω.

8. γελοίοις περιστερεῶσιν] It would be rash to infer from this that the image is not Plato's own. Is Socrates never made to accuse himself of absurdity ? Rep. 354. οὐ μέντοι καλῶς γε εἰστιώμεθα δι' ἐμαυτὸν ἀλλ' οὐ διὰ σέ. Prot. 340. οἴει τις γελοίους ἰατρούς.
The value of such inferences must depend on the tone of the particular passages from which they are drawn.
16. ὁ λόγος] Either this particular argument, or rather the discussion in the form of an imaginary disputant.
18. τὸ δὲ] Sc. ψευδῆν δόξαν τί ποτ' ἐστίν.
24. γάρ που is said to be the reading of Ven. Π., and is probably right. (Cett. πω.)

ΘΕΑΙΤΗΤΟΣ.   189

p. 200.   ΘΕΑΙ. Ἥκιστα, ἐάνπερ μὴ σύ γε ἀπαγορεύσῃς.
ΣΩ. Λέγε δή, τί ἂν αὐτὸ μάλιστα εἰπόντες ἥκιστ'
ἂν ἡμῖν αὐτοῖς ἐναντιωθεῖμεν ;
e   ΘΕΑΙ. Ὅπερ ἐπεχειροῦμεν, ὦ Σώκρατες, ἐν τῷ
πρόσθεν· οὐ γὰρ ἔχω ἔγωγε ἄλλο οὐδέν.
ΣΩ. Τὸ ποῖον ;
ΘΕΑΙ. Τὴν ἀληθῆ δόξαν ἐπιστήμην εἶναι. ἀνα-
μάρτητόν γέ πού ἐστι τὸ δοξάζειν ἀληθῆ, καὶ τὰ ὑπ'
αὐτοῦ γιγνόμενα πάντα καλὰ καὶ ἀγαθὰ γίγνεται.
ΣΩ. Ὁ τὸν ποταμὸν καθηγούμενος, ὦ Θεαίτητε, 10
ἔφη ἄρα δείξειν αὐτό· καὶ τοῦτο ἐὰν ἰόντες ἐρευνῶμεν,
p. 201. τάχ' ἂν ἐμπόδιον γενόμενον αὐτὸ φήνειε τὸ ζητούμε-
νον, μένουσι δὴ δῆλον οὐδέν.
ΘΕΑΙ. Ὀρθῶς λέγεις· ἀλλ' ἴωμέν γε καὶ σκοπῶμεν.
ΣΩ. Οὐκοῦν τοῦτό γε βραχείας σκέψεως· τέχνη
γάρ σοι ὅλη σημαίνει μὴ εἶναι ἐπιστήμην αὐτό.

Sound Knowledge. And, though we can attempt nothing better than our last answer, perhaps if we return and examine it, the object of our search may show itself.

A brief examination is sufficient here.

1. ἀπαγορεύσῃς] Vat. Coisl. Zitt. The Bodl. has ἀπαγορεύῃς with an erasure.

8. καὶ τὰ ὑπ' αὐτοῦ γιγνόμενα πάντα] True opinion guides to right action, but it is a blind guide.

10. ὁ τὸν ποταμὸν] The man who had to show where the river was fordable is reported to have said, Go on, and you will find. For the expression αὐτὸ δείξει, τάχ' ἂν αὐτὸ φήνειε, cf. Phileb. 20. προϊὸν δ' ἔτι σαφέστερον δείξει. Protag. 324. αὐτό σοι διδάξει. Cratyl. 403. τοῦτό γε ὀλίγου αὐτὸ λέγει ὅτι ——— ἐπικεκρυμμένον ἐστί. Hipp. Maj. 288. εἰ δ' ἐπιχειρήσειε ἔσται αὐτῷ——αὐτὸ δείξει. The Scholiast says: δεῖξαι αὐτά. δεῖ τὸν ἐν πείρᾳ γιγνωσκομένων. κατα-

των γάρ των εἰς ποταμὸν πρὸς τὸ διασπερᾶσαι ἔρχεταί τις τὸν προαγόρευον οἱ βάθη ἔχει τὸ ὕδωρ. ὁ δὲ ἔφη, αὐτὸ δείξει.

The explanation is probable, though the authority is uncertain.

See above, πλεῖα δεῖ διασκεπτέα——τὸν ἐξ ἀρχῆς λόγον; and compare Rep. 454. ἐὰν τί τις εἰς πολυμάθειαν μικρὸν ἐμπέσῃ ἐάν τε εἰς τὸ μέγιστον πέλαγος μέσον, ὅμως γε νεῖ οὐδὲν ἧττον.

12. ἐμπόδιον γενόμενον] Those fording the river were feeling the bottom with their *feet*. Compare the way in which Justice 'turns up' in the Republic, 433. πάλαι, ὦ μακάριε, φαίνεται πρὸ ποδῶν ἡμῖν κυλινδούμενον.

ΘΕΑΙ. Πῶς δή; καὶ τίς αὕτη;

ΣΩ. Ἡ τῶν μεγίστων εἰς σοφίαν, οὓς δὴ καλοῦσι ῥήτοράς τε καὶ δικανικούς. οὗτοι γάρ που τῇ ἑαυτῶν τέχνῃ πείθουσιν οὐ διδάσκοντες, ἀλλὰ δοξάζειν ποιοῦντες ἃ ἂν βούλωνται. ἢ σὺ οἴει δεινούς τινας οὕτω διδασκάλους εἶναι, ὥστε οἷς μὴ παρεγένοντό τινες ἀποστερουμένοις χρήματα ἤ τι ἄλλο βιαζομένοις, τούτοις δύνασθαι πρὸς ὕδωρ σμικρὸν διδάξαι ἱκανῶς τῶν γενομένων τὴν ἀλήθειαν;

ΘΕΑΙΤΗΤΟΣ.   185

p. 201.   ΘΕΑΙ. Οὐδαμῶς ἔγωγε οἶμαι, ἀλλὰ πεῖσαι μέν.
ΣΩ. Τὸ πεῖσαι δ' οὐχὶ δοξάσαι λέγεις ποιῆσαι;
ΘΕΑΙ. Τί μήν;
ΣΩ. Οὐκοῦν ὅταν δικαίως πεισθῶσι δικασταὶ περὶ ὧν ἰδόντι μόνον ἔστιν εἰδέναι, ἄλλως δὲ μή, ταῦτα τότε ἐξ ἀκοῆς κρίνοντες, ἀληθῆ δόξαν λαβόντες, ἄνευ ἐπιστήμης ἔκριναν, ὀρθὰ πεισθέντες, εἴπερ εὖ ἐδίκασαν;

c   ΘΕΑΙ. Παντάπασι μὲν οὖν.
ΣΩ. Οὐκ ἄν, ὦ φίλε, εἴ γε ταὐτὸν ἦν δόξα τε ἀληθὴς †καὶ δικαστήρια† καὶ ἐπιστήμη, ὀρθά ποτ' ἂν

3. πεῖσαι μέν] The implied antithesis is δοξάσαι δ' οὔ. Cf. Rep. 475. Οὐδαμῶς, εἶπον, ἀλλ' ὁμοίως μὲν φιλοσόφοις. Τοὺς δ' ἀληθινούς, ἔφη, τίνας λέγεις; Soph. 240. Οὐδαμῶς ἀληθινὸν γε, ἀλλ' ἐοικὸς μέν.

13. καὶ δικαστήρια] Several MSS. read δικαστηρίᾳ. These words have been rejected by the critics, except Buttmann, who conjectured καὶ δικαστικῇ, very aptly for the sense, if the word can be made to signify 'worthy of a good judge.' See the words εἴπερ εὖ ἐδίκασαν— ὀρθά ποτ' ἂν δικαστὴς ἄρχων ἐδόξαζεν. It is in Plato's manner thus ostensibly to restrict himself to the case in point. Cf. p. 152. ἔν τε θερμοῖς καὶ πᾶσι τοῖς τοιούτοις. p. 204. ἔν γε τοῖς ἀνευ ἐξ ἀριθμοῦ ἐστιν.

Possibly καὶ δικασταὶ ἄξια may be the true reading. Cf. Apol. 18. δικαστοῦ γὰρ αὕτη ἀρετή. And see Phileb. 13., where the Bodl. has παραρυεῖσα for παραμενου‐ μένη. Ib. 36, where παραφυο‐ μένοις in the same MS. is a correction for πάσας ἀφροντι‐

νως, which the first hand wrote. But it is after all conceivable that δικαστηρία may be the feminine of an adj. not found elsewhere, except in the neuter substantive δικα‐ στήριον.

To resume the argument from p. 195.

Viewing the mind as a receptacle of impressions (or ideas), we said that to think falsely was to fail in identifying present impressions with the ideas already existing in the mind. And thus it seemed impossible to be mistaken about these ideas themselves apart from impressions from without. But in fact we do mistake in things independent of sensation. E.g. an arithmetician who possesses the knowledge both of 11 and 12, will sometimes say that the sum of 7 and 5 is 11. We resort therefore to a less simple conception of knowing, and to a more complex image. To know is to possess knowledge. We may possess it without

D b

186 ΠΛΑΤΩΝΟΣ

III. Theaetetus now remembers to have heard that true opinion, unless accompanied with an account of its object, is not knowledge.

δικαστὴς ἄκρος ἐδόξαζεν ἄνευ ἐπιστήμης· νῦν δὲ ἔοικεν p. 201.
ἄλλο τι ἑκάτερον εἶναι.

ΘΕΑΙ. Ὃ γε ἐγώ, ὦ Σώκρατες, εἰπόντος του
ἀκούσας ἐπελελήσμην, νῦν δ' ἐννοῶ. ἔφη δὲ τὴν μὲν
μετὰ λόγου ἀληθῆ δόξαν ἐπιστήμην εἶναι, τὴν δὲ d
ἄλογον ἐκτὸς ἐπιστήμης· καὶ ὧν μὲν μή ἐστι λόγος,
οὐκ ἐπιστητὰ εἶναι, οὑτωσὶ καὶ ὀνομάζων, ἃ δ' ἔχει,
ἐπιστητά.

Socrates identifies

ΣΩ. Ἦ καλῶς λέγεις. τὰ δὲ δὴ ἐπιστητὰ ταῦτα

having it in hand. We therefore image to ourselves false opinion thus. We have caught, as it were, (in learning) various species of knowledge, some gregarious, some noble and solitary, (i. e. abstract), and have caged them in the mind, like birds. We try to take in hand one of these birds which we possess, and as they flutter about, we take hold of another instead of it. But then, if we have this one in hand, how can we mistake it for the other? How can Knowledge be the means of error? Perhaps (Theaetetus suggests) there were ignorances flying about amongst the knowledges, and we have taken one of them. But if I have an Ignorance in hand, how can I take it for a Knowledge? Must we imagine another cage or waxen block to contain the Knowledge of the knowledges and ignorances? This would be endless.

4. τὴν μὲν μετὰ λόγου ἀληθῆ δόξαν] Cf. Meno, p. 97, 98. καὶ γὰρ αἱ δόξαι αἱ ἀληθεῖς, ὅσον μὲν χρόνον παραμένωσιν, καλὸν τὸ χρῆμα, καὶ πάντα τἀγαθὰ ἐργάζονται. πολὺν

δὲ χρόνον οὐκ ἐθέλουσι παραμένειν, ἀλλὰ δραπετεύουσιν ἐκ τῆς ψυχῆς τοῦ ἀνθρώπου, ὥστε οὐ πολλοῦ ἄξιαί εἰσιν, ἕως ἄν τις αὐτὰς δήσῃ αἰτίας λογισμῷ.—ἐντεῦθεν δὲ διεξιών, πρῶτον μὲν ἐπιστήμας γίγνεσθαι, ἔπειτα μείμονα· καὶ διὰ ταῦτα δὴ τιμιώτερον ἐπιστήμη ὀρθῆς δόξης ἐστί, καὶ διαφέρει δεσμῷ ἐπιστήμη ὀρθῆς δόξης. See the whole passage. Polit. p. 309. τὴν — ὄντως αὖσαν ἀληθῆ δόξαν μετὰ βεβαιώσεως. Symp. 202. ᾗ οὐκ ᾔσθησαι ὅτι ἐστί τι μεταξὺ σοφίας καὶ ἀμαθίας; τί τοῦτο; τὸ ὀρθὰ δοξάζειν καὶ ἄνευ τοῦ ἔχειν λόγον δοῦναι οὐκ οἶσθ', ἔφη, ὅτι οὔτ' ἐπίστασθαί ἐστιν ἄλογον γὰρ πρᾶγμα πῶς ἂν εἴη ἐπιστήμη; οὔτε ἀμαθία· τὸ γὰρ τοῦ ὄντος τυγχάνον πῶς ἂν εἴη ἀμαθία; ἔστι δὲ δή που τοιοῦτον ἡ ὀρθὴ δόξα, μεταξὺ φρονήσεως καὶ ἀμαθίας. Rep. 506. οὐκ ᾔσθησαι τὰς ἄνευ ἐπιστήμης δόξας, ὡς πᾶσαι αἰσχραί; ἐν αἷ βέλτισται τυφλαί· ἢ δοκοῦσί σοί τι τυφλῶν διαφέρειν ὁδὸν ὀρθῶς πορευομένων οἱ ἄνευ νοῦ ἀληθές τι δοξάζοντες;

7. οὑτωσὶ καὶ ὀνομάζων] i. e. using this strange term ἐπιστητά. infr. τὰ δὲ δὴ ἐπιστητὰ ταῦτα. ἐπιστητός, like αἰσθητὴς and νοητής, was a novel word, formed on the analogy of αἰσθητός.

ΘΕΑΙΤΗΤΟΣ. 187

p. 201. καὶ μὴ πῇ διῄρει, λέγε, εἰ ἄρα κατὰ ταὐτὰ σύ τε κἀγὼ ἀκηκόαμεν.

ΘΕΑΙ. Ἀλλ᾽ οὐκ οἶδα εἰ ἐξευρήσω· λέγοντος μέντἂν ἑτέρου, ὡς ἐγᾦμαι, ἀκολουθήσαιμι.

ΣΩ. Ἄκουε δὴ ὄναρ ἀντὶ ὀνείρατος. ἐγὼ γὰρ αὖ ἐδόκουν ἀκούειν τινῶν ὅτι τὰ μὲν πρῶτα οἱονπερεὶ στοιχεῖα, ἐξ ὧν ἡμεῖς τε συγκείμεθα καὶ τἆλλα, λόγον οὐκ ἔχοι. αὐτὸ γὰρ καθ᾽ αὑτὸ ἕκαστον ὀνομάσαι μόνον εἴη, προσειπεῖν δὲ οὐδὲν ἄλλο δυνατόν οὔθ᾽ ὡς ἔστιν, οὔθ᾽ ὡς οὐκ ἔστιν· ἤδη γὰρ ἂν οὐσίαν ἢ

p. 202. μὴ οὐσίαν αὐτῷ προστίθεσθαι, δεῖ[ν] δὲ οὐδὲν προσφέρειν, εἴπερ αὐτὸ ἐκεῖνο μόνον τις ἐρεῖ. ἐπεὶ οὐδὲ τὸ αὐτὸ οὐδὲ τὸ ἐκεῖνο οὐδὲ τὸ ἕκαστον οὐδὲ τὸ μόνον οὐδὲ τοῦτο προσοιστέον, οὐδ᾽ ἄλλα πολλὰ τοιαῦτα.

the saying thus quoted with what he himself has heard from certain "as in a dream;" viz. that the elements of all things cannot be expressed in a proposition, but can only be named. You cannot give them any attribute, since even such common predicables

1. εἰ ἄρα κατὰ ταὐτὰ σύ τε κἀγὼ ἀκηκόαμεν] Had they both heard from the same source? Or is Plato here, as in the beginning of the dialogue, weaving together two distinct theories? See Introduction.

5. ὄναρ] Cf. Phileb. 20. λέγουσί τινες νῦν δὴ ἐπιόντες ὅπερ ἢ καὶ ἐγγεγραφὼς νῦν ἐντός——. Phaed. 61. Ἀλλὰ μὴν αὐτὸ ἐξ ἀνοίας περὶ αὐτῶν λέγω.

6. ἰδ-ναρ ἀκούειν] 'I heard in my dream.'

οἱονπερεὶ στοιχεῖα] The metaphor is not lost sight of. Infr. 203. τὰ τῶν γραμμάτων στοιχεῖά τε καὶ συλλαβάς. ἢ οἴει ἄλλοσέ ποι βλέπειν αὐτὸ εἰπεῖν τὸν εἰπόντα ἃ λέγομεν.

9. προσειπεῖν δὲ οὐδὲν ἄλλο δυνατόν] 'But it is impossible to go on to predicate any thing of it (the element), either affirmatively or negatively. For in so doing there is added the idea of existence or non-existence: but nothing must be added,

seeing that you can only speak of the element by itself.

14. οὐδὲ τοῦτο] This has given needless trouble. Heindorf thought the article was required as with the other words, and inserted it. Buttmann objected to τοῦτο being so far separated from ἐκεῖνο, and ingeniously conjectured οὐδὲ τὸ τό. Both objections are obviated by observing that αὐτό, ἐκεῖνο, ἕκαστον, μόνον, occur in the preceding lines. For this reason they are put first, and with the article, and οὐδὲ τοῦτο—οὐδ᾽ ἄλλα πολλὰ τοιαῦτα is added afterwards. Cf. supr. p. 157. τὸ δ᾽ εἶναι πανταχόθεν ἐξαιρετέον—οὐ δεῖ—οὔτε τι ξυγχωρεῖν αὑτὸν τῷ αὑτοῦ ἐμοῦ οὔτε τῷδε αὐτῷ ἐκείνῳ οὔτε ἄλλο οὐδὲν ὄνομα ὅ τι ἂν ἰσχῇ. Accordingly in the reference to this passage, p. 205, (which Buttmann must have overlooked) the article is introduced,—οὐδὲ τὸ τοῦτο.

188 ΠΛΑΤΩΝΟΣ

as "this" and "that" are separable from the things to which they are applied. As the elements are combined in Nature, so definition is a combination of names. That which is second is the object of Sensation; the combination of these elements is

ταῦτα μὲν γὰρ περιτρέχοντα πᾶσι προσφέρεσθαι, p. 202.
ἕτερα ὄντα ἐκείνων οἷς προστίθεται, δέον δέ, εἴπερ ἦν
δυνατὸν αὐτὸ λέγεσθαι καὶ εἶχεν οἰκεῖον αὑτοῦ λόγον,
ἄνευ τῶν ἄλλων ἁπάντων λέγεσθαι. νῦν δὲ ἀδύνατον
5 εἶναι ὁτιοῦν τῶν πρώτων ῥηθῆναι λόγῳ· οὐ γὰρ εἶναι b
αὐτῷ ἀλλ' ἢ ὀνομάζεσθαι μόνον· ὄνομα γὰρ μόνον
ἔχειν· τὰ δὲ ἐκ τούτων ἤδη συγκείμενα, ὥσπερ αὐτὰ
πέπλεκται, οὕτω καὶ τὰ ὀνόματα αὐτῶν συμπλακέντα
λόγον γεγονέναι· ὀνομάτων γὰρ συμπλοκὴν εἶναι
10 λόγου οὐσίαν. οὕτω δὴ τὰ μὲν στοιχεῖα ἄλογα καὶ
ἄγνωστα εἶναι, αἰσθητὰ δέ· τὰς δὲ συλλαβὰς γνω-
στάς τε καὶ ῥητὰς καὶ ἀληθεῖ δόξῃ δοξαστάς. ὅταν
μὲν οὖν ἄνευ λόγου τὴν ἀληθῆ δόξαν τινός τις λάβῃ,
ἀληθεύειν μὲν αὐτοῦ τὴν ψυχὴν περὶ αὐτά, γιγνώ- c

1. περιτρέχοντα πᾶσι προσφέρεσθαι] Cf. supr. 198. ἐνίοις δὲ μόνοις διὰ πασῶν δεῖν ἂν τύχωσι ἐντομένοις. Rep. 402. τὰ στοιχεῖα—ἐν ἅπασι—περιφερόμενα.

2. εἴπερ ἦν δυνατὸν αὐτὸ λέγεσθαι] αὐτὸ is not emphatic. 'If it could be spoken of,' λέγεσθαι is the emphatic word.

7. (§η)] i.e. 'When we come to them.'

9. ὀνομάτων γὰρ συμπλοκὴν εἶναι λόγου οὐσίαν] Cf. Sophist. 262, where it is described more accurately as συμπλέκων τὰ ῥήματα τοῖς ὀνόμασιν. See the whole passage.

A passage of Aristot. Metaph. II. 3. is closely parallel to this. He has just shown that sensible reality (αἰσθητὴ οὐσία) consists of matter or potentiality (ὕλη, δύναμις), and form or actuality, (μορφή, ἐνέργεια). ἔστι ἡ ἀπορία ἣν οἱ Ἀντισθένειοι καὶ οἱ οὕτως ἀπαίδευτοι ἠπόρουν, ἔχει τινὰ και-

ρόν, ὅτι οὐκ ἔστι τὸ τί ἐστιν ὁρίσασθαι (τὸν γὰρ ὅρον λόγον εἶναι μακρόν) ἀλλὰ ποῖον μέν τι ἐστιν ἐνδέχεται καὶ διδάξαι, ὥσπερ ἄργυρον τί μέν ἐστιν, οὐ, ὅτι δ' οἷον καττιτέρος. ὥστ' οὐσίας ἔστι μὲν ἧς ἐνδέχεται εἶναι ὅρον καὶ λόγον, οἷον τῆν συνθέτου, ἐάν τε αἰσθητὴ ἐάν τε νοητή ᾖ· ἐξ ὧν δ' αὕτη πρώτων οὐκ ἔστιν, εἴπερ τι κατά τινος σημαίνει ὁ λόγος ὁ ὁριστικός, καὶ δεῖ τὸ μὲν ὥσπερ ὕλην εἶναι, τὸ δὲ ὡς μορφήν. See Introduction.

Locke's 'simple ideas' are not very different from the meaning of στοιχεῖα here.

12. καὶ ῥητάς] There is possibly an allusion to the mathematical use of the word. Cf. Rep. 546. πάντα προσήγορα καὶ ῥητὰ πρὸς ἄλληλα ἀπέφηνεν. But the immediate reference is to ῥηθῆναι λόγῳ, 'Capable of expression.'

14. ἀληθεύειν—περὶ αὐτά] 'Is exercised truly with regard to it.'

ΘΕΑΙΤΗΤΟΣ.

p. 202. σκεῖν δ' οὔ· τὸν γὰρ μὴ δυνάμενον δοῦναί τε καὶ δέξασθαι λόγον ἀνεπιστήμονα εἶναι περὶ τούτου· προσλαβόντα δὲ λόγον δυνατόν τε ταῦτα πάντα γεγονέναι καὶ τελείως πρὸς ἐπιστήμην ἔχειν. Οὕτως σὺ τὸ ἐνύπνιον ἢ ἄλλως ἀκήκοας;

ΘΕΑΙ. Οὕτω μὲν οὖν παντάπασιν.

ΣΩ. Ἀρέσκει οὖν σε καὶ τίθεσαι ταύτῃ, δόξαν ἀληθῆ μετὰ λόγου ἐπιστήμην εἶναι;

ΘΕΑΙ. Κομιδῇ μὲν οὖν.

d ΣΩ. Ἆρ', ὦ Θεαίτητε, νῦν οὕτω ῥᾷδε τῇ ἡμέρᾳ εἰλήφαμεν ὃ πάλαι καὶ πολλοὶ τῶν σοφῶν ζητοῦντες πρὶν εὑρεῖν κατεγήρασαν;

ΘΕΑΙ. Ἐμοὶ γοῦν δοκεῖ, ὦ Σώκρατες, καλῶς λέγεσθαι τὸ νῦν ῥηθέν.

ΣΩ. Καὶ εἰκός γε αὐτὸ τοῦτο οὕτως ἔχειν· τίς γὰρ ἂν καὶ ἔτι ἐπιστήμη εἴη χωρὶς τοῦ λόγου τε καὶ ὀρθῆς δόξης; ἓν μέντοι τί με τῶν ῥηθέντων ἀπαρέσκει.

---

above the object of Knowledge. For that impression deserves not to be called knowledge, which cannot be expressed in a proposition.

Knowledge then is true opinion giving an account of itself. This is our third answer.

Can we prove it true?

1. The answer may be a true one, and yet the

---

2. περὶ τούτου] Sc. οὗ ἂν μὴ δύναται δοῦναι λόγον.

3. δυνατόν—ταῦτα πάντα] Sc. δοῦναί τε καὶ δέξασθαι λόγον. It is a curious form to use in referring to such a simple thing. Possibly γιγνώσκειν and ἀληθεύειν are included.

Contrast with this Arist. Phys. Ausc. I. 1. (who points out that the elements, or simple ideas, are known not by sensation, but by analysis; and that definition distinguishes, while the name signifies an undivided whole.)

"Ἔστι δ' ἡμῖν τὸ πρῶτον δῆλα καὶ σαφῆ τὰ συγκεχυμένα μᾶλλον· ὕστερον δὲ ἐκ τούτων γίνεται γνώριμα τὰ στοιχεῖα καὶ αἱ ἀρχαί, διαιροῦσι ταῦτα.—Τὸ γὰρ ὅλον κατὰ τὴν αἴσθησιν, γνωριμώτερον. Τὸ δὲ καθόλου, ὅλον τί ἐστι. Πολλὰ γὰρ περιλαμβάνει ἐν μέρη τὸ καθόλου. Πίπτωσι δὲ ταὐτὸ τοῦτο τρόπον τινὰ καὶ τὰ ὀνόματα πρὸς τὸν λόγον. Ὅλον γάρ τι καὶ ἀδιορίστως σημαίνει, οἷον ὁ κύκλος· ὁ δὲ ὁρισμὸς αὐτοῦ διαιρεῖ εἰς τὰ καθ' ἕκαστα.

10. νῦν οὕτω] i. e. 'In a casual conversation.'

11. καὶ] Is to be taken with the whole clause as if it were ἐ καὶ—. For instances of this hyperbaton, see Ellendt. Lex. sub voce καὶ, C. 4.

15. αὐτὸ τοῦτο] The definition itself, whatever may be said of the theory that has been put forward. Heindorf's conjecture, εἶδός γ' αὖ τοῦτο, would give a different turn to the sense. 'It is natural to suppose that we have said well.'

ΠΛΑΤΩΝΟΣ

ΘΕΑΙ. Τὸ ποῖον δή;   p. 202.

ΣΩ. Ὃ καὶ δοκεῖ λέγεσθαι κομψότατα· ὡς τὰ μὲν στοιχεῖα ἄγνωστα, τὸ δὲ τῶν συλλαβῶν γένος γνωστόν.

ΘΕΑΙ. Οὐκοῦν ὀρθῶς;

ΣΩ. Ἰστέον δή· ὥσπερ γὰρ ὁμήρους ἔχομεν τοῦ λόγου τὰ παραδείγματα, οἷς χρώμενος εἶπε πάντα ταῦτα.

ΘΕΑΙ. Ποῖα δή.

ΣΩ. Τὰ τῶν γραμμάτων στοιχεῖά τε καὶ συλλαβάς. ἢ οἴει ἄλλοσέ ποι βλέποντα ταῦτα εἰπεῖν τὸν εἰπόντα ἃ λέγομεν;

ΘΕΑΙ. Οὔκ, ἀλλ' εἰς ταῦτα.

ΣΩ. Βασανίζωμεν δὴ αὐτὰ ἀναλαμβάνοντες, μᾶλ- p. 203. λον δὲ ἡμᾶς αὐτούς, οὕτως ἢ οὐχ οὕτως γράμματα ἐμάθομεν. φέρε πρῶτον· ἆρ' αἱ μὲν συλλαβαὶ λόγον ἔχουσι, τὰ δὲ στοιχεῖα ἄλογα;

ΘΕΑΙ. Ἴσως.

ΣΩ. Πάνυ μὲν οὖν καὶ ἐμοὶ φαίνεται. Σωκράτους γοῦν εἴ τις ἔροιτο τὴν πρώτην συλλαβὴν οὑτωσί, Ὦ Θεαίτητε, λέγε τί ἐστι σῶ, τί ἀποκρινεῖ;

ΘΕΑΙ. Ὅτι σίγμα καὶ ὦ.

ΣΩ. Οὐκοῦν τοῦτον ἔχεις λόγον τῆς συλλαβῆς;

ΘΕΑΙΤΗΤΟΣ. 191

p. 203.   ΘΕΑΙ. Ἔγωγε.
b   ΣΩ. Ἴθι δή, οὕτως εἰπὲ καὶ τὸν τοῦ σίγμα λόγον.
    ΘΕΑΙ. Καὶ πῶς τοῦ στοιχείου τις ἐρεῖ στοιχεῖα; καὶ γὰρ δή, ὦ Σώκρατες, τό τε σίγμα τῶν ἀφώνων ἐστί, ψόφος τις μόνον, οἷον συριττούσης τῆς γλώτ- 5 της· τοῦ δ᾽ αὖ βῆτα οὔτε φωνὴ οὔτε ψόφος, οὐδὲ τῶν πλείστων στοιχείων. ὥστε πάνυ εὖ ἔχει τὸ λέγισθαι αὐτὰ ἄλογα, ὧν γε τὰ ἐναργέστατα αὐτὰ τὰ ἑπτὰ φωνὴν μόνον ἔχει, λόγον δὲ οὐδ᾽ ὀντινοῦν.
    ΣΩ. Τουτὶ μὲν ἄρα, ὦ ἑταῖρε, κατωρθώκαμεν περὶ 10 ἐπιστήμης.
    ΘΕΑΙ. Φαινόμεθα.
c   ΣΩ. Τί δὲ δή; τὸ μὴ γνωστὸν εἶναι τὸ στοιχεῖον, ἀλλὰ τὴν συλλαβήν, ἆρ᾽ ὀρθῶς ἀποδεδείγμεθα;
    ΘΕΑΙ. Εἰκός γε.
    ΣΩ. Φέρε δή, τὴν συλλαβὴν πότερον λέγομεν τὰ ἀμφότερα στοιχεῖα, καὶ ἐὰν πλείω ᾖ ἢ δύο, τὰ πάντα, ἢ μίαν τινὰ ἰδέαν γεγονυῖαν συντεθέντων αὐτῶν;
    ΘΕΑΙ. Τὰ ἅπαντα ἔμοιγε δοκοῦμεν.

1. But is it therefore unknown?

First, How is the complex related to it?

5. *οἷον συριττούσης τῆς γλώττης*] This mode of definition reminds us of the Antisthenean saying quoted by Aristotle—*τοῦδε μέν τί ἐστιν ὑπάρχειν καὶ διδάξαι* κ. τ. λ.; and also of Euclides' objection to definition by comparison.

8. *ἐναργέστατα*] Bodl. *ἐνεργέστατα* sed exem.

14. *ἀποδεδείγμεθα*] Heindorf conjectured *ἀποδεδείγμεθα*, for which MS. authority (Coisl. et Par. F. ex corr.) has since been found; and it has been received by Bekker. But Stallbaum rightly defends *ἀποδεδείγμεθα* in the sense 'we have declared our opinion;' in which sense the pf. pass. is used by Xenophon and Lysias. Vid. supr. 180. *ἀποδεδειγμένον*. Compare, however, infr. p. 205. *ἀνθωμολογούμεθα ἡγούμενοι τὸ λέγεσθαι*. But this refers to a part of the theory which is deliberately received in the words *τοῦτο μέν—κατωρθώκαμεν*.

16. *τὴν συλλαβήν*] Arist. Met. H. 3. *αἱ φαίνεται δὴ ζητοῦσιν ἡ συλλαβὴ ἐκ τῶν στοιχείων οὖσα καὶ σύνθεσις*.

The word *συλλαβή* is used probably not without the consciousness of its etymology.

ΣΩ. Ὅρα δὴ ἐπὶ δυοῖν, σῖγμα καὶ ὦ. ἀμφότερά p.203. ἐστιν ἡ πρώτη συλλαβὴ τοῦ ἐμοῦ ὀνόματος. ἄλλο τι ὁ γιγνώσκων αὐτὴν τὰ ἀμφότερα γιγνώσκει;

ΘΕΑΙ. Τί μήν; d

ΣΩ. Τὸ σῖγμα καὶ τὸ ὦ ἄρα γιγνώσκει.

ΘΕΑΙ. Ναί.

ΣΩ. Τί δέ; ἑκάτερον ἆρ' ἀγνοεῖ, καὶ οὐδέτερον εἰδὼς ἀμφότερα γιγνώσκει;

ΘΕΑΙ. Ἀλλὰ δεινὸν καὶ ἄλογον, ὦ Σώκρατες.

ΣΩ. Ἀλλὰ μέντοι εἴ γε ἀνάγκη ἑκάτερόν γιγνώσκειν, εἴπερ ἀμφότερά τις γνώσεται, προγιγνώσκειν τὰ στοιχεῖα ἅπασα ἀνάγκη τῷ μέλλοντί ποτε γνώσεσθαι συλλαβήν, καὶ οὕτως ἡμῖν ὁ καλὸς λόγος ἀποδεδρακὼς οἰχήσεται.

ΘΕΑΙ. Καὶ μάλα γε ἐξαίφνης. e

ΣΩ. Οὐ γὰρ καλῶς αὐτὸν φυλάττομεν. χρῆν γὰρ ἴσως τὴν συλλαβὴν τίθεσθαι μὴ τὰ στοιχεῖα, ἀλλ' ἐξ ἐκείνων ἕν τι γεγονὸς εἶδος, ἰδέαν μίαν αὐτὸ αὑτοῦ ἔχον, ἕτερον δὲ τῶν στοιχείων.

ΘΕΑΙ. Πάνυ μὲν οὖν· καὶ τάχα γ' ἂν μᾶλλον οὕτως ἢ ἐκείνως ἔχοι.

ΣΩ. Σκεπτέον, καὶ οὐ προδοτέον οὕτως ἀνάνδρως μέγαν τε καὶ σεμνὸν λόγον.

ΘΕΑΙ. Οὐ γὰρ οὖν.

p. 204. ΣΩ. Ἐχέτω δὴ ὡς νῦν φαμέν, μία ἰδέα ἐξ ἑκάστων τῶν συναρμοττόντων στοιχείων γιγνομένη ἡ συλλαβή, ὁμοίως ἔν τε γράμμασι καὶ ἐν τοῖς ἄλλοις ἅπασιν.

ΘΕΑΙ. Πάνυ μὲν οὖν.

ΣΩ. Οὐκοῦν μέρη αὐτῆς οὐ δεῖ εἶναι.

ΘΕΑΙ. Τί δή;

ΣΩ. Ὅτι οὗ ἂν ᾖ μέρη, τὸ ὅλον ἀνάγκη τὰ πάντα μέρη εἶναι. ἢ καὶ τὸ ὅλον ἐκ τῶν μερῶν λέγεις γεγονὸς ἕν τι εἶδος ἕτερον τῶν πάντων μερῶν;

ΘΕΑΙ. Ἔγωγε.

ΣΩ. Τὸ δὲ δὴ πᾶν καὶ τὸ ὅλον πότερον ταὐτὸν b καλεῖς ἢ ἕτερον ἑκάτερον;

ΘΕΑΙ. Ἔχω μὲν οὐδὲν σαφές, ὅτι δὲ κελεύεις προθύμως ἀποκρίνασθαι, παρακινδυνεύων λέγω ὅτι ἕτερον.

ΣΩ. Ἡ μὲν προθυμία, ὦ Θεαίτητε, ὀρθή· εἰ δὲ καὶ ἡ ἀπόκρισις, σκεπτέον.

ΘΕΑΙ. Δεῖ δέ γε δή.

ΣΩ. Οὐκοῦν διαφέροι ἂν τὸ ὅλον τοῦ παντός, ὡς ὁ νῦν λόγος;

In that case it cannot have parts: unless we regard everywhole in the same way as something different from all its parts, resulting from them.

With a view to this we venture to assert that the Whole is different from the All.

1. Ἐχέτω δὴ ὡς νῦν φαμὲν μία ἰδέα] There is no occasion to suspect the reading, or to conjecture μίαν ἰδέαν: ἐχέτω ὡς = ἔστω ὡς —. Cf. Rep. 547. τὰ δ᾽ ἐμοὶ φαινόμενα οὕτω φαίνεται, ἐν τῇ γνωστῷ τελευταία ἡ τοῦ ἀγαθοῦ ἰδέα καὶ μόγις ὁρᾶσθαι.

'Let it be then as we have now put it, that the syllable is a simple form arising out of each combination of harmonious elements.' The words Ἐχέτω δὴ ὡς take up the thread of τάχ᾽ ἂν μᾶλλον οὕτως ἢ ἐκείνως ἔχοι. In the conjectural reading the words ἐχέτω — μίαν ἰδέαν would of course refer to ἰδίαν μίαν αὐτὸ ἑαυτοῦ ἔχον.

For μία ἰδέα = εἶδος ἰδίαν μίαν ἔχον, cf. Euthyphr. 6. τὸ εἶδος ᾧ πάντα τὰ ὅσια ὅσιά ἐστιν; ἔφησθα γάρ που μιᾷ ἰδέᾳ τά τε ἀνόσια ἀνόσια εἶναι καὶ τὰ ὅσια ὅσια. Inf. 205. μία τις ἰδέα — συλλαβὴ ἂν εἴη.

19. Δεῖ δέ γε δή.] Sc. καὶ τὴν ἀπόκρισιν ὀρθὴν εἶναι.

20. τὸ ὅλον τοῦ παντός — τὰ πάντα καὶ τὸ πᾶν] Cf. Ar. Met. Δ. 26. 1024. a. ὕδωρ γὰρ καὶ ὅσα ὑγρὰ καὶ ἀριθμὸς πᾶν μὲν λέγεται, ὅλος δ᾽ ἀριθμὸς καὶ ὅλον ὕδωρ οὐ λέγεται, ἂν μὴ μεταφορᾷ· πάντα δὲ λέγεται, ἐφ᾽ οἷς τὸ πᾶν ὡς

ΠΛΑΤΩΝΟΣ

But can we go so far as to distinguish ΑΠ, in the singular, from ΑΠ, in the plural? It is evident that "all of six" is the same as "all six."

ΘΕΑΙ. Ναί.

ΣΩ. Τί δὲ δή; τὰ πάντα καὶ τὸ πᾶν ἔσθ' ὅ τι διαφέρει; οἶον ἐπειδὰν λέγωμεν ἕν, δύο, τρία, τέτταρα, πέντε, ἕξ, καὶ ἐὰν δὶς τρία ἢ τρὶς δύο ἢ τέτταρά ο τε καὶ δύο ἢ τρία καὶ δύο καὶ ἕν, πότερον ἐν πᾶσι τούτοις τὸ αὐτὸ ἢ ἕτερον λέγομεν;

ΘΕΑΙ. Ταὐτόν.

ΣΩ. Ἆρ' ἄλλο τι ἢ ἕξ;

ΘΕΑΙ. Οὐδέν.

10 ΣΩ. Οὐκοῦν ἐφ' ἑκάστης λέξεως πάντα τὰ ἓξ εἰρήκαμεν;

ΘΕΑΙ. Ναί.

ΣΩ. †Πάλιν† δ' οὐδὲν λέγομεν τὰ πάντα λέγοντες;

ΘΕΑΙ. Ἀνάγκη.

15 ΣΩ. Ἢ ἄλλο τι ἢ τὰ ἕξ;

ΘΕΑΙ. Οὐδέν.

ἐφ' ἑνί, ἐπὶ τούτοις πᾶσιν ὡς ἡθροισμένοις· πᾶν οὗτοι ἀριθμός, πᾶσαι αὗται αἱ μονάδες.

5. ἡ τρία καὶ δύο καὶ ἕν] The words ἡ πέντε καὶ ἕν, which were introduced by Cornarius, are anticipated in the simple enumeration ἕν, δύο, &c. They do not occur in the Bodleian or any other MS.

10. Οὐκοῦν ἐφ' ἑκάστης λέξεως πάντα τὰ ἓξ εἰρήκαμεν;] So far the MSS. give a meaning perfectly clear and natural. The words which follow are not so clear. The only way in which it seems possible to construe them as they stand, is by laying an unnatural stress on ἕν. "Again, while we speak of all (in the plural), is there no one thing of which we speak?" This is brought out more distinctly by C. F. Hermann's conjecture, οὐχ ἕν.

But this sense of πάλιν as a mere particle of transition, = ἢ τί δή, is hardly admissible in Plato (contrast p. 197. πάλιν δή, ὥσπερ ἐν ταῖς πρόσθεν παρανοῦ τι ε. τ. λ. — νῦν αὖ — περιστερεῶνα π. τ. λ. infr. p. 205. πάλιν δή, ὅπερ ἄρτι ἀνεχείρουν— Cf., however, Phil. 14. πολλοῖς εἶναι πάλιν.) And this objection is not obviated by substituting the awkward expression πᾶν τὰ ἓξ for πάντα τὰ ἓξ in the previous line. For 'Do we not repeat something when we say τὰ πάντα' would not be a satisfactory rendering. The present passage is one in which a reader of Plato will expect extreme clearness and minuteness of logical sequence. To put πᾶν τὰ ἓξ in the beginning of the argument would be to assume bluntly that which it is intended to prove, viz. that an aggre-

ΣΩ. Ταὐτὸν ἄρα ἕν γε τοῖς ὅσα ἐξ ἀριθμοῦ ἐστί, τό τε πᾶν προσαγορεύομεν καὶ τὰ ἅπαντα;

ΘΕΑΙ. Φαίνεται.

ΣΩ. Ὧδε δὴ περὶ αὐτῶν λέγωμεν. ὁ τοῦ πλέθρου ἀριθμὸς καὶ τὸ πλέθρον ταὐτόν· ἦ γάρ;

ΘΕΑΙ. Ναί.

ΣΩ. Καὶ ὁ τοῦ σταδίου δὴ ὡσαύτως.

ΘΕΑΙ. Ναί.

ΣΩ. Καὶ μὴν καὶ ὁ τοῦ στρατοπέδου γε καὶ τὸ στρατόπεδον, καὶ πάντα τὰ τοιαῦτα ὁμοίως; ὁ γὰρ ἀριθμὸς πᾶς τὸ ὂν πᾶν ἕκαστον αὐτῶν ἐστίν.

But all (plural) implies number, and number implies parts.

gate may be regarded as one thing. With this object it is necessary to reason from the plural to the singular, and to do so by gentle steps. The above argument might lead to the substitution of τὸ πᾶν for τὰ πάντα. But the objection against πᾶλυ would still remain: and there would be needless obscurity in the logical inversion by which, after reasoning *from* the number, we should then reason *to* it. 'In counting six, we said "all six" (in the plural.) Again, in speaking of *all*, in the singular, is there nothing which we express?' 'There must be.' 'And is not this six?' 'Yes.' The desirable sequence is restored if for πᾶλυ (which is itself a source of difficulty), we read πᾶν, (which in the MS. character could be changed into something very like πᾶλυ by the repetition of ν.) The passage may then be rendered, 'Have we not, then, in each expression, spoken of all the six?' 'Yes.' 'But while speaking of them all, is there no one thing *all* of which we express?' 'There must be.' 'And is that any thing but the six?' 'Nothing.' Compare with the resumption of the last admission in τὰ πάντα λέγοντες, Soph. 328. οἴεσθον τό γε εἶναι προσάπτειν συμφερόμενοι ἑκαστοτε τῶν πρόσθεν Πλεγμε; Φαίνει. Τί δέ; τοῦτο προσέπτεται οὐκ ἐπὶ διαλεγόμεθα; After ἀνάγκη, we must understand τῶν τι λέγειν. Compare Symp. 193. εἶδ᾽ ἂν εἰς ἐξαρνηθείη — ἀλλ᾽ ἅπαν᾽ ἂν (sc. πᾶς τις) κ. τ. λ. alib. For what has been said of minute sequence, compare, amongst other passages, supr. 164. Μὴ οὖν ἐγὼ λεγω κ. τ. λ. 188. Ἦ οὖν καὶ φιλεῖ που κ. τ. λ.

1. Ταὐτὸν—ἅπαντα] We give the names πᾶν and πάντα to the same thing.

4. λέγωμεν] Several MSS. have λέγομεν. If λέγωμεν is right, it refers, not to the present sentence, but to the argument which it introduces about the relation of parts to a whole.

10. ὁ γὰρ ἀριθμὸς] i.e. ὁ ἀριθμὸς πᾶς ἑκάστου ἐστὶ τὸ ὂν πᾶν ἑκάστου. 'The number of each taken altogether is each real thing

ΠΛΑΤΩΝΟΣ

ΘΕΑΙ. Ναί. p. 204

ΣΩ. Ὁ δὲ ἑκάστων ἀριθμὸς μῶν ἄλλο τι ἢ μέρη ἐστίν;

ΘΕΑΙ. Οὐδέν.

Therefore all (singular) also implies parts.

ΣΩ. Ὅσα ἄρα ἔχει μέρη, ἐκ μερῶν ἂν εἴη;

ΘΕΑΙ. Φαίνεται.

ΣΩ. Τὰ δέ γε πάντα μέρη τὸ πᾶν εἶναι ὁμολογεῖται, εἴπερ καὶ ὁ πᾶς ἀριθμὸς τὸ πᾶν ἔσται.

ΘΕΑΙ. Οὕτως.

Therefore, if all (singular) and the whole are different, the whole is without parts.

ΣΩ. Τὸ ὅλον ἄρ' οὐκ ἔστιν ἐκ μερῶν. πᾶν γὰρ ἂν εἴη, τὰ πάντα ὂν μέρη.

ΘΕΑΙ. Οὐκ ἔοικεν.

ΣΩ. Μέρος δ' ἔσθ' ὅτου ἄλλου ἐστὶν ὅπερ ἐστὶν ἢ τοῦ ὅλου;

ΘΕΑΙ. Τοῦ παντός γε.

But this is absurd.

ΣΩ. Ἀνδρικῶς γε, ὦ Θεαίτητε, μάχει. τὸ πᾶν δὲ p. 205. οὐχ ὅταν μηδὲν ἀπῇ, αὐτὸ τοῦτο πᾶν ἐστίν;

ΘΕΑΙ. Ἀνάγκη.

ΣΩ. Ὅλον δὲ οὐ ταὐτὸν τοῦτο ἔσται, οὗ ἂν μηδαμῇ μηδὲν ἀποστατῇ; οὗ δ' ἂν ἀποστατῇ, οὔτε ὅλον οὔτε πᾶν, ἅμα γενόμενον ἐκ τοῦ αὐτοῦ τὸ αὐτό;

taken altogether,' or ' each taken altogether so far as it exists.' ἑκάστου would be more convenient, but we cannot venture to say that ἑκάστου is wrong. τὸ ἓν—ἕκαστον = ἕκαστον, ὅ ἐστιν. Cf. Rep. 490. αὐτοῦ ὃ ἔστιν ἑκάστου τῆς φύσεως. But it must be admitted that the text becomes more uncertain in the last few pages of the dialogue.

2. ὁ δὲ ἑκάστων ἀριθμός] The word ἀριθμὸς implies plurality. Hence ἑκάστων, unless it is corrupt. We are now reasoning from singular to plural, as before from plural to singular.

16. ἀνδρικῶς μάχει] Viz. for the thesis he has chivalrously taken up, p. 204. παρακινδυνευτέον λέγω ὅτι ἕτερον.

17. αὐτὸ τοῦτο πᾶν ἐστι] Is this very thing all, just as above, ἐστὶν ὅπερ ἐστίν. πᾶν, being predicate, does not need the article.

21. ἐκ τοῦ αὐτοῦ] Viz. ὅλον = οὗ ἂν μηδὲν ἀποστατῇ = πᾶν.

τὸ αὐτό] Viz. οὐχ ὅλον = οὐ πᾶν.

ΘΕΑΙΤΗΤΟΣ. 197

p. 205. ΘΕΑΙ. Δοκεῖ μοι νῦν οὐδὲν διαφέρειν πᾶν τε καὶ ὅλον.

ΣΩ. Οὐκοῦν ἐλέγομεν ὅτι οὗ ἂν μέρη ᾖ, τὸ ὅλον τε καὶ πᾶν τὰ πάντα μέρη ἔσται;

ΘΕΑΙ. Πάνυ γε.

ΣΩ. Πάλιν δή, ὅπερ ἄρτι ἐπεχείρουν, οὐκ, εἴπερ ἡ συλλαβὴ μὴ τὰ στοιχεῖά ἐστιν, ἀνάγκη αὐτὴν μὴ ὡς b μέρη ἔχειν ἑαυτῆς τὰ στοιχεῖα, ἢ ταὐτὸν οὖσαν αὐτοῖς ὁμοίως ἐκείνοις γνωστὴν εἶναι;

ΘΕΑΙ. Οὕτως.

ΣΩ. Οὐκοῦν τοῦτο ἵνα μὴ γένηται, ἕτερον αὐτῶν αὐτὴν ἐθέμεθα;

ΘΕΑΙ. Ναί.

ΣΩ. Τί δ'; εἰ μὴ τὰ στοιχεῖα συλλαβῆς μέρη ἐστίν, ἔχεις ἄλλ' ἄττα εἰπεῖν, ἃ μέρη μέν ἐστι συλλαβῆς, οὐ μέντοι στοιχεῖά γ' ἐκείνης;

ΘΕΑΙ. Οὐδαμῶς. εἰ γάρ, ὦ Σώκρατες, μόρια ταύτης συγχωροίην, γελοῖόν που τὰ στοιχεῖα ἀφέντα ἐπ' ἄλλα ἰέναι.

c ΣΩ. Παντάπασι δή, ὦ Θεαίτητε, κατὰ τὸν νῦν λόγον μία τις ἰδέα ἀμέριστος συλλαβὴ ἂν εἴη.

Margin notes:

We cannot therefore view the whole as different from the all. But, if the whole is all the parts, the complex, if distinct from its elements, is not the whole of which they are the parts.

And it can have no other parts.

Therefore it can have no parts.

3. *ἐλέγομεν*) The argument is resumed from p. 204. Ὅτι οὗ ἂν ᾖ μέρη, τὸ ὅλον ἀνάγκη τὰ πάντα μέρη εἶναι.

6. Πάλιν δή—ἐλέγομεν] This was said before, pp. 203, 204. πραγματεύεσθαι τὰ στοιχεῖα ὅπως ἂν ἀνάγκῃ τῷ μέλλοντί ποτε γνώσεσθαι συλλαβήν,—οὐκοῦν μέρη αὐτῆς οὐ δεῖ εἶναι.

8. ἢ ταὐτὸν οὖσαν αὐτοῖς ὁμοίως ἐκείνοις γνωστὴν εἶναι] ταὐτὸν οὖσαν αὐτοῖς was proved (p. 203.) to follow from their being parts. For the turn of the sentence, compare Rep. 490. ἡγεῖτο δ' αὐτῷ εἰ νῷ ἔχοις, πρότερον μὲν ἀληθείᾳ, ἐν δεύτερον αὐτῶν πάντως καὶ πάντῃ ἕξει ἢ ἀλάζων ἔστι μηδαμῇ μεττέχων φιλοσοφίας ἀληθινῆς. ib. 503. πλέγομεν δ', εἰ μνημονεύεις, διὰ ——— τὸ ἄγημα τοῦτο μήτ' ἐν πόνοις μήτ' ἐν φόβοις —— φαίνεσθαι ἐκβάλλοντας ἢ τὸν ἀδυνατοῦντα ἀποκρίνειν. ib. 525. διὰ τὸ τῆς οὐσίας ἁπτέον εἶναι γενέσεως ἐξαναδύντι ἢ μηδέποτε λογιστικῷ γενέσθαι.

21. συλλαβή] The absence of the article marks our familiarity with the word, and also gives it a certain indefiniteness: as in the expression πάντων μέτρων ἄνθρωπος. Cf. Rep. 369. Γίγνεται τοίνυν—πόλις—ἐπειδή κ. τ. λ.

ΘΕΑΙ. Ἔοικεν.

ΣΩ. Μέμνησαι οὖν, ὦ φίλε, ὅτι ὀλίγον ἐν τῷ πρόσθεν ἀπεδεχόμεθα ἡγούμενοι εὖ λέγεσθαι ὅτι τῶν πρώτων οὐκ εἴη λόγος, ἐξ ὧν τὰ ἄλλα σύγκειται, διότι αὐτὸ καθ᾽ αὑτὸ ἕκαστον εἴη ἀσύνθετον, καὶ οὐδὲ τὸ εἶναι περὶ αὐτοῦ ὀρθῶς ἔχοι προσφέροντα εἰπεῖν, οὐδὲ τὸ τοῦτο, ὡς ἕτερα καὶ ἀλλότρια λεγόμενα, καὶ αὕτη δὴ ἡ αἰτία ἄλογόν τε καὶ ἄγνωστον αὐτὸ ποιοῖ;

ΘΕΑΙ. Μέμνημαι.

ΣΩ. Ἦ οὖν ἄλλη τις ἢ αὕτη ἡ αἰτία τοῦ μονο- d ειδές τι καὶ ἀμέριστον αὐτὸ εἶναι; ἐγὼ μὲν γὰρ οὐχ ὁρῶ ἄλλην.

ΘΕΑΙ. Οὐ γὰρ οὖν δὴ φαίνεται.

ΣΩ. Οὐκοῦν εἰς ταὐτὸν ἐμπέπτωκεν ἡ συλλαβὴ εἴδος ἐκείνῳ, εἴπερ μέρη τε μὴ ἔχει καὶ μία ἐστὶν ἰδέα;

ΘΕΑΙ. Παντάπασι μὲν οὖν.

ΣΩ. Εἰ μὲν ἄρα πολλὰ στοιχεῖα ἡ συλλαβή ἐστι καὶ ὅλον τι, μέρη δ᾽ αὐτῆς ταῦτα, ὁμοίως αἵ ͵τε συλλαβαὶ γνωσταὶ καὶ ῥηταὶ καὶ τὰ στοιχεῖα, ἐπείπερ τὰ πάντα μέρη τῷ ὅλῳ ταὐτὸν ἐφάνη.

ΘΕΑΙ. Καὶ μάλα.

ΣΩ. Εἰ δέ γε ἕν τε καὶ ἀμερές, ὁμοίως μὲν συλ- e λαβή, ὡσαύτως δὲ στοιχεῖον ἄλογόν τε καὶ ἄγνωστον· ἡ γὰρ αὐτὴ αἰτία ποιήσει αὐτὰ τοιαῦτα.

ΘΕΑΙ. Οὐκ ἔχω ἄλλως εἰπεῖν.

ΣΩ. Τοῦτο μὲν ἄρα μὴ ἀποδεχώμεθα, ὃς ἂν λέγῃ

p. 206. συλλαβὴν μὲν γνωστὸν καὶ ῥητόν, στοιχεῖον δὲ τοὐναντίον.

ΘΕΑΙ. Μὴ γάρ, εἴπερ τῷ λόγῳ πειθόμεθα.

ΣΩ. Τί δ᾽ αὖ; τοὐναντίον λέγοντος ἆρ᾽ οὐ μᾶλλον ἂν ἀποδέξαιο ἐξ ὧν αὐτὸς σύνοισθα σαυτῷ ἐν τῇ
τῶν γραμμάτων μαθήσει;

ΘΕΑΙ. Τὸ ποῖον;

ΣΩ. Ὡς οὐδὲν ἄλλο μανθάνων διετέλεσας ἢ τὰ
στοιχεῖα ἔν τε τῇ ὄψει διαγιγνώσκειν πειρώμενος καὶ
ἐν τῇ ἀκοῇ αὐτὸ καθ᾽ αὑτὸ ἕκαστον, ἵνα μὴ ἡ θέσις
σε ταράττοι λεγομένων τε καὶ γραφομένων.

ΘΕΑΙ. Ἀληθέστατα λέγεις.

ΣΩ. Ἐν δὲ κιθαριστοῦ τελέως μεμαθηκέναι μῶν
b ἄλλο τι ἦν ἢ τὸ τῷ φθόγγῳ ἑκάστῳ δύνασθαι ἐπακο-
λουθεῖν, ποίας χορδῆς εἴη· ἃ δὴ στοιχεῖα πᾶς ἂν ὁμολογήσειε μουσικῆς λέγεσθαι;

ΘΕΑΙ. Οὐδὲν ἄλλο.

ΣΩ. Ὧν μὲν ἄρ᾽ αὐτοὶ ἔμπειροί ἐσμεν στοιχείων
καὶ συλλαβῶν, εἰ δεῖ ἀπὸ τούτων τεκμαίρεσθαι καὶ
εἰς τὰ ἄλλα, πολὺ τὸ τῶν στοιχείων γένος ἐναργε-
στέραν τε τὴν γνῶσιν ἔχειν φήσομεν καὶ κυριωτέραν
τῆς συλλαβῆς πρὸς τὸ λαβεῖν τελέως ἕκαστον μάθημα, καὶ ἐάν τις φῇ συλλαβὴν μὲν γνωστόν, ἄγνωστον δὲ πεφυκέναι στοιχεῖον, ἑκόντα ἢ ἄκοντα παίζειν
ἡγησόμεθ᾽ αὐτόν.

Therefore it is untrue to say that the complex is known, but the simple unknown.

And we have experience to the contrary: for we learnt our letters before we could read, and our notes before we could play the lyre. From this it appears that the element is more known than the syllable, the simple than the complex.

Soph. Ant. 35. ἀλλ᾽ ἐς ἂν τούτων τι δρᾷ, φόνου προκεῖσθαι δημόλευ-στον ἐν πόλει.

1. γνωστὸν] ἄγνωστον Bodl. sed δ erasum.

8. ὡς οὐδὲν ἄλλο] 'That in learning you continued doing nothing else but endeavouring to distinguish, &c.' Cf. Men. 80. ὅτι οὐδὲν ἄλλο ἢ αὐτός τε ἀπορῶ.

24. ἑκόντα ἢ ἄκοντα παίζειν] 'That he is either playing with us, or talking nonsense.'

The tendency of the present passage is to rise from the conception of elementary objects of sense (simple ideas of sensation) to that of abstract ideas, (universals, predicables), as the true elements of Knowledge.

ΠΛΑΤΩΝΟΣ

ΘΕΑΙ. Κομιδῇ μὲν οὖν. p. 206.
ΣΩ. Ἀλλὰ δὴ τούτου μὲν ἔτι κἂν ἄλλαι φανεῖεν ὁ

Cf. Ar. Met. B. I. 995 b. πότερον αἱ ἀρχαὶ καὶ τὰ στοιχεῖα τὰ γένη ἐστὶν ἢ εἰς ἃ διαιρεῖται ἐνυπάρχοντα ἕκαστον.
This may be illustrated from the frequent use by Plato of the example of letters, elementary sounds, etc. to represent the Ideas and the mode of becoming acquainted with them.
The following passage of Rep. p. 402. is an instance of this :—

"Ὥσπερ ἄρα — γραμμάτων πέρι τότε ἱκανῶς εἴχομεν, ὅτι τὰ στοιχεῖα μὴ λανθάνοι ἡμᾶς ὀλίγα ὄντα ἐν ἅπασιν οἷς ἐστὶ περιφερόμενα, καὶ οὔτ' ἐν σμικρῷ οὔτ' ἐν μεγάλῳ ἠτιμάζομεν αὐτά, ὡς οὐ δέοι αἰσθάνεσθαι, ἀλλὰ πανταχοῦ προὐθυμούμεθα διαγιγνώσκειν, ὡς οὐ πρότερον ἐσόμενοι γραμματικοὶ πρὶν οὕτως ἔχοιμεν. Ἀληθῆ. Οὐκοῦν καὶ εἰκόνας γραμμάτων, εἴ που ἢ ἐν ὕδασιν ἢ ἐν κατόπτροις ἐμφαίνοιντο, οὐ πρότερον γνωσόμεθα, πρὶν ἂν αὐτὰ γνῶμεν, ἀλλ' ἔστι τῆς αὐτῆς τέχνης τε καὶ μελέτης ; παντάπασι μὲν οὖν. Ἆρ' οὖν, ὃ λέγω, πρὸς θεῶν, οὕτως οὐδὲ μουσικοὶ πρότερον ἐσόμεθα, οὔτε αὐτοὶ, οὔτε οὕς φαμὲν ἡμῖν παιδευτέον εἶναι τοὺς φύλακας, πρὶν ἂν τὰ τῆς σωφροσύνης εἴδη καὶ ἀνδρείας καὶ ἐλευθεριότητος καὶ μεγαλοπρεπείας καὶ ὅσα τούτων ἀδελφὰ καὶ τὰ τούτων αὖ ἐναντία πανταχοῦ περιφερόμενα γνωρίζωμεν καὶ ἐνόντα ἐν οἷς ἔνεστιν αἰσθανώμεθα καὶ αὐτὰ καὶ εἰκόνας αὐτῶν, καὶ μήτε ἐν σμικροῖς μήτε ἐν μεγάλοις ἀτιμάζωμεν, ἀλλὰ τῆς αὐτῆς οἰώμεθα τέχνης εἶναι καὶ μελέτης ;

At the same time it is hinted that the sensible elements, so far as each of them can be regarded

as one individual thing, are also the objects of Knowledge.
Cf. Ar. Met. a. 994. b. ἔτι τὸ ἐπίστασθαι ἀναιροῦσιν οἱ οὕτως λέγοντες (viz. τὸ ἄπειρον λ.) οὐ γὰρ οἷόν τε εἰδέναι πρὶν ἢ εἰς τὰ ἄτομα ἐλθεῖν.

To resume the argument from p. 201, Theætetus has heard it said that true opinion with a reason was knowledge: and that nothing which had not a reason could be known. This reminds Socrates of a theory which said that of the elements (or alphabet) of things no account could be given— they could only be named. But of their combinations an account could be given, and these could be known. Knowledge according to this consists in being able to give an account of any thing. This, however, may be true, and yet the theory on which we have based it may be unsound. Testing this by the example of letters, we find that of the syllable σω an account can be given (it can be analysed), but not of its constituents σ and ω. But is the syllable known, the letter unknown? If so, in what way are we to conceive of the syllable? As all the letters? How then can I know them all, and yet none singly? Or is it a simple unity formed out of them? It cannot then be related to them as a whole to its parts, unless we can establish a distinction between whole and all. But all (singular) cannot be distin-

ΘΕΑΙΤΗΤΟΣ.   201

p. 206. ἀποδείξεις, ὥς ἐμοὶ δοκεῖ· τὸ δὲ προκείμενον μὴ ἐπι-
λαθώμεθα δι' αὐτὰ ἰδεῖν, ὅ τι δή ποτε καὶ λέγεται τὸ
μετὰ δόξης ἀληθοῦς λόγον προσγενόμενον τὴν τελεωτάτην ἐπιστήμην γεγονέναι.

ΘΕΑΙ. Οὐκοῦν χρὴ ὁρᾶν.

ΣΩ. Φέρε δή, τί ποτε βούλεται τὸν λόγον ἡμῖν
σημαίνειν; τριῶν γὰρ ἕν τί μοι δοκεῖ λέγειν.

ΘΕΑΙ. Τίνων δή;

d   ΣΩ. Τὸ μὲν πρῶτον εἴη ἂν τὸ τὴν αὑτοῦ διάνοιαν
ἐμφανῆ ποιεῖν διὰ φωνῆς μετὰ ῥημάτων τε καὶ ὀνομάτων, ὥσπερ εἰς κάτοπτρον ἢ ὕδωρ τὴν δόξαν
ἐκτυπούμενον εἰς τὴν διὰ τοῦ στόματος ῥοήν. ἢ οὐ
δοκεῖ σοι τὸ τοιοῦτον λόγος εἶναι;

[marginal note:] 5 This need not, however, affect the truth of our third answer. What is meant in it by 'giving an account?' One of three things. Either, III. a. The reflexion of thought in speech.

guished from all (plural); and this, containing all the parts, can scarcely be distinguished from the whole. Hence whole and all are indistinguishable. Therefore either the syllable has parts, and, consisting of things unknown, must be itself unknown; or, not having parts, it is uncompounded, and therefore itself, according to the theory, unknown. But our own memory ought to teach us that we first learnt to know the letters, and then the syllables and combinations of them.

Though the theory is rejected, we gain from it the notion of a simple idea and of a complex whole.

(2.) κἂν ἄλλας φωνῶν ἀποδείξεις] The train of thought, here broken off, is resumed in the Sophist, where the στοιχεῖα τῶν are treated as elements, and combinations of them are shown to be possible.

6. τί ποτε βούλεται] The subject is either ὁ ταῦτα λόγος, (cf. infr. τὸν ἀπεφηνάμενος ἐπιστήμην ὁ νῦν σκοπούμεν), or ὁ λόγος, viz. τὸ μετὰ δόξης ἀληθοῦς λόγον προσγενόμενον τὴν τελεωτάτην ἐπιστήμην γεγονέναι.

τὸν λόγον σημαίνειν] id. qu. τ. λ. εἰπεῖν. σ. 'What are we to understand by this λόγος?' Three meanings are put forward as possible:— 1. Expression in words. 2. Analysis. 3. Definition.

11. ὥσπερ εἰς κάτοπτρον] Cf. Phileb. 38. κἂν τίς γ' αὐτῷ παρῇ, τά τε πρὶν αὐτῷ ῥηθέντα ἐντείνας εἰς φωνὴν πρὸς τὸν παρόντα αὐτὰ ταῦτα ἂν πάλιν φθέγξατο, καὶ λόγον δὴ γέγονεν οὕτως ὁ τότε δόξαν ἐκαλοῦμεν;

12. ἐκτυπούμενον] 'Imaging.' Compare also the saying of Democritus, λόγος ἔργου σκιά.

For τὴν διὰ τοῦ στόματος ῥοήν, cf. Tim. 75. τὸ δὲ λόγων νᾶμα ἔξω ῥέον καὶ ὑπηρετοῦν φρονήσει κάλλιστον καὶ ἄριστον πάντων ναμάτων. Soph. 263.

D d

ΠΛΑΤΩΝΟΣ

ΘΕΑΙ. Ἔμοιγε. τὸν γοῦν αὐτὸ δρῶντα λέγειν φαμέν.

ΣΩ. Οὐκοῦν τοῦτό γε πᾶς ποιεῖν δυνατὸς θᾶττον ἢ σχολαίτερον, τὸ ἐνδείξασθαι τί δοκεῖ περὶ ἑκάστου αὐτῷ, ὁ μὴ ἐνεὸς ἢ κωφὸς ἀπ' ἀρχῆς· καὶ οὕτως ὅσοι τι ὀρθὸν δοξάζουσι, πάντες αὐτὸ μετὰ λόγου φανοῦνται ἔχοντες, καὶ οὐδαμοῦ ἔτι ὀρθὴ δόξα χωρὶς ἐπιστήμης γενήσεται.

ΘΕΑΙ. Ἀληθῆ.

ΣΩ. Μὴ τοίνυν ῥᾳδίως καταγιγνώσκωμεν τὸ μηδὲν εἰρηκέναι τὸν ἀποφηνάμενον ἐπιστήμην ὃ νῦν σκοποῦμεν. ἴσως γὰρ ὁ λέγων οὐ τοῦτο ἔλεγεν, ἀλλὰ τὸ ἐρωτηθέντα τί ἕκαστον δυνατὸν εἶναι τὴν ἀπόκρισιν διὰ τῶν στοιχείων ἀποδοῦναι τῷ ἐρομένῳ.

ΘΕΑΙ. Οἷον τί λέγεις, ὦ Σώκρατες;

ΣΩ. Οἷον καὶ Ἡσίοδος περὶ ἁμάξης λέγει τὸ ἑκατὸν δέ τε δούραθ' ἁμάξης. ἃ ἐγὼ μὲν οὐκ ἂν δυναίμην εἰπεῖν, οἶμαι δὲ οὐδὲ σύ· ἀλλ' ἀγαπῷμεν ἂν ἐρωτηθέντες ὅ τί ἐστιν ἅμαξα, εἰ ἔχοιμεν εἰπεῖν τροχοί, ἄξων, ὑπερτερία, ἄντυγες, ζυγόν.

ΘΕΑΙ. Πάνυ μὲν οὖν.

ΣΩ. Ὁ δέ γε ἴσως οἴοιτ' ἂν ἡμᾶς, ὥσπερ ἂν τὸ σὸν ὄνομα ἐρωτηθέντας καὶ ἀποκρινομένους κατὰ συλλαβήν, γελοίους εἶναι, ὀρθῶς μὲν δοξάζοντας καὶ

p. 207. λέγοντας ἃ λέγομεν, οἰομένους δὲ γραμματικοὺς εἶναι καὶ ἔχειν τε καὶ λέγειν γραμματικῶς τὸν τοῦ Θεαιτήτου ὀνόματος λόγον. τὸ δ' οὐκ εἶναι ἐπιστημόνως οὐδὲν λέγειν, πρὶν ἂν διὰ τῶν στοιχείων μετὰ τῆς ἀληθοῦς δόξης ἕκαστον περαίνῃ τις, ὅπερ καὶ ἐν τοῖς πρόσθε που ἐρρήθη.

ΘΕΑΙ. Ἐρρήθη γάρ.

ΣΩ. Οὕτω τοίνυν καὶ περὶ ἁμάξης ἡμᾶς μὲν ὀρθὴν ἔχειν δόξαν, τὸ δὲ διὰ τῶν ἑκατὸν ἐκείνων δυνάμενον διελθεῖν αὐτῆς τὴν οὐσίαν, προσλαβόντα τοῦτο, λόγον τε προσειληφέναι τῇ ἀληθεῖ δόξῃ καὶ ἀντὶ δοξαστικοῦ τεχνικόν τε καὶ ἐπιστήμονα περὶ ἁμάξης οὐσίας γεγονέναι, διὰ στοιχείων τὸ ὅλον περάναντα.

ΘΕΑΙ. Οὐκοῦν εὖ δοκεῖ σοι, ὦ Σώκρατες;

ΣΩ. Εἰ σοί, ὦ ἑταῖρε, δοκεῖ, καὶ ἀποδέχει τὴν διὰ στοιχείου διέξοδον περὶ ἑκάστου λόγον εἶναι, τὴν δὲ κατὰ συλλαβὰς ἢ καὶ κατὰ μεῖζον ἔτι ἀλογίαν, τοῦτό μοι λέγε, ἵν' αὐτὸ ἐπισκοπῶμεν.

d ΘΕΑΙ. Ἀλλὰ πάνυ ἀποδέχομαι.

ΣΩ. Πότερον ἡγούμενος ἐπιστήμονα εἶναι ὁντινοῦν ὁτουοῦν, ὅταν τὸ αὐτὸ ὁτὲ μὲν τοῦ αὐτοῦ δοκῇ αὐτῷ εἶναι, τοτὲ δὲ ἑτέρου, ἢ καὶ ὅταν τοῦ αὐτοῦ τοτὲ μὲν ἕτερον, τοτὲ δὲ ἕτερον δοξάζῃ;

ΘΕΑΙ. Μὰ Δί' οὐκ ἔγωγε.

ΣΩ. Εἶτα ἀμνημονεῖς ἐν τῇ τῶν γραμμάτων μα- But I may perform this rightly

—Ἀρ' οὖν, ἃ λέγω, πρὸς θεῶν, οὕτως αὐτοὶ μουσικοὶ κ. τ. λ.

3. τὸ δ' οὐκ εἶναι] 'Whereas it is impossible.' Cf. p. 157. τὸ δ' οὐ διά, and note.

5. ἐν τοῖς πρόσθεν] p. 206. ὅτι οὐδὲν ἄλλο μανθάνων διατελέσει κ. τ. λ. is most probably referred to.

15. Εἰ σοί] εἰ is interrogative, depending on τοῦτό μοι λέγε.

21. τὸ αὐτὸ ὁτὲ μέν—] e. g. thinking τ to be the first letter both of τν and θν.

23. τοῦ αὐτοῦ τοτὲ μέν] e. g. thinking the first letter of θν at one time θ, at another τ.

204 ΠΛΑΤΩΝΟΣ

in the case of Theaetetus' name, and yet mistake in the first syllable of Theodorus', which is the same in both.

θήσει κατ' ἀρχὰς σαυτόν τε καὶ τοὺς ἄλλους δρῶντας p. 207.
αὐτά;

ΘΕΑΙ. Ἆρα λέγεις τῆς αὐτῆς συλλαβῆς τοτὲ μὲν ἕτερον, τοτὲ δὲ ἕτερον ἡγουμένους γράμμα, καὶ τὸ αὐτὸ τοτὲ μὲν εἰς τὴν προσήκουσαν, τοτὲ δὲ εἰς ἄλλην τιθέντας συλλαβήν;

ΣΩ. Ταῦτα λέγω.

ΘΕΑΙ. Μὰ Δί' οὐ τοίνυν ἀμνημονῶ, οὐδέ γέ πω ἡγοῦμαι ἐπίστασθαι τοὺς οὕτως ἔχοντας.

This is not to know the syllable.

ΣΩ. Τί οὖν; ὅταν ἐν τῷ τοιούτῳ καιρῷ Θεαίτητον γράφων τις θῆτα καὶ εἶ οἴηταί τε δεῖν γράφειν καὶ γράψῃ, καὶ αὖ Θεόδωρον ἐπιχειρῶν γράφειν ταῦ καὶ p. 208. εἶ οἴηταί τε δεῖν γράφειν καὶ γράψῃ, ἆρ' ἐπίστασθαι φήσομεν αὐτὸν τὴν πρώτην τῶν ὑμετέρων ὀνομάτων συλλαβήν;

ΘΕΑΙ. Ἀλλ' ἄρτι ὡμολογήσαμεν τὸν οὕτως ἔχοντα μήπω εἰδέναι.

ΣΩ. Κωλύει οὖν τι καὶ περὶ τὴν δευτέραν συλλαβὴν καὶ τρίτην καὶ τετάρτην οὕτως ἔχειν τὸν αὐτόν;

ΘΕΑΙ. Οὐδέν γε.

ΣΩ. Ἆρ' οὖν τότε τὴν διὰ στοιχείου διέξοδον ἔχων γράψει Θεαίτητον μετὰ ὀρθῆς δόξης, ὅταν ἑξῆς γράφῃ;

ΘΕΑΙ. Δῆλον δή.

ΣΩ. Οὐκοῦν ἔτι ἀνεπιστήμων ὤν, ὀρθὰ δὲ δοξά- b ζων, ὥς φαμεν;

ΘΕΑΙ. Ναί.

ΣΩ. Λόγον γε ἔχων μετὰ ὀρθῆς δόξης. τὴν γὰρ

---

2. αὐτά] 'What I have described.'
20. Οὐδέν γε] 'Certainly not.'
γε assents to the meaning of the question. Cf. Phil. 38. Οὐδέν γ. ἀλλ' ὅπερ εἰπὼν λέγω.

p. 208. διὰ τοῦ στοιχείου ὁδὸν ἔχων ἔγραφεν, ἣν δὴ λόγον ὡμολογήσαμεν.

ΘΕΑΙ. Ἀληθῆ.

ΣΩ. Ἔστιν ἄρα, ὦ ἑταῖρε, μετὰ λόγου ὀρθὴ δόξα, ἣν οὔπω δεῖ ἐπιστήμην καλεῖν.

ΘΕΑΙ. Κινδυνεύει.

ΣΩ. Ὄναρ δή, ὡς ἔοικεν, ἐπλουτήσαμεν οἰηθέντες ἔχειν τὸν ἀληθέστατον ἐπιστήμης λόγον. ἢ μήπω κατηγορῶμεν; ἴσως γὰρ οὐ τοῦτό τις αὐτὸν ὁριεῖται, ἀλλὰ τὸ λοιπὸν εἶδος τῶν τριῶν, ὧν ἕν γέ τι ἔφαμεν λόγον θήσεσθαι τὸν ἐπιστήμην ὁριζόμενον δόξαν εἶναι ὀρθὴν μετὰ λόγου.

ΘΕΑΙ. Ὀρθῶς ὑπέμνησας· ἔτι γὰρ ἐν λοιπόν. τὸ μὲν γὰρ ἦν διανοίας ἐν φωνῇ ὥσπερ εἴδωλον, τὸ δ᾽ ἄρτι λεχθὲν διὰ στοιχείου ὁδὸς ἐπὶ τὸ ὅλον· τὸ δὲ δὴ τρίτον τί λέγεις;

ΣΩ. Ὅπερ ἂν οἱ πολλοὶ εἴποιεν, τὸ ἔχειν τι σημεῖον εἰπεῖν ᾧ τῶν ἁπάντων διαφέρει τὸ ἐρωτηθέν.

ΘΕΑΙ. Οἷον τίνα τίνος ἔχεις μοι λόγον εἰπεῖν;

d ΣΩ. Οἷον, εἰ βούλει, ἡλίου πέρι ἱκανὸν οἶμαί σοι εἶναι ἀποδέξασθαι, ὅτι τὸ λαμπρότατόν ἐστι τῶν κατὰ τὸν οὐρανὸν ἰόντων περὶ γῆν.

ΘΕΑΙ. Πάνυ μὲν οὖν.

Or, lastly, III. γ. The power of adding a mark which distinguishes it from all other things, i.e. Definition by the characteristic difference, or by the sum of the distinctive elements.

7. ὄναρ——ἐπλουτήσαμεν] Cf. Polit. 277. κινδυνεύει γὰρ ἡμῶν ἕκαστος οἷον ὄναρ εἰδὼς ἅπαντα, πάντ᾽ αὖ πάλιν ὥσπερ ὕπαρ ἀγνοεῖν. 278. ἴσα ὕπαρ ἀντ᾽ ὀνείρατος ἡμῖν γίγνηται.

8. ἐπιστήμης λόγον] λόγος is used here in a double sense. 1. Definition of Knowledge. Cf. p. 149. ἐπὶ λόγῳ προσειπεῖν. 2. That 'account' of a thing which (with right opinion) constitutes Knowledge. The play of words may be preserved, "when we thought we had found the most indubitable 'account' concerning Knowledge."

9. τις] Viz. the nameless author of our theory.

17. ὅπερ ἂν οἱ πολλοὶ εἴποιεν] The two former were inferences from different meanings of λόγος;—to express and to enumerate. See p. 206. τὴν γοῦν αὑτοῦ διάνοιαν λέγειν φαμέν.

206   ΠΛΑΤΩΝΟΣ

ΣΩ. Λαβὲ δὴ οὗ χάριν εἴρηται. ἔστι δὲ ὅπερ ἄρτι p. 208. ἐλέγομεν, ὡς ἄρα τὴν διαφορὰν ἑκάστου ἂν λαμβάνῃς ᾗ τῶν ἄλλων διαφέρει, λόγον, ὥς φασί τινες, λήψει· ἕως δ' ἂν κοινοῦ τινὸς ἐφάπτῃ, ἐκείνων πέρι σοι ἔσται
5 ὁ λόγος ὧν ἂν ἡ κοινότης ᾖ.

ΘΕΑΙ. Μανθάνω· καί μοι δοκεῖ καλῶς ἔχειν λόγον ε τὸ τοιοῦτον καλεῖν.

ΣΩ. Ὃς δ' ἂν μετ' ὀρθῆς δόξης περὶ ὁτουοῦν τῶν ὄντων τὴν διαφορὰν τῶν ἄλλων προσλάβῃ αὐτοῦ,
10 ἐπιστήμων γεγονὼς ἔσται οὗ πρότερον ἦν δοξαστής.

ΘΕΑΙ. Φαμέν γε μὴν οὕτως.

Even this disappoints us on a nearer view.

ΣΩ. Νῦν δῆτα, ὦ Θεαίτητε, παντάπασιν ἔγωγε ἐπειδὴ ἐγγὺς ὥσπερ σκιαγραφήματος γέγονα τοῦ λεγομένου, ξυνίημι οὐδὲ σμικρόν· ἕως δὲ ἀφεστήκη
15 πόρρωθεν, ἐφαίνετό τί μοι λέγεσθαι.

ΘΕΑΙ. Πῶς τί τοῦτο;

ΣΩ. Φράσω, ἐὰν οἷός τε γένωμαι. ὀρθὴν ἔγωγε p. 209. ἔχων δόξαν περὶ σοῦ, ἐὰν μὲν προσλάβω τὸν σὸν λόγον, γιγνώσκω δή σε, εἰ δὲ μή, δοξάζω μόνον.

20 ΘΕΑΙ. Ναί.

ΣΩ. Λόγος δέ γε ἦν ἡ τῆς σῆς διαφορότητος ἑρμηνεία.

ΘΕΑΙ. Οὕτως.

ΣΩ. Ἡνίκ' οὖν ἐδόξαζον μόνον, ἄλλο τι ᾧ τῶν

3. τινες] Probably the Megarians. See Introduction.
9. αὐτοῦ.] This punctuation appears preferable when it is observed that there has been a tendency in the last few pages to accumulate genitives.
10. δοξαστής] Cf. p. 160. ἐπιστήμων ἐν εἴρῃ, ὥσπερ αἰσθητής.
13. σκιαγραφήματος] The image is a familiar one. Cf. Phaed. 69. μὴ σκιαγραφία τις ᾖ ἡ τοιαύτη ἀρετή. Rep. 365. 602.
16. Πῶς τί τοῦτο] 'What do you mean? and why is it so?'
19. δή] According to the hypothesis.
21. ἦν] Is, according to the hypothesis.
24. ᾧ τῶν ἄλλων διαφέρει, τούτων αὐτοῦς] It occurs to Socrates while speaking that the 'Difference' of one person from another is not one but many.

ΘΕΑΙΤΗΤΟΣ. 207

p. 209. ἄλλων διαφέρεις, τούτων οὐδενὸς ἡπτόμην τῇ διανοίᾳ;

ΘΕΑΙ. Οὐκ ἔοικεν.

ΣΩ. Τῶν κοινῶν τι ἄρα διενοούμην, ὧν οὐδὲν σὺ μᾶλλον ἤ τις ἄλλος ἔχει.

b ΘΕΑΙ. Ἀνάγκη.

ΣΩ. Φέρε δὴ πρὸς Διός· πῶς ποτὲ ἐν τῷ τοιούτῳ σὲ μᾶλλον ἐδόξαζον ἢ ἄλλον ὁντινοῦν; θὲς γάρ με διανοούμενον ὡς ἔστιν οὗτος Θεαίτητος, ὃς ἂν ᾖ τε ἄνθρωπος καὶ ἔχῃ ῥῖνα καὶ ὀφθαλμοὺς καὶ στόμα καὶ οὕτω δὴ ἐν ἕκαστον τῶν μελῶν. αὕτη οὖν ἡ διάνοια ἔσθ᾽ ὅ τι μᾶλλον ποιήσει με Θεαίτητον ἢ Θεόδωρον διανοεῖσθαι, ἢ τῶν λεγομένων Μυσῶν τὸν ἔσχατον;

ΘΕΑΙ. Τί γάρ;

ΣΩ. Ἀλλ᾽ ἐὰν δὴ μὴ μόνον τὸν ἔχοντα ῥῖνα καὶ ὀφθαλμοὺς διανοηθῶ, ἀλλὰ καὶ τὸν σιμόν τε καὶ ἐξ- c όφθαλμον, μή τι σὲ αὖ μᾶλλον δοξάσω ἢ ἐμαυτὸν ἢ ὅσοι τοιοῦτοι;

ΘΕΑΙ. Οὐδέν.

ΣΩ. Ἀλλ᾽ οὐ πρότερόν γε, οἶμαι, Θεαίτητος ἐν ἐμοὶ δοξασθήσεται, πρὶν ἂν ἡ σιμότης αὕτη τῶν ἄλλων σιμοτήτων ὧν ἐγὼ ἑώρακα διάφορόν τι μνημεῖον παρ᾽ ἐμοὶ ἐνσημηναμένη καταθῆται, καὶ τἆλλα οὕτως

For unless I can distinguish Theaetetus from Socrates and every one else, how can I be said to have a right opinion of him? If then by the comprehension of a true account is meant "right opinion of the distinctive difference," this is a necessary part of right opinion.

5. *ἤ τις ἄλλος ἔχει*] The verb is attracted by τις ἄλλος.

13. *τῶν λεγομένων Μυσῶν*] The phrase Μυσῶν ἔσχατος is strengthened by the insertion of the article. The editors (under protest from Huttmann) read τὸ λεγόμενον. There seems no reason for this. Cf. supr. οἱ τῆς θαλάττης λεγόμενοι χόες. Arist. Eth. N. VIII. 3. δεῖ γὰρ τοὺς λεγομένους ἅλας συναναλῶσαι. In the examples quoted by the Scholiast the proverb is used to express contempt. Here it means only remoteness.

22. *μνημεῖον — ἐνσημηναμένη*] Cf. pp. 191, 196. This is an instance of the way in which a theory which is rejected is still permitted and intended by Plato to leave an impression on the mind.

23. *καταθῆται*] So Bodl. with Vat. Ven. Π.

208 ΠΛΑΤΩΝΟΣ

ἐξ ὧν εἶ σύ, [καὶ ἐμέ,] ἐὰν αὔριον ἀπαντήσω, ἀνα- p. 209.
μνήσει καὶ ποιήσει ὀρθὰ δοξάζειν περὶ σοῦ.

ΘΕΑΙ. Ἀληθέστατα.

ΣΩ. Περὶ τὴν διαφορότητα ἄρα καὶ ἡ ὀρθὴ δόξα d
ἂν εἴη ἑκάστου πέρι.

ΘΕΑΙ. Φαίνεταί γε.

ΣΩ. Τὸ οὖν προσλαβεῖν λόγον τῇ ὀρθῇ δόξῃ τί
ἂν ἔτι εἴη; εἰ μὲν γὰρ προσδοξάσαι λέγει ᾗ διαφέρει
τι τῶν ἄλλων, πάνυ γελοία γίγνεται ἡ ἐπίταξις.

ΘΕΑΙ. Πῶς;

ΣΩ. Ὧν ὀρθὴν δόξαν ἔχομεν ᾗ τῶν ἄλλων διαφέρει, τούτων προσλαβεῖν κελεύει ἡμᾶς ὀρθὴν δόξαν
ᾗ τῶν ἄλλων διαφέρει. καὶ οὕτως ἡ μὲν σκυτάλης ἡ
ὑπέρου ἢ ὅτου δὴ λέγεται περιτροπὴ πρὸς ταύτην τὴν e
ἐπίταξιν οὐδὲν ἂν λέγοι, τυφλοῦ δὲ παρακέλευσις ἂν
καλοῖτο δικαιότερον· τὸ γάρ, ἃ ἔχομεν, ταῦτα προσλαβεῖν κελεύειν, ἵνα μάθωμεν ἃ δοξάζομεν, πάνυ γενναίως ἔοικεν ἐσκότω μένῳ.

But if it means, "Knowledge of the distinctive difference," the term Knowledge remains still unanalysed.

1. καὶ ἐμέ.] Bodl. εἰ σὺ ἐμὶ καὶ: Vat. Δ. εἰ σὺ ἐμὶ καὶ: Ven. Ξ. et pr. Π. εἰ σὺ ἢ ἐμὶ καὶ (Bekk. Stallb.): cett. εἴσῃ ἐμὶ καὶ: Ven. Σ. γρ. αἴσῃ ἐμί. ἢ is awkwardly remote from its antecedent, and sets aside τἆλλα ἐξ ὧν εἰ σύ, which answers to ἐξάφθαλμον in the previous sentence. And the ἢ may have originated in the similarity of sound between ἢ and ἦ, as in p. 200. many MSS. read αὐτὴν for αὐτάς. Heindorf's conjecture, ᾖ, referring to μνημεῖον, is unsatisfactory, because it is rather the object of sense, which, by fitting the μνημεῖον, would be said to remind. Hence ἂ ἐμὶ καὶ would seem a fair emendation. But the above is chosen as the simpler, and as accounting more naturally for the corruption. If it is right, the sentence must be supposed to revert by a conversational licence to the indicative mood. See p. 149, ποιεῖν καὶ — ἀμφιδλήσκουσιν, and note. Schleiermacher's conjecture, ᾖ, leaves the subject of ἀναμνήσει doubtful. That of the Zurich editors, εἴσῃ σὺ ἐμὶ καὶ ἐμέ, introduces an abrupt and awkward inversion. And the use of οἶδα in this sense is very questionable.

14. ὑπέρου—περιτροπή) ἐπὶ τῶν τὰ αὐτὰ ποιούντων πολλάκις καὶ μηδὲν ἀνυόντων, ἢ ἐπὶ τῶν ταχέως τι πραττόντων. μέμνηται δὲ αὐτῆς Φιλήμων ἐν Ἥρωσι καὶ Ἐπιγέλια Πλάτων. (Schol.) οὐδὲν ἂν λέγοι, i. e. λήροι ἂν εἴη.

ΘΕΑΙΤΗΤΟΣ.

p. 209. ΘΕΑΙ. †† εἴ γε δή τι νῦν δὴ ὡς ἐρῶν ἐπύθου;

ΣΩ. Εἰ τὸ λόγον, ὦ παῖ, προσλαβεῖν γνῶναι κελεύει, ἀλλὰ μὴ δοξάσαι τὴν διαφορότητα, ἡδὺ χρῆμ᾽ ἂν εἴη τοῦ καλλίστου τῶν περὶ ἐπιστήμης λόγου. τὸ
p. 210. γὰρ γνῶναι ἐπιστήμην που λαβεῖν ἐστίν. ἢ γάρ;

ΘΕΑΙ. Ναί.

ΣΩ. Οὐκοῦν ἐρωτηθείς, ὡς ἔοικε, τί ἐστιν ἐπιστήμη, ἀποκρινεῖται ὅτι δόξα ὀρθὴ μετὰ ἐπιστήμης διαφορότητος. λόγου γὰρ πρόσληψις τοῦτ᾽ ἂν εἴη κατ᾽ ἐκεῖνον.

ΘΕΑΙ. Ἔοικεν.

ΣΩ. Καὶ παντάπασί γε εὔηθες, ζητούντων ἡμῶν ἐπιστήμην, δόξαν φάναι ὀρθὴν εἶναι μετ᾽ ἐπιστήμης εἴτε διαφορότητος εἴτε ὁτουοῦν. οὔτε ἄρα αἴσθησις, ὦ Θεαίτητε, οὔτε δόξα ἀληθὴς οὔτε μετ᾽ ἀληθοῦς
b δόξης λόγος προσγιγνόμενος ἐπιστήμη ἂν εἴη.

ΘΕΑΙ. Οὐκ ἔοικεν.

1. εἴ γε δή] So the MSS., except Vat. Δ., which has εἰ δί. The Bodleian continues without punctuation from ἰσνοτομίνῳ, and accents as above. But the accents appear to have been added by a later hand. Is it possible some words may have slipt out? such as Τί οὖν δή; εἴ γε δὴ τι— 'Well, what then? For I presume your question just now implied that you had something to say.' The reading of Vat. Δ. admits of being rendered, however, 'Well, but if,—what were you just now going to say, when you asked the question?' Most of the editors give Εἰνί. The question referred to is τὸ οὖν προσλαβεῖν— τί ἂν ὅτι εἴη; This is a little difficult; and Badham, retaining εἰ δί, most ingeniously conjectures τί νῦν δὴ ἐς ἔτερων ὑπέθου, i. e. 'what was the suppressed alternative implied by the use of μέν?' But this is hardly required. Theaetetus very properly recalls Socrates from his unwonted discursiveness.

3. ἡδὺ χρῆμ᾽ ἂν εἴη τοῦ] The genitive is due to a sort of attractive ethical force in ἡδύ, cf. ἄνυσσε τὴν συμκρολογίαν above. Soph. Phil. 81. ἀλλ᾽ ἡδὺ γάρ τοι στῆμα τῆς νίκης λαβεῖν.

'An amusing sort of creature must be our fairest of the accounts of knowledge!'

8. ἀποκρυνεῖται] Sc. ὁ λόγος.

13. φάσει] ἰσύκων sc.

210   ΠΛΑΤΩΝΟΣ ΘΕΑΙΤΗΤΟΣ.

ΣΩ. Ἦ οὖν ἔτι κυοῦμέν τι καὶ ὠδίνομεν, ὦ φίλε, p. 210. περὶ ἐπιστήμης, ἢ πάντα ἐκτετόκαμεν;

ΘΕΑΙ. Καὶ ναὶ μὰ Δί᾽ ἔγωγε πλείω ἢ ὅσα εἶχον ἐν ἐμαυτῷ διὰ σὲ εἴρηκα.

Though Theaetetus has brought forth more than he knew was in him, the art of Socrates has hitherto rejected all. But he is cured of thinking that he knows what he does not know.

ΣΩ. Οὐκοῦν ταῦτα μὲν πάντα ἡ μαιευτικὴ ἡμῶν τέχνη ἀνεμιαῖά φησι γεγενῆσθαι καὶ οὐκ ἄξια τροφῆς;

ΘΕΑΙ. Παντάπασι μὲν οὖν.

ΣΩ. Ἐὰν τοίνυν ἄλλων μετὰ ταῦτα ἐγκύμων ἐπι- c χειρῇς γίγνεσθαι, ὦ Θεαίτητε, ἐάν τε γίγνῃ, βελτιόνων ἔσει πλήρης διὰ τὴν νῦν ἐξέτασιν, ἐάν τε κενὸς ᾖς, ἧττον ἔσει βαρὺς τοῖς συνοῦσι καὶ ἡμερώτερος, σωφρόνως οὐκ οἰόμενος εἰδέναι ἃ μὴ οἶσθα. τοσοῦτον γὰρ μόνον ἡ ἐμὴ τέχνη δύναται, πλέον δὲ οὐδέν, οὐδέ τι οἶδα ὧν οἱ ἄλλοι, ὅσοι μεγάλοι καὶ θαυμάσιοι ἄνδρες εἰσί τε καὶ γεγόνασι. τὴν δὲ μαιείαν ταύτην ἐγώ τε καὶ ἡ μήτηρ ἐκ θεοῦ ἐλάχομεν, ἡ μὲν τῶν γυναικῶν, ἐγὼ δὲ τῶν νέων τε καὶ γενναίων καὶ ὅσοι d καλοί. νῦν μὲν οὖν ἀπαντητέον μοι εἰς τὴν τοῦ βασιλέως στοὰν ἐπὶ τὴν Μελήτου γραφήν, ἥν με γέγραπται· ἕωθεν δέ, ὦ Θεόδωρε, δεῦρο πάλιν ἀπαντῶμεν.

3. Καὶ ναὶ μὰ Δί᾽ ἔγωγε πλείω] καὶ πλείω, 'even more,' ναὶ μὰ Δί᾽ ἔγωγε is interposed.

9. Ἐὰν τοίνυν] I. e. 'The power of rejection is one of the greatest powers in thinking.'

19. τὴν τοῦ βασιλέως στοὰν] Indictments for impiety were laid before the ἄρχων βασιλεύς, who was the representative of the ancient kings in their capacity of High-Priest, as the Rex Sacrificulus was at Rome. (Smith's Dict. of Ant.) It is at this point that the Euthyphro is supposed to open.

APPENDIX A.

On some peculiarities of style and idiom in Plato.

'Ἀλλ' οὐ πρότερόν γε, οἶμαι, Θεαίτητον ἐν ἐμοὶ δοξασθήσεται, πρὶν ἂν ἡ συμφυὴς αὐτῇ τῶν ἄλλων συμοτήτων ἐν ἐμοὶ ἑαυτὴν διάφορόν τι μημεῖον παρ' ἐμοὶ ἐνσημηναμένη κατάθηται. Theæt. p. 209 c.

The words of Socrates, it is said in the Euthyphro (pp. 11, 15), are like the works of Dædalus; they are endued with motion. This image expresses the most characteristic peculiarity of Plato's style, the source of much both of its beauty and of its difficulty. His thoughts are not fixed and dead, like specimens in a museum or cabinet, but flying as he pursues them, doubling, hiding, reappearing, soaring aloft, and changing colour with every change of light and aspect.

The reader of the Theætetus, for example, is disappointed, if he looks for perfect consistency with the Republic, or if he expects to find the logical statement of a definite theory. The ground is shifted several times. One line of inquiry is abandoned, and yet the argument presently returns from a new starting-point upon the former track. A position is assumed and then relinquished;—the figures are erased,—and yet further discussion is made, not without reference to the hypothesis which has been demolished. The doctrine of sense, for instance, is wholly negatived, and yet it cannot be said that we are not intended to gather something from it.

Plato's metaphors are 'living creatures' rather than figures of speech; he regards them not as airy nothings, but as realities; he recurs to them with fondness, as Lord Bacon does. But no expression is ever merely repeated in Plato. If an image is recalled, it is with some additional or altered feature: if a conception is resumed, it is not merely copied, but a fresh picture is drawn from the life. Even in recapitulating, some modification is often made, or the argument is carried further. Thus the photograph, as it has been called, of the connexion is apt to be blurred, from the thought moving as we read. Even in the same passage, where an ordinary writer would

APPENDIX A.

be contented with referring to an example or illustration just adduced, Plato surprises the reader with a different one, which perhaps gives a new direction to the current of thought. A fair instance of this occurs in Theæt. p. 168, where Theodorus says: 'It was mere nonsense in me to hope that you would excuse me and not compel me to strip for the contest, as the Lacedæmonians do. You are rather to be compared to *Sciron*: for *they* tell one either to strip or go away; but you are rather like *Antæus* in your way of doing business, for you will let no man go till you have *stripped him* (like Sciron) and *compelled him to wrestle with you* (like Antæus).'

The argument itself (ὁ λόγος) is continually personified and is spoken of under a Protean variety of figures.

It is at one time our servant, who must wait our leisure, or who runs away from us, or who seems likely to die and vanish away 'like a tale.' More frequently it has power over us, like a general commanding us, like a sea in which we must swim for our lives, while it rolls its successive waves over us, or like a wind which carries us we know not whither. Sometimes 'its name is legion,' and it is multiplied into a swarm or an impetuous throng. Or it takes a milder form, as the raft, or dolphin, on which we seek to escape from a sea of doubt, or the wall behind which we screen ourselves from the driving shower. The Argument talks with us, it goes through a subject, takes up a position, hides its face from some threatening objection and passes on. It rebukes us for unfair treatment of itself, it can be insulted, it stands in need of help, it has a father, and guardians of its orphanhood.

This movement or plasticity of ideas, which penetrates the whole of Plato's writings, is closely connected with their conversational form, and manifests itself in what may be called his poetical use of language.

The observation of both these elements of Plato's style is of importance to the student, because it saves him from the necessity of resorting to some forced construction, or flying to conjecture, upon each occasion of grammatical perplexity.

1. Conversationalisms. In Plato we often meet with irregularities of construction, which in an oration or set treatise would be referred to looseness or inelegance of diction, but which only make the dialogue more easy and lively and natural.

a. Changes of construction. The following are a few out of several instances in the Theætetus :

(1.) p. 144. τὰ γὰρ εὐμαθῆ ὄντα—πρᾷον οὐ εἶναι—ἐγὼ μὲν οὖν' ἂν

APPENDIX A.   215

φαίνῃ γενέσθαι οὔτε ἀπὸ γεγονότος. Theodorus begins by simply expressing his surprise, but proceeds to dwell upon his previous anticipations and experience to account for it.

(2.) p. 153. ἃ δ' ἐν τῇ ψυχῇ ἕξει—ατίσαί τε μαθήματα κ. τ. λ. cf. p. 173. συνιδεῖν δ' ἑτοιμοτάτων ἐπ' ἀρχάς—αὐθ' ἅπερ πρώτοισι προσίστανται αὐτοῖς.

The emphasis on the first words causes the sentence to begin vaguely, and the construction is determined as it proceeds.

(3.) p. 167. τοιαύτην ψυχῆς ἕξει δοξάζοντας συγγενῆ ἑαυτῆς.

Here, unless something is corrupt, a transition is made to the reflexive pronoun, as if ψυχή were the subject of δοξάζοντας: a transition from the persons who think to the mind which thinks.

(4.) p. 172. οἷα ἂν τολμήσειε φῆσαι (ὁ λόγος) .... ἐθέλουσιν ἰσχυρίζεσθαι. He passes from what the argument would say, to what certain persons do say. So elsewhere there is often a transition from the indefinite singular to the indefinite plural.

To this may be added the occasionally difficult use of the cases of nouns: e.g. Theæt. p. 147 ἐν τῇ τοῦ πηλοῦ ἐρωτήσει, without περί : just as we might say in conversation, 'the mud-question,' for 'the question about the mud.'

β. Resumption. A thought is frequently resumed in the same sentence, for the sake of modifying it, or of particularizing the aspect in which it is considered, or merely for the sake of clearness. The introduction of the pronoun αὐτός, to recall a noun which has been thrown back for the sake of emphasis, is a familiar instance of this.

e.g. p. 155. ἐάν σοι ἀνδρῶν—τῆς διανοίας τὴν ἀλήθειαν—συνεξερευνήσωμαι αὐτῶν.

Perhaps the most marked instance of resumption in the Theætetus occurs p. 171. μᾶλλον δὲ ὑπό γε ἐκείνου ὁμολογήσεται, ὅταν τῷ τἀναντία λέγοντι ξυγχωρῇ ἀληθῆ αὐτὸν δοξάζειν, τότε καὶ ὁ Πρωταγόρας αὐτὸς συγχωρήσεται.

γ. Redundancy. There are other ways in which regularity of construction is sacrificed to fulness of expression.

e.g. p. 153. Ἔτι οὖν σοι λέγω τεκμήρια τε καὶ γαλήνας καὶ ὅσα τοιαῦτα, ὅτι αἱ μὲν ἡσυχίαι σήπουσι καὶ ἀπολλύουσι, τὰ δ' ἕτερα σώζει.

p. 172. τοὺς λόγους ἐν εἰρήνῃ ἐπὶ σχολῆς ποιοῦνται, ὥσπερ ἡμεῖς νυνὶ τρίτον ἤδη λόγον ἐκ λόγου μεταλαμβάνομεν, οὕτω κἀκεῖνοι, ἐὰν αὐτοὺς ὁ ἐπελθὼν τοῦ προκειμένου μᾶλλον, καθάπερ ἡμᾶς, ἀρέσῃ.

APPENDIX A.

p. 199. μὴ γὰρ ἔχειν τὴν ἐπιστήμην τούτου οἷόν τι, ἀλλ' ἑτέραν ἀντ' ἐκείνης, ὅταν ——— θηρεύων ἑτέραν ἀνθ' ἑτέρας ἁμαρτὼν λάβῃ, ὅτι ἄρα τὰ ἕνδεκα δώδεκα ᾠήθη εἶναι, τὴν τῶν ἕνδεκα ἐπιστήμην ἀντὶ τῆς τῶν δώδεκα λαβών, τὴν ἐν ἑαυτῷ οἷον φάτταν ἀντὶ περιστερᾶς.

An occasional consequence of this fulness of expression is the deferred apodosis, which sometimes occurs, especially after ὥσπερ: e. g. Rep. 402 Ὥσπερ ἄρα ———. Ἆρ' οὖν, ὁ λέγω, πρὸς θεῶν, οὕτως κ.τ.λ. Theæt. p. 207. ὥσπερ ἂν —— οὕτω ταῦτα κ.τ.λ.

8. Also connected with the conversational form of Plato's writings, and the plastic, growing condition of his thoughts, is the imperfect kind of argument which he sometimes employs. It is a saying of Aristotle's that Dialectic deals tentatively with those subjects on which Philosophy dogmatizes, (ἡ διαλεκτικὴ πειραστικὴ περὶ ὧν ἡ φιλοσοφία γνωριστική); and Bacon speaks of a Socratic induction. To this, and to a certain economy used towards the respondent, is to be attributed the frequency of the argument from example (the example often covering more ground than seems quite fair,) and of the inference, by means of simple conversion, from particular to universal.

The immaturity of the science of logic no doubt renders this mode of reasoning more easy and natural than it could be in a later age, but it is not explained without allowing for the fact that the inquiry is conducted, at least on the part of the respondent, in a tentative and inductive spirit.

An instance occurs in the Theætetus p. 159, when it is argued that if what is different is dissimilar, then whatever is dissimilar is wholly different, and what is similar is the same. That Plato was fully aware of the inconclusiveness of the form of argument thus ironically adopted, appears from Protag. p. 350, where Socrates is checked for it by Protagoras, who says, "Ἔγωγε ἐρωτηθεὶς ὑπὸ σοῦ, εἰ οἱ ἀνδρεῖοι θαρραλέοι εἰσίν, ὡμολόγησα· εἰ δὲ καὶ οἱ θαρραλέοι ἀνδρεῖοι, οὐκ ἠρωτήθην· εἰ γάρ με τότε ἤρου, εἶπον ἂν ὅτι οὐ πάντες.

And sometimes, even where an instance is really meant to cover a large conclusion, its power is ostensively limited with persuasive modesty: as in Theæt. p. 152. Φαντασία ἄρα καὶ αἴσθησις ταὐτὸν ἔν τε θερμοῖς καὶ πᾶσι τοῖς τοιούτοις. ——— Αἰσθήσεις ἄρα τοῦ ὄντος ἀεί ἐστι.

Ib. p. 204. Ταὐτὸν ἄρα ἔν γε τοῖς ὅσα ἐξ ἀριθμοῦ ἐστί, τό τε πᾶν προσαγορεύομεν καὶ τὰ ἅπαντα.

ε. It is difficult to separate between the conversational and the poetical element in Plato. Their combination gives him the power of 'saying any thing.' Just as there is a freedom of expression

APPENDIX A.

possible in conversation, which we feel to be impossible in writing, or as the poet can express with grace and dignity what by other lips were better left unsaid.

II. This leads us to the *Poetical use of language*. Plato's words have frequently a different value from any that could be given them by a mere prose writer. The language as well as the thought is instinct with a creative power, which gives it a dramatic vividness and refinement; at times even a dithyrambic cadence, or a lyrical intensity. The poet whom Plato most resembles in this is Sophocles; but his style may be regarded as the mirror of all Greek literature.

a. Poetical use of single words.

(1) Choice of a more sensuous expression (πρὸ ὁμμάτων ποιεῖν).

p. 150. ἐναργὲς ὅτι for δῆλον ὅτι ('as clear as day').
p. 154. ταῦτα τὰ φάσματα.
p. 156. συνεστήσουσα καὶ γεννωμένη.
p. 160. μὴ στοίων τῇ διανοίᾳ.
p. 162. διαλύγιος φλυαρία.
p. 165. σφαλεῖς γὰρ ἧττον ἀσχημονήσει.
p. 169. μάλ' εὖ ξυγκατάθεσαι.
p. 171. ταύτῃ ἀν—ίσταιεθαι τὸν λόγον.
p. 172. ἀνάγκην ἔχων ὁ ἀντιδίκος (wielding coercion).
p. 202. ταῦτα—περιτρέχοντα πᾶσιν προσφέρεσθαι.

To which may be added the 'hypocoristic' use of diminutives.

p. 149. φαρμάκια.
p. 195. ἐάν του σμικρὸν ᾖ τὸ ψυχάριον.

(2) Use of Epic words, the meaning of which is sometimes *spiritualized*.

p. 149. ῥαῖσι γενναίαις καὶ βλοσυραῖς.
p. 162. ἄξιος εἶδ' ἑνὸς μόνου.
p. 174. παλὸ βάλλοντα.
p. 189. τοῦτο γὰρ μοι ὑπόλληται διασεσημένη.
p. 194. Ὅταν τοίνυν λάδονδο του τὸ εἶαρ ᾖ.

(3) Playing upon a word.

p. 150. σύρμμα. Cf. Soph. Œd. Tyr. 1108.
p. 152. τὴν ἀλήθειαν.
p. 181. τοὺς ῥέοντας.
p. 194. τὸ τῆς ψυχῆς εἶαρ.
p. 208. ἀμφίστομον ἐπιστήμης λόγον.

Closely related to this is (4) the etymological use of words; i.e. when, by dwelling upon its etymology, a word is made to express something different from, or more than, its ordinary meaning.

216 APPENDIX A.

p. 149. ὅτι ἔλαχον οὗτοι τὴν λοχείαν εἴληχεν.
p. 152. (perhaps) ξυμφερέσθων (let them march one way).
p. 161. τὸ ἀμφιδρόμια αὐτοῦ ὡς ἀληθῶς ἐν κύκλῳ περιθρεκτέον.
p. 193. ὥσπερ οἱ ἡμίαλοι ὑποδούμενοι παραλλάξας.
p. 198. προέχειμεν δ᾽ οὐκ εἶχε τῇ διανοίᾳ.

(5) Poetical use of particles: e.g. the frequent use of ἄρα, helping to keep up the idea that Socrates is repeating what he has heard, the occasionally difficult reference with γάρ (p. 152. οἶα γὰρ—and note), the hyperbaton of καί (p. 154. καὶ μὴν ἔγωγε. p. 190. δατέον δὲ καὶ σοι τὸ ῥῆμα—), and generally the dramatic liveliness, with which successive clauses are contrasted, as if each were put into the mouth of a different person. Speech thus becomes literally a 'self-dialogue.' See especially p. 155, ὃ μὴ πρότερον ἦν, ἀλλὰ ὕστερον τοῦτο εἶναι: and p. 190, ὅτι παντὸς μᾶλλον—ὡς παντὸς μᾶλλον—ὡς παντάπασιν ἄρα—ὡς ἀνάγκη—, with which the supposed answers of the mind to itself are introduced.

Compare Phil. 38. τί ποτε ἄρα ἐστι τὸ παρὰ τὴν πέτραν τουτ᾽ ἑστάναι φανταζόμενον ὑπὸ τοῦ δένδρου.

β. The same poetical energy shows itself in the expansion of some of the ordinary forms of grammar. In this also Plato reflects the general tendency of the Greek language.

(1) Apposition. The use of the apposition of clauses (as a form of epexegesis) deserves to be reckoned among the more salient peculiarities of Plato's style. One example from the Theaetetus will suffice to indicate what is meant.

p. 175. πῶλοι οἱ τὰ ἀντίστροφα ἀποβλέπουσιν—Διογγήσει τε ἐφ᾽ ὑψηλοῦ κρεμασθεῖσ—ἰλιγγιῶσάν τε καὶ ἀπορῶν καὶ βαρβαρίζων—γέλωτα—παρέχει κ.τ.λ.—where another writer would probably have inserted γάρ.

Sometimes a sentence is thus placed in apposition with a pronoun such as τοῦτο (p. 189 ad fin.) or ὅ (p. 158.) Compare the use of τὸ δέ, e.g. p. 157. A slightly different use is that of the accusative in apposition to the sentence, which may be viewed as an extension of the 'cognate accusative.' Instances of this are p. 153, ἐπὶ τούτοις τὸν κολοφῶνα κ.τ.λ.; p. 161, τὸ ἀμφιδρόμια αὐτοῦ κ.τ.λ. (Many of the examples of resumption and redundancy above referred to would fall grammatically under this head.)

(2) Attraction. E.g. where a main verb was to be expected, we find a participle. It can be accounted for; but there is reason to believe that it is partly due to the neighbourhood of another participle, or of some word that is usually construed with a participle.

p. 173. τοῦν δὲ τοῦ ἡμετέρου χοροῦ πότερον βούλει διελθόντες ἢ ἐάσαντες πάλιν ἐπὶ τὸν λόγον τρεπώμεθα; where we should have expected διελθόμεν.

p. 150. τὸ μὲν πρῶτον φαίνονται καὶ πᾶσιν ἀμαθὲς, πάντες δὲ προσιόντες τῆς συνουσίας θαυμαστὸν ὅσον ἐπιδιδόντες, ἐν αὑτοῖς τε καὶ τοῖς ἄλλοις δοκοῦσιν: where, but for the proximity of ὅσον—, ἐπιδιδόντες would probably have been ἐπιδιδόασιν. See also λαβὼν, p. 199. which but for ὅπως—λάθῃ would be λαβόντα.

γ. To the same self-consciousness of language which betrays itself in the foregoing instances may be attributed the minuteness of antithesis, which, though common everywhere in Greek, is strikingly so in Plato.

p. 150. ἐμοῦ δὲ καταφρονήσαντες, ἢ αὐτοὶ ὑπ' ἄλλων πεισθέντες.

p. 151. ἴσως δὲ δή, καὶ πάλιν αὐτοὶ ἐπιδιδόασιν; where the subjects of the two verbs are opposed.

p. 197. εἰ δυνατὸν οὕτω κατημένον μὴ ἔχειν, ἀλλ' ὥσπερ κ. τ. λ.

δ. This power of refining upon language is turned to account in adapting the mode of expression to the exigencies of the argument.

E. g. p. 157, where we are gradually led from the example of the wind, which one man feels cold, and another not, to the position that sensation is the correlative of reality. See also pp. 158, 159, where, as the argument proceeds, (ἕτερον) ἅμα τούτῳ ἅμα ἐκείνῳ is substituted for ἄλλο ἑτέρου.

ε. The care which is taken of the rhythm is a further peculiarity of Plato's style, and may be treated as a poetical element. This is especially noticeable (1) in the manner in which quotations from poetry are shaded off so as to harmonize with the surrounding prose, and, (2) in the occasional elaboration of prose writing to something like a metrical cadence.

(1.) p. 173. In the quotation from Pindar, φέρεται is probably substituted for πέτεται (see note on the passage), the words τὰ ἐπίπεδα γεωμετροῦσα are inserted, and τὸν ὄντα ἕκαστον ἥλιον is added at the close. Thus the poetical language is interwoven with the sentence, so as to embellish it without interrupting its harmony.

p. 194. The substitution of the Attic εἴαρ for the Homeric ἦρ is probably due to a similar motive.

(2.) Dithyrambic and lyric cadences are more frequent in some other dialogues than in the Theætetus. See especially Sympos. pp. 196, 197. the close of Agathon's speech, especially the last few

APPENDIX A.

lines, in which the rhetorical antitheses have more the effect of rhythm than of argument: Phædr. 238, 241, alibi; Rep. 546, 7; 617, 8; and several places of the Timæus, e. g. p. 47, ἐν ᾗ μὴ φιλόσοφος τυγχάνῃ τις ἀθρούμενος ἐν ὀργανῷ μέτρῳ. With such passages may be compared Theæt. 175, 6, οὐδέ γ' ἁρμονίαν λόγων λαβόντος ὀρθῶς ὑμνῆσαι θεῶν τε καὶ ἀνδρῶν εὐδαιμόνων βίον ἀληθῆ.

The same power shows itself more slightly in an occasional inversion of the order of words for the sake of emphasis.

p. 158. οἱ μὲν θεοὶ αὐτῶν οἴονταί εἰσιν.

p. 160. κατὰ δὲ Πρωταγόραν τὸν σοφώτατον πάντων χρημάτων ἄνθρωπον μέτρον εἶναι.

ζ. A few words may be added in conclusion on the artificial structure of Plato's dialogues, of which the Theætetus is acknowledged to be a prominent example.

There is a unity in each of them, approaching to that of a living organism:—the spirit of the whole breathing in every part;—a continuity independent of the links of question and answer, by which it appears to be sustained; which may be viewed apart from the scenery and the changes of persons, and the passages of humour and pleasantry by which it seems to be interrupted.

And while it is comparatively easy to distinguish the principal stages of the argument, yet there is such a dovetailing and interpenetration of the parts, that it is difficult to adopt an exact division without doing violence to the real harmony, or even to mark the exact point of transition from one hypothesis to another.

An instance of this is the way in which the reader is prepared for the argument from the idea of expediency, which may be said to be anticipated as early as p. 157, ἀγαθὸν καὶ καλόν. (Compare the anticipation, at the very beginning of the dialogue, p. 144, ἐπισκεψάμεθ᾽ ἂν εἰ μουσικὸς ἂν λόγοι, of the conclusion arrived at p. 179, σοφώτερόν τε ἄλλον ἄλλου εἶναι καὶ τὸν μὲν τοιούτων μέτρον εἶναι, κ. τ. λ.) The difficulty of reconciling the ideas of goodness and wisdom with the doctrine of sense appears more distinctly in the defence of Protagoras, p. 167, and presses for solution as an element of the common opinion of men, p. 170, καὶ ἔν γε ταῖς μεγίστοις κινδύνοις——περὶ σφίσιν.

These two passages have prepared the way for the statement in pp. 171, 2, of the 'semi-Protagorranism' of those who will not venture to say that every creature knows what is for its own health, nor that every individual and every state knows equally what is expedient in legislation. When a breach has thus been made in the

APPENDIX A. 219

enemy's lines of defence, a rest is afforded to the reader by the vision of the Divine Life which follows, in which, however, the ideas of wisdom and holiness and righteousness have a direct bearing upon the conclusion towards which we are being carried step by step, and its effect upon the tone of the discussion is apparent in the words p. 177, πλὴν εἴ τις τὸ ὄνομα λέγει· τοῦτο δέ πω σκέψωμ' ἂν εἴη πρὸς ὃ λέγομεν οὐχί; κ.τ.λ. At this point the argument from Expediency is fully entered into. But it is difficult to say exactly where it began.

A similar gradation may be observed in the development of the difficulty about false opinion.

Note also the artfulness of the transition from sensation to thought, pp. 184-187, and from 'true opinion' to 'true opinion giving an account of itself,' p. 201.

And while the earlier part is written with a view to what is in reserve, the previous discussion is not forgotten as the inquiry proceeds. See p. 194. ὃ δὴ ὄντα καλοῦσι, compared with p. 152. ὃ δὴ φαμὲν εἶναι, οὐκ ὀρθῶς; and p. 209, μνημεῖον παρ' ἐμοὶ ἐνσημηναμένη κατάθηται,—an application of the (relinquished) conception of the waxen block.

Plato's philosophy has been compared to a building, of which the Republic is the superstructure, while the other dialogues are the pillars and fretted vaults upon which it rests.

The image fails to give an adequate idea of the perfection of Art, —or rather of Nature conscious of itself,—which gives harmony, but not regularity, a growing, not a fixed, consistency, both to the parts and to the whole.

His writings are the creations of a great master, whose sketches are worked up into the larger monuments of his genius, a cycle surrounding an eternal Epic poem, bound together by the unity not merely of a particular age and country, but of an individual mind.

APPENDIX B.

μὴ οὔ.

§ 1. The most familiar use of μὴ οὔ is after verbs of fearing and the like, with the subjunctive[a]: where a fear is expressed that something is not, or will not be; e.g. Plat. Men. p. 89. πρὸς τί βλέπων δυσχεραίνεις αὐτὸ καὶ ἀπιστεῖς, μὴ οὐκ ἐπιστήμη ᾖ ἡ ἀρετή;

But there are other cases of a different kind, in which μὴ οὔ has only the force of a single negative.

These are, (1) With a conditional participial clause depending on a negative sentence, e. g.

Hdtus. II. 110. οὐ αἱ συσσῇσθαι ἔργα οἷά περ Σεσώστρι τῷ Αἰγυπτίῳ, ... οὔκων δίκαιον εἶναι ἱστόρια ἐπιμιστθῆ τῶν ἱππέων ἀναθημάτων, μὴ οὐκ ὑπερβαλλόμενον τοῖσι ἔργοισι.

Hdtus. VI. 106. ἐούσῃ δὲ οὐκ ἐξελεύσεσθαι ἔφασαν, μὴ οὐ πλήρεος ἐόντος τοῦ κύκλου.

Soph. Œd. Rex, 220. οὐ γὰρ ἂν μακρὰν ἴχνευον αὐτός, μὴ οὐκ ἔχων τι σύμβολον.

(2.) With an infinitive or participle dependent on a negative sentence, when the clause so introduced explains or supplements that which is denied. What is so explained has of course something in it of a privative meaning. The commonest instances are those of verbs of refraining, being able (to avoid), admitting (a negative), and denying; e. g.

Soph. Œd. Col. 361. ἥκεις γὰρ οὐ κενή γε, τοῦτ' ἐγὼ σαφῶς ἔξοιδα, μὴ οὐχὶ δεῖμ' ἐμοὶ φέρουσά τι.

Soph. Œd. Rex, 1088. οὐ τὸν Ὄλυμπον ἀπείρων, ὦ Κιθαιρών, οὐκ ἔσῃ * * * μὴ οὐ σέ γε κ. τ. λ.

---

[a] To the same head should probably be referred the use after αἰσχύνομαι with the infinitive, mentioned by Rost (Grammatik, p. 764); of which I have been unable to find an example. But for the converse, see Plat. Gorg. p. 461. ἐσχύνθη μὴ ὁμολογήσεισθαι.

APPENDIX B.   221

Soph. Antig. 540. μή—μ' ἀτιμάσῃς τὸ μὴ οὐ θανεῖν τε σὺν σοι—
Œd. Col. 572. ξένον γ' ἂν οὐδὲν ὄνθ', ὥσπερ σὺ νῦν ὑπεκτραπείμην
μὴ οὐ συνεκσῴζειν.
Plat. Phæd. 72. τίς μηχανὴ μὴ οὐχὶ πάντα ἀναλωθῆναι εἰς τὸ τε-
θνάναι;
Ib. 88. οὐδενὶ προσήκει θάνατον θαρροῦντι μὴ οὐκ ἀνοήτως θαῤῥεῖν.
Ib. ἐκείνῳ μηκέτι συγχωροῖ, μὴ οὐ ποιεῖν αὐτήν—.
Symp. 197. τίς ἐναντιωθήσεται μὴ οὐχὶ Ἔρωτος εἶναι σοφίαν;
Gorg. 461. (l. c.) μὴ προσομολογήσαι—μὴ οὐχί. Ibid. τίνα οἴει
ἀπαρνήσεσθαι μὴ οὐχί—;

(3.) With the infinitive or participle after αἰσχρόν ἐστι, and some
other expressions of reproach.

Plat. Theæt. p. 151. αἰσχρὸν μὴ οὐ παντὶ τρόπῳ προθυμεῖσθαι ᾗ τι
τις ἔχει λέγειν.
Plat. Soph. p. 219. τὴν θηρευτικὴν ἄλογον μὴ οὐ τέμνειν διχῇ.
Plat. Symp. πολλὴ ἄνοια μὴ οὐχ ἕν τε καὶ ταὐτὸν ἡγεῖσθαι τὸ κάλλος.
Plat. Phæd. 85. μὴ οὐχὶ παντὶ τρόπῳ ἐλέγχειν—πάνυ μαλθακοῦ
ἀνδρός.
Soph. Œd. Rex, δυσάλγητον γὰρ ἂν εἴην, τοιάνδε μὴ οὐ κατοικτείρων
ἕδραν.

§ 2.

1. There is a simple and obvious explanation of the two passages
of Herodotus, which may perhaps be found with some modification
to apply to the other cases above mentioned.

Both in II. 110. and VI. 106. the clause introduced with μὴ οὐ
expresses not a merely hypothetical condition, but a condition which
was also a fact. It is not merely said that Dareius should not stand
before the image if his deeds were inferior, it is also asserted that
they were inferior. The Spartans did not say that they would not
come unless it was full moon, but that they would not come on the
ninth day, because the moon was not then full.

The same explanation applies to Soph. Œd. Rex, 220. Œdipus
says, not 'that he could not have made the investigation, unless he
had had some clue:' but that 'not having any thing to guide him, it
was impossible for him to conduct the investigation by himself.'

In all these instances therefore οὐ is clearly significant: not de-
stroying the negative force of μή, but strengthening into a subordinate assertion what might otherwise be understood as an hypothesis.
It gives a degree of objective reality to the clause, and brings it into
prominence as an integral part of the predication.

APPENDIX B.

But why is this only done when the whole sentence is negative? For instance, why could not the priest have said, 'δεῖν αὐτὸν προσενιέναι τὰ ἑαυτοῦ ἀναθήματα, μὴ οὐκ ὑπερβαλλόμενον τοῖσι ἔργοισι'?

The answer is probably to be sought (1) in the tendency of negative particles in Greek to multiply themselves,—which acts here in two ways, the negative turn of the sentence leading the mind onwards to a further negative, and the negation in the principal clause making it necessary to strengthen the subordinate but independent negative expression:—(2) in the indefiniteness of the negative sentence, which makes the necessity of avoiding ambiguity to be more distinctly felt.

2. These last remarks apply equally to the second case, that of negative sentences, (or interrogative with negative meaning,) to which a negative clause is appended, explanatory of that which in the chief clause is denied. But it is less easy here to determine the exact significance of οὐ. The subordinate clause in this case does not run parallel to the whole sentence, but to a part of it, i.e. it corresponds, not to what is negatively asserted, but to what is denied. Still it is a fair hypothesis that it is not merely subordinate, but that it enters into the predication. It is co-ordinate with the predicate, if we do not include in that term the negative particle. It is a fact consistent with this hypothesis, that what is thus introduced with μὴ οὐ is generally dwelt upon with some emphasis, and is often more important to the sense than the preceding verb, which has something of an auxiliary character. Thus Plato Phaed. 72. τίς μηχανὴ μὴ οὐχὶ πάντα ἀναλωθῆναι, might be more briefly expressed thus,

πῶς οὐ πάντα ἀναλωθήσεται;

and ib. 88. οὐδενὶ προσήκει θάνατον θαρροῦντι μὴ οὐκ ἀνοήτως θαρρεῖν, is nearly equivalent to οὐδεὶς ἂν θάνατον θαρρῶν οὐκ ἀνοήτως θαρροίη.

It is not necessary for the validity of an hypothesis of this kind to show that where οὐ is omitted, (as in Soph. Œd. Rex, 1388. οὐκ ἂν ἐσχόμην τὸ μὴ 'ποκλεῖσαι τοὐμὸν ἄθλιον δέμας. Philoct. 348. οὐ πολὺν χρόνον μ' ἔστεχον μή με ναυστολεῖν ταχύ,) the clause is purely subordinate, though the case would be considerably strengthened if this could be proved. And though an account could be given of both the above instances, (in the first the remoteness from fact of an imaginary act in past time, in the second the emphasis being on ἔστεχον, and his 'not sailing' being in this case so purely imaginary), still it is better, especially when dealing with poetical instances, not to seem to strain them to our theory. It is noticeable that οὐδεὶς κωλύει is generally followed by the infinitive without either μὴ or μὴ οὐ. It is in effect an affirmative expression.

APPENDIX B.

3. The last case is in form nearly analogous to the first, with this difference, that the clause introduced with μὴ οὐ, instead of being co-ordinate with the predicate, is itself the subject of the sentence. Here μή indicates that the expression is hypothetical, while οὐ shows that what is thus supposed is conceived of objectively, and as taking place in the region of fact. The supposition generally refers to the case which is immediately before the speaker, and it is usually a supposition of something not done in that case. Here a 'negative instance' comes to our aid. Soph. Œd. Rex, 12. δυσάλγητος γὰρ ἂν εἴην τοιάνδε μὴ οὐ κατοικτείρων ἕδραν. But ib. 76. τηνικαῦτ' ἐγὼ κακὸς μὴ δρῶν ἂν εἴην πάνθ' ὅσ' ἂν δηλοῖ θεός. Again, Plat. Soph. l. c. ἄλογον μὴ οὐ τέμνειν. But, where it is a more abstract supposition, πῶς οὐ πολλὴ ἀλογία—γνῶναι τὴν ψυχὴν μηδέν. (Theaet. 199.) οὐκ ἄλογον μὴ —θεῖν. (Phaed. 62.)

What has been already said of the tendency of negatives in Greek to suggest negatives must be applied to this case also. Thus: καλόν ἐστι, μή—. αἰσχρόν ἐστι μὴ οὐ—.[b]

---

§ 3.

Although the MS. authority for οὐ in Theaet. 151. a. is weak, (Par. C. E. Flor. a. c. Palat. Coisl. ex em. Ven. Π. ex em. Par. B. ex em.), yet the comparison of similar passages, especially Phaed. 88. οὐδενὶ προσήκει θάνατον θαρροῦντι μὴ οὐκ ἀνοήτως θαρρεῖν, tends strongly to confirm the reading which has been retained in the text. According to Hermann, the omission of οὐ in such cases is a frequent error; and, after what has been said above, it may perhaps be added, that the use of μὴ οὐ is in harmony with the general vividness and reality with which the whole passage is conceived.

[b] It is possible that the use of μὴ οὐ after such expressions as οὐκ ἂν δυναίμην, οὐδεμία μηχανή, τίς μηχανή, should have been placed under this rather than the foregoing head.

APPENDIX C.

εἶδος, ἰδέα.

§ 1. The words εἶδος and ἰδέα are throughout nearly synonymous in Greek, but there is a tendency observable to a difference in their use, perhaps in some way connected with the difference of gender.

εἶδος seems earlier to have shaken itself clear of metaphor, and to have settled into an abstract meaning. Thus in Thucyd. II. 50 τὸ εἶδος τῆς νόσου means simply the nature of the disease, but in II. 51 τοιαύτη ἦν ἐπὶ πᾶν τὴν ἰδέαν, should be translated, 'was such in its general phenomena.' Here ἰδέα calls up a picture, while εἶδος simply designates a class or kind of thing. So πᾶσα ἰδέα—θανάτου Thuc. III. 81 is not 'every kind of death,' but 'death in every form.'

§ 2. The word εἶδος occurs frequently in Plato in its ordinary sense. Thus in Theæt. p. 157. ἀνθρωπόν τε τίθεσθαι καὶ λίθον καὶ καθ᾽ ἕκαστον ζῷόν τε καὶ εἶδος, the word is scarcely more abstract than in Herodotus I. 94. τὰ—τῶν πασγνίων εἴδεα.

A more philosophical application of the same use occurs p. 181, where we have the δύο εἴδη κινήσεως.

§ 3. But it occurs also in a more abstract sense, which we may possibly be right in attributing to Socrates, as a distinctly logical term. εἶδος then means a class, or species, as that to which particular things are referred, which contains them, and marks them off from others, and which itself answers to their definition. See Theætetus, p. 148. ταύτας πολλὰς οὔσας ἐνὶ εἴδει περιέλαβες. p. 205. εἰς ταυτὸν ἐμπέπτωκεν ἡ συλλαβὴ εἶδος ἐκείνῳ.

§ 4. It may be doubted whether in Plato the word εἶδος ever loses entirely the association of its earliest meaning (in which he frequently employs it) of outward appearance, form. (See Ast, Lex. sub voc.) But as it approaches to its technical use in his philosophy, it tends to regain metaphorically the association of visible shape, which in a literal sense it has cast off. The metaphor is not perfect, however, until the word has been changed to ἰδέα. Or if we choose to put it so, εἶδος expresses the general shape and contour of a thing; ἰδέα implies also the colour and the whole appearance. εἶδος is a colourless ἰδέα. See Theæt. p. 203. ἦν τι γεγονὸς εἶδος, θᾶτερ

APPENDIX C.

μίαν αυτὸ αὑτοῦ ἴχον. And there is a real difference underlying the figurative one. For a comparison of passages tends to prove that εἶδος is applied to the universal forms of existence as they are distinct from one another; ἰδέα rather as each of them has a unity in itself. Thus in Theæt. l. c. we have ἔν τι γεγονὸς εἶδος, ἰδέαν μίαν αὐτὸ αὑτοῦ ἴχον, ἕτερον δὲ τῶν στοιχείων°. Again, p. 204. μία ἰδέα ἐξ ἑκάστων τῶν συναρμοττόντων στοιχείων γεγονυῖα. Ib. ἔν τι εἶδος ἕτερον τῶν πάντων μορίων. p. 205. μία τις ἰδέα ἀμέριστος συλλαβὴ ἂν εἴη. 205. καὶ μία ἐστὶν ἰδέα. Cf. supr. p. 184. εἰς μίαν τινὰ ἰδέαν—σύνεσιν.

It should be noticed, that in the above passages the use of both words is in a transition state, assuming rather the form of an adaptation of the ordinary use, than of technical phraseology. Plato may perhaps be teaching the doctrine of ideas by example; but he does not avowedly give to the words the 'second intention' with which they are used in many passages to express the eternal forms of Being. There is also an intermediate transition noticeable in the use of ἰδέα, from the abstract to the concrete, i. e. it passes, by a kind of synecdoche, from meaning the sum of the attributes to mean that to which they belong. So in Thuc. l. c. πᾶσα ἰδέα θανάτου = θάνατος πάσης ἰδέας. And in Theæt. l. c. μία ἰδέα is used synonymously with ἓν εἶδος, ἰδέαν μίαν αὐτὸ αὑτοῦ ἴχον. It is more to the purpose, however, to observe generally, that the word εἶδος tends to a use at once more logical (ἕτερον εἶδος, ἀντὶ εἴδη, κατ' εἴδη θάντας, κατ' εἴδη τέμνειν) and more concrete: (the ἰδέα is spoken of as inherent in it); the word ἰδέα to one more metaphysical, (εἰς μίαν ἰδέαν συνορῶντα ἄγειν τὰ πολλαχῇ διεσπαρμένα, μίαν ἰδέαν διὰ πολλῶν πάντῃ διατεταμένην ἱκανῶς διαισθάνεσθαι,) more abstract, and at the same time more figurative.

The word ἰδέα is a fair symbol of the union of reason and imagination in Plato.

° Cf. Rep. p. 544. ἢ τινα ἄλλην ἴχεις ἰδέαν πολιτείας, ἢ τις καὶ ἐν εἴδει διαφανεῖ τινι αὑτῆς.

APPENDIX D.

'Ω θαυμάσιε, ὦ δαιμόνιε, ὦ ἑταῖρε, ὦ μέλε.

These and the like phrases are apt to be slurred over in translating or interpreting Plato, from the frequency of their recurrence and the difficulty of appreciating their exact force in each connexion. They belong to that conversational sprightliness and play of fancy which it is impossible to bind to any rule.

Here, as elsewhere, Plato carries further an existing tendency of the Greek language. Such addresses as δαιμόνιε, δαιμονίη, ἠθεῖε, in Homer (Il. VI. 407, 486, 518, 521. cf. Plat. Rep. 344 ὦ δαιμόνιε Θρασύμαχε) vary in signification according to the mood of the speaker. The same may be said of ὦ δαιμόνιε, ὦ μέλε, in Aristophanes.

In Plato the variety of such addresses is much greater, and the variety of their meaning greater still. They can often be more perfectly rendered by a changed expression of the voice or countenance, than by any words. All that can be said of them generally is, that they give an increased intensity to the tone of the conversation at the moment, whether this be grave or humorous, respectful, ironical or familiar.

ὦ θαυμάσιε in its simplest use conveys a remonstrance, 'I wonder at you.' The most decided instance is in the Phædo, p. 117. Οἷον, ἔφη, ποιεῖτε, ὦ θαυμάσιοι. 'What are you doing! I am amazed at you.' It may also sometimes convey admiration. But it is frequently used where the subject of wonder or surprise has nothing to do with the person addressed: e.g. Cratyl. 439, where it indicates Socrates' intense interest in the mystery of the Ideas. Compare the use of the form of congratulation ὦ μακάριε (see Aristoph. Nub. 167.) to express Socrates' own delight at some great discovery; e.g. Rep. 432, where Justice is discovered; Phæd. 69, where Socrates congratulates himself as well as Simmias on the superiority of the philosophic life.—So when Hamlet says, 'O good Horatio, I'll take the ghost's word for a thousand pound,' the address is prompted not this time by Horatio's worth, but by the relief caused to his own mind by the discovery of the king's guilt. Thus in Theæt. p. 151, ὦ θαυμάσιε can hardly be rendered except by a note of admiration. 'Do you know that many have been ready to bite me!'

Nearly the same is true of ὦ δαιμόνιε, p. 180, though it here retains a slight tone of remonstrance. 'Disciples, my good sir!' 'Disciples, did you say?' While in p. 172 it wears quite a different expression, conveying really Socrates' admiration for the philosophic life, and is more difficult to render. 'Ah! my good friend, this is not the first time I have observed how natural it is that a philosopher should make a poor figure at the bar!'

The affectionate confidence and familiarity expressed in ὦ ἑταῖρε, ὦ φίλε, ὦ φίλε ἑταῖρε, acquires, in ὦ μέλε, a degree of humorous or triumphant gaiety. Theæt. p. 178. Νὴ Δία, ὦ μέλε, 'My dear fellow! I should rather think he did.'

The use of quaint adjurations and addresses in Shakespeare affords an interesting illustration of this feature of Plato's style.

ERRATA.

Page xxiv. line 20, *for* invocation *read* invention

xxviii. line 5, *for* θεσπίῳ *read* θεσπίῳ

xxxvi. line 8, *for* hard *read* had

lxxxiii. line 25, *for* experiences *read* experience

151. c. 84., add note on πλεονεκτεῖς] i. e. 'Wiser even than we esteemed him;' referring to σοφὸν ἄνδρα above.

In the note on p. 155. b. 84., for ἐμοῦ τοῦ ὄγκου read τοῦ ὄγκου ἐμοῦ

208. line 18. ἐσώτατα μέρη *read* ἐσωτεμέρη

BOOKS

PRINTED AT

THE CLARENDON PRESS, OXFORD,

And Published for the University

BY MACMILLAN AND CO.,

29, 30, BEDFORD STREET, COVENT GARDEN, LONDON.

LEXICONS, GRAMMARS, &c.

A **Greek-English Lexicon**, by Henry George Liddell, D.D., and Robert Scott, D.D. *Sixth Edition, Revised and Augmented.* 1870. 4to. cloth, 1l. 16s.

A **Greek-English Lexicon**, abridged from the above, chiefly for the use of Schools. *Fifteenth Edition,* carefully revised throughout. 1871. square 12mo. cloth, 7s. 6d.

A **copious Greek-English Vocabulary**, compiled from the best authorities. 1850. 24mo. bound, 3s.

Graecae Grammaticae Rudimenta in usum Scholarum. Auctore Carolo Wordsworth, D.C.L. *Seventeenth Edition.* 1870. 12mo. bound, 4s.

A **Practical Introduction to Greek Accentuation**, by H. W. Chandler, M.A. 1862. 8vo. cloth, 10s. 6d.

Scheller's Lexicon of the Latin Tongue, with the German explanations translated into English by J. E. Riddle, M.A. 1835. fol. cloth, 1l. 1s.

A **Sanskrit-English Dictionary**, Etymologically and Philologically arranged, with special reference to Greek, Latin, German, Anglo-Saxon, English, and other cognate Indo-European Languages, by Monier Williams, M.A. 1872. 4to. cloth, 4l. 14s. 6d.

A **Practical Grammar of the Sanskrit Language**, arranged with reference to the Classical Languages of Europe, for the use of English Students, by Monier Williams, M.A. *Third Edition.* 1864. 8vo. cloth, 15s.

An **Icelandic-English Dictionary**. By the late R. Cleasby. Enlarged and completed by G. Vigfússon. Parts I. and II. 4to. 21s. each.
  Part III. *just ready. This Part completes the Work.*

GREEK AND LATIN CLASSICS.

Aeschylus: Tragoediae et Fragmenta, ex recensione Guil. Dindorfii. *Second Edition.* 1851. 8vo. cloth, 5s. 6d.

Sophocles: Tragoediae et Fragmenta, ex recensione et cum commentariis Guil. Dindorfii. *Third Edition.* 2 vols. 1860. fcap. 8vo. cloth, 1l. 1s.
  Each Play separately, limp, 2s. 6d.

  The Text alone, square 16mo. cloth, 3s. 6d.
  Each Play separately, limp, 6d.

Sophocles: Tragoediae et Fragmenta, ex recensione Guil. Dindorfii. Second Edition. 1849. 8vo. cloth, 5s. 6d.

Euripides: Tragoediae et Fragmenta, ex recensione Guil. Dindorfii. Tomi II. 1834. 8vo. cloth, 10s.

Aristophanes: Comoediae et Fragmenta, ex recensione Guil. Dindorfii. Tomi II. 1835. 8vo. cloth, 11s.

Aristoteles: ex recensione Immanuelis Bekkeri. Accedunt Indices Sylburgiani. Tomi XI. 1837. 8vo. cloth, 2l. 10s.
Each volume separately, 5s. 6d.

Catulli Veronensis Liber: recognovit, apparatum criticum prolegomena appendices addidit, Robinson Ellis, A.M. 1867. 8vo. cloth, 16s.

Catulli Veronensis Carmina Selecta, secundum recognitionem Robinson Ellis, A.M. Extra fcap. 8vo. cloth, 3s. 6d.

Demosthenes: ex recensione Guil. Dindorfii. Tomi IV. 1846. 8vo. cloth. Price reduced from 2l. 2s. to 1l. 1s.

Homerus: Ilias, ex rec. Guil. Dindorfii. 1856. 8vo. cloth, 5s. 6d.

Homerus: Odyssea, ex rec. Guil. Dindorfii. 1855. 8vo. cloth, 5s. 6d.

Plato: The Apology, with a revised Text and English Notes, and a Digest of Platonic Idioms, by James Riddell, M.A. 1867. 8vo. cloth, 8s. 6d.

Plato: Philebus, with a revised Text and English Notes, by Edward Poste, M.A. 1860. 8vo. cloth, 7s. 6d.

Plato: Sophistes and Politicus, with a revised Text and English Notes, by Lewis Campbell, M.A. 1866. 8vo. cloth, 18s.

Plato: Theaetetus, with a revised Text and English Notes, by Lewis Campbell, M.A. 1861. 8vo. cloth, 9s.

Plato: The Dialogues, translated into English, with Analyses and Introductions, by B. Jowett, M.A., Master of Balliol College, and Regius Professor of Greek. 4 vols. 1871. 8vo. cloth, 3l. 6s.

Xenophon: Historia Graeca, ex recensione et cum annotationibus L. Dindorfii. Second Edition. 1852. 8vo. cloth, 10s. 6d.

Xenophon: Expeditio Cyri, ex rec. et cum annotatt. L. Dindorfii. Second Edition. 1855. 8vo. cloth, 10s. 6d.

Xenophon: Institutio Cyri, ex rec. et cum annotatt. L. Dindorfii. 1857. 8vo. cloth, 10s. 6d.

Xenophon: Memorabilia Socratis, ex rec. et cum annotatt. L. Dindorfii. 1862. 8vo. cloth, 7s. 6d.

Xenophon: Opuscula Politica Equestria et Venatica cum Arriani Libello de Venatione, ex rec. et cum annotatt. L. Dindorfii. 1866. 8vo. cloth, 10s. 6d.

THE HOLY SCRIPTURES, &c.

The Holy Bible in the earliest English Versions, made from the Latin Vulgate by John Wycliffe and his followers: edited by the Rev. J. Forshall and Sir F. Madden. 4 vols. 1850. royal 4to. cloth. Price reduced from 5l. 15s. 6d. to 3l. 3s.

The Holy Bible: an exact reprint, page for page, of the Authorized Version published in the year 1611. Demy 4to. *half bound*, 1l. 1s.

Vetus Testamentum Graece secundum exemplar Vaticanum Romae editum. Accedit potior varietas Codicis Alexandrini. Tomi III. 1848. 12mo. *cloth*, 14s.

Novum Testamentum Graece. Accedunt parallela S. Scripturae loca, necnon vetus capitulorum notatio et canones Eusebii. Edidit Carolus Lloyd, S.T.P.R., necnon Episcopus Oxoniensis. 1869. 18mo. *cloth*, 3s.

The same on writing paper, with large margin, small 4to. *cloth*, 10s. 6d.

Novum Testamentum Graece juxta exemplar Millianum. 1868. 12mo. *cloth*, 2s. 6d.

The same on writing paper, with large margin, small 4to. *cloth*, 6s. 6d.

Evangelia Sacra Graece. *The Text of Mill.* 1870. fcap. 8vo. *limp*, 1s. 6d.

The New Testament in Greek and English, on opposite pages, arranged and edited by E. Cardwell, D.D. 2 vols. 1837. crown 8vo. *cloth*, 6s.

Novum Testamentum Graece. Antiquissimorum Codicum Textus in ordine parallelo dispositi. Accedit collatio Codicis Sinaitici. Edidit E. H. Hansell, S.T.B. Tomi III. 1864. 8vo. *half morocco*, 2l. 12s. 6d.

Diatessaron; sive Historia Jesu Christi ex ipsis Evangelistarum verbis apte dispositis confecta. Ed. J. White. 1856. 12mo. *cloth*, 3s. 6d.

Canon Muratorianus. The earliest Catalogue of the Books of the New Testament. Edited with Notes and a Facsimile of the MS. in the Ambrosian Library at Milan, by S. P. Tregelles, LL.D. 1868. 4to. *cloth*, 10s. 6d.

Horae Hebraicae et Talmudicae, a J. Lightfoot. *A new Edition,* by R. Gandell, M.A. 4 vols. 1859. 8vo. *club*. *Price reduced from 2l. 2s. to 1l. 1s.*

ECCLESIASTICAL HISTORY, &c.

Baedae Historia Ecclesiastica. Edited, with English Notes, by G. H. Moberly, M.A., Fellow of C.C.C., Oxford. 1869. crown 8vo. *cloth*, 10s. 6d.

Bingham's Antiquities of the Christian Church, and other Works. 10 vols. 1855. 8vo. *cloth.* *Price reduced from 5l. 5s. to 3l. 3s.*

Burnet's History of the Reformation of the Church of England. *A new Edition.* Carefully revised, and the Records collated with the originals, by N. Pocock, M.A. With a Preface by the Editor. 7 vols. 1865. 8vo. *cloth,* 4l. 4s.

Councils and Ecclesiastical Documents relating to Great Britain and Ireland. Edited, after Spelman and Wilkins, by A. W. Haddan, D.D., and William Stubbs, M.A. Vol. I. 1869. medium 8vo. *cloth,* 1l. 1s.
    Vol. II. Part I. medium 8vo. *cloth,* 10s. 6d. *Just Published.*
    Vol. III. medium 8vo. *cloth,* 1l. 1s.

Records of the Reformation. The Divorce, 1527-1533. Mostly now for the first time printed from MSS. in the British Museum, and other Libraries. Collected and arranged by N. Pocock, M.A. 2 vols. 8vo. *cloth,* 1l. 16s.

Books printed at the Clarendon Press.

Eusebius' Ecclesiastical History, according to the text of Burton. With an Introduction by William Bright, D.D. 1872. Crown 8vo. *cloth*, 8s. 6d.

Fuller's Church History of Britain. Edited by J. S. Brewer, M.A. 6 vols. 1845. 8vo. *cloth*, 1l. 19s.

Hussey's Rise of the Papal Power traced in three Lectures. *Second Edition.* 1863. fcap. 8vo. *cloth*, 4s. 6d.

Le Neve's Fasti Ecclesiae Anglicanae. *Corrected and continued from 1715 to 1853* by T. Duffus Hardy. 3 vols. 1854. 8vo. *cloth*. *Price reduced from* 1l. 17s. 6d. *to* 1l. 1s.

Noelli (A.) Catechismus sive prima Institutio disciplinaque Pietatis Christianae Latine explicata. Editio nova cura Guil. Jacobson, A.M. 1844. 8vo. *cloth*, 5s. 6d.

The Orations of St. Athanasius against the Arians. With an Account of his Life. By William Bright, D.D., Regius Professor of Ecclesiastical History, Oxford. Crown 8vo. *cloth*, 9s.

Patrum Apostolicorum, S. Clementis Romani, S. Ignatii, S. Polycarpi, quae supersunt. Edidit Guil. Jacobson, S.T.P.R. Tomi II. *Fourth Edition*. 1863. 8vo. *cloth*, 1l. 1s.

Prideaux's Connection of Sacred and Profane History. 2 vols. 1851. 8vo. *cloth*, 10s.

Shuckford's Sacred and Profane History connected (in continuation of Prideaux). 2 vols. 1848. 8vo. *cloth*, 10s.

Reliquiae Sacrae secundi tertiique saeculi. Recensuit M. J. Routh, S.T.P. Tomi V. 1846–1848. 8vo. *cloth*. *Price reduced from* 2l. 11s. *to* 1l. 5s.

Scriptorum Ecclesiasticorum Opuscula. Recensuit M. J. Routh, S.T.P. Tomi II. *Third Edition*. 1858. 8vo. *cloth*. *Price reduced from* 1l. *to* 10s.

Stubbs's (W.) Registrum Sacrum Anglicanum. An attempt to exhibit the Course of Episcopal Succession in England. 1858. small 4to. *cloth*, 8s. 6d.

ENGLISH THEOLOGY.

Butler's Works, with an Index to the Analogy. 2 vols. 1849. 8vo. *cloth*, 11s.

Greswell's Harmonia Evangelica. *Fifth Edition*. 1856. 8vo. *cloth*, 9s. 6d.

Hall's (Bp.) Works. *A new Edition*, by Philip Wynter, D.D. 10 vols. 1863. 8vo. *cloth*. *Price reduced from* 5l. 5s. *to* 3l. 3s.

Heurtley's Collection of Creeds. 1858. 8vo. *cloth*, 6s. 6d.

Homilies appointed to be read in Churches. Edited by J. Griffiths, M.A. 1859. 8vo. *cloth*. *Price reduced from* 10s. 6d. *to* 7s. 6d.

Hooker's Works, with his Life by Walton, arranged by John Keble, M.A. *Fifth Edition*. 1865. 3 vols. 8vo. *cloth*, 1l. 11s. 6d.

Hooker's Works; the text as arranged by John Keble, M.A. 2 vols. 1865. 8vo. *cloth*, 11s.

Jackson's (Dr. Thomas) Works. 12 vols. 1844. 8vo. *cloth*, 3l. 6s.

Jewel's Works. Edited by R. W. Jelf, D.D. 8 vols. 1847. 8vo. *cloth.* Price reduced from 2l. 10s. to 1l. 10s.

Patrick's Theological Works. 9 vols. 1859. 8vo. *cloth.* Price reduced from 3l. 14s. 6d. to 1l. 1s.

Pearson's Exposition of the Creed. Revised and corrected by E. Burton, D.D. *Fifth Edition.* 1864. 8vo. *cloth,* 10s. 6d.

Pearson's Minor Theological Works. Now first collected, with a Memoir of the Author, Notes, and Index, by Edward Churton, M.A. 2 vols. 1844. 8vo. *cloth.* Price reduced from 14s. to 10s.

Sanderson's Works. Edited by W. Jacobson, D.D. 6 vols. 1854. 8vo. *cloth.* Price reduced from 2l. 10s. to 1l. 10s.

South's Sermons. 5 vols. 1842. 8vo. *cloth.* Price reduced from 2l. 10s. 6d. to 1l. 10s.

Stanhope's Paraphrase and Comment upon the Epistles and Gospels. *A new Edition.* 2 vols. 1851. 8vo. *cloth.* Price reduced from 18s. to 10s.

Wall's History of Infant Baptism, with Gale's Reflections, and Wall's Defence. *A new Edition,* by Henry Cotton, D.C.L. 2 vols. 1862. 8vo. *cloth,* 1l. 1s.

Waterland's Works, with Life, by Bp. Van Mildert. *A new Edition,* with copious Indexes. 6 vols. 1857. 8vo. *cloth,* 2l. 11s.

Waterland's Review of the Doctrine of the Eucharist, with a Preface by the present Bishop of London. 1868. crown 8vo. *cloth,* 6s. 6d.

Wheatly's Illustration of the Book of Common Prayer. *A new Edition,* 1846. 8vo. *cloth,* 5s.

Wyclif. Select English Works. By T. Arnold, M.A. 3 vols. 1871. 8vo. *cloth,* 2l. 2s.

ENGLISH HISTORY.

Two of the Saxon Chronicles parallel, with Supplementary Extracts from the Others. Edited, with Introduction, Notes, and a Glossarial Index, by J. Earle, M.A. 1865. 8vo. *cloth,* 16s.

Burnet's History of His Own Time, with the suppressed Passages and Notes. 6 vols. 1833. 8vo. *cloth,* 2l. 10s.

Carte's Life of James Duke of Ormond. *A new Edition,* carefully compared with the original MSS. 6 vols. 1851. 8vo. *cloth.* Price reduced from 2l. 6s. to 1l. 5s.

Clarendon's (Edw. Earl of) History of the Rebellion and Civil Wars in England. To which are subjoined the Notes of Bishop Warburton. 7 vols. 1849. medium 8vo. *cloth,* 2l. 10s.

Clarendon's (Edw. Earl of) History of the Rebellion and Civil Wars in England. 7 vols. 1839. 18mo. *cloth,* 1l. 1s.

Freeman's (E. A.) History of the Norman Conquest of England: its Causes and Results. Vols. I. and II. *A new Edition,* with Index. 8vo. *cloth,* 1l. 16s.

Vol. III. The Reign of Harold and the Interregnum. 1869. 8vo. *cloth,* 1l. 1s.
Vol. IV. The Reign of William. 8vo. *cloth,* 1l. 1s.

May's History of the Long Parliament. 1854. 8vo. *cloth*, 6s. 6d.

Rogers's History of Agriculture and Prices in England, A.D. 1259–1400. 2 vols. 1866. 8vo. cloth, 2l. 2s.

Whitelock's Memorials of English Affairs from 1625 to 1660. 4 vols. 1853. 8vo. cloth, 1l. 10s.

PHILOSOPHICAL WORKS, AND GENERAL LITERATURE.

A Course of Lectures on Art, delivered before the University of Oxford in Hilary Term, 1870. By John Ruskin, M.A., Slade Professor of Fine Art. Demy 8vo. cloth, 6s.

A Critical Account of the Drawings by Michel Angelo and Raffaello in the University Galleries, Oxford. By J. C. Robinson, F.S.A. Crown 8vo. cloth, 4s.

Bacon's Novum Organum, edited, with English notes, by G.W. Kitchin, M.A. 1855. 8vo. cloth, 9s. 6d.

Bacon's Novum Organum, translated by G. W. Kitchin, M.A. 1855. 8vo. cloth, 9s. 6d.

The Works of George Berkeley, D.D., formerly Bishop of Cloyne; including many of his writings hitherto unpublished. With Prefaces, Annotations, and an Account of his Life and Philosophy, by Alexander Campbell Fraser, M.A. 4 vols. 1871. 8vo. cloth, 2l. 18s.

Also separately. The Works. 3 vols. cloth, 2l. 2s.
The Life and Letters, &c. 1 vol. cloth, 16s.

Smith's Wealth of Nations. *A new Edition*, with Notes, by J. E. Thorold Rogers, M.A. 2 vols. 8vo. cloth, 1l. 1s.

The Student's Handbook to the University and Colleges of Oxford. Extra fcap. 8vo. cloth, 2s. 6d.

MATHEMATICS, PHYSICAL SCIENCE, &c.

Treatise on Infinitesimal Calculus. By Bartholomew Price, M.A., F.R.S., Professor of Natural Philosophy, Oxford.

Vol. I. Differential Calculus. *Second Edition*. 1858. 8vo. cloth, 14s. 6d.
Vol. II. Integral Calculus, Calculus of Variations, and Differential Equations. *Second Edition*. 1865. 8vo. cloth, 18s.
Vol. III. Statics, including Attractions; Dynamics of a Material Particle. *Second Edition*. 1868. 8vo. cloth, 16s.
Vol. IV. Dynamics of Material Systems: together with a Chapter on Theoretical Dynamics, by W. F. Donkin, M.A., F.R.S. 1862. 8vo. cloth, 16s.

Vesuvius. By John Phillips, M.A., F.R.S., Professor of Geology, Oxford. 1869. crown 8vo. cloth, 10s. 6d.

Rigaud's Correspondence of Scientific Men of the 17th Century, with Index by A. de Morgan. 2 vols. 1841–62. 8vo. cloth, 18s. 6d.

Clarendon Press Series.

The Delegates of the Clarendon Press having undertaken the publication of a series of works, chiefly educational, and entitled the **Clarendon Press Series**, have published, or have in preparation, the following.

Those to which prices are attached are already published; the others are in preparation.

I. GREEK AND LATIN CLASSICS, &c.

A Greek Primer in English, for the use of beginners. By the Right Rev. Charles Wordsworth, D.C.L., Bishop of St. Andrews. *Second Edition*. Ext. fcap. 8vo. cloth, 1s. 6d.

Greek Verbs, Irregular and Defective; their forms, meaning, and quantity; embracing all the Tenses used by Greek writers, with reference to the passages in which they are found. By W. Veitch. *New Edition*. Crown 8vo. cloth, 10s. 6d.

The Elements of Greek Accentuation (for Schools): abridged from his larger work by H. W. Chandler, M.A., Waynflete Professor of Moral and Metaphysical Philosophy, Oxford. Ext. fcap. 8vo. cloth, 2s. 6d.

The Orations of Demosthenes and Aeschines on the Crown. With Introductory Essays and Notes. By G. A. Simcox, M.A., and W. H. Simcox, M.A., Fellows of Queen's College, Oxford. 8vo. cloth, 12s.

Aristotle's Politics. By W. L. Newman, M.A., Fellow and Lecturer of Balliol College, and Reader in Ancient History, Oxford.

The Golden Treasury of Ancient Greek Poetry; being a Collection of the finest passages in the Greek Classic Poets, with Introductory Notices and Notes. By R. S. Wright, M.A., Fellow of Oriel College, Oxford. Extra fcap. 8vo. cloth, 8s. 6d.

A Golden Treasury of Greek Prose, being a Collection of the finest passages in the principal Greek Prose Writers, with Introductory Notices and Notes. By R. S. Wright, M.A., Fellow of Oriel College, Oxford; and J. E. L. Shadwell, M.A., Senior Student of Christ Church. Extra fcap. 8vo. cloth, 4s. 6d.

Homer. Iliad. By D. B. Monro, M.A., Fellow and Tutor of Oriel College, Oxford.

Also a small Edition for Schools.

Homer. Odyssey, Books I-XII (for Schools). By W. W. Merry, M.A., Fellow and Lecturer of Lincoln College, Oxford. *Third Edition*. Extra fcap. 8vo. cloth, 4s. 6d.

Homer. **Odyssey**, Books I-XII. By W. W. Merry, M.A., Fellow and Lecturer of Lincoln College, Oxford; and the late James Riddell, M.A., Fellow of Balliol College, Oxford.

Homer. **Odyssey**, Books XIII-XXIV. By Robinson Ellis, M.A., Fellow of Trinity College, Oxford.

Plato. Selections (for Schools). With Notes, by B. Jowett, M.A., Regius Professor of Greek; and J. Purves, M.A., Fellow and Lecturer of Balliol College, Oxford.

Sophocles. The Plays and Fragments. With English Notes and Introductions by Lewis Campbell, M.A., Professor of Greek, St. Andrews.

Vol. I. Oedipus Tyrannus, Oedipus Coloneus, Antigone. 8vo. *cloth*, 14s.

Sophocles. In Single Plays, with English Notes, &c. By Lewis Campbell, M.A., Professor of Greek, St. Andrews, and Evelyn Abbott, M.A., of Balliol College.

Oedipus Tyrannus will be published shortly; the others will follow at intervals of six months.

Sophocles. The Greek Text of the Plays. For the use of Students in the University of Oxford. By Lewis Campbell, M.A., Professor of Greek, St. Andrews. *Just ready.*

Sophocles. Oedipus Rex: Dindorf's Text, with Notes by the Ven. Archdeacon Basil Jones, M.A., formerly Fellow of University College, Oxford. *Second Edition.* Ex. fcap. 8vo. limp cloth, 1s. 6d.

Theocritus (for Schools). With Notes, by H. Snow, M.A., Assistant Master at Eton College, formerly Fellow of St. John's College, Cambridge. Extra fcap. 8vo. cloth, 4s. 6d.

Xenophon. Selections (for Schools). With Notes and Maps, by J. S. Phillpotts, B.C.L., Assistant Master in Rugby School, formerly Fellow of New College, Oxford. *Second Edition.* Extra fcap. 8vo. cloth, 3s. 6d.

Part II. By the same Editor.

Arrian. Selections (for Schools). By the same Editor.

Caesar. The Commentaries (for Schools). Part I. The Gallic War, with Notes and Maps, by Charles E. Moberly, M.A., Assistant Master in Rugby School; formerly Scholar of Balliol College, Oxford. Extra fcap. 8vo. cloth, 4s. 6d.

Part II. The Civil War: Bk. 1. By the same Editor. Extra fcap. 8vo. cloth, 2s.

Cicero's Philippic Orations. With Notes, by J. R. King, M.A., formerly Fellow and Tutor of Merton College, Oxford. Demy 8vo. cloth, 10s. 6d.

Cicero pro Cluentio. With Introduction and Notes. By W. Ramsay, M.A. Edited by G. G. Ramsay, M.A., Professor of Humanity, Glasgow. Extra fcap. 8vo. cloth, 3s. 6d.

Cicero. Selection of interesting and descriptive passages. With Notes. By Henry Walford, M.A., Wadham College, Oxford, Assistant Master at Haileybury College. In three Parts. *Second Edition.* Extra fcap. 8vo. cloth, 4s. 6d.

Each Part separately, limp, 1s. 6d.

Part I. Anecdotes from Grecian and Roman History.
Part II. Omens and Dreams: Beauties of Nature.
Part III. Rome's Rule of her Provinces.

Cicero. Select Letters. With English Introductions, Notes, and Appendices. By Albert Watson, M.A., Fellow and Tutor of Brasenose College, Oxford. 8vo. cloth, 18s.

Cicero. Selected Letters (for Schools). With Notes. By the late C. E. Prichard, M.A., formerly Fellow of Balliol College, Oxford, and E. R. Bernard, M.A., Fellow of Magdalen College, Oxford. Extra fcap. 8vo. cloth, 3s.

Cicero de Oratore. With Introduction and Notes. By A. S. Wilkins, M.A., Professor of Latin, Owens College, Manchester.

Cornelius Nepos. With Notes, by Oscar Browning, M.A., Fellow of King's College, Cambridge, and Assistant Master at Eton College. Extra fcap. 8vo. cloth, 2s. 6d.

Horace. With Essays and Notes. By Edward C. Wickham, M. A., Head Master of Wellington College. *In the Press.*

Also a small edition for Schools.

Livy, Book I. By J. R. Seeley, M.A., Fellow of Christ's College, and Regius Professor of Modern History, Cambridge. 8vo. cloth, 6s.

Also a small edition for Schools.

Livy. Selections (for Schools). With Notes, by Henry Lee-Warner, M.A., Assistant Master at Rugby School. *In Parts.*

Part II. Hannibal's Campaign in Italy. Extra fcap. 8vo. cloth, 1s. 6d.

In the Press.

Part I. The Caudine Forks.   Part III. The Disaster of Pydna.

Ovid. Selections for the use of Schools. With Introductions and Notes, and an Appendix on the Roman Calendar. By W. Ramsay, M.A. Edited by G. G. Ramsay, M.A., Professor of Humanity, Glasgow. Ext. fcap. 8vo. cloth, 4s. 6d.

Persius. The Satires. With a Translation and Commentary. By John Conington, M.A. late Corpus Professor of Latin in the University of Oxford. Edited by Henry Nettleship, M.A., formerly Fellow of Lincoln College, Oxford. 8vo. cloth, 7s. 6d.

Pliny. Selected Letters (for Schools). By the late C. E. Prichard, M.A., formerly Fellow of Balliol College, Oxford, and E. R. Bernard, M.A., Fellow of Magdalen College, Oxford. Extra fcap. 8vo., cloth, 3s.

Fragments and Specimens of Early Latin. With Introduction, Notes, and Illustrations. By John Wordsworth, M.A., Fellow of Brasenose College, Oxford.

Selections from the less known Latin Poets. By North Pinder, M.A., formerly Fellow of Trinity College, Oxford. Demy 8vo. cloth, 15s.

Passages for Translation into Latin. For the use of Passmen and others. Selected by J. Y. Sargent, M.A., Tutor, formerly Fellow, of Magdalen College, Oxford. *Second Edition.* Ext. fcap. 8vo. cloth, 2s. 6d.

II. MENTAL AND MORAL PHILOSOPHY.

The Elements of Deductive Logic, designed mainly for the use of Junior Students in the Universities. By T. Fowler, M.A., Fellow and Tutor of Lincoln College, Oxford. *Fourth Edition,* with a Collection of Examples. Extra fcap. 8vo. cloth, 3s. 6d.

The Elements of Inductive Logic, designed mainly for the use of Students in the Universities. By the same Author. Extra fcap. 8vo. cloth, 6s.

Principles of Morals. By J. M. Wilson, D.D., President of Corpus Christi College, Oxford, and T. Fowler, M.A., Fellow and Tutor of Lincoln College, Oxford. *Preparing.*

A Manual of Political Economy, for the use of Schools. By J. E. Thorold Rogers, M.A., formerly Professor of Political Economy, Oxford. *Second Edition.* Extra fcap. 8vo. cloth, 4s. 6d.

The Logic of Hegel; being Part I. of the Encyclopaedia of the Philosophical Sciences. Translated by William Wallace, M.A., Fellow and Tutor of Merton College. *In the Press.*

III. MATHEMATICS, &c.

Acoustics. By W. F. Donkin, M.A., F.R.S., Savilian Professor of Astronomy, Oxford. Crown 8vo. cloth, 7s. 6d.

An Elementary Treatise on Quaternions. By P. G. Tait, M.A., Professor of Natural Philosophy in the University of Edinburgh; formerly Fellow of St. Peter's College, Cambridge. Demy 8vo. cloth, 12s. 6d.

Book-keeping. By R. G. C. Hamilton, Accountant to the Board of Trade, and John Ball (of the Firm of Messrs. Quilter, Ball, and Co.), Examiners in Book-keeping for the Society of Arts' Examination. *Third Edition.* Extra fcap. 8vo. limp cloth, 1s. 6d.

The Scholar's Arithmetic. By Lewis Hensley, M.A., formerly Fellow and Assistant Tutor of Trinity College, Cambridge. Crown 8vo. cloth, 4s. 6d. *Just published.*

Figures made Easy: a first Arithmetic Book. (Introductory to 'The Scholar's Arithmetic,' by the same Author.) Crown 8vo. limp cloth, 6d.

Answers to the Examples in Figures made Easy, together with two thousand additional Examples, formed from the Tables in the same, with Answers. By the same Author. Crown 8vo. cloth, 1s.

A Course of Lectures on Pure Geometry. By Henry J. Stephen Smith, M.A., F.R.S., Fellow of Balliol College, and Savilian Professor of Geometry in the University of Oxford.

A Treatise on Electricity and Magnetism. By J. Clerk Maxwell, M.A., F.R.S., Professor of Experimental Physics in the University of Cambridge. In two volumes. Demy 8vo. cloth, 1l. 11s. 6d.

A Series of Elementary Works is being arranged, and will shortly be announced.

IV. HISTORY.

A Manual of Ancient History. By George Rawlinson, M.A., Camden Professor of Ancient History, formerly Fellow of Exeter College, Oxford. Demy 8vo. cloth, 14s.

Select Charters and other Illustrations of English Constitutional History; from the Earliest Times to the Reign of Edward I. Arranged and edited by W. Stubbs, M.A., Regius Professor of Modern History in the University of Oxford. Crown 8vo. cloth, 8s. 6d.

A Constitutional History of England. By the same Author. *Nearly ready.*

A History of France, down to the year 1453. With Maps and Plans. By G. W. Kitchin, M.A., formerly Censor of Christ Church. *Now ready.*

A History of Germany and of the Empire, down to the close of the Middle Ages. By J. Bryce, D.C.L., Fellow of Oriel College, Oxford.

A History of Germany, from the Reformation. By Adolphus W. Ward, M.A., Fellow of St. Peter's College, Cambridge, Professor of History, Owens College, Manchester.

A History of British India. By S. J. Owen, M.A., Lee's Reader in Law and History, Christ Church, and Teacher of Indian Law and History in the University of Oxford.

A History of Greece. By E. A. Freeman, M.A., formerly Fellow of Trinity College, Oxford.

V. LAW.

Gaii Institutionum Juris Civilis Commentarii Quatuor; or, Elements of Roman Law by Gaius. With a Translation and Commentary, by Edward Poste, M.A., Barrister-at-Law, and Fellow of Oriel College, Oxford. 8vo. cloth, 16s.

Elements of Law, considered with reference to principles of General Jurisprudence. By William Markby, M.A., Judge of the High Court of Judicature, Calcutta. Crown 8vo. cloth, 6s. 6d.

The Elements of Jurisprudence. By T. Erskine Holland, D.C.L., Barrister-at-Law, and formerly Fellow of Exeter College, Oxford.

The Institutes of Justinian, edited as a recension of the Institutes of Gaius. By the same Editor. Extra fcap. 8vo. cloth, 5s.

Authorities Illustrative of the History of the English Law of Real Property. By Kenelm E. Digby, M.A., Vinerian Reader in Law, formerly Fellow of Corpus Christi College, Oxford.

VI. PHYSICAL SCIENCE.

Natural Philosophy. In four Volumes. By Sir W. Thomson, LL.D., D.C.L., F.R.S., Professor of Natural Philosophy, Glasgow; and P. G. Tait, M.A., Professor of Natural Philosophy, Edinburgh; formerly Fellows of St. Peter's College, Cambridge. Vol. I. 8vo. cloth, 1l. 5s.

Elements of Natural Philosophy. By the same Authors; being a smaller Work on the same subject, and forming a complete Introduction to it, so far as it can be carried out with Elementary Geometry and Algebra. Part I. 8vo. cloth, 9s.

Descriptive Astronomy. A Handbook for the General Reader, and also for Practical Observatory work. With 224 illustrations and numerous tables. By G. F. Chambers, F.R.A.S., Barrister-at-Law. Demy 8vo. 856 pp., cloth, 1l. 1s.

Chemistry for Students. By A. W. Williamson, Phil. Doc., F.R.S., Professor of Chemistry, University College, London. *A new Edition, with Solutions.* Extra fcap. 8vo. cloth, 8s. 6d.

A Treatise on Heat, with numerous Woodcuts and Diagrams. By Balfour Stewart, LL.D., F.R.S., Director of the Observatory at Kew. *Second Edition.* Ext. fcap. 8vo. cloth, 7s. 6d.

Clarendon Press Series.

Forms of Animal Life. By G. Rolleston, M.D., F.R.S., Linacre Professor of Physiology, Oxford. Illustrated by Descriptions and Drawings of Dissections. Demy 8vo. cloth. 16s.

Exercises in Practical Chemistry. By A. G. Vernon Harcourt, M.A., F.R.S., Senior Student of Christ Church, and Lee's Reader in Chemistry; and H. G. Madan, M.A., Fellow of Queen's College, Oxford.
Series I. Qualitative Exercises. Crown 8vo. cloth, 7s. 6d.
Series II. Quantitative Exercises.

Geology of Oxford and the Valley of the Thames. By John Phillips, M.A., F.R.S., Professor of Geology, Oxford. 8vo. cloth, 21s.

Geology. By J. Phillips, M.A., F.R.S., Professor of Geology, Oxford.

Mechanics. By Bartholomew Price, M.A., F.R.S., Sedleian Professor of Natural Philosophy, Oxford.

Optics. By R. B. Clifton, M.A., F.R.S., Professor of Experimental Philosophy, Oxford; formerly Fellow of St. John's College, Cambridge.

Electricity. By W. Esson, M.A., F.R.S., Fellow and Mathematical Lecturer of Merton College, Oxford.

Crystallography. By M. H. N. Story-Maskelyne, M.A., Professor of Mineralogy, Oxford; and Deputy Keeper in the Department of Minerals, British Museum.

Mineralogy. By the same Author.

Physiological Physics. By G. Griffith, M.A., Jesus College, Oxford, Assistant Secretary to the British Association, and Natural Science Master at Harrow School.

Magnetism.

VII. ENGLISH LANGUAGE AND LITERATURE.

A First Reading Book. By Marie Eichens of Berlin; and edited by Anne J. Clough. Extra fcap. 8vo. stiff covers, 4d.

Oxford Reading Book, Part I. For Little Children. Extra fcap. 8vo. stiff covers, 6d.

Oxford Reading Book, Part II. For Junior Classes. Extra fcap. 8vo. stiff covers, 6d.

On the Principles of Grammar. By E. Thring, M.A., Head Master of Uppingham School. Extra fcap. 8vo. cloth, 4s. 6d.

Grammatical Analysis, designed to serve as an Exercise and Composition Book in the English Language. By E. Thring, M.A., Head Master of Uppingham School. Extra fcap. 8vo. cloth, 3s. 6d.

An English Grammar and Reading Book. For Lower Forms in Classical Schools. By O. W. Tancock, M.A., Assistant Master of Sherborne School. Extra fcap. 8vo. cloth, 3s. 6d.

The Philology of the English Tongue. By J. Earle, M.A., formerly Fellow of Oriel College, and Professor of Anglo-Saxon, Oxford. *Second Edition.* Extra fcap. 8vo. cloth, 7s. 6d.

Specimens of Early English. A New and Revised Edition. With Introduction, Notes, and Glossarial Index. By R. Morris, LL.D., and W. W. Skeat, M.A.

Part I. *In the Press.*
Part II. From Robert of Gloucester to Gower (A.D. 1298 to A.D. 1393). Extra fcap. 8vo. *cloth,* 7s. 6d.

Specimens of English Literature, from the 'Ploughmans Crede' to the 'Shepheardes Calender' (A.D. 1394 to A.D. 1579). With Introduction, Notes, and Glossarial Index, by W. W. Skeat, M.A., formerly Fellow of Christ's College, Cambridge. Extra fcap. 8vo. *cloth,* 7s. 6d.

The Vision of William concerning Piers the Plowman, by William Langland. Edited, with Notes, by W. W. Skeat, M.A., formerly Fellow of Christ's College, Cambridge. Extra fcap. 8vo. *cloth,* 4s. 6d.

Milton. The Areopagitica, with Notes. By J. W. Hales, M.A., late Fellow of Christ's College, Cambridge. *Preparing.*

Typical Selections from the best English Authors from the Sixteenth to the Nineteenth Century, (to serve as a higher Reading Book,) with Introductory Notices and Notes, being a contribution towards a History of English Literature. Extra fcap. 8vo. *cloth,* 4s. 6d.

Specimens of the Scottish Language; being a Series of Annotated Extracts illustrative of the Literature and Philology of the Lowland Tongue from the Fourteenth to the Nineteenth Century. With Introduction and Glossary. By A. H. Burgess, M.A.

See also XII. below for other English Classics.

VIII. FRENCH LANGUAGE AND LITERATURE.

An Etymological Dictionary of the French Language, with a Preface on the Principles of French Etymology. By A. Brachet. Translated by G. W. Kitchin, M.A., formerly Censor of Christ Church. *Just ready.*

Brachet's Historical Grammar of the French Language. Translated into English by G. W. Kitchin, M.A., formerly Censor of Christ Church. *A new Edition, with a full Index.* Extra fcap. 8vo. *cloth,* 3s. 6d.

Corneille's Cinna, and Molière's Les Femmes Savantes. Edited, with Introduction and Notes, by Gustave Masson. Extra fcap. 8vo. *cloth,* 2s. 6d.

Racine's Andromaque, and Corneille's Le Menteur. With Louis Racine's Life of his Father. By the same Editor. Extra fcap. 8vo. *cloth,* 2s. 6d.

Molière's Les Fourberies de Scapin, and Racine's Athalie. With Voltaire's Life of Molière. By the same Editor. Extra fcap. 8vo. *cloth,* 2s. 6d.

Selections from the Correspondence of Madame de Sévigné and her chief Contemporaries. Intended more especially for Girls' Schools. By the same Editor. Extra fcap. 8vo. *cloth,* 3s.

Voyage autour de ma Chambre, by Xavier de Maistre; Ourika, by Madame de Duras; La Dot de Suzette, by Fiévée; Les Jumeaux de l'Hôtel Corneille, by Edmond About; Mésaventures d'un Écolier, by Rodolphe Topffer. By the same Editor. Extra fcap. 8vo. *cloth,* 2s. 6d.

IX. GERMAN LANGUAGE AND LITERATURE.

Goethe's Egmont. With a Life of Goethe, &c. By Dr. Buchheim, Professor of the German Language and Literature in King's College, London; and Examiner in German to the University of London. Extra fcap. 8vo. cloth, 3s.

Schiller's Wilhelm Tell. With a Life of Schiller; an historical and critical Introduction, Arguments, and a complete Commentary. By the same Editor. Extra fcap. 8vo. cloth, 3s. 6d.

Lessing's Minna von Barnhelm. A Comedy. With a Life of Lessing, Critical Analyses, &c. By the same Editor. Extra fcap. 8vo. cloth, 3s. 6d.

X. ART, &c.

A Handbook of Pictorial Art. By R. St. J. Tyrwhitt, M.A., formerly Student and Tutor of Christ Church, Oxford. With coloured Illustrations, Photographs, and a chapter on Perspective by A. Macdonald. 8vo. half morocco, 18s.

A Music Primer for the use of Schools. By J. Troutbeck, M.A., and R. F. Dale, M.A., B. Mus. Crown 8vo. cloth, 1s. 6d. *Just Published.*

A Treatise on Harmony. By Sir F. A. Gore Ouseley, Bart., M.A., Mus. Doc., Professor of Music in the University of Oxford. 4to. cloth, 10s.

A Treatise on Counterpoint, Canon, and Fugue, based upon that of Cherubini. By the same Author. 4to. cloth, 16s.

The Cultivation of the Speaking Voice. By John Hullah. Crown 8vo. cloth, 3s. 6d.

XI. MISCELLANEOUS.

Outlines of Textual Criticism applied to the New Testament. By C. E. Hammond, M.A., Fellow and Tutor of Exeter College, Oxford. Extra fcap. 8vo. cloth, 3s. 6d.

A System of Physical Education: Theoretical and Practical. By Archibald Maclaren, The Gymnasium, Oxford. Extra fcap. 8vo. cloth, 7s. 6d.

The Modern Greek Language in its relation to Ancient Greek. By E. M. Geldart, B.A., formerly Scholar of Balliol College, Oxford. Extra fcap. 8vo. cloth, 4s. 6d.

XII. A SERIES OF ENGLISH CLASSICS.

Designed to meet the wants of Students in English Literature: under the superintendence of the Rev. J. S. BREWER, M.A., *of Queen's College, Oxford, and Professor of English Literature at King's College, London.*

It is also especially hoped that this Series may prove useful to Ladies' Schools and Middle Class Schools; in which English Literature must always be a leading subject of instruction.

A General Introduction to the Series. By Professor Brewer, M.A.

1. **Chaucer.** The Prologue to the Canterbury Tales; The Knightes Tale; The Nonne Prestes Tale. Edited by R. Morris, Editor of Specimens of Early English, &c., &c. *Third Edition.* Extra fcap. 8vo. cloth, 2s. 6d.

Clarendon Press Series.

2. **Spenser's Faery Queene.** Designed chiefly for the use of Schools. With Introduction, Notes, and Glossary. By G. W. Kitchin, M.A., formerly Censor of Christ Church.
    Book I. *Fifth Edition.* Extra fcap. 8vo. cloth, 2s. 6d.
    Book II. *Second Edition.* Extra fcap. 8vo. cloth, 2s. 6d.

3. **Hooker.** Ecclesiastical Polity, Book I. Edited by R. W. Church, M.A., formerly Fellow of Oriel College, Oxford. Extra fcap. 8vo. cloth, 2s.

4. **Shakespeare.** Select Plays. Edited by W. G. Clark, M.A., Fellow of Trinity College, Cambridge; and W. Aldis Wright, M.A., Trinity College, Cambridge.
    I. The Merchant of Venice. Extra fcap. 8vo. stiff covers, 1s.
    II. Richard the Second. Extra fcap. 8vo. stiff covers, 1s. 6d.
    III. Macbeth. Extra fcap, 8vo. stiff covers, 1s. 6d.
    IV. Hamlet. Extra fcap. 8vo. stiff covers, 2s.

5. **Bacon.** Advancement of Learning. Edited by W. Aldis Wright, M.A. Extra fcap. 8vo. cloth, 4s. 6d.

6. **Milton.** Poems. Edited by R. C. Browne, M.A., and Associate of King's College, London. *Second edition.* 2 vols. extra fcap. 8vo. cloth, 6s. 6d.
    Also separately, Vol. I. 4s., Vol. II. 3s.

7. **Dryden.** Stanzas on the Death of Oliver Cromwell; Astraea Redux; Annus Mirabilis; Absalom and Achitophel; Religio Laici; The Hind and the Panther. Edited by W. D. Christie, M.A., Trinity College, Cambridge. Extra fcap. 8vo. cloth, 3s. 6d.

8. **Bunyan.** Grace Abounding; The Pilgrim's Progress. Edited by E. Venables, M.A., Canon of Lincoln.

9. **Pope.** With Introduction and Notes. By Mark Pattison, D.D., Rector of Lincoln College, Oxford.
    I. Essay on Man. Extra fcap. 8vo. stiff covers, 1s. 6d.
    II. Satires and Epistles. Extra fcap. 8vo. stiff covers, 2s.

10. **Johnson.** Rasselas; Lives of Pope and Dryden. Edited by C. H. O. Daniel, M.A., Fellow and Tutor of Worcester College, Oxford.

11. **Burke.** Thoughts on the Present Discontents; the two Speeches on America; Reflections on the French Revolution. By Edward John Payne, B.A., Fellow of University College, Oxford. *In the Press.*

12. **Cowper.** The Task, and some of his minor poems. Edited by H. T. Griffith, M.A., Pembroke College, Oxford.

Published for the University by

MACMILLAN AND CO., LONDON.

The DELEGATES OF THE PRESS invite suggestions and advice from all persons interested in education; and will be thankful for hints, &c. addressed to either the Rev. G. W. KITCHIN, St. Giles's Road East, Oxford, or the SECRETARY TO THE DELEGATES, *Clarendon Press, Oxford.*

www.ingramcontent.com/pod-product-compliance
Lightning Source LLC
Chambersburg PA
CBHW030733230426
43667CB00007B/699